THE IDEA OF FRATERNITY IN AMERICA

Wilson Carey McWilliams

THE IDEA OF FRATERNITY IN AMERICA

UNIVERSITY OF CALIFORNIA PRESS
BERKELEY, LOS ANGELES, LONDON

UNIVERSITY OF CALIFORNIA PRESS
BERKELEY AND LOS ANGELES, CALIFORNIA
UNIVERSITY OF CALIFORNIA PRESS, LTD.
LONDON, ENGLAND
COPYRIGHT © 1973, BY
THE REGENTS OF THE UNIVERSITY OF CALIFORNIA
SECOND PRINTING, 1974
FIRST PAPERBACK EDITION, 1974
ISBN: 0–520–01650–5 CLOTH-BOUND
0–520–02772–8 PAPER-BOUND
LIBRARY OF CONGRESS CATALOG CARD NUMBER: 73-101339
PRINTED IN THE UNITED STATES OF AMERICA
DESIGNED BY DAVE COMSTOCK

CONTENTS

PREFACE

This book began as a doctoral dissertation, which is warning enough for the experienced. To the usual faults of dissertations I have added other defects, nurtured in the intervening years and perfected by revision. It is pretentious even by the standards of political theory; and since theorists must, like Jacob, wrestle with gods and men, those standards are far from mean. It is intolerably long. Let it stand that I have provided myself the weak excuse of recognizing such faults and forewarning the reader.

The excuse for the book—and every book needs an excuse—is as much political as intellectual. Americans, especially young Americans, cannot find their country in the land about them. Often, in fact, they cannot find the land, hidden as it is by the cancer-growth of concrete and the slow poisoning of air and water. Wealth accumulates, men decay; racism stubbornly, and violence insistently, remain with us; riches and poverty exist in insane juxtaposition. Some turn to the chemical laboratories to provide fevered moments and mad dreams; others delight in the effete pornography of violence found in fashionable motion pictures; sex becomes an industry and a routine, almost a duty devoid of joy. Boredom and rage walk together; and war, with infinite patience, watches every act.

To be trapped in the present is not only to lose perspective. It is to be blinded, by one's own revulsion if not by the blaze of products and illusions which society proliferates. Even resistance, then, is only a wild lashing of blows which as often as not fall on the shelf. Those who would change, or even endure, America must recognize the roots of her agony in themselves; even in their horror, most Americans think, believe, and act in ways that reflect their Americanness and reveal that the same seeds from which the horror grew are planted in their own spirits.

In this condition, memory can be the ally of men. The contemporary American is not unique, and his struggle is not in a historical sense waged alone. The combat, for all its bizarre and peculiar features, is as old as the settlement of the land and possibly older, part of the human inheritance. If the present struggle is more desperate, our perception of it is blurred by the desperation itself; all the more reason to look to those Americans who had the luxury of easier times and a clearer sky to help them think more clearly. Too, by knowing how we have come to our dismal passage, we may be able to find the way out. To restore the past is, perhaps, to recover the future.

It may recover the present as well. Under the blank and brutal masks, behind the strange faces and suspect conduct which Americans have made for themselves, we can learn to see our countrymen. We can recognize that our tensions and torments are common, that the stranger and the enemy are not very different from the self. If one is fortunate, he may even find a brother among his fellow Americans, which opens the path to many things, as Plato knew: "The older I grew, the more I realized how difficult it is to manage a city's affairs rightly. For I saw that it was impossible to do anything without friends. . . ."

Inevitably, this book is dedicated to all my brothers. They will read their names on its pages and will hear in it our conversations and remember our arguments, our libations, and our common victories and defeats. They will also notice their ideas which, with fraternal license, I have appropriated. And they will be generous enough to see where I fall short of what I aimed at, or even fail to start. Thus it is superfluous to name them, saving me both the impertinence and the fault of slighting those of my brothers who are yet unknown.

Some names, however, must be included because of very special debts. My teachers John Schaar, Sheldon Wolin, and Norman Jacobson each gave me in his highly individual way a sense of the excitement of political theory and the realization that great knowledge heightens the capacity for compassion and outrage, as well as wisdom. To John D. Lewis and George A. Lanyi, I owe some years in which they taught me much, as men no less than as scholars, and I treasure especially the example they set by their supremacy in the Olympian gift of humor, combined in them with unexcelled loyalty. I will always be indebted to the late Ewart K. Lewis for the standard she set by her fierce devotion to truth and for her generous willingness to recognize some part of her spirit in another. Benjamin Rivlin of Brooklyn College gave me kindness, understanding and, when needed, reproof; he must always rank with the best of department chairmen.

I also thank my editors: Grant Barnes, for allowing me to pre-

sume many times on our ancient friendship and for his faith in my
work, which helped me through many moments of doubt; and Barbara
Rosecrance, who got down on the semantic mat with me and wrestled
with meaning and substance, page by page, as well as form. And to
Nancy McWilliams I owe a debt—one among many—for proving
the interdependence of sorority and fraternity and for refuting all
misogynists by demonstrating that a man's wife can stand in the first
rank of his friends and brethren.

W.C.M.

ABBREVIATIONS

For brevity and convenience, I have abbreviated the names of publications repeatedly cited here. The abbreviations employed are:

AA	American Anthropologist
AJP	American Journal of Psychoanalysis
AJS	American Journal of Sociology
AL	American Literature
AM	Atlantic Monthly
APSR	American Political Science Review
AQ	Anthropological Quarterly
AR	Antioch Review
AS	American Scholar
ASR	American Sociological Review
CHAL	Cambridge History of American Literature (New York: Macmillan, 1946)
CR	Centennial Review
ESS	Encyclopedia of the Social Sciences (New York: Macmillan, 1931)
HR	Human Relations
IJP	International Journal of Psychoanalysis
JAH	Journal of American History
JAI	Journal of the Anthropological Institute
JAP	Journal of American Psychoanalysis
JASP	Journal of Abnormal and Social Psychology
JEH	Journal of Economic History
JNH	Journal of Negro History
JP	Journal of Politics
JPE	Journal of Political Economy
JSH	Journal of Southern History
JSI	Journal of Social Issues
JSS	Journal of Social Science
MJPS	Midwest Journal of Political Science
MLQ	Modern Language Quarterly
MTJ	Mark Twain Journal

MVHR	Mississippi Valley Historical Review
NAR	North American Review
NEQ	New England Quarterly
P	Psychiatry
Phil.R.	Philosophical Review
POQ	Public Opinion Quarterly
PPR	Psychoanalysis and Psychoanalytic Review
PQ	Philological Quarterly
PR	Partisan Review
Psy.R.	Psychological Review
PSQ	Political Science Quarterly
QJE	Quarterly Journal of Economics
RP	Review of Politics
SAQ	South Atlantic Quarterly
SF	Social Forces
SP	Studies in Philology
SR	Social Research
USDR	United States Democratic Review
VQ	Virginia Quarterly
WMQ	William and Mary Quarterly
WPQ	Western Political Quarterly
YR	Yale Review

INTRODUCTION

THE terms of kinship are written on the gates which guard the mysteries of politics. Modern analysts, content to hawk their wares outside those gates, have assured us that not kin, but the group, is the basis of politics. The existence of a group, however, depends on some sense of being alike, of being "akin." Knowledge of the nature of kinship must logically precede knowledge of the nature of groups, for the sense of kinship is prior both in time and in what the ancients called the "order of nature." Our strongest descriptions of relations between men are analogies to kinship, as when an older benefactor is described as "like a father," or two inseparables as "like brothers." When human relations have meaning to men, we judge them to be at least akin to kinship.

Kinship does more than describe group feeling. It introduces men to hierarchy, authority, and command. The terms of kinship are characterized by implied obligation and subtle gradation, and modern theorists reaffirm that the child's image of authority is shaped in the family.[1] When political theorists seek to account for the origin of political authority and institutions, they are driven back to the nature of kinship. Locke's theory, so important to America, begins with a dissent from Filmer on the nature of patriarchal authority. Among moderns, Freud's Ur-father and De Jouvenel's elders are part of a tradition of thought as old as Romulus and Remus or Israel and his sons. Even Plato, who scorned such historical ventures, introduces Socrates in the *Euthyphro*, a dialogue which centers on the duties men owe to their fathers and to the gods.[2]

Of all the terms of kinship, none has had so enduring an appeal and so firm a place in political symbolism as fraternity. Fraternity is a cry that survives the ages. Men speak in the tongues of Babel, but fraternity sounds sweet to their ears. The Hebrew prophet astonished by God's glory, and the eighteenth-century philosopher who sought

[1] F. I. Greenstein, "The Benevolent Leader: Children's Images of Political Authority," *APSR*, LIV (1960), pp. 934–943.

[2] For a discussion of the *Euthyphro*, see Romano Guardini, *The Death of Socrates* (New York: Meridian Books, 1962).

to slay Him, the medieval knight and the small-town businessman, Martin Luther King and the Dragon of the Klan—all have spoken of fraternity as high, if not highest, among the relations of men. Liberty and equality, honor and obligation: fraternity forms an easy combination with all terms and has a place in the vocabulary of political aspiration, whether ancient or modern. The dream of the revolutionary and the bastion of the reactionary, it is a word to conjure with at all times and by all fires. It may in fact be a proof of human kinship that all men find a need to claim the word as a talisman.

Yet the perenniality of the word must raise doubts in the mind of any concerned with its meaning. Men and gods are like Proteus, changing their appearance and remaining the same. But a word which does not change, like an old law in new times, may change its meaning: science may come to mean what men once meant by religion, freedom may mean rank, and the rhetoric of classlessness may give birth to class hierarchy. The word's form becomes a limiting ritual; by refusing to be Protean it becomes Procrustean, forcing men and relationships into the mold of the word, at whatever violence to meaning or to themselves.

Such doubt has a strong foundation when dealing with fraternity. The problem is made still more difficult by the circumstance that definitions of brotherhood and studies of fraternity are almost entirely lacking. The dictionary proceeds like a rudderless ship, in ever-widening circularity: "Fraternity: a relation of brotherhood, the status of being a brother, an organization based on fraternal relations between members." Nor is the definition of "brother" more helpful. We begin clearly enough, with a reference to the male offspring of one's parents. That clarity is immediately dispelled by a transitive verb, "to brother," surely difficult enough genetically. What characterizes the relation of brothers made and brothers born that makes them alike, gives them their quality?

The dictionary replies that it is an "exceptionally close" relation, but even in this day of operational definitions, social scientists may balk at calling a husband and wife "brothers," though their relationship is surely "exceptionally close." What among the unusually close relations of men characterizes fraternity? On this the dictionary maintains an oracular silence.[3]

[3] *Funk and Wagnalls Standard College Dictionary* (Chicago: Willcox and Follett, 1943).

It is of course not the task of dictionaries to define philosophic and political ideals and concepts. Intellectual historians, though, have done little better. Kingsley Martin's *French Liberal Thought in the Eighteenth Century*[4] refers to fraternity in its first chapter, as any work dealing with the creed of 1789 must. The terms discussed throughout the book, however, are liberty and equality, not fraternity —and in this respect Martin is typical.

Social and psychological scientists are no great improvement, and here it is more astonishing. Freudian analysts have expended almost all their attention on the relations of parents and children; sibling relations have been approached as a secondary question and discussed only in relation to childhood, when they are dealt with at all.[5] American group theorists have made no study of fraternal orders, despite the fact that, until the beginning of this century, fraternal orders were the groups with which Americans were most familiar. The *Encyclopedia of the Social Sciences* (1931 ed.) contains an essay on fraternal insurance and another on fraternization as a technique of warfare (perhaps the best single commentary on modern images of politics). Beyond that, fraternity surfaces in odd corners like a paragraph of Simmel's, a chapter in a work of popular ideology by T. V. Smith,[6] and an essay in an encyclopedia of religion which concerns itself largely with fraternal rituals.[7]

Recently, Lionel Tiger's *Men in Groups*[8] has provided something of a new departure. Tiger's speculative bio-anthropology, however, is concerned with precisely the question implied by the title— the solidarity of male groups generally. Though obviously this is a question intimately related to fraternity, it does not deal with the specific qualities of fraternity as a relationship. It may provide a

[4] New York: Harper and Row, 1956.
[5] D. P. Irish, "Sibling Interaction: A Neglected Aspect of Family Life Research," *SF*, 42 (1964), pp. 279–282.
[6] *The Sociology of Georg Simmel*, ed. Kurt Wolff (Glencoe: Free Press, 1951), pp. 423–424; T. V. Smith and E. C. Lindeman, *The Democratic Way of Life* (New York: New American Library, 1951). A rather specialized exception to the rule is Benjamin Nelson, *The Law of Usury: from Tribal Brotherhood to Universal Otherhood* (Princeton: Princeton University Press, 1949).
[7] A work not relevant to my purpose, because its concern is with the "theory of organization" rather than fraternity or politics, is William A. Scott, *Values and Organizations: A Study of Fraternities and Sororities* (Chicago: Rand McNally, 1965).
[8] New York: Random House, 1969.

foundation, but it does not complete the structure. And there are ambiguities in even that analysis; Tiger traces male solidarity to the needs of the hunt, and is it accidental that the huntsman's deity in Greece was a woman—and a virgin at that? Or that the Hebraic symbol of the hunter, Nimrod, is a patriarchal figure? The hunt is a mystery, a suggestion of incompleteness, not an answer—and especially not for those who would know the meaning of fraternity.

There are no other anchor points for an analysis of the idea of fraternity. Ironically, this is partly the fault of the eighteenth-century theorists who most stridently raised fraternity as a political battlecry. Whatever their motives, their theories were expressed in the individualistic terms of natural right and the "state of nature." To allow kinship terms to enter the discussion would have been to bind "natural man" in a network of social relations. Paternity implies antecedent relations with a woman, present relations with children; fraternity implies relations with brothers presently and parents antecedently. Such terms suggest the "natural sociability" which medieval thought had derived from the empiricism of Aristotle and from the classicists generally. Many social-contract theorists, following the example of Hobbes, devoted themselves to stripping away the mantle of authority that had garbed parents, equating paternal and "despotical" power.

Despite this hostility to ideas of kinship, the eighteenth-century devotees of contractarian theory did appeal to that one significant kinship term, fraternity. It has been argued that they did so because fraternity "implies equality." All kinship terms, however, imply equality within the class of relations involved; all fathers are equal in being fathers, and grandfathers are "grand" only in relation to their children's sons, not to each other. Parental terms do suggest superiority to children outside the class, but for that very reason fraternity implies, not "equality," but common inferiority and obligation to parents. The single kinship term which suggests liberty and equality had already been discovered by the kin-conscious monarchs of Europe: the term is "cousin." All cousins are equal, and none share parents, which leaves each cousin "free" in relation to every other.

The creed of liberty, equality, and fraternity is intelligible only in relation to the idea of a Creator, a Divine "father" who established fraternity among men. Fraternity would emerge when liberty and equality could in some final sense dissolve the lesser fatherhoods and fraternities of men. The men of 1789 were not so blind as to believe that men held fraternal sentiments for all their fellows. They did not appeal to fraternity as a fact or as a method, but as an *end* in the relations of men; liberty and equality were only means. Without all the faith of those who founded the creed, T. V. Smith still called fraternity "the first objective, ethically . . . of the democratic way of life." [9]

The eighteenth-century doctrine can be regarded in many ways. Some have seen in it a moral passion to realize the universal fraternal standards of Christianity in this world rather than the next. With equal force, others have seen it as a nostalgia for, and an effort to recapture, a warmth and social stability which have been increasingly sensed as lost with the advent of modernity. Yet the success or failure of either attempt, and the truth of the creed, depended on the degree to which the theorists who developed the doctrine understood human nature and the character of fraternal relations among men.

A part of the argument in this book is designed to show that the liberal Enlightenment understood men imperfectly at best, and fraternal relations among men little or not at all. Given that misunderstanding, their zeal for fraternity did at least as much to weaken brotherhood as it did to strengthen it. And it is also my purpose to argue that the liberal tradition of the eighteenth century accounts for only a small part of the yearning for fraternity to be found in the history and letters of America.

In more than one sense, my assumptions are "reactionary," for the definition of fraternity that I seek is an essentialistic one. That is, I presume that there is a nature of man, and consequently a nature of fraternity. Fashionable philosophic thought in our times prefers "nature" in quotation marks, for it tends to follow the quest for ultimate particles which requires the dissolving of nature, probing that subatomic chaos which Plato suspected was beneath physical things.

At least, however, fraternity is an organic and not a physical term, belonging to social science because fraternity presumes society.

---

[9] Smith and Lindeman, p. 33. Smith also calls fraternity the "brightest" of the three ideals of 1789 (p. 19). Compare Smith and Lindeman with John H. Schaar, *Escape from Authority* (New York: Basic Books, 1961), p. 11, and James Fitzjames Stephen, *Liberty, Equality, Fraternity* (London and New York: Holt and Williams, 1875), pp. 256–310.

Equality and liberty have their analogues in physical science, but fraternity does not. Gasses may be free; they cannot be fraternal. Any analysis of the relations between human beings must take into account the primary fact of human, if not of organic, life: the consciousness itself.

An additional school of modern philosophers, the Existentialists, beginning with that consciousness, have regarded it as an ultimate, a psychological monad separated from all other things. This too denies that man and his relations have a nature, order, and form. Man, to this school, is he who imposes order on the chaos of the world by choice and will. Existence, their dictum asserts, is prior to essence, which is "made" by man.

It is a touching faith, and one must sympathize with it. It is an attempt to deny the most painful, most evident, lesson of the times. Man is permeable, not a fortress of adamant; the consciousness is malleable within limits, thought is always subject to control. Inalienable rights have proved only too alienable, and today no social scientist would argue, as did so many following Spinoza, that the mind, unlike the body, cannot be chained.

Analytic and Existential philosophies share a common aim, if not a strategy. Both seek man's conquest of nature, his emancipation from and lordship over the world of physical things, and deny his status as a part of nature. Both descend from the once unified battalions of the eighteenth century. Analytic philosophy retains the ancient élan, the belief in *offensif à l'outrance* against nature, with the objective of breaking it up, reducing it to matter in motion subject to man's control. Existentialism fears that the foe is mightier than was believed, and wisely realizes that control of nature by man threatens man with control by man. It seeks, therefore, to fortify the spirit of the individual against that assault, asserting—because it hopes to make it so— that the consciousness is impregnable.

The military metaphor is intentional. Existentialism grew up among the generation of 1916, who learned in the trenches around Verdun to discard the high optimism of individualism and progress. It is appealing in a time in which only entrenchments seem safe amid the forces let loose by the modern world; but that semblance, tempting though it may be, should have perished in 1940. There is no safe place in our world.

Both Existential and Analytic schools, however, continue to contend that nature is a foe, an enemy separable from man. The quotations around "nature" are the writer's tools of attack, but the conception of humanity is excluded from the assault. The dominant usage refers to human "nature," not "human nature," and "human" nature is unheard of and unwritten.

Two facts encourage those who would brave the two great falanges of the army of modern philosophy. First, the portents of man's "conquest" of nature are increasingly grim;[10] second, the research of some social scientists begins to suggest that results may be obtained by assuming once again, as the classics did, that man is a part of nature and that human nature is a fact which affects the life of men. Nor is "nature" restricted, as so much modern thought would have it, to biology and the mechanics of inheritance; and "nurture" is not separate from, but a part of, the nature of man.[11] May it not then be possible to consider a nature of the relations of men, a nature of fraternity, even a natural law?

The question is not its own answer. It only implies, for those willing to ask, that it may be fruitful to begin at the beginning, to examine fraternity as it was seen by those who believed it to have a nature because they felt it as an immediate thing. When we have examined fraternity from that traditional perspective, that perspective in turn may be examined in terms of our own observations. And finally, it will then become possible to trace the labyrinthine path of fraternity as an idea in the life of America.

All these examinations have convinced me that the ancients were right in seeing fraternity as a means to the ends of freedom and equality; and correspondingly, that the modern theorists who reversed this relationship were guilty of a serious error. I will argue that fraternity:

1. Is a bond based on intense interpersonal affection, and,
2. Like all such bonds, is limited in the number of persons and in the social space to which it can be extended; that it
3. Also involves shared values or goals considered more important than "mere life," and

[10] Konrad Lorenz, "On the Virtue of Humility," in *On Aggression* (New York: Harcourt, Brace, 1966), pp. 220–235.
[11] Tiger, *Men in Groups*, pp. 1–17; James C. Davies, *Human Nature in Politics* (New York: Wiley, 1963).

4. Is closely related to the development of "ego identity," since it

5. Includes a recognition of shortcomings and failure in the attainment of ultimate values, but

6. Provides the emotional encouragement and sense of worth ("assurance of identity") which make it possible to endure such tensions without betraying one's own values, and finally,

7. Implies a necessary tension with loyalty to society at large.

This is, of course, to anticipate. Worse, it forces a rigid structure on a relationship which is always a rich fabric woven of states and clans, times and places, dreams and despairs. My argument may seem tortuous; it is, I would claim, necessarily so. But perhaps it is justification enough that, however tangled, the path of the argument is my own. And ". . . when I shall have set down my own reading orderly and perspicuously, the pains left another will only be to consider if he also find not the same in himself. For this kind of doctrine admits no other demonstration." [12]

[12] Thomas Hobbes, *Leviathan*, ed. C. B. Macpherson (Baltimore: Penguin, 1968), p. 83.

> And Cain talked with his brother Abel, and it came to pass, when they were in the field, that Cain rose up against Abel and slew him. And the Lord said to Cain, Where is Abel thy brother? And he said, I know not. Am I my brother's keeper? And he said, What hast thou done? Thy brother's blood cries to me from the ground. And now thou art cursed from the earth.
>
> *Genesis* 4:8–11

CHAPTER I

CLAN, TRIBE, AND CITY

Between Worlds

THE study of fraternity involves the study of kinship; and in both, modern men are at a disadvantage. All of us know something of physics and finance, but for most of us kinship is a kind of "given" which deserves and receives little conscious thought and reflection. The majority of our kinsmen affect us only mildly; kinship obligations are probably best described as a moderate nuisance. And while our intimate families do concern us deeply, they are thought of as peripheral to the "important issues" of the day. The women's liberation movement, for example, concerned as it is with the nature and structure of the family, aims largely at freeing woman for a role in the "real" world. Correspondingly, most of our thought about kinship is at best primitive and undeveloped. Communes and collectives are experiments in a new science, quite as unsophisticated as were the then new natural sciences of the sixteenth and seventeenth centuries. Those who hope for fraternity in society are probing into what amounts to unknown territory.

It was not always so. The unimportance of kinship, perhaps more than any other factor, distinguishes modern societies from those social orders which social scientists often class together as "pre-modern." In those traditional societies (and the term "traditional" is both less pejorative and closer to the fact), the individual is almost defined by his kindred, and his personal virtue is assessed largely in terms of his fulfillment of kinship roles and duties. "Merit," in modern societies, tends to be defined in terms of the ability to manipulate things and men; in traditional societies, it was more likely to imply standing in a "right relation" to them.

It is not necessary to romanticize traditional societies to accept this difference. Human beings in traditional orders have desires for power and dominance and are often manipulative in their relationships. But the existence of the ideal of "right relations" affected practice, however often it was violated. In ancient Israel, it was considered a moral obligation to release one's brothers from debt during the Sabbatarian year, and those who did not (they were many) were considered, and considered themselves, sinners; in modern America, anyone who forgave his debtors every seven years would certainly be a deviant and would probably be suspected of some mental defect. (Marc Swartz found that the Trukese, otherwise admiring, were shocked at the lack of a sense of fraternal obligation among Americans.)[1]

Kinship always implies limitations on the individual. To establish that he has "relations" with others is, once those relations have been defined, to fix his place, his social locale. Discerning those persons who are like the individual, we divide him from those he is not like; the boundary of comparative dissimilarity separates kindred from the outside world. It was logical, then, for modern political theorists, with their emphasis on liberty and universality, to deprecate the claims of kinship. Modern kinship has been reduced to the minimal, if ineradicable, claims of heredity on the individual; "relations" are defined by the genes, and kinship is automatic and purely physical.

Traditional societies have thought otherwise, and it is with that thought that I am concerned here. Of course, ancient and traditional ideas reveal all the diversity of human thought generally, and in seek-

[1] Marc Swartz, "Negative Ethnocentrism," *JCR*, V (1961), p. 79.

ing the general pattern of such ideas I am bound to offend the eth-nologist, who will find what follows too abstract and neglectful of exceptions. It is undeniably presumptuous for an outsider to claim, however tentatively, to have fathomed the thought of very different peoples and cultures. Nevertheless, there is a unity of theme in tradi-tional ideas of kinship, and the claim to have discerned it seems less arrogant than referring such ideas to an undecipherable, qualitatively different "primitive mind." In any case, to learn from traditional so-cieties we must be abstract; unlike the citizens of such polities, we cannot learn their wisdom through experience. And in a sense, ab-straction is appropriate to traditional ideas themselves, for kinship and fraternity were much more ideational in traditional thought than they are in modern imagining.

Traditional ideas of kinship were more expansive than ours. The limits they imposed on the individual were greater, as were the claims they allowed him to make on others. At the same time, kinship was defined less automatically than it is among us. While "blood descent" played a vital role, it was never absolutely definitive. The numerous exceptions to "biological kinship" found in traditional societies cannot be explained away in terms of imperfect ideas of biological and pro-creative processes (though such defective knowledge sometimes played a role). Initiation into adulthood, for example, did not always correspond to physical puberty. And adoption was an almost universal practice, inexplicable in "blood" terms. Recent research indicates that traditional kinship is never without an element of choice; the individ-ual is potentially a member of several kindred, and actual membership depends on the fulfillment of certain key roles and obligations.

Traditional ideas of kinship were definitions of relationships among men. One modern analyst even finds the fault of those ideas to be a confusion of "relations" and "relationship"; semantically, the error would seem to lie with modernity. If modern men lack "rela-tionship" with their "relations," it reflects not only the declining role of families, but the reduction of family to blood-kinship.[2]

The myth of blood-kinship was powerful in traditional society

[2] Crawley, *The Mystic Rose* (1927), vol. II, pp. 62, 179–180, 221; see also Hamilton-Grierson, "Brotherhood: Artificial," in *Encyclopedia of Religion and Ethics*, p. 857. (Discussion of sources, with publication data, can be found in the Bibliographic Notes at the end of this volume.)

because of a simple logical fallacy: the association of ideas. Traditional thought was heavily empirical, inclined to materialistic explanation even when it spoke of "supernatural" things, and the peril of empiricists has always been association. When so many vital functions, especially the care and rearing of children, are vested in procreative groups, the idea that there is some "natural" connection between the two may become overpowering. The performance of function, however, ultimately defined kin.

The meaning of "function" can only be established extrinsically. Activities are "functional" insofar as they further goals or values deemed to be desirable. To the extent that kinship depends on function, it depends on common values; indeed, it consists in the fact that some men share values, outlooks, and ideas of responsibility which others do not.

As parents have always been symbols of authority, so they have been regarded by most as the incarnation of differing values, symbols of the needs of the individual and the community. Maternal authority seems universally associated with warmth, affection, and sensory gratification. Maternal insight is conceived to be Epimethean, associated with the lore of the past and with the projection of the past into the future; cycle is the time-metaphysic of the Earth Mother. In her association with birth and nurture, the mother symbolizes those qualities required for a continuous, ongoing society; her mysteries are necessary if the community is to have a life beyond that of its immediate members.

Paternal authority represents quite different things: the abstract as opposed to the immediate, the uncertain rather than the familiar. Paternity is Promethean, foreseeing, restrictive of immediate desires which the Mother might well gratify, mindful of the dangers of change and chance. Obviously related, and possibly rooted in the needs of the huntsman, the symbols go further: two figures from the Hamangia culture show a woman holding her pregnant belly, the man touching his head—where one supposes he, like Zeus, has his place of conception.[3] Death, the great abstraction, at odds with birth, the empirical fact, has also been associated with paternity: the Mother

[3] Clark and Piggott, *Prehistoric Societies*, plate V, p. 186.

gives, the Father takes away. If maternal authority is derived from functions inside the community, paternal authority derives from what is outside or transcends it, convicting maternal lore of ignorance and its experience of parochiality.

The use of these symbols need not involve a belief in differing psychological attributes of the sexes. Doubtless some such differences do exist, though probably only as end points on a continuum. Actually, traditional societies reveal, in many rites and myths, a desire to create a social barrier against the temptations of the role accorded to the opposite sex, and taboo and envy—even envy of the ineluctable physical qualities of the other sex—are marks of likeness and attraction rather than of difference. In at least one traditional society, the onset of female maturity is viewed as a divine affliction, setting women of child-bearing years apart from the "natural," sexually undifferentiated state of humanity to which old women eventually return.

Those rites and tales, however, also reveal that whatever psychological differences exist between the sexes are reinforced by the needs of society. The different physical characteristics of the sexes seem—until *Brave New World*, at least—to demand some difference in social role, and where technology plays a small role, physical powers must play a large one in the division of labor. Modern societies reduce the difference between the sexes (it would even be possible to argue that a high propensity for "male bonding" now has a negative survival value); traditional societies strengthen it at almost every point.

Sexual solidarity helps, in fact, to decrease the social importance of sexuality. Sexual gratification is self-referential and isolating, and its logical tendency is to create isolated procreative groups or sporadic unions for immediate gratification. The solidarity of sex overcomes that tendency to some degree and serves as a bond which crosses the lines of clan and descent.

More important, perhaps, is the fact that sexual solidarity supports the social system of authority. Age implies authority because, in a society which changes little and which lacks the wisdom of written records, knowledge is based on experience. Yet, no less than in our times, the young outgrow the physical basis of subordination. That, in part, underlies the terrible fear of the young—to some degree, probably, a projection of past guilt—which is the basis of so much rite and precept. ("Honor thy father and mother, that thy days may be long on the face of the earth.")[4]

Since young men and women who share common tasks and intense interaction develop common attitudes and interests, the solidarity of the age-set is a constant threat to the authority of the older members of each sex. Nor does this solidarity occur only within sexual groups. The fact that sisters are subjected to special and extraordinary taboos, and the degree to which strong brother-sister ties are socially acknowledged, alike testify to the bond created by subordination to similar authority. Sexual solidarity creates a likeness between persons otherwise separated by barriers of age, command, and authority, a hierarchical rather than horizontal pattern of communication and community. Encouraging the subordination of young to old, the bond between members of the same sex also renders elders less anxious about the ascent of the young, making the old teachers rather than antagonists. This solidarity of sex helps assure a smooth transition from child to elder and maintains the subordination to authority.

In an important sense, the initiate, the young man who has entered into the exercise of male functions and of authority, is in a fraternal relation with his father. Before authority can be transferred, it must be recognized that it can be conferred; the child must learn that it resides in knowledge and the ability to perform functions rather than in the person of the father. Authority always implies an association of ideal values with a particular person supposed to possess them, or knowledge about them, in unusual degree. For men to assume authority, or for those possessing it to yield part of their sway, that association must be broken down. The authority of the "male principle" must be raised above both father and son. In this sense, they cease to be father and son and become sons of the same parent, subject to the same higher authority, and hence brothers.

The role and the mysteries of woman, and thus the authority and status of the mother, have a solid empirical foundation. The chief mystery of the mother is the incarnate fact of birth; she gives physical proof of her connection with the forces of life and continuity. (And if more proof is needed, the menstrual cycle suggests a relation to the

---

[4] *Exodus* 20:12.

phases of the moon.) Too, maternal authority is rigidly and exclusively feminine; women can perform male tasks and roles, but no man can learn to perform the mystery of conception and giving birth. Even when men discover their contribution to that mystery, the discovery is based on abstract reasoning which connects unlike events separated in time. The male role in procreation remains external, quasi-theoretical, and partly unsatisfying. (Why else did men feel obliged to assert the "homunculus" theory, which deprecated the role of women altogether?)

The male functions are far less certain, dealing with what is outside the expectations and normal order of the community, distinct from the predictable cycle of nature. Man's "estate" is filled with things which defy and threaten internal order—enemies, unexpected events, unknown powers and forces. The ability to perform such functions cannot be taught in any complete sense. A "teaching" could only be based on a set of maxims which, taken as rules, would incapacitate the male in the face of man's dilemmas, which are his precisely because they are outside the sphere of proverbial wisdom.

Male mystery, the esoteric knowledge of the father, is founded not on knowledge but on knowledge of ignorance. Custom and conventional wisdom provide no safe rules for dealing with the unknown or the unexpected. A girl, becoming a woman, learns or grows into the ability to do what her mother does in her public role. To become a man, a boy must learn what his father does not know; he must remove the public mask of certainty that hides the male secret. Male authority is fragile, and its maintenance demands solidarity among men.

That authority is delicate in still another sense: the very functions it claims, the virtues it avows, enhance the danger of division among men. Feminine functions admit of passivity and dependence; society and subordination are written into them. "Masculinity," by contrast, stresses activity, strength, ascetic resistance to pain, and the ability to act outside the comfort and security of society. The male virtues all imply independence and self-sufficiency as an ideal. Men are always tempted by the fraud of claiming to embody that ideal, as women in all ages have known. Passivity and defenseless admiration are the traditional weapons of woman's arsenal, softly beguiling the vanity of men until they will fight for her favor. The solidarity of men, as well as the knowledge of ignorance that is the mark of adult maleness, requires the recognition of imperfection in "masculinity."

Men and women alike are part of the feminine sphere, part of the community and its life, as all men are "born of woman." Only some persons, and only some men, become part of the male sphere. As a man is always part of two worlds, so there is always ambiguity in his loyalty to maleness. (Obviously women are also ambiguously "feminine," but the tension is less marked in traditional societies.) Practice asceticism though he may, man will always have physical needs and weaknesses; wise though he may become, he will not know the law and logic of all that is "outside" the community. Men are "called out" of the community in which they are born, yet remain bound to it, unable to be fully at home in either realm.

Fraternal solidarity has often been associated with matrilineal societies. Here the importance of the father declines; brothers are the closest male relations (a genetic truth, of course), and male authority is vested in the brother of one's mother. Males also share a certain rough equality in being set outside the organizing principle of society; the critical features of a man's life are established by his feminine connections. (Men reside, for example, with their wives' kindred.) However, if fraternity is the most important relation between men in such communities, it is never man's most important relation: that relation is always with his mother, his sister and, to a lesser degree, with his wife.

Patrilineal societies, though they elevate the importance of relations with men, tend to create struggle and competition for paternal status, the effort of each son to obtain the undivided authority of the father, whether by winning his blessing or by slaying him. Sons may, as Freud pictured them doing in *Totem and Taboo*, combine against the father, but such unity is the temporary cooperation of an alliance which vanishes with the destruction of the "enemy." Hostility between brothers, based on the desire for undivided authority and independence, is the logical rule (one which is carried to an extreme, as ancient Israel knew, in polygamous societies, where competition between mothers is an added and reinforcing consideration). Society tends to develop in the direction of independent clans and male households, even where peaceful succession is the rule—the eldest son often succeeds the father, while his younger brothers set out to establish households of their own.

Fraternal solidarity in patrilineal societies, Freud argued, must be based in part on guilt; having idealized the father, sons feel remorse for his murder and need their brothers as sharers of the burden and sources of encouragement and affection. Patricides discover, to put it another way, that the death (and even the devouring) of the father does not confer on them the "male" attributes of knowledge about and power over the forces outside a community which they imagined the father to possess. It matters little whether they believe that the father actually had these powers (and hence, dread possibility, may have survived death in some form) or whether they realize that he, too, was imperfect in knowledge and control; the resulting guilt is much the same.[5]

A society may seek to protect the father and his authority by surrounding him with taboos which make competition for his favor and status impossible, although they also make his authority irrelevant for much of day-to-day life. In such a society, as Firth found among the Tipokia, the relations of brothers are necessarily close and no brother enjoys authority over another.[6] Brothers are thrown back on one another as the only guides and sources of encouragement in a problematic world. In one sense, this only postpones the dilemma of entrance into authority. In another, it emphasizes that perceived distance from authority, imperfection in relation to it, is necessary to fraternity.

At the same time, some tie to authority is necessary. Authority which has no applicability to human life or is so distinct as to be incomprehensible would make no claims on us. Guilt comes only from the conviction that we ought to have acted differently; sin is conceivable only if we have some understanding, however dim, of what is righteous. Maleness, the physical fact, may obscure many of the qualities of "maleness" as a social and psychological principle, but it does provide a tenuous sense of connection between men and the "male knowledge" they know to be important but which they do not possess in full.

[5] Freud, *Totem and Taboo*, pp. 927–930.
[6] Raymond Firth, *We, the Tipokia* (London: Allen and Unwin, 1936), pp. 165–166, 384.

A brother is, however, not simply one who shares a father: in the most absolute sense, he is one who shares a mother as well (*brüder* once implied one of the brood, a product of the same litter or womb). To be fully one's brother, he must share ties to feminine things—to affection, to gratification, to welfare, and to community. A brother is in this sense the only person who shares both the authorities to which men are subject, flesh and spirit, birth and death, community and the outer world. Of all human relationships, fraternity is the most premised on imperfection, the most fraught with ambiguity, the least subject to guidance by fixed rules, the most dependent on choice. All of these qualities make fraternity difficult; they also make it true to the nature of humankind. Traditional societies may have associated fraternity with men, but the appeal of sorority is no less. With all its difficulties, fraternity is vital for anyone who would find himself and who knows that no one can do so alone.

Souls and Secrets

For traditional societies, kinship depended on social relations; this made it possible to create kindred by instituting the proper relationship. Fraternity was thought to be especially susceptible to creation by conscious decision and covenant—hence the plethora of fraternal rites in traditional society. The public and semi-public character of such rituals makes them available for investigation and illuminates much of the traditional idea of fraternity.

All intimate relationships are dangerous. A man bares his soul, revealing his affection and admiration for another; he thereby subjects himself to the risk that his fellow will prove false and will use these acknowledged weaknesses against him. Too, a sincere but weak fidelity may be undermined by conflicting loyalties. These perils, characteristic of all intense relations, will seem greater to those trained to play the traditional masculine role with its emphasis on independence and the corresponding fear of acknowledging the "feminine" side of a man's nature. (James Baldwin's description of the "male prison" is much in point.)[7] That anxiety, moreover, is only one of the problems which beset those who would enter a fraternal covenant.

[7] *Nobody Knows My Name* (New York: Dell, 1961), pp. 125–130.

The rule of reciprocity, which mitigates such dangers, is subject to peculiar difficulties when the parties are on the same status level. Between levels of a hierarchy, complementarity is the rule; the exalted receive deference and extend protection. Within a level, each party must be simultaneously protector and protegé; for the relationship to be reciprocal, each must have strength and acknowledge weakness. Neither ego-gratification nor security is unambiguously available; each must be dependent and responsible.

The "likeness" of a friend or brother, his similarity of status, thus only makes relations with him more difficult. There is no danger in the weak, and there is no defense against the strong, but a brother is a danger against whom I may be able to defend myself and whom I have no assurance of defeating. The barriers of defense must come down at the same time, otherwise there is no fraternity. For one to capitulate to the other is to change the relationship to that of superior and inferior, for neither to capitulate is to leave both in isolation; and a friend who has not acknowledged his concern is "taboo" in more than one society. Nietzsche spoke to the point: "Canst thou go nigh unto thy friend and not go *over* to him?" [8]

Traditional societies generally sought to solve the problem by an "exchange of identities." Reciprocal covenants provided for an exchange of names, of wives, of kindred; commensality gave men a common substance, clothing gave them a similar appearance. Brothers-to-be exchanged things that might divide them in terms of the continuous community and its concern for life. All of those things to which the body is tied by physical need (food, sexuality, clothing) and by which a man is known to others (his name and kindred) might be interchanged. By such sharing, a new relation would be created; only one's covenanted brother might share all of one's kin. Even if it acknowledges the bond, the family to which a man is born shares none of his acquired kin save for his new brother. The fraternal relation is distinct from, yet encompasses, both kindreds. It is an "overlapping" bond in which unambiguous loyalty is owed only to one's sworn brother.

This, however, hardly eliminates the threat of injury: it expands

[8] *Thus Spake Zarathustra*, trans. Thomas Common, in *The Philosophy of Nietzsche* (New York: Modern Library, 1954), pp. 57-59.

that danger by taking another and his kindred into the self. "Any man's death diminishes me," Donne wrote, and the expansion of concern implied by fraternity creates the same problem on a smaller scale, laying the self open to new grief and labor.

Moreover, the individual faces the threat of painful ambiguities which are the source of a perennial drama: if my brother's kindred divide from mine, shall I fight for his father or for my own? Saul turned to Jonathan with a violence that reveals the problem in all its difficulty: "Do I not know you have chosen the son of Jesse to the shame of your mother's nakedness?" [9] The words convey—as in part they conceal—the King's real anger. The choice of David might be tolerable were David loyal to Saul, but David is loyal to (or not at odds with) his father's house and disloyal to Saul; therefore, the King told his son, in choosing David you are choosing the House of Jesse in preference to that of Kish, preferring Jesse to me. The language and the meaning, if unjust, are certainly comprehensible.

Fraternity by covenant, even if it succeeds in creating the feeling that the things of birth and of the flesh have been made common, does not create identity; because it does not and cannot, it only increases the threat to the individual. Men run the risk that fraternity implies only because of a prior sense of greater goods to be gained or greater perils to be avoided by entering into fraternity. Understanding covenant fraternity depends on learning what Crawley called "the categorical imperative of primitive man," the first premise of the covenant and of the idea of fraternity itself. [10]

Men ran the risks inherent in covenant fraternity because that brotherhood was thought to be inseparable from the discovery of one's true self and the entry into man's estate. Man was thought to have a spirit that was in one sense "private," a soul tied to the body and its senses. The sensual, erotic nature of that soul, however, tempted it to attach itself to things in the external world, and because of this it was constantly in danger of falling into the hands of others. Human affection, for men or for things, carried with it anxiety; to be captivated risks being captured, and it often seemed prudent to fight or flee whatever was not safely private.

In societies where the fraternal imperative ran strong, however,

9 *I Samuel* 20:30.
10 Crawley, *The Mystic Rose* (1902), vol. I, p. 258.

the private soul was not man's only soul: it was only the soul of the body, the inheritance of flesh and blood. Man also was conceived to have a second soul, an "external" spirit (originating with gods, natural forces, or ideas) which lodged itself in or was given to particular men. Not restricted to the body, this soul could potentially be shared with others. But this "external soul" was in an important sense more personal than the soul of the body, partly because it could enable men to free themselves from the terrors and needs which enslave the flesh, especially the fear of pain and of death.

Ordeal was normally associated with the discovery of the "second soul," often including (as among the Omaha) a period of isolation. Physical ordeal proved man's ability to rise above pain and pleasure, but isolation reminded the individual of his loneliness and finitude, helping to humble the pride which passing the physical test might arouse. And the humbling of pride was critical to the design of the rites; they aimed at destroying the desire for, not merely the possibility of, individual self-sufficiency.

It was hoped that the climax of the ordeal would reveal his true self to the individual. This revelation might come in a vision in which the spirit manifested itself, like the totem animals of the American Indians. It made the individual a brother of those whose ordeals Alice Fletcher correctly referred to as based on "common right in a common vision." [11] While the soul thus revealed was shared, she went on to observe, it was emphatically more personal than the private soul. The private soul was inherited and bound the individual to all his blood-kin, while the vision-soul could not be inherited and had to be discovered by each individual. The ordeal of the Omaha parallels the general process of learning to dissociate blood and authority, to separate the father from the "male principle." Heretofore, the individual has thought in "female" terms, has associated authority with blood and person, as he has thought of self in the same terms. That has now changed, and he has become a brother of all those set under the same authority, who share a notion of what is most worthy of devotion, emulation, and obedience; indeed, it is sharing these ideas, and having an emotional as well as intellectual comprehension of them, which constitutes fraternity.

[11] For Alice Fletcher's findings, see *Annual Report of the Smithsonian Institution for 1897* (Washington, 1898), p. 582.

There remains the stubborn privateness of the fleshly soul, with its physical attachments and its clan kindred. The covenant ritual, consequently, seeks to conquer or subordinate that soul by reference to its weakness, the ease with which it may be enticed out of the body and lured into locating itself in physical things. Such a ritual aims at creating a community of interests and affections among those already presumed to share an identity of aims and essence. The risks seem minor if one already is of "one soul" with his brother.

The shared soul is the true self of man; yet, the rituals suggest, it is nothing automatically or invariably recognized by all men who share it. It must be voluntarily acknowledged and accepted because it goes beyond what is "necessary" in human life: the continuity of blood and community.

Covenant fraternity presumes a "true identity" which crosses the boundaries of blood, clan, and tribe, and there is no logical reason why the common vision or authority which unites brothers should not be universal. The private soul, however, is resolutely parochial, limited to the empirical environs of the self. Contact with the senses is needed to draw the private soul out into the world, where it becomes vulnerable. Traditional societies attributed to their rites a powerful efficacy, often contending that a rite once practiced made the individuals brothers forever, but they knew that face-to-face meeting is necessary before fraternity is possible. "Brothers-by-nature" whom we do not know are not brothers in any important human sense, for those who are brothers must share emotional bonds as well as spiritual community.

Fraternal ritual symbolizes a new birth, but it recognizes the priority of the old self in time. It presumes a surrounding network of relations, the community of birth and rearing. Brothers owe a debt to that community: without it, they would never reach the stage at which their true nature can be discerned, and would never know one another as brothers.

In an equally important sense, however, fraternity is a violation of that community, an acknowledgment of obligations which transcend it, an assertion that the identity it confers is false or at least lower in the scheme of things. Always in society, brothers are never again of it. The fact that fraternal ritual surrounded itself in secrecy and mystery suggests as much. Whether secrecy is a tool for power or a sacred truth not to be uttered before the profane, the secret presumes those from whom the secret is kept. It is based, as are "rites of passage" in general, on a separation between included and excluded.

Incorporated into a new community, the initiate brother is alienated from an older community. In fact, a recognition of values and truths higher than those of the old community is a prerequisite of initiation. "Becoming a brother," like becoming a man, is not something one grows into by the ordinary processes of a procreative community. It amounts rather to a revolution.

Almost universally, fraternal rituals involve a crime against custom and taboo. The most frequent, and one of the most enduring, is the "spilling of blood," sacred symbol of birth and clan continuity. Such acts may be gestures of contempt toward birth and maternity, a defiance of the goddess and her power. Yet they may also be efforts to remove the stain of Oedipus, to allay the fear of approaching sacred things (or resentment against them), and to replace this with a sense of bond, a positive reverence for holy things and the will to defend them against the profane.

In either case, the act of collective criminality has three elements: (1) it separates the violator from the community of "decent" men; (2) by demanding a risk of life and soul, by making each violator the hostage of the others, it demands that each put his devotion to the test; and (3) it does so symbolically, without asking or allowing the ultimate test which fraternity implies, the willingness to die for one's brother. Deferring that test, it makes possible the coexistence of fraternity and life, softening the revolutionary character of becoming a man by allowing the initiate to be strengthened by the support of his fellows before being put to the final proof of his devotion.

Rising above the norms and mores of the community makes the initiated, or a band of brothers, dangerous men. Freedom from the fear of sanctions which surrounded the old taboos tempts the individual to a life of unrestraint and shamelessness. Before the violator can be a "safe man," the control of the private soul must be assured; hence the insistence on the prior development of an external soul, which because it is a collective property subjects the individual to a new network of restraint. To many societies this seemed insufficient, and special elements of ritual were needed to guarantee the sincerity of new commitments and the passing of the private soul from control of the self.

Death is, in an important sense, the symbol of all the new values to which the individual must dedicate himself. It is the desolator of pride, the strongest taboo of the procreative community, the ultimate frustration of the private, erotic soul. Too, death suggests the unknown and uncertain and at the same time implies *telos*, a law of nature beyond the control of the community and of men. Death in the body easily comes to be associated with the birth of the external soul.

Of course, it is not necessary that the individual should die; for traditional rituals, it is enough if he believes he is about to die. (The element of inducing belief in events which do not actually happen only strengthens, in human ritual, what Lorenz calls "mimic exaggeration.")[12] The secret of the ritual of death and rebirth is among the most zealously guarded, lest its psychological effect be lost. (Eventually, of course, it is revealed, such being the fate of human secrets.) Submission to death is an acknowledgment, by one now intellectually as well as physically independent of the community, of a law and necessity inherent in nature. Willingness to die is a demonstrable triumph over the private soul, and a suggestion of reverence for the unknown, or eagerness to seek it.

Since the individual does not die, he does not enter the unknown, and the private soul, with its material needs, remains alive. In the companionship of his initiate brothers, the individual finds an "unambiguous moment" in which purpose and affection are one, and private and external souls, though not united, are at least fulfilled. Fraternal encouragement may lead the individual to run risks he would otherwise shun. Fraternal bonds both allow and increase the impact of reproof, which guards against pride and reminds each of his imperfection in relation to the ideal.

Politics and Fraternity

If Lionel Tiger's selection of politics as an example of the "male bond" was an obvious choice, the preceding discussion should make equally obvious the intimate, even integral, connection of fraternity

[12] For Lorenz's phrase, see *On Aggression*, p. 76.

and politics.[13] Politics, in the inescapable definition of Aristotle, presumes a separation between "life" and the "good life," between physical and ethical necessity, between custom and authority. It presupposes an idea of justice which rises above the law of blood and clan and is applicable to men of different clans. Rules can be applied in a like manner only to beings judged to be alike, and ethical likeness, being subject to the same moral standards, only strengthens the association of that likeness with kinship.

The social-contract theorists saw the political society as the result of a necessity deriving from threat, and threat doubtless played a role. Whatever the genesis of the idea of an abstract justice, its political relevance could develop only in the context of a generally recognized failure of traditional norms and prescriptions. The social contract theorists aside, however, human folly has confronted such situations as often as human wisdom; the same necessity and threat in different places and times does not always produce a political order. Persistent necessity might tend to produce a confederacy of separate clans, an alliance in the face of threat. As Freud knew, however, there is no basis for obligation and citizenship in an alliance; the primary obligation remains to one's blood-kin. In a confederacy produced by threat, kinship groups are only compelled, for the moment, to cooperate with others, and an alliance collapses whenever its ad hoc justification is removed.[14]

Political society does not exist where two or more clans, each with its own ways and customs, confront one another in moral exclusiveness, if not hostility. It demands more than the sense of shortcoming in traditional norms, more than the suspicion that none of the ways is truly according to nature. Political society requires a belief that there is a law and an authority common to all, whether or not it is precisely known. The idea of the *polis* is based on a law of higher standing than blood-right, one which logically involves a conception of unity in nature behind the multiplicity of appearance and experience. The separation of the "male principle" from blood descent becomes elevated to an explicit status in the construction of the state.

It is not necessary that the idea of justice precede the sense of

[13] Tiger, *Men in Groups*, pp. 60–80.
[14] Freud, *Totem and Taboo*, pp. 927–930.

fraternity among "citizens." In fact, it is more likely that the sense of likeness and kindred raises questions about the origin, the paternity, of this kinship. Covenant fraternity, when it crosses clan boundaries, works to create a political order, even if this is not its original aim. When private kinship obligations are exchanged, conflict between duties can be avoided only if all relevant blood-kindreds are made subject to a single law.

As with covenant fraternity, men in political society retain their ties to a community of birth. This is not simply the result of necessity; it reflects men's imperfect knowledge of justice and of the good life. All human rules and doctrines are uncertain, yet some rules continue to be needed; and custom and blood-right, though based on false premises, pass the pragmatic test as workable principles for a continuous society. Politics is always the art of exceptions. It seeks to know where custom must be violated, where human habits and institutions must be changed to guarantee the survival of what is most important, and where the ideal itself must be compromised or muted so that life itself may endure.

The dawn of political thought was a perception of the human condition as one suspended between two laws: a law of custom, which was in some important sense in error, and a true, natural law imperfectly grasped. Elevated above "mere life" by an intimation of the good, men were compelled to seek a resolution in the "good life," to translate that abstract, partly understood vision of goodness into the language of a world resistant to it. Bound to respect the lesser law on which life depends, men owed a new duty to another.

The Greeks, Plato commented, are wrong to imagine that because the Greek language contains words which draw distinctions between "Greek" and "barbarian," such distinctions are real. Similarly, Hesiod spoke of an evil spirit (Eris) which introduced conflict and competition between men. The gods' effort to remedy this by giving men a sense of justice was defective because justice remained only partly known, only partly able to deflect Eris, and only partly applicable to human affairs, where much depended on chance. Heraclitus, too, spoke of a conflict between the private world of the individual and the *logos* of nature, which men resisted and of which they knew little. Greek philosophy and much of Greek tradition presumed that men understood the limits of custom and of their own wisdom. Politics depended in part on intellectual desolation, the realization that no certain guides existed and that no man could claim final authority.[15] Greek theory was often explicitly fraternal in its descriptions of politics. The truth or godhead which men were to seek, but would never fully know, was a generator or creator, a "father" in the essential sense of "that which causes to be." The love of this "father" united friends; an ultimate love, it made lesser love possible. The love of the body was based on pleasure and profit, on the desire to be loved. Only by seeing imperfection in himself through a love of more exalted things could a man truly love others. The ultimate love was "similar to filial affection" but higher in status, as the "first cause" was more truly a father than the physical parent. The bond of friends united by such a vision thus resembled but was more excellent than the ordinary fraternity of men (though of course this higher fraternity, like all human things, would be imperfect).

It was in this sense that Aristotle could declare that most held fraternity to be the chief good of states, and Plato's Athenian could rebuke his Cretan companion for the neglect of brotherly affection in Crete's law. Whatever the *telos* of human life, the emotions came first in time and needed their own education and satisfactions if the mind was to be able to rule. Men's love of honor and their desire to be loved should be utilized by making love and honor dependent on the practice of virtue. Action did not create but awakened intention; to the extent that such associations could be created, the law of "mere life" was made to support and aid the search for the true and the good. Socrates' criticism of Callicles was that he reversed the process: he gave his hearers an appearance of knowledge and independence in order to receive their affection, and in him, as in so many of the young Athenians with whom Socrates spoke, the higher man was made prisoner by the lesser.[16]

[15] Plato, *Statesman*, 262d–263e, 273–276c; see also Jaeger, *Paideia*, vol. I, pp. 148, 181, 283, vol. II, pp. 197–198.
[16] Aristotle, *Politics*, ed. Barker, pp. 46–47. Aristotle criticizes Plato because, in his view, Plato has made the fraternity of the ideal state too feeble by failing to root it in emotion. This view is tenable only because Aristotle has already rejected Plato's effort to overcome this (pp. 44–45). The reference to Socrates and Callicles is from Plato's *Gorgias* (see especially 507a–508b). It is also useful to compare Aristotle's views in the *Ethics*, Bk. II, chs. 3–5, and Bk. III, chs. 5–8, with his comments in the *Politics*.

Men could not be taught the higher law and the higher love in any formal sense. Teaching presumes authority in the teacher, the association of authority and person; what is taught becomes doctrine to those who accept it, and a knowledge of ignorance is, as a doctrine, a simple contradiction. Moreover, a knowledge of the imperfection of earthly law and knowledge creates no sense of obligation to seek a better or to accept responsibility for formulating uncertain law, no willingness to accept blame and the burden of failure in the interest of one's fellows. A man "free from custom" may only be free from all law save that of his emotions, mastered by the shameless passion of the tyrant for admiration and affection. Philosophy was, in a sense, the most democratic of disciplines: unable to teach, able only to suggest, question, and encourage, it could claim no perfect knowledge and was always tied to the free consent and vision of each individual.

Philosophy's quarrel with democracy was that democracy taught men in childhood to be "free," and hence legitimated their private emotions and desires. Democracy failed partly because it did not attempt to develop the awareness of imperfection in knowledge and virtue. This humbling awareness created a bond among those who participated in it and freed them from the tyranny of the emotions. It is vital to remember that Plato saw Sparta, no less than Athens, as in error: Sparta, like so many traditional societies, believed that fraternity can be taught, can be embodied in iron rules of custom and ritual. Sparta constrained men only externally; if Athens encouraged men to seek pleasure, Sparta could not train them to resist it. Neither saw the necessity for desolation, for destroying pride of custom and pride of self as the first step toward instilling a vision of a higher authority which would allow pleasure to take a necessary if lesser place in the scheme of human life.[17]

Greek philosophy saw fraternity as a necessity of life and politics. Life might be seen as a hierarchy of fraternities—the fraternity of blood yielding to that of association, which in its turn yielded to that of the city. For some, even civic fraternity yielded to the fraternal citizenship of philosophers in "their own" city. Only among brothers was a man free to follow what is best in him at any time, and hence to ascend the ladder of excellence.

Civic fraternity serves the gods and philosophic fraternity serves

[17] Plato, *Laws*, Bk. I, 643c, 653a–b.

what is true, but the gods are not always friendly to man, nor is truth always friendly to the gods. Man may aim at what is noble, but the noble is, in the light of nature, excess: it goes beyond the normal rules of life. Civic and philosophic brethren are alike in being alienated from the community of birth; philosophy is also alienated from the city. In the family or the city, the secret must be kept. Men must pay due homage to the needs of continuity, nurture, and education. Only among his brothers, who have already learned the lesson that the lesser fraternities exist to instill in men, is a man truly free and equal; elsewhere, he must be mindful of the hierarchy inherent in human improvement. If the lesser fraternities failed to educate men or did so imperfectly, then it was the duty of man to learn the arts of education; it was his interest as well, for each man needs brethren. The function of citizens in either city was the same: encouragement and reproof. Criticism was needed, to remind each person of the desolating truth of human ignorance and imperfection, but it was a criticism which held out the promise of affection for those who could accept that burden and still seek the unknown.

Lessons and Legacies

One lesson above all emerges from the analysis of fraternity in "kinship societies" and the ancient city: fraternity exists only in a state of tension, incompleteness, and ambivalence. Alienated from society, men are still in society and are bound to it by lesser loyalty. Fraternity is made both necessary and possible by that tension, providing the only world in which man is free from divided loyalty, in which there is a genuine alliance between emotion and vision.[18]

Given this definition, fraternity always contains the seeds of its own destruction. The values to which it is dedicated tend ultimately to suggest the idea of universal fraternity. If all men are children of a common Father and creator, then logic and duty may seem to demand that all men be united in a single polity. Such a conviction, if pursued with any degree of success, leads to the vast state in which

---

[18] See, for the central idea, Hegel's careful distinction between alienation and estrangement. *Phenomenology of the Mind* (New York: Swann and Sonnenschein, 1910), vol. I, pp. 197–198.

brothers know one another only as abstractions. Emotional comprehension of the state, let alone fraternity, becomes impossible.

If men feel devotion to the state beyond calculations of interest, their emotions will center on the leader, the god-king, authority incarnate. Alexander, who sought to put the idea of universality into practice, was forced into combat with brothers who sought once again to reduce him to equality with themselves. In the quest for universal fraternity, Alexander was forced to deny his fraternity with others and ultimately committed a kind of fratricide.

It was because Greek philosophers knew as much, because they realized the impossibility of making fraternity a universal within the conditions of human life, that they concealed many of the universal implications of their ideas. They sought to retain the limited society which, whatever its defects, formed the emotional basis for fraternity. Aristotle is noted for his defense of slavery (though it is a rather corrosive "defense"), but in citing an example of natural law, he refers readers of the *Rhetoric* to "what Alcidamas says," and Alcidamas, we are told, said that nature has "made all men free," that slavery exists only as a violation of the natural law. The full realization of philosophic fraternity depended on turning men toward the "city" whose justice was never completely possible in the world, though its citizens might find one another within the political orders which were possible.[19]

Only in one situation does the alienation of brothers from the community seem to end. During a period of crisis and war the shamelessness and fearlessness of brethren, their willingness to lose life and their fascination with death, become needs of society, not dangers to it. War and crisis are temptations of those false brothers for whom fraternity is not enough, who would escape alienation in order to re-enter community. War may demand a purification before the soldier, who has dealt intimately with tabooed things, can return to the community, but the defense of the community makes what is otherwise criminal into a source of honor.

Rapid change and permanent crisis, the society based on war and expansion, are at odds with fraternity. Fraternity's ideal of voluntary submission, and its consequent need for decision by debate, are dys-

[19] Aristotle, *Rhetoric*, trans. W. R. Roberts (New York: Modern Library, 1954), p. 78.

functional when the state requires speed of decision, unchallenged obedience, and unity of command. The societies that valued fraternity yet were involved in (or chose) war and expansion sought to avoid the necessity which seemed to demand the god-king, through the institution of double kingship. Yet the dual kings were only slightly more effective than fraternity in dealing with crisis. Worse, the very existence of dual kingship violated the nature of fraternity, for even divided kingship is authority and implies a special relation to knowledge. A king may be made to bear burdens, to die at the end of a term or at the gods' displeasure, but he usurps the functions of fraternity. If two kings occupy the throne, they may be brothers, but only in relation to each other; they are parents to those below.

Brotherhoods in great states must be dependencies of the crown or they become its opponents. Often they are bulwarks of conservatism, embittered and resistant bodies which combat the crown and deny the need for its authority. Sometimes they become smaller groups within the state, groups where men find solace and concern for their persons, as well as a sharing of values. In either case, they become resistances which prevent or limit the ability of the political order to act as one. The only alternative, however, is to submit to the crown.

The residence of brethren in a continuous community also poses a problem—the relation of fraternity to time. Ritual, despite all the arts of man, loses its personal impact. Secrets leak; the young man on the verge of adulthood comes to expect a vision and, expecting it, to claim one whether it has occurred or no; when he sees others return from initiations year after year, the fear of death becomes muted; the father, anxious that his son succeed, whispers a mystery. A hundred conditions conspire to deprive ritual of its impact, to make it a formal teaching devoid of personal truth. Yet ritual is one of the few protections against the fact that fraternity otherwise depends on the accident of personality. Fraternity is in any case at odds with the continuous community; its values include at least the commitment that physical survival can come at too high a price.

The foregoing analysis suggests at least three conditions necessary for fraternity among citizens: (1) the absence of continuous war or crisis; (2) the small state, which makes possible the sharing of affection and emotion; and (3) a nonmaterialistic standard of value, excluding the possibility of individual perfection and setting citizens apart from other members of the community. In the long term, the Hellenic effort to maintain those conditions was a losing one. The men of classical antiquity, like those of all times, tended to slide into emphasis on life as opposed to the good life, for all men experience the former and only some know the allure of the latter. They were led into war and the attempt to build the universal city or, perhaps worse, lapsed into simple individualism. Any of these courses works to destroy civic fraternity. There is, as Plato knew, no permanent solution to the problem of the political: the best city needs peace, but the political unit must be small. However, the excellence of such a city will be envied by its neighbors, which implies the likelihood of war. The possibility of war introduces into the state an imperfection which will eventually threaten fraternity: the virtue of the guardians, in the *Republic*, is that of dogs and not of men.

The problems inherent in the relation of fraternity and the city only demonstrate that the values which create fraternity cannot be identical with political virtues. Brothers hold life as a value which must prove its worth, an instrumental and not an autonomous good, the life of cities no less so than the life of a man. Brothers are never more imperiled than when they become the heroes of the city, never safer than when it scorns them. The most that fraternity can hope from the community and from the *polis* is that their lesser fraternities prepare the way for a fraternity beyond the brotherhoods of blood and politics.

> Then I returned and I saw vanity under the sun. There is one alone, who hath not a second, yea, he hath neither child nor brother, yet there is no end of all his labor, neither is his eye satisfied with riches, neither does he say, From whom do I labor and bereave my soul of good? This also is vanity, and an unhappy business. Two are better than one, for they have a good reward for their labor, for if one fall, his fellow will lift him up, but woe to him who falls when he is alone. Again, if two lie together they have heat, but how can one be warm alone? And if one prevail against him, two shall withstand him, and a threefold cord is not swiftly broken.
>
> *Ecclesiastes* 4:8–11

CHAPTER II

FRATERNITY AND THE MYTHS OF IDENTITY

Eros and Community

SOMETIMES irreverently, sometimes wistfully, modern humanity is prone to dismiss old teachings as irrelevant in new times. Nor can it be denied that, whether the measure is time or social change, a great distance separates us from traditional wisdom. But time and change have often deluded us; problems we thought were solved have returned to perplex us, and old solutions have revealed unsuspected vitality. For that reason alone, history—the record of man and his changeable social arrangements—is of enormous social value; but history is merely the record, not a template for succeeding generations and not itself an agent of change. History does not change human nature. Fraternity is a perennial need of that nature, a critical synthesis of the singularity of the individual and his needs as a social animal. This assertion anticipates the argument, but it may help establish the need to begin once again at the beginning, with man and his efforts to understand himself and his world.

In the beginning of perceptions is the child. It is an objective fact that the child is born dependent and weak, it is a psychological fact that man is "born free"—free, that is, in the sense that the Enlightenment theorists who gave us the phrase meant: the child is the deity of Berkeley's cosmos, without whose thought nothing would be; for to the child, the world exists when he perceives it to be, when it acts on him as the "cosmic entity," the absolute idea. Man is born free, without a sense of exterior limitations to the self, to will, or to desire. The egotism of the child is innocent because it is unaware of the need for evaluation; indeed, it is ignorant of the possibility of evaluation.

The discovery that the self has limitations is painful to eros, the desire for physical gratification and security. The existence of an outside world is learned only grudgingly and resentfully, for it reveals the extent of the child's dependence and insecurity. What is outside is a source of frustration and fear, a fit object for hatred. The preferred solution of eros is the elimination of the external world, the restoration of cosmic aloneness, the destruction of the other.

Physical nature is full of mystery and danger, but in an important sense it is the least menacing of the environs of the self. Nature is subject to manipulation in the literal sense; to some extent it may be touched, and in many cases ingested and incorporated, "reintegrated" with the cosmic self. If man cannot eliminate all the frustrations evoked by physical nature, he can nevertheless moderate many of the fears it creates. Physical nature loses many of its terrors when it is predictable. The delight of the child (as of men in pre-technological societies) is not in the "spontaneity of nature" so much admired by Romantics; it is in the regularity of things, the torpor-producing security of cycle and perenniality. Konrad Lorenz reminds us "how tenaciously little children cling to every detail of the accustomed and how they become quite desperate if a story-teller diverges in the least from the text of a familiar fairy tale." [1] Eros, in its search for satis-

---

[1] Lorenz, *On Aggression*, p. 71.

faction and security, seeks to control—and failing that, to predict—its environment.

The greatest menace to eros comes from animate nature, especially man. Not only is the child's dependence on other humans greater; man seems more mysterious, more prone to unpredictable vagaries. What a man has been one day, he may not be the next; as history attests, man may be possessed by demons. Our dependence on our fellows makes us social beings; it does not make us sociable. Men, as Thomas Hobbes knew, are prone to vainglory, and the greatest obstacle to vanity is weakness, dependence on beings having wills and power greater than our own. Diffidence and vanity alone conspire to create hostility, for the greatest obstacle to the recovery of "oneness" is the existence of the other as a separate being.[2]

This suggests a major qualification to Freud's thesis that eros is the producer of collectivities. Erotic desires certainly presuppose the need for something outside the self: even though the adult may satisfy many of his own erotic needs—may feed, clothe, warm, or even sexually satisfy himself—such satisfactions presuppose action by the individual on himself. Erotic needs presume subject and object: he who needs, and what is needed. But the whole object of such desires is to eliminate that distinction, to make the object "one" with the subject. To want is to be in want, and action to eliminate need always aims at self-sufficiency.[3]

Dependence on others for gratification may compel us to seek or accept "collectivities," but they remain collectivities in the true sense: collections of essentially discrete beings. A "corporate group" metaphorically shares a body; eros presupposes bodies which are separate. Sensation is always perspectivistic and self-referential, referring back to the physical self. Sensation teaches best when it inculcates the lesson of limitation, weakness, and isolation. Indeed, the highest of the sensations drives home more than any other the melancholy truth that physicality is an impassable barrier between human beings. Sexuality seeks hallowing in the language of love, always partly meant if most often insincere: the cry of a longing aroused by the recognition at the moment of ecstasy that insofar as eros is part of the self, men are always alone.

[2] Hobbes, *Leviathan*, ed. C. Macpherson, pp. 160–168, 183–188.
[3] Freud, *Civilization and its Discontents*, pp. 13–18, 25–28, 32–34, 44, 50, 56.

It is remarkable that many social scientists continue to identify eros and community, and to define community in terms of "warmth," physical gratification, and the "original," "natural" desires of pre-cultural, pre-political man. The "natural man" of the late Enlightenment, and the pre-Freudian child, are seemingly invincible against efforts to dislodge them. T. V. Smith, for example, identified brotherhood with a desire to recapture the "sweetness" of childhood.[4] The impression that childhood is a dulcet time suggests how kind are the failures of memory. One forgets the nameless terrors that accompany the cosmic exaltations of the child; only children, it would seem, appreciate the fundamental realism of Lewis Carroll. The process of forgetting—the desperate need to forget—is as interesting as what is forgotten; it explains, in part, how the identification of childhood with community, and eros with fraternity, has been possible.

Human relations, though less predictable than physical nature, are more malleable and subject to our control. The child, unable to escape dependence and unwilling to accept the limitations imposed by a will other than his own, finds his only resource in his relative control over himself. The dilemma can be resolved and the "oneness" of things restored if the child makes the other's will his own. This effort to identify the self with the other by changing the self differs tactically, but not strategically, from the effort to eliminate or control the other. The aim is the same: the recovery of the delusion of omnipotence, that all is as we wish it to be. Man, "everywhere in chains," can become free again if he learns to love the chains and regards them as armor or decoration worn by choice.

The child learns early that demonstrations of affection and obedience gain him a modicum of control over those around him. This effort does not, obviously, make him "like" the other; but it does make him "likeable." By doing what is pleasing, the child feeds the other's vainglory, his sense of control and well-being; servile adulation provides a compensation for adult insecurities. By such tactics, the child becomes an important part of the parent's self-esteem, giving the child some control over the parent's behavior. Yet this is no bond between selves, no likeness or communion in the genuine sense. The child may repress it deeply, but his identification with parental standards and expectations conceals resentment that he must so limit

---

[4] T. V. Smith and E. C. Lindeman, *The Democratic Way of Life*, pp. 25–27.

his desires. To be sure, such limitation may lead to long-term gratification (though that only emphasizes its private quality); but even so, short-term frustrations and indignities are deeply resented.

Parents' love for children has resentments and anxieties of its own, too. It may flatter a parent's self-esteem to be admiringly adored, but children demand sacrifices. Moreover, the parent must pay a price for that adoration; he must conceal his own weaknesses, which may at any time be found out. The old proverb "Do as I say, not as I do" might as easily run "Be as I say, not as I am." But, for the child, the relations with his parents are the oldest form of love-magic, a striving to propitiate a dangerous thing on which one depends.

Blood kinship is, in fact, a beneficent myth designed to buttress the security of parent and child alike. It declares that one's kindred are established genetically, and hence automatically. It is a myth because it attempts to make human relations, in which an element of volition is always involved, appear to be the result of a primal necessity independent of choice. Though it is a restriction, blood kinship more than pays the price in security; if I am forced to acknowledge kinship to others, they are compelled to admit that they owe obligations to me. "Home," Robert Frost wrote, "is when you go there, they have to let you in."

Nonetheless, blood kinship does not eliminate all anxiety. It is difficult to repress the knowledge that those who must accept me may not want to; they may have scant regard for my personality and still love my genealogy. And, since the child is compelled to accept them and their ways without being consulted, he may, in return, be resentful of them. This merely reiterates an old axiom of Simmel's that groups which are necessary, stable, and secure tend to lack meaning to the individuals who compose them; for to be stable over time, a group must be comparatively independent of personalities. Individual irrelevance is, in greater or lesser degree, the price of social security. The bonds of blood kinship are the human relations farthest from personal relations. They are the mark of an insecurity so pervasive that even the sacrifice of personality seems a small loss, analogous to the anonymous animal hordes which cohere because the mass reduces the chance of being singled out by a predator.[5]

As the child grows into the man, he gains a measure of strength

---

[5] *The Sociology of Georg Simmel*, pp. 145–153.

and knowledge, a capacity to do without others. As those capabilities grow, eros struggles to become free of social restraint—for that freedom, as Philip Slater observes, is its constant aim. The identification of the individual with his group is threatened, and society must seek to reinforce the individual's sense of weakness and dependence. The logic of society commands the use of eros against eros, physical fear against physical desire, in the attempt to reduce man to the status of the child.[6]

Such pressures are unlikely to be wholly successful in maintaining the identification of the individual with his group, for the adolescent or young adult is simply not subject to the total compulsion that rules the child. Social constraint may compel him to observe the proprieties, but he is likely to be at least partly conscious of being compelled. The effort to be what others desire, Erich Fromm's "market orientation," follows the belief that we are what others desire.[7]

The manipulation of a public self to serve the interests of a private self which others do not see is as old as man. It is part of the unending strategy of eros, the tactical effort to delude by cunning what cannot be defeated by force. The existence of a private self, however, interferes with the performance of the public roles we must play in order to control our fellows. Seeking privately to be fulfilled and gratified, passively acted on by others, we must appear to be those who fulfill, gratify, and act on others. (The private self often gives the game away in the unguarded word, the "slip" of the tongue, the incautious gesture.) The private self must be tamed, suppressed, even destroyed to protect the public self which was originally developed to serve it. That we are sometimes aware of following this line of conduct is a hint of the numberless instances when we do so unknowingly. Nietzsche taunted,

> Thou wouldst wear no raiment before thy friend? It is in honor of thy friend that thou showest thyself as thou really art? But he wishes thee to the devil on that account! . . . What is usually the countenance of thy friend? It is thine own countenance in a coarse and imperfect mirror. Sawest thou ever thy friend asleep? Wert thou not dismayed to see thy friend looking so? [8]

[6] Philip Slater, "On Social Regression," *ASR*, XXVIII (1963), pp. 339–363.
[7] Erich Fromm, *Man for Himself* (New York: Rinehart, 1947), pp. 67–82.
[8] *The Philosophy of Nietzsche*, p. 58.

The nineteenth-century social theorists who discerned a "group mind" or a *volksgeist* in "primitive" societies were misled by a combination of romanticism and behaviorism. Discontented with the competitive ethics of industrial society, they sought to find somewhere a community of perfect love and interpersonal identification. Against the new world of the bourgeoisie, they sought an *ancien régime*—but one in which the aristocrats were not warriors. Inheritors of the Enlightenment concepts of noble savagery and "natural man," they discounted the "state of war" which was associated with those ideas. They forgot that "primitive man" is basically just man, not characterized by a specific "mind" but by some of the possible variations within our common human nature which may result from differing social organization.

Men in traditional societies are not more "naturally communal" than other men. Exposed to massive peril and insecurity, they are only more conscious of their dependence on other men; predatory man must hunt in groups, a necessity from which it is one of the "achievements" of modern society to have freed us. Such men are often desperately anxious lest they lose their refuge: "My punishment," said Cain, "is more than I can bear." [9]

Traditional societies surround man with iron-clad custom out of individual anxiety, not communal love. Tönnies noted that obedience to rules of custom always requires an individual decision.[10] Habit and inheritance, however, made rules of custom seem impersonal, immutable, and inevitable, concealing that decision. The appeal of custom, like that of blood kinship, is its seeming impersonality; the self is not committed, while the other is controlled. Custom creates a communal self in which all are "one person," rather than a world of relations between one self and another. The price of denying the separate existence of the other, however, is denying our own identity, a price we resent paying. The single "identity" of customary society is not community: communion and common things presume something shared between two or more entities otherwise separate, an essential unity of things divided by their accidents. The "we" of *gemeinschaft* is based, by contrast, on a denial of individual personality and separateness.

The myth of gemeinschaft is exposed whenever one examines a

---

[9] *Genesis* 4:13–14.
[10] Ferdinand Tönnies, *Custom, passim.*

society that proclaims it. The surface may seem untroubled, but rites and taboos announce a hidden fear. The rule of unanimity which many traditional societies employ in decision-making does not suggest that no disagreement exists; as sensible to find a "group mind" in the procedures of the Security Council. The rule of unanimity implies an individualism so sensitive that it cannot tolerate rule by others, and only when there is in fact an identity between each individual and the "single self" of the community is a decision possible.

No better demonstration exists than the "witch hunt." Men are aware that "community" among them is a delusion; they explain it by reference to a malignant spirit which has destroyed or undermined their "unity." Politics, ancient and modern, has sought to relieve men's anxieties by projecting them onto foes outside the state. The witch hunt, however, suggests the truth: the dangers and insecurities men face are inside the gates. And, though it is not admitted, the necromancer is inside the self.

The erotic image of the self, on which gemeinschaft is based, in its quest for physical security and satisfaction conceives death, pain, and limitation as "outsiders," separate from the self. Insofar as the self is identified with the communal "self," those qualities must also be outside it, in the surrounding world. The appeal and the justification of such a society rest on its ability to combat foes. The authority of the warrior results from his strength in turning away beasts and hostile men; the authority of the magician lies in man's desire to bar the gates against death and finitude, the beasts and dark enemies of the spirit.

But of course the limitations on man's security and pleasure, on his knowledge and his life, are not the result of "outside" forces alone. They are part of man himself. Many social scientists have concluded, from discovering the defects and illusions of gemeinschaft, that community among men is impossible. That conclusion does not, however, follow from the evidence, but from the fact that such social scientists share with gemeinschaft its definition of man. Those who do not understand man are incapable of understanding the nature and conditions for community and fraternity between men.

The Dying Animal

Even at birth, the child shows the complexity of human nature. It is certainly painful for the child to discover that his mother is a separate being with a will that resists his. Yet all of us have seen a child delight in the discovery of his foot. However distinct the two phenomena seem, they are connected; both relate to discovering the limitations and boundaries of the physical self. Childhood is the time of surprising and unexpected events, grim horrors and mad joys. The child seems willing to risk the horrors in quest of the delights— helped, doubtless, by the fact that eros is so often blind to the future. Children seemed, to G. K. Chesterton, led by a curiosity so extreme that he was led to postulate an "instinct for astonishment." [11]

The object of that curiosity is certainly the self. Seeking to discover his identity, the child is willing to discover boundaries which separate the self from its environment. The pain he encounters may cause the child to suspend the desire for such learning. Physical survival is a precondition for self-knowledge and must be attended to first, which tends to demand the acceptance of the "reality principle" imposed by parents and society. But the temporal priority of physical need does not change the fact of the search, nor does repression eliminate it from the spirit.

Self-knowledge is purchased only by tribute to *Ananke*, mother of the Fates. Necessity inheres in the self, in the facts of life and nature of which it is a part, and which it can neither change nor manipulate. The major premises of the great human syllogisms are acknowledgments of our duty to the goddess: all men are born; all men have fathers; all men are mortal. Knowledge of self involves a continual discovery of the limits of self, especially of the pettiness and transience of the physical self within the infinitude of reality.

Erotic sensation can teach the same lesson up to a point, but it cannot discover the inevitability of death or even penetrate to the great abstraction of paternity. As Hegel pointed out, the empirical skeptic, relying on sense impressions, is incapable of forming a concept of the self because he cannot see the self as a whole. Seeing the

[11] G. K. Chesterton, *Orthodoxy* (New York: Dodd, Mead, 1959), pp. 95–97.

self as a "collection of experiences," he encounters in the very act of trying to define this collection a new experience and hence a "new" self. The self is viewed in terms wholly Epimethean, as what it has been, and the viewer looks with constant astonishment on what it becomes. The epistemology of empiricism is based on a yearning after origin, an effort to stand still if not retreat to birth, and a refusal to look further toward the self's own end than events compel it to.

Equally damning was Hegel's demonstration of the arrogant credulity at the root of empirical skepticism.[12] The skeptic's pose of humility is impeached by his refusal to accept the world except as his experience "demonstrates" it. The existence of the world is proved by its action on the self, which claims to be the ultimate arbiter. The reward of skepticism is the conviction that only what I know, only what I have experienced, surely exists, that the self and reality are one. (Extreme forms of relativism, more tolerant toward others, are even more insistent on this dogma.) Logically, of course, the doctrine fails because of the skeptic's inability to define a self. Psychologically, it reveals the tenacity with which erotic perception, on its own terms, clings to the "cosmic entity" of birth. (The existence of societies where the inevitability of death was not acknowledged is empirical evidence of the insufficiency of empirical perception.) Yielding outlying areas, it never surrenders the citadel.

Yet if men are to find an identity, that citadel must fall. Identity involves, at the least, the recognition that finitude and mortality are not events which "happen to" the self, but integral parts of the self. Death is merely the omega for which birth is the alpha. The "antithesis" of life and death, so often employed in philosophy and psychology, is a false one. Life is not antithetical to death, but premised on it. Death, to be sure, is a fact which we cannot change; but for that matter, so is birth. Not having been asked whether we desired to be born, we cannot logically take it amiss if we are not asked our wishes about dying. (In fact, since we sometimes have a measure of choice in the time and circumstances of death, it must be judged more compatible with our dignity, more respectful of the self, than is birth.)

If I would "know myself," I must know a self which is mortal and perishing. By the same token, if I would be myself, would love

<hr />

[12] G. W. F. Hegel, *The Phenomenology of the Mind*, vol. I, pp. 197–198; see also *Wissenschaft der Logik* (Leipzig: Meiner, 1923), vol. I, p. 32.

myself, then mortality must be part of what I am and love. If man is, as Norman Brown argues, a "sick animal," it may be because he is impelled to a truer perception of the mortal nature of animality by a greater need to know himself. To the extent that men are endowed with a desire for identity, they include *Thanatos*, Freud's instinct for death, in their conception or understanding of that identity.[13]

The term *Thanatos*, however, is not entirely a happy one. It tends to center attention on death alone, not on death as the archetype of a class of actions and perceptions. The "instinct" that produces a willingness or a desire to perceive the inevitability of death is, in more general terms, a desire to see and have ends and goals. It is the mainspring of that "purposive behavior" which sociologists, more concerned with conduct than with its psychological genesis, have defined as the counterpart of "expressive" behavior. The willingness to die is an ultimate guarantee of moral standards, of purposes, and of the self; it establishes control over the tendency of the passions to seek survival at all costs, not excluding the destruction of the ego, the identity, of man. The tyrant, the Stoic Epictetus remarked, cannot harm me; he can only cut off my head.[14]

To the degree that Promethean motives are incorporated into the psyche, men are freed from dependence on physical needs and on those around them. That is one ground for Freud's argument that Thanatos is productive of individualism, a view which has another important basis. To a large extent, we are frustrated by others in our effort to reach goals, whether because they dislike and oppose our goals or because they themselves want to reach the same end. Purposive action, and purposive motives, frequently create barriers of resentment between our fellows and ourselves.

In a vital sense, however, purposes and goals are the source of unity among men. A physical barrier prevents sensation from ever being common; ideas and values, in themselves, are not subject to the same limitation. Too, if values and purposes free men from dependence on—or even divide them from—others, they may also free men from anxiety regarding others. Any close bond between men depends

[13] Norman O. Brown, *Life Against Death* (New York: Random House, 1960); Sigmund Freud, *Beyond the Pleasure Principle*. New York: Boni and Liveright, 1924.

[14] Epictetus, *Discourses*, trans. T. W. Higginson (New York: Walter Black, 1944), pp. 268-272.

on value, on the capacity to attach worth to a particular human being because of qualities he is thought to, or does, possess. (Robert Merton and others have demonstrated the extent to which friendship depends on "value homophily," common interests and standards of judgment.)[15]

Unity between men can never be discovered empirically. The diversity of the species is united by the idea of "man," and that unity becomes important only as "mankind" is valued among the lesser kindreds of men. A common view of the world, based on values and conceptions, constitutes the essential unity between men who must necessarily see the world with different eyes.

Indeed, it is death, the great *telos* of human life, that makes men most alike. Birth separates men by strength and beauty in biological terms, by class and advantage in social ones; death makes few distinctions. As the ages have always known, the lover of mankind finds a truth (and a delight?) in death. Consider, for example, the lines from Walter von der Vogelweide's "My Brother Man":

> Say you, who knew the living man by sight,
> Which is the villein now, and which the knight,
> That worms have laid their corses bare? [16]

Those sentiments echo in the great cadences of Donne: involved in mankind, there is no need to know "for whom the bell tolls"; perhaps a deep awareness of the tolling bell must precede such involvement.

My Brother, My Enemy

Classical philosophers believed that hostility occurred between men who had common goals when the values and virtues involved were scarce, limited, not shareable in themselves. Physical objects are subject to the law of exclusive possession. Men who seek wealth as a value are led to a struggle to despoil one another; men who desire the same woman are prone to combat. Power, the symbol of control over things physical, is the least shareable of all values; a quest by two par-

---

[15] Paul Lazarsfeld and Robert Merton, "Friendship as a Social Process," in *Freedom and Control in Modern Society*, ed. M. Berger et al., pp. 18–66.

[16] Walter von der Vogelweide, "My Brother Man," *The Idea of Equality*, ed. G. L. Abernethy (Richmond: John Knox Press, 1954), p. 75.

ties for dominion contains a logic of annihilation and enslavement. The law of exclusive possession is, moreover, supplemented by the law of insecurity of possession. Any good in physical nature is subject to being lost; indeed, it is certain to be lost, given the destiny of life. Possession generates envy; if I claim virtue or *dignitas* because of what I own or control, I invite others to despoil me.

Alternatively, the classics advised the quest for abstract values, for the true and the beautiful as such, which, not being limited by space, could be shared in ways that material goods cannot. The greatest classical thinkers, however, never forgot that the *vita contemplativa* was a variety of life, lived by a physical being and involved in the limitations of physical things. Truth discovered becomes wisdom, the knowledge of something by someone. The idea, when it enters physical nature in the mind of man, becomes a possession. Who has not felt the indignation of being robbed when he finds an idea of his in the writings of another—even an author long dead and much revered? The vision of the artist becomes a work, and while the vision may be shared, the work is a matter of rivalry with his fellow artists. When ideas are shared by teaching, it is worse; wealth may be dispensed by charity, but that is likely to produce only resentment—for, like teaching, it implies superior and inferior. Metaphysically, truth and beauty may be abundant; in the physical world they are scarce, matters of pride in the possessor and envy in the beholder. Agathon's desire to "rub off" the wisdom of Socrates reflects an old, cunning tactic: eros would use one of its weapons to gain control over wisdom, which in this world is a weapon to strengthen and enhance pride.[17]

This does not deny an important distinction between abstract values and physical assets. The latter are inherently unshareable, from their nature as things; the former are unshareable because of the defects of men as physical beings. The artist who senses that his vision, placed on canvas, becomes a source of division, even among those who share the vision, should see in this fact a demonstration of human pettiness. In fact, clearsighted devotion to the great abstractions only reveals that those values and virtues cannot be attained; men may create a hint ("example") of truth or beauty, but they cannot embody them; and the work, involving still other limited and limiting

[17] Plato, *Symposium*, 175c–d.

materials, will fail still more. Devotion to the great values involves a willingness to fail, the foreknowledge of failure, the judgment of imperfection on the self and on the world.

That judgment, needless to say, is unpleasant, something men will continue to flee, whether by fevered involvement with the physical world and a "reality principle" that suppresses the issue, or by claiming to know the good they dimly see or to possess the truth that is forever elusive. In fact, even the doctrine of imperfection can be a mark of pride; it presupposes a knowledge which legitimates judgment. The assertion that life is "absurd" can only be based on a claim to know what is not absurd and a knowledge of the ways in which nature and life relate to it.

The recognition of a radical defect in human knowledge, even knowledge of ignorance, is hard to bear, but ideally at least, it levels pride and stimulates only curiosity. It does not eliminate rivalry between men who share the burden of that perception; the effort to learn and to discover is competitive. It does, however, eliminate the possibility of final success in attaining the goal. Degrees of success are possible, but this leaves man part of the same kind and kindred as his fellow, subject to the same authority rather than possessed of it.

This emphasis on defect and shortcoming should not obscure a prior fact; men must first share the value and the goal, must feel toward it an obligation and a conviction that their present imperfection can only be remedied by its perfections. Love, in this ancient sense, is necessary before man can recognize that he is incomplete, and only when the erotic dream of completion is desolated can man fully recognize his fellows, see himself and them alike as parts of a whole.

The law of failure and exclusion is the law, nonetheless, of all bonds between men. Those who pursue physical objects can unite to despoil others, so long as success eludes them or a pooling of strength seems advised by other dangers or opportunities. The major advantage of abstract values in terms of stable social relations is that success is impossible; and if this is recognized to be so, it guarantees the permanence of relations between those who remain true to the goal.

Failure does, however, create frustration; and frustration creates aggression toward whatever impedes success. Among those who share values and common purposes, three objects of aggression exist, as they do for all men: (1) the environment—even those with the most abstract concerns can be hindered by the impinging of other cares; (2) the other, who is thought not to be "carrying his weight," his proper share of the burden; and (3) the self, for similar reasons.

Aggression toward the other is not to be feared entirely; in fact, one of Lorenz' most valuable services is his reminder that aggression is always a component in the relations of those capable of personal attachment.[18] Fraternity does not exclude disagreements; only perfect knowledge can do that, and fraternity rejects such a claim. Indeed, the suppression of disagreement only produces self-contempt in the suppressing individual, and unconditional cooperation results in contempt for him whose eagerness to "cooperate" suggests that he has nothing of value to offer. To hide disagreement is to draw lines of superiority and inferiority between the self and the other; if the disagreement is related to shared values, suppression of it implies that the relationship itself is of more importance than the values which are its nominal basis—and this, as such, is a denial of fraternity.

Nietzsche knew that the kindest office of friendship and fraternity is often criticism; the reminder of how far from attaining their common goals both brothers are is an "arrow of longing," a rebuke to pride which stimulates the passion for the goal, and equally, a reaffirmation of mutual usefulness and need. The existence of intense bonds between men presupposes the ability to see some things as excellent and valuable and other things as base and unworthy; consequently, my brother should express aggression toward me when, with the common fallibility of humanity, I act basely. (The fact that I will not think so at the time only proves that I need his attack.) "If one would have a friend, one must be willing to wage war for him: and in order to wage war, one must be capable of being an enemy. . . . In one's friend, one shall find one's best enemy." [19]

The great danger of romanticism is that it makes a purpose of human relationships; the greatest danger of the eighteenth-century creed is that it makes a goal and value of fraternity. To invest any human relationship with total value, to presume that my "identity" is possible only in that relationship, is to make me totally dependent on the other, who now controls ("is") myself. For the other is mor-

[18] *On Aggression*, pp. 148, 211.
[19] *The Philosophy of Nietzsche*, pp. 58–59, 63–64.

tal: he may be injured or die; worse, he may change toward me. The closer our relations, the more I must acknowledge the fact of physical and emotional separateness and the fact that the other's whim or caprice may at any time carry him away from me. Fear of betrayal and fear of natural processes, both inherent in any human relation, are raised to a psychotic level of anxiety when the relationship is charged with nearly total meaning.

The greater the dependence, the greater will be the desire to control the relationship. In the extreme case, the aim will be the elimination of the separate personality of the other, the achievement of total subjection. In a painful paradox, that control is possible only by the death of the other, for in his death, his private emotions and whims are destroyed and his dying becomes an infliction of my will, not an affliction visited on me by nature. Fratricide is the hidden theme of those who would make fraternity an ultimate value.

The creed of universal fraternity derives much of its appeal from these dangers and deficiencies of the romantic dyad. My relation to mankind is, of all the relations and kindreds of men, that which demands the least psychological risk; it is the most automatic, the most stable, the longest-lasting. If I must grieve whenever the bell tolls, I am never bereft: some of my kinsmen will remain. Indeed, I need not grieve much—even, lest I suggest some preference among my brethren, should not grieve much—for each loss is small compared to what remains. The "love of humanity," too, reduces any fear that I will be injured by access to myself which I have given to another, for I will have given no individual much, if anything. It is possible to love everyone equally only if one loves nothing in particular. And, to the extent that others are won to the creed, I need not fear betrayal. Evaluation of my character will not matter beyond the bare fact of my humanity; and given that, another's love can be commanded.

It is evident that the creed of universal fraternity is at war with the demands of eros. Personal status and recognition are excluded; the security of "human fraternity" is possible only because no individual matters more than another—and, as Sir William Gilbert put it so succinctly in *The Gondoliers*, "When everyone is somebody, then no one's anybody." The dignity of mankind and the dignity of the individual are incompatible terms. Gemeinschaft insists that I give up my claim to special recognition within the "community," but its narrow frontiers at least allow me to feel distinction in relation to outsiders.

Even the most exalted creeds that proclaim universal brotherhood face the problem that men fall short of the ideal. Eros will not be eliminated, and the most cosmopolitan mind is housed in a parochial body. Too, the doctrine is irrational if it asks that we close our eyes to the differences of virtue among men. As an ethical standard, universal fraternity demands either that we level such distinctions or that we find some apparent men to be not "truly" human. If some men, despite our true fraternity, refuse to feel fraternally toward me, should they not be compelled to do so? If I cannot feel as fraternal toward those I do not know as toward those I do, is there not some defect, some perversity, in me? When Chamfort summarized the doctrine of 1789 in the statement, "Be my brother or I will kill you," [20] he might have added with equal justice, "If I cannot be your brother, I will kill myself."

The doctrine of universal brotherhood is only one form of all teachings which, based on pure purpose and ideal, ignore the erotic, private qualities of the individual. Since that private self is hostile to the collective "self" created by unity of purpose, it must be annihilated, along with all immediate reactions and emotions, all aims and judgments different from those of the whole. The kinship of pure purpose and the kinship of pure eros are alike in this: they deny the separate existence of my brother, though at the price of denying my own. As Erich Fromm has argued, the appearance of single-minded devotion in the purely purposive group conceals a terror of dependence, a hatred of the other, a flight from life itself.[21] And, in slightly different form, purges and heresy trials testify that such groups still need the witch and the enemy to account for and control the enemy within each of their members.

[20] Cited in Cyril Connolly, *The Unquiet Grave* (New York: Viking, 1960), p. 78.
[21] Erich Fromm, *Escape from Freedom* (New York: Rinehart, 1939).

Sciences and Sentiments

Fraternity requires acknowledgment of the separateness of each brother from the others and of all from the common ideal. At the same time, it is evident that if what divides men becomes more salient than what unites them, fraternal relations become impossible. The sense of kinship, of which fraternity is a part, will have been lost.

The salience of likeness in any social category is established only by contrast with other, less like or unlike, categories which are visible and important to the individuals within the group. If that likeness is to be valued, it must be thought better, higher, and more exalted than the "unlike" qualities of those who surround us. Black Americans have always sensed a likeness; but, as contemporary militants have realized, it was not a valued one—escape from it was desired more than unity based on it.

Fraternity presupposes alienation, an elevation above some surrounding, salient environment. Even the universal fraternity envisioned by theorists of the Enlightenment postulated the hostility of man toward nature. Those theories, however, neglected the fact that nature is only rarely as salient in the life of man as are his relations with other men. Even in a threatening, bitter environment, this is likely to be demonstrated. Lorenz calls our attention to "polar disease or expedition choler," the hostility and factionalism which appears among groups of explorers braving the icy terrors of the poles; it is characteristic, he argues, of groups which are mutually dependent but which are "prevented from quarreling with strangers or people outside their own circle." [22] Of course, the sense of difference from others can be misleading; it is no better than the group's perception of what is salient, valuable, and true. Even when perceptions are defensible, there is a grave danger of magnifying differences into a version of "pseudo-speciation," racism being the most striking example; it was to deal with that danger that *I Peter* proclaimed that Christians must "honor mankind" in order to "love the brotherhood." [23] One must acknowledge what is human in one's brother, what

[22] *On Aggression*, p. 55; see also pp. 165–219, and Tiger, *Men in Groups*, pp. 165, 191.
[23] *I Peter* 2:17.

is kin between him and all men, before one can claim to have a genuinely higher feeling for him. Even so, although we will always feel aggression toward our brothers, our bond with them requires a more salient alienation from, and potential aggression toward, a (normally) human environment.

If the Enlightenment partly recognized that rule, it left out of account aggression against the self. Yet it is in what is most immediate to man, in the self, that he first feels the sense of shortcoming that is so vital an element of fraternity. That is not a perception which he can tolerate alone.

"I and me are always too many about me, thinks the hermit," wrote Nietzsche; "always twice one makes two in the long run." [24] The awareness of shortcoming will force the individual to war with himself. Left to himself, he will lose this war, for sooner or later he will yield to the temptation to claim perfection or, with the ascetic's delusion, come to pride himself on his sinfulness. As Nietzsche knew, continued striving for what is excellent and continuing recognition of one's faults cannot be endured without a friend. The individual who knows his unworthiness needs the assurance that he has value; he demands the encouragement of affection. The burden of failure is made easier, moreover, if he acknowledges a similar value in the other, for this establishes that some of the burden and some of the blame are shared, that failure does not lie wholly with the self, but is partly one's brother's responsibility.

This need can be seen in fraternities based on values less exalted than the quest for the eternal and true. Men who combine their forces in a temporary alliance, the better to win some material goal, may if the struggle is prolonged and the burden heavy come to find encouragement in their fellows. There is a kind of fraternity among thieves as well as among soldiers. "Honor" may compel what private emotion would flee, and honor presumes those who give honor. In the long run, shared encouragement may make honor more important than the original goal, may make the group and its unity more important than the object it set out to win. In fact, unity may be so valued that what was at first a prudential alliance persists even after the unshareable objects it sought have been gained.

This only illustrates an old truth, that the frustration of purpose

[24] *The Philosophy of Nietzsche,* p. 57.

is made endurable by joys which make the world seem good, short of the ultimate ideal. Who has not discovered that a journey is shorter when it is made with a companion? Eros takes the edge of fanaticism from purpose, and in so doing makes it possible to evaluate purposes, to weigh one goal against another, and even to discover entirely new or unexpected goods and goals.

The weightier the ideal, the stronger the devotion to truth, the greater is the need to subject existing ideas and accepted premises to criticism and attack, to reexamine tentative convictions in the light of ultimate commitments and ultimate uncertainty. And a more intense devotion to truth carries with it a commensurately greater need for the affection and encouragement which can make such evaluation possible. Moreover, the higher the vision, the greater is the compulsion to seek affection wherever one can find it. Lacking fraternity, we will take encouragement from those who neither see nor share our goals, and the price of their admiration may prove to be self-betrayal. In every "born psychologist," Nietzsche observed, "there is a tell-tale inclination for intercourse with commonplace and well-ordered men," an indication that "he too requires healing from what his 'business' has laid upon his conscience." [25]

One may observe that inclination only too easily among the intellectuals of our time. There is little danger that men will fail to understand the defects of purely purposive activity; the cult of *grande passion*, de Rougemont's nemesis, has waned under the critical analysis of psychology, sociology, and even philosophy. What has replaced the cult of purpose, however, is an attraction to the cult of eros, the worship of spontaneity, immediacy, gratification for its own sake, and "creativity." Nathanael West was right to indict a society which produced men with "fevered minds and emaciated bodies," and in contemporary society he would certainly recognize the defects of an overreaction which has produced men, conformist and "rebel" alike, with fevered bodies and emaciated minds. [26]

In a society like ours, where formal institutions tend to be based on purpose rather than immediate gratification, there is generated an almost obsessive demand for what those institutions deny: affection,

[25] *Ibid.*, pp. 593–594.
[26] Denis de Rougemont, *Passion and Society*, and Nathanael West, *The Day of the Locust* (New York: Bantam Books, 1961).

relaxation, personal recognition as against impersonal process. The intellectual's fascination with the creative and spontaneous (and hence, personal), or even with the accidental, is only a counterpart of the fascination of ordinary men with dreams of romance and blood-violence.

Yet if all men are born with and retain a desire for "unbridled gratification," and if some never move beyond it, that desire is still only one part of man. Societies which abound in outlets for emotion, in which individual man is very important, produce citizens who demand escape from the anxiety and isolation of eros. Moreover, such societies rouse a desire for purpose, for escape from the sheer boredom of life according to the "rhythm of nature." That, sadly, is one of the great appeals of war.

Expressive and purposive outlets and institutions are inversely related, and either generates a demand for its opposite. In society or in the individual, integration and stability demand both purpose and expression, the "optimum" represented by the following "cost curve":

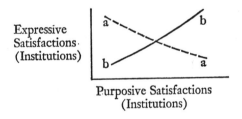

Expressive
Satisfactions
(Institutions)

Purposive Satisfactions
(Institutions)

A society based on either the "individualism" of purposive action or the "merger" of expressive gemeinschaft violates the psychic economy of the individual. (Of course, no society can exist without some element of both; differences are those of degree and not kind.) Men are at odds with a society which frustrates either of their great needs. Anomie is not solely the result of modern society and industrialization, and alienation was known before modern institutions existed among men.

Yet this argument at best only summarizes the typical findings of social science, and at worst does little more than enunciate in professional terms the teachings of common sense. Both social science and common sense are prone to the vacuous belief that emotion and ideal need to be "balanced" against one another. Such analyses have the value of suggesting that personal or social integration is an incomplete and imperfect state, one which invariably contains some element of frustration of both expression and purpose, and hence some element of aggression toward the things which make up the world of man: himself, his environment, his fellows.

The language of "balance," however, is contentless and static. Man, modern philosophers like Dewey and Sartre proclaim in a favorite truism, is "in process" and "becoming"—yet those abstract terms, like "function" or "efficiency," are extrinsic and not intrinsic. To know their meaning, one must establish where, or toward what, "becoming" is occurring; one must also discover the beginning and the ending of the "process"—for process is defined by its end points. Nietzsche, precisian of language that he was, meant more by his use of the borrowed aphorism that man is "eternally becoming" than many have realized.[27] One becomes something, having been something else; to be always becoming implies a beginning and ending which always exist, a fixed alpha and omega unaffected by time.

Modern theorists have often spoken as if change and dynamics were phenomena men of earlier times were unaware of. Actually, classical and Christian theorists were deeply concerned with change and development, but their attention centered on the development of the individual, on his growth from opinion to knowledge or from sin to salvation. In both cases, they were concerned with the individual in the world and with his happiness, and consequently with the emotional support which would make tolerable the eventual shortcomings of the world and would enable men to face and strive to overcome imperfections in the self. The "unhappy consciousness" of failure demanded the joy, solace, and encouragement of friends and brethren.

Modern political theory transformed the question by shifting process and development from the individual to history. Secularism called into doubt any theory that accepted failure in the world; the Reformation's emphasis on sin questioned the validity of worldly happiness. The Reformation retained many of the older concerns, especially that the individual bear the burden of knowledge of defect, but it tended to define defect wholly in terms of the individual himself.

---

[27] Man, Zarathustra declares in his prologue, is a "rope across an abyss" (*The Philosophy of Nietzsche*, p. 8); see also Nietzsche's attack on "objective man" (*ibid.*, pp. 504–506).

Men were strongly tempted to fly the grim and unrelieved sense of their own sinfulness, seeking some affirmation in the life of society. If they did nothing else, many of the teachings of the Reformation helped open the way for acceptance of newer, secular doctrines which oriented analysis more radically.

Modern secular political theory began by conceiving of the individual as morally complete in his "original" condition. This view makes man the erotic animal, rightly aiming at eliminating restrictions on his desires imposed by others, and seeking above all else to preserve his life. Education and personal development consisted in acquiring the skills and the "prudence" needed to accomplish those aims. Notably, prudence acquired a new meaning; still implying excellence in action, it came to be associated with caution, with avoiding risk to life and limb. Life, for such theories, contained no high promise or value, but only frustration and limitation which violate the "natural right" of man. Death ceased to be a "natural end," becoming the frustration of the natural or, at least, of the humanly natural. As death and limitation were facts in the life of the individual, that life was destined to defeat; individual development was a declining path that led to ultimate disaster.

Meaning in life could only be hoped for as the "progress" of science and technology eliminated restrictions from human life. Meaning that an individual life could not have might be found in the great aggregations capable of persisting through time: race, nation, and species.

Concrete fraternity was dangerous because it tempted men to contentment and encouraged "vainglory," a defiance of the limits of life and a reverence for the unknown. Immediate fraternity had to be destroyed, not because fraternity had no value, but because fraternity was conceived as an end, a goal that would complete history. Even the elimination of death would not fully remove the limitations on man; other independent wills, the desires of other men, would always restrict him. Only when all men had identical wills would frustration be removed, and this became the logical, if not always the explicit, utopia of political thought. The erotic dream of merger into perfect unity came to be identified with fraternity, and the hope for such "fraternity" in the future served to justify the lack, or even the destruction, of a different sort of fraternity in the present.

There are many examples of the substitution of historical for individual development in modern thought. The Darwinian thesis that ontogeny recapitulates phylogeny might, especially in view of Darwinistic individualism, be thought to imply individual development, which moved from an undifferentiated man to man as a member of a group, and only finally to genuine individuality. Herbert Spencer, however, applied this logic to the history of the species but not to individual men. Hegel, despite his superb critical psychology, sought a mirror of the dialectic in the processes of history. Even Freud, who restored the knowledge that each generation begins in the caves, sometimes implied that "civilized man" was a different, and better, creature than earlier man.[28] And there are certainly enough illustrations in the literature of "political development."

In a critical respect, contemporary analysis reflects the creed of modernity. Modern social scientists have abandoned any hope for total "objectivity," conceding that it is impossible to eliminate the influence of emotions and sentiments on perception. In fact, if there is one generally accepted principle in social science, it is that individual needs and satisfactions influence what an individual sees and is willing to learn; and because groups play a vital role in satisfying needs, they are recognized as influencing and structuring knowledge and perception. Social scientists, however, continue to treat objectivity as desirable if unattainable, a fact which causes them to center on the distortions of reality produced by group influences. Rarely if ever has social science concerned itself with the positive role which groups or emotions can play in individual perception.

Max Weber, for example, described the types of mental process in terms of their relation to rational action:

	Rational Ends	
	+	−
Rational Means +	Zweckrational	Wertrational
Rational Means −		Affective

[28] Herbert Spencer, *Principles of Biology* (New York: Appleton, 1874), vol. I, pp. 201–209; compare Freud, "Thoughts for the Times on War and Death," p. 221, with Freud and Albert Einstein, *Why War?* (UNESCO, 1946).

Considering Weber's great analytic powers, it is astonishing that he left out of his reckoning the possibility, starkly attested by the gap in the matrix, that emotion might be a means to rational ends. Weber's fourth category, "traditional" action, is almost instinctive and is barely intelligible. (Parenthetically, this is doubtless related to Weber's failure to develop a conception of democratic authority based on the law of nature or a "general will." Rational-legal authority was technological, scientific only in the sense of application to objects, not to any knowledge of the nature of man.)[29]

In his "total conception" of ideology, Karl Mannheim felt it necessary to "unmask" the influences of group and class on the individual mind. Yet Mannheim felt no such need to "unmask" the individual's own distortions. Basic to Mannheim's argument is the notion that, once freed from the distortions of class and group-based ideology, individuals will learn to adjust their differences. History, an "irreversible process" to which man must "adjust himself," would free men from error and "reveal man's essential nature." The only danger to the process was the possibility that, encouraged by group pride and perspective, the individual might resist the "teaching" of history.[30] Such an argument ignores the possibility that the individual himself, not the group, is the greatest distorter of reality, that the residual claims of eros may at once underlie and exceed the distortions of the group.

Psychologically inspired awareness of the individual's own distortions has centered on means for making him "secure." There is truth in the thesis that insecurity is the origin of distortion, but the truth must be tempered by the fact that man's life is insecure and environed by the unknown. The issue is not whether man should be secure, but what he should be insecure about. Men who face insecurity in day-to-day survival are unlikely to face the dubiety of cosmos; they will seize on simple principles which provide courage, and support practical measures, to cope with a world of scarcity and threat. The claims of survival and of physicality come first in time,

[29] For Weber's ideas, see *Wirtschaft und Gesellschaft, Grundriss der Sozialökonomik*, vol. III (Tubingen: J. C. B. Mohr, 1922), p. 12.

[30] Karl Mannheim, *Ideology and Utopia* (New York: Harcourt, Brace, 1956), pp. 13–20, 22, 38–41, 45–46, 55–58, 65–81, 87, 94–95, 118–146, 262–263.

and only when these have found some minimal level of satisfaction is it possible for men to begin to learn the lesson that eros is not enough.

"The secret sits . . ."

The process of individual development begins with the emotions and with the primary social groups which serve them. Society may satisfy basic material and erotic needs sufficiently to enable the individual to doubt society's purposes, to allow ego to put eros to the question. It is then that the influence of society becomes perilous, for morally and psychologically the individual must face the dilemma that Socrates poses in the *Crito*. The individual is in a position to challenge society because society has made him so, and (his moral debt to society aside) he will hesitate to move into a new world at the cost of the goods of the old. Indeed, he cannot do so: eros threatened tends to become eros sovereign, and to go beyond society requires the individual to find new support and security.

It is in this situation that man finds a need for brothers, for "true friends and genuine contemporaries" who share his values and with whom he experiences the encouragement of affection and rivalry. The individual does not find "identity" through his brothers, for identity is not vouchsafed to men in this life. To know the self is to know the whole of which the self is a part; to know identity, one must not only know the self at a given time, but the self over time, something which man cannot "know" until the end. Man's foreknowledge of death, in fact, always wars with his desire for survival until eros finally surrenders its effort to deny death's reality in the moment of experiencing it. The only complete moment of identity is the moment of extinction. Fraternal relations do not reveal identity to the individual: they provide him the assurance of identity which is necessary for him to seek to know its nature.

Man is never assured of identity except in relation to others; in dialogue, all the diverse elements of the personality must speak as one. The crises of our private emotional life often seem foolish when we try to communicate them to others, for the needs of coherent speech force and allow the conscious mind to assume control.

Most men experience the "psyche group" in relation to persons they are unconscious of. What Freud called the "superego" is less a thing than it is other people, predominantly parents and blood kin, who are buried in the psyche. For the individual who would know his identity, however, the superego is not enough, even if its counsels are wise and prudent. But ending the "tyranny of the superego" is also not enough. The possibility of moving forward in the search for identity requires the support of persons who assure our identity anew—not as an authority might, by giving us the conviction of a new, "known" self, but by stimulating us to seek the self which remains unknown.

To many, it seems puzzling that fraternity has so often been associated with the secret society. To be sure, the secret emphasizes the distinction between insiders and outsiders, and hence strengthens the things which unite the former. What is critical, however, is the nature and purpose of the secret as viewed by the members themselves; that, as Simmel knew, is crucial to an evaluation of the claim of a secret society to be a "fraternity."

In most instances, the secret is not valued by members of the secret society. Secrecy is adopted as a means to ends other than the protection of the secret. This is obvious in the case of formal and public "secret" societies. Publicity calls attention to the society and raises the danger that the secret will be discovered. The risk is justifiable only if the members desire the attention which publicity provides, value the interest, curiosity, and attention of the community. That in itself violates the claims of fraternity: the purpose of the secret is to secure the admiration of outsiders, which becomes more valuable than that of one's brothers.

Secrecy may also be used by a revolutionary group which seeks to transform the surrounding society. Then, however, separation from society, let alone secrecy, has no value. The whole purpose of such a group is to end itself; specifically "fraternal" relations are only a mark of defeat.

Most typically, perhaps, the secret is a means to the expression of emotion and the gratification of needs in ways prohibited or inhibited by society. The aim of such secret organizations is freedom *from* purpose and value, and the secret is valuable only insofar as it prevents others from observing their conduct. Such secret bodies normally exist to permit men to live in society without challenging its values; they serve as a safety valve for the shortcomings of society itself. Stanford M. Lyman suggested a classification of secret societies[31] as follows:

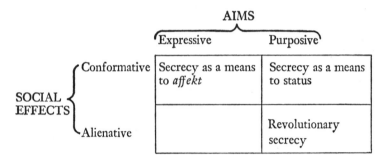

		AIMS	
		Expressive	Purposive
SOCIAL EFFECTS	Conformative	Secrecy as a means to *affekt*	Secrecy as a means to status
	Alienative		Revolutionary secrecy

There remains the final category, in which emotional and expressive functions support a challenge to the values of the surrounding society. There is no necessary revolutionary intention in such a secret fraternity. If anything, the implication runs the other way, for such a society presumes that the specific relations of fraternity are necessary to challenge the dominant values of the social order. Secrecy is a fact, not a purpose; the members are presumed to share a knowledge or truth, and discovery of the secret automatically makes an insider of the discoverer.

The secret is necessary at all, and necessary to fraternity, because fraternity is a personal relation, depending on more than formal doctrines, based on qualities of spirit which cannot be "taught" in a formal sense. Contemporary men may feel, as some Existentialist thinkers have implied, that we "know" the imperfection of things human and of human knowledge, and that consequently we "know" all things necessary to teach fraternity. We cannot, however, claim to know ignorance; we can only suspect and hypothesize it. Our ignorance is no test, for unless we have reached the human pinnacle, it is not necessarily the limit for others. In any case, to teach imperfection is to teach a comforting certainty. Uncertainty, for those who know it, is an agony and not a fact, a torment and not a dogma.

In fact, the doctrine of Nothingness is of all doctrines most suited to trap men in a world of inherited opinion. Making no positive claims, it cannot be subjected to the test of critical reason. God's will, as

[31] In personal discussion.

omnicompetent an explanation of the world as has ever been devised, conflicted with God's justice in the affairs of men and was bound to produce curiosity. Nothingness denies that there is anything about which to be curious, and it conflicts only with the rational perception that nothing with or without a capital letter, is not something.

Ignorance cannot be conceived without some notion of what knowledge might be; injustice is recognized because we have some sense of the just. What can be taught by brothers to society is the perennial possibility inherent in those dim perceptions, the duty and the obligation to seek them out. Nor can they deny the possibility that others will excel them in knowledge, and the teachers become the taught.

Plato realized that a child born to a *polis*, however well trained in its principles, would be a different person from the founders. Founders were men whose emotions had been trained in a past society, and the shortcomings of that society had led them to seek a better way and a good society. What they created was unfamiliar, uncertain, and chosen; what they teach, however, becomes the inherited and accepted, the familiar and established. A perfect social order would be accepted by those who could not have created it, and might be rejected by those most similar in personality to the founders.

Tradition is, at best, a kindly myth whose substance is eroded with time. The only enduring society is that which recreates in each generation the experience of the founders, which begins with man at the beginning and leaves its final secrets for the new generation to discover. Then, perhaps, all generations can be "genuine contemporaries" in following the same aspirations, the goal which is man's by nature. If the emotions are first in time, the quest for identity is first in the order of nature. All men seek knowledge of the whole and of themselves; without that, "self-preservation" is problematic and uncertain. When Frost wrote that poetry was "simply metaphor" and delight in ulteriority, he added:

So is all philosophy—and science too, for that matter, if it will take the soft impeachment from a friend. . . . And there is a sense in which all poems are the same old metaphor always.[32]

[32] *The Poetry of Robert Frost* (New York: Modern Library, 1946), p. xvi.

In that sense, of course, all men are contemporaries and brothers. Metaphor is a likeness, the likeness of ideas to others, of my thought and feeling to yours. The recognition of common meaning demands common language, objects, and experience. So fraternity depends on the ability and willingness to recognize one's brothers if one meets them. In both senses, ability and will, brothers owe some debt, if only a negative one, to parents and *patria*, who shaped their wills and provided them with skills.

In another sense, however, the existence of fraternity depends on chance, on the accident of possessing the necessary skill and desire, and on the greater accident of proximity. All child-rearing, to take only the most obvious element, is a thing of chance. Our imperfect knowledge aside, the moments of life bulk larger to the child, and a forgotten word or incident may be critical in shaping the man. And from such accidents, others proliferate. James Baldwin is accurate enough: "People can't invent their lovers and their friends any more than they can invent their parents. Life gives them and takes them away." [33]

Dependence on chance may seem a burden and a limitation on fraternity, as doubtless it is. Knowing how much we depend on chance, however, is a barrier against pride, a motive for compassion; "there but for the grace of God go I" is the statement, after all, of one who feels the sentiments of pity or of envy that are the marks of common humanity. Chance does more, however. It is a guarantor of fraternity, the assurance that even in the most unpropitious of societies, men are not excluded from the possibility of brotherhood.

Fraternity grows from the recognition of kinship, likeness more important than unlikeness. All the fraternal relationships of man, in his progression from birth to death, teach the same lesson. A man is kin to his blood-brothers, like them more than he is unlike, because dependence and society are more important than physical isolation. His fraternity with those who share value and vision is established because man's recognition of a perfection which he sees but does not embody is a truer measure of human proportions and nature.

In one sense, the law of life is the law of differentiation, the quest for identity; in another, it is the law of likeness. Men may feel that the loss of their illusions of unity and identity, which began with the child's sense of oneness, is the barring of a door which shuts them out

[33] *Giovanni's Room* (New York: Dell, 1964), p. 10.

of home. But if the kindreds of man have done their task of strengthening the individual, he will feel the change to be the result of his opening the gates which shut him in. Alienation is not involuntary exile. It is not the loss of an old home so much as the finding of a new patria which makes the old, valued as it may be in its own way, seem less excellent, less truly "mine."

If ego motives become increasingly dominant, life is a process in which eros, gradually losing the capacity for delight in the world of sense, loses its hostility to thanatos, a "learning how to die" that may be the only means to genuine identity. Death is the supreme moment of human independence, yet it is also the moment at which men are most alike and akin. Then all the bizarre garbs, the kaleidoscopic costumes of the ages and the nations, clans and classes, are swept away. All the panoply of illusion men use to brighten life and darken the blaze of truth—necessary, as Plato knew, if they are to bear it at all—pass, and man is one with man.[34]

[34] Plato, *Phaedo*, IX (64), XVI (71), XII (67).

> It would seem as if the rulers of our time
> sought only to use men in order to make things
> great; I wish that they would try a little more
> to make great men; that they would set less
> value on the work and more on the workman;
> that they would never forget that a nation
> cannot long remain strong when every man
> belonging to it is individually weak, and that
> no form or combination of social polity has
> been devised to make an energetic people out
> of . . . pusillanimous and enfeebled citizens.
>
> De Tocqueville, *Democracy in America*

CHAPTER III

FRATERNITY AND MODERN POLITICS

Aliens and Strangers

BUILDING a fraternal polity is at best difficult, and these are not the best of times. We have come to expect prosperity and to suspect its consequences; as bored as we are insecure, we find our sanctuaries invaded by others and we resort to public places only to meet loneliness. It is natural that many should feel a need for fraternity, and brotherhood is one of the few moral ideals common to the diverse radical movements of the day. But many in recent times have set out to found the fraternal city and have seen their dreams transformed into totalitarian nightmares. More than in the past, we need caution in our political dreaming; we live amid dangers so great that a misstep can be fatal to all the dreams of mankind.

At the same time, we must not be frightened into quietism. Inaction offers no highway to safety; drift may have consequences worse than those of ill-considered zeal. But passivity and frenzy are not the only possibilities, any more than faithlessness is the answer to fanaticism. Action can be clear-sighted, and the requirement for such clarity is greater if one believes that radical surgery is needed to cure the ills of society; it is all too easy, as John Schaar remarks, to "cut off some parts that would be useful later on." [1] When a disease is far advanced, extreme remedies may be necessary, but the need implies the difficulty of cure.

In this chapter, I will speak primarily of the political and intellectual limitations in our environment which make it difficult to realize the hope for fraternity. I do so to encourage those who share this hope, as I do; not to reduce them to despair. Courage is demonstrated, after all, by those who know what is to be feared, not by those who are moved either by a euphoric confidence in easy victory or by the fury of desperation.

The political barriers we face are great; political fraternity, as I will attempt to demonstrate, is impossible in the great industrial states, and even more limited brotherhood is difficult. The intellectual obstacles we confront are equally formidable. We are, after all, the children of the society we assail. Inheritors of its premises and prejudices, we are never more in danger of being trapped by them than when we feel ourselves free of their influence. The intellectual obstructions, in fact, must logically be leveled first; plan precedes construction in the sequence of building. And the worst errors are often committed by those who yearn for fraternity. Need made desperate is often blind, and we begin in a political world in which men often find themselves not only brotherless, but alone.

True, controversialists have repeatedly denied that alienation and anomie are characteristic of modern politics. Social scientists have sought to disprove the idea that feelings of powerlessness, indignity, and unimportance are widespread; similarly, they have rejected the corollary thesis that these feelings are accompanied by resentment, lessened political commitment, and temptations to violence. Yet events in the ghettos, in colleges, on urban streets, and in middle-class suburbs, even in pronouncements by high officials of the land, demon-

---

[1] John H. Schaar, "Rationality and Legitimacy in the Modern State," in *Power and Community*, ed. P. Green and S. Levinson, p. 284.

strate the irony of such findings. It hardly raises confidence that Robert Dahl, among the most sensitive of social scientists, wrote not long ago that "full assimilation of Negroes into the normal system has already occurred in many northern states." [2]

The error of such studies lay in equating the absence of political disturbance with the existence of psychological serenity. It should have been evident that estranged men are not often engaged in political protest; those who feel powerless are more inclined to submit and even to mask their resentments. It should also have been possible to see signs of the development of our present crisis in many aspects of popular culture. Nor was it the limitations of method alone which caused social scientists to ignore such possibilities. The modern and liberal tradition which informs most social scientists sees man as an apolitical animal concerned with the fulfillment of his private desires. In such a theory, abundance and stability are naturally associated; trained in its doctrines, social scientists have felt no need to go beyond the orderly semblance of society.

Even if we accepted the idea that man is only a private being, it would be easy to build a case against modern industrial society. Unparalleled opportunities for fulfilling our material desires are inseparably associated with a technology which grows more threatening with each "advance" and with a system of organization which makes us dependent on masses of unknown others. We become insecure, dependent, and fearful, losing dignity as we gain prosperity. Even our old delights pale with repetition, bringing into sharper focus the still frustrated desires for healthy youth and escape from death. Modern society, in other words, threatens as it rewards, frustrates as it gratifies, and creates dependence where it liberates. The sentiment of resentment inheres in those ambivalent relationships and will appear openly whenever prosperity falters or when state sanctions fail.

But man is more than a private being, just as his self is more than erotic. Recognizing both aspects of the self, classical political theory set out to make a man's private emotions into at least partial allies of his values and reason. It argued that man was a "political animal" because that synthesis could best be achieved in political life. By "po-

[2] Robert A. Dahl, *A Preface to Democratic Theory* (Chicago: Phoenix, 1963), pp. 138–139.

litical," however, it meant specifically the public world of the *polis*. The small state lay within the range of a citizen's senses, maximized by its minuteness his chances for status and honor, and made it possible for a personal bond to exist between him and his fellow citizens. The polis, in other words, maximized the emotional goods to be found in politics, gave man the support of his fellows, and allowed him a considerable share in the shaping of his destiny.

By contrast, modern industrial societies minimize the goods in politics as they increase the goods outside it; politics becomes burdensome for most, honoring only a few and lacking any personal bond between the multitudes who make up its citizenry. True, as Morris Rosenberg has argued, those who do participate in political life find it a source of greater personal security, meaning, and dignity. James Davies, in fact, has identified political motivation as "self-actualization." [3] But although such findings tend to confirm the old proposition that man is political by nature, they do not change the fact that only a tiny fraction of citizens can participate in any significant way in political life. Privatistic values only add to what would in any case be a severe limitation.

Politics, after all, is subject to the restrictions of space and time, and time alone is a radical constraint. Even if we devoted all our waking hours to political matters, the number of us who could address our fellow citizens would be limited. All societies face what Bertrand de Jouvenel calls "the chairman's problem," the task of determining somehow who will have access to the public and for how long. Given the number of citizens in modern states, those allowed access can never be more than a small percentage of the whole. Most are relegated to the role of listeners and spectators, unable to participate in the deliberation which formulates policies and establishes alternatives.

Men are taught to retreat from politics by their exclusion from any active responsibility in it; before we can be held responsible or will hold ourselves so, we must have some significant personal control over events. The retreat is, individualistic theory to the contrary, not

---

[3] Morris Rosenberg, "The Meaning of Politics in Mass Society," *POQ*, XV (1951), pp. 1-15, and "Self-Esteem and Concern with Public Affairs," *POQ*, XXVI (1962), pp. 201-211; James C. Davies, "A Note on Political Motivation," *WPQ*, XII (1959), pp. 410-416.

the result of any generalized desire to be "free" from obligations. Most citizens fill their private lives with numberless petty duties and cares on which tey lavish all the attention, and for which they feel all the anxiety, that a few devote to the issues of the day. It is sometimes pleasant to feel irresponsible, but we also seek responsibility because we desire to be important. "Every man is the hero of the psychodrama of his own life," H. L. Nieburg writes, and sane men are aware that few can be public heroes.[4] If men shut out the knowledge that many of the problems which plague them are political in origin, it is to preserve the illusion of personal responsibility for their own destinies.

In large modern states like our own (if not in others), the individual who feels that he does not matter is the rational man, not the one who believes the opposite. Rousseau pointed out that the citizen is always fully subject to sovereignty, but that he himself is only a fractional part of the sovereign. He went on to observe, with impeccable statistical logic, that as the state grew in numbers, the fraction declined toward a point at which it would be so small as to seem insignificant to the citizen and the sovereign alike. Expansion made the state more and more an external thing, claiming but a small part of the individual and reducing him to a dispensable part of the whole. As men found this to be so, they retreated into smaller circles where they still mattered, and ultimately into themselves. "As the public sphere expands," De Tocqueville wrote, "the private sphere contracts."[5]

Totalitarianism is not an exception to the rule; it is a desperate effort to counteract it by force. It attempts to compel citizens to yield out of terror what they will not grant of themselves. And consequently, totalitarian orders are trapped by a logic that requires the state to provide ever more terrifying enemies if it is not to become the enemy itself. Either totalitarian states march inexorably toward war or they change into simple tyrannies and bureaucratic oligarchies. They have no answer to the privatizing logic of modernity.

[4] H. L. Nieburg, *Political Violence* (New York: St. Martin's, 1969), p. 122.

[5] Rousseau, *The Social Contract*, Bk. III, ch. 1; Alexis de Tocqueville, *Democracy in America*, trans. H. Reeve (New York: Schocken, 1961), vol. II, pp. 256–258.

In localities and private groups, of course, the dynamic of privatization is much less operative. However, if local governments and interest groups are small enough to be meaningful to the individual, they tend to be too small to be effective in solving problems. In larger groups and in the great cities, a gap grows up between speakers and listeners, a fissure between rulers and ruled only a little less wide than that in national politics.

Political pluralists have known this, despite their tendency to identify the interests of a group with those perceived by its leaders. Their emphasis on leaders as upholders of social cohesion and the "rules of the game," their feeling that it is desirable for leaders to have greater discretion and control, and their generalized suspicion of the public, all testify both to a gap between rulers and ruled and to the extent to which the ruled limit their commitment and allegiance. As a result, the "oligarchs" feel themselves unable to call for sacrifice or to do more than serve the most private and parochial of ends.

Local groups and governments have, at least, the advantage of common space, the world of personal interaction. "Functionalist" theory has more than once erred in forgetting that those whom we encounter in day-to-day life play a far more immediate role in our security and emotional life than those to whom we are tied by abstractions. Penetration of one's "turf" remains a matter of concern. Distant others are strangers to the flesh even when they are bound to us in spirit, and more than one study shows the effect of dispersion in inhibiting participation where other factors would encourage it.

Most of the studies which have confirmed pluralists in their theory, moreover, have been local, examinations of limited milieus in which problems are simple and group organization is fairly easy because so many potential members are acquaintances. Even in the Civil Rights Movement, initial concerns, actions, and enemies were local. As the movement's concerns impinged on national politics, it required—though it could not always obtain—discipline, hierarchy, and the like.

In the most local groups, moreover, problems become insoluble. As we have been told repeatedly, local autonomy is impossible in a national and international economy. In this, functionalists are surely to the point: economic process, communication, military and political relations, all the great events of political life, cross the boundaries of local areas and defy control by them. These are the forces that lower the importance of locality in the minds of its citizens. (It is this factor too, as Robert Presthus has observed, that casts doubt on studies of "community power"; those who have power may find it unimportant to rule localities.)[6]

Interest groups have no greater ability to win loyalty and deep commitment. In addition to dispersion, they suffer the equally serious handicap of lacking, in most cases, any shadow of moral or ethical dignity which might justify a claim on the individual. There is nothing in the production of floor wax or burley tobacco to justify individual sacrifice, and the "alienation of labor" is, on the whole, a rational process, a refusal to identify with products of labor which have no claim on man's devotion. Worker community, where it exists, combines isolation in space with at least some highly valued qualities in work itself. (Miners, paradoxically, seem to value the danger and peril of their work—it is the civilian's equivalent of the fraternity of battle.) For the most part, however, the "corporation" is not aiming at a way of life internal to itself (which should end all comparisons to the medieval corporation) but at the production of a commodity for sale by criteria determined elsewhere (for this purpose, "consumer demand" and governmental planning are identical). Its life is guided by external standards and it promises extrinsic rewards.

Finally, "overlapping membership," much praised as the source of political cohesion, works—to the extent that it is operative—by creating tensions of loyalty between groups, divesting membership of meaning for the individual. Frequent tensions and painful choices are in fact likely to cause a retreat from any but the most peripheral "affiliation" into private, expressive groups where no such pain is required. And if those primary groups, where meaning becomes concentrated, come into conflict, the individual is likely to be unable to act at all; paralysis of will, not moderation, will be the result.

In fact, these tensions and the fear of them may account for the unevenness of formal group membership. Estimates vary, but many Americans have no such membership, and group affiliation, like "ac-

[6] Robert Presthus, *Men at the Top* (New York: Oxford University Press, 1964).

tive citizenship," tends to follow class and status. W. Lloyd Warner's data indicate the following:

	Membership in formal associations
Upper class	72%
Upper-middle class	64
Middle-middle class	49
Upper-lower class	39
Lower-lower class	22

This indicates that groups may be much less a cause of the sense of importance in politics than has been argued. Rather, they suggest that a sense of dignity derived from private things may lead men into a demand for membership; those who need access most are least likely to have it. And these statistics may reflect an ability to accept tensions in loyalty which results from a more certain and abundant private sphere of gratification.[7]

The politics of classical antiquity presumed "overlapping memberships" between clans. It was, however, a common overlapping membership, a group of brothers who shared both tensions and loyalties and who could provide a center of unambiguous loyalty and emotional support inside the public sector, rather than apart from it. This is rarely the case in modern life. The complexity of loyalties and division of feelings tend to make the individual unique and alone, and the tensions of his purposive life only magnify the desire to flee from purpose into a private world of emotional expression where the burdens of value and goal are momentarily forgotten.

More than other organizations, political parties resist that logic. The party aims at winning a generalized loyalty, at creating a bond of identification between rulers and ruled, private men and public values. Its success depends on how well it forms a civic identity in its members, a coherent picture of the self in relation to the political community over and above the divisive effects of private roles and life. It lays claim, in other words, to the whole individual, and the partisan act requires a consolidation of reference groups, a decision as to which loyalties the individual values most. It is a matter of common observation that an election, temporarily at least, disrupts some human

[7] William Lloyd Warner, *American Life: Dream and Reality* (Chicago· University of Chicago Press, 1962), p. 229.

relationships and intensifies others, and loyalty to party often over-rides "interest" affiliations (so often that many interest groups wisely proclaim a "nonpolitical"—nonpartisan—stance).

In the ideal case, a party is a hierarchy of overlapping fraternities gradually ascending from locality to the national government, each level of the ladder enjoying personal relations and a common condition of responsibility and obligation. The partisan ideal is identical to what C. Wright Mills described as an "articulated public"; parties, to the extent that they conform to that ideal, are able to deal with substantive matters, because men are assured by a chain of personal trust that those who rule are "men like ourselves," whose judgment will reflect our sentiments and values.[8]

The task of the party was easier, its possibilities greater, when it was rooted in local communities, in societies in which the individual's loyalty had already been given a limited public dimension. The party is no better than the individuals who make it up. Political leaders are most often sensitive men, concerned about public applause as well as the public welfare, and they tend to follow popular opinion even more than the logic of electoral competition demands. Of course, in noncompetitive systems, the party may ignore opinion with greater ease, but then the party becomes a mere bureaucracy, a government over men. (The "iron law of oligarchy," after all, was formulated with reference to parties.)

To provide the emotional foundations of allegiance and political education, the party is dependent on local groups in which participation is possible and on the ability of those groups to offer man something his emotions value. As local politics becomes less important, party loyalty becomes attenuated. And to make matters worse, involvement outside the home has become less necessary as it has become more threatening.

Concerts and plays—even the pleasure of hearing oratory—can be indulged in without crossing the threshold. As families become more permissive, forbidden delights which drove men outside the home (and which the party protected if it did not provide) can be found inside it. Even the bar, which Duverger called "the agora of

[8] C. Wright Mills, *The Power Elite* (New York: Oxford University Press, 1956), pp. 298–324.

modern democracies," [9] yields increasingly to the liquor cabinet. Great political events become more akin to funerals, something entered into only by compulsion (and even the funeral, once, was a social "event"). The roots of loyalty run thin, and partisan commitment with them.

In the new political environment, where bonds beyond the family are weak and the emotional life of the individual closes in around himself, doctrinal and ideological parties become more frequent. In part, these may result from education, but their true basis is not intellectual sophistication (which could as easily argue for compromises to win the "best possible" result), but from an insecurity which demands absolute agreement as the price of trust and commitment. It is the echo of gemeinschaft, in which difference is intolerable, the terrified child's demand for "oneness." Its doctrines may be wise and valuable, but the doctrinal party is based on a self that remains pre-political and pre-fraternal.

Max Weber wrote that civic fraternity ceased to be possible when citizens lost the ability to defend their own walls, but defense was less vital than the wall itself, the symbol of a polity whose boundaries were the emotional universe of the citizen. The classic philosophers would have agreed with Marcuse that the best solution of the political problem demands a convergence of reason and art.[10] That would have emphasized the necessity (though not the sufficiency) of the small state. It is not enough that rulers and ruled share an abstract standard of justice. Art demands knowledge, and respect for the material at hand; so in the state, rulers must have personal knowledge of those they rule, and the ruled must sense themselves as known. The highest justice demands the greatest sharing of value and the deepest mutual knowledge; it demands fraternity.

All that is impossible in the modern state. Even if philosophers were kings, they might know "man" but they would not know *me*. And most often, modern kings are much less than philosophers and are endowed with dreadful weapons and magics. I am aware that new "technologies of control" open new possibilities for decentralization, but these are still systems of control; they only make it possible to

[9] Maurice Duverger, *Political Parties* (New York: Wiley, 1951), p. 20.
[10] Max Weber, *The City* (Glencoe: Free Press, 1958); Marcuse, *One Dimensional Man*, p. 238.

manage men more impersonally and indirectly. In fact, they remove an old limit on central regimes: orders had to pass through officials outside the ruler's span of control. (It was just that limitation which encouraged the traditional bureaucratic emphasis on rigid obedience to rule and procedure.) The new techniques only increase the dispensability of man and give new evidence of individual unimportance, even if they make it more endurable.[11]

In the modern state, civic fraternity is impossible and the best, or rather the safest, approximation of justice is procedural rather than substantive, limited to external conduct, and leaves the development of man's justly fearful spirit to others than the state. This is the irreducible claim of liberalism, one conceded by the most unlikely men. Marcuse, for example, writes that "no tribunal can justly arrogate to itself the right to decide what needs should be satisfied," and goes on to describe the perils of "educational dictatorship from Plato to Rousseau" (an unhappy comment on his skills as an intellectual historian).[12]

Most of *One Dimensional Man*, however, is a demonstration that modern man cannot make such decisions himself. If no "tribunal" acts for him, the remaining logic is that of drift, with fearful and isolated man following the passive and resentful pattern of the child, and technological expansion pursuing its own unguided course. It is at best a Hobson's choice for those who fear that the destination is disaster.

Resistance

The great majority of contemporary social scientists have been only too aware of the citizen's defects, so much so that they have raised stability and order to the status of self-sufficient political values. Terrified of the citizen, they have been only slightly concerned to improve him, falling back instead on the hope that the "system" of "pluralistic" politics would be "self-regulating"—the liberal's dream.

[11] For some possibilities, see Michel Crozier, *The Bureaucratic Phenomenon* (Chicago: University of Chicago Press, 1964).

[12] *One Dimensional Man*, pp. 6, 40; compare the odd consonance, on many points, of Arthur Schlesinger, Jr., *The Crisis of Confidence* (Boston: Houghton Mifflin, 1969), pp. 30–31, 42–45.

Fear blinds, and the arguments of social scientists are a curious potpourri. Having proved that "uncommitted voters" are ill-informed and often irrational, they congratulate America for an electoral system in which such voters hold the political balance. Believing that an inrush of new voters may encourage authoritarianism, they praise apathy; but—liberals to the core—they propose not closing but broadening the legal channels of participation. (To be consistent, they should prescribe participation *before* crises propel men armed only with desperation into political life, in the hope that they would learn greater respect for democratic institutions and procedures.) Finally, though social scientists have praised the representative qualities of groups, they also laud them for avoiding conflicts between "attitude and behavior" which group members might perceive in themselves if they participated. That last argument is only an academic statement of the proposition that the system conceals and avoids issues (especially those which might threaten the position of established leaders). Moreover, good men and good citizens alike are aware when their behavior deviates from what they believe and value ("attitudes"), and to support a system which keeps men in ignorance of that conflict is, implicitly, to defend it for protecting and encouraging baseness and illusion in those who are ruled.

Those who cannot share the sanguine beliefs or the low values inherent in such theories, however, must beware of corresponding errors in their own. The contemporary citizen is trapped between his resentment against modern politics and his desire for the material goods it provides, goods he may lack the skills to do without. Confronted with a dilemma, cunning man seeks a way to grasp both horns without injury. He seeks for assurance that all things are possible according to his desire and will not willingly accept the counsel of those, like De Jouvenel, who warn him that to grasp both horns of this dilemma is to become a victim of the Minotaur.

Contemporary men seek a magic which will enable them to keep the material benefits of modernity while escaping its political costs. Sometimes, of course, they look to "charismatic" leaders to provide miracles, but they also turn to intellectuals for a magic of words which seems to bridge the abyss of choice. If intellectuals are tempted to engage in that magic, it is not only because by pandering to public desire they can maximize their own power. We intellectuals are ourselves contemporary men; the desire and the temptation is in us, not in outside pressures. The increase in the intellectual's political power, as others look to him for answers, only adds to his temptation. And to repeat, the danger is as great for critics of the established order as for its supporters.

In *One Dimensional Man*, one of the subtler works of the time, Marcuse argues that we must complete the "historical project" of winning mastery over nature, assuring us that there are "two kinds of mastery, a repressive and a liberative one." Most of the argument of the book, however, suggests that the two are inseparably connected; the possibility of dividing one from the other rests on the assertion that

> A mature and free industrial society would continue to depend on a division of labor which involves inequality of functions. . . . However, the executive and supervisory functions would no longer carry the privilege of ruling others in some particular interest.

This is a thesis Marcuse would scorn if advanced by another: administration need not affect policy, nor fact, value; technology is "value neutral." His willingness to make the argument turns on the term "free industrial society," for Marcuse asserts that if certain changes are made in modern society we may expect "yet uncharted realms of freedom." The dilemma is resolved and repression is split from liberation, in other words, by mystery, the prospect of "uncharted realms" for which no evidence exists and which no evidence can refute.[13]

This sort of intellectual magic contributes to the frustrations of contemporary politics. Denying the need to face choices, it lessens or destroys the ability to make them; it encourages a concentration of attention on issues which are secondary at best and which leave unchallenged the fundamental problems and processes of modern life. It is understandable that this should be so. As Arnold Gehlen writes, the great processes of modern society have come to seem "meta-human," and we forget that all such developments originate in human decision, even if masses of individuals are involved.[14] Changing such processes comes to seem hopeless; the only hope seems to lie in concentrating the powers of the intellect in an effort to classify and comprehend the

[13] *One Dimensional Man*, pp. 2, 44, 231, 236.
[14] Arnold Gehlen, "L'Avenir de la Culture," *Futuribles*, #50 (March 10, 1963).

forces and direction of change. Thought seems impotent, for ideas persuade men slowly if at all, while a new technological development can transform the life of man in an instant. But understanding such notions does not excuse them. They tend to produce a mind which is receptive, adaptive, concerned with adjustment; reason, as Marcuse writes, becomes a form of submission.[15]

Social scientists even define man in terms of such categories. "The most important and most typically human quality," Nieburg writes, "is generalized adaptability." The critics of social science themselves fall victim. Marcuse, for example, insists that "social theory is historical theory" and that it "opposes all metaphysics by the rigorously historical character of the transcendence. The 'possibilities' must be within the reach of the respective society; they must be definable goals of practice." Truth is what works at any time; Greek thought is "ineffective, unreal," the two qualities being so identical in Marcuse's mind as not even to require a "therefore" to unite them.[16]

The individual who is to "adjust" himself cannot allow himself to be tied to things or to persons; he must be isolated, free-floating. Deprived of any emotional connection to or support from the outer world, such an individual is unlikely to examine his goals or his image of himself. He concentrates on adjustment and must take himself as a given. Modern life is not responsible for the "intolerance of ambiguity" observed by students of the "authoritarian personality." The emotions are always hostile to ambiguity; and in any case, toleration of ambiguity is no intellectual virtue, although the recognition of ambiguity may be necessary. What matters is that in the modern world, forced to tolerate ambiguity in social and political affairs, we tend to reject it in matters involving first premises.

Marcuse has pointed out that tolerance, like the fact-value distinction, tends to reduce values to a special, inferior status which renders them impotent in affecting behavior.[17] But the principle of toleration also places values in a sphere where they need not be defended and cannot be affected by "external" evidence or by events. Social toleration, in fact, is a buttress for private dogmatism.

[15] *One Dimensional Man*, pp. 11, 98–99.
[16] Nieburg, *Political Violence*, p. 51; Marcuse, *One Dimensional Man*, pp. xi, 126 (see also pp. 97, 141, 217–221, 229–230).
[17] *One Dimensional Man*, pp. 84, 146–147.

Classical political theory hoped for individuals who would examine such basic beliefs and values, for not only all conventional wisdom but ultimately all human knowledge was ambiguous and uncertain. But Classicism argued that individuals who could bear such "knowledge of ignorance" were most likely to develop in stable societies which gave them emotional security. Ambiguity was twofold: aware of the defects of customary belief (and those of philosophic doctrines), the philosopher would also see his paradoxical dependence on customs and conventions based on those beliefs. Philosophic knowledge was a good in itself, as "private" as a value could be in the polis; the intellect would deal gently with the ambiguities of "right opinion," aware that the most philosophic of men owed a personal debt to, and shared a bond of emotions and feelings with, the political world. "Know thyself," after all, was a Delphic mystery, not an adjuration to individualism.

Modern society reverses the order of things, its rapidly changing insecurity placing a premium on men who can concentrate the emotions within the self and who can use the intellect as a tool for establishing control over and security in the world of events. The number of men who earn their labor by the intellect has greatly increased, but their labor is increasingly sophistic, involving the use of the mind for ends other than knowledge. Grants and rewards do their work; the "intellectual workman" focuses on problems posed by society, not on questions distinctly his own. Science, as Marcuse observes, comes to identify itself with technology; educators delight in serving as the "handmaiden of industrialism," and social scientists set their hopes on "prediction and control." It is hardly an accident that when intellectual and academic relevance to society reaches a high point, students should suspect that both lack relevance to the personal development of man.[18]

The modern literati are no less specialists than the technicians, fixing their attention on the private emotional life of men. Implicitly and explicitly, they tend to teach that the solutions to man's problems are in himself, and consequently the emotions should be withdrawn from outside objects and concentrated in the self. Individualism comes easily; "radicals" teach and practice withdrawal into drugs and

[18] *Ibid.*, pp. 155–164, 115–116.

sex—acting, Nieburg notes, only as consumers of different products. "Desublimation," Marcuse observes, becomes repressive, and "the avant-garde and the beatniks share the function of entertaining without endangering the good conscience of men of good will." [19]

An exception may seem to exist in the prescription of "love," but to urge men to love per se is to urge them to love something, not any particular thing. It reflects a desire to have love without love's risks and threats; all love is acceptable and no love matters; what is accessible will do as well as, and more safely than, what is demanding. Equally, it reflects a desire to escape the boundaries and limits that surround lovers. "Make love, not war" is sensible only if we do not ask "to whom?" Love become specific becomes limited, potentially scarce, and perhaps the most prolific source of war men know. Men who speak in such terms betray their own emptiness. They are the victims of society, not its teachers and prophets.

Modern society discourages fraternity and, as a result, those who become discontented in its midst are most often alone. It is hard to sustain that loneliness, much less to transform uneasiness and resentment into vision and freedom. What is called "alienation" among us is, in fact, far removed from the older meaning of the term. It does not refer to men who have made themselves aliens because, "called out" by values higher than those of the polity, they are citizens of a better city. Rather, it is used to designate those who are citizens nowhere. And the result is often a desperate scrabbling to find affection and response somewhere, on almost any terms—lest, finding his isolation unendurable, the individual fall into conventionality and respectability. Even "nihilism" is often a request that we bar the door; often, we only open it wider, offering fame and adulation. Unconventionality becomes first notoriety, then fashion, and finally a new style of respectability. The real complaint against modern society is that in so many ways it denies men the ability to become alienated.

Often the desperation of the discontented leads them to postulate a "fraternity" between themselves and the excluded and oppressed, men who would in any case deserve compassion, concern, and support. Those who adhered to the "old left," Ignazio Silone remarked, never understood that the real basis of their revolt was a "choice of

---

[19] *Ibid.*, pp. 70 and 56–83; Nieburg, *Political Violence*, pp. 143, 158–159.

comrades." The comradeship is, of course, often spurious; the excluded resent their outcast state precisely because it lies on them so heavily, threatening their survival and their real needs; their greatest hope is to enter and not to escape society. In fact, they may even resent the values and virtues which they have been able to preserve in and through exclusion. The moral heritage of Jews, Nietzsche commented, would enable them to rule Europe if they wished, but they only aspire to become like others.[20]

Of course, one can hope to "teach" his oppressed comrades, but such a relation is not fraternity; it is paternalism, justified perhaps, but paternalism nonetheless. But the relationship between the uprooted intellectual and the too-rooted oppressed is tainted by more than paternalism. All too often, our feelings for the persecuted result from our fear of others more similar to us. The belief in "superior virtue of the oppressed" results from my belief that they can hardly afford to reject my love, and that it will not hurt me too much if they do. Even the desperately fearful child knows that love can be expressed toward dogs and underdogs. And such feelings are made easier and safer when we know few of those we claim as "brothers" except as abstractions.

That the excluded are often members of traditional groups and communities only adds to their appeal, for traditional cultures and vocabularies often passionately criticize and are criticized by the whole apparatus of modern life and thought. "What any age deems evil," Nietzsche wrote, "is usually the unseasonable echo of an earlier ideal." [21]

Mobilized yet excluded by modern systems, traditional groups become aware of different, even shocking, moral standards in the new order; to such developments rural orders the world over have raised cries of protest. The loss of community, the decline of kinship ethics, the rise of competitive and careerist patterns all win their share of denunciation. Traditional leaders or new prophets call for resistance, seeking to transform or obliterate what is hateful in the new order.

The weapons of traditionalism, however, are few. Its adherents may cling to rites and institutions for emotional security. They may

---

[20] Ignazio Silone, "The Choice of Comrades," *Dissent*, II (1955), pp. 7–19; *The Philosophy of Nietzsche*, pp. 562–565.

[21] *The Philosophy of Nietzsche*, p. 466.

employ the traditional language as a means of winning support inside the group (and, if the traditional culture is part of the heritage of dominant groups, within those as well). If traditionalism persists simply in opposing modernity, however, it becomes burdensome to most of its adherents, and not only because they are likely to suffer sanctions and reprisals, but because they will be asked to forego many of the comforts and rewards which modernity makes available. (Low prices, Marx declared, are the "heavy artillery" of the bourgeoisie.)[22]

In the Middle Ages, when central regimes were weak, such cultures and groups with autonomous standards of value might hope to win contests with the state; in modern states, such successes have been rare indeed. The original "pluralists" were, more often than not, political romantics who sought to apply medieval history to modern times. Laski's "examples" of resistance demonstrated futility more than triumph. The resistance of Oxford Catholics to the doctrine of Papal infallibility, or of the Scottish Church in the 1840s, were hardly proofs that the state was a "myth." In fact, pluralist theory, rising just before and during World War I, was less an argument against the existence of the "omnicompetent state" than a moral protest against the fact.[23]

A group with autonomous values has three options within the modern polity: (1) to preserve values by reducing membership to those to whom its beliefs are sufficiently valuable to make the burdens worthwhile—by becoming a sect or something still smaller; (2) to decrease the burden on its members by reducing claims to those, such as ritual, which do not conflict with dominant social and political claims; and (3) to attempt the seizure of political power.

The last is rare within modernized states, which wield the full arsenal of reward and sanction, but it is frequent enough in transitional communities. Winning power, however, hardly solves the problem. In the first place, both external and internal pressures for change will continue to exist. In fact, power cannot be won or kept without adopting great elements of modern technology. The conquest of the state by the unassimilated, should it take place, would only increase the state's legitimacy by lessening its alien quality. After De Tocque-

---

[22] Karl Marx, *The Communist Manifesto*, in *Marx and Engels*, ed. L. Feuer (Garden City: Doubleday, 1959), p. 11.

[23] Harold J. Laski, *Studies in the Problem of Sovereignty* (New Haven: Yale University Press, 1917).

ville and De Jouvenel, lengthy comment would be pointless; once the excluded take power, traditional values become relegated to the status of distant hopes, and fraternity becomes the forever distant promise of an "unfinished" revolution.[24]

The preservation of traditional values and symbols, even in an "irrelevant" sphere, however, has its effects. Often the only means by which the heritage can be preserved at all, such values and symbols may give individuals some sense of "belonging" which counteracts tendencies toward isolation. They may provide the security which forms the basis of a challenge to the times, and traditional values which indict modern practice may help to define that challenge (whether it is felt as private guilt or social evil). Too, they provide the freedom which comes from having a past and the metaphors which may enable the individual to communicate his vision and feeling to others. But though all these factors may help to initiate later discontent, they are not enough to sustain and develop it. The hand of the past may beckon, but it is dead, too chill to provide the emotional and personal support needed by living men. Ancestors are not a substitute for brethren.

Generation

Men still begin their lives, and first know their past, in families, but men of an earlier day would find home in our world a strange place. Even the most acute of nineteenth-century observers thought they had encountered something generic in the American family, with its explicit acceptance of romance. Debate still exists, but most evidence now appears to support the predictions of De Tocqueville and Beaumont that what they saw might become the general tendency of modern life. Modernity seems to encourage families which (1) are conjugal, with a corresponding rise of emotional intensity and instability; (2) are shut off from a comparatively uniform "outside" world, with blood kinsmen and friends increasingly viewed as outsiders and intruders; (3) expel instrumental and purposive activities into the outer world; and (4) decrease the role of the father, whose position is associated with those activities. When De Tocqueville and

[24] Alexis de Tocqueville, *The Old Regime and the French Revolution* (New York: Doubleday, 1955), and Bertrand de Jouvenel, *On Power*.

Beaumont, with mingled horror and admiration, saw American woman as the critical factor in American life, they thought of her role in the family.[25]

It could scarcely be otherwise. Parents find in the intense, half-closed universe of the family a solace for their feelings of social and political indignity, a source—almost the only one—of emotional meaning. The same forces from which they retreat, however, deny them authority. Under conditions of rapid change, the experience of parents rapidly becomes irrelevant as a guide for the young (America saw this early in immigrant families); where stable societies saw wisdom in age, modern ones see obsolescence and senility.

As the rational basis for parental authority declines, parents seek a new basis for relations with their children which will give them security against change (especially among those who disregarded the authority of *their* parents). That, as De Tocqueville observed, they find in the "natural affections," [26] for the claim of love is not necessarily undermined by change. If the child's duty rests on the parent's love for him, it is the parent who controls that duty, nor does time invalidate the claim that parental "sacrifice" demands love in return.

But the use of the "natural affections" as the basis for authority implicitly (at least) threatens a withdrawal of affection if the child does not obey. Such threats are feared in all societies, but in the family which uses love as authority they amount to an effort to obtain obedience by maximizing the child's emotional insecurity.

It hardly helps that parents desire children as sources of love rather than as economic assets. Children's admiration is an element of dignity in parents' lives, and as the child's independence of the parent increases (and his adulation diminishes), the desire of the parent to emphasize the child's insecurity and dependence keeps pace. Affection is not only conditional; it comes to seem a permanently scarce good, and no amount of present affection secures against the threat of loss.

Brothers, as De Tocqueville realized, are no longer united by a common struggle with their father over the right to become adult or to enter into the family patrimony;[27] each child is encouraged to

[25] Alexis de Tocqueville, *Democracy in America,* vol. II, pp. 229–242; G. de Beaumont, *Marie* (Stanford: Stanford University Press, 1958), pp. 16–22.

[26] *Democracy in America,* vol. II, p. 233.

[27] *Ibid.,* pp. 234–235.

"make his own" and, in societies like ours, each is taught that it is a duty to rise above one's parents. Brothers are always rivals who are admired and feared, but in modern society economic and social life does little to check that rivalry; in fact, it reinforces it.

Told that he must "share," cooperate with, and "love" his brothers, the child (and this, increasingly, includes female children) finds himself compared to brothers or sisters in respect to relative success or failure in the outside world. There is little or no structure within fraternal relations, no authority in older brothers, that might minimize competition. The competition is itself less important than that it aims not at the ostensible prizes of the struggle, but at affection. Hence a deliberately encouraged insecurity impels men to strive against their fellows for the appearance of self-sufficiency or, as a result of particular family situations, for the appearance of failure and dependence. In both cases, the individual will have unconscious awareness, at least, that his action is pretense; his "independence" is motivated by a desperate dependence on affection and emotional support, his "dependence"—if he uses that tactic—by a desire for elevation over his brothers and for greater closeness to his parents.

Under no circumstances can the individual be free from a fear of being "found out," and those who are most like him are the most feared because they are likeliest to discover the secret. Correspondingly, it is necessary to put distance between them and the self; consider only the frequent anti-intellectualism of left intellectuals, the posturing *einigkeit* of those of the right.

Yet men always struggle somewhat against their child-selves and seek the fraternity necessary to manhood. Fraternal affection is passionately desired and desperately feared, and few institutions exist to moderate the extremity of feeling. Frequently, the desire for fraternity as a means becomes so deeply identified with the end as to create the image of a perfect, romantic "liberator" who frees the individual from the emotional world of the "family of orientation." It is a wistful, pathetic theme, especially notable in American letters, pejoratively adolescent. The image of the perfect brother is based on the desire to be free both from the family and from adulthood, Erikson's "moratorium" on adulthood in a literal sense. Behind it is the desire to possess the goods of adulthood without the burdens of responsibility, to have fraternity without the "imperfection" and risk which results from the independent self of the other and the limits of nature.[28]

But the power of romanticism is also the result of the accurate perception that very little in adult life is worthy of emulation. By default, rejection of meaningless adulthood may become a defense of childhood, and the romantic dream of childlike irresponsibility combined with physical maturity may seem the "best of all possible worlds." At least inarticulately, however, such resistance is a demand for values and virtues which modern society and politics do not provide.

Equally inarticulate but quite as marked is society's dumb conspiracy to keep such protests unprogrammatic, disorganized, romantic and futile. In the past, studies of youth by American social scientists focused on the gang, treating it as the "enemy" of society. Recently, greater attention to and sympathy for youth have resulted in a more favorable view which sees the gang as a means to move from passivity to activity, to critically examine conventional values and wisdom. But such analyses, like celebrations of youth generally, neglect the fact that such needs and desires are modal, not substantive. Gangs or students may desire to "escape passivity," to "participate" or to "find choice"; that does not tell us what such groups wish to choose, or even what they wish to participate in. And substantive values are a critical aspect of any youth rebellion.

The ethnic gangs in American cities, for example, provided a center of unambiguous loyalty for youth caught between a disintegrating heritage and exclusion from the dominant society. But the purpose of such gangs has been determined by the desire for inclusion; formal organization was normal and reflected the instrumental thrust of the gang. The successful ethnic gang became the "machine" or the "syndicate," and interpersonal solidarity yielded to something like bureaucracy.

If racial gangs today seem to differ, it is possibly only because more doors are locked shut. Violence often seems the only mode of action, whether it is blindly cathartic or, where hopelessness is less extreme, more selective in its choice of objects and enemies. Even

[28] Erik Erikson, "Youth: Fidelity and Diversity," *Daedalus*, 91 (1962), pp. 5-27.

"revolutionary" ideology may be no more than a logical response to the difficulty of gaining access to the dominant society and the values it inculcates and makes available.

There is no problem of exclusion, of course, for middle-class youth. But its discontents most often take the form of a protest against established purposes and goals which lacks any alternative standard of value. Movements and fashions reject the limitations on immediate gratification which society imposes, but also all intense personal bonds and loyalties which require the hallowing of commitment. "Youth culture" is not fraternity; its basis is the romantic dream of self. And never far below the surface lie the anxieties and terrors which are inseparable from the romantic's lonely flight from the limitations of his own nature.

Set against the hobo-cult, or the religion of hallucination, the organized instrumentalism of the traditional gang seems rational and even noble. But in all the currents among youth, modality tends to replace substance; the chivalry of the gangs is *dignidad* without the Christian ideal, and the "anti-utilitarian values" of middle-class youth are a rejection of utilitarian prudence, not of materialism.

When all that is said, however, it must be conceded that those observers who have discerned alternative values in youth movements —like idealism, radicalism, or nobility—are not wholly wrong. Largely inchoate, such values may be possible of realization. Romantic resistance may, in our times, be a precondition of fraternity. Established social institutions, however, seem almost contrived to prevent such a transition from possibility to actuality. Edgar Friedenberg accurately observes that

> Some schools actively discourage cliques based on "mere friendship."
> . . . Youngsters . . . know that their relations are disapproved as un-
> democratic and become still more guilty and defiant about their own ex-
> clusiveness; the members lose, or never develop, confidence in their right
> to choose their own friends. . . . The school encourages extensive social
> contact, but discourages intensive relations between small numbers of
> self-sufficient individuals.[29]

Social processes in which such educational practices play a role increasingly shift the place of rebellion, the stage of fidelity, to the

[29] Edgar Z. Friedenberg, *Coming of Age in America* (New York: Random House, 1965), pp. 238–239.

college campus. The campus is ideal in another sense: it is one of the last analogues of the *polis*, a society in which there is considerable unity between the expressive and purposive universe of the individual. And, of course, the college cannot help increasing the awareness of alternative values, of ideals lacking in contemporary society.

But student-as-virtue will do no better than gang-as-virtue, though either may be closer to the truth than Joe College and the "delinquent." Student rebellion gradually moves away from social and political sophistication toward symbols which reflect established individualism, "freedom" and the right to unobstructed will and gratification, the romantic love of the victim. This in part simply reflects the necessity of any mass movement to speak to the values and the desires which already exist in the mind of the many.

The need for a mass movement, however, also reflects the guilt of which Friedenberg speaks, the need to justify a desire for brothers in terms of universal fraternity. So long held together by interpersonal bonds, a movement like S.D.S. was led by the hope of success and the universalism of its doctrine to welcome rapid expansion of membership. New recruitment, through the agency of the mass media, far outran the capacity of the movement to socialize and assimilate members into the old understandings, much less into the structure of friendship. Factionalization and formalization became necessary, and the new left became like the old, men once again justifying their "choice of comrades" by the abstractions of ideology.

It is too much to expect those who by their own critique proclaim themselves the emotional and intellectual victims of society to formulate alternatives to it, or to develop a clear understanding of values and virtues which have little or no contact with their lives. Like the gangs, they do their best service when they act as warriors. Their combats and conflicts may do them some damage; they may also do good. At the very least, they compel other men to think, deny the capacity for retreat and evasion, and raise the possibility of clarity, if not an alternative. As Plato knew, the virtue of guardians, savage to enemies and loving to friends, may only be the virtue of dogs, but it is essential to the wisdom of the philosopher who would be king. Based on the awareness that there are such things as friends and enemies, the concept may cause some to ask the true nature of friends and foes, and even to realize that in one's brothers one finds the best of both.

Recognition

Men have always relied on appearances to help them classify and predict the behavior of unfamiliar persons. Beset by masses of such men, modern man becomes a connoisseur of appearances and external symbols; not for nothing do so many battles rage between the generations on the question of hair and fashion. Each man, however, knows that the categories derived from appearance apply only in the crudest way to himself, and experience teaches him the same lesson with respect to others. The "aesthetics of vision," as Rieff calls them, are at best accurate in the aggregate, mistaken in detail, revealing little of the personality behind the facade.[30]

This is especially true because our fellows, fearing what is different and valuing the distinction it conveys, are so prone, when they cannot eradicate perceptible difference, to adopt it. A thousand media advertise costume, massify style, and publicize argot until whatever internal character those things had seemed to betoken is lost amid millions who adopt them only as talismans of status, power, and security. Forced to classify men in such categories, and aware of their inaccuracy, we become cautious in our commitments, defensive in our approaches. Even conversation becomes disembodied, part of the mask, the product of some third and fourth parties to the discussion who are strangers to our real selves.

There is another reason, perhaps more vital. Mobility in space and occupation implies that all relationships are subject to an impermanence which did not pervade traditional society. Deep personal bonds are discouraged by the knowledge of transience; the residence and the personal universe of men are largely determined by extraneous factors like the market. Romantics may believe in a love independent of space and time, but most know only too well that memory and will are feeble instruments, and that in a contest with the senses, the senses usually prevail. Memory and intention guarantee only that drifting

[30] Phillip Rieff, "Aesthetic Functions in Modern Politics," *WP*, V (1953), pp. 478–502.

apart comes slowly and painfully, leaving a sense of regret which serves to warn the individual of danger in deep ties to others.

Save for peculiar cases like school graduations, when one person leaves, the other is left behind. The feelings of bereavement, desertion, and abandonment return one, momentarily at least, to the child's moments of terror. Having felt this, a man begins to look to his defenses, and each instance strengthens his will to avoid a repetition. Commitments consequently become weaker, and he feels the temptation to protect himself by being the first to leave.

Between humans there are always fears of loss and injury. Modern society raises those anxieties to the level of sober fact. At the same time, it is possible for individuals to satisfy their social needs while minimizing the degree to which they are known by or are dependent on any of their friends. Friendship becomes less a relation of whole personalities than a situation based on discrete roles and attributes. We learn to modify the term by adjectives ("business friends"), and to those involved it seems never to occur that the term "fraternity brother" is pathetically redundant.

Men move in circles which are "limited liability communities." Often our social world is little more than the opportunity for emotional expression or for social contact as such. Common values and purposes, when avowed, are frequently little more than an excuse, a justification which conceals and protects personal need and vulnerability. To listen to conversation in such circles can be painful; opinions are tediously uniform and boringly predictable, and the uniformity itself reveals the fragile bond that unites the group. It is, in fact, a pseudo-gemeinschaft, like its genuine counterpart unable to endure disagreement, but different from it in that the "liability" and investment of each individual are so small.

Where traditional societies made self-concealment comparatively difficult, modern societies make it easy. Few men know the individual's past or more than a part of his present, and those who know him today may not tomorrow. His life becomes divided into a series of isolated periods of time as well as into separate roles. Small wonder if the individual finds it hard to maintain a coherent sense of self. His innumerable selves, in fact, may grow too great for his "span of control"—here, at least, still tied to personality—and some may become "external" forces which control him. Men raised in traditional communities may find it a liberation to enter modernity, but even for them, the doubt comes early. Man cannot conceal himself from others without losing a part or all of himself, and privatization more than any single fact destroys the possibility of genuine privacy. There are no secrets where everything is a mystery.

Even riches embarrass us. Modern society makes life cosmopolitan, throwing us into contact with thousands and making it far more likely that we will meet those who might become our brothers. If we should recognize such potential kinsmen, however, their numbers may make us think of fraternity as something easily found, discouraging the deep personal commitment necessary to the development of fraternal relations. But it is much more likely that no such recognition will occur, for our lives and emotions are not shaped for fraternity. Unlighted ships, we pass by or collide violently, all too often without hail.

But even if we did call out, would we be understood? Language is a thing of metaphor, and to communicate we require not merely a common idea but similarity in the emotions associated with words and sounds. Men whose pasts differ greatly and who share few emotional symbols may find it difficult to develop a common language, or even to recognize as common words and symbols they would not themselves employ. And, as Marcuse points out, men are increasingly separated from their pasts. Language becomes radically self-centered, operating on individualistic presuppositions which tend to foreclose the possibility of communion and fraternity. Those who recognize a need for fraternity may, balked by the lack of common emotional associations, be tempted to see emotion and the senses as the answer to their need. But to make a purpose of emotion and the senses is to deny the very nature of fraternity, to isolate the individual in himself. Under the best circumstances, the emotions can be made fraternity's ally. The relation of brotherhood, however, is impossible without common symbols and values that can cross the gap which the senses always leave between men.[31]

It is never easy to identify one's brothers, and for modern man the task may seem impossible, or not worth the cost. Brethren have always required "proofs" of one another, and being put to the test is

[31] *One Dimensional Man*, pp. 174ff., 211–215.

an essential element of growing into fraternity. The ultimate test, of course, was the willingness to sacrifice life. In modern societies, where trust and its risks require so much, and where—far from being a relation one "grows into" over time—fraternity often seems a thing which must be seized at once or lost altogether, that final test may seem the only adequate proof. Violence and romanticism are twins, as the wise have always known.

The temptations of violence, however, cannot be discarded so simply. In the modern state, the threat of violence has been the core of legitimacy, able to break the walls of withdrawal and privatization and to call for sacrifice from citizens. War and the threat of war come naturally where legitimacy is threatened or is otherwise inadequate, when the productive apparatus fails or when faith in the future decays. Consider the definition of legitimacy put forward by H. L. Nieburg: "Raw physical power becomes legitimate in the hands of some kind of centralized authority as a means of promoting internal and external security." [32]

Most social scientists, in fact, would agree. War is not the "instrument of policy" of modern states; it *is* their policy. Politics itself is only war conducted by other means. The modern state arose as an instrument for the conquest of nature and of other men, and when the conquest is completed, the state will no longer be needed. In its promise that the state will "wither away," Marxism merely follows the logic to its conclusion, just as Herbert Spencer did. But it is essential to see that the conquest of all men is involved; while some resist others, the state is still needed. Marcuse makes himself the prophet of the "pacification of existence" (at least partly aware, one hopes, that "pacification" was a nineteenth-century euphemism for imperial conquest), basing his hope on the proposition that human aggressiveness along with misery and injustice, is "superimposed . . . by particular social interests." [33]

Yet aggressiveness, even if we accepted Marcuse's theory, still remains an essential element of precisely the freedom that Marcuse most admires: the effort to discern truth behind appearance. Equally, it is an element of man's freedom and of his capacity to value, for to

[32] *Political Violence*, p. 11. See also Marcuse, *One Dimensional Man*, pp. 155–164.
[33] *One Dimensional Man*, pp. 5, 16, 236.

love or value something is to deprecate and be aggressive toward other things. If anything, modern man has been pacified too much, and his resentment of the fact is a major element in his fascination with violence.

No one need be told the uses of disobedience and violence (or the threat of violence) within the state. They retain some capacity to shatter the private fortresses of men, to make citizens aware that a problem exists, and to enable a devoted few to obtain some hearing from the diffuse indifference of the many. Though the reaction of citizens may be hostile, it is at least less ignorant than what preceded it, and in so many cases, violence can activate the conscience of man and force him to be free. The terrible qualities of violence—the waste of its destructiveness, the danger that it will grow out of control and even become a pattern of life—need not blind us to its educative functions.

Violence has, however, other and intrinsic appeals. It is a means for testing one's friends and proving one's self to them. More important, it helps men find solidarity. The greater fear of the enemy enables them to override the fears and suspicions of everyday life, and they find in their fellows a virtually essential source of support and encouragement. There is no doubt that the fraternity of battle has produced moments of nobility, nor that, once known, it long endures in the mind of man. Not for nothing does Lewis Coser call attention to the "rebirth" that men seem to feel in situations of violence.[34]

Yet the fraternity of battle is radically defective as fraternity. Those who must fight or "confront" others to find solidarity leave the essential decision—what is being fought about—to the enemy. The values and goals of combat are determined by what the enemy thinks worth fighting for; male hair styles become a vital issue and a source of conflict only when the enemy is asinine enough to make them so. And as we know only too well, in war and conflict the life of one's own people becomes shaped by the requirements of victory, by what conquers and not by what is right. In the simplest sense, any army can find fraternity in battle, whatever its cause. The fraternity of combat lacks the essential of true fraternity: standards and values by which the self is judged defective and guilty. At root, though the fraternity

[34] *Continuities in the Study of Social Conflict*, p. 81.

of battle may produce heroism, its basis is the fear of death, not the inadequacy of life; guilt and blame reside in the enemy, not in the selves of the individual and his brethren.

The fears which prevented the same sense of solidarity from developing in time of peace are quieted in time of conflict, but not because one risks his own life—that he could always do. The risk seems tolerable in war because others risk their lives as well. The solidarity one was too cowardly to seek in peace is purchased at the price of brothers' blood.

Moreover, "confrontation" and conflict tend to compel a recognition of the humanity of those we fight. Such is the melancholy condition of man, in fact, that his definition of "soul" might well be "that which resists my violence by violence." So often we fight those we admire, whom we wish to admire and notice us; so often we come to admire those we fight. And those feelings frequently become clear to us only when it is too late. All these guilts, unlike those of fraternity, the individual must bear alone.

I hardly deny the sad truth that war and violence are sometimes necessary. I only deny the proposition that they produce fraternity. Brothers may march to defend something they value already, and it may strengthen both their bonds and their devotion to the valued thing that they do so; it creates neither. Why else the mournful lesson of battle fraternity, that it lapses with the end of war?

The temptation to violence is greatest among those who feel the need of fraternity most. It is necessary to tell them the grim truth of the matter: that political and civic fraternity are impossible under modern conditions; that the chances of fraternity within the polity, in lesser groups, are small enough; that there is no simple tactic which can produce brotherhood. And certainly, one must persuade as many as will listen that following modernity still another distance down the path will lead to universal fratricide more surely than to the realization of universal fraternity. That vision, the highest dream of modern politics, is exalted indeed; for as the old sages knew, it is supremely beyond the abilities of men, yet always tantalizing because it has a measure of truth. But it is not a truth which can find application in this world.

The grim lessons must be learned to teach the brighter. Fraternity may be unlikely in modern society, but likelihood is never certainty.

Accidents of character and rearing, the traditions of culture and people, the chance events of meeting and moment, all qualify the logic of modern life. Predictable in the whole, they remain uncertain in the particular. And because fraternity is a need of man, it is always possible while man remains; society does not make nature or nature's laws any more than individual will does.

Those who hope for fraternity in these times face three imperatives: to recognize fraternity when it occurs; to broaden the chance for others; to feel compassion for those denied the opportunity of fraternity. All include the obligation to set an example, the oldest duty of fraternity, in whatever sphere falls to us and our brothers. And all embody a duty to preserve, recreate, and add to the old tradition which made the idea and the language of fraternity accessible to humankind, so that those who come after may find a world in which the chances and hopes for fraternity are broader and less faint. These may seem massive duties in view of what must, for us, be slight possibilities, but a devotion to improbable visions and a willingness to bear great burdens are among the qualities that most deserve to be called human.

America! America!
God shed his grace on thee
And crown thy good
With brotherhood
From sea to shining sea!

Katherine Lee Bates,
America The Beautiful

I'd hammer out danger,
I'd hammer out a warning,
I'd hammer out love between
My brothers and my sisters
All over this land.

Pete Seeger

CHAPTER IV

THE AMBIGUOUS IDEAL: FRATERNITY IN AMERICA

Inheritances

POLITICAL thinkers in America have spoken of liberty and equality, decentralization and bureaucracy, law and violence, but they have rarely spoken of fraternity. Yet in political life, the word still has magic: an advocate of racial equality appeals, not to equality, but to the fact that we are "brothers under the skin"; a racial militant refers —sometimes without knowing he refers obliquely to the same principle—to his "black brothers"; and the word resounds in songs and oratory. In this case, Robert McCloskey's thesis does not hold true;

political thought has, in relation to fraternity neglected the politics and practice of America.[1]

This touches our political thought in a place of weakness. The great concern of American political philosophy has been the development of "democratic theory." That concern has focused on formal institutions and organizations, even when it rejected "formalism." In so doing, it has neglected the fact that democratic theory must always be primarily a theory about a *demos*, about the character and relations of citizens. What we have been taught to call political life and opinion reveal only part of the picture. Indeed, what most never notice, or what they never conceive to be political, may be more important than the issues and events which engage them most.

> These three great causes serve, no doubt, to regulate and direct the American democracy; but if they were to be classed in their proper order, I should say that the physical circumstances are less efficient than the laws, and the laws subordinate to the customs of the people.[2]

Louis Hartz' seminal *The Liberal Tradition in America* has demonstrated beyond the need of further argument the degree to which conscious and formal thought about politics has shaped itself in terms of the categories of Enlightenment liberalism. In fact, "conservatism" in America has been little more than a dessicated variety of liberalism, bereft of faith but clinging to the institutions supplied by the liberals of the past. In the contemporary right, we can still hear the "steel chain of ideas" that Eric Goldman found in the liberal orthodoxy of the nineteenth century, now even more embittered and lacking the generous hope of the eighteenth-century founders of the creed.[3]

That nearly unchecked dominance is not difficult to explain. The United States government was, after all, founded on liberal doctrines, and deviation from them has had a suspect, alien quality. The massive instrument of public education has been at pains to teach the creed to

[1] Robert G. McCloskey, "American Political Thought and the Study of Politics," *APSR*, LI (1957), pp. 115–129; Carey McWilliams, *Brothers under the Skin* (Boston: Little, Brown, 1951).

[2] De Tocqueville, *Democracy in America*, vol. I, p. 383 (see also pp. 340–392).

[3] Louis Hartz, *The Liberal Tradition in America* (New York: Harcourt, Brace, 1955); Eric Goldman, *Rendezvous with Destiny* (New York: Knopf, 1954).

generations of school children. Too, the liberal philosophy was, and to an extent remains, the basis of modern science and reason, and those who argued from different premises or motives were forced to state their case in liberal terms in order to be listened to by rational men.

"Irrational" arguments, to be sure, have never been absent from political theory, and the great theorists have never hesitated to depart from reason as understood by their contemporaries. But, as Hartz points out, the monuments of political custom and tradition led straight to liberalism in America; "presumptive reason," appealing to the past against the present, refers more directly to Madison and Jefferson than to St. Thomas or Aristotle.

And so much of the American experience seems to confirm the great liberal theses. The creation of American institutions was almost the visible demonstration of the struggle against nature, the social contract, the superiority of individual decision, science and contrivance over custom and natural law.

Those who turned from the individualism of "natural right" often sought their explanation of American thought and practice in the environment itself, crediting geographic isolation, the Mississippi River, or the "frontier" with distinctive and essential contributions to the making of American culture.[4] Such doctrines were appealing at those times when the philosophy and metaphysic of the eighteenth century seemed hard to defend, for they enabled men to reach the prescriptions of liberalism without its theory. If man were not "by nature" and universally free, equal, individualistic, and democratic, then something "in nature" must make him so in America. (Nor were such theorists much different from *The Federalist*, whose authors appreciated their unique opportunity, or from Jefferson, passionately eager to defend the salubrity of the American clime.)

Yet De Tocqueville was right; too little is accounted for by either the laws and doctrines or the environment of America, or by both together. Neither can really explain the American reverence for the Constitution, which invests it with a moral value independent of its value as a device for obtaining results. More important, they explain nothing of the theory of man as an "individual personality,"

---

[4] Frederick Jackson Turner, *The Frontier in American History* (New York: Holt, 1920); James Truslow Adams, *The Epic of America* (Boston: Little, Brown, 1947).

requiring and depending on others for the development of his moral being, in sharp contrast to Enlightenment individualism which saw man as morally complete. Where the liberal theorist saw individual freedom and equality as means which would produce good policy, others have insisted on civic freedom and equality as ends which good policy should produce. The vision of the political order as an educational community has never been entirely displaced by the technological vision of the eighteenth century. G. K. Chesterton spoke with truth when he declared America was based on

> . . . the pure classic conception that no man must aspire to be anything more than a citizen, and that no man shall endure to be anything less. . . . [T]he idealism of America . . . still revolves entirely round the citizen and his romance. . . . [T]here is an army of actualities opposed to that ideal, but there is no ideal opposed to that ideal.[5]

The most perceptive students of American politics have always seen that American culture is deeply dualistic, that the domination of its formal thought by the Enlightenment does not exclude an informal tradition in symbols, rituals, and arts and letters based on very different notions of man and politics. The immigrant was, after all, not a *tabula rasa* on which the environment could write at will. The isolated America of Hartz and Boorstin was isolated before the Enlightenment became dominant in the field of ideas, certainly before the new science and politics derived from it had influenced the mass of men. As Harriet Martineau observed, the state is new in America, but the people are old; older, one might add, than many of their European counterparts who have seen their traditions broken so often.[6]

Obviously, Americans did not bring from Europe and Africa any sophisticated understanding of medieval thought or ancient philosophy. Most, then as now, were not intellectuals. But that only made

---

[5] G. K. Chesterton, "What I Saw in America," *The Man Who Was Chesterton*, ed. Raymond Bond (Garden City: Doubleday, 1960), pp. 132–133.

[6] Harriet Martineau, *Society in America* (New York: Sanders and Otley, 1837). In *The Revolution of the Saints* (Cambridge: Harvard University Press, 1965), Michael Walzer writes that "Lockean liberals found it possible to dispense with . . . controls . . . because the controls had already been implanted in men" (p. 303).

the majority of Americans, as opposed to their more intellectual leaders, resistant to change in ideas. The traditional ideas they brought did not come arrayed in the impressive but vulnerable garb of a philosophic system. They came in a culture, in institutions, festivals, tales and songs of love and glory. Preeminently, of course, they came in religion; the United States drew its first great wave of immigrants from what was the last migration of the religious age, and subsequent immigrants to America were largely traditional peoples who embodied or readily imbibed the religious heritage.

Opposition to liberal theory and secular life in America, however, has had at least two distinct forms. The first is the myth of *gemeinschaft*, the dream of community which, seemingly so different from the liberal creed, blends easily with it. Like the romantic undertow that Europe felt in the eighteenth century, it has more than once helped support the effort to conquer nature in the hope that, by a devious route, it might lead humanity back to "oneness."

The second is the Judaeo-Christian idea of fraternity which, however attenuated and distorted, has perpetuated ideas which contravene both liberalism and its romantic symbiote. It has seen man and the world as inadequate, but has recognized that man's quest to transcend nature is critically dependent on society and politics, and on a fraternity which shares alienation from nature and estrangement from God. The Judaeo-Christian tradition gave America its sense of a natural law which enabled it to speak, as the theory of natural right could not, of duties and obligations above those imposed by positive law and beyond its command. John F. R. Taylor sees in America a Hebraic "aspiration for covenant relations made visible in our every day's most quiet act." And Americans have felt more than a little sadness that so often such hopes only appeared in their quiet acts.[7]

The religious tradition has not been uniformly beneficial. Deprived of their basis in faith, misinterpreted and twisted, religious ideas of fraternity have encouraged violent millennialism, revivalist frenzy, and political quietism. At their best, however, they have expressed a wisdom and truth which the Enlightenment did not possess, and they have always provided the emotional and symbolic basis for

[7] John F. R. Taylor, *The Masks of Society* (New York: Appleton-Century-Crofts, 1966), p. 46.

the appeal to fraternity in American politics as an immediate need rather than a distant goal.

The Homes of the Homeless

The nostalgia for community derives much of its power from the conditions in America which some imagined would dispel it. The environment did not "free" men from the beliefs and attitudes of the past. It commanded that they conduct themselves according to unwonted rules of behavior. The promise it offered was probably congenial, and even the freedom may have been welcome, but the passing of time made it clear that this "freedom" was not a matter of choice.

Certainly, the pioneer or immigrant had little time, in his fevered struggle to master an alien world, for the examination of his basic beliefs or feelings. Too, the alienness of the land and the loneliness of the frontier or the industrial city made men likely to feel warm about their past, and inclined them to try to recreate the old country, at least to teach its traditions to their children. Too much depended on the individual in the new world, and it is understandable if he harkened to a time when, subject to authority and surrounded by community, each man mattered less and life was more secure.

Old expectations perished rapidly as guides to action, and with them passed secure expectations about the behavior of men. Even men one had known in the old country became potentially unpredictable in the new. The atmosphere of America drew barriers of prudence and caution between men. Uncertainty made the suspicion of motives which men always feel something immediate and vital rather than peripheral and residual.

Making dependence on others unwelcome, American life also made it less necessary. Abundance of land made self-sufficiency a possibility. The compulsion of scarcity operated only in the first days, and after nature had yielded to taming, the tenuous alliances of the battle against her lost their basis. To be sure, abundance often fell short of what men hoped for, but the promise of abundance combined with the fact of scarcity only increased tendencies for suspicion and envy between men.

Moreover, as many have observed, in a land where there were few social limitations to prosperity, success seemed the test of man's worldly virtue. In early America, that might be moderated by rough equality and by the fact that prosperity and ill were often the result of general conditions shared by all; weather, for example, made a year "good" or "bad" for all farmers in a region, great or small. When inequalities of wealth became massive and when some acquired independence of general conditions ("fortune"), differences of success became measures of personal worth and dignity, failure a reproach to the self.[8]

The competitive personal relations and insecurity of status which characterize American life have, however, only intensified the American's desire for emotional security and assurance. They encouraged the tendency to manufacture a nostalgic Eden in the old world and a romantic Eden in the new.

Americans came from Europe seeking escape from something, whether bondage and oppression, the indignity of servitude, or limited hopes. One of the greatest appeals of mobility, however, lies in the fact that it enables the individual to escape his actual past and those who have known him in all his weakness and folly. It enables him to create a past, to tell fictitious tales of his own or his ancestors' glory, to make out of fantasy a past which protects in the present. The American who found insecurity and indignity in America often used that tool to tell his children of a time and place when he was happier and more exalted; pseudo-memory, sometimes the collective delusion of sizeable groups, has safeguarded the fragile esteem of the self.

All Americans have known that temptation to "psychic emigration"; the "roots of American loyalty" are always shallow. Indeed, those roots are often shallowest in those who fear and attack "foreignness" and allegiance to peoples and "potentates" abroad. The immigrant could not deny that he had chosen America, and his nostalgia was mitigated by the fact of a too-true memory of the old homeland. The native, having chosen less, may be forgiven if he regrets more. It has been among very American names and families that the tendency to emigrate has been most notable: Adams, Eliot, James come easily to mind.

For most, however, the choice has been to come or to remain. Men might create the myth of a necessity which compelled them to

[8] David Potter, *People of Plenty* (Chicago: University of Chicago Press, 1957), pp. 91–110, 126–141.

quit the old world: foreign masters, persecuting faiths, tyrannical kings. Nonetheless, they left behind them those of their blood kinsmen who had felt no such necessity. "Compulsion" is always a relative term, and the brave may withstand what compels the coward; in that sense, compulsion is always the result of partial volition. (It is ironic that those who were most clearly compelled, the blacks, have shown least nostalgia, and continue to do so even today. It also speaks to the fact which Baldwin knows so well, that blacks have "another country" in their tradition.)

Those who break the ties of blood and base their loyalties on choice must accept the fact of instability. It was no small motive for nostalgia that it made parents more secure, obscuring in part the precedent set when they deserted their kin. But only in part; in America, all the relations of men become charged with impermanence. Individuation and insecurity have been the first premises of life; native and immigrant alike lacked the symbols of emotion and security that cluster around the term *patria*.[9]

Individual isolation produces that sense of weakness which De Tocqueville realized was one of the legacies of equality in America. Masses of strangers environ men, and if equality seems the fact, inequality is the fear and suspicion. Indeed, equality becomes feared lest it should deprive the self of all excuse for failure and reveal our true weakness.[10] Nothing is more feared than the secret, esoteric community "set apart" which may combine solidarity with hidden hostility; yet nothing is envied more, for in solidarity there may be a security, a joy, and hence a strength, which the isolated individual lacks.

For racial minorities and immigrant groups, "community" has served as a solace amid exclusion, a retreat from slights and prejudice (and too often, this has made it only the mark of failure, something resented for all its helps). The "assimilated," however, may find something lacking in their greater abundance; permanent insecurity and lack of warmth seem characteristic of life, and those whose lives seem communal and affectionate are envied. Americans have passed through alternating cycles in their attitudes toward the ethnic culture of immi-

---

[9] Perry Miller, "The Shaping of the American Character," *NEQ*, XXVIII (1955), pp. 435–454.

[10] Robert E. Lane, "The Fear of Equality," *APSR*, LV (1959), pp. 35–59.

grants and the "simpler ways" of racial minorities. From fear and hatred, they pass to nostalgia and romanticism. The negative sentiments, however, appear first; only when our superiority is proved in *kulturkampf* is it safe to express sentiments and regrets. Americans, as Frost knew, remain aliens on the land, fearful of nature and their fellows alike.

The "myth of Empire," as Henry Nash Smith calls it,[11] consists in the belief that fear can be mastered by power. Personal aggrandizement becomes thought of as a means to a safe, risk-free "community" with others, the old romantic hope. The quest for power in America always hints at a longing for something lost or absent in American life, a desperate need for admiration and concern.

Children in America may turn to that myth in place of nostalgia for the old world; they may also, especially when they have met with defeat, substitute a simpler version of that myth. The locale of the dream changes from the romance of Europe to romance per se. In the first instance, the Garden may seem to lie in one's childhood; the two romances merge here, for the symbols of Europe were powerful because they were associated with childhood. And they were all the stronger because of what parents taught and remembered: the old world things are associated with joy. Festival and feast and tale and romance: even the grim stories of persecution become exciting adventures which the child knows have now turned out all right for those he knows—and for himself.

Increasingly, the nostalgia lost its roots in Europe and settled in childhood itself. The old country becomes the old place. Defeated by or discontented with the myth of Empire, indignity and insecurity, individuals quietly or verbally walk those old acres and paddle the brooks. That this is illusion, that it shuts out the terror and the horror of the child, may be true. But it is a soft illusion, one which binds the individual to certain men and locales, if only in memory. And that, at least, makes him more fortunate than those who must concentrate everything within the self.

Wanderer's Star

Having chosen to cross an ocean did not separate most immigrants from God as it shut them away from the social environment and cul-

[11] Henry Nash Smith, *Virgin Land* (New York: Vintage, 1950).

ture of the past. The Puritans, with their acute self-consciousness, had momentary doubts as to whether the continent was meant for Christian men. They could not, and would hardly have wished to, deny the claims of God Himself to feel as much at home on this continent as on any other in His creation.

Protestant religion, providing some contact with ideals not encountered in the struggle with nature, contributed even by its sternest and most forbidding qualities. God made earthly things and attainments of lesser importance, and His judgment of sin on all men leveled men far more effectively than physical similarity, the secular standard, could possibly do. Those who felt themselves estranged from God, moreover, drew closer to men for comfort; fear was overridden in part by fear of judgment, and in the common doom and fatality many of the barriers between men seemed less important. Helping to set aside barriers of anxiety and pride, God's judgment offered the least exalted man the assurance, if not of his own dignity, at least of the equal indignity of others.

It did more, of course. It bound men by a law which transcended the right of custom and the law of blood. The negative basis of community was weak in America, where a man might hope, at least, to stand alone. God created a positive basis for community, a set of obligations beyond physical necessity, claims on the spirit of man. Men were obliged to mirror, so far as they were able, the City of God; the best earthly city had no place for pride, and brotherhood was the principle of life. Worldly goods, useful enough for men, should be bent to the task of winning and perpetuating fraternity.

That subsequent generations of Protestants fled their burden of obligation and guilt is well known. And if the Church came to terms with society, that only points to the fact that, as an organization, the Church must come to terms with it. Though not of this world, the Church must deal with men in it, and if it can and does affect the way in which men behave and conceive their duties, it cannot ignore the effects of society and the environment on men.

Many traditional social scientists have regarded religion as "epiphenomenal," reflecting the interests of groups, classes, or the state. There is much in American religious history to sustain that view. Pietism identified Sin with petty sins of the flesh which could be avoided without interfering with the quest for wealth and power.

It translated the political and social ethics of religion into the "next world," away from the status of duties to men. Fraternity was identified with a vague, condescending, and not very serious obligation to charity, seen as gratuity rather than duty, accepted at the cost of dignity and not as a right. A complacent cosmic optimism identified what passed with the Divine will, assuring men that America was as perfect as conditions permitted, and might become better through "progress" combined with faith.

Yet the "inner-worldly asceticism" which led Weber to identify Protestantism with the capitalist spirit derived less from Protestantism than from the environment of the Church's life. Weber's sources were often American and, as a glance at the history of other faiths will reveal, they suffered from the same tendencies in the American setting.

The new doctrines were tributes to sophistry; they remained but badly correlated with the words of Scripture. Even if the ethics of fraternity were relegated to the "next world," they remained a standard of excellence, a symbol of high virtue. When faith in the next world was weak, or when hopes for progress corresponded badly with developments, men might appeal for the immediate realization of those values which had been relegated to the long term. Moreover, for groups whose weakness did not allow for any effort to realize the ideal in practice, even the pietistic style kept the ideal in being. Religion may, for example, have retarded social protest among Negroes, though that is debatable; what is certain is that it helped protect against the internalization of "inferiority" which almost all other institutions conspired to teach and command. Benton Johnson's studies have demonstrated what common sense knew—that religious ethics were never without those who sought to apply them, and that the tradition led members of the upper classes toward reform, just as it led the less fortunate to accept the established state of things.[12]

Especially among immigrants and in rural areas, where Enlightenment ideas and modern institutions touched lightly, the religious standards of evaluation stayed strong. When "mobilization" drew such groups into contact with the dominant institutions and groups, the traditionalistic protests were certain. Not for nothing was "assimilation" a concern of American politics long before it found its way

[12] Benton Johnson, "Ascetic Protestantism and Political Preference," POQ, XXVI (1961), pp. 35-46.

into Karl Deutsch's terminology. And democratic institutions only made the values and concerns of the "mobilized and unassimilated" groups relevant political facts. For the established groups, such values might be deflected or defeated, but they could not be ignored. Immigrants, to be sure, were uncertain, and first generations often reacted submissively, but internal assimilation was often a difficult matter; the great protests against the dehumanizations of industrialism came first from the farms.

So long as the society made few claims on the devotion and values of men—so long, that is, as prosperity made it possible to meet most demands and avoid sacrifices—assimilation might proceed on its gradual course. Economic failure, however, released the resentments and the moral self-doubts of many. Millennial movements have been frequent, more secular radical ones only a little less so. Their defeat in the effort to transform the environment led to disillusionment and often to a weakening of the faith.

Their struggle, however, strengthened the hand of those who had been moved to protest and action before the crisis by their own moral doubts and needs. In many cases, in fact, the protest awoke those doubts, often in apparently unlikely bosoms. Less desperate, as well as more prudent, the "social gospel" and similar groups helped to humanize industrialism, though what they established was at best the shadow of a fraternal polity.

Some, seeking to close the gap between fraternity and modernity, have turned to violence, and the history of such conflicts would make a sizeable part of the history of the land. That testifies to the hold which the idea of fraternity has on Americans, even in our times. It has kept its hold, in part, because it rested first in religion, then in custom. Fraternity, Myrdal noted, retained appeal here long after the universalism of "humanity" in Europe had yielded to nationalism and class.[13] God, unlike "humanity," need not promise success to create a duty.

But where the earlier idea of fraternity was coherent, clearsighted, and rooted in a deep understanding of men and political things, today the idea of fraternity has become attenuated, for most, to a vague and confused symbol. Less aware of the limitations of their

[13] Gunnar Myrdal, *An American Dilemma* (New York and Evanston: Harper and Row, 1962), p. 757.

alternatives, Americans are less able to choose between them. Such choices, however, would always have been painful, and our present confusion is due, in part, to a prolonged attempt to deny or obscure the necessity of choice.

Misleaders and Guides

American political theorists have, as Daniel Boorstin argued, been anti-theoretical in most cases, aggressively "pragmatic" and concerned with "interests" rather than ultimates.[14] Hartz accounts for this by reference to "irrational Lockeanism," a system of thought so deeply ingrained as not to seem theoretical at all, but only to represent simple fact. Boorstin's argument, that there existed a unified "pre-formation ideal" in America, follows a similar logic.

Both are perceptive, but neither fully explains the active aversion of Americans to theory, their distaste for any attempt to go to first principles or ultimate values, or their preoccupation with accommodation. So aggressive a pragmatism may rouse the suspicion that there exist basically contradictory principles, not only among groups, but more importantly, within the individual himself. There may exist an American creed, but it is a compendium of convictions hardly consistent with one another.

Perry Miller, more concerned with the religious tradition than Hartz or Boorstin, noted the "habit of ambiguity" which grew up among New England divines under the combined impact of social change and Enlightenment theory.[15] With some justice, one could refer to a general principle of ambiguity in the culture. Certainly, more than one liberal and secular theorist found it useful to mute or disguise his departures from traditional religious theory; radicals and reformers have found it equally sensible to cast their argument in terms of "irrational Lockeanism." Conscious efforts, however, are less important than the normal desire of men to retain both traditions, to avoid the necessity of choosing between values and deeply held beliefs.

[14] Daniel Boorstin, *The Genius of American Politics* (Chicago: University of Chicago Press, 1953).

[15] Perry Miller, *The New England Mind* (Boston: Beacon, 1961), vol. II, pp. 199, 382–383.

Pragmatism is an ideal doctrine to that end; William James was eloquent in proclaiming that it allowed men the best of both worlds.[16] Decisions in practice are matters of emphasis and direction rather than sharply defined "choices." They are "balanced" in the sense that for sane men they are points along a broad continuum. The most ethereal of men must give some heed to the flesh, the most sensual must engage in some thought. When pragmatism is raised to the level of a doctrine, it does not imply the inability to distinguish best from worst, for that is implied by the prescription that we choose the better rather than the worse. Rather, it suggests an unwillingness to consider such questions deeply, a desire to blind oneself to the fact that all decisions imply direction and that, while we "balance" values at any time, we are moving toward and strengthening one and weakening and moving away from the other.

American politics has eschewed any claim to control more than external behavior; the "oaths" which it has imposed on newcomers and themselves have not been concerned with doctrinal orthodoxy— one is not required to swear by the Declaration or *The Federalist*—but with obedience to law and the rejection of "force, violence, or other unlawful means." Yet external behavior is always regulated by internal norms. Rules of ethics prescribe certain forms of conduct and proscribe others. Moreover, actions and behavior affect the thought of men. Institutions do more than channel the "outer man"; they reward certain attitudes and punish others, shape habit and expectation. If the courts use the "bad man" theory to interpret laws, then the law must be read in light of that theory and, if the individual is not to be victimized, he must expect that his fellows will act toward the law and toward him as "bad men" do. And the optimal result demands that he limit his own feelings of obligation to those of bad men. Obviously the conscious elements of the process are less important than what shapes the unconscious, especially through the socialization of new generations. If you cannot "legislate morality," you cannot legislate without moral effect.[17]

The American unwillingness to face that fact, our aversion to realizing that we are shaping the personalities of men by our political

[16] William James, *Pragmatism* (Cleveland and New York: World, 1968).

[17] Harry Ball, George Simpson, and Kiyoshi Ikeda, "Law and Social Change," *AJS*, LXVII (1962), pp. 532–540.

life, results in a decision about how that life is to be shaped. The assumption of American politics has been that the external behaviors prescribed by the legal and political system either eventuate in good results or are good in themselves; correspondingly, the private character most consonant with those behaviors should be encouraged.

The separation of "public" and "private" spheres is, in the long term at least, a fraud; our efforts to deal with racial inequality and poverty, for example, take us ever deeper into the private sphere, while our ingrained "public" habits of mind make our invasions ineffective, ungracious, and dehumanizing. The concept of such a separation originated in part as the attempt to wall our personal lives off from men we did not know and feared, and as a social aim this retains validity. In another sense, it arose as a denial of the relevance of our public conduct to our private principles, and vice versa. We could have both without choice and without conflict.

That, however, is not the case. The "system" is not a "value-neutral" set of techniques; the Framers would have been offended at the mere suggestion. Our public institutions have been based on the assumptions and theories of the liberal Enlightenment. Law contains a bias toward individualism, a hostility to communities, an assumption that material well-being and technological advance are in the high interests of man. (Almost the only positive aim set forth in Article I of the Constitution is the "progress of science and the useful arts.") In this sense, "working within the system" has weakened the strength of the informal and religious tradition, as opposed to the formally established and "rational" doctrines of modernity.

Nowhere is this more vital than in relation to "fraternity," an idea common to both the Enlightenment and the religious tradition which touches the most delicate point of distinction between them. The traditions differ on the nature of fraternity, and the paternity which is its basis, because they differ on the nature of man. That first principle is, in relation to fraternity, immediately relevant in the relations and conduct of men; it cannot be dispensed with as a "metaphysical" question irrelevant to conduct.

Whatever may be thought of the liberal idea of fraternity, the liberal tradition proposed to discard fraternity as a means to human perfection and a norm in everyday political and social life. In fact, it set aside the premise that man was a political animal who required civic relations for his perfection. (It was this, after all, that allowed the idea of a viable theoretical distinction between public and private things.)[18]

It is not so easy, however, to set aside older traditions that demand different things of man and of the state. Competitive ethics, privatism, political impersonality, and concern for material power above other values must be viewed as immoral in the light of the ancient imperatives. Though the goods of modernity appealed to Americans enough to direct the lives of most, traditional values were restraints that limited their enthusiasm and made them uneasy at heart in the "new order." Loyalty and commitment required the belief that traditional values were compatible with, were indeed forwarded by, obedience to the "rules of the game."

That assurance was provided by the myth of progress which, as Michael Rogin comments, "allows a relaxation of moral standards" in the convenient belief that old standards will not be destroyed, and that values denied expression now will become possible in the future.[19] The goal of a universal fraternity, or at least a fraternal society, is the bribe which progress offers to tradition. Yet the ideas of fraternity and fraternal society characteristic of the religious tradition, when seen clearly, clash with those of the liberal tradition. Religious theory, in the simplest sense, presumes that fraternity is a means and not the end of human striving. The ability of "progress" to harmonize religious and Enlightenment ethics depends on the ability to obscure the ultimate aim, allowing men to close their eyes to the fact that the goals differ, and the paths with them, and that what is progress toward one becomes, after a certain crossroads, retrogression from the other.

Obscuring this, pragmatism and anti-theory have yet another effect. Prescribing bargain and compromise, they play down the fact that the bargainer can be so absorbed in the process as to forget the goal, ignoring the fact that deals are either good, bad, or indifferent, not valuable in themselves. Too, though he is able to find accommodation within a system and situation, he is likely to ignore the possibilities for changing either. Groups which must endeavor to change not merely the distribution of values, but the values them-

---

[18] Sheldon S. Wolin, *Politics and Vision*, pp. 286–381; John H. Schaar, "Some Ways of Thinking About Equality," *JP*, XXVI (1964), pp. 885ff.

[19] Michael Paul Rogin, *The Intellectuals and McCarthy: the Radical Specter* (Cambridge: M.I.T. Press, 1967), p. 43.

selves, not their position in the system, but the moral assumptions of the system, find themselves at a disadvantage. The bias of the system works against them. What else is the lesson of race relations in American life?

If direction rather than drift is to be possible, if clarity about values—to say nothing of change in them—is to be conceivable, a leadership is needed to remind men forcefully of what they do, and possibly teach them to do better. Religious groups, though their performance has been spotty, have sometimes performed that service, and religious men have often done so grandly. Philosophers and intellectuals, captivated by the charms of modern philosophy and modern pelf, have done far less. Perhaps the greatest service for the old tradition was performed by novelists, poets, and tellers of tales, who kept its ideals alive when the influence of Scripture waned and the old philosophies ceased to move men. Sometimes too, political men and statesmen, whom the proud scientism of the Enlightenment sought to displace, performed similar tasks in the struggle to retain as much as might be of the idea of fraternity and the vision of the city. Those who would accept a similar duty in the unpromising present would be well advised to seek inspiration and wisdom in their example.

> The short space of threescore years can never
> content the imagination of man; nor can the
> imperfect joys of this world satisfy his heart.
> Man alone, of all created beings, displays a
> natural contempt of existence, and yet a
> boundless desire to exist; he scorns life, but he
> dreads annihilation. . . Unbelief is an ac-
> cident, and faith is the only permanent state
> of mankind.
>
> De Tocqueville, *Democracy in America*

CHAPTER V

PURITANISM: THE COVENANTS OF FRATERNITY

"This nation, under God . . ."

"LAND where my fathers died," the song intones, "land of the Pil-
grims' pride." The reference is more than local; the Pilgrim and the
Puritan lay claim to the collective fatherhood of America. The claim
is disputed, and the argument still fires the temper of academia to an
unusual heat.[1]

Behind scholarly passion lies the more theoretical proposition
which De Tocqueville asserted. In all nations, he wrote, "the circumstances which accompanied their birth and contributed to their rise

[1] An excellent discussion of the dangers of partisanship is David Lewis, "The
Hazing of Cotton Mather," *NEQ*, XXXVI (1963), pp. 147-171.

affect the whole term of their being." [2] Puritanism, whether it encouraged liberty or repression, democracy or autocracy in America, was here first. What is best in America may have required that Puritanism be superseded, but it cannot be forgotten.

The intensity of debate also testifies to both the contemporaneity and the perenniality of Puritan thought. The Puritan thinkers struggled with perplexities which are important not only to an understanding of man in the seventeenth century, but to a knowledge of man himself. The answers may be deemed wrong; the questions merit a concern equal to that which the Puritans gave them. On this much, assailants and defenders of the Puritans and their creed agree.

Too often, however, the disputants speak of different aspects of Puritanism. Supporters discuss doctrine, teaching, and philosophy; opponents wish to fix attention on the spotty practice of Puritanism in America.[3] The "failure" of Puritanism, however, can be adjudged only by its own standard, for by the standard of secular thought New England was an almost unambiguous success. Critics forget that they judge American Puritanism by its own hopes and promises; that alone is a mark of the influence of Puritanism on American life and thought.

Even so, it is hard to judge the failure too harshly. As sympathetic critics have noted, the doctrine and the teaching required an extraordinarily muscular psyche. The Puritans were never sanguine on this point; they did not expect that more than a few could follow their teaching. That even the most devoted deviated from the logic of Puritan theory would have been no surprise; none ever foretold their own shortcomings more accurately than the spokesmen of New England.

In fact, the danger of failure and the requirements of the teaching established, for the Puritan, the importance of fraternity. Whatever chance men might have for excellence required rearing in community and encouragement from fraternity. Whenever great things are at stake, the Puritan argued, short of the Grace of God, man depends upon his brother man, or at least on those of the species who recognize in him a part of the great fraternity.

[2] *Democracy in America*, vol. I, p. 13.
[3] For example, see John Cary, "Statistical Method and the Brown Thesis on Colonial Democracy," with an excellent reply by Robert E. Brown, *WMQ*, third series, XX (1963), pp. 251–276.

"The fault of dullness is within us . . ."

The most neglected element of Puritan thought is the triumphant affirmation that was the first premise of its theology. The rigors of God's law and plan did not make the universe grim and forbidding. The Puritan insisted that creation was good, that man as a part of creation was most excellent, and that the Divine order was beautiful as well as determined.

The Puritan theologians were well aware that predestination and Free Grace, the principles of their doctrine of salvation, did not appear beautiful to men. If men felt themselves unjustly dealt with, however, they insisted that this was the result of a defective perception of reality which was the fault of man himself.

God had provided man with a prudent desire for physical security and well-being and, at the same time, with a desire for the true, the perfect, and the eternal, the *imago dei*. Yet, at least since the Fall, man was born with a desire to deny his own mortality and ignorance. Puritanism echoed Augustine: man willed that "God should not be," choosing rather to perceive an omnipotent self and detesting reality. Nothing in nature could repair that defect. Facts might argue against the will; natural necessity might compel men to yield. Neither could erase entirely the will to illusion which led men to resist and resent the truth, and which always distorted their perception of it. In living men, means tended to become ends and vice versa: the emotions struggled for sovereignty and men yearned for a physical safety and permanence denied them by God's creation. Man, as Perry Miller comments, was a "maladjusted mechanism." [4] If God redeemed some men, He did so by a "Grace" outside the order of nature which man could neither merit nor fathom.

The grim antithesis of Grace and nature did not, however, exhaust human possibilities. Man might always be imperfect, but that did not preclude degrees of imperfection. The imago dei remained the "law of man's being" and sought to turn to its proper object, seeking the right and meditating on truth. Deflected and distorted, unable to grasp the positive vision of Divine justice, it retained sufficient power to reveal man's defects. Men might at least become "displeased with

---

[4] *The New England Mind*, vol. I, p. 256.

themselves," and in the best circumstances they might feel at fault. The fact of sin was universal; the perception of sin was not. It was the fortunate man who acquired a sense of sin; short of Grace, this was the highest excellence of man's spirit.

Even profane men, moreover, might be given "special gifts" by God above the ordinary "gifts of nature." Such talents were excellent in themselves, though they did not reflect any merit in the recipient. Because of this excellence, a talented man who failed to develop such gifts only added to his burden of guilt.

Between Grace and damnation, God and Nature, the Puritan established two hierarchies of value:

	Natural Excellence	Spiritual Excellence	
Nature	Special Gifts	Grace	God
	Gifts of Nature	Sense of Sin	

Though human efforts could not reach the saving pinnacle, they could develop the excellencies of nature and could encourage men toward the lesser good of the spirit. The flaming sword which barred man from paradise did not prevent him from breaching the wall between nature and spirit; God had broken that wall when he placed His image in man.

The road between nature and spirit was found in reason, the most excellent of the faculties of nature which also united man to God—the "highest reason," *logos*, and final cause. Reason was a bond between God and man, though human reason could not reach the Divine altitude. For men, it was always *technologia*, a method for approaching, though never attaining, Divine wisdom.

The Fall had not irreparably damaged reason as it had damaged the will. To be sure, man's corrupt will led him to reject the force of well-taken argument. Yet in some degree, reason was impersonal, separate from the will. The Puritan delight in logic was based on logic's iron and inescapable quality which enabled it to govern the will more effectively than other forms of argument. Logic, in other words, could partly free reason from the corruption of the human psyche. Calvinists were simply prudent rationalists, conscious of the numberless failings and limitations of reason. Their suspicion of inspiration, however, was more basic and thoroughgoing.

God's Elect could never be certainly known. Works, the only standard by which human beings can judge one another, were no test of motive or merit. God might favor His Elect by Divine intervention and miracle, but He might afflict them by identical means. He might give prosperity to the unrighteous who were destined for damnation. Nor could the individual judge his own election. Faith was not an adequate proof; even the best faith is tested by doubt and uncertainty, and no faith can be called perfect until the end, which no man can foresee. Moreover, God may grant in the future a faith now lacking.

The Scripture, the foundation of Calvinism, also had problematic elements. The Word must be the sole and final source of authority, but all Calvinists knew that there were many interpretations of Holy Writ. Even the language of the Scripture could be misleading. Moses, Calvin contended, had not meant to teach astronomy; he intended a moral lesson and "descended" to language suited to popular understanding. Scripture, John Winthrop wrote, must always be the rule, "yet not the phrase." [5]

The need to interpret Scripture, however, reintroduced uncertainty. First, it depended on fallible man, and human judgment, however schooled and disciplined, was never safe. Second, a complete understanding of Scripture would require a knowledge of the Divine plan; some mysteries, consequently, could not be understood even by the Elect. The chosen might will correctly, but even they lacked the wisdom of the Most High. Despite his desire to emphasize reliance on Scripture, Calvin conceded that "without Him we cannot understand anything that is shown in His Word." [6]

The ultimate uncertainty which Puritan teaching imposed proved too much for any to tolerate comfortably. Even Calvin, arguing that church membership was no test of salvation, hinted that excommunication might be "ratified" in heaven. Puritan theorists went further, seeking "usual" signs of election; surely, they reasoned, even if God is free to make exceptions, there must be some general rules by which He guides himself. Often, they argued like trial lawyers, hoping for "reasonable assurance" of salvation or speculating that good conduct might be necessary to "prepare" the soul to receive Grace. These

[5] Calvin's comment is cited in McNeill, *History and Character of Calvinism*, p. 213; Winthrop's statement is from *The Winthrop Papers* (Boston: Massachusetts Historical Society, 5 volumes, 1929–1947), vol. IV, p. 348.

[6] Cited in Ronald Wallace, *Calvin's Doctrine of the Word and Sacrament* (London: Oliver and Boyd, 1953), p. 103.

efforts to nibble at the apple of certainty only indicate, however, that until the last days the Puritan Commonwealth kept uncertainty at the center of its theology even as it probed the periphery.

In the days of vital faith a Puritan minister would proclaim the folly of believing that "God must go by our rule." [7] If doctrine and inspiration were no test of salvation or of ultimate truth, both were also inadequate in the organization of human life. Thomas Hooker wrote:

> He that will estrange his affection because of the difference of apprehension of things difficult must be a stranger to himself one time or another. . . . (W)hen men set up their sheaves (though it be but in a dream as Joseph's was) and will fall out with everyone that will not fall down and adore them, they will bring much trouble into the world but little advantage to the truth or peace. [8]

Advantage to truth and peace demanded that men avoid pride of thought or person, even in private reflection. In this life, "things difficult," the darkened mysteries of theology and metaphysics, are not a standard for action. Even in its persecuting days, Puritanism felt compelled to argue that it was not "for cause of conscience" that men were punished, but for actions detrimental to the well-being of the community. [9] (It was, in fact, the persecuted who normally claimed revelatory certainty.) The standards of life in the world were to be found in the comparatively simple and accessible truths of the natural law and the common good.

"No neglect of means . . ."

Ultimate uncertainty and imperfection did not excuse men from the effort to improve their knowledge or to lead better lives. "The good of which we are destitute," Calvin said, should be the chief goal of human life. This "doctrine of works" seemed paradoxical to those sectarians who asserted that the irrevocably saved elect were not bound by lesser laws; it has seemed a simple contradiction to secular

---

[7] John Preston, cited in Miller, *The New England Mind*, vol. I, p. 18.

[8] Thomas Hooker, "A Survey of the Summe of Church Discipline," in *The Development of American Political Thought*, ed. J. Mark Jacobson (New York: Appleton-Century-Crofts, 1932), p. 67.

[9] See Calvin, *Institutes*, III:xix:14–16.

critics who see little point in urging men to work if they cannot be redeemed by works. Even a sympathetic student like Haller contends that the doctrine has not "metaphysical but . . . moral" validity.[10] Both types of critic have presumed, however, that salvation is the only goal suggested by theology, which it assuredly is not. The doctrine of works in Calvinistic and Puritan thought is founded on the excellence possible in life in this world.

Man, the Calvinist argued, is estranged from the world of nature. Seeing nature's law as a grim necessity, men confront it with futile resentment or sullen passivity. Their enjoyment of life and its pleasures is always hampered by an anxiety more or less extreme, for they fear the loss of what they possess at the very moment when they possess it.

Man is simultaneously subject to three laws: (1) the Law of Nature, common to all created things; (2) the Law of Man's Nature, based on man's specific faculties, which reveals the shortcomings of mere life and commands an effort to overcome them ("laws commonly called political," in Baxter's phrase);[11] and (3) the Law of Regeneracy, which sets the terms on which living men may find fulfillment.

All three laws operate continuously in human life. God does not suspend the two laws of nature for His elect. Like all men, they will experience pain, defeat, and death; like all men, they will desire knowledge and goodness and find themselves ultimately lacking in wisdom and virtue. The unredeemed, however, will live with illusion and anxiety; unable to obey the highest law, they cannot fully obey the lesser laws, and unhappiness is their only destiny. Natural reason cannot make man capable of fulfilling the Law of Regeneracy, but it can discern that only the statutes of that law make the best life possible. The faith of the elect enables them to live without anxiety, for they are not bound and enslaved by the things of the world; it enables them to live truly, for their will that the world should be as it is and as God created it frees their perceptions from the resentment of the world that darkens the understanding of natural man.

Moreover, though reason cannot enable man to obey the highest law, it is not wholly impotent. Only God can grant the psychological

---

[10] William Haller, *The Rise of Puritanism*, p. 89; see also George Santayana, *Reason in Religion* (New York: Scribner's, 1905), pp. 93–96.

[11] Richard Baxter, *The Holy Commonwealth*, theses 202, 213.

attitude necessary for redemption. Action, however, is subject to natural regulation and to human control. Reason can structure man's behavior, and can use its power to develop the highest approximation of regeneracy possible within man's sphere. Calvinistic ethics begin, then, with the question, "How can the effects of sin be minimized in the human psyche, short of the redemptive action of Free Grace?"

Stated as a therapeutic problem, that question was easily answered: sin is lessened when the faculties are directed to their proper objects. The emotions and desires must be prevented from controlling the spirit and be directed toward fulfillment in the natural world. So too, the spirit must be turned toward God and away from the effort to discover or impose perfection on the natural world.

Miller is right in observing that the Calvinist "revolt" against traditional Judaeo-Christian thought was very limited; as analysis and as therapy, the Puritan view of the human soul was part of that tradition. If the Calvinist laid somewhat greater emphasis on the final imperfection of any therapy than had been traditional, he did not doubt the diagnosis or surrender the effort to cure.

The "cure" was far from ascetic or pietistic. The emotions were, in their place, both good and useful. "Delight" had been designed by God as a "help" and encouragement to man. Emotion is only a danger, the Puritan argued, when it becomes an end in itself. Man, Calvin cautioned, should avoid any severity greater than God's: the road of asceticism is the road of impiety and not of virtue.[12]

The monks and the perfectionistic sects which sought to "withdraw" from the world received Calvin's severe denunciation. They were too "morose," refusing to see the excellence of the created order and underrating the possibilities of human improvement within the limits of nature. At the same time, they were too "giddy," overestimating the degree to which man by his own efforts might attain or be assured of salvation.

Both monks and sects were guilty of a prideful concern for personal salvation and an unconcern for their fellow man. The truly chosen, Calvin pointed out, need not fear contamination by any man, and hence need not commit the sin of indifference. Even if it were possible for man to be saved by his own efforts, it would be unlikely

[12] Miller, *The New England Mind*, vol. I, p. 102; Calvin, *Institutes*, III:iii:12, ix:3, x:1–5.

that the first step toward salvation should be a violation of the rules of ethics and morality.[13] Finally, all such doctrines were based on illusion; the Laws of Nature continue to operate in man, and "escape" from them is neither possible nor necessary.

To be sure, the Calvinist employed the language which Weber was to call "inner-worldly asceticism." He urged men to regard the world as a "place of exile"; he proposed that men "use the things of the world as though you used them not"; he termed life a "pilgrimage" in which men should not "settle" on the land which their task was to "pass through." Yet all these propositions have a positive, if muted, side: the exile has a homeland, the pilgrim a direction.

John Cotton wrote that each man should regard life and labor as a "calling" in which the goods of the world are sought only insofar as they aid men to glorify God. We are, Cotton contended, stewards of God charged with the management of life.[14] The perception of a righteousness beyond that of men does not call man out of the world, it calls him into it, providing him with a reason for struggling with life's frustrations, a dignity that cannot be shaken by disappointment or defeat.

> He who would Valiant be, 'gainst all disaster,
> Let him in constancy follow the Master.
> There's no discouragement shall make him once relent
> His first avowed intent to be a pilgrim. . . .
> Since, Lord, thou dost defend us with Thy spirit,
> We know we at the end shall life inherit.
> Then fancies flee away! I'll care not what men say,
> I'll labor night and day to be a pilgrim.[15]

Calvinist and Puritan ideas of the good life can be summarized in a simple proposition: the good life consists in transforming estrangement from nature, created by the Fall, into alienation from nature.

The human malaise, in the Puritan's view, centered in the will or "heart" of man. Reason was the guiding light of men's natural

---

[13] *Institutes*, IV:xiii:16.

[14] John Cotton, "A Christian Calling," in *The American Puritans*, ed. Perry Miller, pp. 173–182.

[15] John Bunyan's hymn is cited from *The Hymnal for Youth* (Boston and Chicago, 1956), #233.

faculties, but it required will to preserve a right order in the soul. Since Adam's fall, the will had become irrevocably defective. Consequently, improvement in man and his condition required the development of external substitutes which would compensate for the will's defect.

A powerful support might be found in the expression of emotion, for the passions might be led to accept their proper role if they found their natural objects in the world. Calvin had noted that sentiments shut up in the self poison the spirit, and for that negative reason if no other, joy and communion were "helps" to man. In an even more negative sense, the passions might be used to help man: the power of fear could, at least, discipline man's conduct. (For both reasons, the Puritans distrusted isolation and compelled single men to live with families.) The use of fear, however, was never more than a melancholy necessity; it imprisoned the passions but it did not free the spirit.

States and societies might be judged good to the extent that they were able to substitute positive motives for the negative impulses of fear. The Holy Commonwealth, Richard Baxter asserted, is that which punishes vice and rewards virtue.[16] God judges the actions of states toward sin as much as he judges the sins themselves; as individuals, we are not accountable for the sins of our fellows, but as members of a community we can be made to answer for our treatment of them. Even more is this the case in our treatment of virtues. The state which punishes virtue encourages vice: it is not only an accomplice in sin, but the instigator of evil. It was the clear duty of the state to encourage man toward virtue and understanding, and to discourage any departures in the direction of pride or sensuality.

Puritanism always saw the community as a creative force, part of the necessary development of man's nature and the good life. The ideal of the state contained an educational goal in the shaping of the individual spirit. The Puritans, living in an atmosphere of religious strife and social change, had an understandably heightened fear of disorder. Yet they never ceased to insist that punishment should only be designed to "win one's brothers" back to fraternal attitudes and conduct. (Characteristically, when Richard Baxter was led, in 1656, to say a good word for tolerance, he wrote of the inferior effect of

16 *The Holy Commonwealth*, thesis 204.

punishment and of the danger that it would lead men to "being forward to impose on others," but he continued to insist that even if punishment of dissenters was abandoned the state should assist the orthodox.)[17]

It exaggerates the case, however, to argue as Miller does that the Puritan emphasis on community represents an anachronistic tribal instinct which had survived into a new era.[18] That underrates too much the very sophisticated analysis of community and society that much of Miller's work sets forth. It slights, too, the general atmosphere of dubiety in which the Puritan conducted his discussion of politics.

Certainly the laws governing political organization and the knowledge of political things could be ascertained more easily than Divine things. That did not make political knowledge a simple thing. Reason could discern, in some degree, the Natural Law, the best organization of the state under the best conditions. Knowledge of the Natural Law, however, was no guide to the best laws possible in particular circumstances. Indeed, the Calvinist insisted that there were no absolute rules of positive law. The Scripture might seem final; the Covenant with Noah had made at least the last seven commandments binding on all men. Yet, Calvin pointed out, those commandments deal only with the "carnal appetites" of men and must change as those appetites vary, constantly aiming to produce the best man from changing conditions. The degeneration of states once good is the rule of human history, and any improvement requires a constant effort to recover lost virtue. Baxter wrote:

> The end, being more excellent than the means, is to be preserved by us, and no means to stand in competition with the end.

That "Machiavellian" statement underlines the fact that for the Puritan, the organization of political community was not to be left to custom, instinct, or tradition: it demanded the application of all of the rational faculties of men.[19]

[17] *The Holy Commonwealth*, theses 238, 239, and *Letter to Sir Edward Hartley* (London, 1656), pp. 48–51.

[18] *The New England Mind*, vol. I, pp. 416–417.

[19] Baxter is cited in Schlatter, *Richard Baxter and Puritan Politics*, pp. 25–26, 162; see also Calvin, *Institutes*, II:ii:13–17, III:x, IV:xx:15–16.

"Without despising life . . ."

In Puritan analysis, every society or polity was based on a "Covenant." Not a utilitarian contract, the Covenant was defined by the values and goals to which its members committed themselves and which gave to the individuals within it a "common soul." Covenants made men brothers, in however limited a degree.

Only one Covenant, the Covenant of Grace, established a perfect fraternity, but degrees of excellence could be distinguished in the lesser covenants and fraternities of men. Four covenants and their corresponding fraternities were delineated in Puritan theory:

1. The Covenant of Grace and the Brotherhood of Man.
2. The Covenant of Nature and the Brotherhood of Blood.
3. The Church Covenant and the Brotherhood of Visible Christians.
4. The Political Covenant and the Brotherhood of Citizens.

It is useful to begin with the extremes, Grace and Nature, because these "limiting cases" or "ideal types" provided the Puritan with the structure he employed in discussing the human covenants.

(1) *The Covenant of Grace and the Brotherhood of Man.* Like Grace itself, the Covenant of Grace was concerned with inner and not outer things. The Elect pledged a pure faith and a pure intention to do good; the Lord pleased, in return, to promise them the will to fulfill their pledge. It was a covenant based on purity of intention, not success in action. (That suggests why Winthrop took so dim a view of clerical participation in politics; a well-intentioned amateur, even if his salvation is assured, is of dubious benefit to men here below.)

Entering the Covenant of Grace, man joined the fraternity of the Elect, the *corpus mysticum*. Unlike all other forms of fraternity, the Elect did not require the physical presence of their brothers. God had granted a perfect will, and the passions could be left to take care of themselves. The passions did not detract from, nor could they enhance, the perfect communion of spirit shared by the chosen. In this freedom from concern for the passions, the brotherhood of the Elect was the only true fraternity, the only complete covenant; only the

Elect were without the trace of self-concern which tainted even the best of human fraternities.

Though this concept of fraternity is an aristocratic one, Calvin also insisted that election alone gave man true knowledge of the brotherhood of all men. As an intellectual or religious dogma, the proposition that all men are brothers can be taught to any man, but nothing in the world of nature can lead him to *feel* that fraternity. Puritan mystics, like the Familists, devoted to the spiritual brotherhood of all men, felt compelled to disregard the illusory "outer man." Characteristically, Calvin and Puritan orthodoxy differed, noting that the way to love for those one has not seen does not lie through indifference toward those one has seen. Men have a "special" duty to those with whom they have special relations. The freedom of the Elect from control by the passions is precisely what enables them to accept and obey the duty to love all men equally. In loving those who are close, they do not neglect or undervalue those who are far away; loving the distant, they do not ignore those who are at hand, to whom their love can be of immediate efficacy. That ability, however, is never present in natural, unredeemed man.

(2) *The Covenant of Nature and the Brotherhood of Blood.* Most societies and groups, the Puritan acknowledged, were based on covenants which were only implicit. The majority were guided by the nearly instinctive commandments of the Covenant of Nature. Closely connected to the family, which the Puritan regarded as the only "natural" group, the Covenant of Nature consisted of the specifically limited obligation to assist one's fellows in the task of physical survival. Aid against enemies, assistance in providing for material gratification and security, affection, and emotional support exhausted its duties.

The fraternity of the Covenant of Nature is also the lowest of the human brotherhoods. It is based, for most men, not on choice but on the accident of birth. The only common value is the desire for individual well-being, narrow and private in character. Of all the fraternities, it is weakest in "common soul," for its community is only a fragile and variable belief in the common interests of private souls.

However, there must always be an element of "natural fraternity" in the lives of unredeemed men. Thought is never removed from the senses, and those who are to share intellectual communion or receive encouragement of the spirit must, to some degree, share common joys and fears. When Calvin wrote of the need to "put the order of nature underfoot," [20] he did not imply that man can abolish nature but that he must subordinate emotion (and his behavior toward natural groups like the family) to higher goals and fellowships.

(3) and (4) *The Human Covenants.* The covenants of state and church represent the conscious effort of men to determine, within the conditions of nature, the best means to the good life. Taken together, they form a course of education for the whole life of man, intended to teach the individual to "yearn for death without despising life."

Church and state were intimately linked in Puritan theory because they were part of a single endeavor to produce the best life available to men. A "separation" of the two presupposes not only a church unconcerned with this life—a manifest absurdity, since its members are living men—but that a state can be complete if it is concerned only with worldly things. Given the Puritan view of human nature, that concept was no less absurd: human happiness, to the degree that it is possible at all, demands alienation from the world, and the means of encouraging that alienation become of direct concern to the state. The purely secular state, Baxter wrote, is to the true commonwealth as "an idiot is to a reasonable man"; lacking a true understanding of man's nature and his perennial discontent with the world and worldly things, such a state cannot treat him with justice.[21]

Two other qualities are common to the human covenants. First, they seem to be based far more on individual choice than are the covenants of Grace and nature, creating obligations that previously did not exist between men. Philosophically, Puritan theorists argued that men only "discovered" the existence of bonds already in existence and written in the character of those who made the covenants. Yet they were willing to concede that the formal act of deliberation and agreement had a function: it pledged men in the flesh to obligations which had previously existed only as abstractions. Duties which might have bound the individual to any set of like-minded men now bound him to the particular set of like-minded men with whom he had en-

[20] John Calvin, *Sermons on the Fifth Book of Moses* (London, 1583), sermon 194.

[21] *The Holy Commonwealth*, theses 190, 198; Schlatter, *Richard Baxter and Puritan Politics*, pp. 21–22.

gaged in the act of covenanting. Flesh could no longer claim ignorance of obligation.

Second, political and ecclesiastical covenants lacked the certainty of the two other varieties of covenant and fraternity. Considerable flexibility in positive law must be allowed to the state because of the variability of human affairs; the same uncertainty applied to church organization. Reason was the best test, but the best reason might err. (Hence the Puritans' reluctance to "separate" from the Anglican Church, even when they believed it to be wrongly organized.) Hooker summed up:

> We doubt not what we practice, yet it's beyond all doubt that all men are liars and we are among the number. . . . We do, or may, err though we do not know it. Yet what we have learned we do profess, yet profess still to live that we may learn.[22]

Uncertainty was a matter of means; the end, the good life for man, was not in doubt. Both covenants were "political" in the Hellenic sense, and the relation of brethren was a civic one. However, to the Puritan mind, the Hellenic view of politics was itself incomplete. The state could not attain its own end. The church, however, demanded at least minimal support from the state. The best life for men demanded the best organization and the best harmony of both.

"Integral and conservant causes . . ."

The simplest way to define the difference between church and state is to distinguish the positive and negative aspects of politics. The state exists to punish vice, to spread "salutary terror" in the hearts of men. The church performs the educational task of teaching men a willing obedience, a genuine reverence for the law. "To conciliate men" and to "form civil manners," Calvin put it in an attempt at summary.[23] Yet the simple statement is an oversimplification: the church also threatens men, and the state cannot be content to punish vice, but must also reward virtue.

Economic regulation, the control of wealth and prices, the effort to provide employment and to guarantee the individual against natural

---

[22] Hooker, in Jacobson's *Development of American Political Thought*, p. 67.

[23] *Institutes*, IV:xx:2.

catastrophe, were all part of the duty of the Puritan state. Social theorists, bemused by the theories of Max Weber, have misinterpreted many of the critical statements of Puritan "economic theology." Puritan analysis, in fact, is often directly opposed to the formulations of those who would see Puritanism as a precursor of capitalism.[24]

The Puritan theorists regarded property as antecedent to government, but not therefore noble. Children and the "just acquisitions" of man were parts of the Covenant of Nature, tied to carnality and passion. Given human nature, they could not be eliminated and were a necessary concession to man's lower nature. Government, however, as a later and higher form of human organization must regulate all of man's "propriety" for the public good.

John Cotton developed the concept of "calling," in which all labor is equally dignified in serving the Lord's end. Certainly an admonition to labor, Cotton's doctrine may seem to preach quietism to the lower classes. Cotton's purpose, however, was to infuse labor with value, to insist that work and gain are not ends in themselves. Men, he wrote, should not be "anxious" about the result of their enterprise. Moreover, men must use their talents according to God's will, and are limited, consequently, to "good means." Men have obligations to love and to seek the good of their brothers; hence competitive ethics, the "undermining of others," or any success in competition obtained at the expense of other men, must be prohibited.[25]

Puritan principles involved more than a limitation of business practices; they also implied positive economic legislation. The aim of legislation is to teach men to "yearn for death without despising life." Despising life is sinful, for life is God's creation. Hence the desperately afflicted of this world, the poor and the diseased who encounter only misery, cannot attain the best state of the human spirit. Yet in part, these conditions may be remedied by human action. Calvinism saw no virtue in poverty. The Calvinist was compelled to grant that poverty might be "happy," but only if the Lord chose;

[24] Max Weber, *The Protestant Ethic and the Spirit of Capitalism* (New York: Scribner's, 1958); see also *Protestantism and Capitalism*, ed. R. W. Green (Boston: Heath, 1959).

[25] John Cotton, "A Christian Calling"; it is not observed often enough that Cotton's argument is part of a larger work (*The Way of Life*, London, 1641) and, like all the closely reasoned treatises of early Calvinism, especially liable to quotation out of context.

his theology compelled him to acknowledge the possibility of miracles, but miracles were not the standards for human legislation.

To be sure, Calvin argued that poverty has an educational value, teaching that mortal things are perishing and insecure and that life is not enough. His argument, however, was that poverty teaches the rich, not the poor. Prosperity, he pointed out, dulls men's sense of sin. It makes them feel secure and contented, and worse, it makes the practice of human virtue too easy. The "vaunted constancy" of the rich, Calvin argued, is exposed for the sham it is by a taste of the conditions which the poor must endure daily.[26] Calvin's thesis, in other words, was virtually identical to the "environmentalist" theories of later social reformism. Though man must expect inequality in this life, a minimal degree of prosperity for all is necessary. (Calvinism implicitly argued that some degree of well-being might improve the moral conduct of the poor.)

There was, moreover, an element of egalitarianism in Calvinistic and Puritan teaching. In one sense this was negative, all men being equal in the "Democracy of the Fall." But also, all men were made equal by the Divine image in their souls: that fact made them deserving of damnation. To secular eyes, differences in ability and virtue must always seem important; to one who sees human attainments measured in the Divine scale, the differences among men are insignificant variations on a common condition of imperfection.

The opposition to "sovereigns" which was always strong in Calvinism and Puritanism can be traced to that egalitarian element of both theories. Only in part was opposition based on a fear of the weakness of man when granted power. Men, the Calvinist argued, "need leaders and not sovereigns." Men, that is, need those who can help them toward improvement, not those who will bear their burdens. Christ, the only true "sovereign," was also the true leader: he showed the way and did not excuse the failures of men.

Christ's sovereignty on earth must be divided among several holders. Powers spiritual, then, may be separated from powers temporal. This division is not a "check and balance" theory: the two powers exist to strengthen and not to limit one another. To be sure, given man's corruption, reproof and admonition are necessary between the powers, but that is a departure from their primary educa-

[26] *Institutes*, III: viii, ix: 1, I: xvi: 8, II: viii: 45.

tional task. The relations of rulers of church and state should be fraternal, for they owe each other the brotherly duties of assistance, instruction, and reproof.

The "generality" of citizens must also have some share of sovereignty. The private citizen cannot be presumed to be as fully a part of the civic fraternity as the magistrate or pastor, because the citizen's private concerns lead him in directions other than the service of the state. Nonetheless, the "unity of humanity" must find some expression in practice.

Calvin was more tolerant in matters relating to the state than the Puritans were to be. Neither, however, considered that the explicit consent of all citizens was necessary to the state. Both argued that consent was preferable, that a "mixed government" was probably the best of political systems, and that implicit consent, at least, was required by all states. All government is bound by some covenant, even if that agreement is tacit. Hence Calvin's thesis that magistrates charged with duties under the law and custom of the state may rebel against a usurping monarch: they act only in obedience to the implicit covenant. Implicit covenants, however, are clearly inferior; they stand closer to the Covenant of Nature than to the higher forms of human association.

The church, however, was required to maintain an element of explicit consent in the choice of pastors and the conduct of church business. Since the moral standards of the church are more exacting than those of the state, and less rooted in nature, the church requires a more conscious decision to bind the individual. Moreover, since the obligations and the standards for membership are more demanding, the membership of the church is more worthy of consultation than the citizenry at large.[27]

The Calvinist, in other words, reserved the highest political standards for the church alone. Calvin and his followers did not insist, as Plato or Aristotle would have, on the small state. Calvinists might prefer the small state, but they did not consider it of the highest exigency. But the church, or at least its congregations, must be comparatively small, so that the membership may participate in its affairs.

Given the aim of transforming estrangement into alienation, Calvinists never believed that the church was or could be coextensive

[27] *Ibid.*, IV:xx:8, 12, 22–23, 31.

with the state or society. The human covenants arranged themselves
in a progressively narrowing hierarchy. In each of the "stages of
alienation," the Calvinist pilgrim found his fraternity with actual men
constricted and limited, until in the last stage he was reunited in
fraternity with all men, a true fraternity purged of the dross of imperfection and sin.

Covenant of Grace	Pure intention	Brotherhood of man
Church Covenant	(1) Conscious conviction	
	(2) Formal profession (including hypocrites)	Brotherhood of visible Christians
Political Covenant	(1) Positive aims: reward of virtue (presumably including magistrates and active citizens)	Civic fraternity
	(2) Negative aims; punishment of vice	
Covenant of Nature	Prudent emotions; families, blood kin. Accidental; not based on personal choice.	Brotherhood of blood
Original Sin	Sub-bestial man. No ties to particular individuals.	Individualism

Calvin presumed that the Church would exist within state and
society, not that it would replace them. The members of the church
have a role in the state, but they are permanently alienated from their
fellow citizens. Given the educational nature of life it could not be
otherwise: born in sin, man acquires virtue only later and through
travail.

The relations between Christians and the rest of society made a
problem of "Christian liberty." Liberty is obviously "safe" for the
elect, and it is required by merely visible Christians. To maintain a
personal conviction and profession they must be free to examine their
own beliefs and to probe and question the foundations of the faith.
That obligation to re-examine the self and its creeds rises above the
law of even the best society.

Yet, Calvin noted, the use of such liberty is dangerous, for it
may "frighten" those of "weaker faith." Presumably the young, as
well as others, need an environment in which the "fundamentals"
are not openly questioned. So too, certainty and dogma are useful
in restraining those who are still only members of the political covenant. Wiser than liberals, Calvinists feared that given the ignorance

and carnality of men, error tends to prevail in the "marketplace of ideas." Liberty of conscience, Calvin argued, is a thing of the spirit, inward and not outward, which need not and should not be "used in the presence of men." [28]

An immediate qualification must be attached. In the best circumstances, liberty of conscience is the concern only of the individual; the Elect can restrict themselves to that enjoyment of liberty. Merely visible Christians, however, will need the support of concrete individuals, will need to discuss, consider, and weigh the arguments and the admonitions of their fellows. Visible Christians need the presence of some men, both to encourage them to use their liberty and to prevent them from losing their way in a sea of doubt.

Ministers especially, Richard Baxter observed, need the support of their fellows against all the temptations which would seduce them from doing their duty—the anger of those they censure, their own desire for ease, the painfulness of confronting doubt. The church, Baxter concluded, must sacrifice something in the way of dogma to preserve its fraternity. Ministers must not be allowed to "rail" at one another over difficult points of doctrine. The church would do well to avoid "too great a precision," for the effort to obtain unity in "human and doubtful things" can only result in "presumptions and impositions" which divide men from their fellows. In all things, the church should limit itself to matters where "common consent" is possible.[29]

Few Puritans went as far as Baxter, but most insisted that liberty of conscience is necessary for the covenanted members of the church. Of all human fraternities, the brotherhood of the church is highest. It is, in fact, the best earthly city, the anticipation of the City of God. Because of the liberty it requires, the church can neither replace nor embrace state and society. Devoted to values beyond human things, the church demands of its members a standard higher than can be asked of or is safe for merely civic man. Fraternity in the church is vital, because the members of the church are exiles in a foreign world, surrounded by strangers.

Yet the church is also part of state and society, for it represents

[28] *Ibid.*, III:xix.
[29] *Letter to Sir Edward Hartley*, pp. 48, 51–53, 56, and *The Holy Commonwealth*, theses 238, 239, 243.

the ideal which alone can fulfill the hopes of humanity's lesser fraternities. The Christian finds his brethren in the political order. The church has an interest in the best politics, because Christ's reign in the church is surer when men have seen and learned the defects of even the most excellent aspects of earthly life and conduct. And the state should recognize that the churches are, as John Cotton put it, "integral and conservant causes" of political virtue.[30] In the best city, the church is guardian of the legitimacy of the state, the custodian and defender of its highest values. Exalted above other human organizations, the church is still part of the political order's endeavor to perfect its citizens to the extent that God and nature permit.

[30] John Cotton, "The Bloody Tenet Washed (etc.)," in *The Bloody Tenet of Persecution for Cause of Conscience,* ed. Underhill (London: Haddon, 1848), pp. 19–30.

> The principles of New England spread at first to the neighbouring states; they then passed successively to the more distant ones. . . . They now extend their influence . . . over the whole American world. The civilization of New England has been like a beacon lit upon a hill, which after it has diffused its warmth around, tinges the distant horizon with its glow.
>
> De Tocqueville, *Democracy in America*

CHAPTER VI

JOHN WINTHROP: THE STATESMAN

"More than nature demands . . ."

JOHN WINTHROP was a political man by vocation, a reflective man by nature and faith. None defended more strenuously the prerogatives of a specifically political wisdom distinct from that of the church. Yet Winthrop never conceived of a political understanding which did not depend on religious teaching; he relied on scriptural and religious authority rather more, and secular classical writings rather less, than did his clerical contemporaries.

His thought consists of a series of reflections on practical politics. It does no violence to Winthrop's ideas, however, to see in them an order and consistency amounting to systematic theory. In fact, Winthrop merits the supreme accolade which can be given a theorist: his diagnosis of his own times is relevant to others. He is a permanent contemporary.

Man, for Winthrop, was above all a social animal. The "paradise" of his spirit was love, which could be found only where there was likeness. Akin to his fellows both in the flesh and in the image of God common to all men, man found his delight in their company. Love, however, was no longer easy for men. Adam's fall had destroyed the instinctive sense of likeness which God had granted him. Men were now left with a darkened understanding which made them feel separate from God and different from their fellows.

Although his emotions now barricade him from others, man may be led by nearness, familiarity, and affection to acknowledge likeness for some of his fellows. The soul may then be enabled to grasp a partial love, imperfect because it is distorted and incomplete. Only Christ's redemption can make possible a sense of likeness without contact and intercourse. Among men in general, distance causes a slow attrition of affection. Memory causes a momentary awareness of the weakness of human will; prayer may cause a miraculous revival of affection and concern. Both memory and prayer, however, offer fleeting exceptions to the rules which testify to the nature of man.

Natural law indicated, Winthrop argued, that all men should be regarded as friends. Race, ethnicity, and nationality had no status in nature. The earth was given to men in common, belonging to no man to the exclusion of others. The increase of men and their flocks, however, produced scarcity in the natural environment. Not all men could be helped in their need; some distinctions were necessary to determine priorities of aid.

Hence, the Covenant of Nature: men formed an implicit agreement to divide the world and to establish barriers, rights of property, special obligations due to some men and not to others. All this derived from a rule of natural justice: that man should aid his fellow to the limit of his own necessity. When all men cannot be aided, Winthrop argued, man acts "by way of commerce," lending where repayment is possible, giving up to that point which endangers his own needs and survival.

The sinful nature of man, however, dominated by corrupted passions, evades the constraint of reasoned natural law. Fallen nature in man, dominated by self-love and the desire for security, is "worse than beasts." Realizing that the goods of the world are perishing and scarce, men are not content with satisfying their needs. They feel driven to "lay up treasures" against some future calamity, and demand more than they need. Scarcity makes the fraternity of nature imperfect; the anxiety of fallen man magnifies the imperfection, making men rivals more than nature requires.

Nonetheless, the rule of natural justice remains the law. All men are to be considered friends and brothers where possible; the expansion of fraternity is a standard of ethics and an aim of civil policy. All relations of natural men require an element of prudence; no perfect trust or fraternity is possible. The existence of evil demands precautions, and scarcity requires that a man look to his own needs. It is still essential, Winthrop argued, that we treat men as worthy of trust until there is a probability that they are unworthy. Mere possibility is not enough; to this extent, the burden of proof lies with the accuser. To adopt suspicion as a first principle is to poison the relations of all men. Even men in nature owe one another an obligation to distrust only as a last resort, and a duty of assistance until their own needs are certainly or probably endangered.

Natural justice, being based on the nature of man, contains no rules for enemies. By nature, men are not enemies, and given the fall, an established enemy is outside the law: natural man owes no obligations toward his foe. Christian man is "set apart" from other men by the existence of a law which regulates his dealing with enemies. The Christian law, however, frees the Christian from the excuse of natural necessity and prudence. It commands him to give even when his survival is endangered, requires him to love his enemies and to show them charity. It orders him, in other words, to be more perfect than nature. To natural men, these duties will seem burdensome; only to the Elect will they seem privileges. Nonetheless, to the extent that the "exclusive" standards of the Elect can be made applicable to human affairs, they consist only in a more intense obligation to establish fraternity among men.

Citizens and Magistrates

Politics must be guided by the fraternal imperative, subject only to the limitation that institutions, though they can instruct man, cannot be "effectual" in changing man's nature. Ends and means tend to overlap in Winthrop's analysis; the good city becomes a series of inter-locking fraternities, binding magistrate and magistrate, magistrate and minister, and magistrate and citizen.

The central role of magistracy is hardly accidental, given Winthrop's view of the nature of his profession. Economic management, which demanded the knowledge of man's material needs and the means to fulfill them, was clearly lower than statecraft—which, because it was concerned with man's humanity, must know man's whole nature, including his spirit.

The church shared that concern, but the church's concern with the temporal world is less demanding than that of the magistrate. Unlike the minister and his congregation, the magistrate cannot select his "members"; he must take men as he finds them. Moreover, while the church need make no promise of material rewards, the magistrate is charged with caring for the public good.

Politics, in other words, demands both a knowledge of the good and a knowledge of the means of attaining it, both good intention and successful action. Thus, to perform his task, the magistrate needs the knowledge and the power of God. The demands on him are more exalted, the certainty of failure clearer, than for any other "natural man." Indeed, the obligations of the magistrate are greater than those of the Elect, while his ability to fulfill them is less. Magistrates, then, have a special need for encouragement and reproof from others in their position who can be expected to feel and understand the burdens of office. The Elect enjoy a special fraternity; the magistrate calls out to his fellow governors from the depth of his personal need.

Minister and magistrate also shared a fraternal bond; despite their distinct skills, their aims were identical. The magistrate should seek the counsel of the clergy in matters of faith and morals (his concern for worldly success made the magistrate especially prone to errors of moral judgment). The clergy, in turn, should accept a part of the burden for the inevitable failures of magistracy in its impossible task. Each, too, owed the other the duty of encouragement and support.

Against the "check and balance" theory of many of his con-temporaries, Winthrop asserted the necessity of "friendship and affec-tion" among those charged with the governing and the guiding of men. The fear of friendship among governors, he noted, is a counsel of division and not of love, and is based on a Machiavellian and not a

Christian theory of politics. It violates the natural law, elevating suspicion over trust, and if enforced will inevitably wreak havoc with the community by raising distrust to the highest level of civil relations.

Moreover, such a counsel and policy violates the responsibility which the citizen owes the magistrate. That responsibility is greater than that which the Visible Christian owes his minister. Since politics has fewer givens than the church, the citizen should allow the magistrate a greater latitude in choice of means and a greater indulgence in failure than he grants to the minister.

Legal and formal restrictions of magisterial power are simply foolish. There is no point in seeking to eliminate the temptation to evil; men should avoid the prideful effort to be "more severe than God." The temptation to tyranny will exist whatever legal devices men create. Yet such rules, though they do not eliminate the danger of tyranny, may make it impossible for the magistrate to perform his functions. Seeking to prevent merely possible evils, Winthrop argued, is folly if it requires a cost to present good (an excellent rebuke to many "tests" of permissible speech later adopted by the United States Supreme Court). It is as much as men can do, Winthrop pointed out, to render tyranny improbable.

Many commentators intent, like Parrington, on seeing Winthrop as an autocrat, have neglected the specific restraints he advocated and the powers he conceded to the people at large. First, he argued that the community may limit the magistrate by statements of purpose and by general rules, for the right of the people in "giving or withholding their covenant" is not to be abridged. This constituent power did not exhaust the sphere of public liberty. At least in Massachusetts, Winthrop conceded the right of annual election of magistrates, and himself expanded the suffrage beyond that implied by the original charter. Finally, the people had a right to offer "counsel" on all laws and taxes, "counsel" having the expanded meaning often associated with premodern usage: no law or tax might be levied without the consent of the public or its representatives.

The people, exercising the power of God "mediately" in civil affairs, create commonwealths, elect governors, and judge their performance. Winthrop insisted only that those who hold divine power show some minimal approximation of divine charity toward those they elect. In modern terms, Winthrop's "autocracy" consisted of no more than a modern executive expects as a matter of course: the right to apply general policy to particular cases fairly free from restraint. His arguments did not presume a naive faith in magistrates; they were directed against a naive faith in legislators.

Winthrop had a more fundamental reason for opposing extensive formal limitations of executive power. He realized that the effort to eliminate all the possible evils of government, especially at the cost of many of its possible goods, is an indication of a desire to retreat from civic responsibility. In the first place, such a course rejects any share of collective responsibility; it regards the people always as victims, and never as victimizers. Secondly, it seeks to protect private concerns from interference at a cost to public goods. Natural man is always prone to self-concern, always likely to forget that "particular estates cannot subsist in the ruin of the public." Some minimal risk of tyranny may be useful in inducing men to take some concern for the community. Moreover, the private interests of magistrates are more closely bound to the interests of the whole than are those of citizens engaged in private pursuits. "Mere democracy" tends to encourage privatism, faction, and disunity; some magisterial power is needed if the interest of the community is to be upheld—not because magistrates are radically different in nature from citizens (though hopefully of greater political ability), but because they are of the same nature. Both citizens and magistrates assume the burden of guilt that comes to the finite man who wields the power of the Infinite. They too owe one another the fraternal duties of encouragement and reproof, admonition and affection.

Profession and Action

Like most Puritans, Winthrop emphasized the natural limitations which compel men toward association and covenant. His assertion of the interdependence of private and public estates is of this order. So too is his argument that God had created differences of talent so that "all men might have need of one another." Differences in special gifts force men to seek association, because no one man can be self-sufficient.[1]

---

[1] *Winthrop Papers*, vol. II, pp. 283–287.

There were, however, two defects to natural scarcity: (1) unless all citizens have at least that abundance necessary to life, conflict between them is bound to occur, and (2) natural scarcity operates more strongly against the poor than the rich, against the weak than the strong. Differences of ability may compel men toward association, but the less able are subject to greater compulsion than their more fortunate fellows.

The remedy for these shortcomings of nature must be sought in law and political action. Nature is inadequate because nature does not recognize, as men must, that differences in special gifts reflect no differences of merit. Winthrop carried his fraternal principles into economic policy; the state must guarantee minimal sustenance to all, and curb the excesses of the wealthy.

There was no doubt that wealth was perilous. Affluence led man to a dangerous feeling of independence, tempting him to believe that injury to the public might benefit his private fortune. The state, in Winthrop's view, must always prevent "oppression," which included usury and excess profiteering. The rich in Germany, he observed, had ignored the plight of the poor, and in their subsequent ruin could be read the moral lesson that each is bound to all.

His economic analysis went further than moralism. The state of English affairs had always disturbed him. "The land grows weary of her inhabitants," he had written; depression, poverty, and unemployment seemed to lie over Britain like a decree of judgment. Winthrop perceived, however, that this was the result not of nature but of defective civil policy. An early form of the "revolution of rising expectations" was sweeping England. A "riot of intemperance" was sweeping the land; men demanded more than was necessary and desired "fripperies" and luxuries of all kinds. The old upper limits to ambition had been swept away, and men were forced to struggle merely to maintain their station. "No man's estate is enough to keep sail with his equals." Compelled to seek an expansion in wealth and revenue, the aristocrats laid an increasingly hard hand on the poor. Change had introduced anxiety and insecurity, and had reintroduced the rapacity of man in the state of Original Sin.[2]

[2] *Winthrop Papers*, vol. II, pp. 111-119, 122-124, 139, 287-288; *Life and Letters*, vol. I, p. 310.

Not all the ramparts of the English conscience had been destroyed. Rather, Winthrop observed that when some men practice acquisitive ethics with impunity, all men are confronted with a choice between imitating the unrighteous or suffering from their greed and lack of scruple. The Elect might choose to lose sustenance rather than engage in evil; unredeemed man must defend his own needs. The task of the state, which the royal government had not performed, is to avoid the necessity of such choices by preventing the unrighteous from acting with impunity. Failure to act is encouragement of evil. The failure of the state also laid a burden on the Visible Christian, who must do his duty and seek to set his fellows an example, even at the cost of suffering. In a fine rebuke to Roger Williams' separatism, Winthrop wrote that most Englishmen were doubtless corrupt but

whores and drunkards they are not. Weak Christians they are indeed, and the weaker for the want of that tender care that should be had of them, (1) by those that are set over them to feed them and, nextly, for that spiritual pride that Satan rooted into the hearts of their brethren, who when they are converted do not and will not strengthen them but also censure them to be none of God's people nor any Visible Christians.[3]

Fortunately, men did not need to face the choice between unrighteous action and natural suffering. A continent lay open in which God had made it possible for man to enjoy the earth's fruits without despoiling his fellow. Moreover, the example of a fraternal community might stir the hearts of men in England. England, apparently, was hopeless. Puritans could not bear adequate witness to God's word, let alone to their social principles. The unredeemed must judge men by their works; the Visible Christian, limited by the natural law, could only guide himself by what was possible in the environment of acquisitiveness. Isolated in scattered communities and surrounded by hostility, the Puritan in England could not be expected to set a standard much beyond that of his fellows. At best, he could suffer with them; he could make little demonstration of the positive goods that might be men's. In America, Puritan political principles might receive an adequate test.

Martyrdom was not infrequent in England, but the cause of

[3] Cited in Morgan, *The Puritan Dilemma*, p. 118.

martyrdom itself illustrated the limitation of the English environment. Persecution was based not on Puritan action, but on Puritan profession. The church could not require its members—most of whom would not be of the Elect—to go much beyond a statement of intellectual conviction. Action lies in the sphere of physical nature; profession is the public statement of an intellectual creed. Being free from emotion's control, the Elect may be expected to act rightly in both respects. The merely Visible Christian has made a statement of his conviction, but he cannot be assumed to control his emotions and physical desires so long as he is isolated. Lonely man, without his brothers, Winthrop implies, is cowardly man, and while he is alone no more than profession can be expected of him. Profession itself, at best half a faith, becomes an "agony" and a virtue; those who fall away do no more than might be expected.

In New England, however, Winthrop argued that "cohabitation and consortship," the intimate, daily support of brethren, raise men above what is to be expected of the average Puritan in England. "What most do in their churches by profession only," he admonished his fellow colonists, "we must bring into familiar and daily practice"; surrounded by his fellows, the New Englander had less excuse than his persecuted brother at home for falling short in the practice of fraternity.

> We must entertain each other in brotherly affection; we must be willing to abridge ourselves of our superfluities for the supply of others' necessities; we must uphold a familiar commerce together in all meekness, gentleness, patience and liberality. We must delight in each other, make others' conditions our own, rejoice together, mourn together, labor and suffer together; always having before our eyes our commission and community in the work, our community as members of the same body.[4]

Winthrop was to write Hooker that New Englanders were brothers in three senses: (1) in peril and envious observation, (2) in consociation, and (3) in the work of God. The three correspond to the humanly-possible covenants of Puritan theology: the Covenant of Nature for "mutual encouragement and succor" against peril; the Civic Covenant, made possible by delight in association; the Church Covenant, produced by an intellectual conviction of the truth of the Word.

[4] *The American Puritans,* ed. Perry Miller, p. 83.

In at least two senses, New England differed from other states. First, there was no necessary conflict between the higher and lower covenants. Second, although the pattern of narrowing exclusiveness would apply—not all would be citizens or churchmen—it would be much softened. New Englanders would be far more equal in dignity and obligation than most communities. We, Winthrop asserted, are part of a fraternity closer than that which bound Israel to Moses, for with us there are no intermediaries between us and the Lord.

Winthrop's standard for New England was based on the theory that the standards of the Church Covenant, the best of all human covenants, can be made applicable as a standard for political practice if there is no hostile political environment to be taken as a given. Winthrop added to the traditional covenant theology of Puritanism the belief that, in the best circumstances, the magistrates and citizens of a Christian community could be elevated to a plane of equality with the church covenant itself; the secular and sacred could be of equal dignity where profession became the standard for action.

Promise and Peril

New England's opportunity partly depended on her peril, a situation which had led many to wonder whether the new continent had been meant for Christian men. The entire structure of covenant theology had been premised on natural scarcity and a hostile environment. Within the covenants, man learned to see his fellows as his chief support against the rigors and insecurities of the world. At the same time, the rigors were required to drive men into the covenants. Indeed, whatever obligations it imposes, a hostile environment can make the community a thing of joy. Lacking an adverse environment, the duties of community may appear an onerous burden to be avoided where possible. And the Puritans encountered such a situation in New England; after an initial period of hardship, the force of natural scarcity was drastically reduced.

Winthrop had rebuked his English critics, who saw migration as a pursuit of ease and comfort, by asserting that life in New England would be hard, and success unsure. Winthrop was right about the early stages, but he never believed that those early conditions would last long (hence his belief that men might enjoy the fruits of the earth without conflict in New England). Before the colonists landed, he stressed the danger that they might pursue "carnal intention" and "fall to embrace this present world, seeking great things for ourselves and our posterity."

Life in America may have been hard, but land abounded, which to a traditional people meant wealth. In America, unlike England, intensive cultivation was not necessary and cooperative agriculture added little to individual well-being. John Cotton, in a phrase that was to have echoes, later denounced those who sought "elbow room" to the detriment of the community. Winthrop felt that punishment was deserved by those who would "enlarge their ease and safety" by deserting their fellows. Yet Winthrop had no doubt that in the new world such a course of action was possible; in America nature no longer compelled men into the civic covenant.

Winthrop's use of the phrase "ourselves and our posterity" was also a portent. Even in America, the Covenant of Nature was necessary for the individual, and the family retained a positive meaning. In England, the Puritans had seen the family as more exalted than the state, the arena where social reformation might begin. That emphasis, however, was only negative; since a corrupt state prevented action in the political sphere, the Puritan must make do with what he had by seeking to reconstitute the family in terms of the higher covenants. In America, the traditional Puritan emphasis on the family could serve to justify a different belief: that the family is more exalted than the state —or, however muted, than the church. The temptation to raise the status of the family arose from the primary temptation to remain a member of the Covenant of Nature alone.

The political community and the church could, of course, force the individual into membership in default of natural scarcity. Yet Puritan theorists understood fairly well that force applied by the community might constrain the individual from yielding to the temptations of nature, but it could not create the sense of political obligation. His consent, freely given, was always necessary. If the community were a burden and not a joy, a man's allegiance would lie with the Covenant of Nature, even if his body were compelled to serve the Civic Covenant.

Winthrop never slighted that understanding. His sterner colleagues always found him lenient. His generosity was partly due to his realization that in America, nature is unreliable; since it does not compel men into the political community, they must be induced to enter it. He feared harshness for the same reason he feared a "mere democracy." To transfer rule to the many is to give scope to their desire to reduce obligations; to treat the many harshly is to increase their resentment and thus heighten their desires to be rid of political obligation.

Most of the institutions of Puritanism were framed on the expectation of persecution by (or at least, alienation from) a surrounding political community. Congregational organization and class distinction argued for conflict as soon as the Puritan lost a sense of the salience of the factors which, uniting him to his fellows, set him apart from others. The Puritan institutions were designed to maximize intensity among a people already set apart from their kindred-in-blood and their kindred-in-politics, to provide support against the older ties and the threats of persecution which might lead a man to betray his own convictions. Winthrop did not always realize the significance of the change in political context which New England confronted, but its dissolutive tendency only emphasizes his thesis.

Winthrop understood that where neither the negative forces of nature nor a hostile community exist, the force of cohesion must be sought in positive moral obligations. The conscience of the individual must compel where man and nature do not. From the beginning, Winthrop defined the peculiar covenant of New England in terms which by the standards of Puritanism made it virtually impossible to fulfill. He demanded that New England produce the best possible human state, the best possible men, the most perfect of human fraternities.

His phrases were not the result of confident self-righteousness. In part, Winthrop's anxiety about the result explains his eagerness to pursue the "errors" of Roger Williams or Anne Hutchinson out of the Commonwealth. To many of his admirers, such as Morgan, Winthrop's conduct in the Hutchinson trial is the weakest moment of his career. Yet Mrs. Hutchinson, like Williams, taught a doctrine whose implications led directly to individualism. Against the positive moral obligations and the negative force of guilt which Winthrop hoped to inculcate as supports for man and for fraternity in New England, both

Williams and Hutchinson appealed to a private moral insight which could justify men in their desire to remain in the Covenant of Nature.

Roger Williams and Anti-Politics

Roger Williams was Winthrop's most painful opponent, as much because of the affection the two always felt for each other as for the danger that Winthrop saw in Williams' teaching. Williams' human virtues and his metaphysical orthodoxy only added appeal to doctrines which threatened the good of the state and the development of the individual.

Williams' heterodoxy lay in the fact that he broke down the synthesis between Grace and nature, this world and the next, which the Puritan had been at such pains to build up. A fairly ordinary variety of religious mystic, as Perry Miller points out, Williams saw the New Testament as a repudiation of the Old and denied any parallel between the physical, material Israel and the "holy mystic nation" of the chosen of Christ.[5]

Against that thesis, John Cotton argued that "the reason of the law (which is the life of the law) is of eternal force and equity in all ages." [6] Reason, as much as revelation, seemed a proof of continuity. Williams' radical dualism, however, was based on a far greater distrust of human reason and conscience than Cotton's; the Fall seemed to him graver and blacker in its consequences than it appeared in even the far-from-cheerful version of Puritan orthodoxy. Williams expressed that view in his best moment, when he opposed Cotton on the question of persecution. Cotton's theological rationalism led him to conclude that Christians, at least, could not in conscience persist in heresy if the true doctrine were explained to them; therefore, they might be punished, not "for cause of conscience" but for "sin against conscience." Yet, Williams pointed out, Cotton acknowledged, as he must, the imperfection of even the orthodox. The conscience of man —and Williams was careful to include his own—is no test at all:

[5] Perry Miller, *Roger Williams*, pp. 150–151; see also pp. 32, 169, 172, 198, 239.

[6] Cited in Miller, *Roger Williams*, p. 181.

This conscience is found in all mankind, more or less: in Jews, Turks, Papists, Protestants and pagans. . . . I have fought against many several sorts of consciences; is it beyond all possibility and hazard that . . . I have not persecuted Jesus in some of them? [7]

Cotton or Winthrop would almost surely have agreed, but they would have insisted on the importance of the "more or less" which Williams treats casually, and on the distinction of possible and probable which Williams does not consider worth noting.

Whatever the defects of Cotton's case, Williams showed none of the concern, on which Winthrop always insisted, for human improvement within the limits of nature. In this sense, Williams was the precursor of a tradition: he was the first American to be so enthralled by the hope of perfection and of a pure and universal brotherhood as to be almost indifferent to conduct here and now. He demanded, as Miller put it, "the real thing or nothing at all." [8]

Realistic enough to believe that salvation and the brotherhood of man depended on Divine, not human, intervention, Williams' devotion to the corpus mysticum led him to deny that there was any application of Christian standards to politics. The testament of Christ, he wrote, is

opposite to the very essentials and fundamentals of the nature of a civil magistracy, a civil commonweal or combination of men, which can respect only civil things.

What is mistaken for "liberalism" in Williams is his dualism, his denial of any connection between the world and the spirit:

Civil weapons are improper in this business and are never able to reach the soul . . . being of a material civil nature . . . (they) cannot extend to spiritual and soul causes.[9]

For that matter, Williams' concern for conscience did not extend beyond the inner world. No less than Cotton, Williams argued that it was proper to restrain those who acted contrary to the public peace. Arguing against a right of conscientious objection, he asserted that on shipboard,

[7] Miller, *Roger Williams*, pp. 158–164.
[8] *Ibid.*, p. 28.
[9] *Ibid.*, pp. 85–86, 132–133.

if any should preach or write that there ought to be no commanders
. . . because all are equal in Christ . . . the commander may judge,
resist, compel and punish.[10]

Moreover, the use of "spiritual weapons" against a recalcitrant conscience was always permissible. Conscience and action were separate
spheres; the political truth that the Puritans always understood, that
the two are interdependent, find no place in Williams' thought.

Williams lowered the political world, by Puritan standards, to the
Covenant of Nature, asking no more of the political order than reason-
able prosperity. Christian values are not necessary to politics, Williams
argued, because the Turkish Empire succeeds without them; indeed,
God often favors "infidel cities" in political life. Williams was no
Machiavellian: he made his case to attack politics, not to praise
Turkey. His well-known argument that the church is "like a corpora-
tion" which

> may dissent, divide, break into schisms, yea, wholly break up . . . and
> yet the peace of the city be not in the least measure impaired or
> disturbed. Because the essence . . . of the city . . . is essentially dis-
> tinct. . . . The city was before and stands entire when such a corpora-
> tion . . . is thrown down.[11]

argues only that a secular city can survive the ruin of the church in
peace. Yet this, like his other arguments, is relevant only in terms of
his dualism. Winthrop and Cotton did not argue that Christian values
and the church were necessary for politics, but that they were necessary for the best politics and the best life available to natural man.

Williams overlooked that argument because all politics seemed
dismal to him, and other men unworthy of the concern of pious men.
There could be no argument, he wrote, that without Christian examples and institutions other men would become diseased in the soul;
"dead men cannot be infected. The civil state, the world, being in a
natural state dead to sin (whatever the state religion . . .) it is impossible that it should be infected." To tie the church to the state,
since civil power came from the people, would be

to pull God and Christ and Spirit out of heaven and subject them to nat-

[10] *Ibid.*, pp. 225–226.
[11] *Ibid.*, p. 117.

ural, sinful, inconstant men . . . and so, naturally, to Satan himself, by whom all peoples naturally are guided.

Given an evil world, a Christian should not concern himself with its affairs or with the good of his fellow men. "Abstract yourself," he wrote Winthrop, "from the dung heap of this earth." [12]

Groups were dangerous, for they might strengthen the individual in pride and security. Nor could the Christian safely associate with the impious: "I durst not officiate," he wrote, "to an unseparated people." Williams was nothing if not extreme: he sought to eliminate the term "Goodman" from everyday speech, seeking to restrict it to those who were truly good. He could not even pray with unregenerate men, and wound up being able to take communion only with his wife—eventually, revolting against that restriction, he welcomed everyone into the church regardless of profession.[13]

As Winthrop and the Puritans had feared, Williams ended with the Covenant of Nature. The uncompromising devotion to an inner and unseen fraternity, beyond the power of man to produce, ends with the isolation of the individual or the destruction of all distinction between men, and the loss of any particular fraternity between concrete men.

It was sadder, perhaps, because Williams was more of a Puritan than he knew. Denouncing the Quakers for claiming a union with God, he denied that such union was possible and contended that their enthusiasm convicted them of deceit:

> The Spirit of God was most purely rational, and a spirit of pure order, and did not prompt or move men to break hedges and leap over one ordinance into another.[14]

In part, it was the lesson orthodoxy had tried to teach Williams himself. Moreover, he denounced the Quakers for denying the existence of a visible kingdom; he, Williams announced, had not found a true church among the many "pretenders," but that did not prove that one did not or could not exist.

Despite the severity of his concept of sin, Williams fell short here

---

[12] *Ibid.*, pp. 127, 147–148, and Roger Williams, *Letters to John Winthrop,* Old South Leaflet #54 (Boston: Old South Association, 1896).

[13] Morgan, *The Puritan Dilemma,* pp. 117–118, 120, 130–131.

[14] Miller, *Roger Williams,* p. 252.

of the Puritan standard. Puritan orthodoxy, Winthrop not the least, would have reminded Williams that all churches of natural men must be "pretenders"; Williams' hope for the pure church and the pure fraternity had engendered his idea of a world of evil, and both had betrayed him. For the Puritan saw the heresy: the world is good, and though the efforts of men be only pretensions, these too are good on their own terms. Rejection of God and truth lies hidden in those who reject the world and their obligations to their brother man.

Puritan Statecraft: The Legacy

Winthrop feared Williams' teachings because they might encourage what was base in New England, might cause her to lose her glorious opportunity and become no better than the human average.

The permanent legacy of Winthrop to American thought is his realization of the American promise and the conditions under which Americans labor in seeking its fulfillment. Winthrop could have echoed D. H. Lawrence. Heretofore, he might have said, all fraternity save that of the Elect (and to a small degree, the church) has been based on the effort to escape from the mastery of nature and of men. America, freed from such mastery, must now essay a giant stride, must seek to be mastered by a higher vision. Struggle against fathers in the flesh must yield to duty to the Father in the spirit of men,

> but if our hearts will not obey but shall be seduced and worship other gods, our pleasures and profits, and serve them, . . . we shall surely perish out of the good land whither we pass over this vast sea. . . .[15]

That prescription was not one in which the Puritan, by his psychological or political theory, could maintain much hope. It was an intellectual last resort, almost a counsel of despair. Winthrop's own forebodings found confirmation in practice, and his influence, like the religious tradition in general, lies in its effects on the ideas and guilts of Americans more than the conduct of American life. Yet symbols have their power. The duty to establish the best city, short of which no failure is adequate or excusable: is that not the definition of the American dream?

[15] *The American Puritans*, p. 84.

> The Americans not only follow their religion from interest, but they often place in this world the interest which makes them follow it. . . . The American preachers are constantly referring to the earth; and it is only with great difficulty that they can divert their attention from it. . . . It is often difficult to ascertain from their discourses whether the principal object of religion is to procure eternal felicity in the other world, or prosperity in this.
>
> De Tocqueville, *Democracy in America*

CHAPTER VII

THE FRUITS OF THE EARTH: CAIN IN NEW ENGLAND

"Say not, I am a child . . ."

NEW ENGLAND's special opportunity was possible because the civic and the churchly fraternities were initially almost identical, since the community was pre-selected; its members were men who had already experienced, in England, alienation from both nature and the state.

The attempt to establish a permanent fraternal community reversed the original Puritan argument. If, the older thesis contended, civic fraternity can be limited to men already members of the churchly fraternity, the best possible polity will result. When the permanent existence of the Commonwealth is taken as a first premise, it is necessary to begin with citizens; in fact, it is necessary to begin with the

Covenant of Nature. Birth in New England carried a presumptive right to membership in the higher covenants. The Half-Way Covenant (which baptized the young, deferring the acceptance of covenant obligations until later) merely codified the fact. The ministers conceded the point grudgingly, realizing the change and the danger which "birthright" implied for New England's standard of fraternity. The culmination of the change, as Miller observes, could be seen when Cotton Mather defended the practices and institutions of New England as her "own," part of an inherited patrimony.

Such an argument insists to the individual that his political obligations are inborn and automatic. Consequently, it argues against the temptation to "go it alone" and to reject duties altogether. Yet, of course, the disadvantages are very great. The argument suggests, contrary to Puritan theory, that the Covenants are not based on personal choices resulting from an individual pilgrimage. It hardly reduced the risk that New Englanders would regard the community as a burden with little personal meaning in the life of the individual. E. S. Morgan writes:

> The Puritan system failed because the Puritans relied upon their children to provide the church with members and the state with citizens.[1]

Originally, Puritans had been preoccupied with keeping hypocrites and deceivers out of a church that would be "speckled" at best; at the same time, they had wondered how "outsiders" might be contented with exclusion from citizenship. Both problems rapidly became irrelevant. The Half-Way Covenanted did not complete the process of covenanting. In politics, although the political order was comparatively democratic—the famous oligarchy was never more than a "speaking aristocracy" faced with a "silent democracy"—apathy, indifference and unwillingness to perform civic duties were more notable than any sense of exclusion. (Robert and Katherine Brown have estimated that a very high percentage of New Englanders, 75 percent or more, qualified to vote if they desired.)[2]

---

[1] Morgan, *The Puritan Family*, p. 185.

[2] Robert E. Brown, *Middle Class Democracy and the Revolution in Massachusetts* (Ithaca: Cornell University Press, 1955); and B. Katherine Brown, "Puritan Democracy: A Case Study," *MVHR*, L (1963), pp. 377–396. The Browns' studies have been frequently criticized without, in my judgment,

The new problems of the New England ministers were to discover means to make inherited duties felt as personal obligations, and
to give inner meaning to outer practices. Rarely indeed did they consider that the old spirit might be rediscovered, if at all, only in new
ways designed for new men. New England was their inheritance, too,
and most sought to find or develop meaning within the old patterns.

The ministers had great faith in the efficacy of doctrine and
preaching. Education became the major hope for maintaining fraternity. Yet it was a naively intellectual education. Puritan doctrine
could only express what the Puritan knew; it could not produce that
knowledge in others. The sense of sin, the conviction of an inherent
inadequacy in human things, may be experienced by men who have
struggled for perfection and failed to gain it or who have known the
best of this life and found it not enough. The doctrine of sin is a self-
contradiction (we know that man cannot know); Hooker wrote that
knowledge of sin "in the notion and conceit only" is radically inadequate. The sense of sin may produce humility, a sense of identity with
all things human. The doctrine of sin, paradoxically, becomes a mark
of pride. It carries a certainty which the sense of sin must always lack,
for the conviction of sin suggests that we may not even be certain
about uncertainty.

The problem of education was indicative of the fact that established practice, not personal relations, had come to provide New
England's solidarity. Personal relations, being among the "givens,"
could even become less valued than personal standing. In such circumstances, reason ceased to be a device for healing disputes among men
who would happily agree; it became a source of dispute, one of the
tools for gaining personal distinction.

New England became more and more a gemeinschaft, with automatic rules against which the individual struggled, hoping to regain
an independence even earlier than the Covenant of Nature: the prideful aim of individual sufficiency.

The institution of the Jeremiad was designed to fill that gap. It
consisted of orations which threatened that God would punish New
Englanders with "providences" outside the course of nature if they
did not fulfill their obligations to Him. The Jeremiad was a dubious

weakening their central thesis. See G. D. Langdon, "The Franchise and Political
Democracy in Plymouth Colony," *WMQ*, XX, 1963, pp. 513-526.

device at best. Faith could only be weakened if disaster failed to materialize and, if prosperity attended New England, it was hard to argue that this was not at least a negative demonstration of Divine favor. Self-righteousness being preferable in the eyes of the clergy to loss of "faith," it is not surprising that they accepted that horn of the dilemma. Yet even if the disaster appeared, the Jeremiad hardly made the community a thing of joy. Men will always resent it if their own efforts may be set at naught by the vices of their fellows even where there is a strong bond of affection; and that bond was increasingly weak in New England.

The growing sense of separation from England offered a more promising source of unity. As the "bowels of affection" that tied the migrants to Britain became attenuated, ministers and political leaders made increasing use of political threats to induce a sense of common peril and involvement. (It mattered little whether the threat came from England or from another source, like France, but Britain was a more permanent danger.)

Winthrop and other early Puritans had always argued that New England would be surrounded by "envious observation." Yet though Winthrop and his fellows might see special providences and miracles about them, they saw them in comparatively petty events. Winthrop was contemptuous of the argument that success is a test in philosophy or ethics. New England's example would be her morality, not her prosperity; the City on the Hill created a duty of fraternity, not a guarantee of power.

If New England's peril was political, however, God might be expected to provide political proofs of his favor or displeasure, signs of success and prosperity which might not only convince New England, but reach across the ocean. In part, this conviction and expectation of political superiority explains the growing and catholic sense of hostility to things foreign, to outside creeds and states and all the related xenophobic phenomena that characterized New England. The hostility toward outsiders must, however, be explained partly as a projection of internal division and hostility.

The early Puritans had felt responsible as Englishmen for the sins of England. They occupied the position of the *ecclesia*, tied both to God and to a this-worldly community. Attempting to bear witness as Englishmen, they also attempted to bear witness for England in the eyes of God. This effort might fail because of the sins of New Englanders or of Britons; and though the first were more serious (considering New England's Covenant), the second were more likely. For the early Puritan, his fellow was a help more than a stumbling block; alienated man meets his brothers with joy.

All this changed as New England began to conceive of herself as a separate nation distinct from others. As God's people, her inhabitants were responsible to God for the "example" they set others, but they were not responsible for other peoples. Hers the credit before the Divine bar, and hers the judgment for failure: this is the price of unique status. Obviously, this helped to foster self-righteousness. Also, however, it meant that the only obstacle to New England's moral success was to be found in New Englanders themselves. Men looked at their fellows with greater or less alloyed suspicion, and with it rose resentment against the collective guilt of the Jeremiads. New England expressed that suspicion and resentment in attempts to ferret out the evil-doers who had or might lead her astray; these efforts culminated in the witch trials which signified the end, not the apogee, of New England doctrines. It is a proof that the older ideas had not wholly died that the trials ended so quickly and that some of the witch-hunters confessed their folly. New Englanders were still enough aware of their own sins to be uneasy in laying blame on others.

Camels and Needles

The insecurity of the individual and his resentment of his fellows provided much of the motive power which worked to expand the doctrines of "special providence" and the "signs" of salvation. First, "special providence" ceased to be directed primarily at the community and was gradually discerned in the life of the individual. Second, the degree of certainty and assuredness possible to the individual through such "signs" was continually expanded.

The materialistic emphasis of "special providence," whether collective or individual, helped to weaken New England's fraternities. In general, it implied a turning away from the relations of men in community toward individual purposive action, the "inner-worldly ascetic" effort to accumulate wealth and power. The distinction of individual and collective providence is important nonetheless, for it suggests that a decline in community precedes doctrine, and not the reverse. The doctrine of "individual providences" did little more than register a fact.

Traditional Puritanism had always suspected wealthy men, and insisted that affluence was justified only in terms of service to the public good. It had always hedged commerce round with regulatory legislation, moral inhibition, and the traditional welfare legislation brought from Europe.

Puritanism still depended, however, on the proposition that distinctions of economic class are compatible with fraternity. This is undoubtedly true, but only if money is not highly valued by either rich or poor. In Europe before the migration, persecution had muted material concerns. In early America, the struggle for survival excluded class from anything more than a peripheral role in men's lives. Even in the first days of prosperity, though tension may have grown, few signs were apparent; the community shared good times and bad, and though some profited more than others, individual and public estates still seemed interdependent.

The first depression which followed the great decrease in immigration, after Cromwell's victory, shattered that unity. Some prospered while others became poor. Growing distinctions of class combined with disparities of destiny; each man would be wise to look to himself, for the community's prosperity was not necessarily his own. Such feelings were exacerbated by the desire of the business and commercial classes (and other men of wealth, to some degree) to be free from the restrictions with which law and custom surrounded the pursuit of gain. Lower-class elements had no notable "fraternal" virtue in seeking to uphold and expand traditional economic regulation; their motives were nearly as individualistic as were those of the more fortunate. At least, however, their economic motives led to an appeal to the ideal of fraternal relations between citizens; they became custodians of the idea, whatever their motives.

The established classes, however, could easily appeal to newer ideas and symbols. "Toleration," fashionable in Britain in the late seventeenth century, arose in part from a concern for the liberties of the individual, in part from a Williams-like dualism which placed nature and faith in different worlds; but it also appealed to those who sought to remove religious fetters from action. In this world, the basic doctrine asserted, necessity ruled by an iron hand indifferent or opposed to human virtue. Man can only conquer nature—his natural aim—by obeying it. He must be "freed" to follow natural necessity in order to achieve his conquest. The major concern of religion is with the next world; it can have little or nothing to say regarding the conduct of political or economic life. That toleration might advance freedom of the mind may have given it appeal to some, but at least equal numbers were attracted by the liberties it promised to the body.

Earlier, similar doctrines had received short shrift. When in the 1640s Henry Parker—on the authority of Machiavelli—identified natural law with the necessities of physical nature, as opposed to the teleological view which tied it to man's "true" or whole nature, the clergy met him with hostility (owing to both his authority and the teaching itself).[3]

The Revolution of 1689 put matters on a different basis. James II had been New England's unambiguous foe, an enemy to provincial autonomy and a Roman Catholic. Pardonably, the clergy could not resist the temptation to regard the Glorious Revolution as a "special providence"—which gave a certain legitimacy to the doctrines of the victorious party, in which individualism, property rights, secularism in the state, and toleration in religion all played a part, and the state was conceived as a contract between discrete individuals for the purpose of utility. The liberalism of John Locke found much of its way cleared in America by the doctrine of "special providence."

In the late seventeenth and early eighteenth centuries, the men of substance like Denison who cited Machiavelli as a great teacher of "civil prudence" wrote to a different audience and met a different reception than had Parker. Thomas Bannister advocated toleration because diverse sects "can never form any idea of combination to the prejudice of the land of our forefathers," the theory of divide and conquer in matters of religion.[4] (Unfortunate as a prophet, Bannister had a happier fate as a precursor of political theory; his argument certainly anticipates Madison's.)

The commercial classes formed the Brattle Street Church, which dissolved all the covenants, regarding religion as a matter between

[3] Haller, *The Rise of Puritanism*, p. 367.
[4] On the "reception" of new doctrines, see Miller, *The New England Mind*, vol. II, pp. 140–141, 156–171, 372–388.

God and the individual. No moral basis existed, in this view, for either political or congregational fraternity. The church was conceived as an assembly of individuals gathered for the utilitarian purpose of supporting individual needs for Divine worship. Men, especially men of substance, need not be subjected to the "indignity of profession," confessing sins and submitting to the test of a congregation of fellow believers. In this individualistic system, no constraint existed on the individual other than his calculations of utility and his own conscience; the only group which retained a moral basis was the family.

The political, economic, and intellectual atmosphere of the late seventeenth and early eighteenth centuries assailed the doctrines of New England. Rationalists by training and temper, the ministers found it hard to argue against a secular doctrine which seemed to have pre-empted the field of reason. Often they attempted to meet the new philosophy on its "own terms," without realizing that he who defines the terms defines the debate.

Cotton Mather, for example, initially sought to capture the new science and the new philosophy for Puritanism. This was only traditional; Puritanism had conceived of science, as well as reason, as a support for theology. Proud of his own "scientific" achievements, Mather sought to couch his explanations in scientific terms subject to the test of experience. Yet although Mather might, like his predecessors, provide "natural" proofs of religious doctrine, the doctrine itself was based on a God outside of nature, a final as well as a first cause. "Natural religion" sought to limit God to nature, while Mather and the Puritans had only seen Him in it.

Moreover, the new philosophy implied a new morality based on the passions of man. The older virtues might be useful to man's preservation or well-being, but the new age regarded them as the results of "convention" or of human artistry, having no status in nature.

Only belatedly (Miller puts it at 1719) did Mather recognize the distance between the new philosophy and his own beliefs. Yet Mather had accepted much of the new philosophy already. Regarding Lockean philosophy as erroneous in reducing man to experience without understanding his spirit, and believing the morality of self-interest to be a "calumny" on mankind, Mather still identified that philosophy with "reason." He attacked empiricism by reference to innate ideas and "self-evident" truths which allegedly reflected the final or true nature of man. Identifying these truths with reason (citing, characteristically, the authority of Newton), he felt obliged to argue that they were "more" than reason—for reason was only the formal mental process which arose out of experience. Mather turned from reason to emotion, from natural religion to the religion of the "heart."

Early Puritanism had protected itself from sentimentality by its conviction that the "heart" was the frailest of reeds; the Puritans had turned to reason as the best of man's faculties. Mather's doctrine was not only prone to mawkishness, it was fundamentally anti-rationalistic. More and more, Mather devoted himself to exposing gaps in science and weaknesses of reason. God became the holes in the veil rather than the capstone of the pyramid, and understanding was best obtained by a sound heart which scorned the mind in its weakness.

Descendant of the founders, Mather had been trained in a political order in which the doctrines of religion had been familiar from childhood. He spoke truly when he asserted that he found a certainty in those truths which was never vouchsafed to reason. His "heart" and the truths he felt self-evident led him to faith, and he found confirmation in his fellow New Englanders. But this misses the point: heart, conscience, and instinct may be reliable tests in a community educated from birth in certain values and beliefs. Mather mistook political for metaphysical truth; that alone suggests the danger which had always been implicit in New England's effort to establish a continuous fraternal polity.

Nor was Mather alone. Religious "conservatives" like Bulkley might argue that religious discipline was "natural" to men. Yet Bulkley's authorities were modern, secular philosophers: Hobbes, Locke, Machiavelli. No less than the secularism he sought to oppose, Bulkley saw nature as the "original" tendencies of man, took the individual as the ultimate political fact, and sought to base religion on utility to the individual himself. So too, the "liberal" Colman argued for religion on utilitarian grounds, but not because it was "natural." Rather, the very unnaturalness of religion made it a useful support of society in promoting peace and obedience. For Colman too, however, "nature" consisted of man's innate tendencies, and only the individual exists "by nature." Colman's argument is wholly concerned with individual conformity, not with setting the conditions under which fraternity is possible. Both Bulkley and Colman dissolved the Covenants, and reduced man from a political animal to isolated, "economic" man.[5]

Yet those who sought to defend the fraternal ideal gave it some of its worst blows. Against those, like Stoddard, who sought to salvage the political influence of the church by centralizing its organization and ruling through a ministerial elite, Cotton Mather wrote that he upheld

the Liberty of the Fraternity in the things of common concernment; for the fraternity to be governed, not as mere brutes or mutes. . . . [I]t may be that in some churches matters have been carried in a strain too democratical, [but] these gentlemen will do well to remember who they are. . . . [T]hey speak of the people in terms [like] . . . the Pharisees of old, whereas indeed, sirs, this people is the Lord's heritage.[6]

Yet Mather's zeal to defend the traditional ideal of Christian fraternity led him to abandon the political, which Stoddard sought to control. If, amid political dissidence and disharmony, the church could keep her political influence only by changing her own organization, politics should be surrendered. The church would stand as an example of voluntary unity and fraternal cooperation above the competitive and conflict-ridden arena of politics.

Yet Mather did not give up a concern for conduct and behavior in society. Since the church had abandoned politics, and politics had fallen in status, "non-political" organizations might fill the gap. First, Christians might form societies for the "reformation of manners," seeking to advance adherence to accepted codes of personal and social conduct. These societies, however, were limited to the consensus among professing Christians on the nature of morality; difference of opinion would make matters "political." This suggestion, then, reduces to the proposition that where mores are uniform among Christians, pressures for conformity may serve to strengthen them.

Second, voluntary associations might be organized for charity

---

[5] Miller, *The New England Mind*, vol. II, pp. 432–433, 380–381, 397–398. Colman argued that the judgment of contemporaries might be preferred to that of the founders because the early Puritans were not "men of the world" and were not "concerned with the natural body." No more inaccurate comparison between seventeenth-century Puritans and eighteenth-century preachers could be imagined.

[6] Cited in *The New England Mind*, vol. II, p. 259.

and benevolence. This possibility, developed in Mather's *Essays to Do Good*, was the positive side of the aim to reform manners; charity adds the inducement of kindness to the force of conscience and conformity. This is, perhaps, the first expression of Puritanism as most Americans know it: pietistic morality and vague benevolence.

Mather's system was forced to shun any area where conflict existed in the church. The church lost its role as guide and became simply expressive of existing agreements. Nor does the exclusion of conflict suggest that such matters are unimportant; it assumes that they are essential and cannot be raised without fragmenting the church. The "fraternity" of Christians is, in these terms, illusory; it depends on excluding any question which might reveal that the "brethren" lack a common spirit and vision. Moreover, the voluntary societies Mather proposed were not aimed at any internal goal; Mather's societies felt duties to outsiders, and their orientation was condescending and not egalitarian. They were not concerned to strengthen or improve those who made them up and were no part of a fraternal pilgrimage. They aimed only to improve the efficacy of the individual in pursuing his benevolent aims.

Those, like Benjamin Wadsworth, who sought to defend and praise *Mutual Love Among Christians* did little better. Wadsworth spoke of the "natural sociability" of man, and used that quality in conjunction with man's desire for "peaceable living" as the basis of his defense. Yet on these terms, Christian love, let alone civic relations, lose any distinctive claim. The hierarchy which Winthrop had built up from the general human hope for love is abolished; fraternity is made identical with warmth and emotion as such.[7]

Eventually the leaders of the clergy came to argue that material success was an "individual providence" and the chief mark of a "visible saint," and worse, that failure was often a proof of vice. This argument served to retain the wealthy in the churches. It provided a religious justification for attacks on the older economic regulations. Yet it also marked the fact that difference of class had come to seem almost a difference of kind. Winthrop's worst fear had come to pass: seeking great things for themselves and their posterities, men sacrificed the

[7] *Ibid.*, pp. 248–249, 397.

fraternal relations which were more to be valued than anything in the "present world."

It was probably inevitable that the modern age would triumph in the political and economic world. If the Puritan divines failed to prevent it from dominating the intellectual world as well, it was a failure they shared with all men of the mind. In fact, the divines did better than most: even if they became abstracted from the world of events, they nevertheless succeeded in preserving the symbols and values of the Puritan polity. The Puritans often likened themselves to Israel, and nowhere was similarity stronger than in the fact that so much of their law and hope survived the demise of their state.[8] After all, the failure of an experiment where conditions are not controlled (as they never are in politics) is no disproof of a theory.

John Wise: Statecraft Revisited

John Wise has had many recent admirers. Parrington, for example, saw him as a precursor of the Enlightenment and a sort of proto-Jefferson. Most of his modern admirers have failed to recognize him for what he was: a most persuasive defender of Puritan political theory. Not that Wise was a reactionary; he realized, far better than most, that old institutions must be changed to preserve old values in new times.

Wise himself, however, contributed to the misinterpretation of his thought. Like most Puritan writers, he was not content to argue from traditional or religious authority, but sought to incorporate the authority and argument of contemporary philosophy. Wise's "modern" authorities, such as Hobbes and Pufendorf, tended to be a bit dated even then, and their ideas do not always sit well with his theories, but they affect the presentation of his argument. Critics, however, have most often failed to note that Wise is equally comfortable in citing Increase Mather, not the most modern thinker of his own times.

Wise spoke of "human nature," for example, in two senses. One he derived from his modern authors, the "original" state of man in

---

[8] See W. C. McWilliams, "America's Two Israels," *Chicago Jewish Forum*, XXII (1963), pp. 18-22.

physical nature, possessed of "original liberty." The tone of his discussion, however, suggests that Wise thought in terms of nature after
the Fall. In an argument derived from Hobbes, Wise argued that all
men must be presumed equal because "human nature agrees equally
with all" and no man wishes to change his own nature. In Wise or in
Hobbes it is hard to miss the irony of that argument; stated more
directly, Wise's contention is that all men are equal in self-love and
self-satisfaction. No man is outside the human heritage of imperfection.[9]

But Wise also referred to a teleological human nature, the law of
man's being, which was part of the "order of nature." Identified with
"right reason," this second "nature" is a "law immutable" in man,
"instamped upon his frame." This is man's true nature because it is
bound up with the order, form, and harmony that comprise the
"beauty and safety of the universe." Despite his modern authors and
sometimes modern language, Wise's idea of man was well within the
canons of traditional thought.[10]

The two natures demonstrate two connected propositions. The
"original" nature eliminates any claim by particular individuals to
special consideration (especially to any distinction based on descent);
the second establishes the claim of each individual to equal consideration in the making of public policy.

Equal consideration, however, does not demand equality. Men
are part of a single species, kinsmen within a kind; except in an essential sense, they are not equal nor brothers. In supporting his case for
equality of consideration, Wise cited *II Peter* 2:17, "Honor mankind." Notably, Wise omitted the second half of the apostolic injunc-
tion, "Love the brotherhood." Men are due equal consideration because of their nature, whether it be realized or not; fraternity is limited
to those who have achieved some measure of virtue.

Admitting the necessity of "just distinctions" among men not
equal in ability, Wise argued, as had the tradition, that the test of

[9] Wise, *Vindication of the Government of New England Churches*, pp.
32–43, 50–53.
[10] *Ibid.*, pp. 42–44, 54–60. Few note the distinction between the idea that
natural rights are "inalienable," which suggests a sort of external, proprietarian
relation, and the notion that they are "immutable," rooted in the order of nature
and hence in man; see *The New England Mind*, vol. II, pp. 288–297, 329.

the justice of distinctions is the public good, with which all distinctions must be at least "agreeable." Just distinction must be based on human excellence, and man's virtues require the political order. The "contemplation of the human condition" reveals that man naturally requires both "sociability" and the "civil state."

His assumption of man's political nature sets Wise apart from his modern authorities and the later theorists whose predecessor he is thought to have been. Wise had no love for pre-political man, and no tendency to derive "right" from his condition. Though he lacked the pathological fear of emotion and nature that was creeping into the thought of his contemporaries, Wise did regard the frontier as almost wholly evil. Like Winthrop, he saw the frontier forcing men to a kind of individualism, preventing settled social and civic relations, and hence obstructing man's hope for excellence. The "equality" of the frontier levels men down to the equality of self-love that is the law of original nature.

Wise himself faced neither the instability and fear of anarchy which the frontier had produced among the first Puritans, nor the new urbanity and secularism which confronted Cotton Mather. He came from a small, long-settled New England town, which enabled him to do what the original migrants and their reverential successors could not: to take the community as a fact, and to see man as developing within it—yet, with the assistance of fraternity, rising above it.

The city was more than social because there it was possible to found distinctions on consent based on an idea of the public good. The ministry should and must concern itself with politics, Wise wrote, because "men trusted to steer in all weather" must not fear the waves. The distinction granted the ministry was a trust; all men had a common, essential nature, but some men could be responsible for that nature. There was a timeless art of piloting above the "waves" of events and politics; that art was based on a truer sight than most could possess. All men should be "honored," but the brotherhood was special and distinct.

Most of Wise's writing consists of injunctions to his ministerial brethren not to fear "imbroylment" with the political world. Wise saw that Mather and his followers did fear that world and sought to protect the church by separating it. Wise suggested that there is a middle way between allowing the church to become identified with the needs of a continuous community and withdrawing the church from political life and concern. The way lay through true statecraft, the insistence that choices in politics be guided by moral purpose, by the "public good."

The aim of government, Wise wrote, is "to cultivate humanity, promote the happiness of all, and the good of every man." Tyler identified this formulation with Jefferson's, but Jefferson was to see the "pursuit" of happiness as an original, individual right; government existed to protect that right and its purpose was, in that sense, negative only. Wise's government is far more active: it must promote happiness and cultivate a humanity which in most men is only a seed of potentiality. Wise sought a fraternally united public which might live to the "height of Religion and right Reason." In preventing evil, the efforts of government to chastise the wicked are always premised on the good which men are to share. "For none so good to man as man," Wise wrote; and added "yet none a greater enemy" as a necessary, but secondary, observation.[11]

Wise defended paper currency, not from considerations of economic prosperity, but from an idea of the moral purpose of the state. Freer currency is needed because a limited medium of exchange would damage the relations of citizens. Wise even conceded that paper currency might cause economic difficulties and loss of wealth. Material well-being, however, was a secondary consideration. He lectured the creditors and the wealthy, "You must do by your Bills, as all wise men do by their wives: make the best of them." [12] The humor is suggestive. Wise indicates that the laws of marriage are determined by the needs of human relations, whatever defects one's spouse may have; and currency, a human institution, is no different. Material satisfactions must be found within the limits within which good relations among citizens are possible.

Not that Wise was ascetic. Commercial prosperity, pursued as an end, was to be deplored, but material prosperity which served the public good was desirable. Indeed, it was essential to excellence that

---

[11] Wise, *The Churches' Quarrel Espoused*, p. 53, and *Vindication*, pp. 42–44; Moses C. Tyler, *A History of American Literature* (New York: Collier, 1962), p. 360.

[12] *The New England Mind*, vol. II, p. 318.

men be able to "banish sordidness and live Bright and Civil, with fine Accomplishments." [13]

Traditionalist that he was, Wise was at least tactically original in being willing to appeal to the public for support. Perry Miller called Wise "the first American Populist," and the term refers to more than Wise's ideas on currency.[14] A populist believes in the people; an American populist believes in the American people. The latter is a specific, not always philosophic, believer in democracy. Democracy in the church, Mather had said, is part of New England's "way." Wise "espoused" the quarrel of the churches because the *demos*, though distinct from the ministers who may "espouse" it, is the best ally of the ministry in seeking to uphold the teachings of the church.

Established men of standing might regard "profession" as an "indignity"; their less fortunate fellows regarded it as a symbol of the equal dignity of "brothers in Christ." To the men of commerce, welfare legislation might appear a misguided mixture of sacred and secular; spokesmen for the poor could argue that only such laws protected the charitable man of commerce from his own bad impulses and the rapacity of the ungodly. Winthrop had felt his ideal could be most safely entrusted to magistrates; in the latter days, the traditionalist turned to the people.

Statesman and people are separate, Wise observed, for the fraternity of statesmen is founded on their devotion to the goal. The people may cling excessively to tradition; secular men may be too ready for change. The ministry, as true statecraft, must "steer in all weather" and keep the course, not a particular setting of the sails. Fraternity is as necessary to keep the ministry from fearing to change as it is to keep them true to the ideal. The unchanging ideal is the fraternal city where man is able to rise from an original nature which is fragmentary and incomplete to one which senses the "beauty and safety of the universe." [15]

Edwards: "God must be near . . ."

The name of Jonathan Edwards, to many Americans, is almost synonymous with Puritanism. Certainly Edwards' passionate defense

[13] *Ibid.*, pp. 320, 329.
[14] *Ibid.*, pp. 300–301; Wise, *Vindication*, pp. 54–55.
[15] Wise, *Churches' Quarrel*, pp. 53, 116, and *Vindication*, pp. 54–55.

of the doctrines of Original Sin and Free Grace appears traditional enough, and his assault on the apparatus of individual and special providences may seem a return to early Puritanism. Appearances, as Edwards would have been the first to assert, can be deceptive. Frederic Carpenter discerned a new teaching under the traditional terminology which Edwards employed.[16]

Edwards gave little attention to the ethical standards of either providential theology or natural religion. His concern centered on abstract questions, especially the problems posed for religion by the "new science" and the new philosophy. Finding his beliefs challenged by the new learning, Edwards resolved with creditable intellectual integrity to accept any teaching which proved demonstrable, even if incompatible with traditional religion. Since the new science did seem "demonstrable" to Edwards, it never ceased to monopolize the world of "mere reason" and "natural knowledge." A defense of religion depended, then, on the argument that religion was a form of knowledge "higher" than reason; the new discoveries, the new ethics, and the new politics were allowed the conquest of the natural world, but they would be incorporated in a broader structure of religious truth.

Edwards began by conceding Locke's premise that sensation is the basis of all human understanding. Yet, he argued, sensation is prone to error and cannot in any case discover a firm ground of Being, a point of certainty. A train of skeptical reasoning reminiscent of Berkeley or Descartes led Edwards to the proposition that Being exists in the ideas in the Divine Mind. In an idealism that came perilously close to naturalistic pantheism, Edwards suggested that sensation called an analogue of those ideas into the mind of man. Given the imperfection of man's animal spirits through sin, error is inevitable, but it is the "heart" (or will) and not the senses which cause men to err.

Edwards was traditional enough in his idea of sin. Man is prone to "dissent from Being," to deny the reality of things outside himself. Men do not see the beauty of things as they are; men only value and will only perceive things in relation to themselves. The seeming virtues of men are always based on instinct, "secondary beauty," or

---

[16] Frederic Carpenter, "The Radicalism of Jonathan Edwards," *NEQ*, IV (1931), pp. 629–644.

association; they are always founded on self-concern and self-reference. Accurate perception and true virtue both depend on a "love for Being" which replaces the self-love of natural man.

Edwards' Lockean psychology, however, commanded him to seek the force which might purify the will of natural man in sensation; traditional Calvinism, though it took due account of the senses, always considered them secondary to reason. Edwards believed he had discerned a "spiritual" or "supernatural" sense which appeared in the regenerate individual. This "sense of the loveliness of God's holiness and justice" was an "affection," but one which was "gracious" in that it was free of physical desire or erotic need.[17] Whatever use traditional Calvinism had had for the emotions, they were in the world and "delights"; Edwards' "gracious affections" were free from the fleshliness of the world.

To the critic, Edwards' argument must seem a barely masked advocacy of sublimation. Certainly it did to Charles Chauncey, who always contended that Edwards had mistaken a "fire in men's bowels" for "light in their minds." Wary of the peril, Edwards always attempted to distinguish the natural and the "gracious" affections, calling the latter "more excellent," "entirely different," and "utterly diverse" from the former. Natural men, he argued, might "mortify their lusts," but it would be vain; such affections would remain impure.

Edwards' case required him to demonstrate an essential difference between the affections, to prove that carnal sentiments and feelings were not the origin of the "gracious" emotions directed toward God. It cannot be argued that he ever made this demonstration. Though in one passage he may refer to the "utter diversity" of the two, in another he will concede their "similarity" or even unity of kind. He will argue at one point for a qualitative distinction, saying that although senses, the two are as different as taste and sight; at another, he will fall back on a distinction of object: the natural affections were produced by "external impression" and the gracious sentiments were "inward," a difference not in the faculty of perception but in the location of the object or impression.

The weakness of Edwards' argument was the psychological

[17] Faust and Johnson, *Jonathan Edwards*, pp. 102–111, 207, 220–227, 238–245, 349–371.

theory which forced him to rest all knowledge on sensation. Certainly in his preaching he used techniques which suggest that the worldly senses can be terrified enough to arouse the gracious affections, for his metaphors were thoroughly physical. In practice, he implied an identity of the "senses," except as to object, that he denied in theory.

Moreover, resting on sensation, Edwards' doctrine was necessarily individualistic. It prompted men explicitly to seek "personal" salvation through private, if "gracious," affections. The sin which he denounced was a relation between God and the individual, not between man and his fellows or a community and its God. It is less important that Edwards, like Mather, advocated charity, than that the works were to be performed by individuals as a result of individual regeneration. Edwards conceived of a duty to give, but not of a right to receive. The duty is owed to God and not man; obligations are exclusively hierarchic and not fraternal.

Indeed, Edwards was actively hostile to relations of fraternity or of community. The bonds of man with man served to provide the individual with a security which enabled him to escape the "troublesome and vexatious" senses that revealed the world's corruption. He did not see or did not believe that in a community guided by common values, emotional security may enable and compel one to look beyond the world. For Edwards, emotional ties in the world weakened the tie to God because the emotions bound man to the Divine. In his social more than his philosophic theory, Edwards stands out as the prophet of the pietistic asceticism which Protestant America came to identify with virtue, and the spokesman for political quietism which left political and social life to the guidance of material aims and secular theories.

The fraternity of living, unredeemed men was bound to be imperfect; traditional Puritan thought, accepting that fact, had sought to distinguish degrees of imperfection. Edwards painted all such fraternity with a black brush. Between the "love of self" and the "love of humanity" there was no intervening gray.[18]

Edwards was not without hope that God might provide another connection between a sinful world and His kingdom. Pondering the origin of evil, Edwards concluded that He must have had a "higher

[18] Edwards, *Works*, vol. II, pp. 18ff., vol. V, pp. 317ff.

purpose" in allowing men to sin. That conclusion, as old as theology, traditionally belonged to the realm of dark mystery, and Edwards did not (as did his naturalistic contemporaries like Mayhew) proceed to identify natural necessity with God's plan, and hence success with virtue. Edwards was willing, however, to argue that historical evil might tend to historical good. In a very modern teaching, he and his disciples could see "self-interest," base in itself, as tending to the public benefit. The ultimate brotherhood of man, which Edwards saw as the ideal, might be brought to pass on earth out of historical evil. However, Edwards described the "coming Kingdom" in terms so millenaristic that any human effort to produce the kingdom was almost excluded. Nonetheless, his argument provided a convenient justification for leaving secular affairs to the logic of material necessity and self-concern.

Too, Edwards did find one prescription for the earthly city. America, he asserted, might hope to become the redeeming nation which would "make all things anew." This patriotic sentiment was possible because America was a "new land" free from superstition and traditional community. Men might then remove the barriers to God's kingdom (as Locke had hoped to clear "rubbish" from philosophy's path?) by destroying superstition and community, leaving the individual to face the "troubles and vexations" of the world alone.

In Edwardian theology, the Christian vocabulary remains but the substance has been transformed. The world is given over to a psychology which all but eliminates the political and communitarian elements of Puritanism. Whatever Edwards' intent, his theory allows the resplendent image of God's city to serve the tawdry purpose of assuaging the conscience of those troubled by their own departures from the immediate, this-worldly practice of fraternity. If Edwards aroused fear, it was fear for self, not for one's fellows. Man was to man a danger and a snare, and the best hope of safety lay in being unsnared. That gospel was qualified only by the duty of charity. In Edwards' thought, the high duties and brotherly obligations which Winthrop had proclaimed found a last pale echo in the ethics of condescension.

> The principle of interest-rightly-understood
> is not a lofty one, but it is clear and sure. . . .
> By its admirable conformity to human weak-
> nesses, it easily obtains great dominion; nor is
> that dominion precarious, since the principle
> checks one personal interest by another and
> uses, to direct the passions, the very same in-
> strument that excites them.
>
> De Tocqueville, *Democracy in America*

CHAPTER VIII

THE AMERICAN ENLIGHTENMENT

Old and New

ORIGINATING in Europe, the doctrines of the Enlightenment entered America through the port cities and the great plantations, the "ports of entry" for ideas as well as trade. Their extraneous origin did not hamper them; it was the age of a cosmopolitan elite, concerned to stand well in European circles. The new theories, moreover, had appeals which specifically commended them to Americans.

The new theories were flattering, appealing to the uncertain pride of America. For more than one theorist of the Enlightenment —Herder and Blake, among the still prominent—America was the redemptive land which had escaped European corruptions and re-covered the liberty of nature. Free to experiment with the new social and moral teachings, America was "the first lodge of humanity," and from her example might arise the freedom and brotherhood of man.

The Enlightenment, too, offered an expanded sphere of moral

possibility. It was not simply that the new ideas were "practical," though usefulness in practice was an important criterion in American eyes. Rather, the Enlightenment offered new and "scientific" means to the realization of social visions heretofore held impossible. Winthrop had feared the loss of natural constraints; the Enlightenment removed the constraints from human imagination and seemed suited to the openness of the continent. Social and political goals became separated from the old constraints of experience and history and, indeed, from those of reason; what man could conceive, he might achieve, especially in America, where the hand of the past fell lightly. Small wonder that Jefferson could write, "I like dreams of the future better than the history of the past."[1]

Indeed, those who turned to the doctrines of the Enlightenment were so captured by the vision of human improvement that they were often unconcerned with the theoretical content of the new creeds. Many have discerned a "Newtonian" influence in eighteenth-century American thought, but Adrienne Koch's reference to "the workshop of liberty" is more to the point.[2] The American intellectual of the eighteenth century was more concerned with technique than theory, interested more in the principles of political mechanics than in the law of gravitation. Jefferson and the Puritans had both revered Newton, but the latter's concern was theoretical: Newton provided part of the path to the "first cause," a glimpse of the laws and mind of God. Jefferson's interest in science, emphasized by many historians, centered on the tangible and utilitarian aspects of the new science, especially on the guidance it might give for the achievement of a more moral humanity.

Concern for practice often led Americans to overlook differences in theory between the Enlightenment and their older heritage, a tendency magnified by the fact that both creeds employed a similar language, though radically different substantive meaning.

Both, for example, spoke of the Law of Nature, but the older tradition implied by that term fixed ends which were "natural" to

[1] Thomas Jefferson, *Writings*, ed. H. A. Washington (Washington, D.C.: Taylor and Maury, 1853–1854), vol. VII, p. 27; compare *Writings*, ed. P. L. Ford (New York: Putnam, 1892–1899), vol. II, p. 80.
[2] Adrienne Koch, "James Madison and the Workshop of Liberty," *RP*, XVI (1954), pp. 175–193.

man, established by an Authority beyond mankind. The new philosophy denied the existence of fixed ends and affirmed infinite possibilities for men. The "laws of nature" were the laws of motion, and man's nature was determined by the desires by which he was "moved." Authority was dissolved by the inference that the individual might appeal to his desires and his conscience as a matter of "natural right."

"Natural right" was innate in the individual; he was born morally complete. Hence, the state did not exist to develop man as a moral personality; it could only be justified in terms of its utility to the individual, a doctrine expressed in the theory of the "social contract." Man's rights were negative and external to his personality, not bonds to his fellows; society and the state either permitted or did not permit the expression of his desires. Thomas Paine drew a sharp distinction between the voluntary cooperation of society and the coercive apparatus which, to him, distinguished government; but even society, Paine argued, "grants nothing" to the individual. "Each man," he wrote, "is proprietor in society." [3]

Puritanism and the Enlightenment both spoke of equality, but where the former conceived of a democracy of the Fall which yielded to an aristocracy of redemption, the latter believed in an original equality modified by different degrees of science and understanding. For the religious tradition, a "natural aristocracy" was defined by personal moral character which belonged to the individual. The newer *aristoi* were defined by technical mastery, the ability to manipulate nature and history; the benefits of their knowledge, if not the knowledge itself, could be disseminated and perhaps established as the basis of a progressive historical movement.

Similarly, the ancient idea of "balance" as a harmony within the individual or the polity was replaced by the conviction of the creative power of competition and balance in conflict. That doctrine reached what was perhaps its highest statement in *The Federalist*'s thesis that competition between individuals and groups on a scale

[3] Thomas Paine, *Common Sense and Other Political Writings* (New York: 1953), p. 4, see also pp. 84–85; and Bernard Bailyn, *Pamphlets of the American Revolution, 1750–1776* (Cambridge: Harvard University Press, 1965), vol. I, pp. 169–202.

wide enough to guarantee a "balance" between them is almost a self-sufficient use of justice.

Yet in practice, their American advocates almost always modified Enlightenment ideas. Serving as useful tools or as sources of inspiration, the new ideas could not wholly displace older precepts from the consciences of men trained in the religious tradition. Defending the British soldiers who had participated in the Boston Massacre, John Adams appealed to the law and right of self-preservation and self-defense—a principle, Adams declaimed in magnificent self-contradiction, "I would not give up for my right hand, nay for my life."

Whatever the logic of their theories, almost all the Framers were advocates of charity and benevolence. Franklin, in fact, revealed that he had learned this obligation from Cotton Mather's *Essays to Do Good*.[4] This only suggests the truth that the Framers and their contemporaries were reflective men of practice, not theorists in action. They lacked the zeal for the concept and the terrifying logicality that mark the doctrinaire. Hamilton was something of an exception; but it was in part his devotion to the idea that made him "the singular Mr. Hamilton" who felt himself an alien in America.[5]

The American Enlightenment transformed the meaning of Christian symbols but felt obliged to retain the old language; discarding the concept, it retained the precept. American theorists sought for some element of fraternity, some suggestion of bonds uniting man and man. Yet the Enlightenment doctrines made the object of that search difficult to attain. Reason, conceived as the "servant of the passions," could not unite men. The empiricism and individualism of the new theories tended to portray man as radically isolated from his fellows. If some bond of brotherhood were to be discovered among men, it would have to be found in the "natural"

[4] Adams is cited in Catherine D. Bowen, *John Adams and the American Revolution* (Boston: Little, Brown, 1950), p. 398; for Franklin's debt to Mather, see Curti, *Growth of American Thought*, p. 73.

[5] Saul Padover, "The Singular Mr. Hamilton," *SR*, XXIV (1957), pp. 157–190, and J. Livingston, "Alexander Hamilton and the American Tradition," *MJPS*, I (1957), pp. 209-224.

qualities of mankind, the senses and "instincts" with which men were born.

Heredity: The Bonds of Race

The idea of a "fraternity" particular to members of a given "race" sat badly with traditional Christianity. The Scripture derived all men from Adam; Ezekiel and Jesus had spoken harshly of heredity; St. Paul had denied that Jew or Greek exists "in Christ." If the elaborate sophistry which derived modern races from the descendants of Noah had been spun out, few theologians employed it. The soul, man's essence, was the same, however fantastic or even deformed the bodies which contained it might appear to be.

Feudal law and custom, of course, emphasized descent and blood-kinship, but even feudalism stressed lineage within classes and stations, not races. A prince was a princely man, whatever his race; a peasant who could claim Roman genes was nonetheless a peasant. Malory found nothing strange in Sir Palomides being a member of the Round Table, though Palomides was a Moor; Shakespeare's Doge described the racial argument against Othello as modern in origin. As Oscar Handlin suggests, feudalism was so hierarchical in concept that it did not entirely degrade the slave in relation to his fellows; he still remained part of the great hierarchy of submission that ended in God.

Both religion and traditional law tended to soften slavery in America. Baptism was initially regarded both as an automatic basis for manumission and as something to be encouraged among slaves. Puritan writers sometimes identified the enslavement of one's fellow man with "original sin," though this did not necessarily lead them toward abolitionism, being only another proof of the world's depravity. Slavery had, however, more thoroughgoing opponents like Samuel Sewall, whose *The Selling of Joseph* went so far as to doubt the authenticity, not merely the applicability, of the "curse of Canaan" text;[6] and Quakers like George Keith took an early lead in anti-slavery propaganda.

---

[6] Samuel Sewall, *The Selling of Joseph: A Memorial*, *Proceedings*, Massachusetts Historical Society, VII (1863–1864), esp. pp. 162–163.

Since Enlightenment thought tended to begin with the premise of "original equality," it had little affinity with racism. However, it also affirmed the right of property and the legitimacy of interest so strongly as to blunt any opposition to the existing institution. Madison argued, for example, that slavery was not in the "true interest" of slave-owners, but he was willing to rely on historical developments to teach the lesson.[7]

The available justifications of slavery, however, seemed inadequate to many who felt the institution justified by the needs of the American economy. Locke's defense of slavery "by right of capture" might be applied to adults, but it could hardly be a basis for enslaving their descendants. In any case, the doctrine was of dubious relevance to the American situation. Moreover, it tended to base slavery on force, and it roused fears that superior force might not always be available to hold down the slave.

Growing anxiety regarding the possibility of slave rebellions, however, was not wholly the result of an analysis of physical capabilities. It reflected a tension and moral uncertainty in the slave-holder himself. Significantly, slave-owners showed an increasing fear of the effects of religious teaching among slaves and in some cases sought to prevent efforts to convert them. The draft constitution for the Carolinas, often attributed to John Locke, forbade the practice of freeing baptized slaves as dangerous to civil order.

Enlightenment empiricism, however, suggested a firmer basis for the institution of slavery. It was impossible to deny the existence of differences in appearance between men, nor could it be argued that these did not correspond to differences in behavior. The Enlightenment theorist might sympathize with the plight of the "naturally free" and uncorrupted Indian; but the qualities associated with blacks —submission and patience, together with a "sullen" resistance and sporadic "risings"—were not qualities that the Enlightenment valued highly. (If it occurred to any that these were the rational responses of civilized men to an impossible situation, as opposed to the futile combativeness of the aborigine, it doubtless only strengthened feel-

[7] Note the progression of the argument in James Madison, *Notes on Debates in the Federal Convention*, ed. A. Koch (Athens: Ohio University Press, 1966), pp. 77, 224-225, 275-276, 295, 365.

ings that the Negro had been corrupted from the path of nature.) Even those who detested slavery, like Jefferson, were inclined to invidious comparisons between races.

Moreover, Enlightenment theorists sometimes argued, the whole idea of a "common origin" of mankind is supported only by a myth, a part of the structure of superstition. Following Lord Kames, more than one argued that the races might have resulted from separate origins and might, in fact, be almost different species, the Negro being an "intermediate" between man and the apes. Even those who would not go so far might be willing, as was Benjamin Franklin, to concede that hostility between races was "natural" to men.[8]

Organized religion compromised more than once with slavery. Despite John Wesley's anti-slavery sentiments, Methodist ministers in the American South tended to remain silent on the question. Yet nothing could make the doctrines of traditional religion compatible with racism. The Bible stood as a firm barrier against ideas of "separate creation," and ministers often declaimed against the atheistic implications of the thesis. Indeed, Federalists employed Jefferson's anti-Negro asides as a proof of his irreligion. Writers like Adair used Scripture to prove the humanity of the Indian (and, more fantastically, to suggest that the Indians were the Ten Lost Tribes).[9]

The Quaker John Woolman carried the anti-slavery message to the non-slaveholding classes of the South. Slavery, he wrote, derived from primal sin; it was self-exaltation, the desire to master nature and escape God. This was a futile effort which would result only in anxiety, the need for greater and greater power and, eventually, the oppression and subjection of man, the noblest part of Divine creation. Quakers, like other Christians, were involved in the establishment and perpetuation of slavery, but their record, especially in the early history of abolition, in the South and elsewhere, was by no means a negligible one.

Opponents of slavery tended almost automatically to cast their

[8] *The Papers of Benjamin Franklin*, ed. L. W. Larabee et al. (New Haven: Yale University Press, 1959), vol. IV, p. 234.

[9] James Adair, *History of the American Indians* (London: Dilly, 1775); L. Tyerman, *The Life and Times of the Rev. John Wesley* (New York: Harper, 1872), vol. II, p. 132, vol. III, pp. 114, 183, 650; D. G. Matthews, *Slavery and Methodism: A Chapter in American Morality* (Princeton: Princeton University Press, 1965), pp. 3–29.

arguments in religious terms. In perhaps the strongest anti-slavery statement made in the Convention of 1787, Mason of Virginia fell into the language of the Jeremiad. Slavery is not only a sin, he argued, but one which will result in a calamity for the nation. The sins of one man may be punished in the next world, but nations have no souls and must expect retribution here below.[10] For once, at least, the grim prophecies of a Jeremiad hit the mark.

The point is not that Enlightenment theorists in America were racial zealots, which they certainly were not. Rather, Enlightenment theory raised the possibility of racism, called the unity of mankind into question, in a way which traditional religion had not allowed.

Even the most humanitarian theorists of the Enlightenment could contribute to racism without intending it. Paine, fervent opponent of slavery that he was, so hated racial exclusiveness that he referred to the "instance of the Jews" as demonstrating that inbreeding results in degeneracy—an argument which tended in almost every direction but the one Paine intended. A staunch environmentalist like Benjamin Rush argued that Negritude was the result of disease; doubtless hoping to vindicate the blacks' humanity, Rush's argument conceded that blackness was a defect, a decisive mark of inferiority, however acquired.[11]

It would in any case have been next to impossible to prevail against the slavocracy. Not only their own power but the rights of property, the concern for order, and the interests of a multitude of merchants were bound up with the institution. The doctrines of the Enlightenment sometimes helped, however, to undermine the moral claims that might have constrained slavery. Indeed, the anti-slavery sentiments of many theorists and publicists lapsed after Whitney's invention in 1793. The theories of the eighteenth century followed the logic of interest and utility and not of liberty, and biology offered the major hope for removing that inconvenient contradiction. Racism was a whispered note in the American Enlightenment, but it was a portent, hidden in a Pandora's box, for which scientism offered a key. Enlightenment theory, alas, did not always march to the drum of progress in the relations of men.

[10] Madison, *Notes*, p. 504.
[11] Paine, *Common Sense*, p. 91. For Rush's and related arguments, see Stanton, *The Leopard's Spots*, pp. 4-12.

Environment: The Brotherhood of Place

Arguments from blood or heredity, however, were not normal in the eighteenth century. The sense of human equality was too strong for that. Man had a single nature which was shaped by his environment; his surroundings either allowed him to develop according to nature's design, distorted him out of his natural pattern of growth, or improved on the inefficient methods of nature by human science. It was natural, given the role which was assigned to environment, that Enlightenment theorists should argue that a common environment created a common nature. "Men are like plants," wrote Crevecoeur, ". . . We are nothing but the air we breathe, the climate we inhabit." [12]

It was natural, too, for American theorists to turn to the environment as the source of American identity, the fraternity of all Americans. The environment, after all, had been the basis for the messianic hopes that European visionaries held for America. Ours was the environment of nature, where man could begin again. Thus, John Adams argued that the seas had broken our ties to our former brethren in England; in the new land, Americans were subject only to the laws of nature and possessed all her rights. [13]

"Natural man," reduced to dependence on his innate abilities and propensities, was only partly a symbol of simple and uncorrupted virtue. There was a darker side to nature—savage, cruel, and unrestrained. The child of nature lacked the ability to master her; innocent in his desires, he had not learned reason or restraint. Crevecoeur commented on the "hideous parts" of frontier life which had been covered over by a "more improved situation": the war of all against all and against nature. Though Crevecoeur wrote that the American chafed in more settled conditions, feeling a "lost repose" and the yearning call of nature, he only emphasized the thinness of the civilized veneer, the anarchy that lay close to the American surface. [14]

Not until the nineteenth century did Americans come to regard nature as a place of unambiguous virtue. Thoreau, from the rather tame wilds of Walden, might regard it so; Cooper, on the Palisades,

[12] Hector St. John Crevecoeur, *Letters from an American Farmer* (New York: Doubleday, n.d.), pp. 50–51.

[13] Adams, *Works*, vol. III, pp. 416–462, vol. IV, pp. 99–121.

[14] Crevecoeur, *Letters*, pp. 230–235.

might spin his fantasies of natural white and red men united in battle against the corrupt of all races. The facts were too close at hand to allow eighteenth-century Americans to go so far in fancy.

There were, however, progenitors of the later romanticism. The fraternity of a common environment seemed, to many, to unite Americans in a mystic bond to the Indian. Jefferson rushed to defend both the Indian and the American clime against the aspersions of Buffon. Colonel Byrd saw the Indians as "untainted by Lewdness and not enfeebled by Luxury," and advocated intermarriage with them.

Neither Jefferson nor Byrd, however, had any hesitation in regarding Indian culture as inferior. Byrd contended that the inferiority of Indian life was due to "different opportunities of improvement" and advocated Christianizing, as well as marrying and assimilating, the Indian. Jefferson, in line with his more general theory, held that if the Indian received fraternal treatment from Americans his feelings would rise "from the immediate to the remote" and link him to a national fraternity. United by a common environment, only the barrier of culture prevented a fraternity of place between white and red.[15]

The Indian hardly benefited from this admiration. The complex institutions and beliefs which produced fraternal patterns among the Cherokee or Iroquois were passed off as the result of an uncorrupted "natural fraternity." Caucasian America was determined to regard its red brethren as moral archetypes and, as a result, lost the sense of their humanity. The seventeenth-century theorist did not admire the Indian, but he had no doubt that the Indian, like all men, had suffered from Adam's Fall. He did the Indian the honor of treating him as an enemy, acknowledging thereby a deeper kinship with the Indian than the gentler theorists of the eighteenth century could know.

Yet environmentalist theory, like the idea of race, played only a secondary role in eighteenth-century thought. Environment was local, a deeply personal thing, tied to the frontiers of the individual's senses and experience. Crevecoeur contended that America had made

[15] *The Writings of Colonel William Byrd of Westover in Virginia*, ed. J. S. Bassett (New York: Doubleday Page, 1901), pp. 8ff.; Jefferson, *Writings*, ed. H. A. Washington, vol. VIII, pp. 66, 107.

a new people by providing security and comfort for the distressed of Europe: *ubi panis, ibi patria.* That thesis, however, is only a veiled form of interest morality, based on the variable standard of personal utility. Gratitude for bread lapses among the well-fed and among those who aspire to cake; if Americans needed proof, Crevecoeur sided with Britain during the Revolution.

The environment might produce some peculiarly American habits like the eating of maize; few theorists were willing to regard it as an adequate basis for fraternity. The call of the patria had little to recommend it to those whose visions reached for the infinite. Conceding the strength of local sentiments, Paine identified them with the failure of men's emotions to reach the compass of their thought.

> It is the good fortune of many to live distant from the scene of sorrow; the evil is not sufficiently brought to their doors to make them feel the precariousness with which American property is possessed.

Paine praised the American environment, but because it tended to free men from the limiting sense of place.

> In this extensive quarter of the globe, we forget the narrow limits of three hundred and sixty miles [the extent of England] and carry our friendship on a larger scale; we claim brotherhood with every European Christian and triumph in the generosity of the sentiment. It is pleasant to observe with what regular gradations we surmount local prejudice as we enlarge our acquaintance with the world.[16]

Paine admired the "generosity of the sentiment," not the tradition which limited the feeling to European Christians; even Americans might yet extend their feelings of fraternity. For Paine, as for most of his fellows, there was no stopping-place short of the brotherhood of man.

The Brotherhood of Man

Human fraternity was a truly congenial concept. It coincided with the language and precepts of inherited morality and at the same time, unlike racial or environmental theories, it paid due attention to the physical fact that man as a species had the capacity to interbreed.

[16] *Common Sense*, pp. 24, 26, 32–33, and *The Political Works of Thomas Paine* (Chicago: Donohue, 1904), pp. 22–23.

The combination of appeals suggests the truth that although the protagonists of the Enlightenment borrowed many symbols from traditional religion, they transformed the meaning of those symbols by making them this-worldly. The Christian ideal of human fraternity was changed into a retreat to Eden or at least a recovery of the old paradise at a higher level of human power. The alienation from nature of the Christian pilgrim yielded to the mastery of nature by estranged man.

In an early work, Franklin argued that the desires of men are all designed for some purpose, and consequently that evil does not exist. The essentially innocent desires pointed the way to human happiness; removing obstacles to their fulfillment was the logic of human life. Franklin later doubted the "prudence" of this work, and retracted the denial he had made of the immortality of the soul; but his ideas of man remained bound to physical nature. The echo of his early "imprudence" can be heard in his hope that science would, if not eliminate death, at least permit human life to be "lengthened at pleasure." [17]

Innocent as the desires were, they hardly seemed an adequate guide for human progress, let alone for fraternity. Interests frequently seemed to divide men, but paradoxically it was the affection of man for his fellows which seemed most likely to threaten the goal. Affection frequently misled men as to their interests; feelings of solidarity were local, parochial, varying with society and climate. John Adams threw it up, at least as a practical measure: man differs from man, he wrote, as much or more than man differs from the beasts, and the "Author of nature" doubtless intended these inequalities to exist.[18] Even Franklin, optimist that he was, doubted the prospects of a "moral science" of human cooperation.

Any number of "natural religions," however, provided an answer. Free to accommodate themselves to the new science and philosophy and to the idea of original nature as the source of right, they could also hold to the "simple ethical teachings" of Christianity. The

[17] Benjamin Franklin, "A Treatise on Liberty and Necessity, Pleasure and Pain," *Select Works* (Boston: Phillips and Sampson, 1857), pp. 124–125, 147, 167, and *Writings*, ed. A. H. Smyth (New York and London: Macmillan, 1905–1907), vol. III, p. 10.

[18] Adams, *Works*, vol. I, p. 462.

new teachings—the Universalism of Murray and Ballou, Deism, Theophilanthropism, and a multitude of similar sects—differed widely from the old, especially in the degree to which the individual's sentiments were made the ultimate test of obligation.

The older doctrines had suggested that man look outward as well as inward: that society and polity might contribute to fraternity. Moreover, they had insisted that a moral man was one in whose soul mind was master over sense. The Quakers, of course, had appealed to an "inner light"; yet the source of that light was external to man, nor did all men necessarily receive it. To the protagonist of natural religion, the source of universal morality was internal and inherent in all men; it was this-worldly, for the world and man had no inherent defects. The language varied, but the idea was common: a "moral instinct" or "sentiment" found in every man directed him toward universal fraternity. Uncorrupted man, Paine wrote, is "naturally the friend of man." [19]

Sentiment for all men required the willingness to overlook differences of principle, even of morals. The "moral instinct" was also at odds with affection in any intense sense, for intensity narrowed the loyalties of men. It was simply a diffuse fellow-feeling, based not on deep bonds but on the suppression of anything which might divide. Friendship, Franklin wrote, should avoid disputation and argument which can produce only "disgust" or hostility; division in any form is a reproach to fraternity.[20] Franklin's prescription suggests a friendship too weak to endure despite disagreement, with an affection hardly profound and a commitment to common goals too enfeebled to tolerate debate. It is the "friendship" of the individualist who demands the semblance of "perfect unity," too proud (or insecure) to bear contradiction, too weak and isolated to do without human support altogether.

Yet this leveling of human relations down to a standard of indiscriminate kindliness cannot serve as a standard for action where real differences of opinion and interest cannot be suppressed. It can

---

[19] *Common Sense*, p. 51.

[20] Franklin, *Select Works*, pp. 128–129, 490. Franklin's praise of fraternity in the parable of Reuben (pp. 396–397) is not strengthened by the fact that he makes fraternal action result in reward and praise, but the utilitarian claim is of a piece with his general theory.

at best remain parallel to politics, in an adjacent sphere of life which affects politics only peripherally and makes no demands on it; the most salient example is the apolitical "fraternity" of the lodges and clubs of modern America.

Human fraternity, however, remained a goal of action if not a guide to it. The friendliness which Franklin advocated was only an immediate tribute to the ultimate goal, a City of God brought into nature as a parallel to the progress of the City of Man. Historical progress would reach toward human fraternity, a situation in which the "moral sentiments" would be the living reality. Even the skeptical Adams referred to the "grand scheme and design of history"; and Franklin, whatever his doubts of the short-term capabilities of men, looked with confidence to the future.[21]

Interest—man's individual pursuit of power—was the motive power and safest guide for historical progress. Even those eighteenth-century theorists who doubted that premise were not inclined to attack material progress or technological innovation. Science and acquisition would lead man to a state of plenty which would remove the shortcomings of the "state of nature." His desires satisfied, his sources of hostility removed, man would find a new and free trust for his fellows, a genuine brotherhood of man.

Paine, who saw man as natural friend to his fellows, and who wrote that man needs society because his strength is "unequal to his wants" and his mind is "unfitted for perpetual solitude," still regarded self-interest and survival as the first and highest laws of human nature. Man felt affection for his fellows only when interest and solidarity walked hand in hand. In the original state of scarcity, man's weakness had made him need others; just so, in modern times,

> The intimacy which is contracted in infancy and the friendship formed in misfortune are, of all others, the most lasting and unalterable.

Consequently, Paine, unlike many of his contemporaries, saw prosperity and not scarcity as the source of conflict among men. "Duty and attachment" would relax when difficulties were overcome; the "social affections" were the source of justice and unity for man

---

[21] Franklin, *Select Works,* p. 338; Adams, *Works,* vol. III, p. 452, vol. IX, p. 420.

but they were not "necessary to his existence," and interest ruled wherever it was able.[22]

To some, that might suggest the desirability of a simple and necessitous society, but Paine drew no such inference. Not only was "interest" the first law and original right of man, the tendency of "duty and attachment" to decline only indicated the blindness of men's affections. Men suffered from a "confusion" of interests when relieved of the spur of necessity; clinging to parochial things and failing to perceive common interests, men could be divided from their fellows and deprived of their natural rights.

The decline of morality amid prosperity did not lead Paine to denounce material gain; a major virtue of continental unity, in his eyes, was that it would promote the "opulence" and power of Americans. Rather, the threat which affluence posed to rectitude suggested to Paine the need to take advantage of sentiments of solidarity while they exist and to provide common institutions that may guard against the fact or effects of future decline. To Paine, the logic of his argument demonstrated that there is no safe resting place for man short of the mastery of nature, when interests could no longer be "confused" and men's natural fraternity could emerge without interference.[23]

Progress—even progress guided by an America imbued with the mission of seeking the "illumination and emancipation of the slavish part of mankind"—demanded a certain savagery, a willingness to put aside demands for immediate fulfillment and especially for fraternal relations on a scale more limited than that of humanity. In the interests of the ideal, the impermissible might be hallowed: competition and conflict, channeled by institutions, might be the norms of action.

Paine was far gentler on this and other points than many of his contemporaries, but he struck the same note. Government, like nature, should be simple, Paine argued, and he followed that postulate with arguments which might have suggested direct democracy: the people, the source of civic virtue, cannot fathom complex systems and confused interests; frequent elections and the highest sympathy with representatives are required for good government. Yet Paine

---

[22] *Common Sense*, p. 40; see also pp. 4, 5, 116.
[23] *Ibid.*, pp. 40, 46, 68; and *Political Works*, pp. 261–264.

supported unity in America even though the size of the state would make a "simple democratical form" impossible. States, like individuals, must surrender part of their rights to obtain the advantages to interest that combination provides. In any event, larger units were truer to the nature of man: "Our great title is Americans; our inferior one varies with the place." The ultimate mission of America is historical; "a new creation is entrusted to our hands," for we may "begin the world again," teaching men the way to "exhibit . . . a character hitherto unknown." [24]

Often, political discussion between advocates and opponents of the Enlightenment seemed only a debate over means, for the goal of human fraternity was common to both. On that assumption, the theorists of the Enlightenment had a decisive superiority. Free from "superstition" and possessed of the new science, they offered a hope for greater progress toward the goal. Jefferson might cling to an older political morality rooted in religion and classical thought, but he felt obliged to adopt the new argument on many points. Morally, doctrines of the critics of the Enlightenment might be appealing; intellectually, they seemed unreasonable and "unscientific" to commentators in their own and later times.

The technical distinctions, however, only concealed a distinction of ends. The city of innocent affection, the goal of the Enlightenment and of partial critics like Jefferson, differed sharply from that of the older tradition, which had sought a man not "one" with nature but alienated from it, not freed from restraint but restrained by obligation. The fraternity which aided man toward that city was vastly different from the fraternity which the Enlightenment saw as a goal in itself; and the muting of the debate, though it may have contributed to American unity, worked to undermine the older tradition. It allowed the American to ease his conscience while he pursued gain, to be convinced that his duties to his brother and to his affluence were one and the same.

Politics as Mechanics

Apart from its intrinsic importance, *The Federalist* may be the best illustration of American thought in the age of the Enlighten-

[24] *Common Sense*, pp. 6, 9, 83, 40, 46, 51, 64, 68–69, 130.

ment. The work of several men, it emphasizes their common agreement and shades over their individual peculiarities. A political tract, *The Federalist* was designed to speak to the active and educated New Yorkers (if not other Americans) of the time. Its axioms and assumptions are a fair codification of the consensus of the times; its more contentious arguments reveal areas of division and debate. Too, the rhetoric of *The Federalist* may not be a true reflection of the convictions of its authors, but it indicates the highest hopes and ultimate values of educated men in eighteenth-century America.

In this last aspect, *The Federalist* abounds in fraternal imagery. Jay refers to Americans as destined by Providence to be a "band of brethren" united by geography, culture, principles, and common struggles. Madison appeals to the "kindred blood" of the nation, the duty of its citizens to think of themselves as members of the "same family." It had been the same in the Convention, where James Wilson had lamented the loss of the Revolutionary unity which had made America "one nation of brethren" and other delegates had voiced similar sentiments.

Nor was the "conservative" Hamilton an exception. For him, human fraternity demanded an American union to "vindicate the honor of the human race" by teaching "moderation" to that assuming brother, the European subspecies, which had unjustly claimed pre-eminence. "Reason, benevolence and brotherly affection" can be said to have occupied a high place in the aims of the Framers.[25]

The symbols of fraternity seem sharply at odds with the view of human nature expounded in *The Federalist*. That conception seems based on the Enlightenment at its grimmest, the daemon of nature in its pure form. In "the transcendent law of Nature and of nature's God" the first statute is "the great principle of self-preservation." Surrounded by scarcity, man is driven to expand his power and is led by his deepest instincts into conflict with his fellows. "The fiery passions of war," Hamilton wrote, "reign in the human breast with a much more powerful sway than the mild and beneficent sentiments of peace. . . ."[26]

Government must impose some order in the life of man if it is

[25] *The Federalist*, pp. 6, 53, 65–66; Madison, *Notes*, pp. 90, 217; Koch, "James Madison . . . ," pp. 180, 187.

[26] *The Federalist*, pp. 160–161, 135, 225, 267.

to serve any purpose ("you must first enable the government to control the governed," Madison wrote in establishing an order of priorities). Yet the object of government is to allow man to preserve as much of his natural liberty as possible, conserving the diversity of faculties established by nature. Fraternal harmony is an equally valid aim. *The Federalist's* theory of human nature does no more than indicate that the achievement of these aims is no easy task.

The Framers constantly inveigh against "utopians" who fail to realize that we are "yet remote" from the day of virtue and fraternity. American constitutions have been ill-designed because they were drafted during the revolutionary struggle wihch "repressed the passions most unfriendly to unity and concord." The complaint, however, is against the measures and not the goals of these constitutions.

Fraternal unity cannot be established by expecting men to behave fraternally. Attaining the goal may require unfraternal means. It is an axiom of *The Federalist,* which Marshall was to enshrine in the law, that the good end authorizes every means "necessary to do it," just as good methods which have bad results are not justified by any rule of logic or reason.[27]

In the main, the Framers argued, government in the past has resulted from force and fraud, perverse means employed in the service of base ends. Only rarely and accidentally have "enlightened statesmen" come to power to rescue it from that corruption, and their work did not endure. The "science of politics," however, has been much improved; still imperfect, it is more trustworthy than individual judgment, less exposed to chance than systems depending on the virtue of statesmen or citizens. Madison expressed the hope that America's lack of veneration for the past would enable her to be the first nation to "display the full efficacy" of the "great mechanical power" recently developed by political theory.[28]

The political machine was intended to be universally applicable, and hence it must not rely on excellent qualities in man. It must be based on his worst propensities because, given that assumption, it could meet the worst situations, not merely the best. Political technology, moreover, would strive to use, not eliminate, those less

[27] *Ibid.,* pp. 259, 20, 24–25, 147–148, 177–178, 231.
[28] *Ibid.,* pp. 1, 37, 44, 62–66, 148, 179–183.

desirable impulses; reliable as virtues never could be, these could be trusted to provide the motive power of the machine.

The fundamental psychology of *The Federalist* is based on the characteristic distinction between *affection,* a simple and natural feeling prone to parochiality and unnecessary to survival, and *interest,* not natural but derived from the principle of self-preservation in a world of scarcity.

Men tend to give their affections to those who satisfy the demands of their interest, but affection has an autonomous tendency. Because affection is weakened by "distance" and "diffusion," men are subject to an emotional temptation to sacrifice a greater fulfillment of their interests in favor of a more intense affection or a more familiar and seemingly more secure one. Conflicts between governments and political bodies are not simply a conflict of interest—for interest, rightly considered, might cause them to combine; they result from the concentration of affection in one unit as against the other.[29]

The hope for avoiding such conflicts lies in understanding interest rationally and in compelling the affections to follow it. Interest points the way to combination as well as to competition, toward an elimination of scarcity as a source of conflict, and toward a schooling of the affections in the large school of humanity. In viewing human nature, Hamilton had remarked earlier, it is essential to observe the "whole volume," not merely the record of individual men in a particular time. As men proceed from interest to affection, so the same course should be followed by the state. The "irresistible and unchangeable course of nature" not only defines necessity, it ties moral and physical necessity together. The efforts of utopians to separate the two, or to reverse the order of priority, can only eventuate in disaster.[30]

Taming the Great Beast

Only a small part of the animus of *The Federalist* is directed at utopians. Far more hostility is evinced toward state political elites and toward all those who have an interest in the system established by the Articles of Confederation. In general, these obstructive groups

[29] *Ibid.,* pp. 3, 25, 69, 80, 87, 97, 76–77, 110, 147–148, 215, 260, 319, 323, 348, 366, 446, 448.
[30] *Ibid.,* pp. 48–53.

are linked by the opprobrious term "politicians." Politicians are said to show a "pretended zeal for the rights of the people," to pay "obsequious court" to the public, and to "flatter" its prejudices and vanities. Though the implication is strong, the perversities of politicians need not be attributed to evil motives; they may result from want of intelligence, courage, or vision. "The little arts of little politicians" are practiced, in part, because of a petty morality and a lack of science.[31]

Politicians are dangerous because they appeal to the public's weakness; and the public, the authors of *The Federalist* never doubt, should be vested with ultimate sovereignty. Since man is a morally complete being by nature, the public's moral judgment is at least as good as that of any elite. Indeed, the public judgment is superior because as a collectivity it cannot monopolize the goods of wealth and power (not that individuals, members of the public, would not). The public never finds its interest fully satisfied; unlike elites, it is not tempted to a complacency which obstructs progress. Hamilton's famous comment that the public is "turbulent and changing" was partly praise.[32]

Yet equally, the public "seldom judges right." Able to judge ends, the public rarely judges means with accuracy. Never knowingly injuring its own interest, the public is tempted by the desire for immediate affection to demand immediate fulfillment in ways which menace the long-term claims of interest and affection alike. Madison described the danger of a "levelling spirit," for example, which was threatening and tempting because of its immediacy and which sacrificed the dynamics of progress associated with the operation of the market. The public, in other words, is perennially "utopian," and in flattering this tendency politicians commit their greatest sins.

The public, the never complacent and always turbulent whole, is always subject to the temptation to dissolve into individuals and groups, each powered by passions and affections more intense than the whole can afford, seeking a privileged and complacent position. Residence, Hamilton declared in the Convention, may produce a powerful "attachment," and precautions must be designed against

[31] *Ibid.*, pp. 2-3, 260, 323, 366.
[32] *Ibid.*, p. 319; Diamond, "Democracy and the Federalist."

the tendency. The public's affections war with the public's interests and threaten the moral functions of the public itself.[33]

From this arises the peril of too frequent changes of law or too frequent appeals to the public in elections. Either menaces the sense of continuity and permanence and creates "confusion" and uncertainty. In part, Hamilton argued, this is dangerous because it benefits the "sagacious few," able to take advantage of change against the "uninformed many." That, however, also adds to public uncertainty and to a mistrust of citizens by their fellows. Either danger leads the public to repose less confidence in the future and in far-removed persons, and increases the tendency to seek short-term solutions and narrow the compass of the affections.[34]

More importantly, the general theory helps explain the Framers' boundless hostility to "faction" and to intermediary bodies between the individual and the general government. Their answer to the dilemma of intermediate groups is, of course, well-known. The large state, and its proliferation of groups and associated factions would leave the government with a multitude of competitors, albeit disunited, for civic affection. Even if a group managed to monopolize the loyalty of its members, it would be unable to "concert" its schemes with the other groups necessary for a venture at control.

"The reason of man, like man himself," Madison commented in one of the more significant sentences in *The Federalist*, "is timid and cautious when left alone, and acquires firmness and confidence in proportion to the number with which it is associated." Madison had excluded as impracticable and undesirable the policy of seeking unity by giving all citizens the "same opinions." The next alternative was to diminish the "firmness and confidence" of individual opinion, leaving the individual, though free from constraint, "timid and cautious," a decent and prudent citizen. That aim is best achieved through the division and fragmentation of loyalty so that few men are associated with others—too few, at any rate to disturb the political order. In this chaos of interests, each unable to fulfill the interests of the individual, the general government would emerge as the sole guardian of interest and the sole object worthy of genuine affection.[35]

---

[33] Madison, *Notes*, pp. 194, 216, 273.
[34] *The Federalist*, pp. 376, 276–278.
[35] *Ibid.*, pp. 258, 267, 124.

Nowhere is this better illustrated than in the "division of powers" between state and federal governments. *The Federalist* spoke to a constituency fairly ready to concede the need for a stronger central regime, but doubtful of the wisdom of direct contact between individual citizens and the central administration. The most dangerous opponents of the Constitution were those who argued that a stronger union could be achieved without violating the principle that the state, and the state alone, should govern the individual citizen and claim his loyalty.

On this point the Framers were insistent. The central regimes must be brought closer to the people in order to "attract to its support those passions which have the strongest influence upon the human heart." To be sure, the authors hasten to reassure the states: local governments will have the support of affection, and like so many "baronies" will be able to resist encroachments. It was an unfortunate allusion in the late stages of absolutism; European baronies had proved singularly unable to retain loyalties against the allures of interest provided by central governments.

In fact, the authors of *The Federalist* give the game away. States could only be injured if the federal government proves to have a better administration than the states and is better able to serve the public's interest. The people should not be prevented, they remark, from giving confidence where it is due. Yet the whole burden of the argument suggests a confidence that the federal administration will be superior. In any event, the federal regime will have a decisive advantage in any competition. The states will not suffer from usurpation, Hamilton contended, because their powers are too limited to serve as "allurements to ambition": yet where ambition cannot be allured, the interest satisfied must be small. *The Federalist* anticipates that if the individual citizen is brought into direct contact with the federal regime and feels personally the rewards and punishments of federal policy, there will be a gradual accretion of loyalty to the nation as a whole. The "division of powers" is in fact a division of citizens, and it is expected that the loyalties of the divided individual will follow the path which interest indicates toward a broader affection.[36]

---

[36] *Ibid.*, pp. 76–82, 130–132, 151, 156, 195, 231, 240, 406, 420, 422.

Unlike many of their later admirers, the Framers were aware that paper constitutions mean little in themselves. Ultimately, republican government depends on the character of the people; hence the concern of *The Federalist* for political mechanisms designed to shape public attitudes suited to the task. It was equally needful, however, to guarantee the republican nature of institutions—to prevent the domination of the central government by a coherent elite.

James M. Burns has recently argued that the "check and balance" system among the institutions of government is rendered pointless by the pluralistic social order envisioned in the papers. The Framers, however, argue that the danger of affection exists at the federal as well as at the local level; social pluralism does not necessarily prevent representatives from developing solidarity and becoming a "faction" themselves. Writing of the states in terms which apply to the national government, Madison warned of the dangers of a "compact and advantageous" position against a "superior number so situated as to be less capable of prompt and collected exertion." The public, in other words, must be protected against any tendency of its agents to usurp sovereignty, and the system of checks is designed to assure that result ("ambition must be made to counteract ambition").[37]

It is noteworthy that Hamilton argues that a great state, in addition to multiplying groups, increases the strength of the people. Implicit is the argument that while a great state weakens the status of individual men and groups, it strengthens them as a whole; becoming "timid and cautious" in isolation, they acquire "firmness and confidence" when they feel themselves associated with the values and attitudes of the great mass of citizens. To be sure, a great public is likely to be passive, and active only under extreme provocation. But this only emphasizes the role of the public; once the "great beast" is tamed and its affections harnessed, it becomes a conservative force which acquires confidence and national sentiment through the greatness of the nation as a whole.[38]

Whatever belief in human fraternity the Framers possessed is muted in the papers; the vision is dimmed, without any aura of

[37] *Ibid.,* pp. 37, 46–47, 223, 307–308, 323, 367; James M. Burns, *The Deadlock of Democracy* (Englewood Cliffs: Prentice-Hall, 1963), pp. 8–23.

[38] *The Federalist,* pp. 135–136, 168, 191, 267, 310, 319, 374, 398, 439, 446, 448.

optimism except, perhaps, for the "regions of remote futurity" to which they only allude. There is a vision of a national "fraternity," but one in which all particular loyalties and local affections must be shattered and deprived of "confidence." *The Federalist,* in that sense at least, foreshadows mass society, a world of superficial relations where all bonds are reduced to the "diffuse" and "diminished" affection that is tied to interest.

Perhaps the beast was made too tame. Adam Ferguson warned the eighteenth century that its version of "political science" might mis- lead legislators until "the barriers they raise against evil actions of men would prevent them from acting at all." Ferguson feared, with a vision perhaps too true, the result of the new theories of politics:

> Men will gather together in public only in the resorts for commerce and for mere amusement in the form of the crowd. The private family be- comes a retreat in reserve away from competition for status and posi- tion. . . . This humor is not likely to grow in either Republics or monarchies. It belongs to a mixture of both where . . . the subject is tempted to look for equality but finds only independence in its place. . . .[39]

James Wilson: The Moral Instinct

Classical American historiography divides the eighteenth century between Hamilton and Jefferson, but James Wilson fits into neither camp: a Federalist in party, Wilson was a democrat by conviction, supporting democracy as a means to centralization. Wilson was no political maverick (as Hamilton, for example, certainly was); he played a vital role in the Convention and later, as a Justice of the Supreme Court, he helped shape the early principles of Constitutional law.

It is even less promising to regard Wilson as an intellectual eccen- tric. His formal education was more extensive than that of many of his contemporaries. At Glasgow, he had been exposed to an atmos- phere made heady by Robertson, Burgh, Ferguson, and Adam Smith; his works bristle with names, great and obscure, from the annals of political philosophy. Wilson could bridge the gap between Jefferson

[39] Adam Ferguson, *Essay on the Origins of Civil Society* (London: Cadell, 1782), pp. 320, 344, 369.

and the Federalists because there ran through his thought the great current of the Enlightenment which was common to both, and because the Scottish Enlightenment, his stock-in-trade, was peculiarly adapted to the moral and intellectual necessities felt by educated Americans.[40]

In one respect, Wilson seems more traditionalistic than modern: he affirmed God's will as the supreme basis of law and obligation. On closer analysis, this appearance dissolves; religion is justified not by its distinct truth but by its utility.

Beginning with the premise of Divine omnipotence, Wilson asserted that such a quality "can never be disjoined" from supreme goodness, but he did not rest there. He began an apparently gratuitous speculation by supposing that power and goodness might be separated before insisting that "the supposition cannot be made" and that "we cannot—must not—proceed to the inference." [41] Evidently there is a contradiction in contending that a supposition which has been made cannot be made, and the argument that we "cannot" proceed from it must have been a red flag to the liberated spirit of the eighteenth century. Wilson was simply, in a public utterance, employing a mildly guarded rhetoric; the "inference" was a stock item of Deistic thought.

An omnipotent God could order men's affairs as He willed, whatever His goodness, but Wilson saw an important moral reason for insisting that His will was good. Law, for Wilson, became obligatory only through the consent of the individual. Natural law, however, must be presumed to be always obligatory because it is "engraved in men's hearts" and has their "true" consent even though they do not always perceive it clearly.[42] Wilson was too politic, however, not to recognize a political if not a moral distinction between a "true" and an apparent consent. The appeal to religion was calculated to remove that distinction.

The law of reason, Wilson commented, is not always clear nor does it reach everyone, being limited both by education and the natural ability of the individual. Revelation can reach those who

[40] *Selected Political Essays of James Wilson*, ed. Ralph G. Adams (New York: Knopf, 1930), pp. 5–8, 81, n.44.
[41] *Ibid.*, pp. 264, 270.
[42] *Ibid.*, pp. 221, 224.

would be "dark and ignorant" by the standard of reason alone and, moreover, it is more certain than reason can ever be, adding new sanctions to those of mere prudence.[43] In all of this, there is no suggestion of a distinct content to revelation; the revealed word is only characterized by greater social and political utility.

Wilson did postulate a Divine Law above the standards of natural reason, but it was composed of God's Inscrutable Will and of the Law for Perfect Beings such as angels—both irrelevant, obviously, in human affairs. The "law of nature and of nations," the highest form of human law, was guided by the end of "happiness" and rested on free consent. (Wilson also deduced from God's "paternal concern" the commandment, certainly liberal and modern enough, "Let each man pursue his own perfection and happiness." [44]

Wilson found both reason and traditional revelation inadequate, however; neither could serve as a "pole star" to guide human striving. Inanimate and irrational nature was guided by the "laws of motion and attraction" such as the automatic movements of instinct. Men, possessing reason, can "find or make" a system of rules which improves their life beyond what was possible in the "state of nature." Even if useful, however, such rules are abstractions, artificialities, the products of convention. Reason enables man to control nature, but it also enables him to err. Reason is always tempted to regard its devices as truths, claiming to "circumscribe" nature in ways which limit human progress; by itself, reason sets too low a standard to serve as a guide for men.[45]

The goals of human life, Wilson contended, were fixed by an inherent "moral sense." Morality and obligation were things which men could only "feel"; reason itself could assign no reason for preferring pleasure to pain. Philosophers, Wilson asserted, had confused the issue by assigning too low a standing to man's instincts. The "moral sense" was different from man's physical needs and emotions, for as man was higher by nature than the beasts, so he possessed certain higher instincts which found expression in his conscience and were reflected in certain truths perceived to be "self-evident." Reason was useful in deducing subordinate means to

[43] *Ibid.*, pp. 266, 286, 287.
[44] *Ibid.*, pp. 255–257, 265.
[45] *Ibid.*, pp. 49, 206, 217–221, 255–257.

the ends determined by the "moral sense," but "a man may be very honest and virtuous who cannot reason." For Wilson, man was not a "rational animal" but only one who reasons in order to obtain a higher fulfillment than was possible in his "original" state.[46]

However, Wilson's treatment of the moral sense was not based on the assumption that all men possess that sense in equal degrees. Moral sentiments "mature" only gradually, and depend in part on education and environment. His insistence that the "moral sense" is inherent implied that there was no qualitative change: maturation made the instinct stronger, and extended it through the refinements of reason. The child felt the impulses of love, gratitude, and sympathy which were the foundation of all morality, but he would feel them only within the limited compass of his senses and experience. The "dawn of reflection" in youth led the individual to think of moral "forms" or "ideals"—but he was still prone to think of immediate times and environments, and unaware of the "distant inferences of action." Maturity presumably existed when men were freed from the constraints of physical nature, such as space and time, in the expression of their moral instincts.[47]

Wilson: The City and the World

It followed from Wilson's theory that the political order existed to ensure the development of moral sentiments according to the law of man's nature. Wilson was willing to insist on this even when it led to radical conclusions; at the Convention he asserted that the improvement of the human mind, not the protection of property, is the purpose of the state, and must have precedence over property in its laws.[48]

There is more than an echo of classical teleology in this idea of politics; but for Wilson, the aims of the state and the legitimacy of the political were founded on consent and construction, not on the nature of man as a "political animal." The first principle of natural law was freedom, and it was in perfecting his individual freedom that man "matured" his moral instinct. Equality, the second

---

[46] Ibid., pp. 261, 270, 272–277, 282–285.
[47] Ibid., pp. 273, 285, 311.
[48] Madison, Notes, p. 287.

principle, was derived from the equal moral nature of men. Both implied that no man is bound without his consent (as did the further "laws" that Wilson derived from these).[49] Government is created by two contracts: (1) the *contract of community*, which forms a people by their agreement to pursue certain aims, and (2) the *contract of government*, which establishes the form of regime which the people believe best adapted to their ends.

These ideas allowed Wilson to speak of political society in language which was often extraordinarily solidaristic, for no "state" is genuine unless it possesses a contract of community, and no state is legitimate unless the principles of that contract prevail against private or partial loyalties. A union, he observed, is more than the individuals who make it up. He scorned the Netherlands as a model for America as a mere "assemblage of societies" and insisted that America, by creating a new, national "people," could combine the "freedom and beneficence" of republics with the "vigor and decision" of monarchy and the power of the large state.[50]

His language might be Rousseauistic, but Wilson would never have conceded that the community adds to—much less creates—the moral excellence of men. Lacking a "moral instinct," the community can derive whatever morality it possesses only from the individual, and it remains morally inferior to him. Thus, Wilson observed, although a community creates a people which is almost a "new person," this abstract person is composed of moral persons and may destroy itself for their benefit—as the individual, according to the "law of nature," may not destroy himself.[51]

Unlike many liberal contractarians, Wilson was willing to be absolutely consistent in applying these doctrines. Men not represented in the making of rules are not bound to obey them; no rule of tacit consent exists. Resting power with the people is the "panacea in politicks" because it is not only the best method of ensuring that the government pursues legitimate ends, but also because it is the only "radical cure" for disorder, depriving men of most legitimate reasons for disobedience. Wilson agreed that if wide differences of property existed, the impoverished might be excluded from the

---

[49] *Selected Political Essays*, pp. 225–232, 251–252, 255–257, 262.
[50] *Ibid.*, pp. 132–133, 166–174.
[51] *Ibid.*, pp. 49, 61, 91, 93, 96–97, 101, 112, 234–247, 305.

suffrage, being subject to "undue influence" and having "no will of their own." [52] The poor might be shut out then not because they are rebellious or anarchic, but because they are not free. Nor are they, if excluded, obliged to obey rules; Wilson's case rests on the fear that they will be too ready to obey commands, not the reverse. Therefore, though the best government must be democratic, it demands the moral freedom which follows the liberation of the moral instinct from physical need. Equality and well-being are social prerequisites for democracy; rightly organized, an increase of human power over nature is an advance for human morality. Thus, although American laws were not purely democratic, Wilson justified this by reference to the greater "convenience" they afforded in obtaining the universal aim of "happiness."

It is a law of nature, Wilson stated, that societies no less than individuals must discard the past for the future. Having accepted from the classics the idea that the nature of a thing is seen truly only in its "improved" state, Wilson transformed that idea decisively by adding a historical dimension. The law of nature is essentially immutable, but is realized progressively in history. "Young affections" must be taught to move in the direction of history and away from their own times and environments. Age and well-being helped develop the individual; time and the conquest of nature developed man-in-history. [53]

Devoted to international law, Wilson saw the state as quite as free as an individual in the "state of nature" to "do itself justice," this justice demanding that men cultivate the earth. Hunting nations, consequently, are culpable of holding "excessive" land and may be deprived of it, for reasonable compensation, if they refuse to give it up. Hunters, moreover, have a duty to learn agriculture and to adopt civilized ways. Self-preservation is a part of the liberty of societies only when it fulfills nature's "intent"; only so long as they further the mastery of the earth do states reflect the true selves of men. [54]

It is a duty of men and of nations, Wilson insisted, to love mankind above the dictates of "jealousy" or "crooked policy." The moral instinct is not tied to the narrow compass of men's emotions;

[52] *Ibid.*, pp. 50–56, 59, 68, 180–181, 311.
[53] *Ibid.*, pp. 164, 206, 290–291.
[54] *Ibid.*, pp. 310, 325, 332, 280–281.

it is capable of being abstracted, the loyalties and capacities it creates enlarged. Wilson's faith became almost mystical; "the capacity of our natures is enlarged; men otherwise invisible are rendered conspicuous and become known to the heart and to the understanding." [55]

The fraternity of mankind is an authentic demand of man's moral instinct, Wilson urged, but only recently has it been recognized in other than intellectual terms. Interest, ambition, and war have previously barred the way to the universal brotherhood we may now aspire to see realized. The hope for fraternity, however, demands that we eliminate conflicts of interest and ambition, and war as a derivative of them. Since that result demands the conquest of nature and the fulfillment of human demands, the victory becomes a duty commanded by human fraternity. If men are deaf to the calls of the moral instinct, they may be forced to take up the struggle; such war, part of the intent of nature, is sanctioned by nature's high law.

Wilson achieved an articulate statement of a moral theory, often muted in *The Federalist*, which inspired many of his contemporaries. Doubtful in many ways, his theory is most suspect in its first premise: the existence of a moral sense apart from man's physical senses and his reason. Serene in the confidence that it existed, Wilson developed a theory which in the hands of men less generous and humane could serve to justify more than one form of inhumanity to men, and which surrendered much of man's moral judgment to the course of history.

[55] *Ibid.*, pp. 312–318.

> It is incontestably true that the love and the habits of republican government in the United States were engendered in the townships and provincial assemblies. . . . But it is this same republican spirit, it is these manners and customs of a free people which are . . . nurtured in the different states to be applied afterward to the country at large. The public spirit of the Union is . . . nothing more than an abstract of the patriotic zeal of the provinces.
>
> De Tocqueville, *Democracy in America*

CHAPTER IX

THE JEFFERSONIANS

"Limited to a narrow space . . ."

In the late eighteenth century, Americans spoke and wrote more to other Americans; the sense of difference from Europeans grew; the symbols common to the leaders of all the colonies became more numerous. The unity which resulted was a prerequisite of the Revolution, the Articles, and the Union. All this is true, but such a description omits those who wrote little if at all and whose voices were not loud enough to catch the ear of the historian—the majority of Americans.

Most lived within the boundaries of locality, shut off from their fellows by barriers of space and time. Even economic life took place, for the most part, within that little circle. The local passage of immigrants and the flux of residents were probably more important than the movement of goods in bringing men into contact with a wider world. But peripheral or sporadic though the manifestations might be, there were echoes of change.

Government, whether parliamentary or congressional, began to search the interior for new sources of revenue, and confronted with Indian menaces, the interior sought protection in return. In the towns and the seaboard, the older, quasi-medieval regulations were lapsing, to be replaced by modern commercial "ethics" and law; in shops, master and journeyman were becoming employer and employee. The most rugged individualist among the frontiersmen needed a spot of cash to pay for powder and shot, and the gently optimistic farmers borrowed to start a new project or to see their families through until the harvests. All were touched by the hand of the new economy. They were made aware of their dependence in hard times, if no other, when debtors cried out for a currency that would protect them against "speculators" and frontiersmen protested—covertly or with rifles—against taxes on liquor.

They did not understand that wider world well, these more isolated Americans, for it was outside their sphere of personal acquaintance and control. What they did understand they did not much admire: expanded central control for the more efficient pursuit of power, economic ethics suited to the acquisitive, laws and regulations which subordinated the immediate relations of men to abstractions like the state or the distant goals of history. The urban merchant or the great planter, the lawyer and the tax collector, were all legitimate objects of hostility to the lower-class or rural American.

The politics of the late eighteenth century were oriented around the conflict between educated, commercial America and her underlying population; the real struggles lay, as Clinton Rossiter puts it, between "the involved and the isolated." [1]

The Revolution had cut across those lines of cleavage with an essentially irrelevant issue: the question of ties to Britain. Even then there had been signs. In the South, where the planters tended to support the Revolution, the up-countrymen, who had clashed with the planters more than once before 1776, often supported the crown. The merchants and the professionals disliked much in British policy but they had no quarrel with "modern" legislation as such and demanded only that it respect their interests. Most had been surprised by the agitation against the Stamp Act; even the shrewd Franklin had accepted it and sought only to secure the appointment of his

[1] Clinton Rossiter, 1787: *The Grand Convention* (New York: Macmillan, 1966), p. 27.

friends as collectors. From the unexpected protest, most learned that their own position could be secured only if they took the leadership of the multitude and turned it to their own account. The Revolution won, the "passions most unfriendly to unity and concord" made their appearance again.

The Federalist to the contrary, more was involved than mass emotion. Confronting the new and wider world, brought increasingly into relations of contact and dependence, Americans from the isolated areas brought with them the older culture of the land. In rural America, the ideas of Locke or DuPont penetrated but little: religion was almost the sole cultural agency. In some areas, religious culture reached a high level of sophistication; for most, it was little more than a set of precepts and proverbs, a few songs, a faith in Scripture. Literate or illiterate, however, it was something chosen, something "our own" and clung to in the face of a world of mysteries and threats.

Political language suggested as much. The leaders of the time might speak of the British tradition and the law of nature, and the mass of Americans could find such references congenial. Whatever their own beliefs, however, when propagandists hoped to hit a deep strain among Americans, they spoke in the language of Israel and Biblical polity. Even Paine deferred, using "Mahomet" as his example of superstition, calling the doctrine of hereditary monarchy a mark of original sin, and asserting that the only King of America "reigns above." [2]

The older culture of America suggested more than symbols, however; related to it was a fairly coherent doctrine of politics, based on the rights of local privilege and autonomy, which was common to North and South alike. If, as De Tocqueville remarked, "democracy came out of the towns" to conquer the state,[3] it did so in the form of demands for government by "our own kind."

The Anti-Federalists, whatever their motives, formulated their opposition in highly traditional terms. The "political science" of the century aroused little enthusiasm. They were "men of little faith" indeed, and to them the work of the Framers bespoke naivete, not pessimism, regarding human nature. Man's depravity was too deep,

[2] *Common Sense*, pp. 10–18, 32.
[3] *Democracy in America*, vol. I, p. 49.

his cunning too great, to be trapped by "devices." The only safe-guard of republican government was a virtuous, active public which could keep agents and citizens alike under a watchful eye. Moreover, civil society was a "blessing," part of the education of men; they needed, not a distant government to guide their interests, but a community which could shape their characters. A government shaped by the requirements of human nature would have to be, like man's per-ceptions, "limited to a narrow space," and no "government of strangers" could be either safe or educational.

Most agreed that a larger union was needed, but they were in-sistent that it be tied intimately to the people, which required that it be built on the basis of locality. They were aware that a large state not only limits the number who can participate but makes it easier for the well-to-do and the educated to organize, and more difficult for the poor (a consideration not lost on those, like Gouver-neur Morris, who had very different ends in view). And, some con-tended, that very fact will make the people suspect a central govern-ment: without a basis in local loyalty, formal powers would only conceal feet of clay; the sense of security in what is close is required for any trust in what is distant.

Anti-Federalist arguments were as diverse as those who pro-pounded them, and the themes discussed here were only some among many objections raised. The tenor of their argument, however, was that of a conservative democracy which feared innovations and which, like the mass of the people themselves, sought guidance from custom and the wisdom of the past.

Awakenings and Architects

The new times, however, would not be denied, and the older values and qualities of life, if they could be preserved at all, would require new forms. To cling to the letter would be to lose the spirit.

Certainly it seemed so in the church, where the ministers of orthodox professions seemed too concerned with subtleties to be relevant to life. Certainly too, the older churches, whatever their virtues, left many Americans with only formal church affiliations, and others isolated from communion altogether.

It was among those who shared such sentiments and situations that the Great Awakening spread its evangelical fervor. With his individualism and fear of community, Edwards had never quite understood the political quality of evangelism. Wesleyanism, with its concern to reinstitute practices like the "love feast," came closer to the mark. The fire of the Awakening was a demand for community and a protest against the new order in terms of the values of the old. It led frequently to a demand that Christian standards be applied in political life. James Davenport, denouncing the hard-heartedness of wealth, was jailed for utterances deemed inflammatory by the well-to-do; Elias Smith defended Jefferson against charges of infidelity, seeing in Jefferson's politics something closer to the Christian standard of fraternity than was characteristic of his foes.

There was of course a more negative side to the "Protestant Counter-Reformation." Emphasis on the spirit and deprecation of the secular could result in the familiar pattern of revivalism: a diversion of attention from problems at hand, an outlet for frustrations whose natural object was political.

That tendency, certainly, led Alexander Hamilton and Benjamin Talmadge, hardly fervent gospelers, to welcome evangelists who preached congenial doctrine.[4] This policy, aimed to discredit those whom the Federalists called "materialistic" (i.e., politically concerned) evangelists like Thomas Cooper, paid surprisingly few dividends. Evangelism in the eighteenth century was too close to tradition to be altogether diverted from political and social content, and Hamilton found a more comfortable alliance with the established denominations.

But the preachers of the Awakening, like Edwards, were convinced that the emotions, contrasted with the supposed amorality of reason, were the fount of moral judgment. Their appeals consequently placed them in the camp of obscurantism and weakened their case against the Enlightenment. Worse, though the appeal of evangelism to isolated Americans lay in the experience of community, it brought that experience about through what is most individual and isolating in men. Frenzies and fervors it gave aplenty, but these passed leaving lonely men with only a memory of momentary warmth.

---

[4] Curti, *Growth of American Thought*, pp. 200–204.

In the towns, the yearning of men took a more organized form. The cities of the time were small enough, but even in the eighteenth century men discovered that they were cast on their own resources and that a more commercial spirit reigned when they entered the towns. Friendly Societies could provide men with a place for emotional expression and for fairly reliable interpersonal relations, and they could perform some of the traditional services of village and parish. Too weak to change the course of political development, the societies, like the abortive workingmen's societies that were even more a portent, were a reflection of nostalgic traditionalism on one hand and, on the other, a desire to preserve some of the older values in a new age.

There was far less traditionalism in the doctrine of Masonry which, opposing "superstition," inclined to Deism and libertarianism and toward a "scientific" spirit in politics. Rooted in the middle and intellectual classes, it provided a means of contact between "enlightened" men for cooperation against diverse foes. The Masons were, after all, a small minority, holding a doctrine that most Americans viewed with fierce hostility. Secrecy was not a frill: "Talking against religion," Franklin warned, "is unchaining a tiger. The beast may worry his liberator." [5]

The metaphysics of Masonry, however, were not the whole story. Its members were less comfortable in the established order than were the elites, and they were allowed, or driven, to see more clearly the conflict between older ethics and newer practices. The explosion of the Order's membership in the late eighteenth century was part of a general growth of Deism after the Revolution; it reflected the desire of men shaken out of old habits and dogmas for an ethical religion which would apply old rules of conduct to an environment in which the old theological abstractions seemed untenable.

Masonry provided such men with an almost indispensable means of becoming aware of their similarly-inclined fellows; it afforded a basis for national political organization and, inclining to the more humane side of the Enlightenment, led straight to Jeffersonianism.

[5] Franklin, *Selected Works*, p. 488.

The elites, by contrast, had ties through business and social relations which made fraternal orders superfluous in politics—and worse, a potential source of embarrassment. The Society of the Cincinnati, for example, was not only needlessly conspicuous and identifiable; its hereditary membership clause raised such a storm of protest, which even a good Federalist like John Adams joined, that it lapsed rapidly into political impotence.

Federalists were slow to see a threat in Masonry. Pre-Revolutionary Tories like Joseph Green had found it dangerous enough, if easy to satirize, but initially the Federalists saw only that Masonry was identified with the same "scientific" political spirit which found favor in many of their own circles. Even fervent anti-Deists like Jedediah Morse were persuaded to treat the Masons as political allies of order and property.

As that illusion vanished, Federalists made up in fury what they had lacked in celerity of perception. Masons were denounced as defamers of marriage, opponents of property, propagators of infidelity, apostles of discord and revolution. Morse, reversing his earlier stand, purported to see in Masonry a "French conspiracy" against the Republic, and Seth Payson, following the dubious disclosures of the Abbé Barruel, discerned a Satanic conspiracy against God in the "Illuminist" doctrines supposed to have infiltrated the Order.

Perhaps the Federalist polemicists were not serious and were only striving futilely for mass appeal, for their expressed fears were hardly justified by the real facts of the case. Combining Enlightenment secular libertarianism with a mystical faith in human fraternity, a periodic bow to brotherhood which did not interfere with the pursuits of life, Masonry was an ideal vehicle for relieving the tensions of men caught between inherited ethics and temporal interests. It might become identified with Jeffersonianism as a protest, but it worked to assimilate Americans to the new order of things.

Perhaps too, however, the horror of a Morse or Payton was not wholly beside the point. They may have sensed in the Order, whatever the reality of its particular case, a truth that had been hidden in Franklin's warning: that released from the chains of orthodoxy, the ethical and millennial promises of religion might yet make claims on the enlightened which would worry the liberators.

"We are all Republicans . . ."

Political organization at the formal level had been superfluous for the Federalists. Securely united by the personal connections of their leaders, and possessing a coherent doctrine, they had found it easy to create an initial coalition of all those who were deeply involved in the commercial economy: merchants, the wealthy planters, and commercial farmers. To these, they had added some who were tied by friendship, interest, or clientage, such as the established clergy of New England and workers in industries like shipping. Theirs was, in fact, the ancient pattern of Anglo-American politics, a reflection of the pre-Revolutionary days when great families, like the DeLanceys and Livingstons of New York had marshalled their kin and satellites for the causes of Crown and Patriot.

Yet change, though tortoise-paced to the modern eye, was undermining that almost immemorial pattern of politics as surely as it was pervading the other institutions of men's lives. New men, outside the circle of clientage, were being drawn into politics; others were becoming discontented with their dependence within it. Still others, like Aaron Burr, sensed in feelings of discontent and exclusion an opportunity for hopes and ambitions of their own.

At first the forces of protest suffered from an insuperable handicap: dissatisfaction, like the men who felt it, was limited by local horizons. Like all coalitions of outsiders, even if the discontented had a common object of animosity and a common body of values, they had to sift such essentials out from a body of attitudes which also included hoary suspicions and hallowed antipathies. Middle ranks among farmers shared little with men who followed subsistence agriculture; and neither shared much with the more radical elements among the slavocracy; agriculture of all varieties had no clear ties to workers or to members of the discontented middle class. With all these were combined distrust and rivalry between state and region and the history of dispute and bloody contest that divided Presbyterian, Catholic, Baptist, and Methodist. The disadvantage of the excluded, in other words, was exactly that pluralism to which Madison had called attention in the tenth *Federalist*.

Federalist party arrogance helped to unite these groups, and so, of course, did the patience and cunning with which Jefferson and his friends in the capital sought support for their policies. Yet, as William Chambers has demonstrated, as much or more was due to movements which originated among the citizens themselves.[6] The Democratic–Republican Societies, of which Tammany is our major surviving reminder, not only united voters to the local political activists; correspondence and communication brought about a sense of unity among societies, creating by organization and effort the web of trust which position had given the Federalists.

Moreover, the Republican party did more than tie national to local leaders and these in turn to citizens, by a hierarchy of interlocking personal ties. Such a hierarchy, as old as feudalism, the Federalists possessed too. The horizontal bonds with one another which the societies gave local leaders provided the party with a stronger note of equality, a slight hint of fraternity which their rivals lacked and whose language they never learned to master. It is a pity that when "modern" political practices made their appearance, political scientists often preserved the old names—patronage was not new; what was unique was the substitution, at local levels at least, of the confidence and complaisance of friends for the obligations of patrons. (Chambers rightly pointed out that the South, where Republicanism was led by a section of the elite, was an exception, persisting in the old patterns).[7]

Jefferson's theory might give his perception a peculiar coloration, but he saw in the party organizations the first steps toward national civic fraternity. He viewed the societies as the place where trust might be gained and affections won which would free men even from the defective environment of the cities.

Ironically, Jefferson's victory blunted any such tendencies, as it removed the sting of protest throughout America. It calmed the anxieties of his opponents—even the orthodox of New England were delighted to discover that Jefferson was not, after all, a devil's disciple—and delighted his supporters.

Jefferson's own hope for national unity betrayed him, making his "cause" a bit too flaccid, his trust—and that of his successors—a

---

[6] Chambers, *Political Parties in a New Nation*, pp. 40–41, 120.

[7] *Ibid.*, pp. 85, 164.

bit too accessible. Combined with the hopelessness of the Federalist cause, that easy tolerance caused his opponents to repair in increasing numbers to the Republican standard. The growth of a consensus among the elite, mirrored in what was to be misnamed the "era of good feeling," deprived the excluded of a vehicle for protest; the lack of contest deprived party organization beyond the local level of its reason for being, and voters of their reason for interest. (The percentage of voters participating fell roughly fifty percent in the first quarter of the nineteenth century). For the moment, America's underlying culture was politically silenced.

Jefferson represented, for Americans, a guarantee of older ethics; his victory allowed the previously suspicious to trust the modern state. It is an indication that the cultural conflicts produced by change in the eighteenth century were minor in scale that calm descended so easily. Yet this also marked the fact that Jefferson guided America toward a new economic and social system in the rhetoric of the old. Jeffersonianism merely postponed the cultural conflict of America until the impact of commerce and the slow growth of industry should be more generally felt and men might see more clearly the passing of once-hallowed practices and values.

Jefferson: "The Great Principles . . ."

Thomas Jefferson has been claimed by almost all political historians and, seemingly, by every political movement. It has become a truism that the images of Jefferson held by later generations only reflect aspects of a complex and not always consistent personality. Man of thought and man of action, moralist and political pragmatist, Jefferson presents a character which seems to be made up of warring antitheses.

As a moralist, Jefferson was consistently devoted to traditional doctrines which varied from those of many of his contemporaries. He was inclined to judge actions by their immediate effects on the life and relations of men, not as they contributed to distant ends. His concern lay foremost with the lives of individuals, not the life of the nation or of the race.

Jefferson believed in and was devoted to human progress, but he suspected the penchant for seeking that goal by devious routes.

If humanity was to move toward higher things, it would be on the foundation created by good men. The political order was designed to develop and improve man as a moral being, without which all progress would be hollow. In that task, the state would find good relations between man and his fellows an indispensable means to human growth; fraternity, as Jefferson defined it, was not just an ultimate goal, but also a present need of men.

This picture of Jefferson, like all others, must be shaded as soon as it is painted. The basic themes of Jefferson's life arose from his adherence to traditional values and to political ideals which corresponded badly with the creeds and the environment of modern politics; but he formulated his doctrine in terms of the thought of the Enlightenment. Part of his political appeal, as has already been suggested, lay in his ability to provide for the inarticulate a modern foundation for ancient hopes. In part, by doing so, he distorted the substance of his symbols, confused his audience, and failed in his self-set task as a political educator. But he also, in a hostile intellectual climate, managed to preserve the symbol of fraternity and shape in its image some institutions of the Republic, no mean contribution whatever his faults.

Jefferson the moralist unites all the Jeffersons, for he insisted that the world was simple and that the distinctions and gradations, theses and antitheses, spun out of the ratiocinations of theologians and intellectuals, lost sight of its essential unity. We must, he wrote Adams, eliminate from language "Logos and Demiurgos, Aeons and Daemons, male and female." Most especially must we do so in morality, returning to the creed of the "unlettered apostles" freed from the "interpretations" with which men have surrounded it.[8]

Jefferson was intensely aware of the role played by society and education in developing—or distorting—man in terms of the law of his nature ordained by Creation (and it is significant that he referred to nature in terms of its "Creator," and not of stark impersonality). Yet given the science of the Enlightenment, Jefferson neither could, nor would have wished to, define nature teleologically. Nature was original, and hence the law of nature was inherently accessible to men by means of a "moral instinct":

[8] *Letters and Selected Works of Thomas Jefferson*, ed. Adrienne Koch and William Peden (New York: Modern Library, 1944), pp. 632, 567.

The great principles of right and wrong are legible to every reader; to pursue them requires not the aid of many counsellors. The whole art of government consists of being honest.[9]

Jefferson accepted the characteristic view that reason only follows emotion, seeking to avoid pain or to strike a calculating balance between pleasures to be gained and pains to be avoided. Left to itself, Jefferson reasoned, reason leads man to avoid attachments to his fellows—who may injure him, depart, or die—beyond the prudential and transient terms of an "alliance." Reason by itself is "miserable," lacking "benevolence, justice, sympathy, and friendship."

Man's moral sentiments not only value all those things which reason wants, they have an impulsiveness that enables man to run risks, especially in relation to his fellows. His moral instincts realize that there is no pleasure without pain, and that for mortal man there is no joy without danger of injury.

Reason exists to provide greater opportunities for the expression of moral sentiments (and in the process, though secondarily, to protect them from excess). Though Jefferson could intone that "Interests, soundly calculated, will ever be found inseparable from our moral duties," his meaning was that sound calculation, even a judgment of what man's interests are, must begin with an assessment of his moral aims and duties.[10]

Man was made a "social animal," and the first principle of his moral instinct is compassion and love for his fellows. These sentiments, however, are limited by the affections; Jefferson realized, no less than did the authors of The Federalist, that affection becomes weaker as it extends outward from the individual. Given the weakness of moral impulses when placed in conflict with man's affections, the Jews and the ancient philosophers had, in Jefferson's view, strengthened his worst impulses by their teaching, inculcating narrow ideas of obligations toward kindred, friends, and the state. (The morality of the Jews was one which Jefferson, no great intellectual historian, regarded as peculiarly "repulsive" and "anti-social.")[11]

It was reserved for Jesus to discover the truth that all men are

[9] Ibid., pp. 310, 636–640, 703, 706.
[10] Ibid., pp. 401–405, 339, 637–638; Koch, "Jefferson," pp. 477–481, 486.
[11] Ibid., pp. 211, 586–590.

members of "one family," Jefferson believed, and to make it possible to educate men according to the true promptings of their moral sentiment. This would be achieved by broadening the circle of duties to include all (though different obligations were suitable for different categories of persons).

Rightly developed, the affections were the allies and not the opponents of moral instinct. The affections relieved life of dreariness; they led man out of himself and toward others. Affection was at odds with morality only when it became a barrier to further expansion, and Jefferson was inclined to blame that situation on affections which were too weak. America's British brethren were "unfeeling"; the measures of the King in Parliament gave the "last stab to agonizing affection." America, with her strong affections, was forced to abandon her "former love" for the Britons, whose feeble ardor could not span the Atlantic.[12]

There was a strong note of romanticism in this view, and certainly direct opposition to *The Federalist*, for it implied that lesser loyalties and affections should be strengthened and not fragmented. Jefferson praised the Indian for his loyalty to his friends to the "uttermost extremity," seeing no conflict between such intense feelings and sentiments of love for mankind. So too, Jefferson felt obliged to attack Buffon's thesis that the Indian was inferior in ardor and sexual potency. Jefferson's motives for the defense were mixed (Buffon having contended that America was unhealthy), but he considered that it would be serious and telling if Buffon could make his case: strong passions were necessary for a full and equal status in the human community. Jefferson does not appear to have considered that Buffon's argument might be irrelevant to the Indian's virtues, still less to treat it, as an ascetic might, as a mark of virtue in the aborigine.[13]

Despite his belief in an instinctual morality, Jefferson was neither sanguine regarding the prospects for men nor entirely a leveler in matters of morality. Morality was the normal case, but exceptions would always be found; men had proved to make "interested uses of every right and power." Moreover, in history, "rogues

---

[12] *Ibid.*, pp. 26–27, 211, 637–639.
[13] *Ibid.*, pp. 210–213.

tend to be uppermost," being able to take advantage of moral men and hence able to corrupt others by their example.

Part of the reason, in fact, for postulating a moral instinct lay in his thesis that society tends to level men down to the worst, for Jefferson wished to affirm that there are always moral resources in man. Even more important, however, is the fact that while the "moral instinct" revealed to man the broad outlines of his due and duty, there were still gradations and degrees of virtue within the category of moral actions.

Heredity established some moral distinctions among men. In the extreme case, Jefferson reasoned, a man might be born without a "moral sense" just as some were born without a sense of hearing. Even in less extreme cases, Jefferson sometimes employed physiological explanations of political and moral conduct, tracing Toryism, for example, to a "sickly, weak and timid" disposition.[14]

Jefferson distrusted the principle of heredity in human affairs because of the effects which institutions based on it had on the development of men. Hereditary aristocracy, primogeniture, and especially slave-holding tended to incite in the individual feelings of egotism, arrogance, complacency, and license. These environmental effects, however, are not a part of "nature" and say nothing of the true effects of heredity on man. Indeed, one of Jefferson's arguments against primogeniture was the contention that it is "unnatural" to raise the first-born over his blood-brothers.

Certainly Jefferson was willing to concede that a "variety of ability" existed among races. Though he did not believe they justified slavery, Jefferson did not see these differences as indifferent to virtue: the Negro was deficient in beauty, reason, and imagination. Though he later modified these views, Jefferson went further than an examination of the evidence would have required of him; seeing much to be disliked among the Indians, he always referred these "undesirable" traits to culture and environment. Too, Jefferson conceded more to heredity than orthodox religion would have demanded; it was part of the "scientific" necessity that made him seek the "nature" of man in what is physical and original rather than in a moral "essence." [15]

[14] *Ibid.*, pp. 238, 277, 534, 638–639, 712.
[15] *Ibid.*, pp. 51–52, 256–257, 278–279, 323, 632–634; Jefferson, *Writings*, ed.

Intellectually necessary perhaps, given his premises, arguments from heredity were almost an aberration in Jefferson's thought, so great was the importance he attached to society and to education. Man, the social creature, depended on society for whatever excellence he might obtain. If society could not legitimately bind a new generation by agreements made in the past, it could educate them to accept those agreements voluntarily. Man had only one claim against the state, though a major one: since the state was designed for the purpose of developing the virtue and expanding the true happiness of individuals, its measures must be adapted to that end.

Some rights were inherent in man's nature, like those rights to freedom of expression made necessary by the requirements of free moral agency. A right like property, however, was more conditional. "The earth belongs in usufruct to the living," Jefferson declared, and the material wealth of society is the property of society, to be assigned in each generation by convention and agreement. Property is of importance to men and to their relations with their fellows, and must be judged as it contributes to these two truly natural phenomena.[16]

All social relations, however, are designed for the development of the individual. Social discipline may be needed as a beginning, but to the extent that circumstances permit—Jefferson always knew that circumstances may force a modification of principle—society must develop the "moral agent" able to discern and accept his obligations voluntarily on the basis of personal reflection and choice.

In fact, it might be necessary to forego many institutions otherwise convenient for society in order to advance the moral education of the individual. Jefferson felt that the safest basis for rights lay in a public conviction that they were "gifts of God," and that a belief that God would punish injustice was a desirable foundation for morality. (Jefferson held both himself, if in unorthodox form.) Yet true or desirable, such beliefs must be subjected to the test of free inquiry. The fallible mind of man errs; religion must often be purged of

---

Bergh (Washington: Jefferson Memorial Association, 1903–1905), vol. XI, pp. 254–255.

[16] *Letters and Selected Works,* pp. 488–491.

corruption. Uniformity of opinion is no more desirable than uniformity of "face and stature." [17]

Beliefs and loyalties could not be inherited without challenge, for to do so is to lose the senses of uncertainty and choice which are part of man's nature and condition. Similarly, Jefferson's statement that he "would not go" to heaven if forced to go there with a party did not imply hostility to parties, which he regarded as founded in temperament and nature. He was assailing loyalty to party given without the awareness of choice, without the sense of a decision based on political goals and moral feelings.[18]

That attitude lay behind the exalted status Jefferson assigned to fraternity as a relation between men. The "moral instinct," as Jesus had discovered it, made men a "family," but so long as it remained at the level of instinct, it was not a basis for fraternity among even the most affectionate. By contrast, Americans and Britons were "brethren" in one sense even if they were in conflict: they shared principles, and it was a fault of affection and not belief that underlay the struggle.[19] Fraternity was the relation with his fellows that an individual attained when he acquired moral freedom and attained the ability to guide his affections on the basis of principle. Moral instinct made fully articulate became moral awareness, and led each to his brothers within the family of men.

These ideals, however, were ends and not beginnings; the free individual might be the raison d'etre of politics, but he was the last result of political life and law. That rule of sequence was behind Jefferson's sympathy for the narrower groups and loyalties that Hamilton scorned; they were means essential to the end. Aware of the perils to his universalistic morality which local loyalties and attachments entailed, Jefferson accepted the risk as necessary, part of the nature of man, not to be eluded by device or overstepped by hope.

"The plain common sense . . ."

Jefferson's sense of the importance of the social and political

[17] *Ibid.*, pp. 275–279, 539.
[18] *Ibid.*, pp. 460, 712–713.
[19] *Ibid.*, pp. 322–323. See also Jefferson's remarks on friendship among students, pp. 386–387, 578–580.

environment to human education made him more able than many theorists of the time to recognize the impact on men of the customs and traditions of particular cultures. True to the vogue, he spoke in universals more often than now seems justified: too often, a characteristic of Americans is attributed to "man"; too often, American beliefs are declared to prove the virtues of commonness rather than the excellence of the beliefs which American common men, by historical accident, happen to hold. Yet as often as not, such phrases in Jefferson's writings were an accident of rhetoric, not an essential of thought.

The Courts of Europe would certainly have been astonished to learn that the Declaration of Independence set forth no "new principles" and merely asserted the "plain common sense" of the subject. The apparent absurdity of Jefferson's comment, however, dissolves if it is remembered that, references to the "opinions of mankind" notwithstanding, the Declaration was intended for domestic consumption. And if Loyalists were a rather striking exception, a case can be made that the Declaration's doctrines and phrases appealed to the "harmonizing sentiments of the day" on this side of the water.[20]

Jefferson never neglected the unique aspects of American culture as they bore upon politics. Even his general acceptance of democratic institutions was premised on the safety with which Americans could demand such rights for themselves. Given their experience and training, Jefferson asserted, the "canaille of the cities of Europe" could not possibly be trusted with political power. (He admired the art and high culture of those cities, but felt they cost too much in moral and political terms; no simple agrarian, he spent some energy attempting to plan towns which would combine the best of both worlds.)

Jefferson's fear of immigration and his support for the deportation of Negroes were based on his solicitude for the American cultural consensus, and the danger to American values which both groups posed. The slave is separated from his master by "habit and opinion," and to leave him in America only invites racial conflict. Immigrants, corrupted by the servile principles of monarchy "imbibed in their early youth," are hardly suited for democratic citizenship.

Jefferson later accepted immigration only because he felt it a higher duty to provide a place of refuge. America must become "an-

---

[20] *Letters and Selected Works,* pp. 449, 719.

other Canaan" where the victims of "Egyptian oppression" may come and be "received as brothers." (As was often the case, his language took on a Biblical tone, only more marked because he spoke of a precept of universal morality which overrode the risk to the political order.) This departure from *Notes on Virginia*, however, hardly bespeaks any declining sense of the uniqueness of America (though it may reflect a greater confidence in her cultural and political stability).[21]

America was, in Jefferson's eyes, "chosen" by what the Creator had given her: economic abundance sufficient to support each citizen in freedom; a sophisticated political inheritance derived from the "freest" principles of Britain; a people raised in the belief in Providence and in religious ethics which stressed the "love of man." All this, he felt, the authors of *The Federalist* and their supporters had tended to ignore, relying too much on "European authorities" who could not understand the American public, whatever the value of their ideas in European settings or as maxims of a universal prudence.

Much was possible in America that was out of the question elsewhere. Since, however, America had given the "signal of arousing man," European states would be wise to read the signs in time. Jefferson realized that the effects of the American example might not be unambiguously desirable if unprepared men tried to imitate it. He could resolve such doubts only by a faith in progress; governments would change, the education and attitudes of men would improve.

Jefferson reasoned, for example, that "time and truth" would prove that the effort to secure the "liberty of the earth" had been worth the blood shed by the Terror. He was, however, unsuited to the role of historical zealot. Denouncing the folly and blindness of the Jacobins, he praised the "cordial friends" of the French Revolution who had been slain by it. These last, he argued, had always been willing to sacrifice their lives for human liberty; and like similar sacrifices in battle, theirs might be justified if the great cause prevailed and the people gained a new wisdom. Yet Jefferson was uncomfortable with such arguments; they did not, after all, account for

---

[21] On the political environment, see *Letters and Selected Works*, pp. 217, 632–634, 51–52, 543; *Writings*, ed. Bergh, vol. XI, pp. 66–67, vol. XV, pp. 139–142, 469; and *The Papers of Thomas Jefferson*, ed. J. P. Boyd (Princeton: Princeton University Press, 1953–1955), vol. VIII, pp. 568–570.

the true innocents slain by the Terror whose deaths could not be shrugged off as merited by crime nor glorified as lost in the human cause. The calculation of the least inhuman method for reaching remote ends was alien to his temper; his belief in progress was a faith, akin to the old doctrine of Providence, and radically different from the creed of "scientific" history.[22]

In any event, America, whatever the effects of her example, posed no such problems. "It suffices for us," he wrote Adams, "if the moral and physical condition of our own citizens qualifies them to select the able and the good for the direction of their government. . . ." In contrast to the authors of *The Federalist*, his major concern was to maintain, not to change, the character and attitudes of Americans.[23]

Jefferson had an ample sense of the uses of continuity and authority. He believed the safest foundation for liberty was a belief in the law of God, not contractarian natural right, and he lamented that the men of Philadelphia had not seen fit to preserve the "venerable fabric" of the Articles of Confederation as a "religious relic" for subsequent generations, if not for other virtues.

To be sure, Jefferson asserted the need to reaffirm institutions and laws in each generation. But that need was, for Jefferson, as much a fact as a prescription. A government is based on the character of its citizens, not on institutions and parchments; if a subsequent generation were to accept without conscious reflection the laws of its fathers, it would by that servile act have destroyed the state's foundation of free and rational consent. Each generation in fact builds anew; a community which would preserve its ancient spirit must design the education of the latest generation to build a character identical to the first. (Hence, in part, the need for a Bill of Rights.) In a free community, all men are founders; he quoted easily:

Not cities proud, with spires and turrets crown'd
No: men, high-minded men;
Men who their duties know
But know their rights, and knowing, dare maintain.
These constitute a state.[24]

[22] *Letters and Selected Works*, pp. 522, 543, 672; *Writings*, vol. VII, p. 450, vol. IX, p. 274, vol. X, p. 324.
[23] *Letters and Selected Works*, p. 634.
[24] *Ibid.*, p. 671, see also pp. 436, 441, 491–492, 714; Chinard, *Thomas Jefferson*, p. 86.

"*The hopes of the world . . .*"

Jefferson felt that America might hope to realize the ideal of a fraternal citizenry. Cognizant of the existence of division, rivalry, and faction, he believed there was nonetheless a consensus on values, an agreement on standards, which overrode such divisions. The problem for America was not one of principle; it was rather a problem of affection. "We have called by different names brethren of the same principle," he asserted in the First Inaugural. "Let us restore to social intercourse that harmony and affection without which liberty and even life are dreary things." [25]

In a state with the size and divisive tendencies of America, it was necessary to oppose anything which threatened the trust and affection of citizens for each other. A staunch Jeffersonian like Livingston opposed the Alien and Sedition Acts because they would excite mistrust and jealousy between men, cause citizens to guard their words and retreat into isolation. So too, Jefferson suspected the separation of powers; based on European theory, it created needless divisions to meet imaginary dangers and it would tend to divide the country and minimize the citizen's sense of responsibility.[26]

Trust and affection were no less important in the states and localities. National unity and fraternal affection should rise out of local devotion, concern for the general interest should be founded on the security of the particular. Jefferson suggested that government be based on "wards," small local units within the range of interpersonal affection and capable of direct democracy. From these an overlapping hierarchy of representation might be built, culminating in the national government. Each body in the hierarchy would be small enough for internal direct democracy and fraternal relations among representatives. This design was Jefferson's effort to combine the virtues he saw in the New England town with a concern for the whole nation which the town, in its "insularity," had lacked.[27]

Never established as a constitutional principle, Jefferson's plan

[25] *Letters and Selected Works*, pp. 322–323.

[26] *Ibid.*, pp. 84–85, 121, 126, 435–436, 442, 447, 460, 462.

[27] *Ibid.*, pp. 661–662, 670, 676, 682, 221, 532, 539; see also J. Reps, "Thomas Jefferson's Checkerboard Towns," *Journal of the Society of Architectural Historians*, XX (1961), pp. 108–114.

did find some expression in the organization of political parties. His impact on the party system deserves emphasis, but it is inaccurate to credit Jefferson with the "strategy of parties." Party, though necessary, was subordinate to the fraternal relations of all citizens. Jefferson abhorred any organization which, like the Order of the Cincinnati, seemed "self-created," exclusive, and desirous of withdrawing its members' affections from the civic brotherhood. If he praised Tammany, he did so because it was a vehicle for civic education; drawing men together out of their isolation into relations of affection, it expanded rather than contracted the sphere of civic fraternity.[28]

Jefferson was closer than many realize to the single-party theorists of the new nations today. The Democratic-Republican party, if it followed the ward scheme, did so because in one sense it was the state-in-becoming; establishing an internal fraternity, it extended its feelings to all Americans and aimed to bring them within the relations of fraternity as well. Without the general affection which Jefferson hoped to establish, party would only result in dangerous or disastrous division.

Jefferson was no formalist; he did not consider political institutions a sufficient condition of public benefits. His hopes for civic fraternity were intimately tied to conditions in the whole environment of politics, the domestic economy, and the international order. There should be reasonable economic security so that individual citizens need not fear or suspect their fellows; there should be none of the massive inequality and hierarchy in economic life which could lead to a re-emergence of feudalism though in different guise; towns and cities should remain of a size to enable personal feelings of involvement and affection. It was these general principles derived from his fraternal ideal, and not any irrational "mystique," that made Jefferson suspect industry and favor agriculture. Finally, there must be a comparative absence of external involvement and war, for Jefferson never doubted that such conditions would demand speed of decision, secrecy, and centralization; foreign policy, if it became perilous and vital, might reduce devices like the "ward" system to obstacles to national survival. And Jefferson, if he asked a nation like America for decency, did not expect nobility.

[28] *Writings*, vol. IX, pp. 180–209, 293–297.

The times were unkind. Eastern agriculture was in decline, partly because of competition from the Western lands and the dispossessed found their way to the cities and into new places in commerce and manufacture (though some, of course, "went West" as well). Jefferson had in any case given up his prescription that America "abandon" the ocean. Commerce was a part of the American heritage —unfortunate, but to be borne because of the unique virtues of that heritage itself. If commerce implied an important role for diplomacy, Jefferson hoped that international life would at least continue to become more moral, more guided by law, less prone to war. Yet it became clear to him that the "republic" of European diplomacy which Gibbon had hailed had yielded to "Machiavellian" statecraft. The devices of his "new diplomacy," like the embargo, died stillborn.

Jefferson was a statesman, not a doctrinaire. New times, though disappointing, required new measures (like a hesitant approval for manufacture). His argument rested with the proposition that changes be made with the reticence that must bow to necessity, that the inevitable compromises at least seek the closest approximation of the ideal.[29]

Even so, part of the blame falls on Jefferson himself. He did not, as Henry Adams was to point out, seem to perceive how much the purchase of Louisiana would change the Union—not only by opening the West, but by making the new states the creations not of local affections but of federal policy.[30] Yet Adams' comments were part of a "case" of his own. More important, Jefferson does not seem to have considered that economic security and equality might demand more of government than measures against "speculation," and might require positive action to defend "productive labor."

However conservative his political morality, the sense of possibility is a dominant theme in all of Jefferson's thought. That sense built into his theory and measures an aversion to the establishment of limits to thought or action. This was praiseworthy when it led him to oppose restraints of human thought and imagination, but this opposition resulted from a sense of the limits of human wisdom as well as from the benefits of freedom. Applied to economic life and action,

[29] *Letters and Selected Works*, pp. 285, 443, 533, 615–616, 621, 626, 654, 657–658, 673–674.

[30] Henry Adams, *History of the United States*, vol. II, pp. 77–115.

or even to politics, the results of this preference for openness were far from uniformly beneficial. Though Jefferson knew better, he came close to the belief that if "artificial" restraint is swept away, the moral nature of man will "emerge"; willing to destroy the restraints of religious orthodoxy (whose teachings he valued), he was unwilling to restrain the passion for economic gain and innovation which he found in American "habits."

Also, although Jefferson's plans represented creative efforts at synthesis, he did not and knew he could not completely resolve the tension between the intense local and diffuse national sentiments of fraternity. Feeling the second to be more exalted, he regarded the first as indispensable, an ambiguity which allows partisans of centralization and states' rights to war over his memory. There was, however, one means to unite the local polity and the Enlightenment dream of the great state in an affectionate whole, though it was a means Jefferson abhorred: hostility toward the foreign, unity forged from abstraction into feeling by the greater difference of the alien, fear and suspicion muffled by the menace of war. Mr. Madison's War and Manifest Destiny—like Unionism and Secessionism—were descendants of that unresolved dilemma.

Finally, Jefferson was misled in part by his sense of the possibilities of America. Led by his theory to stress sentiment, he was moved to greater emphasis by his belief that Americans were united in principle though estranged in affection. Affection became, consequently, almost a self-sufficient good; distinctions of policy were regarded as secondary and unimportant. This uniform caress of affection neglected the possibility that the original assumption might be wrong. The theories of traditional religion and of the Enlightenment were not easily compatible; the tortuous effort of Jefferson's theory to combine local fraternity as a means and universal fraternity as at least part of the end of human endeavor suggests how difficult any synthesis is. Jefferson, in fact, refusing to recognize differences of principle because on the whole they lay within and not among individuals, tended to a policy which buried differences by appeals to sentiment, but which could not hope to resolve them.

Jefferson in the end saw the tide of disunion as national "suicide" and "treason" to the "hopes of the world," produced by the "unwise and unworthy passions" of the sons of the Constitutional generation. The slavery issue, however, could not be resolved: "We have the wolf by the ears, and can neither hold him, nor safely let him go." [31] Jefferson's implication was that the issue should be avoided, that America should agree to overlook that vital difference of principle in a renewed affection (overcoming, notably, "unwise and unworthy passions," not unwise principles). Yet that hope, however despairing, made the symbol of the "fraternity" of Americans a tawdry thing, a cloud of sentiment which would obscure injustice to a race. It was a sad ending for Jefferson's attempt to resolve the two traditions of America, for it bespoke a surrender of principle to affection; and fraternity—for Jefferson—seemed closer to the reverse. As a portent, it revealed the degree to which the Jeffersonian unity, avoiding conflicts of principle, lost the guidance of principle and yielded slowly to the forces of drift.

[31] *Letters and Selected Works,* pp. 698–699.

> ... (W)hile man takes delight in this honest
> and lawful pursuit of his well-being, it is to
> be apprehended that he may in the end lose
> the use of his sublimest faculties; while he is
> busied in improving all around him, he may
> at length degrade himself. ... (A)ll who feel
> an interest in the future destinies of democratic
> society ... should make joint and continual
> efforts to diffuse the love of the infinite, a
> sense of greatness, the love of pleasures not of
> the earth.
>
> De Tocqueville, *Democracy in America*

CHAPTER X

THE DIVIDED HOUSE

Excelsior

JOHN W. BURGESS called the years from 1817 to 1858 the "middle period" of American history, meaning that those years balanced uneasily between the old Republic and the new.[1] His was a truer image than that which sees the "age of Jackson" as a time of expansive confidence and radiant optimism, for the very passion of the optimists of those years bespeaks a doubt and a desperation, and confidence is more often than not only the visible sign of uncertainty.

The brightest writing of the time is rarely without its moments of shadow; in some men, that cloud became a permanent pall, a feeling that old virtues were passing and new vices succeeding. Even Zebulon Pike allowed himself a Winthrop-like reflection, seeing the

[1] John W. Burgess, *The Middle Period, 1817–1858* (New York: Scribner's, 1902).

Western prairie as a desert which would help to limit a people excessively "prone to rambling." [2] And at the end of the era, Longfellow left his youth who had borne the banner of aspiration frozen in a gray twilight.

Hope and anxiety reflected a sense that a fundamental change was occurring in the life of America after 1815—if not a change, as Henry Adams would see it later, in the life of man. In one sense, the change was small: America remained an agricultural country; though manufacture grew steadily, the percentage of the population engaged in agriculture remained virtually constant between 1818 and 1840, falling only from 81 percent to 79 percent. The great transformations of the time were wrought by a revolution in communication and transportation. Railroad mileage increased a hundredfold between 1820 and 1840 and doubled every five years until the war; travel between Pittsburgh and Philadelphia which had required 144 hours in 1812, took 91 hours in 1834 and 13 in 1854. Newspaper readership underwent a similar expansion and the telegraph—which so disturbed Thoreau—spread over the land.

Subsistence farming declined rapidly in favor of an agriculture linked to national and international markets. Once a land of semi-sufficient localities, America was becoming part of a new, inter-dependent economic order. The old ethics, based on the personal relations of men in small communities, squared badly with a market become radically impersonal. Mobility in space and society destabilized the relations between men who knew each other, and bound their fortunes to other men they knew not at all. "Slowly," Arthur Schlesinger writes, "private morality and business morality grew apart. Slowly the commercial community developed . . . devices and ceremonials which enabled businessmen to set aside the ethics which ruled their private life [sic] and relations." [3]

Even that understates the case—first, because the "personal relations" of men were affected by and indistinct from their business connections; second, because the condition affected more than businessmen. It touched the whole country. Charles Dickens noticed in

[2] Elliot Coues, *The Expeditions of Zebulon Pike* (New York: Harper, 1895), vol. II, p. 525.

[3] Arthur Schlesinger, Jr., *The Age of Jackson*, pp. 334–335.

America a spirit of "universal distrust" in which "smart" dealing was valued as proof of a shrewd ability to "take care of oneself." [4]

It was a disturbing time because the old morality had not disappeared, even though it might be banished temporarily to "private" life and "personal" affairs; the requirements of economic and political success clashed with the rooted precepts of religion. Jefferson might reluctantly recant his opposition to manufacture; others saw the new age with horror. A Massachusetts legislature would shudder at corporations: "artificial creatures . . . not chastened and restrained . . . by human sympathy or direct personal responsibility. . . ." [5] Mass and market were seemingly producing a satanically distorted "fraternity": at best an impersonal fiction; at worst, personal relations which debased men.

Prosperity, as De Tocqueville realized, did not decrease the uneasiness of Americans. In one sense, he observed, restlessness rose from materialism itself.

> He who has set his heart exclusively on the pursuit of worldly welfare is always in a hurry, for he has but a limited time at his disposal. . . . The recollection of the brevity of life is a constant spur to him. . . . This thought fills him with anxiety, fear and regret and keeps his mind in ceaseless trepidation which leads him perpetually to change his plans and his abode. [6]

In another sense, however, prosperity increased anxiety simply because it was associated with success in the "amoral" world of the economy; affluence was only too likely to convict a man in the eyes of his less fortunate fellows, and but little less likely to convict him in his own. The seductions of well-being might be enough to pacify both discontents, but panic or depression could catalyze them into expression. The fantastic variety of religious and political movements which followed the economic crisis of 1836–37 was a mark of American uneasiness and of the desperate need to find at least a truce between public man and his private soul.

New England, always a comparatively commercial region, felt

---

[4] Charles Dickens, *American Notes* (New York: Fawcett, 1961), pp. 278–281.

[5] Schlesinger, *The Age of Jackson*, pp. 18, 335.

[6] *Democracy in America*, vol. II, p. 162.

the impact of mobilization most heavily, as the slow decline of her agriculture drew more and more of her citizens out of the farms and villages. Her influence was far more than regional: New England migrants made up a large proportion of the new inhabitants of New York, Oregon, California, and the Old Northwest. And New Englanders felt more sharply than others the moral crisis and the psychic tension of the times. The towns preserved much of the heritage and atmosphere of the Puritan polity and the old culture reigned with a powerful sway in the mind of man. Religion, Van Wyck Brooks noted, was the "romance" of New England:

> They named their children after the biblical heroes, and the Bible places . . . were stations on the map of their El Dorado. The congregations followed the web of the sermons with a keen and anxious watchfulness, eager to learn the terms of their damnation. And they talked about fate and freedom and how evil came, and what death is, and the life to come, as familiarly as they talked of their crops and the weather. . . . Blacksmiths and farriers, youths and maidens argued about free will and predestination, about "natural ability" and "moral ability" and "God's efficiency" and "man's agency". . . . The conscience of New England was precocious.[7]

Man, his virtues and his obligations, his role in community and polity, was still central in the life of the towns, and the displaced townsman could hardly be expected to live easily with the processes of the market or the impersonal cities.

Those who stayed behind were hardly immune. There had been a personal sense of obligation in the older wealthy classes. The Lowell factories, though never models of fraternity, had prided themselves on a charitable paternalism which at least softened the rigors of industrial life, and as late as 1853, a business leader like George Hilliard could tell the Massachusetts State Convention that "only by a constant recognition of . . . a common brotherhood" could property avoid dangers to itself, for only by that "moral element, flowing from Christianity and humanity," could a community escape the division and disorder that must follow when some grow richer and others poorer.[8]

---

[7] *The Flowering of New England*, p. 61; see also pp. 1–7, 58, 60–63, 220, 539–542.

[8] Commonwealth of Massachusetts, *Official Reports of Debates and Proceedings of the State Convention of 1853* (Boston, 1854), p. 131.

The market, however, especially in the straitened conditions of 1836, took its toll. Low-wage immigrant labor and child workers displaced former employees; affluence and a desire to escape personal responsibility led owners to migrate to the cities leaving factories in the hands of "efficient" managers (which had something to do with the fact that Harriet Beecher Stowe made Simon Legree a Vermonter). Increasing competition from the national market forced agricultural prices down, put pressure on local merchants, deprived crafts of local monopolies. The locality could no longer protect its own.

The old town democracy won De Tocqueville's admiration but, as he suspected, it was losing its hold. Cities were forced by expanding population and extended suffrage to abolish the town meeting, following the example set by Boston in 1822. More important, the local world was losing its importance to the individual; it could no longer play any critical role in determining the conditions of his life, and while participation in local affairs might be pleasant (though often a burden), it was losing its previous force as a shaper of individual personality. (The case was even worse in the Western cities, which lacked New England's inherited culture and institutions.) As localities became ineffective, the individual was left to his own devices in dealing with the nation at large.

New England had inherited an insulating culture which other sections lacked; what she could not do, they would find impossible. The case of New England suggests the unifying theme of the fantastically diverse movements of the Jacksonian era: driven by a need to unite the divided house of man, they sought a means by which private morals and public conduct could be harmonized. Behind the violent moods of the time, its millennial hopes and apocalyptic forebodings, lay the desire of men to discover some way to dignity and personal importance in the new world, some fraternity sufficient to enable man to be himself. The political and intellectual rumblings were a documentation of De Tocqueville's maxim: "The soul has wants which must be satisfied; and whatever pains are taken to divert it from itself, it grows weary, restless and disquieted amidst the enjoyments of sense." [9]

---

[9] *Democracy in America*, vol. II, p. 160.

Romance and Transcendence

The estrangement of the intellectuals from American politics, which struck the young Henry Adams after the Civil War, began, as the older Adams would realize, with the defeat of Quincy Adams, not with the election of Grant. The Jacksonians among the younger intellectuals kept up hope until the defeat of Van Buren; after 1840, disenchantment's chill spread steadily.

Not that the public was unreceptive to the work of artists and writers: with the spread of literacy, the United States developed an eager literary "class," driven to the arts by its own uneasiness and by status motives alike. The intellectual might be gratified; he was also disturbed. In the first place, the expansion of the "reading public" made him part of the vast apparatus of publishers, copyrights, and commercial considerations; literary livelihood was obtained at a cost in autonomy. Second, he discerned without difficulty that the eagerness of the public was in direct proportion to its lack of taste and critical judgment. Finally, he could not ignore the fact that his work had little effect on the lives of men caught up in an expanding commercial society. Art and the mind had become "other worldly"; there was in the mid-nineteenth century almost none of that sense of guidance and leadership which had informed intellectuals a century earlier.

Few American intellectuals developed the combination of vision and emotional strength which transforms estrangement into alienation. Most found fraternity impossible; living in an atmosphere of individual isolation, their emotions were denied expression under the combined constraints of individualism and pietism. Doctor Holmes' comment on New England's intellectuals applies generally; they were, Holmes said, a "great procession of the unloved," their affections hidden behind a wall of pretense. And those concealed emotions took possession, gradually, of the mind and spirit.[10]

The majority of American intellectuals were driven by a desire for admiration, an almost desperate craving to find a "place" in American life. De Tocqueville had realized that the equalitarianism

[10] Oliver Wendell Holmes, *Elsie Venner* (New York: Grosset and Dunlap, 1883), pp. 1–5.

of American society made it difficult for intellectuals to develop a
sense of identity and a corporate style distinct from society as a whole;
the literarian of democratic times, he commented, would be oriented
outward, toward the taste of the public, not inward toward his fellows.
And the literary nationalism of the period, the effort to create a
"homogenous national life" (Margaret Fuller's phrase), was little
more than the effort to define America in such terms that the intellectual would have a place in it.

The intellectual, of course, had deep doubts as to whether he
wanted a place in America as it was. Few were without some sense
that there was something unlovely and joyless in American life. Most
had considerable doubt about the formal American creed; eighteenth-
century rationalism, which had used the skeptical weapon against the
traditional ideas of the religious, was suffering from that impartially
destructive device, as historical analysis and utilitarianism combined
with disappointed hopes in an assault on "natural right." Doctor
Holmes, in his novel *Elsie Venner*, satirically portrayed a liberal
minister of the period, the Rev. Chauncy Fairweather, gradually
drifting into Roman Catholicism as he became progressively bored
by discourses on the abstract beauties of abstract virtue, obsessed with
a sense of sin and doubtful of the moral consequences of individual
freedom. There was a general tendency to sense something lacking in
the immediate relations of men, to become suspicious of institutional
as well as metaphysical rationalism, and to grow less hostile toward
the emotions, the "natural sentiments" of man.

Most intellectuals, however, remained well within the eighteenth-
century creed; they merely added to the old theory a new, spiritualized
rhetoric (or, more gently, a new formulation). The intellectual could
find a "place" in American life by assuaging the doubts of the literary
classes more easily than by challenging them. ". . . We forget," Perry
Miller comments, "against what a background of loud hosannas
Thoreau and Melville wrote." [11]

Curti sees the intellectual conflict of the age as lying between
"utilitarianism" and "romanticism," though of course few Americans
chose either extreme. [12] Both doctrines, notably, are definitively individualistic and anti-political, carrying individualism to new heights
in a world where the individual counted for less, substituting ideology

[11] Perry Miller, *The Life of the Mind in America*, p. 300.
[12] Merle Curti, *Growth of American Thought*, pp. 371-376.

for fact. Both, too, are naturalistic; and in America most of the votaries of both believed—if with a twinge of uncertainty—in progress and the conquest of nature. In fact, as Miller remarks, the most vaulting claims for a new sphere of the mind, an escape from older limits, were only "a notice served that the mind need no longer apologize for devoting itself to utility, that, in fact, such seeking for practical improvement was *the* true life of the mind." Between the two great schools of the time, Romanticism and Transcendentalism, there was considerable difference in the amount of attention directed to this world; yet as teachings and doctrines, both were very much of the world of the age.[13]

Of the two, Romanticism offered the simpler analysis of the malaise of American life. Man had lost contact with nature, had become entangled in a civilization which stood between him and his fellows and which denied him access to the roots of human genius and understanding in the intuitions. It provided a simple negation as cure: the remedy for gesellschaft is gemeinschaft. It rejected the grays of civil life, the artificialities of thought, in preference for the starker contrasts, risks, and adventures of "nature," where choice was made simple and the agonizings of reflection were unnecessary. Freed from the artificial, more than one Romantic proclaimed, man would be able to express his "natural" fraternity for his fellows.

In its most extreme forms, Romanticism argued for a flight from purpose and from thought alike, glorifying the direct expression of the feelings, identifying fraternity with a "simple and spontaneous" relation between simple and spontaneous men. Even at his most sanguine, however, the Romantic could not wholly ignore the dark possibilities which the Enlightenment had known lay in untamed nature. In some cases, like Charles Brockden Brown's, there was even the hint that the "darker passions" were themselves, perhaps, the only road to genuine communion.

Fenimore Cooper might make his Indians speak in classic cadences; he did not disguise the savagery of the frontier. He made no attempt to argue that the mere environment of America, freeing the white man from custom, would make him brother to the red. Rather, Cooper constructed a no-man's land, "neither East nor West," between the old barbaric and the new commercial societies, in which Natty Bumpo and Chingachgook—towers of virtue far above their

13 Miller, *Life of the Mind*, p. 311 and pp. 300-313 generally.

respective cultures—could find fraternity. There was more than a note of sadness in Cooper's novels as civilization pushed Natty farther and farther West and threatened to extinguish that utopia forever. Like most Americans, Cooper could not admire the savage in any simple sense: he admired a "noble" savage, the idyllic Indian or Polynesian who reappears in the literature of the period. In the same sense, Cooper admired, not the frontiersman per se, but the noble hunter—simpler, no doubt, but more constrained than civilized man. Cooper may have hoped to present his readers with a picture of "natural fraternity"; in fact, he drew a portrait of alienation, a suggestion that the noble man is always a wanderer and without a home.

Yet few American Romantics could accept alienation. Not many went even so far as advocating a return to rurality and agrarian simplicity; Americans might sacrifice the goods of an expanding economy in daydreams and fantasies, but not otherwise. They might yearn after release from restraint and purpose; but precisely because they were devoted to that Erotic ideal, they turned away from doctrines which suggested scarcity or the leisurely simplicity which might leave too much time in which to contemplate their own finitude and mortality.

Romantic theorists tended to prefer the cult of heroic action, the image of creative transformation of the world, cast in terms of the orthodox values of individualism and historical progress. Politically, Romanticism was mostly confined to a warm sentimentality with which, in a literary tour de force, the Romantic vested America, and to the no-less-agile rhetoric which endowed technology with all the qualities the Romantic valued. Perry Miller comments that

> Down to the crash of the Civil War the mind in America could happily interpret the railroad and the factory not as rejections of natural grandeur but as legitimate offsprings of its spontaneity. . . . For . . . George Bancroft the railroad proved that mechanics, science, Nature and genius could come together in a single triumph which, in its ultimate meaning, was a work of art. . . . In this philosophy, which dreamed of all things possible on earth if not in heaven, there was no remotest chance that things could mount the saddle and ride mankind, for man's conquest of the mountain was not a violation of Nature but an embrace.[14]

14 *Ibid.*, p. 306; George Bancroft, *History of the United States*, vol. II, p. 325.

Even in modified form, however, Romanticism departed far enough from traditional moral language to shock many Americans. Transcendentalism, with its rhetoric of spirituality, its hint of asceticism, its impeccably traditional private moral doctrines and—not the least—its acceptance of the political aims and ethics (though not the "science") of the eighteenth century, struck a more responsive chord.

Despite its talk of the spirit, however, Transcendentalism's metaphysics were entirely naturalistic. William Ellery Channing, who stood at the passage between Unitarian rationalism and the new doctrine, still felt it necessary to place God and the human spirit in a sphere separate from nature.[15] Transcendental theory, by contrast, saw nature as an encompassing whole, a "oneness" which included spirit and flesh alike. It did little more than "spiritualize matter"; it was in fact an ascetic Romanticism, erotic in content though abstract in form.

Transcendentalists doubted the rationalistic science of the previous century, but they kept the basic political norms of the liberal tradition, especially in the shape which Channing's reformulations had given those ideas. Drawing from eighteenth-century Deism, Channing had asserted that man possessed an "innate moral sense" which required human fraternity for its fulfillment.[16] The Transcendentalist merely broadened the "fraternity" to include the cosmos, and though he might speak of the "universal soul," he expected to find a microcosm of that soul in the individual. In fact, it might be better to state that he expected to find the cosmos a macrocosm of the individual soul. Doctrines of "cosmic fraternity" and of universal "oneness," the Romantic's dream of perfect brotherhood, served only to degrade and refute the claims of the imperfect fraternity that men might find in the world. Liberty, not fraternity, was the chief political prescription of Transcendentalism; its creed was epitomized by Emerson's comment that the moral basis of the new age must be the "sufficiency of the private man."[17]

If the seeds of universal morality and fraternity lay in the indi-

[15] Channing, *Works* (Boston: American Unitarian Assn., 1896), vol. II, pp. 31–36, 161, and *Unitarian Christianity and Other Essays* (Indianapolis: Bobbs-Merrill, 1957), pp. 3–38, 60–65.

[16] *Unitarian Christianity*, pp. 84–108, 118.

[17] Ralph Waldo Emerson, *Essays* (New York: Hurst, n.d.), vol. II, pp. 135–136.

vidual, they were often kept from germination by the weeds of physicality. Scarcity, force, and passion all combined to narrow the loyalties of the individual to the limited groups that satisfied his needs rather than the cosmic fraternity his moral instinct yearned after. The Enlightenment theorists in America had shared much of that analysis, but they had hoped to win man's allegiance away from narrow groups by appealing to the same interests that had brought those groups into being. It was a faith that endured among the ideologists of Whiggery, the Everetts, Websters, and Storys: interest, technological advance, "circulation of information," commerce, and exchange would, given time, create a fraternal spirit in the nation.[18] That faith Transcendentalism rejected: interest was base, leveling, destructive of spiritual excellence.

However, material progress did have redemptive possibilities for the Transcendentalist. He believed in history, seeing it as a drama in which man's spirit gradually prevailed over his fleshly weakness not through mortification but through the conquest of nature. Where he differed from the eighteenth-century doctrine was in denying that the amoral pursuit of interest could, through scientifically designed institutions, be transformed into the general good. The emergence of the moral instincts could not be thought of as an automatic by-product of something else, for they required an education of their own. To leave most men the unconscious instruments of process was too low a standard of morality, and though the Transcendentalist might accept Channing's notion that only great men see through the delusions of physicality to the reality of fraternity, he insisted that those great men could teach others.[19] He did not, however, reject the environment of individualism, competition, and technological advance; he only desired to add to it a new state of mind. Men should become conscious that they were playing parts in a universal drama; there was no need to change either the setting or the plot. Sometimes a Transcendentalist might concede that a changed environment might imperil a culture ("Mexico," Emerson wrote, "will swallow us"), but he was

[18] Miller, *Life of the Mind*, pp. 292, 298–300; Joseph Story, *Commentaries on the Constitution* (Boston: Little, Brown, 1872), vol. III, pp. 346, 455, 461–462, 477.

[19] Channing, *Works*, vol. II, pp. 7, 17, 29, 35; *Unitarian Christianity*, pp. 60–85, 109–120.

confident that "mental culture" and the "education of the spirit" were enough in themselves to change the life of the individual.[20]

In fact, the greatest Transcendentalist hostility toward "interest" was not directed at private individuals but at the political and especially at the concrete groups and limited loyalties which stood between the individual and the universal. Trade unions were likely to be called "artificial," and the leading Transcendentalists, Emerson in the van, scorned Brook Farm, sometimes with patronizing sympathy, as much for its "political" character as for its impracticality. Of all the less-than-universal groups, only the nation won Transcendentalist sympathy. Sometimes identified as an "innate" quality of the individuals who made it up, the nation was also often seen as a step above the petty groups of men, a link in the ladder which would lead to the universal. Organic nationalism found much in Transcendental writing to support its case.

Yet despite the intellectual influence of Transcendentalism, it developed little mass following; traditional religious men suspected it, common-sense men of affairs scorned its "effusions." Certainly, like Romanticism, if it had political effects they tended to be only an easing of the American's burden of doubt. Counseling men to "rise above" the perspective of the earth, it enabled men to live more easily within that compass. Its visions of a universal fraternity worked as the allies of a process which disregarded or assaulted the limited fraternities of men.

"Brothers will you meet me . . . ?"

For most Americans, the moral conflict of the middle period was fought between religion and the new order; "supernaturalism," in Gabriel's terms, contested with "naturalism" for supremacy.[21] The newly-mobilized brought with them a religious heritage to which they turned when they were baffled and disappointed by a society which was unfamiliar and powerful, full of wild prospects and unpredictable cruelties.

Doubt, of course, came easily. Material rewards were tempting; religious thought and belief were undermined by the sophisticated

---

[20] Emerson, *Essays*, vol. II, pp. 140–141.
[21] R. H. Gabriel, *The Course of American Democratic Thought*, p. 26.

doctrines of the times; the strange gods beckoned and attracted. If the fortresses of the old creed were breached, however, the Citadel remained for those who had been reared in it. The older moral ideas had their adherents even in good times, and when the cornucopia of prosperity ceased to flow and the confidence of the established leaders was shaken, those ideas became the basis of protest against the new order.

Elias Magoon spoke of Christianity as the "patron of the aspiring" and the "deliverer of the oppressed" with some reason.[22] To be sure, religious appeals by the excluded were often little more than a seizing of the weapon at hand, and Christianity as an implement of political warfare was a perversion of the teaching of the Nazarene which suggested that what the aspiring and oppressed resented about the commercial system was not its moral shortcomings but their exclusion from its benefits. Nonetheless, language and symbol are not without power; both played a role in shaping the content of programs and the personalities of those who appealed to them.

There was often a painful inarticulateness to protest. The newly mobilized only dimly recognized their discontents as political, and had little awareness of common involvement, especially since rural communities were tied not to each other but to lines of communications which ran to the urban centers. There was only a minimal understanding of the new social forces, and the passionately discontented and abysmally unsophisticated tended to see their own tensions and outrages as signs of the long-promised millennium. William Miller gathered his converts to prepare for the advent; others, inspired by visions of the world's end, joined the Shaker communities in which celibacy replaced the "sins of the flesh." Even in folly there can be wisdom: the Shakers at least appreciated the value of concrete community and knew that sexuality was a threat to it; there was something to be said for the goal if not for the Shaker route to it.

Religious protest, however, also found articulate leadership, sometimes among the established classes, sometimes among the newly-mobilized themselves. Rarely without some element of Enlightenment doctrine drawn from and mediated by the popular social science and political philosophy of the day, numberless movements addressed themselves to the task of reforming or transforming the American

[22] Elias Magoon, *Republican Christianity* (Boston: Gould, 1849).

polity. Few, even the most prudent, avoided setting forth their programs as panaceas, and the age is filled with the rival declarations of impassioned "true believers." Vegetarians and natural food cultists, pacifists, abolitionists, socialists, total abstainers, advocates of free love—they agreed about little except that America suffered from some malaise and must change her ways.

The key word of the time, however, was not utopia but revival. In one sense, it was a misleading word; often what the revival sought to "revive" had never existed, and there was newness even in the traditionalism of the revival. Its aim, as Perry Miller recognized, was not merely resisting the incursions of infidelity. Rather, it sought to create a national community, a fraternal polity that could give moral direction to the forces of the age.

> The steady burning of the Revival, sometimes smoldering, now blazing into flame, never quite extinguished until the Civil War . . . was a central mode of this culture's search for national identity. . . . After 1800, the vast literature in defense of the Revival is unabashedly communal. . . . The driving concern was that the ecstasies had to assure, not only the conviction of innumerable individuals, but the welfare of the young country. . . . It soon becomes evident, though seldom acknowledged, that anxiety over the future, not of the individual soul in heaven, but of this nation on earth, lies at the center of the movement.[23]

The revivalist could be sophisticated in his political analysis. The rise of prosperity released the spirit of speculation and the passion for gain; the size of the country and its growing population made it difficult for men to know or to feel community, and hence the country was beset by selfishness and sectionalism alike. Patriotism, a matter of feeling, could not unite citizens; it was too unreliable, too local. "Philosophy," the rational recognition of interdependence and obligation, was too cerebral. With that powerful set of negations, it is no surprise that the revivalist felt he had made his case: revived religion was needed to bind the country together. In fact, he still needed to demonstrate that evangelical religion could overcome the limitations of reason and feeling alike, and that task was to prove impossible.

Charles Grandison Finney's doctrine of "Christian Perfectionism" never sought to deny the fact of sin, and if Finney insisted on

[23] Miller, *Life of the Mind*, pp. 5–6, 11, 12, 21.

the ability of men to be saved it was because, more concerned than most with action, he sought to demand responsibility and right conduct from men. His teaching was in part a reinstitution of the doctrine that no Christian can be content with sinfulness or complacent in the face of evil, and that he must do his utmost to better the life of his fellows. Finney rejected the other-worldly sects as well as Unitarian rationalism, "alike concerned more with property than piety," and insisted on fraternal action as the relevant standard of Christian life.

Finney tended, however, to accept the definition of reason as no more than a "felicific calculus," and though it was not hard for him to make the point that merely intellectual knowledge, separated from the "heart," is not enough to make men virtuous, he went further, deprecating the intellect itself. His sermons and writings tended to suggest that not only is the mind inadequate alone, but that it is decisively inferior to the "heart."

Finney knew, of course, that the emotions are privatizing and tied to the physical self and its well-being. Consequently, it was necessary for him, as it had been for Edwards, to argue that the "heart" was separate from the "feelings," that it was a separate mode of knowledge. (The argument, of course, was made necessary by the democratic character of evangelism itself; high metaphysics and cold logic would not stir those audiences that Finney and his fellows sought to redeem.) Finney succeeded no better than Edwards had. His effort to convince resulted in the importation of individualistic and Romantic concepts into his teaching; "innate instincts" for morality and appeals for "true utility" played a major role in his teaching and that of his disciples. In any case, as the evangelist John Woodbridge was to realize, a union of men based on feeling alone, which all evangelism tended to produce, was mere "neutrality and insipidity." It hardly improved the case when the feelings were sublimated into "heart."

Finney himself is reasonably exempt from the charge. His disciples and converts were certainly leaders in the quest for social reform (as were those of other evangelists and sometimes the preachers themselves: Peter Cartwright, for example, once ran as a Jacksonian against Lincoln in a race for Congress), and if Finney's legions had a strong trace of self-righteousness, it was not because they were unified insipidly and without principle. Acquit the man: the ambiguity remains in the teaching. And Finney was a giant among the evangelists.

The revival was one of feeling, especially in the lonely West, which had little in the way of institutional religion; it was almost a Dionysian rite, suggesting the desperate desire for communion that may beset isolated men, the desire to be freed if only for a moment from suspicion of one's fellows, struggle, and hypermasculine pretense. Carl Sandburg knew the appeal:

> Beyond Indians there was something else; beyond the timber and the underbrush, the malaria, milk sick, blood, . . . hands hard and crooked as the roots of walnut trees, there must be something else.[24]

And not only "beyond": the revival produced a tantalizing moment here and now.

To be sure, the revival was more catharsis than redemption. Against the appeals of gain and the dream of progress, the church could not move the age. Moreover, churches took on the individualism of liberal ideology, revivalists spoke of theirs as a "voluntary principle" of association and even began to argue that the pursuit of wealth might be justified if a redeemed America used it to evangelize the world. Nevertheless, the high moments of revivalism brought men "very near the apocalyptic kingdom," rousing a sense of the possibility of renewal in social life which lingered when the moment passed. If it calmed many, the revival made others impatient with the state of the land. And it built a psychological barrier which prevented full identification with the ethics of materialistic individualism. De Tocqueville was sympathetic even with what he could only regard as "religious insanity":

> If their social condition . . . and their laws did not confine the minds of the Americans so closely to the pursuit of worldly welfare, it is probable that they would display more reserve . . . whenever their attention is turned to things immaterial. . . . But they feel imprisoned within bounds which they will apparently never be allowed to pass. As soon as they have passed these bounds, their minds know not where to fix themselves, and they often rush unrestrained beyond the range of common sense.[25]

The utopians were more "commonsensical" than the revivalists in that they knew the importance of social conditions. They rejected

[24] Carl Sandburg, *Abraham Lincoln* (New York: Harcourt Brace, 1954), p. 17.

[25] *Democracy in America*, vol. II, p. 160.

the Revivalist faith that America could be redeemed simply by a mental transformation, though they often shared the goals of the revival itself. The luxuriant variety of New Jerusalems grew out of the conviction that for men who found no support in daily life and relations, the demands of faith were too great. For the utopians, change demanded a "coming out," a withdrawal from American life which was not entirely flight; it was in large part an attempt to teach by example a lesson which could not be taught in the old home. New land, new men, the City on the Hill: the utopians were Puritans in that much. But they were Puritans without prudence in most cases, without sophistication in many; and most forgot, as the Puritans never did, that they took with them the Old Adam they sought to escape.

One utopia, at least, endured: the Church of Jesus Christ of Latter Day Saints. Mormonism's appeal was not founded on its theology, though its doctrines may have offered, by their very bizarreness, a sense of distinct identity. The great attraction of Mormonism lay in its institutions, in the firm discipline of community, common property, and the duty to assist one's brethren. Yet Mormonism did not establish fraternity: it was built on an individualistic premise, the struggle to combine isolated and fearfully assertive men under the iron rule of gemeinschaft.

When Bernard de Voto compared Mormonism to the Puritan covenant, he misconstrued both. Mormonism was not based on a covenant between brothers; rather, it was an organization held together by the subordination of discrete individuals to the autocratic power of the "prophets." After the death of Brigham Young, in fact, even Mormon sources called attention to the rise of individualism and the concern for economic gain. Prosperity and success seemed, more and more, the chief supports of unity. (Congress, in the Edmunds–Tucker Act of 1887, individualized property holdings, apparently hoping to break up the church as well as to make things more consonant with the doctrines of laissez-faire; that the church survived is a mark of the degree to which it had become an institution and an indication of the fact that common property was not the sole basis of Mormon community).

More sophisticated movements were little better in theory and far less successful in practice. Many of the Utopians accepted an essential principle of eighteenth-century political science: the belief that political problems are best solved by technology and not education. New Harmony and the "phalansteries" of Brisbane's dutiful Fourierism, for example, were both confident of the sufficiency of their "scientific" institutions in shaping men, however men had developed before. They paid little attention to the skills of recruits; their concern for values was limited, at most, to a professed faith in the doctrines on which the communities were based. In addition, both ideologies made an ideal of personal relations as such. The onset of the Romantic agony of jealousy and suspicion was inevitable even among the most devoted, and all too many were devoted in word only, and that only for a time. Efforts to impose control followed, and control was at odds with the individualistic equalitarianism of the creeds, let alone the self-concern that moved the lukewarm. Schism, defeat, the collapse of the ideal: these are the normal patterns of the utopian communities of the time.

Brook Farm was probably the most influential of the communities; it was also perhaps the most distinctly American. Its doctrines were a mixture of Christianity, Channing's Unitarianism, and Emersonianism. In one sense, Brook Farm represented an advance on Transcendentalism, suggesting that fraternal social relations as it understood them were necessary for individual perfection. Yet it was always, in theory and practice, fiercely individualistic. The experiment, its founders promised, would reveal the "benign effects of liberty," for its "common faith" was the "universal man" with "no law over his liberty."

As Hawthorne was to comment, the Brook Farmers had little in common beside their hostility to the surrounding society. Like the "Socialist" experiments, Brook Farm aimed at a perfect community, a unity of sentiment and belief that would eliminate all conflict and hence would make solidarity compatible with individualism. None of the Brook Farmers seemed prepared to tolerate a check to his will or abide by group decision. The Constitution of Brook Farm provided that "love, purity and justice" should be its regulating norms but the members were responsible only for their overt acts; the community claimed no concern with opinions or "private" character. Even within the public sphere, the trustees were forbidden to make contracts which made the shareholders "individually or personally responsible" without their express consent.

Brook Farm's unity depended on the will and ability of the residents to ignore the more obvious imperfections of their "fraternity" or to paper them over with sentiment. For example, given the conflict between physicality and both the dream of perfect communion and the belief in a "transcendent self" or "universal man," it is no surprise that Brook Farmers had the usual Transcendental hostility to sensuality. As in many other utopias, the effort to maintain unity on the basis of illusion and repression was destined to fail at Brook Farm. It does the original doctrine too much credit to blame the demise of the experiment on the subsequent Fourierist takeover, for that coup itself is a demonstration of the schism and disharmony that were already at work.

If the utopian communities had a creative political thinker, it was John Humphrey Noyes, who recognized the roots of failure in the individualism of the utopians, itself based on their refusal to recognize imperfection in man and his creations. Man had divinity, Noyes argued, but he was not divine, and his bond with his fellows lay in a common ideal beyond the separate selves of men. "Wisdom and spiritual power" were the goals he set at Oneida, and fraternity was to be a means and not an end.

Too, Noyes was well aware that even where property is common, the emotions would be a source of tension. Rivalry for affection or sexuality (which Hawthorne's picture suggests was rife at Brook Farm) were the most powerful and enduring sources of division among men, and the sexual prudery of most utopians denied physical outlets to self-referential emotions, making them only more powerful in the psyche of the individual. Noyes knew, moreover, that "free love" is perhaps the most inequitable of all standards; it tends to follow the lines of physical attractiveness, which itself has no relation to merit. Hence Noyes insisted on a "dutiful promiscuity" in which choice of sexual partner would be eliminated and each would be linked to all. The requirement was designed to eliminate sexual rivalry while permitting sexuality, hopefully eliminating the emotional frustrations which might impede the spirit's quest for wisdom and, at the same time, strengthening the fraternal support available to the individual.

The paths of the emotions are devious, and despite the sophistication of Noyes' scheme, it is likely that the claims he made for it were excessive. However, unlike its rivals, Oneida maintained a record of solidarity if not fraternity and in practical terms was a model of success. Too much so, in fact: the prosperity of Oneida combined with its deviance made state intervention to break up the community inevitable. That Oneida perished only because of external intervention gives some verisimilitude to Noyes' ideas. But it is very doubtful if Oneida was more than a radical's Mormonism: it depended on the autocratic personality of Noyes himself, and the basic relationship in Oneida was the tie between citizen and leader, not citizens with their fellows. Even so, Oneida remains a tantalizing question in the annals of utopianism, a might-have-become which rouses curiosity if not imitation.

Utopia and revival, the gentle school of example and the fierce assault on the spirit, were both demands for fraternity. Both, too, were movements partly founded in despair, differing only in their estimate of how corrupt the country had become; the fact was never in doubt. And as the converts lapsed and the Arcadias died, the despair flourished. "Brothers," the old camp-meeting song asked, "will you meet me over on the other shore?" That hazy other shore was vital because it came to seem less likely that a man would meet his brothers on this side. Even that other shore was receding: the religious wisdom and morality which underlay so much of the thought and passion of the utopians and the revivalists was already running thin, being diluted by the waters of more modern doctrine. In the atmosphere of defeat, many became paralyzed; others simply learned to lower their standards, contenting themselves with the achievable political gains which might at least comfort men while the clouds gathered.

Old Romans, New Liberals

In politics, it was the age of Jackson and the Whigs alike, a time of unfamiliar faces and new ways. The mobilization of new masses created pressures for the "democratization of society," the need for a new political identity for citizens drawn into a larger world. Under that pressure, and the even more relentless pressure of age, the "Constitutional Generation," guardian of the uneasy synthesis between religious morality and Enlightenment theory since 1787, disappeared from the seats of power.

Its place was taken by men who lacked the older grace and balance, new men whose presence reflected and helped to shatter the old alignments. Whiggery was not the "rich, good and wise" of Hamiltonian rhetoric; it spoke for a new commercial elite, increasingly unabashed in advocating the unrestrained ethics of the market. Many old Federalists were horrified at the new "vulgarity" and as conservative a man as Fenimore Cooper felt a disgust so deep that he could only portray the new elites as characters in a rustic comedy. Jacksonians attacked Jefferson for being more democratic in theory than in practice (they were more violent with Jefferson's "federalized" successors) and yearned to sweep away the old compromises with republican purity.

The politics of the period were complex. Writers like Lee Benson and Thomas Flinn have destroyed the old assumption that the Jacksonians alone represented the lower classes or the newly-mobilized, and party alignments were always complicated by the politics of region and section. (The newly mobilized American had a limited perspective, after all, and the sections corresponded to important differences in economics and culture.)[26]

Jackson had support from the political elites of New York and Virginia, and he was himself a member of an elite faction in Tennessee. In the first two cases, however, support for the General seems to have resulted from a desire to avoid defeat rather than from a passionate zeal for his cause, and while the New York party became progressively Jacksonian and democratic, the Virginia "Junto" refused to support Van Buren and engaged in erratic alliances with the Whigs. In Tennessee, as in Kentucky, Jackson's policies gradually cost him elite support, and both states tended toward the opposition in later years. The core of Jacksonianism was composed of an "anti-elite" of editors and professionals hostile to the mercantile leaders, who appealed to the immigrants, the dispersed and disorganized, and to important elements among the increasingly assertive craftsmen. Jacksonian support was strong, for example, among the new, unstable white populations of Alabama and Mississippi. As late as 1851, a "straight out" Jacksonian Unionist defeated Jefferson Davis in a race for the governorship of Mississippi. In more stable South Carolina, if

[26] Lee Benson, *The Concept of Jacksonian Democracy*, and Thomas A. Flinn, "Continuity and Change in Ohio Politics," *JP*, XXIV (1962), pp. 521–544.

Jackson's name remained a household word, the word itself was probably unprintable.

Jackson's opponents were strong among those who retained some viable social organization, some sense of tie to inherited loyalties, institutions, and symbols. The Whigs, for example, won the allegiance of the New England settlements in the Western Reserve of Ohio and in Northeast Illinois, of much of Ohio's Virginia Military District, and of the Louisiana Creoles. Jackson's party appealed to the more nakedly exposed, those who confronted the times with no sense of "place" in America. It drew the immigrants; equally, it won intellectuals of varying degrees of alienation and quite various political persuasion, like Hawthorne, Cooper, Bancroft, Whitman, and Melville. It spoke to the excluded in established communities, to those who were isolated and lacked communities, to those who turned to older values as a weapon for winning a place in America, and to those who, because of devotion to those values, sought to make a new America.

Jacksonianism was, as Marvin Meyers calls it, a "persuasion," a set of attitudes united by little save discontent with the existing state of things. It was a major element of Jackson's strength in 1824 that his position on the issues was largely unknown; men who shared only common objects of hostility could rally to the hero, sure at least that he would battle the foe.

To this extent there is truth in the old view that saw Jacksonianism as a "Western" movement. A distortion in any empirical sense, that interpretation did touch the fact that the West was the uninsulated region, possessing no established community, more sharply revelatory of the economic and social forces of the time. And in the sheer lack of an inherited set of institutions, the mental set of the Westerner was likely to resemble that of those isolated and excluded men who followed Jackson himself.

The West was individualistic, but man depended desperately on man. Individualism grew out of institutional weakness, the fact that customary and legal restraints were thin if not absent. Men were necessarily suspicious in neighborhoods which were little more than accidental gatherings, ever on guard against insult and injury, equalitarian out of touchiness more than love. Yet the combination of the need for cooperation and the insecurity of social relations produced an ethic suited to the situation: the doctrine of rigorous personal loyalty.

Democracy in politics meant, too, the rule of the "public" in ways less qualified by individual "rights" than a Jeffersonian would have allowed. If men took the law into their own hands, it betokened less a lust for liberty than a passion to end it, a desire to establish a "wholesome" order even at the cost of individual freedoms. (It was this sort of attitude, of course, that struck at local and state's rights when the Jacksonians gained national power, despite their nominal ideology.)

Fraternity in the West, as in the Jacksonian party, was the by-product of battle; combat required from men sentiment and trust. The enemy, feared more than one feared his fellows, was necessary to cement any relationship. (The Western view of Easterners as sharp dealers, speculators, and immoral men was a fair picture of what Westerners feared in their fellows and themselves.) It was no accident that Western politics so often centered around meetings of the militia where men found an opportunity for friendship under the nominal shadow of danger and the memory of old struggles. Still less was it by chance that Josiah Quincy could see in General Jackson a "knightly" character.[27]

Jackson was a symbol for the movement to which he gave his name because he was in fact the "Old Roman," a man of intense private virtues and personal honor, inclined to place his trust in men rather than institutions or abstractions—jealously ready, however, to scent betrayal. The stern code by which he lived concealed the religious morals that were never far below the surface and were revealed in the paradoxical tenderness he showed to individual Indians who had survived his victories or in his private comments that the wars with the Indian were a violation of "humanity." Sometimes the code actually excused humanitarianism; Jackson defied local opinion in New Orleans by allowing "free men of color" to enlist and fight in his army. And if only from deference to Lafayette, he supported Frances Wright's attempt to create a school for freedmen.

Certainly the image of military fraternity gave Jacksonianism much of its language of imperialism. (Jackson himself was hesitant, fearing that expansion would endanger the Union.) More importantly, it shaped the Democratic party. Raising the value of personal loyalty, intensifying party competition, the image of military fraternity

---

[27] Marquis James, *Andrew Jackson: Portrait of a President*, p. 348.

helped justify the Spoils System which, more than being a way of eliminating the "superannuated" or establishing "democratic participation," was a system which associated (or identified) "merit" with personal loyalty and friendship. This was certainly the root of the otherwise curious confidence and fondness which grew up between Jackson and the urbane and cosmopolitan Van Buren, and between Jackson and the New York Democracy, with its already doubtful standards of rectitude. "If I were a politician," Jackson declared, "I would be a New York politician." Seeing something a bit amoral and shifty in the political vocation, the General thought that New York Democrats had made their profession more acceptable by insisting on loyalty to comrades in arms.[28]

Recent critics, concerned to debunk the notion of Jackson as the "precursor" of modern liberalism, have stressed his economic conservatism. They have a good case: Jackson's formal political beliefs were often Jeffersonian, individualistic, reflecting Enlightenment liberal ideas of man and the state. The critics, however, neglect two important considerations. First, the iron traditionalism of Jackson's code put him at odds with the new commercialism; he detested "artificial wants" and despised the disloyalty of businessmen toward their fellows. Second, he was devoted to the Union, and he hoped for a fraternal citizenry united by public virtue. This was always his talisman in morality. Admiring Jefferson, he thought the Virginian too unwilling to carry democracy into practice, too pusillanimous to sufficiently assert the rights of the citizen against foreigners. Even Jackson's opposition to "internal improvements" was more ambiguous than many believe it to be. He supported those improvements he thought likely to cement the Union, drawing surplus labor from the land and providing a market for agricultural produce. He opposed "local" projects which he believed were designed to benefit only "special interests" or likely to contribute to inflation. And though he retained the old moral opposition to slavery, he regretted the Missouri Compromise as tending to divide citizens who ought to be brothers.

Jackson was certainly no modern liberal. He was, as Meyers argues, a traditionalist who saw himself as the guardian of civic rectitude. His opposition to the Bank (partly influenced by the fact that the Bank had been against his election) was moral, not economic.

28 Woodrow Wilson, *Division and Reunion*, p. 32.

"Perish commerce," he wrote, rather than allow the "tyranny of an irresponsible corporation." Stewardship was a part of his theory; the people must be protected against their baser instincts which made them willing victims of the Bank and the "monied capitalists" who sought the "corruption of human nature," man's submission to materialism and self-concern.[29]

In contrast to the ideas of his more radical supporters like the Locofocos, Jackson's economic ideas often seem archaic. That doubtless only commended them more to a public hardly advanced in its understanding of modern economies. Jackson was in fact a political revivalist, one who attempted to unite public life and private morals by imposing the latter on the former; and his belief in the possibility of a fraternal Union was the political analogue of the evangelist's belief in the powers of the "heart"—with all the defects of that belief.

Jackson and his party did represent a protest against the working of the commercial system and the character of nascent industrialism, but one which was deeply ambiguous. In the simplest sense, the Democrats were obliged as a political party to offer the promise of material gain if they hoped for success. Moreover, Jacksonians tended to see nature, in America certainly, as abundant, and while this enabled them to see poverty as the result of exploitation, it also combined with a laissez-faire tendency which led them to see government as the chief promoter of exploitation. Eliminate "special privilege," allow the "voluntary principle" to work (especially in the "free chartering" of corporations), trust "human nature," and abundance and fraternity would result of themselves.

Walt Whitman recorded that creed:

In this wide naturally rich country, the best government indeed is "that which governs least." One point . . . ought to be put before the eyes of the people every day; and that is, although government can do little positive good to the people, it may do an immense deal of harm. . . . Why we wouldn't give a snap for the aid of the legislature in forwarding a purely moral revolution! It must spread from its own beauty and melt into the hearts of men, not be forced upon them. . . .[30]

Even Orestes Brownson, who could be so eloquent in arguing that without social and economic equality political democracy was

---

[29] Marvin Meyers, *The Jacksonian Persuasion*, pp. 16–32.
[30] *Social Theories of Jacksonian Democracy*, ed. J. Blau, pp. 131–133.

pointless, who demanded that man be made supreme over property, offered only the prescriptions of destroying the priesthood, so that the "original" spirit of Christianity could emerge, and repealing inequitable laws. (To do him credit, Brownson included the law of inheritance among these.) "Its first doing must be an undoing. There has been thus far quite too much government. . . ." [31]

Even in such arguments, the Jacksonian intellectuals proclaimed the need for a "moral revolution" to make human character and relations dominant over things in American life. But they were too well trained in liberal theory, too wedded to the times and the dream of progress; their therapy, militant individualism, was often worse than the disease. Eventually, many lost their faith in the untaught conscience of man; Brownson turned to Catholicism for an answer. Others became more strident in their hope for the future, making history the repository of deferred visions, values which the present denied.

George Bancroft was their poet, a historian who could speak persuasively to Americans because he felt all the same tensions of spirit. Bancroft's father, though "liberal" in attitude, remained a Calvinist, and Bancroft always avowed himself a Trinitarian Christian. Inevitably, though, Bancroft's education was shaped by the academically-dominant rationalism of the eighteenth century, and he sought the resolution of heritage and education with the assistance of Jonathan Edwards—who had confronted the dilemma so long before—and of the early Romantic and late Enlightenment thinkers like Herder and Schleiermacher whom he encountered at Göttingen.

Bancroft was too liberal to believe in the inevitability of sin, but he conceded in practice much of what he rebelled against in theory. All men sinned; their lapses were errors of judgment resulting from the conflict between man's "limited nature" and the "better life of which he conceives." Man lived happily and well only if he could "conform the passions of the human breast to the conditions of human existence" and to the Divine Will. These, despite Bancroft's quarrels with the old language, are deeply traditional ideas, and they are the basis for Bancroft's too-little-remembered critique of Romanticism. [32]

---

[31] Orestes Brownson, "The Laboring Classes," *Boston Quarterly Review,* III (1840), pp. 358–395.

[32] George Bancroft, *Literary and Historical Miscellanies,* pp. 44–102.

The Romantic, Bancroft argued, errs in his excessive individualism, from which derive his tendencies to enthusiasm and sensuality, his taste for the sensational as a means of gaining attention, and his lack of self-control. Ignoring the dependence of the artist on the political order, which he needs to develop his gifts and provide him with some sort of audience, the Romantic lacks a due sense of political obligation. Romantic posturing, Bancroft concluded, deludes the artist and may poison the polity upon which art depends.

Bancroft himself, however, was not entirely free from such faults. Aware of the effects of environment, custom, and "national genius" in shaping men, he never conceded that these factors might have a creative impact on man. God, he contended, is a "creative spirit indwelling in man"; man is born with all the requirements of moral excellence. Hence Bancroft's view of the human race as a "whole," a single fraternity: the universal elements of human nature contained all that was humanly valuable.[33]

Excellence derived from the proper use of intuitive "reason," which gave men the capacity for moral decision and self-government. In the heights of enthusiasm, Bancroft's language became Romantic in the extreme. Patrick Henry was a "child of the forest"; Andrew Jackson was the "nursling of the wilds . . . pupil of the wilderness," free to imbibe "first principles" and "natural dialectics" unencumbered by science or tradition.

Bancroft was, however, no partisan of "natural man." While his individualism did not blind him to the effects of culture and rearing on men, it led him to assign some of them, at least, to heredity. Despite his belief in human fraternity, Bancroft thought that the Indian might be prevented from using the moral powers God had given him by some peculiar genetic defect, and despite his anti-slavery convictions he regarded Negroes as inferior. Beyond heredity, too, Bancroft's view of sin demanded that he distrust the judgment of individuals in a way which limited his admiration for spontaneity.

Not the individual, but the public, became Bancroft's high court of moral appeal. Men might err, especially in their own cases, but since

[33] Ibid., pp. 103–247; Russel Nye, George Bancroft, pp. 65–66, 113–115, 128. See also Bancroft's review, "Van Dohm's Memoirs," North American Review, XXVI (1828), pp. 285–316.

all men possessed identical moral intuition, the safest tribunal was the "combined intelligence" of the people.

> . . . true political science does venerate the masses. Individuals are of limited sagacity; the common mind is infinite in its experience. Individuals are languid and blind; the many are ever wakeful. Individuals are corrupt; the race has been redeemed. Individuals are time serving; the masses are fearless. . . . The decrees of the universal conscience are the nearest approach to the presence of God in the soul of man.

Bancroft never feared the logic of his argument. The artist, he declared, should not only recognize his responsibility to society but should regard society as the arbiter of excellence, "the highest possible authority on earth." Even the creative hero, in Bancroft's view, did no more than perceive the ideas inherent in his people and his time.[34]

True, Bancroft admitted, the people can err, but such mistakes cannot persist historically. Momentarily, the public may yield to the emotions of man's "limited nature"; ultimately, moral conscience will prevail. In part this is because the people learn from error, but that limited foundation was too uncertain for Bancroft. God, he asserted, governs history, and Providence works "not merely in the distant heavens but here among men."

> The movement of the species is upward, irresistibly upward. The individual is often lost; Providence never disowns the race. . . . No truth can perish, no truth can pass away. The flame is undying though generations disappear. . . . Each generation gathers together the imperishable children of the past and increases them by new sons of light, alike radiant with immortality.[35]

The march of history was the advance of liberty, the freeing of man's inherent powers. Bancroft was well aware that much in American history was unique, and as a nationalist he valued that aspect of American life. He combined universal and particular by the simple expedient of regarding the American heritage as uniquely libertarian: what is specifically American is freedom from the diversities of custom and culture that draw other nations away from the "universal conscience."

[34] Bancroft, *Literary and Historical Miscellanies*, pp. 408–435, 444–480, and *History of the United States*, vol. I, p. 177.

[35] *Social Theories of Jacksonian Democracy*, ed. J. Blau, pp. 272–273.

Bancroft was accurate when he drew attention to the lack of feudalism in America, but facts did not always deter him. In a magnificently illustrative pair of distortions, Bancroft revealed both the passion of his faith and the defect of his thought: first, he professed to find Calvinism a doctrine characterized more than Lutheranism by "freedom" and the willingness to appeal to individual decisions; second, he managed to convince himself that slavery was a European imposition which Americans had always disliked.

America, then, did not represent a distinct national culture but was rather the vanguard of a history which would eventuate in human fraternity. "The heart has its oracles not less than the reason," Bancroft wrote, and the "good time is coming when the spirit of humanity will recognize all members of its family, when man will dwell with man as his brother."

His faith in history made it unnecessary for Bancroft to depart from eighteenth-century political theory. There were times when he suggested the need for a more immediate fraternity; defending Jackson's bank veto, he declared that the claims of Want are as legitimate as those of Have. But he went no further than the characteristic Jacksonian prescription of removing privilege and monopoly from the books of law. The Constitution was a triumph of historical providence, based on the truth that government exists to maximize individual freedom and must be limited to specific purposes. A nationalist who could refer to the need to balance the "organic unity" of society against the claims of individual liberty, Bancroft meant by "organic" no more than a Newtonian metaphor. Moving atoms, he pointed out, each free of the other, create an attraction and repulsion that constitutes "the whole," and this entity is a matter of "balance" and adjustment.[36]

Bancroft saw appalling things around him: greed, materialism, egoism, indifference. His historical creed, however, enabled him to regard those things less as by-products of the new society than as things which would pass away. Technological advance was almost poetry to Bancroft; he was loud among the hosanna-singers noted by Perry Miller. History offered an ultimate reconciliation, a means of drawing together the old faith and the liberal creed, a method of

---

[36] For Bancroft's ideas of history, see his *History of the United States,* vol. I, pp. 159, 175, 190, vol. II, p. 451, vol. III, p. 408; and Nye, *George Bancroft,* pp. 87, 93–94, 130, 158. See also *Literary and Historical Miscellanies,* pp. 481ff.

achieving the impossible. Even the fire of Bancroft's faith, however, betrays the truth: political fraternity was impossible in the times, for men could not bring themselves to discard the benefits of the age—yet they dreamed of fraternity too much to abandon it. A historical artist like Bancroft might at least paint the vision in colors so bright that the vision would glow more brilliantly as it vanished into the future.

At best, however, history was only an abstraction. The demand for political fraternity, the moral force behind all the great movements of the middle period, did find some expression in devotion to the ideal of the Union. Status and dignity were tied to the Union: in citizenship and party the citizen might discover a shadowy suggestion of fraternity that would partly redeem its absence elsewhere in life. It was a Whig as well as Democratic creed; Webster and Jackson, with almost identical passion, espoused it. The Union was an ideal which sought to substitute fraternity's pale imitator, devotion, for the thing itself.

The old Union proved unable to survive regionally divisive issues. It could endure only by ignoring or postponing them. (As Jackson guessed, each "compromise" only gave stronger formal recognition to the division itself.) Forced to choose between the lofty ideal of the Union and the men with whom they lived their lives, American citizens preferred the latter. Not even by Jackson's will could the Union avoid the legacy of the flesh.

Cries of Race and Clan

Many Americans, though disturbed at the state of the country, were too identified with existing economic and political institutions to blame them for the ills of the land. Interest tied many to those institutions, and others were bound by theory. Still others, especially men drawn from among the newly mobilized in the long settled communities (predominantly rural Protestants from the Southern Piedmont and upper New England), believed themselves to be losing a place they had once had in America, and clung desperately to all that they had inherited from their fathers.

Defending or never questioning existing habits and practices in a changed time, they were, of course, undermining old values, helping to change the content of American life. Preserving outer semblance, they lost inner meaning. But it was a simple response, easy for unsophisticated and self-ignorant men. They blamed what they disliked in America on malefactors who sought to change the old ways, or who seemed the visible symbols of those changes. The stranger, the enemy, defined the boundaries of morality; the quest for fraternity stopped with the demands of gemeinschaft.

Freemasonry was one of the first "enemies" to command attention. Having inherited suspicion from the eighteenth century, it was a traditional symbolic foe for traditional man. Paradoxically, the suspicion had lost whatever basis it once possessed. With expanded membership, the Order had abandoned most of its original deism in favor of a nondenominational Protestantism. Masonry had never lost its associations with heresy and the occult, however, although this might never have mattered had it not been for the "mystery" of 1826 in which Masons were accused of murdering one Morgan for revealing the secrets of the Order.

The interest aroused made Masonry a logical center of political attention. Anti-Jacksonian (and anti-Jeffersonian) politicians found Anti-Masonry a convenient basis for acquiring mass support, one which paid better dividends than their own political doctrines. Masonry had been vaguely associated with Jefferson, and though many Whigs were Masons, the primary political tendency of Masonry was Democratic. The lodges were a setting in which members of the professional and middle classes, and to some degree "mechanics" and artisans, could form emotional bonds and organize for political action. The commercial elites were in much less need of such formal organization.

It is impossible to concede much sincerity to the Anti-Masonic political leaders. John Quincy Adams, elected as an Anti-Mason in 1831, had been an active member of the Order not long before; Thaddeus Stevens had been sympathetic to Masonry before climbing on the new bandwagon. William Wirt, the only presidential nominee of the Anti-Masonic Party, was a survival from the age of Federalism who brought to the Anti-Masonic crusade a strong anti-Jeffersonian flavor. Whiggish criticism of Masonry was often revealingly mild. Doctor Holmes admired Masonry's freedom from religious sectarianism; he felt distaste for the Masonic preoccupation with ritual, its concern for the outer man. For urban and educated Whigs, attacks on Masonry were easiest as jests at its flummery and pretension. Such criticism, however, did not touch the chord of mass response.

The major theme common to Anti-Masonry and Jackson's opponents was hostility to the "narrowness" and "exclusiveness" of the Order, to the fact that it set itself apart from the civic fraternity of all Americans in a special brotherhood. In that hostility, Whig nationalism could find a bond with the newly-mobilized and with evangelical religion. The same theme united the unsuccessful attacks on the Greek-letter fraternities that began to grow up in American colleges in imitation of Masonry. Outlets for the expression of emotion, college fraternities were also a revolt against the "impracticality" and other-worldliness of religious and classical education. Whig leaders could hardly find such sentiments reprehensible, but they could unite with the revival against the "special" fraternal loyalties, which gave the crusade a doctrine with a clear indebtedness to the Enlightenment.

There is some justice in seeing the anti-secret-society movements as diversions of the newly-mobilized's hostility from its logical object, the commercial order. In New England, where anti-Masonry was strong, new voters drawn to the polls seem to have become Democrats when the crusade lapsed, and similar signs existed elsewhere. That the union of newly-mobilized and elite existed at all was due in part to the fact that Masons were often the local business and professional leadership, and the local agent could become the scapegoat for the distant leaders of commerce. That Anti-Masonry had so short a career and so little impact is itself a reflection of the fact that the Masonic Order was not a plausible enemy and was at best an unlikely cause of America's troubles.

In any case, a more likely foe than Masonry was readily at hand. It was the age of the Irish migration; six thousand Irish arrived in 1825, a hundred and seventy thousand in 1850. With the Irish came Germans, many of them Catholics; four hundred arrived in 1825, sixty thousand in 1850. The massive increase in the number of immigrants was paralleled by a change in class. Earlier immigration had showed a considerable percentage of merchants and professionals; by the end of the period, 90 percent were farmers, mechanics, and laborers—the last growing in proportion throughout the period.

Protestant religious leaders and intellectuals like Samuel F. B. Morse discerned a Catholic menace which was endangering and demoralizing American life. Morse saw Catholic power as a threat to all the traditional institutions he identified with America: republicanism, reason, individual liberty, and the Protestant religion. Catholicism was authoritarian, exclusive, secretive, "loyal to a foreign Potentate"; aside from its corrupting effects, the critics charged, it refused to join a fraternal citizenry, preferring special loyalties.

Yet the anti-Catholics were faced with the fact that the norm of religious tolerance was well established. Too, many Americans, especially in the cities, had friendly contacts among the Americanized Catholic population. It was far easier to direct hostility toward "foreigners" in general than to single out a religion. Moreover, anti-foreignism could enlist the support of the "scientific" theories of "race" then coming into vogue.

George Perkins Marsh, beginning a long career, located the "ancient virtues" of New England in the supposed democratic, rational, anti-sensual qualities of the "Gothic race" he believed to have settled the area. "Roman" influences, Marsh feared, would erode those virtues, menace her religious spirit, and shatter her civic fraternity and public spirit. (Marsh was a true pragmatist; he would later see Italians as "realistic" nationalists and denounce the "Teutons" as metaphysical, anti-democratic, and aggressive. To the end, however, Marsh remained staunchly anti-Catholic and saw immigration as leading to materialism and civic decay.) Other anti-foreign spokesmen directed attention to the "conspiratorial" and "exclusive" fraternities which were the foreign counterpart of Masonry: the Hibernians, the Turnerbund, the Sokol. Anti-Masonry was limited to an attack on foreign "ideas"; the Know-Nothings could focus resentment more empirically, on the foreigner himself.

Nativist arguments were oddly ambivalent. At one point, they seemed exclusivistic, hoping to bar the gate to the foe; at another, they denounced the foe—immigrant, Catholic, Mason—because he was excluding them, refusing to become a part of the one life that was America. The assault was tinged with wistful admiration, a belief that others possessed some special community or fraternity. Equalitarian individualist that he was, the American nativist did not propose to let others be better off, or to admit that he feared they were better off, than he was; they must join the rather chill brotherhood of Americans or stay away. (Many Know-Nothings, somewhat unexpectedly, were anti-slavery; their devotion to the American creed was less purely verbal than it might seem.)

Behind all these movements lay the hope for community, a dream also expressed by those Americans who tried to find some automatic basis for American brotherhood, kinship in place and blood, the pure logic of gemeinschaft. Some resurrected the old idea of an environmental fraternity, born of the land itself, with the attendant belief in a special kinship with the Indian. The Masonic lodges of upstate New York were emptied by Anti-Masonry, only to be filled by the impeccably American "Order of the Iroquois," which had the positive result of helping to start Lewis Henry Morgan's ethnological researches. More bizarre was the belief, stimulated by the discovery of the civilization of the mound-builders, that the Indians were Jews, descendants of Noah. (This antediluvian theory, obviously, found its way into Mormonism.) It was surely a strange route to the affirmation of America as Israel; it was also not a little racist, suggesting that one wanted an Indian for a kinsman only if he were something other than an Indian.

On the whole, however, environmentalism was a survival from the eighteenth century. If men were more prepared to romanticize the Indian, they were less able to believe that the land itself created fraternity. The environmentalist was, in any case, interested in America's future as often as her past, and was seeking a guarantee for her destiny by looking to her origins, her "state of nature." Much later, Morgan was to state his own creed:

> The human mind stands bewildered in the presence of its own creation. The time will come, nevertheless, when the human intelligence will rise to the mastery over property. . . . Democracy in government, brotherhood in society, equal rights . . . and universal education, foreshadow the next higher plane of society to which experience, intelligence and knowledge are steadily tending. It will be a revival, in a higher form, of the liberty, equality and fraternity of the ancient gentes.[37]

Jacksonianism's creed and Bancroft's history—Morgan found a surer foundation for both in anthropology. Such a belief, however, offered brotherhood to future men; men in the present would have to get by with that "brotherhood" which Morgan discerned in the existing order of things, until the "next plane" was reached and history came full circle.

[37] Lewis Henry Morgan, *Ancient Society* (Chicago: Charles Kerr Cooperative, n.d.), pp. 561–562.

There were more sinister ideas at work in America. The idea of blood brotherhood, the kinship of race which Marsh invoked, was receiving the support of science and pseudo-science. Samuel Morton's cranial capacity "test," which "proved" blacks inferior, was united with the incantations of phrenologists. Josiah Nott demonstrated to his satisfaction that racial mixture produced only a "hybrid," a degraded form of both. And of course the theory of separate creations, and hence separate "species," reached a new apex of strength.

These ideas, obviously, were eagerly received by Southern ideologists. In the North, more than a few showed an equal enthusiasm. The old difficulty remained, however: racism makes bad monotheism. Racist theorists were regularly assailed for their "materialism" and their departure from scriptural orthodoxy. Abraham Coles, for example, found a parallel between Christianity and equality, and consequently one between infidelity and slavery, and helped forward his argument by citing the heretical views of racist ideologues. These arguments, and others like them, had their effects. The pious Louis Agassiz, though he accepted the "scientific" accuracy of Morton's test and of many of Nott's ideas, held that these must be interpreted in the light of the "scriptural" truth of human unity. Thus, though there are "very different degrees" of excellence among the races, there is an "essential humanity" in all men. It was not a very easy position to defend, perhaps, but Agassiz preferred it to the attacks of theologians or anxiety about his soul.[88]

Racism had its attractions, and few Americans were genuine equalitarians. The "brotherhood of whites," however, was a pale ideal in the North where other brotherhoods beckoned and other whites seemed more suspect. That fact alone made it easier for religious leaders to oppose racism, keeping their own heritage pure. On all sides, the case was different in the South.

White Hopes, Dark Presences

The South was the land of the individual, the place of isolated men. The town and village yielded in the South to the county, a larger

[88] Edward Lurie, "Louis Agassiz and the Races of Man," Isis, XLV (1945), pp. 227–242.

unit composed of a number of isolated, almost self-sufficient units: plantations and subsistence farms. Isolation, of course, was not unknown elsewhere; it characterized the farms of the Middle states and much of the life of the frontier. In the South, however, social organization was intertwined with the "peculiar institution," which had individualizing and isolating effects of its own.

In the older South there had been some restraints. A certain sense of equality existed; although inequalities of wealth were greater than in the North, the isolated character of Southern life left men less conscious of them than was possible for the inhabitant of the closer-linked New England town. Too, Southern wealth had about it a certain roughness, an insecurity deriving from new tenure. The successful were often old comrades, or kinsmen, of the unsuccessful. And, like the Westerner, sheer need for the assistance of others modified the individualized pattern of economic life along the Southern frontier; rules of personal loyalty became even more rigid because they were needed to master the divisiveness of the environment. Even the gently contemptuous creed of the "yeoman farmer" helped; as an ideal, at least, it placed the "freeman" in a political context, a republican community.

Those restraints, however, were always weaker than they later seemed to nostalgic historians. "Yeomanry" presumed that free birth was the only basis of dignity and status; but such a condition never existed in the South. Slavery introduced a distinction between the owning and the non-owning free which produced resentment and a feeling that labor degraded man. The Southern farmer was an imperfect yeoman indeed; a rapacious cultivator, he showed all too many signs of temptations to betray a friend despite the restrictions of the ethical code. The distinction between owner and non-owner could cut two ways; in the early South, rural areas were the country's center of anti-slavery sentiment. On the whole, however, slavery made the owning whites models for emulation, setting standards that pervaded the region.

As Jefferson had realized, slavery taught the children of the owning classes to define freedom as dominion, liberation from restraint, and unlimited power. Allowed an imperious liberty as a child, the young owner would be savagely resentful of all subsequent restraint.

What Henry Adams was to see in Randolph was characteristic of the class: group loyalty was almost wholly lacking, and their image of the state was contractarian in the extreme, accepting the state only if it was useful in meeting the desires of the individual.[39]

In fact, that absence of group loyalty was responsible for some of the equalitarian feelings of Southerners. Upper and lower classes alike developed no loyalty to class, no special bonds to set one group of men off from another. Equality may grow out of such relations, but it is an equality in which all men are equally irrelevant to the self, not one in which they are brothers.

It was thus no "aristocratic" class that grew up in the South. The manners of the elite remained largely "democratic"; their status and power lay in wealth and human capital. Its concerns were commercial; far from being contemptuous of trade and business, the owners were distinctly a part of the mercantile community. Anti-business sentiments, in fact, were mostly confined to those who remained part of the local, subsistence sector of the economy. In fact, until the slavery issue reached its apogee, the slave-holding areas of the South were dominated by the Whigs; as Arthur Schlesinger points out, the defense of property was best achieved by avoiding alliance with the Democrats who, though advocating states' rights, were commercially unreliable. The owners turned to the Democratic party only when their Whig allies in the North, under the pressure of anti-slavery feeling, became untrustworthy friends of property.

The life of the South made Enlightenment ideas of man and the state the natural ideology of the owning class. That those ideas were fashionable and highly persuasive only added to their appeal. It was hardly strange, however, that the owners should adopt a doctrine which, though it might argue for a theoretical equality, provided both a defense of property and a justification of the fierce individualism that slavery and social organization built into the Southern psyche.

The writings of John C. Calhoun, for example, are entirely based on Enlightenment concepts. True, Calhoun could refer to man as "naturally social," but he meant by that phrase no more than Hamilton

[39] Jefferson, *Letters and Selected Works*, pp. 278–279; Henry Adams, *John Randolph* (Boston and New York: Houghton Mifflin, 1882); see also De Tocqueville, *Democracy in America*, vol. I, p. 471.

or Madison had when they referred to the "affections" and those weaker sentiments which inclined men to harmony and peace. Sociability, Calhoun argued, warred with man's feelings for himself, and his self-concern was more powerful, more truly natural; self-preservation is, he declared, "the all-pervading and essential law of the animated universe."

Again, like the authors of *The Federalist*, Calhoun regarded the social affections as dangerous. Society was needed to breed and rear the young, to "preserve and protect the race," but it led to complacency and to an excessive interference with individual liberty, the more fundamental need of race and individual alike. Hence, men must be encouraged, or even forced, to be selfish if "progress" is to ensue; they must be driven to take up the struggle with nature which advances them.[40]

Calhoun defended slavery, in fact, as a "spur to competition" which helps, like all inequalities, to drive men to better themselves by making liberty a "reward to be earned." Obviously, Calhoun's argument provides no basis for the permanent enslavement of a race, but Calhoun had no intention of arguing that eventual liberation was the object of the slave system. His defense of chattel slavery rested on a different basis: the "scientific" case for Negro inferiority. Calhoun's case is no more than a defense of inequality of wealth and property. His contention, simply, is that when ownership is made the condition of genuine liberty, men are spurred to engage in the struggle to possess. It is a doctrine whose justification lay in its presumed effects on non-owning whites, not on blacks. Slurring over the fact that the property in question is human, it represents only a typical form of eighteenth- and nineteenth-century theories of competition and the market. (Equally, Calhoun's eager acceptance of scientific racism is due in part to the fact that, unlike the old sophistry about the sons of Ham, "scientific racism" allowed the belief that blacks are a separate species, hence outside the principle of human equality.)[41]

Calhoun's ideas on government and politics were also based on the presumed danger of the affections. Government, necessary to prevent violent conflict among warring men, must be kept weak to force

---

[40] John C. Calhoun, *Works* (New York: Appleton, 1863), vol. I, p. 10, vol. II, pp. 1–10, 58–59, 507.

[41] Calhoun, *Works*, vol. I, pp. 55–57.

men to be concerned for themselves, compelling individual self-assertion. It exists only to prevent the destructive aspects of human aggressiveness from making themselves felt.

Calhoun spoke of his theory of the "concurrent majority" as an "organic" theory, but the image of an "organism" is curious indeed, being wholly mechanical. The argument is simple enough: the traditional "separation of powers" is defective because it does not represent regional interests, therefore each region must have an "organ" which represents it and can veto the decisions of others. Calhoun's theory presumes that Madison was wrong in fact, not in principle. Accordingly, Jackson's age had introduced a merely "numerical" majority, a national majority which ignored and overrode local and regional interests, and the "self-regulating" idea implicit in *The Federalist #10* must be replaced by formal, institutional recognition of regional diversity.

Calhoun was never a doctrinaire secessionist. Willing to withdraw from the Union in the last extremity, he hoped always to preserve it. Nullification and concurrent majority were devices designed to protect the minimal interests of the South. His aim was to guarantee that the Republic would continue to be a useful, non-menacing instrument, prevented from discriminating against the South or its "capital." The great concern was to combat the secular faith of Jacksonianism, to deny the Union or any government the status of a moral ideal or any claim to represent a corporate public. Calhoun's "organic" theory was based on the proposition that organic theories of the nation were no more than dangerous delusions, that the state must be kept a passive instrument, limited to the utilitarian purposes of private interests and private men.[42]

Yet though Calhoun's ideas were rooted in the Enlightenment, he spoke for a new South and a new generation. There is a ruthlessness in Calhoun's doctrine which Jefferson and most of his Southern contemporaries never knew. Absent in Calhoun is any generosity of spirit or breadth of vision; certainly lacking is the high dream of universal brotherhood. That dream finds a last, pallid survival in Calhoun's concern for the preservation and protection of the "race." Even that concern, founded on the exclusion of the dark brother from

[42] Herman von der Holst, *Calhoun* (Boston and New York: Houghton Mifflin, 1882), pp. 62–183; Wilson, *Division and Reunion*, pp. 56, 60, 66, 171.

humanity, leads only to the prescription that men should be driven to compete with their brothers, forced to limit the social affections until they are scarcely seen outside the walls of domesticity.

Jefferson's spirit lingered awhile in some of the more stable and settled areas where the gentility of the Old South was not quite mythical. In Virginia, a John Taylor kept up the old devotion to the small community and the old hostility to mercantile ethics, condemning the new individualism and inequality of wealth which led, as Taylor saw things, only to the "democratization of aristocratic vice" and the loss of civic spirit. Yet Taylor was only acting out an ancient ritual, repeating maxims which were largely inapplicable in the new context. No wonder perhaps: Virginia was in decay, and with it the South for which Taylor spoke; the economy of the Old Dominion was becoming based on the breeding and export of slaves, a domestic Africa safe from the slave patrols.

The South had a social crisis of its own. The impact of the cotton gin made itself felt toward the end of the second decade of the century, raising the marginal profitability of the slave system by making extended cotton acreage possible. The plantations spread onto the better lands of the old "yeomanry," leaving the displaced farmers the alternative of retreating into the hills or migrating north or west. Migration was encouraged, too, by the slow exhaustion of the soil in the old states; man rapes the land only to his cost.

The tide of social movement destabilized the already tottering social system. For those who stayed in the South, the economic foundation of the slave system marked sharper lines of class; mobilization drew men into a life in which almost all dignity and honor were tied to the possession of slaves, into a world where the inequality among whites—always considerable in fact—became agonizingly clear.

The new spokesmen of the South were often, like Jefferson Davis, men whose origins lay in the "yeoman" class, but who had gained access to the more productive lands in the old Southwest. There they were joined by others who had fled the slowly decaying plantations farther east. Both groups were attracted by the aristocratic image of the Old South, although in practice both were too caught up in the battle to succeed to be more than entrepreneurs, concerned to keep profits high and, accordingly, seeking to escape the restraints of both governmental interference and civic ethics.

They were harder, more determined men, and even their affections made them so. Those who remembered ties of blood and old friendship to the non-owning whites of the South were the most extreme among Southern advocates of slavery expansion. The demand for room to grow, expressed in the imperialism which sought Cuba and Nicaragua and in the more symbolic insistence on a Kansas open to slavery, reflected the massive pressure to create at least the image of opportunity for the poorer whites to enter the governing classes.

Concern for the slaveless white—75 percent of Southern whites at the beginning of the war—was moved more by calculation than by altruism. Social mobilization created a need to assimilate these men to the plantation system and to keep them from losing their hope of dignity within it. If the blaze of opportunity ceased to blind him, the poorer white might take up the anti-slavery banner he had once held. Already, free soil enthusiasm was marked among Southern families that had moved north and west, Abraham Lincoln being a salient figure. Such men might not love the slave, but they hated his competition and, to some degree, his owner. Southern representatives had once favored a Homestead Law; as late as 1851, most of the Southern members of the House voted for such a bill, and even Hayne of South Carolina could co-author it with Andrew Johnson. As the crisis deepened, Southern leaders recognized such bills as a menacing alternative to slavery expansion; only three voted for passage in the House in 1859. Ben Wade, the anti-slavery radical, put the question in exactly the terms in which militant Southerners saw it: "Shall we give niggers to the niggerless, or land to the landless?" [43]

Hinton Helper's prediction of an "impending crisis" in the South was premature, but there was enough Unionism and hostility to secession during the war to be disquieting. No state with a slave population of less than 25 percent was to secede; the whole Appalachian belt tended—sometimes militantly, as in East Tennessee or West Virginia —toward the Union; the Confederacy was forced to introduce conscription early in the war. Southern Whigs were often leaders in the anti-secession struggles, but their support came from poorer whites in the Democratic hill country.

Helper and similar prophets erred because they discounted the strength and appeal of the "brotherhood of whites." There were a

[43] Cited in Hans Trefousse, *The Radical Republicans*, p. 127.

few positive bases for that feeling of fraternity: the kinship ties between men, the somewhat condescending kindliness an owner might
show his non-owning fellow whites, the equality that reigned during
election time. The real bond, however, was negative: white unity was
aroused by the menace of the Negro. Whiteness became salient in a
sea of black, an ocean always disturbed by resentment against slavery;
the threat of insurrection and the motive of status were the cement of
white "fraternity." Jefferson Davis admitted as much, conceding that
white brotherhood was united largely by the "presence of a lower
race." That alone suggests the spuriousness of white "brotherhood";
it lacked unity in either value or joy and was no more than an alliance
of individuals driven by fear and hostility into a semi-permanent confederacy.

White unity received additional support from the external crisis
of the South. Better communication brought the South into closer
contact with the rest of the country at a time when the economic
status of the South was falling relative to the rest of the national economy. That, and such additional frictions as the tariff, made many feel
victimized by the North. Contact also made Southerners aware of the
isolation of their ideas and institutions from the culture of the time.
Certainly the "self-sufficient" individualism of Southern life and culture placed the region at a disadvantage in a world of increasingly
complex market organization. Economic and social marginality created a hostility to the North in all classes which were exposed to the
commercial system (notably, Unionism was strongest in the most isolated areas). It was a feeling common to Southern commercial and
business classes as well as farmers. While in agriculture the decline
was more felt than real, it was hard fact in business and trade. By the
1850s, New Orleans had already lost the trade of the West; ports on
the Atlantic sometimes showed absolute gains, but even they suffered
relative to the North.

Increasingly, Southern orators abandoned appeals on behalf of
particular states, or even defenses of slavery, in favor of advocacy of
the cause of "the South" as a whole. To some, sectional feeling was
natural; others appealed to it more consciously to divert attention
from differences within the South. Functionally, antipathy to the
North combined with antipathy to the Negro in overcoming much of
the hostility that Southern whites felt for each other.

Newly mobilized and poorer whites might have been less willing allies of the slave-owning militants if their own lives had not been isolated and individualistic from the beginning. And in the South, unlike the North, traditional religion did little to oppose the individualizing effects of the social and economic order.

In the interior of the South, organized churches, like all other forms of permanently organized life, were few, and the frenzy of revivalism, almost the only outlet for "half-perceived miseries" and "nebulous discontent and obscure longing" tended to fix attention on the next world. The more orthodox churches were even more otherworldly. Cash called the life of the South one of "social schizophrenia";[44] its daily activity was patterned on individualism and materialism, while its spiritual vision was an abstracted ideal of love, justice, and authority.

Traditionally, religious thought had sought to connect those two aspects of man's nature through communion, but community and fraternity were lacking in the Southern milieu. God was shaped to the needs of the individualist, emerging as a terrifying deity able to frighten suspicious and self-seeking men into a modicum of decent social behavior. God judged individuals guilty and extended mercy, but only the individual was involved. Even the pietistic insistence of the Southern churches on sexual taboos and the restraint of fleshly desires appealed in part to the fear of involvement which guides the pure individualist. Fearing passivity, weakness, and submission, the needs and dependences of the flesh, the isolated Southerner easily combined a materialistic life and an ascetic romanticism. There was in the mind of the white South a greater unity than Cash realized: the dream of the sufficient self.

Even so, religion did pose some challenge to Southern institutions. John Bachman, though a defender of slavery, felt obliged to oppose the "scientific" case for racism and for separate creations, pointing out not only the irreligious implications but also the fact that Morton's tests showed no racial variations so great as those between animal species (and arguing too that Negro intelligence had been underrated). Bachman was content with the well-known Biblical "justifications" of slavery, but others were not. Moncure Conway could see no way out: the Negro must either be an "inferior animal" or a "man

<hr />

[44] W. J. Cash, *The Mind of the South*, p. 70.

and a brother." Eventually coming to accept the truth of the latter alternative, Conway felt a deep sense of his own inferiority and lack of humanity in having ever doubted, and spent much of his life trying to make up for it.[45] Even the evangelical and Quaker-inspired anti-slavery societies, which perished with the political and economic changes of the late '30s and the '40s, had their effects on the consciences of men.

George Fitzhugh, one of the most strident defenders of slavery, felt obliged to argue that there was a "fraternity" between masters and slaves.[46] Taken at face value, of course, Fitzhugh's argument confused paternalism with brotherhood and, because such kindliness rarely extended to poor whites, the assertion served to illuminate Southern self-concern as much as it did to defend slavery. The obvious sophistry of Fitzhugh's claim is less important, however, than the fact that he felt a need to make it; the religious heritage made it necessary even for a slavery zealot to avow some bond with the Negro as a man.

Without economic or political institutions to support them, however, such moral beliefs, often painfully confused and half-recognized, were bound to be swamped. The function of the religious heritage was to make rationalization necessary. Since rationalization is always vulnerable, its effect was to leave the individual beset, consciously or unconsciously, by feelings of obscure guilt. The new crisis in relation to the North exacerbated such feelings. Southerners were aware that international opinion generally regarded slavery as a survival from a dark and ignorant age. Slavery isolated the South morally without shielding it (as Wilson erroneously believed) from the "nationalizing" forces of commerce and technology.

Conscious of the weight of outside opinion, secretly uncertain of their own, Southern elites became increasingly defensive and fearful of ideas. Gone was Jefferson's libertarianism. The control of outside ideas became severe, using the pressures of law and social conformity alike, and pro-slavery doctrine became more rigid. Southern churches became more intolerant and other-worldly; at the same time,

[45] William Stanton, *The Leopard's Spots*, pp. 135–136, 166–172; Moncure D. Conway, *Autobiography* (Boston and New York: Houghton Mifflin, 1904), vol. I, pp. 87, 90.
[46] George Fitzhugh, *Sociology for the South, Antebellum*, ed. Harvey Wish, pp. 58–59, 95.

they fled their Northern brethren, founding separate churches designed to protect the South and its institutions. Churchmen defended separation on the grounds that the North was a hotbed of scientism and infidelity, her churches touched by the general decay. The fact, however, is that the separation only calls attention to the intellectual isolation and moral defensiveness of the South. And the enlistment of the churches in defense of the region, advancing the radically inaccurate belief of a conflict between Northern commercialism and infidelity and Southern gentility and piety, greatly contributed to the sense of a "brotherhood" among Southern whites.

What a mad myth it was! The Southern upper classes could hardly serve as models of spiritual resistance to materialism or of personal relations against individual self-assertion. Fitzhugh's defense of slavery, for example, rested heavily on the right of property, and though Fitzhugh made the argument that the South eliminated a conflict of interest between labor and capital because the two were identical in the South, his argument is clearly commercial and materialistic. So too, Harper's defense of slavery "in the light of social ethics," like Calhoun's, defended slavery as a spur to progress. Life, Harper argued, was the supreme good, the end of all creation; existence was good in itself. Since slavery at least preserved this for the slave (most of the time), it could not be called bad; since it contributed to economic growth, it must be good. The materialism which is the basis of Harper's argument would be difficult to outdo. Nor was it the soul to which Hammond appealed in his famous contention that "cotton is king." (In fact, Hammond's reference to the "mud sills of society" applied to the poorer Southern white as well as to the Northern laborer, its nominal object, suggesting how spurious was the ideology of "white fraternity.")

The most striking characteristic of Southern ideology, in fact, was its individualism, which in some expressions was implicitly amoral. Fitzhugh felt that he had scored a point with his argument that the North, no less than the South, drew its sustenance from an oppressed class. *Cannibals All* was persuasive to many because of the moral obtuseness of some of Fitzhugh's Northern opponents, who could so easily discern the South's guilt and ignore their own. The suggestion of *Cannibals All* is not, however, that "cannibalism" should be given up: rather, it argues that the oppression of labor in the North justifies slavery, that one sin excuses another, that "cannibalism" is the law of the race.[47]

The innocent individualism which pervaded Southern doctrine avoided too much, ignoring both the weakness and insecurity of life and man's desire for passivity, affection, and communion. Compelled to deny much in himself, driven to conceal more, the Southerner felt a pervasive anxiety and insecurity. The result was a constant touchiness regarding "honor" which could only be defended by the individual himself—for it would be unmanly to depend on the state—and, hence, the *code duello*. In more isolated areas, the blood feud was equally eloquent testimony to the defects of individualism.

Beneath the codes of violence, however, lay a desire for affection and admiration so passionate as to possess, so overlaid with fear as to be fratricidal. Woman, the symbol of passivity and the senses, was set apart lest her contagion spread to man, and the fear of contagion implies temptation. Southern idealization of women suggests the romantic individualist's desire for an affection "purified" of the senses, liberated from the limitations of mortal flesh. (The idealization was fairly new: in the seventeenth century, much anxiety about white women had openly centered on their supposed lust for Negro males.)

The Negro, set apart no less than women, could not be idealized. Yet blacks were nonetheless credited with a mysterious power of communion and joy, a quality that was discussed with a note of envy and more than a hint of fear. The Negro symbolized all the attractions of passivity, the temptations of emotionality and affection with which the white male struggled in himself. The Negro male was even more threatening, being virtually the alter ego, the "dark self" of the white.

Social and political conditions only increased these anxieties. The North was dynamic; the South was passive, seemingly compelled to accept a backwardness in economics and politics, slumbering rather than gaining wealth and mastery. Ideological vauntings aside, the Southern individualist did not value leisure and repose; his was a cult of action. Over the South there settled a kind of boredom which created a ready enthusiasm for the chivalric opportunities of war. The War provided a chance to prove individual and regional manliness,

[47] Fitzhugh, *Sociology for the South* and *Cannibals All, Antebellum*, ed. H. Wish, pp. 63–85, 97–156.

to assert will and vitality against the organizational power of the North. And so Southern youth went out to keep a rendezvous with unknown hills and little-known towns, into a war that made glory "out of date." [48]

Sadly, the War did little, especially when viewed nostalgically, save to cement the brotherhood of whites, that miasmic imitation of fraternity. The battle-brotherhood of individualists, it needed a foe to overcome the fear of each toward the other; for the open fratricide of the duel, it substituted the concealed fratricide of war. It bears pathetic witness to the fact that individualism is not enough, and that men will seek for some modicum, even a phantasm, of fraternity.

Battlecries of Freedom

The North met the sectional crisis hesitantly, reluctantly; zealots and devoted men it had, but few were eager for conflict. Many feared for the Union, the Jacksonian ideal, and hated the "extremists" in both sections who would disrupt it. Others, sober and urbane men, deplored violence and fanaticism; they raised skeptical eyebrows at the moralists and spoke of adjustment and compromise. Many saw the slavery question as a secondary issue: the real question was the right of property, the right of the individual to pursue gain.

Not all were conservatives; the moderate-to-liberal Stephen Douglas declared of slavery that "I don't care whether it be voted up or down. . . . It is merely a matter of dollars and cents." The greater number were worried because they saw in anti-slavery agitation a phenomenon intimately connected to all the other protests of the age, a reaction against individualism, materialism, and the creed of the eighteenth century. It was to these that Fitzhugh and his cohorts really spoke: do you imagine, Fitzhugh was asking in effect, that you can free our slaves and not be asked to free yours? Anti-slavery advocates often made the same argument, in early days, to the horror of Whigs and respectable men of all parties. Noyes had seen a link between revivalism and socialism, and more than one

[48] The phrase is from Bruce Catton, *A Stillness at Appomattox* (New York: Doubleday, 1953), p. 1.

utopian went the next step, seeing slavery as only another form of "capitalist greed." [49]

There was sufficient stirring among Northern workers to rouse the fears of the propertied classes, though hardly enough to justify them. Developing industrialism was slowly eroding the old monopolies of craft; machines were driving the artisan out or forcing him to take relatively lower pay; all workers suffered under poor conditions and arbitrary authority. But there was little feeling of class, less even than the sentiments, always weak, which were to develop later. Craftsmen were not eager to be classed with unskilled men; natives and immigrants suspected each other; and the belief in opportunity—a dream more than a fact—led men to see themselves as individuals, not as tied to a group destiny.

Even the unions which existed or grew up tended to be local, with workers clinging jealously to the autonomy of organizations in which they counted for more and were among friends. Certainly there was little "class" dimension in politics; workers divided between the parties, and the National Trades Union, itself an experiment to see whether national economic unity could not be gained, learned from experience to avoid "political" involvement.

The ideal of the unions, the organized and articulate spokesmen for worker resentment against industrialism, was tied to the idea of civic fraternity and to the brotherhood of craft. Worker spokesmen often spoke of employers as "slaves of the capitalists" like themselves (though they did not excuse them; when one rejects servitude, his condition is not improved by being a servant's servant). From Europe, Marx denounced the "petty bourgeois individualism" of American workingmen and counseled that the "capitalist evil you are trying to avoid is historically good," but such logic was too circuitous for American workers.[50]

The attitudes of workingmen's organizations were complex, however. They demanded those reforms which would enable labor and

---

[49] *The Anti-Slavery Vanguard*, ed. M. Duberman, p. 61, and J. H. Noyes, *History of American Socialisms*, p. 26. See also Duberman, pp. 241, 242, 245, 247, 254, 256, 267.

[50] Marx's comment is cited from V. I. Lenin, *Selected Works* (New York: International Publishers, 1930), vol. XII, p. 302.

the public to maintain citizen status in a larger, more complex society. This idea was linked with the claim to a right of association so that workers might not be the helpless dependents of a "master." The theme of citizen status was equally present in the demand for public education, designed to eliminate the "supineness" of poorer citizens, resulting from their bewilderment and ignorance. There were some advanced demands—regulation of hours, abolition of child labor— which reflected the desire for a society free from distinctions "independent of merit." "Eliminate inequities" was a Jacksonian phrase; the claim to recognition of "merit" was an amalgam, some of its associations being drawn from liberal political theory, some from the traditional ideal of civic fraternity. Vagueness was useful; it could bridge gaps which clarity might widen.

The hostility of even articulate workers to industrialism was ambiguous; private material ambitions warred with the fear that the cost of fulfilling such ambitions might be too high. Some sought a new way in cooperative workshops operated on fraternal principles. Slower in action and decision, these shops were driven out of business or forced to adopt the techniques of the competitive market they had tried to resist. (Successful cooperatives, in fact, often hired additional workers who were treated much the same as were the employees of more orthodox businesses.) The tensions within industrial society tempted workers to a flight of their own, a retreat like that of the Mormons and the Utopians, to the "independence" of agriculture, though little movement actually took place.

George Henry Evans, who preached the slogan "Vote Yourself a Farm" as a panacea, founded his case on "natural right," but he limited those rights to the things of nature, essential to man's simple needs: air, water, light, and soil. All other needs, Evans argued, are artificial; all other rights are "conventional," the result of community decision. It was an argument cast in eighteenth-century language; and Evans, a thorough individualist, regarded groups as a menace to liberty. His argument, however, rejected much of the traditional theory, especially in conceding to the community a greater role in shaping man; others would turn that idea to more radical ends. That Evans' ideas gained political force which culminated in the Homestead Act was a reflection of their greater acceptability to most Northern workers and employers. For both workers and businessmen, free land seemed a way of postponing conflict, of avoiding painful decisions. (Southern opposition was moved, in part, by the fear that free land might lessen Northern labor problems in ways dangerous to Southern interests.) And that, after all, was what most Americans desired.

Others in the North found in the anti-slavery movement a means of dealing with their dichotomous heritage. It was, of course, easy to defend the movement in terms of Enlightenment doctrines of "natural right," individual freedom, and equality (or even, as Olmstead did, by attacking the "inefficiency" of slavery). The basis of anti-slavery passion, what mass support it won, and surely the moral ardor of its leaders, was founded in religion. What else, for example, could have shaken the Calvinistic Wendell Phillips so thoroughly out of his Federalist–Whig heritage? Charles Finney, T. D. Weld, Orange Scott, James Birney: all were evangelists or evangelist-trained. Moreover, the movement was rooted in ideas of collective guilt and corporate responsibility, in the belief that there can be no escape from responsibility for one's brother man and that no individual rights exist which can justify indifference. Such ideas, alien to liberalism, derived from religious ideas of sin and of community, especially from the spirit of the revival.

There were differences among the early abolitionists. Garrison, close to the Transcendentalists in theory, was ferociously anti-political, insistently individualistic; the more orthodox Orange Scott lectured him on the folly of leaving matters to God without human agency, pointing out that government was a powerful enemy to a cause it opposed precisely because it was a strong help to those causes it favored. Many, like Phillips, straddled these positions. Phillips' refusal to participate politically had a political root; it was, he said, a man's duty to "live where God sent you and protest against your neighbor," but it was no duty to join him in sin. Drawing on De Tocqueville, he commented that Americans had lost the sense of public, the ability to do or say what they knew right: "More than any other people, we are afraid of each other." Phillips resisted the temptation to see slavery as the paramount evil; greed and inhumanity were, as he knew, characteristic of the "free market" as well. The great danger was that Americans would be "melted in luxury," caught up in their fearful isolation in the cult of material gain.

The diversity had a common element, however. The early abolitionists were kin to the revivalists in technique as well as belief, seeking to convert men by preachment and example. Even Phillips rejected the claim of a right to rebel, claiming only the minority's right to convert its opponents. Donald G. Mathews is cogent in arguing that there was a basic inconsistency in the abolitionist case: "If men are sinners . . . then their wills are as sinful as any part . . . they could not change their lives wholly by self-will." [51] The abolitionist sometimes knew as much. Garrison might vaunt and evidently delight in his isolated stance; James Birney lamented the fact that duty had left him without the support of friends. The real case of most was the belief that Americans would not have to depend solely on "self-will," that the conscience of the country was clear and that example and preaching would win for the individual the support of his fellow citizens. The conscience of the country, however, was divided and unclear, and disillusionment was bound to grow among the abolitionists as time passed.

Moreover, there was among the abolitionists an individualistic moral confidence which was never far from self-righteousness and often passed the boundary. It was revealed in the conviction that evil and guilt lay in tolerating the existence of slavery in the external act and not in the self. Revivalism's techniques exhibit the same danger, for they are based on the thundering insistence that individual salvation is possible. The desperate desire for purity, for being "in the right," was illustrated by the "fratricidal conduct" (Frederick Douglass' description) of anti-slavery men toward each other, against which black advocates inveighed more than once. This defect appeared most perhaps, in the Garrisonian demand, which others echoed as they became disenchanted, for the dissolution of the Union, which would purge the North of slavery's taint. Douglass knew that for what it was, a flight from responsibility, a desperate search for innocence; the movement, he sneered, "started to free the slave: it ends by leaving the slave to free himself." [52]

The decline of abolitionist hopes for a reborn Union was paralleled by the waning of utopianism as the experiments failed. This de-

[51] Donald G. Mathews, "Orange Scott: the Methodist Evangelist as Revolutionary," in *The Anti-Slavery Vanguard*, p. 95.

[52] Frederick Douglass, *Life and Writings* (New York: International Publishers, 1950–1955), vol. II, pp. 52–53, 149–157, 524.

velopment, which John Thomas has traced very ably,[53] was accompanied by the sharpening of the sectional crisis, as the South for her own reasons pushed expansion into Texas and beyond. As the utopian passion faded, the cause of slavery became more threatening to Northerners and the cause of anti-slavery became safer, more respectable, and less involved with ideas of social transformation. Former utopians and disillusioned revivalists helped by lowering their sights and concentrating on practical goals.

Commenting on anti-slavery arguments, James McPherson observes that the Biblical argument, used so freely by both sides, had been relatively "played out" by 1860. The fact is that it had been "played out" sooner, in terms of winning national support; those who had felt it in their soul found it no less compelling now. The change in argument was moved by a desire to persuade, to find ways which would speak to the interests and the "scientific" beliefs of men—to liberalism as well as Puritanism, "reason" as well as faith. Doing this attenuated the movement, cut it off from its own roots, appealed to men who did not share its commitments. The arguments themselves were sometimes quite unfortunate. Moncure Conway, for example, had been wise enough to see that poor whites in the South showed the same response to education as did blacks, a few years of interest followed by a gradual lapse of concern, and inferred that environmental factors like the absence of opportunity were critical. But Conway and others, even Theodore Tilton, found the "scientific" case for racism too difficult to refute and simply turned it on its head, arguing for the moral value, or the superiority, of "black" qualities. McPherson writes: "The belief of Tilton, Conway and others in the inherent superiority of the Negro in the 'feminine' virtues—religion and the arts—implies an assumption of Negro inferiority in the 'masculine' virtues of reason and enterprise." And to anxious Northerners, the "feminine" virtues commended themselves but little more than they did in the South; these and similar arguments might justify freedom for the slave but not equality for the man.[54]

Increasingly, as the slavery question became a sectional issue and

[53] John Thomas, "Anti-Slavery and Utopia," in *The Anti-Slavery Vanguard*, p. 266, and pp. 240–269 inclusive.

[54] J. McPherson, "A Brief for Equality: the Abolitionist Reply to the Racial Myth, 1860–1865," in *The Anti-Slavery Vanguard*, pp. 158, 168, 172.

the basis of a politics which involved no greater commitment than being a Northerner, the moral dimension of the movement grew weaker. It had never been too exalted; even most abolitionists showed no real zeal for equality or feelings of brotherhood for the Negro. Republicans showed even less, especially since they were concerned, for good political reasons, to turn aside charges that they advocated "amalgamation, equality, and fraternity" with the dark race. Some abolitionists did see the need to do more in education and economic life than merely free the slave, but their voices became less audible. Black spokesmen, in fact, were more inclined to see the need of economic reforms, better able to see the urgency of making something other than wealth the "God of the American heart." The experience of slavery may in fact have freed them from more than one delusion, given them a "more inclusive sense of human brotherhood" than was possible for whites. Certainly white commitment was superficial enough.[55]

The anti-slavery movement in its later years provided an outlet for moral protest which did not touch the conditions of industrial development and social change that were the basic facts of American life. It avoided the need for choice; God and Mammon marched in the same army, although many business leaders remained hostile to abolitionism until the end. It served the psychological needs of ordinary Americans, and the results of the war would serve the interests of the industrial order. War against slavery, pacifists were to argue, was not war; industrialism against slavery, reformers were to echo, was the arsenal of liberation. Obviously, these arguments are partly true, which is why they persuaded; the passion of the crusade, however, too easily turned grudging acceptance into elated cheer, compromise into righteous zeal. That, in the end, is harder to forgive, if easy to understand.

The vision of an American political fraternity, the ideal of the Union: these might still sway men, but they had come to seem more distant from, if not at odds with, the existing realities of American life. Lincoln was to become a hero in the myth that grew out of the times—a most unlikely result to many of his contemporaries who could see only his ordinariness and typicality. Yet Lincoln was extraordinary precisely because he was "common" plus something more, the unusual strength and clarity with which he felt and saw the divisions that were wracking the country and the American himself. And too, it helped the myth that, having struggled heroically to overcome those divisions, he met the assassin before he knew defeat.

There was a deep religiosity in the man, a nondoctrinal faith in God and human brotherhood that few missed, and an ethical creed that demanded action here and now. Sometimes his ideas were quite traditional, as when he spoke of a conflict between man's "selfishness" and his "love of justice" which could not be removed and which expressed itself in a sense of wrong. It was, perhaps, natural enough in one who had read *Pilgrim's Progress* as a boy and had grown up in a society fired by the revival.[56]

The boy had graduated quickly, though, to Gibbon and Paine; and the code of Jesus and the language of Scripture lay alongside the theory of liberal secularism in Lincoln's mind. He was a passionate believer in individualism, in thrift and the struggle to advance oneself, and most of his political ideas had a Lockean cast. If he insisted that each should have the reward of his labor, this meant little more than the Jacksonian interest in removing abuses and a willingness to support unions as an extension of the "voluntary principle" of self-help. His exultant description of the Thirteenth Amendment as the "king's cure for all evils" is pardonable, but his insistence on the ultimate unity of self-interest and love is less so, and more questionable still was his faith in industry, the cities, the growth of technology, as steps of progress toward a fraternal goal.[57]

Despite all that, Lincoln had a need for intimacy and friendship and knew man's need for both. Loyal almost to a fault, he constantly needed encouragement and affection as he struggled with moral dilemmas almost too great for any man. He knew, for example, that persuasion and reason will have little effect until men are friends, or willing to be. And too, he had the great dream of a fraternal Union, a vision of man as a political animal which led him to reprove those who argued, like Madison, that government results from vice alone:

---

[56] Carl Sandburg, *Abraham Lincoln*, pp. 14, 575, 641.

[57] *Collected Works of Abraham Lincoln*, ed. R. P. Basler (New Brunswick: Rutgers University Press, 1953), vol. I, pp. 408–416, 438, 484–485, vol. II, p. 493, vol. III, pp. 477–480, vol. IV, pp. 7, 24, 25, 202–203, vol. VII, pp. 259–260, vol. VIII, p. 254.

men, Lincoln declared, would need government even if they were just to do those things they can only do together.[58]

There is great insight in his diagnosis of the Union's crisis. He always knew the "vigor" of slavery, understood the social pressures that made economic common sense and statute law no barrier to expansion. Worse, he saw a breakdown in the attachment of the people to the government, a weakening of the emotional bonds of the polity. Those who seek glory will no longer feel the state to be their own creation, as their fathers did, and men will find no satisfaction of the need for glory in keeping up a house built by others. The "family of the lion and the tribe of the eagle" will be ranged against the old Union. The old Union had made the passions either "dormant" or "active agents" of liberty because it directed unfriendly passions against Britain. Then too, most men, being "living histories," felt themselves tied by the moving experiences of battle, sacrifice, and shared devotion to the Republic and its principles. This, Lincoln argued, is a state of feeling which "must fade, is fading, has faded. . . . What invading foemen could never do, the silent artillery of time has done." All that remained to hold the Union together was "cold, calculating, unimpassioned reason" and an iron adherence to law as the "political religion of the nation." [59]

It was a sentiment which Sherman was to echo, and an analysis which foreshadowed the famous Weberian classification of the three types of authority (glory–charisma; the erosion of tradition; the need for rational legality) but with greater insight than Weber's into the ways of the emotions. Lincoln, too, had Weber's note of sadness, even of despair. His hopes might silence him, but he knew cold reason is not enough, especially when men part company on basic principles. The lawyers of the time knew it too, departing from the eighteenth-century creed in imitation of the revival, seeking to go beyond reason to invoke God as the fountain and Christ as the water of American Constitutional Law.[60] That also was a doomed effort: the God who sent Dred Scott back to slavery was the God of property and not of man, and for the various reasons of each individual, He found few worshippers in the North.

When the war came, it came not sadly but with a cheer. It re-

[58] *Ibid.*, vol. I, p. 273, vol. II, pp. 220–221, 271.
[59] *Ibid.*, vol. I, pp. 108–114, vol. III, p. 130.
[60] Miller, *Life of the Mind,* p. 206.

leased many from the chains of self-doubt and ambiguity, gave to many, in retrospect if not at the moment, the sense of a battle-fraternity in a holy cause, provided a dimension of life that had been lacking. Dr. Holmes, skeptical, urbane, lightly amused, wrote Puritan war songs; the moral passions which had found no due object before found them in the war. And Fredericksburg, Cold Harbor, and Petersburg have an even grimmer memory if one remembers the popular song:

> We are filling up the ranks
> Of our brothers gone before,
> Shouting the battlecry of Freedom.
> We will fill those thinning ranks
> With a hundred thousand more,
> Shouting the battlecry of Freedom.

Freedom it was, and a high cause. Yet like so many high causes, it hallowed too much, Jay Cooke with the fallen, the arms factory with the slave. Charles Francis Adams, anti-slavery radical to the core, knew that the war must be fought and gave lion-service to the cause, but felt compelled to write that

> No man who dips his hand in this blood will remember it with satisfaction. And I confess my aversion to see any of my blood either a victor or a victim in this fratricidal strife.[61]

An inaccurate prediction, a sound sentiment: Adams' remark is not so much a verdict on the war as on Americans and on man, and a comment on the blind stumbling which is so often a part of man's search for self and for fraternity. But the cause itself had dignity enough to give a measure of truth to the proudest boast of the crusaders,

> I have seen Him in the watchfires
> Of a hundred circling camps,
> They have builded Him an altar
> In the evening dews and damps,
> I have read His righteous sentence
> By the dim and flaring lamps. . . .

And the song was more prophetic than its singers knew; part of the "righteous sentence" fell on the victors and their descendants, not on the vanquished alone.

[61] Cited in Edward Chase Kirkland, *Charles Francis Adams, Jr., 1835–1915* (Cambridge: Harvard University Press, 1965), p. 22.

> When the conditions of society are becoming
> more equal and each individual man . . . more
> like all the rest, a habit grows up . . . of over-
> looking individuals to think only of their kind.
> . . . The idea of unity so possesses a man . . .
> that if he thinks he has found it, he readily
> yields himself up to repose. Nor is he content
> with the discovery that there is nothing in
> this world but creation and Creator; still em-
> barrassed by this primary division . . . he
> seeks to . . . simplify his conception by in-
> cluding God and the Universe in one great
> Whole.
>
> De Tocqueville, *Democracy in America*

CHAPTER XI

EMERSON AND THOREAU: THE ALL AND THE ONE

America's Philosopher

AMERICANS of the nineteenth century acclaimed Ralph Waldo Emerson with an impressive unanimity. They lavished on him all the accolades that the schoolmen had reserved for Aristotle; he was non-pareil, the sage, the philosopher, the metaphysician. Even Julian Hawthorne, carrying on a family tradition of distaste for the seer of Concord, felt obliged to call Emerson's work "enlightening"—though, he hastened to insist, Emerson was at best only a collector of truths.[1]

[1] Julian Hawthorne, "Ralph Waldo Emerson," *Harper's*, LXV (1882), pp. 278–281.

Prophets, however, are not honored in their own houses, and the genius who is praised in his own time is frequently no genius at all. He is likely to see too much as his own contemporaries see: parochiality is more often than not the price of applause. This is not to imply that Emerson engaged in fulsome flattery of America and Americans. He was often a critic, sometimes a powerful one, of American life and conduct. Flatterers win laurels as rarely as prophets; men at any time have doubts about their own conduct and even more about that of their fellows. The popular sage may be a critic, but he will see the virtues and vices of a people as it sees them, ascribe them to causes it finds persuasive, and prescribe remedies congenial to the public mind.

"I love a prophet of the soul," Emerson wrote, and he came at a time when America needed just such a prophet. Like most New Englanders, he was troubled by the industrial order he saw emerging, distressed by its impersonality, doubtful of its aesthetics and morality. In that, as Parrington realized, he reflected the "submerged idealism" of his region. In thought, however, he stayed close to the surface; he "came out" of the Unitarian church, but he retained the Enlightenment liberalism which was the basis of its doctrine.[2]

As Santayana (and others) saw, Emerson's philosophy was decisively influenced by Locke and the theorists of the eighteenth century. German thought in the nineteenth century influenced him less than critics like Frothingham imagined; the European authorities were added as footnotes to a doctrine already developed and articulated. His political prescriptions show if anything an even greater dependence on eighteenth-century ideas. The Enlightenment was the source of all his key premises: existence of a deity in and not outside nature, the rejection of authority, and a belief in individualism and the creed of progress.[3]

In his attitude toward personal morality and conduct, Emerson never doubted the precepts of traditional religion. (Small wonder that Whitman, otherwise boundlessly admiring, thought him "blood-

[2] *The Complete Works of Ralph Waldo Emerson* (Boston: Houghton Mifflin, 1883), vol. IX, pp. 15–17; Parrington, *Main Currents in American Thought*, vol. II, p. 372.

[3] *The Journals of Ralph Waldo Emerson*, ed. E. W. Emerson and W. S. Forbes (Boston: Houghton Mifflin, 1909–1914), vol. X, p. 195.

less.")[4] Yet he did not see his own moral attitudes as the result of culture and institutions. Himself undoubting, tutored in the doctrines of individualism, he was satisfied that the morality he accepted was founded in individual "instinct" and that self-honesty would suffice to produce it

In the same spirit, he accepted the theory of progress. Rejecting any authority beyond the individual, he was led to reject a God beyond nature. Emerson changed the angle of man's vision: where once man had sought right by trying to steal a glimpse of what lay behind the veil of human things, Emerson insisted that the good was to be found in the scrutinizing of this-worldly process. In that sense, Emerson was not "transcendental" at all. His vision remained bound to the immanent world; his conceptions were not those of the great prophets of the soul, but the beliefs of a typical if talented American intellectual.

Living in the All

Chance was absent from Emerson's universe; all things were part of the great design. Man, however, could not see the aim or the plan; he could only observe motion. Faith in the "oneness" of the universe, which the Enlightenment had believed it could demonstrate by reason, Emerson derived from intuition; the critical doctrines of Hume and Kant (not to say Jonathan Edwards) had bitten deeply into the crust of eighteenth-century rationalism. Emerson carried that critical tradition to its logical conclusion: since man could not discern nature's logic, neither could he discern nature's laws. The scientism of the Enlightenment—its belief that the laws of motion could be learned and then directed—had now to be rejected. For Emerson, man was limited, so far as reason was concerned, to the knowledge of motion itself, ignorantly adrift in the currents of nature and history.

It was a fatalistic but optimistic doctrine. Emerson argued that man's intuition of the wholeness of things should lead him to a faith or realization that all the movement of history worked for the good, that present ills, if seen truly, were part of a process which tended

[4] Edmund Wilson, *The Shock of Recognition*, pp. 277–278, 286–287.

toward unity and harmony. His panglossism was stern and unyielding; he set it as a dogma to rule against all the dark perceptions of men, including his own, and he established sunniness as a test of reason and poetry alike.

His optimism, moreover, was naturalistic. Hence he rejected any idea that there were limits to the goods for which men might hope or any natural restrictions of human desire. He censured the great orthodoxies, Calvinism and Catholicism, because they insisted on the seemingly rational proposition that men were "born to die." Emerson never accepted death as a natural end, even though he doubted the existence of a future life. There were at least two possibilities for this-worldly immortality: the historical immortality of the "success of that to which we belong" and, more importantly, immortality through the "oneness of nature itself." Men, Emerson counseled, should "accept the tide of being which floats us into the secret of nature." The Mother who was Emerson's Nature reabsorbs, and all dilemmas and choices, values and qualities, disappear.

> If the red slayer think he slays
> Or if the slain think he is slain,
> They know not well the subtle ways
> I keep, and pass, and turn again.
> Far or forgot to me is near;
> Shadow and sunlight are the same;
> The vanquished gods to me appear;
> And one to me are shame and fame.[5]

On a less exalted level, Emerson did not disdain fame and success "of that to which we belong." Indeed, although the "natural" soul, with its physical and involuntary needs, was lower than the "transcendent" soul which saw something of the nature of the cosmos, Emerson conceded that man must first develop his "practical" faculties. The lesser immortality of success might be a necessary stage to the attainment of the higher.

Emerson transferred that permissive, naturalistic optimism to his analysis of history. He never lost his conviction of progress, even in the gloomier reflections of old age. The task of philosophy, he

[5] *Works*, vol. IX, p. 170; see also vol. I, pp. 87, 96, vol. VI, pp. 43, 100, 306, vol. X, pp. 130, 149, 189, and *Essays* (New York: Hurst, n.d.), vol. I, pp. 42–46, vol. II, pp. 108–111.

wrote, is to "console" men who suffer "under evils whose end they cannot see," which, when rightly understood, will prove not evils at all but only stages to some unseen good.

Consequently, Emerson could never bring himself to participate in politics. Even when the issues of the day seemed to involve questions of great moral import, they were not truly serious. History was moving to abolish slavery (hence, abolitionism was needless and possibly imprudent), to establish peace (hence pacifism was ill-timed and short-sighted), and to create conditions of equality. Reformers and utopians should realize that their advocacy merely described "that which is really being done." [6]

In this sense, Emerson was a "progressive" and might, as Daniel Aaron argues, be considered some sort of forerunner of the movement which took that name. He did formulate many of the relativistic doctrines that later reformers used to challenge the "steel chain of ideas" of late-nineteenth-century liberal orthodoxy. American institutions were suited to their historical period, he commented, but will someday have to pass away; the doctrine that "property writes its own laws" will have to yield to a more equitable standard. Emerson, however, firmly believed that progress did not require a movement; it was written in the motion of nature, and would come of itself.

At the end of history, Emerson was certain, he could discern man's ultimate destiny. His political ideal was a "nation of friends," a "political brotherhood" based on inward unity of spirit and the power of love. Beyond that ideal lay the final city, the brotherhood of man. The issues that divide men, their wars and conflicts and agonies, he wrote, are merely "the melting pot," just as the calamities of the Dark Ages brought forth a new Europe. One day "all men will be lovers," pain and catastrophe will cease, and all mankind will stand "in the universal sunshine." [7]

It is tempting simply to classify Emerson's doctrines as only the most noxious example of the meliorism of the nineteenth century.

[6] *Journals*, vol. IV, pp. 430–431, vol. V, p. 288, vol. VIII, p. 449; *Works*, vol. VI, p. 306; *The Early Lectures of Ralph Waldo Emerson*, ed. S. E. Whicker and R. E. Spiller (Cambridge: Harvard University Press, 1959), p. 22; and *The American Transcendentalists*, ed. Perry Miller (New York: Doubleday, 1957), pp. 5–20.

[7] *Journals*, vol. III, p. 235, vol. V, p. 380, vol. VI, p. 336, vol. VII, pp. 115–116, vol. VIII, p. 456; *Works*, vol. I, p. 242; *Essays*, vol. II, pp. 116–117, 142.

Yet Emerson could also write of fraternity in eloquent language. Friendship, he said, was man's ultimate ideal, but because it is, men are tempted to romanticize—to believe that the other is "tantamount" to the self and not separate, or to "idolatrize" the other to the detriment of vision. The "ultimate friend" is a "dream and fable," Emerson counseled; men are always separate and imperfect, though the ideal remains valid. Actual friends must be honored, not resented, for their independence. Anticipating Nietzsche, Emerson insisted that a friend must be a "beautiful enemy" and not merely a "trivial conveniency." [8]

Emerson drew much of this wisdom from the traditional doctrine whose moral precepts he always followed. His concept of fraternity, however, was placed in a context which subtracted almost all its content from that teaching. Wisdom taught by a fool can become folly.

First, Emerson distrusted personal friendships, not from a concern for the common values which should be the basis of a "common soul," but in the name of universal fraternity. Fraternity itself is the ultimate ideal, not a means to it. Each friend is the "harbinger of a greater friend" in the sense that the circle of friendship gradually grows wider. The "transcendental friend" is the "other me" which unites me not only to humanity, but to all of nature. Friendship, Emerson believed, was the great leveler, which strode over all barriers of age, sex, religion, circumstance, and character. Friendship abrogates, in other words, all personal judgment of value and quality. Hence, personal friendships based on qualities of personality hamper men in their efforts to "merge" with the all. [9]

Second, Emerson's universal fraternity was premised on a radical individualism and privatism. Indeed, his was a doctrine so extreme that despite his own practice it could serve to moralize disloyalty and self-seeking. For Emerson, Ralph Barton Perry observed, "humanity" often seems an "automatic by-product of selfishness." Emerson might and did denounce "egotism," but he insisted that the "universal soul" was to be found in the individual. Moreover, he felt that this "higher" soul could best be sought in the "spirit of infancy," the erotic sense of "oneness." Friendship, he warned, is

[8] *Essays*, vol. I, pp. 104–114, vol. II, pp. 140–141.
[9] *Works*, vol. I, p. 96, vol. II, p. 304, vol. X, p. 136.

never as "large as one man" if he truly understands himself; all society is a "descent" into parochial and "animal spirits" for one of vision. The good man must separate himself from class or party; he must regard all association as only "natural," "momentary" and hence suspect. "All private sympathy," Emerson intoned, "is partial." The individual should reject the "material limitations" which unite him to particular human beings and places; Emerson went so far as to argue that an impoverished environment which holds no temptations is peculiarly conducive to the growth of thought. The path of greatness, Emerson declared, is the road that will most swiftly unite the individual with the race. In effect, Emerson's was a teaching of sublimation, offering a sense of "union" with the race at the price of a separation from individual men.[10]

> Give all to love;
> Obey thy heart;
> Friends, kindred, days,
> Estate, good fame,
> Plans, credit and the Muse—
> Nothing refuse. . . .

> Leave all for love;
> Yet hear me, yet,
> One word more thy heart behoved,
> One pulse more of firm endeavor—
> Keep thee today
> Tomorrow, forever
> Free as an Arab
> Of thy beloved.[11]

Each Man a State

Many have been misled by Emerson's rhetorical use of the symbols of fraternity. More than one critic has argued that Emerson was, in some sense, a philosopher of democracy. But the divinity which Emerson saw in man was a deified self, independent of other individu-

---

[10] *Works*, vol. I, pp. 9, 272, vol. III, p. 276, vol. IX, p. 11; *Essays*, vol. II, pp. 78, 116, 140–141; *Journals*, vol. V, pp. 310–311; Wilson, *Shock of Recognition*, p. 626.

[11] *Works*, vol. IX, pp. 84–86.

als and the democratic public alike. Government and politics moved
him only to disdain. While Emerson valued success in the human
attempt at "making the world," he traced it to the "spiritual impulse"
of a man who "trusts himself" and seeks to make the world in the
image of his own will. The world, Emerson held, is "realized will,"
emanating from the One of which man is a part. The individual, in
Emerson's view, can be said to have self-knowledge when he wills
what must be; but it is also a valid demonstration of that exalted state
that what he wills, must be. Since Emerson's was a doctrine of activity, individualistic romanticism, not democracy, was the logical
result of his teaching. He hoped to make "each man a state," not all
men equal citizens of a democratic polity.[12]

Emerson left to the state only the task of designing ways for his
assertive individuals to live in reasonable concord. Even so, the state
exists to minimize itself; coercion and compulsion, which Emerson
identified with politics, are evil because they violate the autonomy of
the individual will, and the task of political wisdom is to decrease
them. The state has a passive role; believing that only education could
change men's "hearts," Emerson saw education as something separate
from politics. Political life was merely a negative, almost accidental,
factor in man's life, not a part of his nature.[13]

Valuing an expanded sociability, Emerson saw the growth of
the city as part of the development toward universal fraternity. In
the hectic streets he saw the meeting and mingling of all classes and
peoples. He was aware of the isolating effect which urban life could
have, and at times it troubled him. His greater fear, however, was
characteristic: he worried that the city might be too collective, too
social, too political. "He who should inspire . . . his race," he
warned, "must be defended from travelling with the souls of other
men." [14]

[12] *Journals*, vol. III, p. 369, vol. IV, p. 95, vol. V, pp. 302, 307; *Works*, vol.
I, pp. 46, 102, 323, 328, vol. VI, pp. 44, 295, 302.

[13] *Works*, vol. I, pp. 115, 347–348, vol. III, pp. 253–254; *Essays*, vol. II, pp.
107–108, 114–115; *Journals*, vol. VII, p. 220, vol. X, p. 144.

[14] *Works*, ed. E. W. Emerson (Boston: Houghton Mifflin, 1903–1904), vol.
VI, pp. 56–57, 148–149, 153–156, vol. VII, pp. 10–11, 153–154, 244, 424–425; *The
Correspondence of Thomas Carlyle and Ralph Waldo Emerson* (Boston:
Houghton Mifflin, 1883), vol. I, pp. 269–270.

Private character, not public virtue, formed the core of Emerson's ethics, and the theme of his political teaching is that the second must be shaped in the image of the first. That doctrine, stated abstractly, always seems defensible; doubtless it seemed even more reasonable in the early industrial age, when private morals rooted in smaller, stabler communities and in the religious tradition were contrasted with the amorality and rapacity that often characterized public life. Emerson's own standards for private character, however, were far from exacting. He did denounce "self-oriented" action, insisting that the individual act for the "good of man." Yet what Emerson was demanding was an intention, a mental attitude, not a type of conduct; provided the intention was pure, he could and did justify many private derelictions. It is too extreme to say, as did Paul Elmer More, that Emerson was indifferent to personal responsibilities, but it is close to the truth.[15] Emerson had one test for intention in action, one measure of ethics and conduct: the standard of success. This was, of course, the logical result of Emerson's faith in individual will and in the morality immanent in historical process, but it can hardly be argued that such a standard made many demands on the conscience of the individual.

Even when Emerson defended the intellectual against the deprecations of practical men of action, he did so on the grounds that "the most abstract truths are the most practical." Men of practice are misled by what is temporary and transient, while philosophers have a sense of movement and of the impermanence of existing institutions, an insight into nature's processes and goal. (This includes the fact that philosophers sense, as practical men may not, the relativity of standards of ethics.) Intellectuality was necessary to genuine *virtu;* Emerson offered a philosophy of action which purported to be a guide superior to the practical knowledge of men who do not see the philosophy in their own action, the moral meaning of events.[16]

Emerson made a near-cult of "spontaneity," of unreflective and instinctual response to situations resulting from the "simple" and "original" talents of men, which he found superior to the "external refinements" of education and culture. Yet knowledge of the superi-

[15] Paul Elmer More, "Emerson," pp. 354, 360–361.
[16] *Works* (1883), vol. I, p. 10; Wilson, *Shock of Recognition*, p. 654; Henry Nash Smith, "Emerson's Problem of Vocation," *NEQ*, XII (1939), pp. 52–67.

ority of unreflective spontaneity is a wisdom which, for Emerson, was not an "external refinement" but a true philosophy and insight into human things. Those who possessed only the spontaneity could not appreciate or use it rightly.

Hence, though Emerson trusted the moral direction of the people (and of the Democratic Party), he did not trust their judgment of means. The United States was a young and "barbaric" country, and its instincts were "rough," deficient in true "grandeur of character." The barbarian people lacked the long view, the vision of history; they were too prone to demand immediate goods and fulfillments, too sensitive to merely apparent evils. The need of the land was for a great man who would not "obey the laws too well," who would obey the law of movement, not the statutes of a moment —and who, overcoming the rough public instincts, could guarantee America's destiny.

The "openness" and "opportunity" which Emerson saw in the United States, would if allowed free competitive play guarantee "success to the best." This in turn would lead to progress in trade and commerce and in "science and computation," and through such material advances lay the path to the final goal of history. Groups, localities, and even fraternal relations might encourage men to follow a by-road which would delay the course of things. True statecraft would give these concrete groups scant and hostile attention; it would seek to make it easier for "events born out of prolific time" to enter and shape American life.[17]

Restating the Enlightenment ideal in the language of will and intuition, Emerson retained the essential prescriptions of that ideal, especially its hostility to fraternity among men in the name of the fraternity of mankind. Certainly his doctrine helped to ease the conscience of industrializing America, and the ebullience of American development, aided or not by the teaching, was such that even Emerson in the end had momentary doubts. Yet only for a moment: Emerson at length retained the curious mental glasses that blinded him to cruelty, stupidity, and sordidness and convinced him that what he saw was in truth the dawning of the "universal sunshine."

[17] *Essays*, vol. II, pp. 109–111, 115; *Works* (1883), vol. I, pp. 150, 221–222, vol. X, pp. 132, 149, 153, vol. XII, p. 60; *Journals*, vol. VIII, p. 449.

Time and Eternity

Henry David Thoreau has become something of a secular saint. A prime authority among advocates of "confrontation politics" and resistance to the draft, his individualism and his woodsiness are admired by many others as well. Thoreau's appeal indicates that the law of nature may be violated, but not with impunity, and that an Emerson can console but not quiet men's feelings of uneasiness. In the midst of affluent industrialism, men feel a disquiet, a murmur of something lost, a fear that they have taken a wrong direction and lost their way. Thoreau had felt and given voice to this feeling at the beginning of the industrial age, and hence his voice persists in our own time.

Emerson, puzzling over Thoreau's inability to say "yes" to the world, called him a "protestant *a l'outrance*," and for once at least the sage of Concord came close to the mark. Thoreau's doctrine was prophetic, his vision traditional. His rhetoric has deceived many who, unlike Emerson, did not know the man. He used words for their effect on his audience, which makes misinterpretation easy. Too, having learned at the feet of Emerson, he often fell into the master's style even when he most rejected his ideas. Emerson's cadences came easily, and Thoreau could identify God with nature and speak of a willingness to "float wherever the river carries" so naturally that even Van Wyck Brooks referred to the "oriental" qualities of his thought.[18]

Thoreau himself, however, believed that the Bible spoke "more sharply to the human condition" than either Emerson or the Eastern texts did. That condition, as Thoreau saw it, was an ignorance more radical than Emerson had been willing to admit. God and nature might in ultimate terms be "one" or at least "at one," but there was no way to know that unity. The law which governed the world could not be discerned by mystical insight or conceived as operating automatically by an inevitable "process." Either claim, Thoreau would have argued, is an impossible presumption. Any sense of unity for Thoreau lay at the end of the intellectual quest and could not be presumed from the beginning. Even then it would remain a hope

18 Ralph Waldo Emerson, "Thoreau," *AM*, X (1862), pp. 239-249.

and not a matter of knowledge. The first facts were singularity, particularity, and diversity; small wonder that Thoreau, as Emerson observed, did not "feel himself except in opposition" to all orthodoxies.

Man, Thoreau argued, is the animal who seeks to know, the beast who craves reality. Human desires for things and for possessions are only misdirected impulse, for men are by nature "students and observers." Men are for the most part simply swept away by the cares of the world, and if they exercised a "bit more deliberation in their choice of pursuits," few indeed would pursue wealth or power as goals.[19]

Note, however, that "deliberation" is required. The desire to know, although a law of man's nature, is not something which develops automatically: it requires conscious thought. In fact, Thoreau accepted the traditional religious doctrine that man's first desire is to deny his finitude, to blot out the awareness of his own limitations. He rejected traditional mythic religion (Emerson noted that Thoreau was religious but never sectarian) because he believed that it pandered to that desire, encouraging a "pious infidelity" in which men were allowed to "fall back on innocence" rather than "falling forward" toward the unknown and the true reality of human life.[20]

Man was born a savage. He never completely overcame this part of his nature; tendencies toward self-indulgence, self-centeredness, pride, and complacency were always present. Outward simplicity might conceal an inward ignorance, for the self of man is neither simple nor known, but complex and a bit mysterious.

> I am a bundle of vain strivings tied
> By some chance bond together,
> Dangling this way and that, their links
> Were made so loose and wide,
> Methinks,
> For milder weather.[21]

[19] *The Writings of Henry David Thoreau* (Boston and New York: Houghton Mifflin, 1906), vol. I, pp. 11, 408, vol. II, pp. 106–110, 121–122, 320, 352; *The Journal of Henry David Thoreau* (Boston: Houghton Mifflin, 1906), vol. III, p. 157.

[20] Thoreau, *Writings*, vol. I, pp. 7ff. and 140–165.

[21] *Collected Poems of Henry Thoreau*, ed. Carl Bode (Chicago: Packard, 1943), p. 81.

Civilization was at least a response to a sharper consciousness of man's nature, a partial expression of his purpose.

Morton and Lucia White are typical of many critics in calling Thoreau an "assailant of civilization." They make this assertion on the basis of the following passage:

> I wish to speak a word for Nature. . . .
> I wish to make an extreme statement. . . .
> for there are enough champions of
> civilization.[22]

Thoreau's quarrel with civilization, in fact, lay in his charge that civilization was insufficiently civilized. Modern civilization forgot the permanent existence of the savage in man, which can still be discovered when we "dredge down into the murk" of man's nature. Fascinated with technological achievements and institutional restraints, civilization has not overcome the savage; it has not changed man's motives or desires. Hence, though it may outwardly have restrained savagery, civilization has placed the savage "at the place of honor" as source of the motive power of life and society. The very accomplishments of civilization, consequently, make it more dangerous than barbarism.[23]

There was, in short, no dogma of progress in Thoreau's thought: "history" intrigued him less than it did most thinkers of his time. History was itself relative to character. "Time" was the self-centered illusion of the savage and all those who measured events in relation to the self. "Eternity" was the whole of time seen accurately, the compendium of all times. To know himself, man had to overcome the contradiction between time and eternity.

Self-knowledge demanded that a man become alienated from his own times, his body, and his life. We cannot know ourselves, Thoreau wrote, so long as we are "afraid of the dark"; we must "drive life into a corner" until we "hear the death rattle in our throats and feel the cold." Man is a mass of "thawing clay," a dying animal, and

---

[22] Morton and Lucia White, *The Intellectual vs. The City* (New York: New American Library, 1964), p. 43.

[23] *Writings*, vol. I, pp. 55–56, vol. II, pp. 44, 132, 236, 242, 315, 320, 368; *Journal*, vol. I, pp. 253, 337–338, vol. XI, pp. 212, 410–412, 424–425.

there can be no reconciliation with life so long as man clings to life and fears himself.[24]

> . . . here I bloom for a short hour unseen,
> Drinking my juices up,
> With no root in the land
> To keep my branches green
> But stand
> In a bare cup.
> Some tender buds were left upon my stem
> In mimicry of life,
> But ah! the children will not know,
> Till time has withered them
> The woe
> With which they're rife.
> But now I see I was not plucked for naught,
> And after in life's vase
> Of glass set while I might survive,
> But by a kind hand brought
> Alive
> To a strange place.[25]

The path to knowledge, then, was obstructed by some of man's deepest emotions; and because of that fact, Thoreau emphasized man's need to be driven along it. In part, the emphasis is rhetorical, in part a reflection of Thoreau's own mental processes. In any case, the primary coercion on a man was exercised by friends, precisely because friends have a positive appeal to the individual's own emotions and values.

Caught between his emotions and the law of his nature, the desire to know, man dreams of discovering a friend who is his "Friend," a "real brother" who can resolve the tension and drive him to self-realization. Friendship which is genuine, Thoreau argued, expects the best and lays a demanding price on affection. "Friendship is not so kind," Thoreau wrote; "it has not much human blood in it." We love what is best in our friend, hoping that it will free what is best in us; his imperfections not only remind us of our own, they deprive us of a chance at freedom. The very fact that friendship is formed on

[24] *Writings*, vol. II, pp. 235, 238, 244, 344, 356.
[25] *Collected Poems*, pp. 81–82.

the basis of common values makes it something stern and hard. "We have not so good a right to hate any as our Friend."

Not surprisingly, then, men's desire for friendship is ambivalent. We are, Thoreau observed, constantly tempted to choose friends on the basis of affection or utility, in which case they become a comfort which is also a snare. Equally, we are tempted to reject friendship with individual imperfect men in favor of some "ideal" friend who does not exist; what we reject in that case is not our friend's imperfections but our own. For most purposes, Thoreau wrote, a man prefers to be treated as "no better than I should be," escaping demands for a greater excellence than the self has already attained.[26]

As he never discounted man's needs for friendship, so Thoreau did not underrate his need for society. He felt a distaste for conventional ideas of society and politics, as he did for ordinary ideas of friendship, which partly accounts for his appeal to "conscience." Thoreau's protest, however, was based on his conviction that conventional society and friendship exist to protect men from genuine social life and fraternity. Modern government, he wrote, is only a "device for letting one another alone"; as he viewed all civilization in his times, Thoreau saw government as a reflection of the hidden savage and his fears.

The Radical in Politics

When Thoreau called modern government a "complicated mechanism" concerned only with restricting the outer man, he was not criticizing it for being too strong: he was denouncing it for being too weak. It left undone the major task; it did not concern itself with the development of the human character. Most Americans wanted to limit the government to the fulfillment of their individual desires. That only emphasized the fact that the government lacked real loyalty and the authority to perform the significant political role Thoreau demanded. "What is called politics," he wrote, "is . . . something so superficial and inhuman that I have never recognized that it concerns me at all."

This is a typical overstatement, for Thoreau's civil disobedience

[26] For Thoreau's comments on friendship, see *Writings*, vol. I, pp. 280–307.

alone indicates that he did feel some concern about political decisions. He intended to stress that very little could be accomplished through politics as it existed. The law, he reminded reformers, cannot free men who are unwilling to be freed.

> Even if we grant that the American has freed himself from a political tyrant he is still the slave of an economical and moral tyrant. Now that the republic—the *res publica*—has been settled, it is time to look after the *res privata*—the private state. . . . The chief want in every State . . . (is) high and earnest purpose in its inhabitants. . . . When we want culture more than potatoes and illumination more than sugar-plums, then the great resources of the world are taxed and drawn out, and the result, or staple production, is not slaves, nor operatives, but men. . . .

America, Thoreau observed, was a "slave state" in more ways than one. The course of economic life was enslaving man to commerce and the machine, impoverishing social intercourse, isolating and trivializing men. Thoreau was not merely a moralist; he had an almost Marxian hardheadedness about economic life.

> To have done anything by which you earned money *merely* is to have been truly idle or worse. If the laborer gets no more than the wages his employer pays him, he is cheated, he cheats himself. . . . Those services for which the community will most readily pay, it is most disagreeable to render. You are being paid for being something less than a man. . . . (I)t would be economy for a town to pay its laborers so well that they would not feel they were working for low ends, but for scientific, even for moral ends. . . . It is remarkable that there is little or nothing written . . . on the subject of getting a living; how to make getting a living not merely honest and honorable, but . . . inviting and glorious; for if *getting* a living is not so, then living is not.

Man's means of earning his living lacked dignity and so, in his own eyes, did man himself. He fled that sense of inner unworthiness and sought to conceal it from his fellows. Social life became a place where "surface meets surface," in which a display of passion and political interest touches no real commitments but is only words, a kind of gossip.

> The excitement about Kossuth, consider how characteristic, but superficial it was! Men were making speeches to him all over the country, but each expressed only the thought, or want of thought, of the multitude. . . . They were merely banded together, as usual one leaning on

another and all together on nothing. . . . For the fruit of that stir, we have the Kossuth hat.

Genuine concern, Thoreau implied, might have taken the form of some action to relieve the sufferings of Hungary, but that would have required a depth of relationship which was lacking between citizens. He offered a final comment on American "fraternity":

> The American has dwindled into an Odd Fellow, one who may be known by the development of his organ of gregariousness and his manifest lack of intellect . . . who . . . ventures to live at all only by the aid of the mutual insurance company, which had promised to bury him decently.[27]

All this criticism was hardly the result of a doctrinaire individualism. It was born, as Thoreau asserted, from a desire to redirect the state and its citizens, to shift the goal of politics from the purposes of commerce and the machine to the goal of human development.

No man with a "genius for legislation," Thoreau contended, had yet appeared in America, a rebuke to the Framers which even then approached blasphemy. Yet it reflected his conviction that whatever their mechanical skills, the Framers had lacked a true knowledge of human nature and had hence been unable to design a polity which would assist men in the path of virtue. Their state, in fact, led rather in the other direction.[28]

Thoreau rejected the Framers' doctrine of a large state, preferring the small political order which was better suited to educating men, especially their emotions. He preached the limited horizon, the place where a man could be "monarch of all I survey." The emotions, as Thoreau knew, insist on that regal security, and given a sense of safety and delight in locality will allow freedom to the mind. When broader horizons make an incursion, the emotions shape men to meet the threat. Thoreau's comment that the telegraph did him no good because he had nothing to say to anyone in Texas was partly fear that the telegraph would lead men to know someone in Texas, only so that they would have something to say. And the great state, aiming at the mastery of nature, led men to destroy locality, cutting

---

[27] All the citations are from "Life Without Principle," *AM*, XII (1863), pp. 484–495.

[28] *Writings*, vol. II, p. 236.

off the emotional roots of virtue in pursuit of a delusory safety through "progress."

> If a man walk in the woods for love of them half of each day he is in danger of being regarded as a loafer; but if he spends the whole day as a speculator, shearing off those woods and making the earth bald before her time, he is esteemed an industrious and enterprising citizen. As if a town had no interest in its woods but to cut them down! [29]

In the same spirit Thoreau assailed those who abandoned their home places for new lands, especially the migrants who rushed to California in quest of gold. They abandoned the true "gold" of their native soil, fleeing a life which could be great vertically, in the depth and height of the spirit, for one which could only be great horizontally, on the surface. Reviewing the brutalizing conditions of the gold fields, Thoreau pointed out that men accepted such inhumanity and dehumanization for a chimera. Success would bring no true rewards and was uncertain at best. The gold rush, Thoreau affirmed with a Protestant note, was gambling and nothing more.

Emerson attacked Thoreau for "referring every minute fact to cosmic laws," but that too was part of Thoreau's caution. He distrusted the great generality which neglected the particular fact, the fraternal ideal which could justify fratricidal conduct. When the "villages are universities," he commented, America would be close to the ideal; the small polity, suited to man's emotions, was the best soil in which to grow the great mind. [30]

Thoreau was not "anti-political"; he was a political radical. He began with the conviction that fundamental changes were needed for things to be put right, and hence that laboring within existing institutions was likely to be as pointless as adopting the prevailing consensus as a basis for discussion. His political values compelled him to adopt the role of challenger, to become the prophet who seeks to point the way by setting an example.

> As for adopting the ways which the State has provided for remedying the evil, I know not of such ways. They take too much time, and a man's life will be gone. . . . A man has not everything to do, but something; and because he cannot do everything, it is not necessary

---

[29] "Life Without Principle."

[30] On the small state, see *Writings*, vol. II, pp. 50, 92, 250, 312, 321, vol. VI, pp. 157, 300; *Journal*, vol. V, pp. 310–311.

that he should do something wrong. . . . (I)n this case, the State has provided no way: its very Constitution is the evil. This may seem harsh, and stubborn and unconciliatory, but it is to treat with utmost kindness and consideration the only spirit that can appreciate or deserves it.

The last sentence suggests how far Emerson missed the mark with his comment that "It cost him nothing to say No. . . ." It cost Thoreau a good deal, shutting him from much communion he might have enjoyed and depriving him of quiet that he might have found productive.

> I seek . . . an excuse for conforming to the laws of the land. I am but too ready to obey them. Indeed, I have reason to suspect myself on this head . . . each year . . . I find myself disposed to review the acts and disposition of the . . . governments and the spirit of the people to find a pretext for conformity.[31]

"Something military . . ."

The radical stance, as the twentieth century hardly needs to be told, is not without its dangers. James Russell Lowell commented that Thoreau "condemned the world without knowing it," and in a sense, though not the one he had in mind, Lowell was right.[32] Thoreau may have known the "secret of friendship," as Emerson said; certainly he desired sympathy and companionship with great intensity. The extremity of his passion itself made him wary, too conscious of the dangers of temptation.

Thoreau protected himself by insisting that a man should "succeed alone" before truly seeking out friends; he set for himself the ideal of a soul that was proof against temptation.[33] It was a contradiction of his theories, but it also grew out of them. His recognition of the savage and the sensual, and his distaste for both, created a respect for the power of the emotions so great as to verge on fear—if, in fact, it cannot be categorized as fear.

He argued, quite properly, that Americans laid too much stress

---

[31] The citations are from "Civil Disobedience," *Writings*, vol. IV, pp. 358–367.
[32] Wilson, *The Shock of Recognition*, pp. 223, 227, 234–236.
[33] *Writings*, vol. IV, p. 299.

on proximity in friendship, affirming that communion is more than mere warmth of contact. Constant closeness, he pointed out, is not necessary for those who have true communion of spirit. He moved on, however, to a position which virtually rejected the need for contact and proximity, advocating a communion so spiritual that it denied the body. It was part, too, of the stern nature he saw in friendship and his emphasis on the sanctions imposed by the friend almost to the exclusion of any concern for the joys his friendship might offer.

There is more than a suggestion of Melville's Pierre in the "noble purity" that Thoreau took as his goal. Too sharply separated from the existing world and the relations of men, Thoreau was constantly in danger of seeing them only in the stark light of sin and shortcoming. He was, as Sherwood Anderson was to write, always a "judge" and not a "lover." [34]

The prophet is always in danger of being tempted by violence in his rage against the obtuseness of men. He needs the softening of fraternity, of delight bound to his vision, more than most men. Thoreau's sensual contact with Nature was not enough; like Pierre the idealist, he was tempted to strike out at those things which barred him from a realization of his vision and from a "pretext" for relations with his fellows.

There was, as Emerson said, "something military in his nature not to be subdued." Convinced of the evil of his times, he could come close to arguing that all that was necessary was to sweep away the defenses of a corrupt civilization. "So is all change for the better, like birth and death, which convulse the body." Too, his theory, if not his understanding, should have told him that an appeal to the consciences of men acknowledged to be corrupt is at best likely to have ambivalent results. [35]

For Thoreau, however, the burden became heavier, and frustration was increasingly difficult to endure; he became more impatient, more insistent on some result. "I have lain fallow long enough," he wrote at one point. Time had gradually overwhelmed Thoreau's sense of eternity.

[34] Wilson, *The Shock of Recognition*, p. 1285.

[35] Emerson, "Thoreau"; Thoreau, *Writings*, vol. I, p. 320, vol. II, pp. 115, 119, 123, vol. IV, pp. 358–367; *Journal*, vol. I, p. 132, vol. IV, p. 410.

Gradually he came to place more emphasis on the possibilities of technology rather than its ugliness or its destruction of social relations. The thrust of his political theory had advocated an outer simplicity as a means to an inner complexity; more and more he looked for a deliverer, a messianic man of action, who would combine inner simplicity and certainty with the ability to command the complex external world. Finally Thoreau came full circle, moving from the soft leadership of example and reproach to an accord with the violence of the crazed John Brown and a hope for apocalyptic transformation. Futile, the younger Thoreau might have asserted, and so it proved. John Brown's example may have helped to produce the Civil War, but both events changed only the constitutional mechanism of American politics, and not its values and motives.[36]

Any criticism of Thoreau must be mild, however; the cause of the slave was one that cried out for solution by almost any means. Moreover, Thoreau, even in his worst moments, never struck the note of the historicists like Emerson. "No convulsion could shake him," John Jay Chapman said of Emerson's serene faith in history. Emerson saw the Civil War not only as an evil remedy for a still greater evil but also as a "cure for cowardice," a smashing of "character-destroying civilization" which would leave a "nation of heroes" in its wake. "Now," Emerson exulted, "we have a country again." [37]

The faith in history, alas, is watered by the blood of martyrs. If Thoreau defended violence, his defense was still tied to individual choice and the martyrdom of example. It was not in Thoreau to have greeted war with a shout of joy. War and violence might be judgments on the sins and follies of men, but Thoreau could never manage the twisted reason that sees fratricide as a means to fraternity.

[36] *Writings*, vol. III, p. 333, vol. IV, p. 185, vol. IX, pp. 410–412, 449; R. C. Albrecht, "Thoreau and His Audience: A Plea for Captain John Brown," *AL*, XXXII (1961), pp. 393–402.
[37] Wilson, *The Shock of Recognition*, p. 621.

> When the public is supreme there is no man who does not . . . endeavor to court it by drawing to himself the esteem and affection of those amongst whom he is to live. Many of the passions . . . which keep asunder human hearts are obliged to retire and hide below the surface. Pride must be dissembled; disdain dares not break out; egotism fears its own self. . . . Men learn . . . to think of their fellow-men from ambitious motives; and they frequently find it . . . their interest to forget themselves. . . . The Americans have combated by free institutions the tendency of equality to keep men apart.
>
> De Tocqueville, *Democracy in America*

CHAPTER XII

NATHANIEL HAWTHORNE: THE CITIZEN

Puritanism Revisited

FROM Henry James to the present, a line of critics has attempted to explain Hawthorne in terms of his "Puritan background." This is an improvement on the spurious theory that Hawthorne's work derives from transcendentalism (which Hawthorne once described as a "heap of fog and darkness"),[1] but it too misses the point.

Certainly Hawthorne wrote often of Puritans and even more

[1] "The Celestial Railroad," *Mosses from an Old Manse*, vol. I, pp. 228–229.

often in Puritan terms. But the emphasis on his "background" makes Hawthorne too passive a figure and reduces his thought to a reflection of his social origins. In a narrow sense, Hawthorne's background was not Puritan at all: he was raised in the liberal-rationalist canon of Unitarian orthodoxy. Hawthorne did, in the end, become something of a Puritan, but his doctrine was so logical as to have balked many of the original Puritans despite their delight in logic, for he espoused a Puritanism without Election. In any case, a result is not a cause; Hawthorne's own variety of Puritanism developed out of his own observation and reflection on the nature and condition of man.

It was important, of course, that Hawthorne lived in a society with a Puritan history, one in which the monuments and relics of Puritanism were everywhere at hand. Hawthorne's New England made seventeenth-century culture easily available as an alternative to the ideas of the eighteenth and nineteenth centuries. The Puritan past was the raw material for Hawthorne's romance, partly because it gave him a language and metaphor both congenial to his own ideas and familiar to the public at large.[2]

This kind of emphasis, little as it may seem to differ from that of James and the critics who followed him, not only gives greater concern to Hawthorne's art and originality but places both in a more political context. And in considering Hawthorne, emphasis on politics is critical. If we have failed to appreciate the degree to which Hawthorne was a political man, it is partly because he played down his own political interests for his own somewhat guileful purposes. Dedicating *Our Old Home* to his friend Franklin Pierce, he apologized to the ex-President because the book did not deal with "matters of policy and government"; its essays belonged "entirely to aesthetic literature."

Perhaps he felt it did, but to most of us Hawthorne's "aesthetic literature" will seem to have a decidedly political dimension. In the first chapter of *Our Old Home*, Hawthorne discusses a catalogue of politically relevant subjects: his fears for the Union, then engaged in the Civil War; the pain that the War caused European exiles who had seen America as "their own in the last resort"; McClellan's Pen-

<hr>

[2] Herbert Schneider, *The Puritan Mind*, pp. 256–262; Joseph Schwartz, "Three Aspects of Hawthorne's Puritanism."

insular Campaign (his comments on the General and his strategy are shrewd); the inadequacy of the spoils system in providing diplomatic personnel, and the insufficient resources made available to consuls; injustices to seamen and the recruitment of foreign and criminal elements as sailors, which resulted in insecure and hence brutal captains; and finally, English and American national character. If a writer who insisted that all of man's life and personal development is involved with politics can legitimately be called political, then Hawthorne was a political man.

Recent studies have nearly dispensed with the picture of Hawthorne as an "ethereal," shy, and sensitive introvert. The new Hawthorne is almost two personalities; the older image must vie with a Hawthorne who is vigorous, cheerful and a man of the world. Hawthorne himself called attention to the duality. The lonely aesthete, he wrote, seemed a "character" he had been assigned to "play," an "amiable outline" which many of his writings were designed to fill in.[3]

Hawthorne always insisted that the self had an inner, "secret" reality which struggled to be revealed—first to the individual, then to his fellows—despite all of society's rewards and threats. Society might develop or distort man's nature; it could never change it.[4] Yet that private, inner self was not the whole of man's nature or personality; political and social life were part of his humanity and his identity. There was no contradiction for Hawthorne between soul and society; the contradiction lay in man, and the task of society was to resolve that conflict rightly. In the ancient ideal, the best society produced the best men; politics was human education.

Fraternity, the best relation between men, was neither an innate "fact" nor an ultimate ideal. (His attack on the utopians in *Blithedale Romance* was partly based on their failure to realize that fraternity may be a relation which results from common purposes, but it cannot be a purpose in itself without distorting men's relations.) Fraternity was something learned, and an essential means to

[3] *The Marble Faun* (New York: New American Library, 1961), pp. vi, 325; *Twice Told Tales* (New York: Washington Square Press, 1960), pp. xiv–xv.

[4] *The Marble Faun* (1961), pp. 98–99; *Twice Told Tales* (1960), pp. xii, 258–265.

individual identity and virtue. Hawthorne's idea of fraternity was certainly "Puritan," at least in outline; it was also that of a political man.

Blackness

Sin was undoubtedly Hawthorne's most frequent subject. The "blackness ten times black," the symbols of darkness and evil, have struck Hawthorne's admirers and deprecators alike as the most arresting feature of his work. Yet few have remembered that sin is never a simple concept—and never less simple, perhaps, than in Hawthorne's writing. Sin was ubiquitous because it was complex, insinuating itself into the diverse situations of human life.

Hawthorne followed the Protestant tradition in identifying "original sin" with the concern for the security and gratification of the physical self with which man is born. In one sense, of course, "original sin" is lawless; the demand for pleasure strains against law, duty, and obligation to one's fellows. Yet, Hawthorne observed, original sin is also law-abiding; the desire for comfort and security may lead a man into conformity and the betrayal of ideals. Ease of life, reputation, "place" (both social and spatial)—all are reflections of original sin. Original sin is inescapable because it simply reflects the frailty of flesh.

"Ultimate sin," by contrast, is the sin of ends and not of beginnings. It is based on the seductions of the ideal and the temptations of pride which lead men to claim they have laid bare the mysteries of the cosmos, and that they have achieved freedom from human limitations and dependence. As individualistic as original sin, ultimate sin is based not on flesh but on the ascetic's dream of escaping the flesh. It aims at "objectivity"; that is, it disdains the subtle webs that bind spirit and body, man and man, man and his world, and would regard all things outside the spirit and will as "external" and separable. The great nemesis of ultimate sin is death. The sinner wills to deny death's power over him and must in the end become self-destructive; the "elixirs" of eternal life that Hawthorne's characters so often brew always turn out to be deadly poisons. Ethan Brand, the discoverer of ultimate sin, hurls himself into the lime-kiln he once operated, as a gesture of defiance to the cosmos itself.

Either sin, of course, violates man's nature, for man can no more be independent than he can attain a world of total gratification. Yet while original sin is a fact, ultimate sin is a folly. Ethan Brand's remains, found the next morning atop the lime, only enrich the product. His melodramatic suicide serves only to demonstrate that man is always bound to his fellows and the world. The romantic (and the romantic-scientific) ideal of "objectivity" is a joke on those who pursue it.[5]

Neither sin can be carried to completion, but man can, especially in youth, approach a kind of innocence. It is only in later life that the grace and beauty of the Donatello clan yields to grossness and subhuman sensuality. For humankind, however, original sin is inevitable, and Hawthorne suggests that this is well: Donatello is never quite real, certainly not human, until he acquires guilt. Ultimate sin is less humanly plausible and not inevitable; it is approached only through self-delusion. (Hawthorne's villainous men of ultimate sin are unbelievable; they serve as moral archetypes whose diabolism can be conceived only in a character monstrously inhuman.)[6]

Hawthorne saw that those whose lives are devoted to one or the other sin find great attractiveness in those who seek the goal they shun. Man violates the law of nature, but never with impunity; nature demands her own, and the self, unbidden, seeks those things the "sinful" mind rejects. Hence, in *The Marble Faun* and *Blithedale Romance*, Hawthorne created twin temptresses, mistresses of the two sins. The women of purity, innocence, and conventional morality (Priscilla and Hilda), with their European names, are contrasted with the dark mystery and passion of the "Eastern" women (Zenobia and Miriam). The Goddess of Purity has her sins; Hilda's willingness to disown Miriam in order to keep herself undefiled is a lesson in the betrayals and the disloyalty of innocence. Hilda, no less than Donatello, needs the education of sin to attain any real humanity. The dark ladies have ultimate sin: Zenobia harbors a fanatical pride,

[5] "Ethan Brand," *The Snow Image*, pp. 102–124; *The Marble Faun* (1961), pp. 131–133, 148–151, 190–195, 204, 311, 328; *Mosses from an Old Manse*, Vol. II, pp. 30–48, 111–138. For Hawthorne's use of the "elixir of life" as a theme, see *The Dolliver Romance* and *Septimius Felton*.

[6] Henry S. Kariel, "Man Limited: Nathaniel Hawthorne's Classicism," *SAQ*, LII (1953), pp. 528–542; Sister J. Marie Luecke, "Villains and Non-Villains in Hawthorne's Fiction," *PMLA*, LXXVIII (1963), pp. 362–381.

Miriam is consumed by the desire to monopolize and cherish guilt.

The intellectuals, Kenyon and Coverdale, are fascinated by the pure woman; the artist and the intellectual are drawn by innocence, for it marks their need for affection and a bond with their own times. Self-observation and analysis reveals failure and shortcoming, which make innocence seem desirable. To the men of innocence and action, Donatello and Hollingsworth, it is the dark lady, the hidden truth, who has the power of attraction. There is a clear lesson in Dona-tello's feeling for Miriam and in his effort to win her by killing her mysterious pursuer. The innocent seeks to free Miriam from her conscience; and being innocent, he can only perceive conscience as a physical force, an exterior threat. Thus Donatello too acquires guilt, learning that conscience is not exterior force but interior reality, that guilt is personal and not foreign.

Hollingsworth seems purpose incarnate. Yet he is nearly without any self-critical faculties. His incarnate purpose is only a combination of egotism and naivete, his strength of character merely a mixture of dogmatism and vitality. Hollingsworth's "strength" is itself based largely on a desperate desire for admiration and affection. Hence his passion for Zenobia: she is unsettling because she is unknown and self-directed, and Hollingsworth is driven to humble her pride, unveil her secrets, and subject her to his will and control.[7]

Inevitably a discussion of Hawthorne's idea of sin must come to *The Scarlet Letter.* Hawthorne opens the novel by reminding his readers that the two sins, symbolized by the prison (original sin) and the cemetery (ultimate sin), followed the Puritans even into the Holy Commonwealth. The chief male characters are analogues of the pairs in *Blithedale* and *The Marble Faun*—Dimmesdale, the intellectual, and Chillingworth, the man of action. Here, however, the intellectual is the "original" sinner, while the more worldly Chillingworth commits the ultimate sin.

Chillingworth's role is determined by his desire to avenge the

---

[7] *Blithedale Romance* (New York: Norton, 1958), pp. 21–22, 34, 38, 58, 78, 108–110, 113–149, 150; *The Marble Faun* ((1961), pp. 58, 131–133, 148–157, 204, 208, 277. See also F. C. Crews, "A New Reading of *Blithedale Romance*," *AL*, XXIX (1957), pp. 147–170, and Philip Rahv, "The Dark Lady," *PR*, VIII (1941), pp. 362–381.

injury to his pride caused by Hester's betrayal. He seeks to restore his sense of potency and control by illogically punishing not Hester, but her lover. Yet the illogic is logical enough; Hester remains the goddess, the object of love for Chillingworth. She must be punished through her lover, brought to see her error in giving her affection to another. It was not Hester's physical charms that Chillingworth adored, as Hawthorne is at some pains to make clear. His delight was in affection and admiration divorced from physicality; Chillingworth is a man of ultimate sin. The scientific detachment with which he sets about his efforts to possess Dimmesdale's soul only reflects that fact. Magic and science are tools by which Chillingworth would master or destroy all wills independent of his own which menace him in his pride.

Dimmesdale's original sin is, of course, symbolized by his relation with Hester. Dimmesdale was seduced less by Hester's sex appeal than by the "dreams of happiness" he associated with her. (Leslie Fiedler is right to point out that the letter "A" symbolized Adam's fall as well as a violation of the Seventh Commandment.) But the demands of original sin are contradictory; Dimmesdale is trapped between his desire for forbidden delight and his need for position and reputation. He is thus an easy victim for Chillingworth's single-mindedness. And it is part of Chillingworth's satanic science to cure the ills of Dimmesdale's body, realizing that bodily health only aggravates the disease of the minister's soul.[8]

Stories of sin, the three novels are also stories of fraternity unrealized or perverted. There are close ties between Kenyon and Donatello, and between Hollingsworth and Coverdale. Hollingsworth, however, demands intellectual submission as a price of friendship, and that Coverdale cannot grant. Donatello's bond to Miriam sweeps him into a dark world of romance and atonement where Kenyon need not and will not follow. The sorority of Hilda and Miriam is no less abortive; and so long as each clings to her original role, the sisterhood of Zenobia and Priscilla is destructive and evil. Even the comparatively sane intellectuals show a fatal hesitancy, an unwilling-

[8] *The Scarlet Letter, passim*; H. Maclean, "Hawthorne's *Scarlet Letter*: the Dark Problem of Life," *AL*, XXVII (1955), pp. 12–24; Irving Howe, *Politics and the Novel*, pp. 164, 167, 170–171, 175.

ness to run the risks of commitment or affection. There can be no recognition of likeness, and hence no fraternity, Hawthorne suggests, while men cling to either of the sinful dreams of self.

The relation between Chillingworth and Dimmesdale is the negation of fraternity. Dimmesdale's body is comforted and his social position is protected, thus fulfilling the minimal demands of original sin, while Chillingworth attains the spiritual control of another on which ultimate sin insists. It is precisely the relation which Coverdale feared might develop if he bound himself to Hollingsworth. In *The Scarlet Letter,* however, Dimmesdale and Chillingworth are united by their mutual relation to Hester. In her person, the dark woman and the pure lady become one. And if the two temptresses have a fundamental identity, it is because original and ultimate sin also have a common root.

Both sins are simply the desire to be independent of others and of the world, expressed in demands which are only the insistence that others submit to the will and desire of the self. Ultimate sin, more learned and intellectual, grander if not as appealing, is only more perverse because it has become separated from physicality. Devotion to Hester leads both men to deny God's demands on their consciences. Ruled by the emotions, men twist their minds; adoration of the Mother is denial of the Father; and shut up within themselves, men shut out the perception of likeness.

Hawthorne's treatment of an idea is often clearest when he writes of its dark negation, and he comes closest to a definition of fraternity in the context of fratricide. In *Alice Doane's Appeal,* the temptresses are again one. Leonard Doane kills his sister's "unknown admirer" only to discover that the victim was his brother, his father's son; but he does not see the "likeness" of their common father until the moment when he slays his brother. The brothers were originally separated by different mothers and environments (one is a rustic patriot, the other a Tory cosmopolite), but difference of origins is the common lot of men and nations. The tragedy results from their desire to win the affection of a single object, a conflict of goals and not of origins.[9]

[9] "Alice Doane's Appeal," *Works* (Boston: Houghton Mifflin, 1883), vol. XII, pp. 279–295; *Mosses from an Old Manse,* vol. I, pp. 43–66, 203; S. O. Lesser, "The Image of the Father," *PR,* XXII (1955), pp. 370–390.

Likeness in the father, the basis of fraternity, Hawthorne knew was not enough. The "heart" of man must be willing to see likeness of spirit and to bestow affection on it. Those who seek to escape the weakness, ignorance and dependence which is man's lot will hate what is most akin. For not only will a kindred spirit remind them of what they would forget in themselves, but because a brother is like the self, he is the most dangerous and knowing of all rivals. (Hawthorne lamented the fact that men of genius, who need social relations and support, are led by vanity and ambition into conflict with those who might genuinely provide them.) It is the logic of the sinner's dream of independence that he must strive to control whatever is outside and distinct from his own will, whether his immediate goal is wealth, fame, or affection. Sin denies fraternity because sin denies humanity and dehumanizes. And since sin is the first condition of man, man by himself is a stranger to his brother.

Veils and Masks

Man, however, is not "by himself." The fourth party in *The Scarlet Letter* is the Puritan polity, and if Arthur Dimmesdale is led to self-betrayal by his desire for repute, it is because the basis on which the community granted honor was a defective one. Puritanism, as Hawthorne saw it, was psychologically blind; in its attempt to deny the heritage of imperfection which is the lot of all men, it became hypocritical, emphasizing external conformity and ignoring the spirit. Hester sinned physically and was judged; Dimmesdale sinned internally and escaped social sanction. Yet Hester's is the easier role; she is protected by the scarlet letter from the temptations of hypocrisy and is allowed to remain a member of society on the basis of her own personality. Forced to be aware of original sin, she moves toward self-knowledge and eventually attains a greater humanity. Society is, after all, not unjust to Hester; she is guilty of the offense with which she is charged. It is unjust in failing to punish Dimmesdale, and the failure results from the fact that to punish Dimmesdale, it would have had to understand itself. Hawthorne found Puritan society defective because its judgments were too few (if he also thought its penalties too severe, he was aware that severity was tied to the delusion that the criminal was unusual).[10]

Knowledge of sin is necessary to knowledge of self; until he sins, Donatello cannot grow toward humanity. A society which encourages the delusion of guiltlessness; whether from Puritan hypocrisy or the more modern belief in the "goodness" of man, in fact prevents human development. The natural law of man's life, as Hawthorne saw it, was to rise from innocence to knowledge, to journey through the recognition of original sin toward that state of excellence which ultimate sin falsely claims to have attained.[11]

To such development, political life was essential. Politics begins with the recognition of the fact of original sin and the destructive consequences of that sin. Yet sin is only the negative side of the positive vision. Hawthorne knew that a society in which men see in their fellows only a reflection of their own guilt would be full of suspicion, resentment, and hostility. Political life demands a "holy sanction" for its justice, a common vision and a shared purpose. Those who share the goal will be aware that they fall short of it, but knowledge of imperfection is endurable precisely when all have that knowledge. Sin derives from a desire for unconditional affection, a demand to be loved for what one is now, not because of what one strives to be. Affection and concern, the sense of communion, are necessary in great endeavors because men need the "upholding" of their fellows; social encouragement is the precondition of any growth toward humanity.[12]

Both original and ultimate sin were the more to be detested because they were sins against the political, affecting not only the guilty but their fellow citizens and subsequent generations. The denial of shortcoming and dependence was necessarily self-deceptive

[10] H. Macpherson, "Hawthorne's Mythology: A Mirror for Puritans," *Toronto Quarterly*, XXVIII (1959), pp. 267-278; R. Haugh, "The Second Secret of *The Scarlet Letter*," *College English*, XVII (1961), pp. 161-172; and L. J. Merrill, "The Puritan Policeman," *ASR*, 10 (1945), pp. 766-776.

[11] *Twice Told Tales* (1960), pp. 19-33, 135, 165, 379-393; *The Marble Faun* (1961), pp. 190-195, 222, 234, 274, 277, 311, 328; *American Note Books*, vol. I, pp. 32-33; *English Note Books*, vol. I, p. 35.

[12] *Twice Told Tales* (1960), pp. 4, 19-33; *The Marble Faun* (1961), pp. 88, 234, 325; Van Doren, *Nathaniel Hawthorne*, pp. 6, 220.

and demanded the effort to deceive one's fellows; pride or the retreat to innocence imposed barriers to communion and to genuine relations between men. Of the two, ultimate sin was by far the more heinous, for original sin is always subject to education by the facts of nature and the perceptions of the mind. When the mind itself is corrupted and the individual shuts himself off from physical communion with his fellows, even that hope is denied. A Dimmesdale may be redeemed, a Chillingworth never. Wakefield, the extreme case of objective man, retained his "sympathies" with his fellows but divorced his feelings from concrete relations and satisfactions; as a result, he became progressively less substantial. Idealism and perfectionism, the greatest forms of pride, lead men to reject what is possible and attainable in human relations, and while one may feel the beauty of an impossible (or temporally impossible) ideal, "it is not wise to intermix fantastic ideas with the reality of affection. Let us content ourselves to hold communion of spirit in such modes as are ordained to us." Perfect unity of spirit is impossible while men have bodies, and delight for the emotions is needful for any bond among men in the flesh. Hence the almost savage attack Hawthorne leveled at the gentle Shakers: by denying the emotions, and by their self-righteousness, they placed impossible barriers to communion.[13]

The polity is founded on the needs of man qua animal, even if its goals are given by the human spirit. That perception was the basis of Hawthorne's suspicion of revolutionaries and reformers. The danger posed by either was simple—that he might shut off the possibility of improvement in an impossible effort to "remake" the world. The world cannot have a new beginning; one begins with what exists and with nature as it must be. The idea alone cannot reshape the emotions, and the human heart is a limit to all change.[14]

So many of the "brethren of love and righteousness" revealed, in their warring sectarianism, a hatred for mankind. So many others, like Emerson, failed as teachers because, unaware of the impact of the political order on themselves, and they appealed to the spon-

[13] *American Note Books*, vol. I, pp. 10, 21, 77, 97, 220; *Twice Told Tales* (1960), pp. 90–99, 165, 330–336.
[14] *Blithedale Romance* (1958), pp. 14, 17, 85, 92–93, 97, 138–141, 193; *Mosses from an Old Manse*, vol. II, p. 189.

taneous education of "Nature" and the untaught heart of man. Despite Emerson's own morality, Hawthorne observed, his teachings left his students with no way to distinguish good from evil.[15]

The doctrine of progress was no better, for it taught men to confuse the "triteness of novelty" with moral improvement; Hawthorne knew there is no necessary connection between being avantgarde and having advanced. Worse, once the "titan of innovation" is thought valuable in itself, it will go beyond attacks on the corrupt and accidental aspects of a polity to lay hands on the pillars of the temple.[16]

Social and political beliefs, Hawthorne argued, can only be tested by their impact on men, and his tenderness toward tradition and existing institutions was based on his recognition of the shortcoming of even the best political systems. Beginning with man as he is born, concerned to govern and improve all, the polity must fall short of the standards of the best men. It must partially violate man's true nature because it begins with his original nature. Hence Hawthorne's clear understanding of the Puritan failure:

> The earliest settlers were able to keep within the narrowest limits of their rigid principles because they had adopted them in mature life, and from their own deep conviction, and were strengthened in them by that species of enthusiasm which is as sober and enduring as reason itself. But if their immediate successors followed the same line of conduct, they were confined to it . . . by habits forced upon them.[17]

The test of a polity is not whether it mirrors the ideal of life and relations which the best men hold for themselves, but whether it encourages the development of such men.

The political order which would rear excellent men will, even in the best of circumstances, need an element of myth. Myth notably, and not untruth, is required. There is always a tension between the best men and society, but society needs the example of excellent men. It is "not everyone who can steal the fires of heaven" and "kindle a thousand hearts," but those who can have drives and standards

---

[15] *Mosses from an Old Manse*, vol. I, pp. 37–38, vol. II, pp. 171, 183, 185; *American Note Books*, vol. II, p. 20. Despite his distrust of those who appealed to "nature," Hawthorne admired Thoreau. (*American Note Books*, vol. II, pp. 97–98.)

[16] *Mosses from an Old Manse*, vol. I, pp. 37–38, vol. II, pp. 175, 181, 185.

[17] *Dr. Bullivant*, p. 151.

which may be at odds with those of society at large. Hawthorne wrote of Shakespeare:

> It is for the high interest of the world not to insist on finding out that the greatest men are, in a certain lower sense, the same kind of men as the rest of us, and often a little worse; because the common mind cannot properly digest such a discovery, nor ever know the true proportion of good and evil, nor how small a part of him it was that touched our muddy . . . earth. Thence comes moral bewilderment and even intellectual loss in regard to what is best in him.

Hawthorne's moral was simple. "A veil," he noted, "may be needful but never a mask." Men who look closely must be able to see through the public personality and discern the real one, if example is to play its highest role; the public personality is needed for the most general role. And, if excellent men are forced to mask themselves completely, they neither set an example nor can they find the help and support that they—"in a certain lower sense, the same kind . . . as the rest of us"—require.[18]

Certainly his belief in the imperfection of all polities was one of the reasons that Hawthorne avoided belief in great states or world government, even as ideals. If America had not separated from Britain, he declared, "the earth might have beheld the intolerable spectacle of a sovereignty and institutions imperfect but indestructible." [19]

Yet Hawthorne never prescribed political quietism. Acutely aware of social evils, he believed in a duty to improve even the best society, and he knew too that decorum, prudence, and respect for convention may only be a mask for moral cowardice; a retreat, like Dimmesdale's, from the burdens of judgment. Political men, he wrote in his *American Note Books*, too often had "consciences . . . turned to india rubber." The purist, however, fled moral responsibility as much as the compromiser. Praise was owed the political men who could stand between the ideal and political necessity and forget neither. Hawthorne found virtue, for example, in Jonathan Cilley, who told no lies but left parts of the truth unspoken in his

[18] *American Note Books*, vol. I, p. 24; *Our Old Home*, p. 117; *Mosses*, vol. II, pp. 179, 181.
[19] *Our Old Home*, p. 24; Hawthorne was often a shrewd judge of world politics. (See *English Note Books*, vol. I, pp. 70, 137.)

public utterances. Cilley "loved the people and respected them, and was prouder of nothing than of his brotherhood with those who had intrusted their public interests to his care," and his guile reflected "a much higher system of morality than any natural integrity would have prompted him to adopt." Natural integrity was suspect in politics, for the "natural sympathies" of a political man—his love for and desire to be loved by the people—always tempted him to articulate the "lower feeling of the multitude" without regard either for truth or for the goals of political life.[20]

Excellence in political art and political morality alike required the improvement of men and the conditions in which they lived, and such improvement justified the means by which it was achieved. Bettering political conditions required change; for Hawthorne, the existing state of politics was unacceptable, and any teaching failed which did not go beyond it. Hence, although he conceded that Franklin's maxims were "suited to condition of the country" and on the whole probably had good effects, Hawthorne found them seriously wanting. Franklin's precepts were too concerned with money-making, he declared, and in any case "teach men but a very small portion of their duties." Critical as he was of reformers, Hawthorne thought they deserved credit for at least attempting to produce a better life; he was always, as Hall asserted, preeminently a "critic of society." [21]

The mission of the political order was, as Hawthorne saw it, to encourage and allow men to develop the highest excellence of which they were capable. The state existed to educate man, and it acted justly to the extent that it understood each man and his needs, especially his need for fraternity. Nature, Hawthorne declared, has "constituted for every man a brotherhood wherein it is the one great office of human wisdom to classify him." [22] But the state of his own times, in Hawthorne's view, classified men superficially at best. American society was blind to the real qualities of men; it reasoned

[20] *American Note Books*, vol. I, pp. 67, 211; *Biographical Sketches*, p. 239; "Civic Banquets," *AM*, XII (1863), pp. 204–205.

[21] *Mosses*, vol. I, pp. 208–209; L. S. Hall, *Hawthorne: Critic of Society* (New Haven: Yale University Press, 1944). Hawthorne's comment on Franklin, made at the height of Franklin's vogue as a child educator, occurs in a children's book (*Biographical Stories*, p. 82).

[22] *Mosses*, vol. I, p. 241; see also *American Note Books*, vol. I, p. 15.

from external qualities and attainments, creating false hierarchies that rewarded vice and punished virtue, ignoring many and corrupting the favored. The poor suffer from "the tainted breath of cities, scanty and unwholesome food, destructive modes of labor and the lack of those moral supports which might partly have counteracted such bad influences." The upper classes are encouraged to bodily and material excess and are left spiritual pygmies; their sorrows—Hawthorne thought lovelorn romance and frustrated ambition the most typical—are insubstantial, for they mourn not something lost, but something never won; their love lacks the sacrifice which marks devotion. (Hawthorne commented that wealthy men who leave their money to good causes prove that their ghosts have love, but not their bodies.) In general, most are miscast for their social roles; many are unjustly honored while others, more worthy, are in such "sluggish circumstances" that only a radical transformation could do them justice.[23]

Hawthorne's egalitarianism was radical, going beyond the doctrine of "moral equality." Even the intellect, he asserted, is probably "only a higher development of innate gifts common to all," and is based largely on the ability to articulate and express ideas and perceptions which remain mute in most men. The bitter experience of Brook Farm taught him (if he had not known before) that men will vary in preferences and choice of pursuit even if environmental influences are neutralized. Those devoted to the mind's goods will find manual labor unsuitable; identical status does not comprise justice. All must have the maximum opportunity to develop what is best in each, which demands a society of variety, not of sameness.[24]

Human virtue depended on obedience to the logic of human life: a growth of knowledge and a growth toward death. (Knowledge of death was, as Hawthorne saw it, the most difficult and possibly the most essential form of self-knowledge.) The good life was, in part, a thing of movement, of alienation from childhood and the past, in which nostalgia bespoke only a lust for innocence and a fear of mortality.

[23] *Mosses*, vol. I, pp. 242–245; a less sophisticated and more moralistic version is *American Note Books*, vol. I, pp. 23–24.

[24] *Mosses*, vol. I, p. 245; *American Note Books*, vol. I, pp. 9–12, vol. II, p. 162.

Yet Hawthorne's "conservatism" considered movement for its own sake as only flight in another sense, and rejected it quite as much as his "radicalism" rejected nostalgia. Clifford Pyncheon might seek to escape the "blood curse" on his house, but his first escape led to prison, not freedom, and he ended by an adulation of movement for itself and without goals, purposeless and ephemeral. The attempt to escape the heritage of sin and doom led first to original, then to ultimate sin. The railroad was Pyncheon's ideal, his hope for endless motion; the electric telegraph would spiritualize matter, making the whole country—or even the world—a nerve throbbing with love.

Clifford Pyncheon's creed was the faith of the nineteenth century: technological pride and the doctrine of progress. The builders of "The Celestial Railroad," however, forgot that the movement and development of life is not movement in space. It is movement and struggle in the spirit of man, knowledge and personality prevailing slowly over delusion and sin. No stages could be skipped, for the emotions must learn, as well as the mind: "worldly wisdom" was a means to "wisdom not altogether of this world." Too, since there was no final resting place for man, there was no necessity for flying the place where he began. The pilgrimage of life might be lived, might even be easier, if lived in one place and with one people. Ultimately, Hawthorne wrote, with a touch of sadness, earth is "not an abiding place," and the pilgrimage which is human progress gradually alienates the individual from childhood, the past, the dream of place, and finally from the world itself.[25]

The march of the pilgrim is quite different from the "independence" of ultimate sin. As men become alienated from the societies of birth, time, and politics, they do not lose their bonds with their fellow men. Those who see their own nature truly will be aware of a "brotherhood with the guiltiest," a lesser likeness within the greater. Too, they will be aware of a debt to the societies which they have gone beyond; excellence depends on a society which, consciously or not, develops the faculties and the will to excel. At each stage of his development, man needs the support of some of his fellows ("a brotherhood wherein it is the one great office of human

---

[25] *The House of the Seven Gables* (New York: Dell, 1960), pp. 261–269; *French and Italian Note Books*, vol. II, p. 187; *American Note Books*, vol. I, p. 212; *Mosses*, vol. I, pp. 216–239; *Blithedale Romance* (1958), p. 193.

wisdom to classify him"). Indeed, the more exalted his purpose, the greater his need for communion. The emotions will struggle to hold the pilgrim back; overcoming them depends on the support of friends who share his goals and can thus understand and share the individual's happiness and woe.

Man's "ascent" demands that he classify some friends as greater and others as lesser; old friendships may lose their fraternal quality if they no longer share a common purpose. That hardly means that one ceases to care for them (Hawthorne's own stubborn loyalty was proverbial). Men do not lose their debt to those who have aided, their bond to those who have encouraged. Though they may be alienated, the highest men live their lives in and not out of society. (Even during an idyll with friends in Maine, Hawthorne saw and was disturbed by the lot of the poor Irish in the district.) And, since knowledge of his own original sin is the first step of his pilgrimage, the excellent man always remembers that guilty fraternity in which he is bound to all humanity.[26]

Hawthorne came only hesitantly and unhappily to recognize his own alienation from society and to acknowledge that the world did not afford a "true place" in which he could openly and completely express his personality "as Nature intended." He believed, however, that the tension between individual and social needs could be palliated if not cured. Alienated man could discover his brothers without menacing the relations of men in society by a private language. Allegory and symbol, the artistic construction, might provide a veil through which the brother might see the intention and recognize his fellow. The failure of the work of art had to be taken for granted; words and pictures cannot convey ultimate vision. Yet, Hawthorne argued, to the "beloved reader" and true brother, the failure suggests the impossible success that was its aim, and it is to find such a brother that the work is written. Hawthorne wrote of himself that "he must necessarily find himself without an audience except here and there an individual or possibly an isolated clique," and it was the moments shared with such individuals and groups that were the unambiguously

---

[26] On the need for fraternal communion and the continuing obligation of compassion, see *Marble Faun* (1961), pp. v–vi, 88, 272–273, 337, 341–342; *Blithedale Romance* (1958), pp. 47–48, 85, 88, 91–92, 97; *American Note Books*, vol. I, pp. 51–52; and Van Doren, *Nathaniel Hawthorne*, pp. 32, 88, 181, 195.

real times when the veil could be set aside. "It is not that I have any liking for mystery and darkness," he declared, "because I abhor it." Hawthorne affirmed a desire to be understood, and called the reserve that impelled him toward allusion and allegory "involuntary," but he knew that the reader "must find his own way there. I can neither guide nor enlighten him." [27]

D. H. Lawrence understood that side of Hawthorne well enough; "blue-eyed Nathaniel," he commented, always seemed more innocent than he really was. The aesthetic and sensitive character which seemed to Hawthorne his most "amiable" relation with society demanded that he conceal forceful sentiments behind the veil of delicacy. Hawthorne, who disdained nostalgia, wrote most often of the past. The allegorical story which speaks of the past conceals more than one which treats of the present; it conceals the contemporaneity of the moral, the perenniality of the analysis. (His fictions, Hawthorne noted, whether present or historical, "have little or no reference to time and space.") [28]

Hawthorne rested his hope on one of the great arts of political man, the art of metaphor, which allows the discerning reader to see meaning in what may seem only a pious affirmation. The socially useful and the theoretically valid were for Hawthorne, never wholly contradictory. Rightly understood, in fact, they were the same, although they must speak in different languages to different men; allegory and symbol merely combined the two languages in the same words.

One Twenty-Millionth of a Sovereign

Progress was never part of Hawthorne's creed. He mocked the science which sought to destroy earthly imperfection, confident that true wisdom did not lie in technological advance. Knowledge of building tools is not understanding of how to improve men; the machine for "the wholesale manufacture of morality" built by the partisans of "The Celestial Railroad" was a fraud, and Hawthorne's

[27] *Marble Faun* (1961), pp. vi, 162–169, 234, 325; *American Note Books*, vol. I, p. 215, vol. II, pp. 214–215; *Mosses*, vol. I, p. 106; Van Doren, *Nathaniel Hawthorne*, pp. 43, 57, 59, 62–64.

[28] D. H. Lawrence, *Studies in Classical American Literature*, p. 93; *Mosses*, vol. I, p. 107.

scientists, over and over again, destroy what they hope to perfect.[29]

Hawthorne did, however, most certainly believe in the possibility of improvement in man's lot. Change for the better depended on the realization that history had already carried men beyond the optimal midpoint between sentiment and purpose. Modern life was characterized by a "sad severity" and a "too earnest utilitarianism"; social life had become grim and gray, and men's emotions retreated from it into private and romantic dreams. This was especially true of America, which lacked the physical symbols to tie romance to the present, or the institutions to bind the emotions to living men. Hawthorne noticed a fatal sign in the propensity of Americans for the romantic delusion that they were heirs of English estates; the emotions were slipping into nostalgic reveries.[30]

Finding much to dislike in Great Britain, Hawthorne nonetheless thought it an advantage in one sense that Britain seemed more material, closer to the flesh than America. Romance lay before the eyes, and Hawthorne found the institution of the civic banquet still more constructive, for it encouraged civic congeniality and allowed the "virulence" of political dispute to be dissolved in a glass (and even more in glasses) of wine. Americans might die for their institutions and beliefs, but "the principle is as cold and hard in an American bosom as a steel spring." Britons had a "closer feeling of brotherhood, a more efficient sense of neighborhood"; and, as Hawthorne had expected, stability and security in local relations allowed Britons to feel a greater devotion for the more distant nation.[31]

That Hawthorne found Britain's ideals defective, her politics lacking the proper standards of purpose and morality, only strengthened the point. The higher the ideal, the more necessary was emotion. Democracy could not be built on man's past or his present; it required a faith in what men might become. It could not allow the emotions to pull men toward a past or private world, but needed those sentiments in the public life of citizens to encourage their efforts and warm their faith. In fact, the whole process of valuing demanded a

[29] Conquering nature, Hawthorne once commented, is "naturally impossible." *American Note Books*, vol. I, p. 97; see also *Mosses*, vol. I, pp. 44, 54, 231.

[30] *Marble Faun* (1961), pp. 101, 122–123, 175, 219–220, 337–342; *Mosses*, vol. I, pp. 206–207, 216–258; *Our Old Home*, pp. 20–30; "Civic Banquets," p. 209.

[31] "Civic Banquets," pp. 198, 202, 210; *English Note Books*, vol. I, pp. 135, 139.

stable and even a limited horizon; evaluation was examination in depth and quality, not breadth and quantity. "The world is accumulating too many materials for knowledge," he observed; "we do not recognize for rubbish what is really rubbish." Men could relate to the world and their fellows only with a "weary torpor or passion of the heart." [32]

America, as Hawthorne saw it, had probably always been too large a state, and had certainly become too impersonal and too rapidly changing, to mirror the political ideal. Men will be drawn to public life only when they feel their own personalities to have weight in events. Gains and rewards are not enough; without personal ties, men seek gains for private motives and resent them at the moment of receiving them. His own appointment by Franklin Pierce, Hawthorne wrote, was tolerable because it came from "friend to friend" and would have been unendurable from a benefactor. Men will find meaning in public life in those smaller spheres where they are known and where their true virtues (and vices) are recognized. In the small towns, Hawthorne observed, the mere fact that each is known to all bestows fame on many who are less rich, intelligent, and wise than others who go unnoticed in the larger world.[33]

The American empire tore man in two. The Confederates were guilty of treason, Hawthorne asserted, but only because they had followed the human qualities of generosity and sympathy instead of an "airy mode of law." America was "too vast by far to be taken into one small human heart." If Americans loved their country, it was because "the singularity of our form of government contributes . . . a form of patriotism by separating us from other nations"; the emotional meaning of patriotism was negative, and feelings of difference were overcome by feelings of still greater difference. Hawthorne was too sophisticated to ignore the xenophobic potential in such sentiments (and as a loyal Democrat, he was certainly aware of the degree to which his fellow partisans sought to use jingoism to shore up the Union), and he was wise enough to realize that if other countries became democratic, the moral content of even that negative patriotism would disappear. Privatism was an even greater danger

<hr>

[32] *Mosses*, vol. I, pp. 36, 208.
[33] *French and Italian Note Books*, vol. II, p. 241; *American Note Books*, vol. I, p. 26.

than parochialism; in Europe Hawthorne could comment ironically
that

> in America, I had an innate antipathy to constables, and always sided
> with the mob against the law. This was very wrong and foolish, con-
> sidering that I was one of the sovereigns but . . . the twenty-millionth
> part of a sovereign does not love to find himself included within the
> delegated authority of his own servants.[34]

Hawthorne may not have spoken for himself when he called
America too vast to love, but he certainly spoke for the average citizen whose pilgrimage had only begun. America had sacrificed the
immediate relations of citizens to its great hopes of size, wealth, and
power. Having overstepped the limits of man's emotions, America
had forfeited political education and much of what lay beyond it.
Republican Florence, Hawthorne observed, had been able to strive
for the best in art and architecture; America sought only the average.
It was an inevitable result of a society where commercialism and
change shattered the bonds which mere size would have left intact,
and left men alone—some envious and fearful of excellence greater
than their own, others fearful of envy itself, and all desirous of fame
won from mediocre men. America was becoming a land of appearances, "mean and shabby," in which men were the prisoners of roles,
conventions, and socially "functional" activities, its citizens too suspicious of their unknown fellows to speak, too fearful of losing an
acquaintance to seek to discover a friend. The emotions were becoming locked within the self, shut up in a prison ruled by the sins
of humankind.[35]

Hawthorne saw that tendency most clearly in modern society's
treatment of the poor. Any man whose sentiments were not diseased
should have reacted to early industrial poverty as Hawthorne did,
finding it "polluting my entire being with the sense of something
grievously amiss in the entire condition of humanity." His analysis
of poverty was more than sentimental. Poverty, he realized, was more
than material deprivation, which was bad enough. Rather, material
scarcity made trust impossible, left men grasping to survive and yet

---

[34] *French and Italian Note Books*, vol. II, p. 46; see also vol. II, p. 189, and
"Chiefly About War Matters," *AM*, XII (1863), p. 48.
[35] *The Marble Faun* (1880), vol. II, pp. 7–20; *Blithedale Romance* (1958),
p. 110; *French and Italian Note Books*, vol. II, p. 155.

despairing. The poor had neither revolutionary potential nor genuine resignation; they suffered from a "diseased flaccidity of hope."

Even those who were charitable kept their emotional distance from the poor, denying their humanity by a sympathy which barely concealed disdain, a kindness which was often no more than a sense of superiority.

> We are apt to make sickly people more morbid and unfortunate people more miserable by endeavoring to adapt our deportment to their especial and individual needs. . . . It is like turning their own sick breath back upon themselves.

Horrified by British indifference to the poor—poverty was so normal it had lost its capacity to shock, and so final that Britons sought to shut the possibility from their minds—Hawthorne still found even unconcern better than the contempt (and worse, ridicule) with which Americans treated the poor. And Hawthorne spoke to more than his own time in finding American "expert officials" by far the most at fault. Charity had ceased to be a mark of love or of concern to improve and had become no more than a buttress of smugness.

Hawthorne's radicalism was apparent in his discussion of poverty. If he hated paternalism, he still saw the material need of the poor as demanding remedy. His antipathy to the nostrums of laissez-faire individualism carried him to attack the "right of property" itself. Something, he commented, is "imperfect in the title" of property which exists amid human misery; in any case, the acquisitive faculties result from an "imperfectly developed intelligence."

> I would listen to no man's theories but buy the little luxury of beneficence at a cheap rate, instead of doing myself moral mischief by exuding a stony incrustation over whatever natural sensitivity I possess.

The center of Hawthorne's case was simple: poverty is worse for the poor, whom it injures in body and spirit, but not much better for those who stay aloof. It dehumanizes both. Each man is

> responsible in his degree, for all the sufferings and misdemeanors of the world and . . . not entitled to look upon a particle of its dark calamity as if it were none of his concern: the offspring of a brother's iniquity being his own blood-relation. . . .

What an intimate brotherhood is this in which we dwell, do what we may to put an artificial remoteness between the high creature and the low. . . . How superficial are the niceties of such as pretend to keep aloof! Let the whole world be cleansed, or not a man or woman of us can be clean.[36]

The Symptom of Brotherhood

His criticism of the emerging qualities of mass industrial society accounts for much of Hawthorne's reverence for America's tradition. Far from being at one with the creed of progress, individualism, and technology, the American tradition was in fact a necessary modifier of American liberalism.

Nothing is so . . . odious as the sense of freedom and equality pertaining to an American grafted on the mind of a native of another country. . . . Nobody has a right to our ideas unless born to them.

The habit of political participation, Hawthorne realized as well as De Tocqueville, gave to liberty a public dimension and an element of restraint which other cultures lacked; the English habit of trusting others to rule, he commented, makes the mass of Englishmen turbulent and difficult to control. (Like De Tocqueville, too, he regarded the rise of democracy as probably inevitable and, despite his trepidation, probably for the best.)[37]

It was his sense of the American tradition that led him to ally himself so loyally to the Democracy. The commonality was less misled by new currents of fashionable error and more rooted in the older culture which emphasized individual relations with others and placed the highest value on the goods of the spirit. Always drawn to the rural areas, he had taken from them his tales and symbols. A limit, but also a safeguard and a source of wisdom,

The great conservative is the heart which remains the same in all ages so that the commonplaces of a thousand years' standing are as effective as ever.

[36] The citations are from Hawthorne's "Outside Glimpses of English Poverty," *AM*, XII (1863), pp. 42, 44, 48, 47 respectively; the title is suggestive, Hawthorne implying that he saw poverty only from the "outside."

[37] *English Note Books*, vol. I, pp. 137, 141–142; "Civic Banquets," *passim*.

In an age which change holds few prospects, the heart and not the head may be the firmest basis of political action. Hawthorne, like Cooper, was a Democrat because of, not despite, his "conservatism." [38]

Hardly anti-intellectual, he was hostile to intellectuals in politics. "Men of words" were unlikely to be men of deeds; like General McClellan on the Peninsular Campaign, they were likely to be paralyzed by seeing too many alternatives and to lapse into the vacillation which is drift. Hawthorne, with his distrust of the tendency of history, could hardly approve of this. Speaking of Jackson, he wrote that the highest administrative ability is intuitive, a revelation of the right course felt so strongly that "very likely it cannot be talked about." If this emphasized the need to seek leaders with the right intuitions, even more did it reveal the shortcomings of a government like England's which sought leaders from among the oratorically skilled. In an age of change, "it is only tradition . . . that assigns any value to parliamentary oratory. The world has done with it, except as an intellectual pastime." [39]

Hawthorne was loyal to Pierce, though acutely aware of his intellectual shortcomings, because he trusted Pierce's moral judgment and because he hoped for much from Pierce's personal charm and skill in human relations. But he never imagined that Pierce's habits of conciliation and compromise were enough in themselves. Hating abolitionism, Hawthorne was nonetheless an opponent of slavery. Like Melville, his racial attitudes were far in advance of the time; he was sensitive to the "shame, sorrow, and humiliation" blacks felt when they were compelled by the threat of white anger to conceal even "deep wisdom" by comic antics, and he wrote of Liberia's President Roberts (who impressed him favorably) that "his face is not . . . so agreeable as if it were jet black." [40]

Hawthorne was simply a Unionist who believed that the local governments and the states were America's closest approximation to the political ideal and regarded the Union as a fortress against

[38] *English Note Books*, vol. I, p. 66; see also *American Note Books*, vol. I, p. 55, and Van Doren, *Nathaniel Hawthorne*, pp. 19, 54, 98, 196–197.

[39] *French and Italian Note Books*, vol. II, pp. 87–88; *Our Old Home*, p. 37.

[40] *French and Italian Note Books*, vol. II, pp. 234–235; *English Note Books*, vol. II, p. 62; *American Note Books*, vol. I, pp. 154–155; and Hawthorne's campaign biography, *The Life of Franklin Pierce*, *Works* (1883), vol. XII, pp. 347–438.

privatism, to be defended as the best hope for human improvement afforded by the time. Slavery was a corruption which deeply poisoned the relations of men in the South; racism helped to hold the Southern "peasants" in "thralldom," and sent them out to die for a cause which was not their own. (One of Hawthorne's few hopes was that the Civil War might free the poor Southern white from his spiritual slavery; the blacks, Hawthorne wrote, are already better off in their souls.) Slavery, denying the common humanity of men, was based on a delusion which destroyed virtue; Hawthorne sneered at Buchanan's comment that the Southern leaders could not "in honor" desert Pierce, noting that the South "had been guilty of such things heretofore." Moreover, slavery affected the North too; if nothing else, it allowed the abolitionists the luxury of self-righteous fanaticism. Hawthorne hoped, simply, for a middle way. Men like Pierce might keep the Union together by charm and compromise, moving at the same time toward the goal of ending slavery. (He came closest to a criticism of Pierce when he admitted to himself, in response to Buchanan's comment that Pierce had drawn his Cabinet from the political "extremes," that Pierce had not included any anti-slavery men.)[41]

It was a forlorn hope, as Hawthorne probably realized, but he held it as long as possible, because he saw that in the conflict of cultures the issue of slavery was essentially peripheral to the far more significant tendencies of industrialism and technology. War, he was to comment in the event, blinds men to moral issues; a nation must be "humbugged . . . to keep its courage up," and the logic of combat allows it to humbug itself. Science was busily destroying "noble possibilities"; mechanized war revealed "the tendency of modern improvement," yet men exulted when it brought them victories.

Hawthorne never doubted that the North deserved his support when the War came. Yet he saw the War as the sad result of America's failures in political education and of the great size and perverse institutions which prevented her from developing civic fraternity. The hatred of the South for the North, he wrote, "is only the symptom of brotherhood (since brothers hate each other best)." Being

[41] "Chiefly About War Matters," pp. 55–56; *English Note Books*, vol. I, p. 294; *Twice Told Tales* (1960), pp. 3–11; and Randall Stewart, "Hawthorne and Politics," *NEQ*, V (1932), pp. 237–263.

quite sure that the War would not have the result that either side expected, he allowed himself the faint hope that it "may make our country dearer"—for sadly, poetry, like affection, "thrives best in the spots where blood has been spilt."

The hope, however, was very faint. War reveals that barbarous "touch of nature" that makes all men kinsmen, allowing them to "kill blamelessly" (original sin) or to "be killed gloriously" (ultimate sin). Treason to the values and ideals of the Union, he saw in Washington, had become pervasive, not specific to a region; the capital was ruled by lobbyists, speculators, and political careerists fattening on the Union's agony—which, ironically, seemed to legitimate their practices. He expected that America could look forward to a politics dominated by "military notoriety" and a succession of "bullet-headed generals" for forty years after the War (he was too pessimistic, but not much), and any hope rested with "another generation."

The one clear good he saw from the conflict was the abolition of slavery. Blacks were among the earliest inhabitants of America, he commented, with a title as old as the Mayflower, and rescue was theirs by right even if "the character of our sacred ship is hurt." Yet even abolition promised little, because those who were most zealous for it underestimated the task. The freed slaves would be "fauns and rustic deities," innocents in need of education and assistance; the odds, however, were that a belief that abolition was a solution in itself would combine with indifference, and leaving the freedmen to "fight a hard battle . . . on very unequal terms." [42]

Hawthorne had few prescriptions, though those few were sound. More notable was his diagnosis of the needs of the intellectual and the artist in mass society. Alienated men would need a private language of allegory to enable them to speak and to find their brothers in spirit without harming the lives of their civic brethren. Not for Hawthorne the brotherhood of the bohemian expatriate; in Rome, he found the world of artists in decay, and the artists themselves in flight backwards from their own goals toward the delusion of innocence. Of his own exile, he wrote that "taking no root, I soon weary of any soil in which I may be temporarily deposited." The

[42] "Chiefly About War Matters," pp. 55–56; also, pp. 45, 49, 51, 60, 61. See also *English Note Books*, vol. I, p. 362, and Randall Stewart, "Hawthorne and the Civil War," *SP*, XXXIV (1937), pp. 91–106.

exile is forever deferring "reality" to some future time which never comes; if he returns home, he will find that the reality preserved by nostalgia no longer exists and that what was real was "the country where we deemed ourselves only living temporarily." [43] The intellectual and the artist always have a social role and a bond with their time; they hold up for their fellows the image of the ideal, however ill-reflected. And when society teaches lessons which are perverse, the duty of the artist is greater, not less.

Hawthorne wrote his essay on the War despite opprobrium (Lowell deleted several pages from the article in *The Atlantic Monthly*, and even accused Hawthorne of "impolitic" sympathy with the rebellion).[44] He could face such penalties because "there is a kind of treason in insulating one's self from the universal fear and sorrow," and a corresponding need to reprove the folly of the sorrowing. It was the mark of his citizenship, his status as a political man. But the highest obligations of the artist and the intellectual were not political in the narrow sense of the word; they were owed to the ideal itself. Living up to those obligations required the communion of fraternity, and since the polity shaped one's self and one's brothers, that need also demanded a political role. Though he had doubts and fears, Hawthorne never accepted the grimmest possibility inherent in mass society: that the common language of symbols may disappear, and hope both for the polity and for discovering brothers may be lost in a world where allegory goes uncomprehended and symbol remains peculiar to the self.

[43] *Marble Faun* (1961), pp. 85, 100–101, 122–123, 337; *French and Italian Note Books*, vol. II, p. 161; *Our Old Home*, pp. 19–20.
[44] "Chiefly About War Matters," pp. 46–47, 49, 54, 56, 61.

> Although man has many points of resemblance
> with brute creation one characteristic is pe-
> culiar to himself—he improves. . . . His re-
> verses teach him that none may hope to have
> discovered absolute good—his success stimu-
> lates him to the never-ending pursuit of it.
> Thus, forever seeking, forever falling to rise
> again, often disappointed but not discouraged,
> he tends toward the unmeasured greatness so
> indistinctly visible at the end of the long track
> which humanity has yet to tread.
>
> De Tocqueville, *Democracy in America*

CHAPTER XIII

HERMAN MELVILLE: THE PILGRIM

"A monstrous allegory . . ."

BATTALIONS of critics have attempted to read the riddle of Melville's work, and have agreed on little except the object of their attention. Lawrence saw Melville as a perennial dreamer, addicted to undying optimism; Parrington classified him as a pessimist; and so it goes. Each man finds his own Melville.

A search for some unity among the many paradoxes of Melville's thought must begin with Melville himself. Hawthorne, who knew him best, wrote that Melville was unable to "rest in anticipation"; his demand for truth was both absolutistic and unfulfilled. Hawthorne tells us that Melville, unable to believe, could not endure unbelief, and he was "too honest and courageous" to give up the search for answers to the paradoxes and the riddles of creation and of the self of man.[1]

Ultimately Melville's quest could end only in failure, yet his pilgrimage had a measure of success. He could not comprehend nature and the self, but he found an order in their incomprehensibility. That structure was a flickering light in the darkness of human ignorance which enabled a man to know truths, even if he could never discern the Truth. Melville's pluralism ultimately resolved itself into absolutism, but he had too much love for the absolute, too passionate a devotion to the Truth, to allow any man the claim to possess it. His pessimism regarding man was a measure of his exaltation of the beloved Truth, beside which all human truths were revealed as shabby. His hope for men, his sense of fraternity, was founded on the same feelings of devotion and failure, and on the fact that the beloved absolute was reflected, however dimly, in his fellows.

Melville's father had died insane while Melville was still a boy; not for nothing were so many of his protagonists and characters fatherless men. His mother had always seemed to favor his younger brother, and it is no surprise that Melville initially sought to displace his brother by demonstrating his prowess and by winning success in the world. But Melville very early escaped this normal, if fratricidal, pattern. He rejected, from whatever cause, the standards of maternity and worldly acclaim, and set out on the quest for paternity that was to dominate his life.

Lawrence Thompson, in his seminal *Melville's Quarrel with God*, understands all this and is wise enough to realize that any quarrel with God must be a lover's quarrel. His thesis—that Melville eventually came to regard God as a malevolent spirit and the author of evil, and that he concealed this teaching in ironic allegories—has, however, the unfortunate result of reducing Melville from a literary giant to a village free-thinker. The attitude Thompson attributes to Melville is not only hardly unique, it is in part impeccably orthodox: the prophet Isaiah affirmed that God was the originator of evil. Worse, if Melville hoped to conceal this "doctrine" he failed as a

[1] *The English Notebooks of Nathaniel Hawthorne*, ed. R. Stewart (New York: Oxford University Press, 1941), p. 433.

literary craftsman, for the early reviewers of his work often "discerned" and denounced it.[2]

Melville, as Thompson is aware, wrote at many levels, and Thompson is guilty of stopping a level too soon; indeed, his own comment that Melville passed and repassed four "quadrants" of belief sits badly with his discovery of three "levels" in Melville's meaning.[3]

Consider Melville's description of Pierre as a writer: "With the soul of an Atheist, he wrote down the godliest of things; with the feeling of misery and death in him, he created forms of gladness and life." [4] Surely this suggests that an author may have a secret, and even a secret intent, though in Pierre's case it only illustrates Melville's doctrine that "all men who say YES, lie." Applied to Melville's work, however, the description produces an interpretation directly contrary to Thompson's. Melville's works are, after all, hardly the "godliest" of works and most certainly not "forms of gladness and life." Might Melville's soul, like his books, be the opposite of Pierre's? Melville, after all, admired Shakespeare because of the darkness he found in his works, but also because the Bard was "gentle" and "full of sermons on the mount." The yea-sayers write of light out of their own darkness; the negators write darkly in order to reveal light.[5]

Melville combined heterodoxy and traditionalism. He despised all orthodoxies as pretentious claims to know what man could not know. Calvinism he rejected because it claimed to know the form and structure of life and of the world, if not their meaning, but he also rejected the doctrinaire formlessness of transcendentalism. Orthodoxy was a soporific, rationalizing away evil in the world and seek-

[2] Thompson, *Melville's Quarrel with God* (Princeton: Princeton University Press, 1952), pp. 30, 124, and *passim*. Contemporary critical reactions are described in *Moby Dick: Centennial Essays*, ed. Hillway and Mansfield, pp. 106–107, 109, 118–119. The Biblical reference is to *Isaiah* 45:7. A fine argument, especially in relation to Thompson's thesis, is Perry Miller, "Melville and Transcendentalism," *Nature's Nation*, pp. 184–196.

[3] *Melville's Quarrel with God*, p. 149.

[4] Melville, *Pierre*, pp. 471–472.

[5] *Herman Melville: Representative Selections*, ed. Willard Thorp (New York: American Book Co., 1938), p. 370. In 1885, Melville wrote that his pessimism had been a "counterpoise to the exorbitant hopefulness . . . that makes such a bluster in these days" (Metcalf, *Herman Melville: Cycle and Epicycle*, p. 268).

ing to put man's doubt to rest and damp the fire of his quest for paternity.

He also rejected, however, the findings of the "higher critics" and the geologists' critique of creation; all his life he continued to regard Solomon as the author of the three books attributed to him by tradition. The Bible was not, as he saw it, a source of metaphysics or a historical record. It was a myth which had captured the perennial quality of human life and experience. The new critics might touch and break what was quantitative and external; they could not affect the internal, qualitative dimension which was the source of all meaning. The Scripture was not "truth," it set down cases and concrete experience; and man, reflecting on these, might catch a glimpse of a truth beyond. Melville regarded Emerson, as he did orthodoxy in the Church, as "unchristian," because Melville classed Jesus, who "saw what made him weep," with the nay-sayers. In the Sermon on the Mount, as Melville knew, lies the dark teaching that, in this life, anguish is bound up with wisdom and joy alike.[6]

The Church had failed precisely because it had lost or rejected that understanding of man. Thompson is right to see Father Mapple's sermon as indirect ridicule of the church, wrong in the lesson he draws. Father Mapple defines Jonah's motive in fleeing God's command as a fear of punishment should he go and prophesy at Nineveh; he was, Mapple says, "appalled at the hostility he should raise." Reduced to obedience by God's chastisement, Jonah is able, in alliance with Divine power, to "preach Truth in the face of Falsehood" and to stand forth as "his own inexorable self," which Mapple sees as "delight." Mapple's doctrine is identical with that of the "rebel" Captain Ahab except for the fact that Mapple has been beaten, that he knows the futility of struggling against God and has submitted. The doctrine is concerned with power, with the self, and has not lost its savagery in submitting to God's will: "Delight is in him who gives no quarter in the truth, and kills, burns and destroys all sin. . . ." When the *Pequod* meets the *Delight*, later in the novel, the *Delight*

6 Wright, *Melville's Use of the Bible*, pp. 12–13, 17–18, 45, 114–115; Bowen, *The Long Encounter*, p. 94; Melville, *Clarel*, vol. I, pp. 126, 247; *Mardi*, vol. II, pp. 71, 306, 307; *Poems*, p. 267. On the seventeenth-century nature of Melville's concerns, see Thompson, *Melville's Quarrel with God*, pp. 18, 123–124.

advises Ahab to submit, to avoid the contest—but the *Delight*, like the "delight" of Mapple, has already fought the white whale and been beaten. Father Mapple is in fact concerned only with the struggle of wills between man and God, man and man; he is not concerned with the meaning of good and evil except in relation to dominance or submission. "Never mind now what that command was . . . ," he declares, for the issue is one of mastery.[7]

The significant fact, however, is that Mapple's "theology" is wrong in every critical respect. Though he explicitly refers to the four chapters of *Jonah*, he apparently has not read the last chapter in which Jonah's motive for disobedience is revealed, not as fear of the Ninevans, but as distaste for God's compassion. Only too willing to see "all sin" killed, burned, or destroyed, Jonah is "displeased . . . exceedingly" that God should forgive it. Even the experience in the belly of the great fish has taught him only to obey; the lesson of mercy and compassion remains to be learned. Implicitly, Father Mapple and the Church are in the same position—as are perhaps the majority of men: beaten Ahabs, who have submitted without a change of motives, retaining full force their pride of self, savagery against nature, and fanaticism in the "truth." [8]

The Church, too, still rejected much of this world. The Cetology chapter of *Moby Dick* (an elaborate spoof on theology) presents Ishmael defending the "old-fashioned" view that the whale is a fish. But though Ishmael announces his acceptance of Linnaeus' delineation of the differences between whales and fish, he omits from his explanation any discussion of the whale's mammalian (mammarian) nature (Linnaeus' comment on the fact is given in Latin). Taken together with the later discussion of the "misnaming" of the sperm whale, the irony suggests that the Church has overestimated the masculine power of the "head" and spirit and neglected the force of the feminine and emotional in man. More than one lesson waited to be taught.[9]

In *Pierre* Melville presented three faiths: the shallow Christianity of conventional Christians, the idealism of Pierre, and the "virtuous

[7] *Moby Dick,* ed. Luther Mansfield and Howard Vincent (New York: Hendricks House, 1952), pp. 39–48, 531–532; Thompson, *Melville's Quarrel with God,* p. 163.

[8] *Jonah* 4:2–3.

[9] *Moby Dick* (1952), pp. 129–142.

expediency" of Plotinus Plinlimmon—a partisan of a sort of Deism which relegates Christian morality to the next world. Melville despised them all, and his distaste suggests the fourth possibility—the fourth level of his writing—an "expedient virtue," a righteousness founded on a recognition of the nature and limitations of man and of this world.[10]

Dark that world and that nature might be, but they could not be escaped by man, nor could he embrace them, and to attempt to do either would only be to produce a darkness which was man's own folly. They must surely be understood, probed, and examined; and once this had happened—who knew?—they might reveal a spark of light.

"A poor unit . . ."

Melville wrote of the sea because it so perfectly symbolized his conception of man. The life of the seaman is endless pilgrimage, and each voyage is ended only to begin another. Man, like the sailor, never ended the journey or the seeking. Strive though he might, man never attained unity of self. He was "a poor unit at best," always in part an "incomprehensible stranger" to himself, confronting an element of "unravelable inscrutableness" like that of his God. If man felt, at one level, a sense of personal unity and selfhood, at another he seemed constantly to fall apart into body and soul, heart and head. Like Pierre, man was mixed and uncertain; he might aspire to heaven, but he was never freed from the earth.[11]

The heart of man sought gratification and joy without travail. Man's "masculine" element, the head, might strive to read the meaning of the world and struggle with it, but the heart preferred to remain unaware and unengaged, for the world contains mystery and pain, neither of them pleasant things.

In spite of early temptations, Melville could never accept the idea of a community of pure love and sentiment. Certainly there is much

---

[10] *Pierre*, pp. 293–300.

[11] *Pierre*, p. 199; *Moby Dick*, vol. II, p. 246; *Mardi*, vol. II, pp. 86, 155; *The Portable Melville*, ed. Jan Leyda (New York: Viking, 1952), p. 674; *Stories, Poems and Letters of Herman Melville*, ed. R. W. B. Lewis (New York: Dell, 1962), p. 33; Bowen, *The Long Encounter*, pp. 14, 15, 26, 27.

"noble savage" in his Polynesian novels, yet Typee's world of primeval innocence contained a hidden horror. Even in *Omoo*, where he
came close indeed to a defense of "natural man," Melville unmasked
self-concern in the "natural fraternity" of the Polynesians. Under the
impact of civilization, the limitations to self-seeking imposed by nature
disappear, and without them the Tahitians become "spongers," content to receive without giving. The warm unity of innocence is
artificial in being based on a limited horizon of thought and a limited
chance for gain. The heart cannot sin because it cannot know good;
a world without sin is a world of men blinded in the "inner eye"
that is thought and imagination.[12]

Time only made Melville more certain of the defects of the
heart. Man's emotions were savage as well as gentle, and men found
satisfaction in inflicting pain out of their own resentment at the limitations inflicted by the world. Nor was there a possibility of separating
the savage and the gentle. In *Mardi*, Taji's pursuit of Yillah, the
symbol of innocent love and purified sensuality, is as much a flight
as a pursuit; Taji is pursued by avengers who are never far behind.
The hero has sought to separate Yillah from Hautia, who represents
death and carnal sensuality; and as Melville realized, the two prove to
be ultimately inseparable, even indistinguishable. The Mother has
two faces, creator and destroyer; Taji is pursued by his own unconscious awareness that the two are one.[13]

But *Mardi* still showed Melville toying with dreams of universal
fraternity and salvation: "Better that we were all annihilated than
that one man were damned." The sense of a common human responsibility and involvement in evil never left Melville, but *Moby Dick*
made clear that he had abandoned the hope for universal responsibility
and fraternity. Ishmael, squeezing spermaceti on the deck of the
Pequod, burlesques the idea of universal brotherhood: "Let us squeeze

[12] *Omoo* (Boston: Page and Company, 1892), pp. 172–179, 216–221; *Typee*,
pp. 262, 275; see also Mayoux, *Melville*, pp. 38–44. For Melville's hostile view of
"natural man," see *The Confidence Man*, pp. 106, 140–141. (The essential study
of *The Confidence Man* is Elizabeth Foster, *Herman Melville's* The Confidence
Man: *Its Origins and Meaning*, unpub. Ph.D. dissertation, Yale University,
1942.)
[13] *Mardi*, vol. II, pp. 400, 351. See also *Pierre*, pp. 127, 246, 252; *The Confidence Man*, pp. 78, 289; *Moby Dick*, vol. I, pp. 176, 233; and Stern, *The Fine
Hammered Steel of Herman Melville*, pp. 12–13, 100–103.

ourselves universally into the very milk and sperm of kindness." The sexual implications of "milk and sperm" are hardly accidental, for the next paragraph comments: "Now . . . by many prolonged, repeated experiences I have perceived that in all cases man must eventually lower, or at least shift, his conceit of attainable felicity." Ishmael educated mocks Ishmael naive; man's emotions are limited by the strait boundaries of the senses.[14]

The appearance of man's ship, Melville wrote, is a lie; most of it is below the surface where the "sick-bay" is hidden from surface view. Yet man begins in the sick-bay, "seasick" on his first embarcation, his emotions hostile to the condition in which he finds himself placed. His heroic triumphs are mostly vauntings, efforts to overcome a nature that will not be denied (and, Melville noted, he hides the dead by dropping them overboard lest they remind him of too much).[15]

Like his mentor Ecclesiastes, however, Melville concluded that it is no answer for man to "fold his hands and eat his own flesh." The effort to remain uninvolved and unconcerned with the world is as much a delusive effort to recover innocence as are the hero's poses. Bartleby confronted the world with the mild negation of his preference "not to," but he escaped the blankness of the office only to find the blankness of a living tomb. He is found in a position which suggests only too clearly the innocence which was his inner desire, "strangely huddled at the base of the wall, his knees drawn up." [16]

So powerful are the emotional yearnings for innocence and self-gratification that they can, and most often do, capture the minds of men. Men become pretentious, affecting a knowledge of the world they do not possess, setting up their creeds and doctrines in a petty effort at self-deceit. We are inclined to think, Melville wrote, that God is ignorant of his own secrets and "would like a little information"; we set up abstractions and then act on them. "Being . . . Me . . . God . . . Nature"—all in a final sense are unknown and may have no reality. Worse, the abstractions serve, as they are intended, to provide men with an excuse and justification for self-concern.

[14] *Moby Dick*, vol. II, pp. 171–172. Note that the Confidence Man regards all strong emotions as "mad" (*The Confidence Man*, p. 232).

[15] *White Jacket*, pp. 502–504.

[16] *Piazza Tales*, pp. 21, 29, 64; the Biblical reference is to *Ecclesiastes* 4:5.

"Take God out of the dictionary and you would have him in the street." Indeed, whatever his pretense, Melville wrote, the idealist is essentially an atheist; he projects his own ideas onto the cosmos and demands that God's creation conform to his categories, seeking to escape the fearfulness of mystery. Optimism and pessimism were both follies (in *The Confidence Man*, both the trusting and the suspicious fall victim, for both have blind spots), and only the "judicious, unencumbered traveler" obeys the logic of the pilgrimage.[17]

The would-be innocent denies in effect both heart and head; Melville insisted on the full development of both. Any truth about man will have to be sought out by the head; it does not exist "in" man, waiting to be discovered. When Pierre sought the "captive king" in his soul, he found only a tomb; the first father, the old Adam, "natural man," is dead if he ever existed. Man's paternity is a secret, as the fatherless men who dot Melville's work suggest, and must be found out.[18]

Melville was no empiricist, for he never underrated the sometimes passionate desire for unity which exists in man. He did insist, however, that men must begin with the diverse and fragmentary perceptions and experience of what is close at hand. Melville rapidly outgrew his early attraction to Emerson because the Sage of Concord sought to overleap experience to reach unity; he did not see life, as Melville did, as a veil through which man must catch the only glimpses of the absolute he can ever see. Striving to see too far, Melville observed, men become blind; beginning with absolutism in tone and teaching, Emerson ended with relativism in practice. Staring at a distant whiteness in *Moby Dick*, the eyes of men cannot distinguish the rapacious squid from the whale, just as Emerson found a unity between good and evil in the cosmos. In fact, the whale may seem to "merge" with its predatory opponent at the moment when the two are locked in mortal combat. Perhaps, Melville implied, there is ultimately a single purpose and goodness in the cosmos, but men here below make their greatest contribution to good in the destruction of concrete evils which they can see. Men need the diverse colors

[17] Lewis, *Stories, Poems and Letters*, p. 58; Thorp, *Herman Melville*, pp. 387–389; *Pierre*, pp. 290, 476; *Moby Dick*, vol. I, pp. 3, 4; and Jan Leyda, *The Melville Log* (New York: Harcourt, Brace, 1951), vol. II, pp. 649, 651.

[18] *Pierre*, pp. 122, 361, 397; *Moby Dick*, vol. I, p. 343.

of fleshly experience to see at all; black may be absorbed in white, evil in good, but gazing at the stark colors of abstraction without the relief of green drives men to madness, not to understanding.[19]

Man's search for truth is set in motion by the defeat of innocence and the experience of pain and defeat, grief and guilt; the head is liberated by the agony of the heart which has been driven to surrender its belief in a simple, painless unity. For that reason alone, man needs a fully developed heart which is able to feel pain. Even more, however, does he need the heart after thought has begun. The head has its compulsions, too; thought sets up a demand for answers. Yet the quest of thought has no final resting place; the life of the head is one of frustration. Once the folly of the innocent heart has been set aside, man must resist the folly of the head, the prideful innocence that will lie and claim to know what it does not. Man needs material pleasures if the intermediacy of his existence is not to overbear him.[20] Joys of sense—especially those shared with one's fellows—make man unwilling to surrender the earth; they provide a balance for the passion of the head. Ambiguity is not an infliction but a necessity of human life and understanding; but a positive ambiguity must be born of twin joys and desires. Once man begins to think, it is the "vernal sense" which provides the "patient root" which enables man to endure failure.[21]

Life is forever incomplete, a thing of pain and frustration; ironic, self-mocking Ishmael insists, with "Solomon," that "All is vanity. ALL."

> But even Solomon, he says, "the man that wandereth out of the way of understanding shall remain" (even while living) "in the congregation of the dead." Give not thyself up, then, to the fire, lest it invert thee, deaden thee, as for a time it did me. There is a wisdom that is woe, and there is a woe that is madness.

The madman has felt pain in the world and knows its woe, but that

[19] Lewis, *Stories, Poems and Letters*, p. 63; *Pierre*, pp. 231, 445; *Mardi*, vol. II, pp. 322–323; *Moby Dick* (1952), pp. 195–200; Metcalf, *Herman Melville: Cycle and Epicycle*, p. 109.

[20] *Clarel*, vol. I, p. 131, vol. II, pp. 139–141, 269, 274, 298; *Redburn*, pp. 120, 237; *Moby Dick* (1952), pp. 104–105; *Piazza Tales*, p. 42; Stern, *Fine Hammered Steel*, pp. 10–11, 157, 159.

[21] *Pierre*, pp. 363–364; *Moby Dick*, vol. II, p. 172; E. H. Rosenberry, *Melville and the Comic Spirit* (Cambridge: Harvard University Press, 1955).

only leads him to anger at the world of which he does not feel himself a part. Those who have known compassion, affection, and the stronger emotions Melville thought inseparable from them have also known woe: the sense of imperfection in even the best, the transience and loss of human things. Yet this is a woe which results from the fullness of joy and binds men to the world; it is a sorrow with, and not because of, nature and one's fellows. Ishmael's citation from *Proverbs* is preceded by more didactic and less oracular verses:

> The soul of the wicked desires evil; his neighbor finds no favor in his eyes. . . . Whoso stops his ears to the cry of the poor, he also shall cry and not be heard. A gift in secret pacifies anger, and a reward in the bosom, strong wrath. It is a joy to the just to do judgement, but destruction shall be to the workers of iniquity.

The Solomonic wisdom which Melville valued was clear enough; the just are not promised success but joy. The wicked, who reject the common lot of man, will reap destruction in any case, but they will miss much; wrath may be cured by a reward for the heart. The ancient "way of understanding" was for Melville just that: it represented the path to the only wisdom man might gain.[22]

The self remains ambiguous to the end: no pure heart, no pure thought, no ability to persevere alone. The would-be innocent, who desires a complete, sufficient self, threatens life and wisdom alike. The crew of the *Pequod* are nearly all "Islanders . . . 'Isolatoes' . . . not acknowledging the common continent of man but each Isolato living on a separate continent of his own." Alone, even a good man is powerless against evil, supposing him able to recognize it; Starbuck, "mere unaided virtue," must yield in the end to Ahab. The other Isolatoes, who share Ahab's desire to protest against the "world's grievances," are like most lonely men held in thrall by any individual whose will and anger are stronger, more maniacal than their own.[23]

The Innocents

The "secret motto" of *Moby Dick*, Melville wrote Hawthorne, was "*Ego non baptizo te in nomine*—but finish the rest for yourself." An obvious reference to the frenzied scene in which Captain Ahab

---

[22] *Moby Dick*, vol. II, pp. 179–182; *Proverbs* 21:10–16.
[23] *Moby Dick*, vol. I, pp. 149–150.

baptizes his spear *"in nomine diaboli"* rather than in the name of the Father, Melville's comment has been used by more than one critic to argue that Melville secretly agreed with Ahab's attitude and doctrine. This position, however, leaves out the significant half of Melville's sentence to Hawthorne: "finish the rest for yourself." If Melville had wanted to identify his position with Ahab's, he need hardly have been so cryptic; moreover, he must have known that given that riddling comment, Hawthorne the allegorist would have sought another "motto" which Ahab's comments might reveal to him. Melville constantly tested himself and his friends, and the comment seems in part a challenge to see if Hawthorne would read him rightly, in part a private joke among friends.[24]

Emerson had written in his essay "Self-Reliance" that "if I am the devil's child, I will then live only from the devil." Melville had regarded this comment as insane and truly diabolic; it reflected one so desperately bound to affirm the self as to make "yea-saying" out of negation itself. Yet Emerson's position is different from Ahab's only in that Emerson was more innocent still than the Captain; he had not yet conceded that he was the devil's child.[25]

There is more than one similarity between the philosopher and Ahab. In Melville's view, Emerson was an archetype of the man who sought to live solely by the head; Emerson began with the neck and went up, Melville commented, and there was nothing of him below. Ahab falls in the same category, although his case is more extreme.

> All loveliness is anguish to me since I can ne'er enjoy. Gifted with high perception, I lack the low enjoying power; damned, most subtly and most malignantly . . . in the midst of paradise.[26]

Fatherless like many Melville characters, Ahab is motherless as well. He is the pure case, in this sense, of "natural man"—like Adam, to whom he likens himself: "I feel as though I were Adam, staggering beneath the piled centuries." The defect of Ahab's situation (like that of the Old Adam?) is that the heart comes first in human life. Ahab's

[24] Lewis, *Stories, Poems and Letters,* pp. 65–67; R. M. Weaver, *Herman Melville: Mariner and Mystic* (New York: Doran, 1921), p. 274.

[25] Emerson, "Self-Reliance," *Selected Poetry and Prose* (New York: Rinehart, 1954), p. 168; Metcalf, *Herman Melville: Cycle and Epicycle,* p. 59; Stern, *Fine Hammered Steel,* p. 12.

[26] *Moby Dick,* vol. I, pp. 209–210.

heart remains untrained, and his emotions are wholly concentrated in himself. The often-noted fact of Ahab's "symbolic castration" is itself a symbol of his separation from his lost mother and the world of concrete sensuality. Ahab is erotic enough, but it is a sublimated eros which is not tied to another human or to mortal flesh. Ahab remains a worshipper of the Mother, as he implies when he complains to and derides the Father:

> Thou art but my fiery father; my sweet mother, I know not. Oh cruel! what hast thou done with her? . . . Thou knowest not how came ye. . . . There is some unsuffusing thing behind thee, to whom . . . all thy creativeness is mechanical.

Eden is forever lost, and Ahab must acknowledge the existence of a power beyond that of the womb and the self. His affirmation, however, centers on a Oneness ("an unsuffusing thing") which unites all diversity and which creates organically; confronted with a Father between him and the Mother-Goddess he believes to exist at a higher level, his instinct is to master the Father erotically.

> Yet while I earthly live, the queenly personality lives in me and feels her royal rights. . . . Come in thy lowest form of love and I will kneel and kiss thee, but at thy highest, come as mere supernal power . . . (to which) there's that in here that still remains indifferent. . . . I burn with thee; would fain be welded with thee; defyingly, I worship thee.

It is more than the ritual of the Eastern Mother used against the Western Father. It is also the cadence of Emerson, who would likewise be "welded" to the higher powers, and whose "indifference" of personal autonomy addressed to "mere supernal power" is belied by the passion of his address.[27]

Ahab's heart, lacking any bond with the material, mortal world, has mastered his head. In all things which show a will or power not his own, he sees something to be hated and conquered. He can show seeming kindness to what he has mastered, but only because he sees the mastered thing as a part of himself. Movingly, he tells Starbuck,

> Let me look into a human eye; it is better than to gaze into sea or sky, better than to gaze upon God. . . . This is the magic glass, man.

[27] *Ibid.*, vol. II, pp. 281–282; see also vol. I, p. 100, and Henry A. Murray, "In Nomine Diaboli," *NEQ*, XXIV (1951), pp. 435–452.

Better indeed for Ahab: sea, sky and God have a common defect in that unlike the human eye they do not reflect oneself.[28]

Ahab's quest for mastery, however, is a monstrous folly. It is "that inscrutable thing" which Ahab "chiefly" hates, but the ultimate unknown does not come within the range of his arm. He can strike only the inscrutable things that are "visibly personified and practically assailable," the living things of this world; but since Ahab rages against all that eludes his control, he will strike whether these be "agent" or "principal." Yet even in the natural world there are powers that elude Ahab's control. "I'd strike the sun if it insulted me," Ahab declares, "for if the sun could do that, then I could do the other, since there is ever a sort of fairplay herein, jealously presiding over all creations." There is no concept of justice here; if there had been, Ahab might have thought it just that Moby Dick had deprived him of a leg after his lifetime of whaling. Ahab is only concerned with his right to strike: "But not my master, man, is even that fair play." Ahab, like all innocents, is in error, for the sun does injure him ("even as these old eyes are . . . scorched with thy light"), and he can vent his anger only on the accessible quadrant. He even insists that this man-made tool must bear the blame because it casts "men's eyes aloft." For innocent Ahab, blame must always lie with something outside the self.[29]

Ahab is not without a measure of humanity, and his effort to master the forces of nature and the unseen speaks deeply to his crew. The crew responds, however, to Ahab's knowledge of "unconscious understandings" and of the "subterranean miner who works in us all"; he speaks to the untrained heart that yearns for innocence. He works with the lowest forces of man's nature (that he uses gold as a lure is hardly accidental), because he seeks not the good of men but mastery over them. "Ay, he would be a democrat to all above; look how he lords it over all below." In the climactic moment, he denies his crewmen humanity altogether; "ye are not other men, but my arms and legs." Even his pathos is full of the folly of individualism. "Oh lonely death on lonely life!" he cries, forgetting that whatever else his death is, it is not lonely; he has taken a whole crew with him.[30]

---

[28] *Moby Dick*, vol. II, pp. 327–330.

[29] *Ibid.*, vol. I, pp. 204–205, 229–230, vol. II, pp. 273–275, 300.

[30] *Ibid.*, vol. I, pp. 149–150, 211, 229–230, 253, vol. II, pp. 314, 316, 329–330, 366.

In part, Ahab is not to be blamed. The circumstances of his birth would have made it difficult for him to form emotional bonds with the world, and his education had little effect for the better. Reared a Quaker, taught to be a man of "stillness and seclusion" and to seek the inner light, when he is struck by lightning—God's outer light—while praying, he retains the faith in the inner light while hating all outer things. He becomes a "Quaker with a vengeance," still certain that he is the lieutenant of fate and absolved from all responsibility. Education has only strengthened the defects of the heart (and Melville knew only too well what Ahab would have learned during his sojourn in the universities).[31]

In another sense, however, Ahab is guilty. For the "unbidden and unfathered birth" which his purpose has become, striving against "common vitality," fights the deepest forces in man's nature. Ahab has made himself over in the image of the imagined machine-god he hates; his "fixed purpose" is "laid with iron rails whereon my soul is grooved to run." He has crowded out humanity, made himself a machine. Vitality will not be denied so easily, however, and the "vultures" of the heart reveal themselves and seek to claim their own during his dreams (one of the frequent "psychoanalytic" insights in Melville's thought).[32]

His predecessor, King Ahab of Israel, had many false prophets and one true one who sought to conceal his truth; self-doubt led the King to reject the comforting lie, to demand that Micaiah prophesy truly. The Captain has many true prophets and one false one—the Parsee who tells a "truth" with a lying tongue (like Macbeth's witches). Though Ahab is skeptical, he chooses to accept the comforting interpretation of the riddling prophecies, and that too convicts him. He joins the ranks of those who say "Yes" without knowing.[33]

Of all the Captain's sins, none is more heinous than his destruction of the "quadrant" (symbolic, in Melville, of religious belief) which tells the seaman where he is. Ahab destroys the quadrant because it could not foretell where he will be tomorrow. He seeks to master time, to find the law and logic of progress in history, in that too resembling the Emerson who may have been his prototype.

---

[31] *Ibid.*, vol. I, pp. 91, 99, vol. II, pp. 281, 352.
[32] *Ibid.*, vol. I, p. 253.
[33] *Moby Dick* (New York: Modern Library, n.d.), pp. 713–714.

D. H. Lawrence saw the *Pequod* as a symbol of America,[34] and there is much in the individualistic crew driven by a desire for gold and the lust for mastery that would sustain that view. That symbol, however, neglects Melville's more vital lesson: that America had a mad "captain," a false affirmer, yet one of sufficient force to master the crewmen and to turn them, like himself, into subhumans with souls fixed to run on iron rails to a destination which could only be disaster.

Ahab was hardly Melville's only innocent; in Pierre he created a younger and more realistic character of the type. Pierre is, in fact, so realistic that one meets him—more or less—every day in the street.

Pierre too is fatherless, in that his father is dead. Raised by a pietistic mother who deplores and seeks to punish the sins of the flesh, Pierre develops a highly idealized picture of his father which is shattered by evidence of his father's early transgressions. Pierre's heart has received no education; his has been a childhood of wealth, without want or suffering; his mother is self-righteous and without compassion. (Later, when Pierre breaks with her, she will send him into the world "an infant Ishmael . . . with no maternal Hagar"—as, in a sense, he has always been.)[35]

It is small wonder, then, that he reacts to his "discovery" by reversing his previous ideas and determining that the world and his father are evil, corruptly allied with fleshly things, hypocritical and false. He does not see this as part of man's nature and his own, but rather as evidence of the polluted character of men who lack "godly freedom," and he resolves to reject the world and his ties to it. ("I will no more have a father.")[36]

Even here, however, there is a suspicious note. Pierre accepts without question Isabel's assertion that she is his father's illegitimate daughter because "nothing but truth" could "move me so." [37] There is no evidence other than the girl's word. Leaving aside the fact that Pierre can show compassion for the victim but not for the victimizer, he is all too ready to convict, to retreat from the innocent faith of childhood to a still earlier faith in the self.

[34] Lawrence, *Studies in Classical American Literature*, p. 174.
[35] *Pierre*, p. 125; Thompson, *Melville's Quarrel with God*, p. 250.
[36] *Pierre*, pp. 89–90, 277; Bowen, *The Long Encounter*, p. 163.
[37] *Pierre*, p. 90.

Rejecting his earthly father, Pierre proclaims an immediate bond with the Heavenly Father. "I will know what is," he vows, "and so what my deepest angel dictates," and later, "I will see the hidden things and live right out in my own hidden life." The truth and what is hidden exist in Pierre himself. In fact on at least two occasions, Pierre identifies himself with the Christ, and on the critical decision— whether it is moral to lie by pretending marriage to Isabel and fleeing with her—Pierre commits the ultimate act of pretension, taking the silence of heaven for approval. The burden of proof, apparently, lies with God and not man—or at least, not with Pierre.[38]

Pierre never loses that assurance of self. After many painful experiences Pierre sits down to write "some thoughtful thing of Absolute Truth"—though, lest we miss the point, the narrator tells us that his poetic talents are chiefly suited to the production of "beautiful imaginings." His reading on this project is cursory and random; to one like Pierre, the narrator suggests, books are apt to be "an obstacle hard to overcome" because one must see beyond the work to the idea in the author's mind. The danger here can scarcely be that Pierre would be imitative; he has too much pride for that. Rather, it must be that such a one as Pierre cannot see beyond the book because he sees his own reflection in it.[39]

Of course, Pierre's "idealism" is a delusion; it consists only in an inability to see beyond appearances. His "brotherly" concern for Isabel would hardly have developed if she were not beautiful, and even Pierre suspects as much. It is in fact sexual, and the elaborate rationalization of his deceits as truly moral is followed by a scene in which passion is nakedly revealed.[40]

More than carnality is involved, however. The shadow that fell on Pierre, the narrator writes, did not only fall "backward, hinting of some irrevocable sin" but "forward, pointing to some inevitable evil." Pierre fears and hates whatever is outside himself, and wills to injure it. Although the whole elaborate plot with Isabel is justified by the need to protect his mother from knowledge of his father's sin, it gives her a greater injury and Pierre later confesses that he "foreknew" it would hurt her. Isabel seeks to avoid his sacrifice for her, knowing

---

[38] *Ibid.*, pp. 98, 149–150, 228, 265–268.
[39] *Ibid.*, pp. 393, 402, 342.
[40] *Ibid.*, pp. 151–152, 229–230, 248–249, 265–268.

it to be a "poison" that would make her an "accursing thing." Of course that is exactly what Pierre seeks; feeling a guilty desire, he must convict Isabel by means of sacrifice. Suffering for her sake, he can be assured of greater purity. Lucy, his blonde and pure light-of-love, is even more dangerous, for she lives up to the idealistic–romantic creed. The world cannot be wholly false if Lucy is not; Pierre hurts her more than once and breaks with her because he fears she will be a snare and a temptation which would lead him (in contemporary usage) to "sell out" to the world.[41]

That not-so-secret hostility to life outside the self is always present in Pierre. In early life he believed that the absolute existed in life; later he is willing to do combat to recover it, violating life to make it stand the test of will. Pierre threatens the "Invisibles" that if they "forsake" him (this on the same page where he parallels himself to Jesus) he will "declare myself . . . free to make war on Night and Day and all thoughts and things of mind and matter." He will follow virtue "where common souls never go," even if this lead to hell; if virtue proves to be vice, he insists that the heavens should "crush me" and "let all things tumble together." This is the logic of "idealism"; Pierre must perish for his idea of virtue, as must the world, for nothing could induce him to change it. Even greater hatred of life is hidden there. The "heavens" will crush Pierre in any case, and—just as he cannot abide a world unresponsive to his ideals—he cannot tolerate the existence of a world in which he is not.[42]

The fact of mortality only drives Pierre into desperate purpose in his work, cutting all his ties to humanity, seeking to defeat death by becoming dead. He was—reversing the pilgrimage of Socrates— "learning how to live by rehearsing the part of death." For a living man that effort is impossible, and eventually Pierre voices his resentment openly. "All things that think, or move, or lie still" were "created to mock and mourn him." "He seemed gifted with loftiness merely that it might be dragged down to the mud. Still, the profound wilfulness in him would not give up." [43]

Pierre has already felt himself to be one of the Titans when he dreams of being Enceladus, striving to retain his "paternal birthright"

[41] *Ibid.*, pp. 58, 148–149, 249, 412–413.
[42] *Ibid.*, pp. 150, 380–381; Stern, *Fine Hammered Steel*, pp. 161–166, 176.
[43] *Pierre*, pp. 425, 471–472.

but still tied to the earth by "o'erfreighted feet," the product of a mixed union, "uncertain, heaven-aspiring but still not wholly earth-emancipated." Pierre has hated those earthbound feet and tried to ignore them. The bohemian idealist with his pen (like Ahab with his spear) has chosen to fight with his arms; Enceladus is armless and fights his battle with legs and body.

Pierre cannot endure the dream and the permanent ambiguity it portends. The deprivation he has inflicted on his heart leaves him too little strength to bear failure. He becomes "hate shod," rejecting the "bread and breath" of the world, spurning both Lucy and Isabel and striving to be "neuter"—which means, for Pierre, rejecting both his "angels." For a man who rejects both heart and head, there is nothing left but death.[44]

Pierre must, as he has always threatened, take someone with him. His mother is already dead; he murders his cousin (who has inherited his estate) for rebuking his conduct; Lucy and Isabel die with him in prison. Melville has a final comment on the murderous innocence of idealism; Isabel outlives Pierre and asserts at the end that she alone has "known" him. Pierre—like Ahab—has all along been the captive of his heart; the head, the "good angel," has never been able to compete.[45]

For his last great tale of innocence, Melville returned to the sea. Captain Vere in *Billy Budd* is more fortunate in his narrator than was Ahab; his story is told sympathetically by one who shares most of Vere's attitudes. There is a Burkean tone to the narrator's discussion of political events, a Whiggish distaste for the revolution and a marveling wonder that it resulted in a "general political advance" for Europe. Surely the narrator disliked the Nore mutiny which menaced England—then "the sole free conservative power"—which is likened to a strike by firemen were London threatened with "general arson." The unanswered question, however, is the aptness of the metaphor: was the threat of the Revolution general, menacing a whole people, or did it threaten a class and a system of rule? For the narrator, no such dilemma exists, nor is he bothered by the contradiction of asserting that the Revolution was a "crisis in Christendom" when he also defers to the "enlightened" spirit he expects to find in his audience,

---

[44] *Ibid.*, pp. 471, 483–484.

[45] *Ibid.*, p. 502; Pierre comes full circle, realizing that in surrendering his birthright, he gave up what he most wanted (pp. 397–403).

seeking to avoid the "charge of being tinctured with the Biblical element." Indeed, like Vere, the narrator sees a gulf between "custom and convention" and virtue, the last being "out of keeping" with the first two. The historian is, like Vere himself, a secular innocent, the product of the age of genteel rationalism, seeking to paper over the dark labyrinths of life.[46]

Vere's is another story of a man seeking to recapture an innocence which his mind should tell him was always an illusion—and one now lost forever. At bottom, he too is diseased at heart, fearing emotion and the world. Vere had trained himself to be "the most undemonstrative of men," one who disliked "mere humor." The heart, denied an outlet, has captured the mind; Vere lapses, from time to time, into a certain "dreaminess of mood" from which he is recalled to reality only reluctantly and with a momentary show of "irascibility."

There are other indications, clear, though indirect. Described as "intellectual," Vere shies away from art and theory, seeking practical works; if he shows a fashionable interest in "unconventional writers" who are free from "cant and convention," he admires those who "philosophize upon realities," accepting the apparent world of "common sense." Vere has "settled convictions" and he uses his mind to find defenses for these, which he has "vainly sought in social converse." He had arrived at doctrines which were, for him, proof against the "invading waters of novel opinion." Vere's mind, in other words, is used to erect securities, to protect Vere against doubt and uncertainty. Nor is it encouraging to be told that, unlike those who defended established institutions because they saw those institutions as part of their privilege and status, Vere "disinterestedly" opposed new ideas as contrary to man's good. Vere is not disinterested, of course: not only is he a high ranking officer, he partly owes his rank to his connections with the nobility, and it hardly speaks well of his moral self-consciousness that he is unaware of the fact.

In those cases where his rationalizations do not protect him, Vere

---

[46] All citations from *Billy Budd* are taken from *Typee and Billy Budd,* ed. M. R. Stern (New York: Dutton, 1958). On the narrator's character, see pp. 276, 285, 286, 304, 305. Notably, he regards the Nore and Spithead mutinies as a "distempering irruption" in a "frame constitutionally sound which anon throws it off" (p. 287). But the "natural" recovery involves the savage imposition of discipline.

is "far from embracing . . . the perils of moral responsibility," preferring always to refer decisions to higher authority, to the book—or, failing that, to his inferiors.

Concerned to preserve his innocence, Vere is at best insensitive to others. In conversation with his peers, he is prone to use literary allusions which they do not understand; the narrator argues that he is simply "unmindful," which would be bad enough, and an uncharitable witness might imagine Vere to be making a subtle effort to establish superiority. Even the narrator compares him to a "migratory fowl" that "never heeds when it crosses a frontier," in this case suggesting that Vere is unaware of concerns, feelings and personalities other than his own.[47]

The Captain is, however, certainly "aware" of his crew. Although there has been no sign of mutiny or disaffection, his attitudes toward the crew are close to paranoia. He is deeply concerned and disturbed by Claggart's artful reference to an incident during the Nore mutiny when the life of a ship's commander was endangered; his first reaction to Claggart's charge against Billy Budd is a fear of keeping "lingering disaffections alive," and his reason for dealing with the charge secretly is fear of the "matter getting abroad." Like his passion for secrecy, his reason for demanding Billy's execution is the danger of mutiny and of a reawakened spirit of the Nore. In the end, his course of action proves utter folly: the only mutinous disturbance, which itself comes to nothing, is provoked by his execution of Billy.[48]

Vere has always shunned the harshest responsibilities of command, and his master-at-arms, Claggart, has willingly assumed them. Throughout the book, the "mystery" of Claggart's iniquity is much discussed, but part of that mystery is not hard to penetrate. Claggart, a man with a dark past ashore, has fought his way up from the bottom

---

[47] On Vere's character, see *Billy Budd*, pp. 291–294, 328; for an excellent discussion, see Thompson, *Melville's Quarrel with God*, pp. 370–373.

[48] *Billy Budd*, pp. 319, 322, 336, 339, 347–348. In an aside, the narrator observes that certain men of the world develop an "undemonstrative distrustfulness" which is so habitual as to be unconscious. He exempts businessmen, who presumably are aware of the nature of the market; his argument applies much better to those in positions of authority (p. 314). The digression on Nelson, who offered himself "for the altar and sacrifice" (pp. 288–291), is clearly meant to contrast Nelson's leadership with Vere's; Nelson would sacrifice himself, Vere would sacrifice another. (Compare *White Jacket*, p. 184.)

ranks and remains an ambitious man. Discussing his iniquity, the narrator comments that among civilized men able to dissemble with one another, outward rationality may conceal a heart run riot, a phenomenal pride and self-concern, in which conduct seems "dominated by intellectuality" but in which reason is only a tool of passions concentrated on the self (with no sign of anything "sordid or sensual"). That description, however, applies to Vere as well or better than it does to Claggart, and the two are also likened in that only Vere could intellectually comprehend the "moral phenomenon" of Billy Budd.

In fact, Claggart's subordinates are said to be compliant "almost to a degree inconsistent with entire moral volition." This also applies to the "ingratiating" Claggart in relation to his Captain. Claggart must feed Vere's fear to advance himself; he is no more than the reflection of the Captain's anxiety.

Nor is Vere free from responsibility for Claggart's plot against Billy. The narrator believes that perhaps the very "harmlessness" of Billy stirred Claggart's hate. Yet Billy is not harmless for Claggart. Dependent on his Captain's favor, Claggart has recognized the fact that Billy had "attracted the Captain's attention from the first" because of his striking beauty. The Captain intended to appoint the far-from-brilliant Budd to captaincy of the mizzen-top to bring him "more frequently . . . under his own observation." Envy of that winning beauty is only a part of Claggart's hostility. Billy is, as far as man may be, an innocent, and Vere longs for that quality and admires it in another. Claggart's position makes innocence impossible, for he must be able to plan and scheme. He would fain have shared innocence, we are told, but despaired of it; Claggart's "elemental evil"—the subtle reminder of intertwined responsibility—causes Vere to feel a "vaguely repellent distaste."

Indeed, it does not affect his actions that Claggart could not "annul" his evil. He could hide the evil and regulate his conduct; when the narrator says that not Claggart but his Creator is responsible for Claggart's actions, he suggests more than he knows. For Claggart's "creator" in a social sense is Vere: if the Captain had expected or rewarded different conduct, Claggart would have provided it.

Gazing at Billy, Claggart grows sad, his face "suffused with incipient tears," revealing that he could have loved the seaman but for "fate and ban." Already, it has been said that Claggart's hostility and envy were not like the "apprehensive jealousy" with which Saul eyed David. Hardly: the case is eventually rightly compared to Joseph and his brothers. The cause is paternal authority, which divides men who might have been brothers by unjust distribution of favor, not—as was the case with Saul—a jealousy aroused by another's fraternity. The case between Claggart and Billy Budd is a re-enactment of the rivalry between Cain and Abel. The one charge rightly laid against Claggart is that he had no idea of an "unreciprocated malice," and that he justi- fied his envy and hatred of Billy by imagining it to be returned in kind —but that sin is derivative and not primary.[49]

Billy's attack on Claggart has been prefigured during his service aboard the *Rights of Man*, where he is taunted, from envy, by another seaman. (The seaman, by the way, calls Billy a "sweet and pleasant fellow" just as Claggart is later to do.) The difference, however, is in the Captain: the genuinely paternal, morally responsible Captain Graveling sees the case for what it is. When Billy strikes his tor- mentor, it luckily does not result in death (for Billy's fate it hardly matters that Claggart dies, as the military offense would have been as serious), for that first blow leads to a sequel: Billy wins the "apparent love" of his erstwhile foe. But there, no Vere divides them.[50]

Billy himself is something of an enigma. He is not quite perfect, but he is likened to a reborn Adam in innocence and he is too pure to be convincingly human. Theological allusions surround his birth, and when Vere likens Billy to an "angel of God," the description is apt. Billy is innocent like the angels, not like the child—for unlike children, he understands what death is, yet doesn't fear it "irrationally." In the great moment of crisis Billy, like God, is voiceless; like the angels, his actions are involuntary, and his fatal blow is not willed. Billy's func- tion is clear if his nature is not: he serves to smash the defenses of Captain Vere.

Vere's response to the crime is a kind of madness; his surgeon thinks him "unhinged," and even the narrator leaves the question open. Despite his normal tendency to avoid responsibility, he insists, con-

---

[49] On Claggart's character, see *Billy Budd*, pp. 297, 304, 306, 307, 308, 314, 318, 320, 321; compare *White Jacket*, pp. 32, 233–234.

[50] *Billy Budd*, p. 280. Vere is "starry" or heavenly, but Graveling's name suggests mortality, earthiness, and probably the heart.

trary to the advice of his subordinates and against the professional judgment of other captains, on trying the case rather than referring it to the Admiral. He departs from custom in selecting the Captain of Marines as one judge, feeling him likely to be more severe than other officers. In fact, Vere interposes throughout the trial and eventually dictates the verdict to his hesitant juniors who are, nominally, the "judges." All of this bespeaks desperation, the feeling that Budd's existence somehow menaces Vere's own mental balance.

Aside from his fear of mutiny, Vere may have some sense of his own culpability; the greater threat, however, is his attraction to Billy, which undermines not only his devotion to the military code but his ability to remain free of involvement with emotional commitments and fleshly things. Melville leaves little to the imagination. That there is nothing "sordid or sensual" in the "depravity" discussed in Billy Budd is ambiguous at best; as an "assurance" from the narrator, it is a mark of his belief that readers will suspect it, and certainly it is part of the problem. Billy and Vere shared "radically . . . the rarer qualities of one nature," because neither is a complete human being. Billy lacks any qualities of mind, his gentle heart cannot guide him, and naturally enough he admires in the Captain the virtues he lacks. Vere's mind, however, is the prisoner of his own corrupted heart, and he sees and fears in Billy a possible balance for his own defect. The narrator speculates that in his visit to Billy after the trial, Vere may have "developed the passion sometimes latent in an exterior stoical and indifferent" which expresses itself in a "sacrament" scarcely ever "revealed to the gadding world." [51]

Even if the "sacrament" took place, it was possible only because Vere had shored up his defenses with the fatal verdict. Vere, judging Billy, sought to avoid all personal responsibility: he appealed to the duty to obey without question the law of the king and to put aside the law of nature. Yet even Vere felt that solution to be unsatisfactory, and he passed the final burden of responsibility to the "Last Assizes"

[51] *Billy Budd*, pp. 326–328, 337–338. Sexual allusions are frequent. They range from the veiled comments regarding the "ambiguous smile" Billy's appearance produced in the hardened veterans of the crew, through the comments on the feminine nature of his beauty, and Vere's imagining him nude, to the reference in which Billy reacts to Claggart's charges like a "Vestal priestess" being buried alive—a punishment normally reserved for cases in which a Vestal lost her virtue. (See pp. 283, 320, 324; compare *Pierre*, pp. 674–675, 680.)

which would acquit Billy. Not only is religion made to serve the state: both politics and religion, the supreme expressions of man's need and search, are converted from reflections of human responsibility to means for evading it.[52]

Perhaps unaware, Vere refers to the sea as that "where we move and have our being"—a quotation from *Acts* 17:28. In context, the citation destroys Vere's argument, for Vere has made God into something removed from men and His law into an ultimate standard which redeems life, but has no application to it. Man's duty, for Vere, is passive: obey the King, have faith in the Lord. Paul, however, had said that men should seek the Lord Who is not far from any man; and if he would have agreed that they should eschew paternal sentiments, it was because they were brothers with a common father: "We also are His offspring." The teaching insists on the possibility and the duty of fraternal justice among men, but it is a lesson Vere could not possibly learn: he who creates fratricide does not know fraternity.

Vere's frenzy was futile; Billy goes to his death still trusting, crying, "God bless Captain Vere." In the final crisis, Billy finds the voice he lacked in the first; it is one which irrevocably involves Vere with Billy's death and rightly suggests the Captain's need for divine blessing. Perhaps unaware, Billy has erased social distance: he assumes the right to bless his superior. His manner of meeting death, too, convicts Vere's own fears. The effect of the blessing is to judge Vere guilty in the tribunal of his own mind. Yet it is, in that very judgment, a true blessing: responsibility and guilt are human facts, and when Vere later dies a hero's death, Billy's name is on his lips.

Dwelling Among Brethren

In Melville's mature view, the sweet in life was wedded to the bitter. The good was rare, a thing of chance and transience, but it was not less real for being so. Men must be aware of the rarity of good to recognize it or to set it at its true value; the excellent, almost by definition, is the abnormal. An "enchanted calm" is a delight to those who have sailed amid tempests, a bore to those who have not. Failure to understand leads men to allow the good that falls to them to slide

---

[52] *Billy Budd*, pp. 333–334; compare *White Jacket*, pp. 196–197.

away, imagining it easy to surpass or recover. Men can, like the coral, build against the tempests and protect their lagoons of calm; but to do so, they must realize that the tempest is to be expected and that man, like the "coral insect," lacks the strength to build alone. Men must yield the defenses by which they would separate themselves psychologically from anguish and mortality, if they are to know or defend good.[53]

Orthodox Christianity, as Melville saw it, was a failure precisely because it enabled and encouraged men to regard death as an illusion.[54] Life, Melville insisted, does not "vanquish" death. Rather, the emotional as well as intellectual knowledge of death sets life at its true value. As an emotional certainty, death loses much of its peril; by becoming a fact, it ceases to be a risk. This enables men to form bonds with their fellows more easily, for while risk is involved in any relationship, we are more willing to risk or to lose when the loss is inevitable. A harpooned whale draws Ishmael into the center of a school of whales where he witnesses the miracle of birth. The bond between him and suffering creation is still involuntary and artificial, but the lesson is clear: awareness of one's connection to creation in its agony is the way to a "rebirth" which is the fullness of life. In *Clarel*, Melville made his premise clear:

Emerge thou mayest from the last whelming sea
And prove that death but routs life into victory.[55]

Man by himself could not support the truth that the self, like all things, is limited, perishing, and without safe haven. Yet that truth is the first great discovery of man's quest for answers and his search to find out the great mysteries of life and being. The discovery of human limitation merely opens the way to one's brothers, making dependence on men seem mild in a universe still more alien, and causing responsibility for them to appear as an affirmation of the worth of the self that was lacking elsewhere. Melville reversed Thoreau's assertion that a man must "succeed alone" before he can find his brothers; man must

---

[53] *Poems*, p. 241; *Clarel*, vol. II, pp. 127–128, 137–141, 284–285, 295, 296, 298; *Moby Dick*, vol. II, pp. 135–136, 143–144, 181; *Piazza Tales*, pp. 188–189.

[54] *Clarel*, vol. II, pp. 51–53.

[55] *Ibid.*, p. 298. See also *Omoo*, pp. 48, 49, 79, 364–372, and *Moby Dick* (Modern Library edition), pp. 558–562.

fail alone, for the heart's hope for innocence must be shattered first.[56]

By himself, man would misread the riddle of meaning. God would be silent and would not reveal his "heart." If he did not abandon the riddle altogether, man was likely to surrender to his pride and claim that the heartless silence he had encountered was itself the "answer." The void would become the thing: he would define God as nonexistent or as an indifferent machine. But this definition would only prove man's ignorance. For whatever voice and heart God would reveal to men must necessarily come through men and their relations with each other. Rejecting "the lee shore for the howling infinite" is no better than its reverse. Melville was cunning; the narrator of Moby Dick, ironic and detached from his former self, urges us to "call" him Ishmael. Yet *Yishmael* means God has heard (or shall hear) whether or not he speaks, nor was Melville unaware of the connection between the name and the Biblical promise that Ishmael shall "dwell in the presence of all his brethren." [57]

"Two together may see," Melville underlined in his edition of *The Iliad*. Fraternity was essential for the realization of man's nature. Man needed both the shore and the infinite, and he required joy and encouragement to support him in his quest. If, however, such supports came from any source but one who shared the quest, they would pull him away from the course of his pilgrimage. Only with a brother could the self find integration, however momentary, and all a man's faculties sail on the same tack.[58]

Yet as Melville came to know, even awareness of the need for fraternity can be a snare. Precisely because his need for his brother is so great, a man may be tempted to seek a perfect fraternity in which the other is without fault and the union of spirits complete. Despairing of himself, he may transfer his hope for innocence to another, finding in their relation the "answer" denied elsewhere.

Melville's own early relationship with Hawthorne was close to idolatrous. He spoke of it in passive terms, using the only-too-compre-

[56] *Pierre*, pp. 402–403; *Clarel*, vol. I, p. 131; *Stories, Poems and Letters*, pp. 7, 48; *Omoo*, pp. 126, 290, 375; Parrington, *Main Currents*, vol. II, pp. 250, 255; Thoreau, *Writings*, vol. IV, p. 299.

[57] *Genesis* 16:12; see also *Stories, Poems and Letters*, p. 62, and Thorp, *Herman Melville: Representative Selections*, p. 392.

[58] *Stories, Poems and Letters*, p. 4; the plural in *Clarel*, vol. I, p. 131, is significant.

hensible metaphor of himself as a "southern soul" with a "hot soil" which longed to receive the "New England roots" of Hawthorne. The adulation made Hawthorne uncomfortable; he had no desire to be Melville's terrestrial deity. The lack of equivalent response made Melville feel slighted, and he doubted whether Hawthorne had an adequate "heart." Hawthorne, however, knew that genuine fraternity demanded a recognition of imperfection in the other and an understanding that the relation of fraternity would be as incomplete and imperfect as were men themselves. "Fraternity of feeling" he could understand; Melville's assertion that his fraternal feeling was "infinite" was out of the question. Nor could Hawthorne have been comforted by Melville's assertion that he was more "persuaded of immortality" by knowing Hawthorne than by reading the Bible.[59]

His estrangement from Hawthorne may have helped teach Melville's emotions what his intellect already knew: that no man is deserving of complete adulation. His sense of loss certainly led him to regret having rejected the more limited terms on which fraternity might have been possible. In "Monody" he wrote that neither he nor Hawthorne had been "in the wrong." Perhaps he blamed the separation on the imperfection of the world; perhaps he meant that his own youthful enthusiasm could be excused, as could Hawthorne's refusal to gratify it. Either possibility makes the same point: time had taught Melville better than to ask for too much.[60]

Fraternity can raise men above what is normally human, but its highest fulfillment is logically an outgrowth of the relation itself, not something to be demanded in the first instance. The accidents of character may enable one's brother to express this fulfillment, but to insist on it is to end in pathos. The "proof" of fraternity and its highest act of devotion is dying for one's brother. All other proofs are suspect. One may be willing to share another's guilt and responsibility in order to escape part of one's own. The willingness to die for the other goes further: it amounts to a willingness to be damned for him, to accept the whole burden of human imperfection and mortality: to sacrifice oneself so that the survivor may receive the greatest revelation of the "heart" of God available to men, and be given the strongest

[59] *Stories, Poems and Letters*, pp. 8–9, 38–81, esp. p. 51; see also Metcalf, *Herman Melville: Cycle and Epicycle*, pp. 99, 108.
[60] *Stories, Poems and Letters*, p. 81.

encouragement and responsibility to continue the human quest. (It is perhaps in this sense that *Moby Dick* is "baptized in hell fire": that it teaches men to court the "curse" of man's condition for their brothers.) For those who seek a perfect fraternity, that sacrifice may come as an awakening shock, the sad recognition that they have not known their brothers until too late.

Nothing could be further from Melville's early demand for a universal, innocent fraternity. "Better that we were all annihilated than that one man were damned" gradually became the opposite: better for one man to be voluntarily annihilated than that his brother be damned. The reversal parallels Melville's realization that not only are universal innocence or universal perfection impossible, but that even the best possible relation among men, fraternity, depends fundamentally on chance and example.

Fraternity demanded the sense of imperfection which resulted from a passion for truth, which in turn Melville found correlated to the chance event of "fatherlessness." Fraternity demanded as well a heart schooled in its own need which would allow men to recognize their brothers. The relationship depended on preconditions which it was impossible for brethren to create: on two souls willing to see and accept the true nature of the human condition.[61]

Society might help with the training of souls, but it could not go beyond its own average, somewhere between the best which man might be and the savagery with which he began, and its weight would tend to fall in the latter direction. Savagery was, after all, a universal, and one which required curbing; concern for excellence could be delayed. The "popular conservatism" with which Melville believed "Solomon" to have "managed" *Ecclesiastes*—diluting its unpalatable truths—would always be a fact. Most men would fear and reject the truth, and a decently behaved innocence might be the best that could be expected.[62]

[61] *Typee*, p. 286; *Stories, Poems and Letters*, pp. 59, 66–67; Mayoux, *Melville*, pp. 91–94. Melville satirized fraternal "orders" under the camouflage of describing the "fraternity" of Tahitian tattoo artists. For Melville, fraternity was not so easy to establish. (*Omoo*, pp. 30–34.)

[62] *Stories, Poems and Letters*, pp. 60, 63; Julian Hawthorne, *Nathaniel Hawthorne and his Wife* (Boston: Osgood, 1885), vol. I, pp. 401–405; Metcalf, *Herman Melville: Cycle and Epicycle*, p. 168; Hillway and Mansfield, *Moby Dick: Centennial Essays*, pp. 73, 75.

This did not lead Melville into political quietism. Rather, it convinced him that the relation of fraternity must always be found outside society and established culture, among men who were "warm amid the world's cold." Reflecting on the painful fact of his failure to receive public esteem and understanding, Melville came to the conviction that an author is always isolated from his public if he has merit. Especially if he wrote in allegories, he must expect to be misunderstood.

Melville wrote allegories even at the cost of misunderstanding because he, like Solomon, "managed" the truth. In one sense, this was because he had no desire to suffer opprobrium, but in another, it was because he had no wish to undermine the decent elements of an imperfect society. He wrote in a manner which he hoped would reach his unknown brothers, and the depths of his disappointment came from the discovery of how few these were and how difficult it was to teach men.

With time, Melville's eagerness to reach his brothers—always his primary aim—increased; his fear for society declined, especially as his own estimate of the virtues of the American polity plummeted. After Hawthorne had read *Moby Dick*, Melville wrote him:

> A sense of unspeakable security is in me . . . on account of your having understood the book. I have written a wicked book and feel spotless as the lamb. Ineffable socialities are in me.

On its face, this passage says that Hawthorne's understanding has relieved Melville of the anxieties he might have felt because of his "wicked" book. Hawthorne's understanding, then, meant that the book had served its moral purpose regardless of the effects it might have on others. It had strengthened Melville's feeling of fraternity, of not being alone: "ineffable socialities are in me."

The "wickedness" of the book may refer simply to the expected public reaction; *Moby Dick* was frequently denounced as immoral and perverse. Yet Melville may also have felt a deeper doubt, a fear that his book might injure society. That may be the meaning of the succeeding lines of his letter.

> It is a strange feeling—no hopefulness is in it, no despair. Content—that is it; and irresponsibility but without licentious inclination. I speak now of my profoundest sense of being. . . .[63]

[63] *Stories, Poems and Letters,* pp. 66–67; Thorp, *Herman Melville: Representative Selections,* pp. 394–395; Metcalf, *Herman Melville: Cycle and Epicycle,*

Hawthorne's understanding allowed Melville to feel "irresponsible" for the consequences of *Moby Dick*; given that understanding, there was no need for hope or despair. Melville had risked doing an injury to find fraternity (a risk Hawthorne would have been loath to run); he was prophet, not priest, in the house of Israel. Yet Melville was a moralist too, which only emphasizes the importance to him of the prophetic teaching he presented in *Moby Dick*.

The novel is prophetic through both characters and events. Ishmael can tell the tale because his "education" has led him to see the threads which tied his destiny to others, because he has escaped from individualism in his view of persons and events. Superficially, for example, there is a great difference between the desertion of Pip by a boat crew and Ishmael's survival of the sinking of the *Pequod;* the first is a conscious decision, the second an "accident." To the now-discerning narrator, however, the events are linked, and Pip's disaster foreshadows Ishmael's: a "like abandonment befell myself." The two are united by nemesis; "the thing is common in that fishery." [64]

Similar in fate, Pip and Ishmael were radically dissimilar in beginnings. Pip was black, but this was hardly the critical difference. (Melville could speak the language of our time. "Nor smile so," he commented, "while I write that this little black was brilliant, for even blackness has its brilliancy; behold yon lustrous ebony, panelled in king's cabinets.") Ishmael was "wolfish" in his anger at the world, while Pip was a child of nature. In his "natural lustre" he had "enlivened many a fiddler's frolic on the green"; he was a lover of life "and all life's peaceable securities," and thus fearful of danger, cowardly in the face of risk. Pip's cowardice is central; it is what leads Stubb to abandon him when he leaps from the whale boat in panic, but it is also the quality which keeps him from falling under Ahab's spell. Being "very bright" he sees, as the crew does not, the perilous folly of Ahab's quest, and he is still close enough to his emotions and realistic enough in his innocence to be able to "feel fear." [65]

---

pp. 128–129. The narrator in *Billy Budd* notes that unpleasant historical truths which injure national pride "cannot be ignored, but there is a considerate way of historically treating them" (p. 287). Melville adapted that prescription for his own purposes.

[64] *Moby Dick* (1952), pp. 409–413.

[65] *Ibid.,* pp. 227–230, 409–413.

When Pip is abandoned, he undergoes an experience not "meant" for men: it is, in fact, a symbolic death. Pip sees into the nature of things, the "joyous, heartless, ever-juvenile eternities," and feels himself "uncompromised, indifferent as his God." The dream of innocence is fulfilled; Pip abandoned is alone with infinity and the naked awareness of the finitude of man and the world. "Death is . . . the first salutation to the possibilities of the immense Remote, the Wild, the Watery, the Unshored"—and the ocean, which is all of these, beckons to the innocent. "Here is another life without the guilt of intermediate death; here are wonders supernatural, without dying for them. . . . Bury thyself in a life which, to your now equally abhorred and abhorring landed world, is more oblivious than death." This, of course, is the real call Ishmael answered in going to sea, and with him most of Ahab's crew. Pip's greater fearfulness led him to accept the embrace of the ocean; accepting the last temptation of innocence, he found out its last fraud, discovering that the "first salutation" of the infinite is death itself.[66]

Not for nothing did Melville have Pip's laugh mock Ahab's "baptism" of his spear, adding that Pip's "strange mummeries" were not "unmeaningly blended with the black tragedy of the melancholy ship." Pip's reappearance is never adequately explained, and yet it is asserted from the first: "He saw God's foot upon the treadle of the loom, and spoke it; and therefore his shipmates called him mad." Melville wrote that Pip's experience "fictitiously" increased his natural brilliance tenfold. It is a curious word; Melville certainly did not believe that extreme or gloomy experience was "unnatural" to the development of man's intelligence. The "unnatural" element is said to be the light which is used to illumine brilliance: in fact, of course, the unnatural light is the license of the novelist, the writer of fictions. Melville "fictitiously" re-introduces Pip, bringing him back from "the bourne from which no traveller returns" in order to suggest what a man might learn who had, in fact, endured the last lesson of the race.[67]

Pip returns as a prophet, one who "spoke" of the Divine order; even Starbuck, who misconstrues his cryptic comments, thinks that he "brings heavenly vouchers of our heavenly homes." Emphasizing both his death and his rebirth as a prophet, Pip denies his past identity

[66] *Ibid.*, pp. 479–481.
[67] *Ibid.*, pp. 410, 413.

("Pip? whom call ye Pip? Pip jumped from the whaleboat. Pip's missing. . . . One hundred pounds of clay reward for Pip . . .") and
asserts a new identity as "ship's crier." Ahab is touched by this madness and chooses the moment to denounce the gods, and to declaim
that man's nature is good—"full of love and gratitude"—even when
he is "idiotic, not knowing what he does."

Pip, however, is far from unaware, and rebukes Ahab at the
moment when the Captain gives him his hand. "Ah, now, had poor
Pip but felt so kind a thing as this, perhaps he had ne'er been lost";
the hand is "a man-rope; something that weak souls may hold by."
The lesson is twofold: given love and concern, Pip might have been
able to face his peril; but also, more generally, Pip's constant mocking
of those who scorned his "cowardice" suggests that they too are "weak
souls" who need the man-rope, despite their vauntings.[68]

Certainly Ahab's comments are fatuous. It was not the gods but
his own zeal for the whale oil, shared by his crew, that led to Pip's
abandonment. His remarks are only another instance of the Captain's
insistence on blaming the cosmos for his own guilts. Even his "compassion" for Pip is partly charged with fear: "I see not my reflection
in the vacant pupils of thy eyes. Oh, God! That a man should be a
thing for immortal souls to sieve through! Who art thou, boy?" The
dead, reborn Pip, with his knowledge of human weakness, makes
Ahab aware of his own limitations; he cannot, as he can with Starbuck,
see his own reflection. Another's death is a reminder of the imminence
of one's own. His desire to be "one" with Pip is his desire to dominate;
Pip's response is a desire to be made whole. For Pip's prophecy leaves
him still incomplete: he is as "mad" with knowledge of human weakness as is Ahab with imagined strength.[69]

Ahab, as the sequel shows, does not learn the lesson that human
sanity demands a sharing of qualities which—taken in isolation—lead
to madness; and he eventually turns away from Pip in pursuit of his
own quest. "There is that in thee, poor lad, which I feel too curing
to my malady." Pip seeks to dissuade him by an appeal to Ahab's
maimed heart, offering it flesh ("ye have not a whole body, Sir; do ye
but use me . . .") and fidelity. Ahab rejects both, spurning the ac-

[68] *Ibid.*, pp. 512–515, 472–477.
[69] *Ibid.*, pp. 512–515.

knowledgment of weakness and dependence they imply. His reply is the fratricidal response of one who cannot endure weakness in himself or independence in another: "Weep so, and I will murder thee!" In the end, Ahab deserts Pip, too; the captain is too far gone to accept Pip's prophecy from the ocean's wilderness.[70]

Pip's prophetic awareness is not limited to his perception of Ahab. Seeing Queequeg in his coffin awaiting death, he cries that "Queequeg dies game!" It is an example to all the crew, from Pip to Ahab, who have been cowards, seeking to escape life's terms and end, and Pip calls for "a game cock . . . to sit upon his head and crow," surely a reference to the fact that the lesson of dying game has been lost on men before, even though the cock crowed twice.[71]

Melville surrounded Queequeg with not-so-mysterious allusions. He is the heir to a "kingdom not of this world"—an island which is "not on any map" because "true places never are"; his "mark" is the symbol of infinity, his name nothing but the repetition of the question "who?," and his god, Yoyo, bears a name which is, similarly, a repetition of "I." The cabalistic symbols with which his body is covered hint at mysteries—the question of man's origin, his identity, his place in the infinite. Small wonder, then, that Ahab regards him as a "devilish tantalization of the gods," for the temptation is to seek the answer to the mystery of self and paternity, one which might sway even Ahab from his war with the world.[72]

Melville repeatedly had presented Queequeg as a "savior," recklessly risking himself to preserve others, and the incident in which Queequeg orders the building of his own coffin is part of that design. It is another tale of death and rebirth, for Queequeg remembers a "duty" ashore, rises suddenly from the coffin, and announces that he cannot die as yet. To his incredulous shipmates, he asserts that if a man "made up his mind to live" he could only be killed by a whale (as Queequeg eventually is) or some other "violent, ungovernable, unintelligent destroyer." Since that "exception" covers much ground, the whole incident more relevantly suggests that Queequeg's real doctrine is that a man must have a reason to live, a duty or tie that

[70] *Ibid.*, pp. 525–526.
[71] *Ibid.*, pp. 472–477; *Mark* 14:66–72.
[72] *Moby Dick* (1952), pp. 54–56, 87–90; (Standard Edition), vol. II, p. 251.

binds him to life. The "neutral" state, for Queequeg, is the will to die, mortality being the normal condition of man.[73]

Certainly this doctrine accounts not only for Queequeg's bravery but for his generosity and ready affection; his is the true insight into the condition of the dying animal, and it frees him to see that life and its goods are things not to be hoarded, but expended. When Ahab later pondering Queequeg's example, rejects it with the assertion that he is too "far gone" in darkness to accept the "theoretic" bright side of life, he is only partly right. It is because Ahab will not accept the darkness that the brightness remains for him "theoretic." [74]

The vital element in the coffin incident is the "duty" ashore which leads Queequeg to opt for life. Queequeg left his "kingdom" to learn from Christians how his man-devouring realm might be improved; he discovered only that Christians were, if anything, worse than his own folk, and that this is a "wicked world in all meridians." Yet the cannibal's Calvinistic perception is also connected to the last "duty" which he is said to have felt before boarding the Pequod. Enroute to Nantucket, after saving several fellow passengers, he seemed to be reflecting, Ishmael tells us, that it is a "mutual, joint stock world in all meridians," as well as wicked. And because of that, "We cannibals must help these Christians." [75]

That knowledge of man's fraternal condition and duties which calls Queequeg back to life comes to be associated with the coffin from which he "rises." Built to serve the need of a lonely, personal death, it comes to symbolize living and dying with and for others. Eventually it is converted into a lifebuoy—an unlikely use which Queequeg contrives to suggest by "strange signs and innuendos." This coffin leads Ahab to his reflections on dark and light; eventually, rising from the wreck of the Pequod, it saves Ishmael. The tomb becomes the means to life; in this sense, Queequeg has died to save his brother and to teach him, in turn, the lesson of human fraternity. It was perhaps his "mission" from the beginning; his god, for a purpose

[73] Moby Dick, vol. I, pp. 75–76, 269–270, 284, vol. II, pp. 77–79, 98–99, 305, 368.

[74] Ibid., vol. II, p. 310.

[75] Moby Dick (1952), pp. 54–61. Who would know better than a cannibal the truth of man's dependence on man, especially the fact that all men are cannibals, "living off" one another?

of his own, had told Queequeg that Ishmael was to select the ship on which both would sail.[76]

The lesson is one which Ishmael has been slow to learn. He begins as an individualist, preferring a bench to sharing a room with another, and when he first glimpses Queequeg he identifies him with death and a "phantom" of his early childhood. (Doubtless that was accurate enough; one phantom of childhood is the threat posed by other men.) Even his "marriage" to Queequeg is marred by an elaborate sophism which, by the "Golden Rule," justifies worship of the pagan's idol as part of a desire to convert Queequeg to Presbyterianism—in other words, to make him like Ishmael. (The narrator says, with hindsight, that Presbyterians and pagans are alike "dreadfully cracked about the head and sadly need mending.") As against the unconditional vows of devotion which he receives from Queequeg, Ishmael's own motives are self-regarding. He decides to sail with Queequeg because the latter, as an experienced whaler, will be useful; he vows to cleave to Queequeg after seeing the latter save several lives in an emergency. In fact, tied as he is to Queequeg, Ishmael is equally attracted to Ahab, his wolfishness drawn to the king of wolves, and only the accident of being thrown from Ahab's boat keeps him from sharing the Captain's fate.[77]

Ishmael's most "fraternal" act, his decision to make Queequeg his heir, is itself suspect. The will is a response to fear, part of an effort to banish death by courting it, desperate bravado employed to deal with threat. Having made his will, Ishmael says, "I survived myself; my death and burial were locked up in my chest." He is "resurrected" and able to take a "cool, collected dive at death," an immortal who is sure of death's impotence against him. The narrator describes his own state of mind:

> Nothing dispirits and nothing seems worth disputing. He bolts down all events, all creeds, and beliefs . . . all hard things visible and invisible, never mind how knobby. . . . Prospects of sudden disaster, peril of life and limb; all these, and death itself, seem to him only sly, good-natured hits and jolly punches in the side bestowed by the

[76] *Moby Dick*, vol. II, p. 305; (Modern Library Edition), p. 99.
[77] *Moby Dick*, vol. I, pp. 32–33, 101, 222–223; Thompson, *Melville's Quarrel with God*, p. 151.

unseen and unaccountable old joker. . . . There is nothing like the perils of whaling to breed this . . . desperado philosophy.[78]

Only the experience of being cast, like Pip, into solitary communion with death and the deep, shakes Ishmael's self-sufficiency. That last torment makes the narrator into "Ishmael"—he who dwells among brethren. The "devious-cruising *Rachel*" finds "another orphan," one who has learned—too late—the bonds that tied him to his fellows. Yet possibly it was not too late: *Rachel* sought the lost children and found only an orphan, yet her cruise is "devious"; the survivors are mother and child, and from the sense of loss both may learn enough to begin again.

As man never escaped the need for fraternity, so he was never free from a brother's duties. How much more was this true for those who learned the lesson of fraternity only through the sacrifice of others! Even in the worst of circumstances, man had the ability to affect the small sphere of life that touched him. Those who saw most truly acquired the duty that men once defined as the *imitatio Christi:* that of standing as an incarnation, an example in the flesh to men who live in fearful innocence of the real nature of man's condition. And there was always the chance that he who stood forth as an example might discover brothers of his own.

"Sitting up with a corpse . . ."

Melville believed that societies made the lot of man better or worse. His interest in metaphysics—which always annoyed Hawthorne—was inseparable from his concern for political life. Melville never lost his early belief that most, if not all, of human iniquity resulted from defective governance, and that men contributed the most to good by eliminating concrete evils. He came to see the United States as a society which made humanity difficult to attain: "Its wood could only be American!" Ahab cries as the *Pequod* sinks.[79]

In early life, however, Melville had seen America in messianic terms, regarding Americans as the "estranged children of Adam"

[78] *Moby Dick*, vol. I, pp. 286–288; see also vol. II, pp. 48–49, vol. I, pp. 273–285.

[79] *Moby Dick* (1952), p. 565; see also *White Jacket*, pp. 381–382; *Stories, Poems and Letters*, p. 67; Stern, *Fine Hammered Steel*, pp. 5, 6, 94.

destined to recover the "hearthstone in Eden." Free from custom and the past, guided by the genius of individual liberty, Americans were achieving a "practical" application of Christianity, a "universal paternity" reaching toward the brotherhood of man.[80]

Even then, Melville had distrusted ideas of progress or of Providential history as too likely to lead men to inaction and to rationalization of present evils. That distrust became stronger with time; it is only a very naive Pierre who is allowed to contend that the "fierce things" of the world are "hourly going out." [81]

Too, Melville more and more distrusted demands for perfection. Absolutism was likely to make men undervalue the real, if imperfect, goods that life made available. Worse, it was often a mask for indifference. A proclaimed, abstract love for all men was too often the mark of unwillingness to sacrifice for or be committed to particular men. It was possible, in ideal terms, to defend Emerson's precept that one should not lend money to friends; but in this world, friends are often in need, brothers in adversity. Contrary to friendship in its most pure state, temporary dependence might make it possible to attain or resume that higher level. Emerson's principled hard-heartedness would only engender resentments that would destroy altogether the bonds among men. Worse still, the hope for perfection may lead men to violence against whatever seems to stand in the way; Melville was only too aware of the degree to which disappointed rationalism is tempted by force. That temptation is only made more severe when combined with faith in progress, for confidence in history allows men to be careless of means to the ends they pursue.[82]

Progress justified the ethics of success, perfectionism moralized noninvolvement; both concealed a hatred of the present world and self which could break out in violence. Rendered by an Emerson, the doctrines and hopes of the Enlightenment became "bogus beatitudes" supporting a false individualism. They destroyed or threatened the possibility of trust among men in the interest of a this-worldly salva-

---

[80] *Redburn*, p. 216; *Stories, Poems and Letters*, p. 47. Americans, Melville wrote in *White Jacket*, are "the chosen people, the Israel of our time" (p. 189).

[81] *Pierre*, pp. 44–46; *Mardi*, vol. II, p. 250; *Poems*, p. 21; *Clarel*, vol. I, p. 172; *The Confidence Man*, pp. 85, 334.

[82] *The Confidence Man*, pp. 253, 271–273; *Poems*, p. 411; *Clarel*, vol. I, p. 189; *Mardi*, vol. II, pp. 276–277.

tion that was impossible in an imperfect world whose only hope and joy lay in the relation of fraternity.

Melville held to the ancient belief that the excellence of its citizens, not its wealth or power, is the test of the state. Politics was part of the education of man, to move him from isolated self-concern toward virtue through the agency of a community united by common values. Even in his days of optimism, he had cried, "The public and the people! . . . Let us hate the one and cleave to the other." Melville knew, in fact, that democracy above all systems of government demands moral standards by which the relative possibilities of this world may be judged. The belief in "liberty and equality" can all too easily become an excuse for innocence, a refusal to judge that at best results in mediocrity and at worst comes to find good and evil indistinguishable. Freedom and equality were means only; elevated to the status of ends, they deprecated the need to seek truth and virtue.[83]

There is a measure of truth in the criticism which sees Melville's later attacks on American life as the overreaction of a disillusioned man who still saw America in absolute terms. Melville realized that if democracy might hope to raise men to new heights, it could also allow them to fall to greater depths.

Myriads playing pygmy parts
Debased into equality:
In glut of all material arts
A civic barbarism may be.
Man disennobled—brutalized—
By popular science—atheized
Into a smatterer.

[83] *White Jacket*, p. 239; *Stories, Poems and Letters*, p. 60. Melville's criticism of civilization and his relative approval of "barbarism" were based on the belief that civilization only governed the outward demeanor and conduct of human beings, and that it did so by fear. ("Barbarism" had a distinct meaning for Melville; he included classical Greece in the category.) Hence, close community (the ship) magnifies aggravations, affections, and attractions alike, because it increases knowledge of the other. The "open society" ashore, however, is one in which individuals are "brought into promiscuous commerce with mankind where unobstructed free agency on equal terms—equal superficially—soon teaches one that unless . . . he exercises a keen distrust . . . some foul turn may be served him." (*Billy Budd*, p. 314. See also *Typee*, p. 273; *Moby Dick*, vol. II, pp. 16–17; *Poems*, p. 64; Humphreys, *Herman Melville*, pp. 32, 55, 88, 105.)

America required a constant confrontation of promise and performance, needed to be reminded relentlessly of the moral goal, in order
not to lose her direction. Melville admired the prophets of the Old
Testament with good reason: theirs was the task he had set for himself.[84]

Prophecy became more necessary as Melville became convinced
that America had lost her way. Excessive individualism—including
the eagerness to profit from the calamity of others—had shattered the
bonds among men. Shut off from their fellows, men were incapable of
collective action and had lost the capacity to direct their lives. Paradoxically, the effort to "conquer nature" had resulted in an impotent
individual isolation which had "extended the empire of necessity" and
made men prisoners of drift.[85]

Prosperity only encouraged feelings of self-sufficiency combined
with feelings of "unity" which would vanish at the touch of adversity.
In the West, with its unparalleled freedom from the past, Melville
saw only misanthropic men whose hearts had descended to the bestial
level; the West revealed nakedly what Eastern hypocrisy concealed.
The East identified business success with personal merit rather than
the venality and good fortune Melville regarded as its more normal
causes. That belief led to a studied inhumanity toward those who
failed, even those who had once been friends. Commercial society
raised success and power to ultimate standards and almost wholly
neglected personal character and the relations among men.

In "The Paradise of Bachelors and the Tartarus of Maids," Melville drew a stark contrast between the "band of brothers" in the
Medieval Inns of Court, possessed of comradeship and comfort, and
the unhealthy, cruel, and impersonal purposiveness of the modern
factory. Melville chose his symbols with care, and it seems likely that
Mayoux is right to see the paper factory in "The Tartarus of Maids"
as an allusion to Locke's theory of man as a *tabula rasa*. The belief
that man can "make himself" and the world, the modern attempt to
master nature, Melville saw more and more as worse than folly; it

---

[84] The citation is from *Clarel*, vol. II, pp. 249–250; see also vol. I, pp. 281–
282; *Mardi*, vol. II, p. 242; and Metcalf, *Melville: Cycle and Epicycle*, pp.
107–108.

[85] *Selected Writings of Herman Melville* (New York: Modern Library,
1952), p. 355; *Redburn*, pp. 230, 315–318, 379; *Pierre*, pp. 9, 16, 33, 321.

was based on hatred of man as he was. The secret logic of the age of the machine was distaste for the self and its human fellows.[86]

Melville's "Man from Missouri" in *The Confidence Man* is less vulnerable than his naive fellow-passengers. Having been blind, he has been made to see by an "oculist" from Philadelphia (Benjamin Franklin?). His new, "scientific" sight, made necessary by the loss of a natural sense, gives him only a misanthropic "vision," a "confidence in distrust" of his fellows. Yet that is no protection; he is duped, eventually, by the Confidence Man. Guised as the representative of the "philanthropic" Philosophical Intelligence Office, the Confidence Man offers the Man from Missouri men and boys as workers for his farms, slavery under the mask of piety. Initially, the Missourian refuses the offer because he prefers machines which are cheaper and more efficient; he eventually succumbs to the desire to be part of a "pure scientific experiment" to determine whether this human labor cannot be made more economic than the machine. This is a sharp commentary indeed on the inner motives of the "science" of the time, with its promises of improvement in man's condition and its professions of devotion to the good of the race.[87]

Yet the effort of men to defy the laws of nature and master her was doomed to failure. The mechanization of life had been founded on artistic pride, on the belief that man could design and "create" the world anew. One result, ironically, was the alienation of the artist from society; and there was a far more radical flaw in the design. The age of mechanization had been unable to change the nature of man, and it ignored the need to school the heart; at best, it had only temporarily repressed that heart. Beneath the surface of civilization, those suppressed passions were at work, mining the resentments that would bring the tower of modern man down.

> You are but drilling the new Hun
> Whose growl e'en now can some dismay:
> Vindictive in his heart of hearts
> He schools him in your mines and marts . . .[88]

---

[86] *Stories, Poems and Letters*, pp. 178–211; *Moby Dick*, vol. I, p. 198, vol. II, p. 172; *White Jacket*, pp. 96–98. On "natural man," see *Pierre*, p. 361; *Moby Dick*, vol. I, p. 343.

[87] *The Confidence Man*, pp. 143–171.

[88] The citation is from *Clarel*, vol. II, p. 246; see also *Stories, Poems and*

Melville came to admire the medieval sense of man's limitations and the concern of older times for the interpersonal relations of men. Yet, despite his distrust of modern thought and institutions, he did not fall into nostalgia. His precepts were perennial, affected by history only as circumstances made them more or less possible of realization. Hence he was never blind to the defects of the past; he rejected ideas of class and inherited worth as firmly as he did those of individualism and the free market.[89]

Too, Melville was almost entirely free of any racial prejudice, so free that his opposition to abolitionism may seem paradoxical.[90] Detesting slavery, Melville saw the pre-war Union as a partial restraint on the industrial age. He admired its pluralism of region and culture as a barrier against the mass society he feared, and long after his youthful enthusiasms lapsed he saw in the Democratic party a reticence toward the industrial age quite different from the approbation of Emerson and his Whig associates.

More seriously, Melville distrusted abolitionism because of its innocent perfectionism and because it concealed a racism quite as marked as the overt Southern variety. In *Benito Cereno*, written in 1855, Melville's chief characters—Delano, the New England captain, and Cereno, the slave-owner—are both blind to the facts of the slave rebellion on the latter's ship. Cereno's "testimony" describes only the savagery and violence of the blacks; he cannot see that the violence is the result of human resentment at being reduced to a thing, part of the flame of man's desire for freedom. Yet although Delano can understand that slaves desire to be free, he is completely obtuse to the evidences of their violence and brutality. Delano suspects evil, but he identifies it with Cereno not only because he assumes the blacks as "natural men" must be good, but because he presumes that the white man must be the master. The inability to see evil in the subject race amounted to excluding that race from sinning humanity—a racism, and potential slavery, gentler but not less real than that which came equipped with iron fetters.

Letters, pp. 298–312; *The Confidence Man*, pp. 263, 264; *Mardi*, vol. II, p. 241; *Clarel*, vol. I, pp. 250, 252, 275, vol. II, pp. 36–37.

[89] *Omoo*, pp. 26, 206–216; *Typee*, pp. 251–252; Mayoux, *Melville*, pp. 44, 52–53, 123.

[90] In *Redburn* (pp. 259–260) he portrayed an interracial couple favorably; see also his treatment of Pip.

Melville saw that the emotions of Americans, North and South, had been crippled. Cereno is not a monster, as Delano assumes. What appears as iniquity is the mask of a man who fears for his life, and who, in seeking physical safety, has been led to self-betrayal. The North—for which Delano is the symbol—could only express emotion toward what could not injure it. It too was fearful, concerned for the protection of life and property, suspicious of its fellow men. It could express emotion and seek solidarity only with nonhuman things, with a personalized "Nature" or with "natural men" deprived of human personality.

The motives of the South in keeping its slaves and those of the North in striving to free them arose from a common source: anxiety for self. At a distance, it was safe to feel sympathy with the oppressed; at closer range, brutality seemed necessary. The sympathy, however, grew out of the impoverished anxiety of Northern life; the North was not willing to recognize kinship, let alone fraternity, with the slave.[91]

Melville supported the Northern cause when the War came. It was, for him, a mixture of hope and crime. The crime was the War itself; the hope, the bare possibility that a new awareness would grow between black and white which might benefit the Union as a whole. It was not a possibility in which Melville had much confidence. At best, the War was a "bad means" to possibly good ends, made necessary by the criminal history which had allowed the growth of slavery.

Melville was not stirred, as Emerson was, by the moral ardor—dormant in industrial society—which awoke with the War. Men's only duty and moral obligation was to avoid the crimes and follies which had resulted in the War. Instead, "duty" had been made "the mask of Cain." The impulse which led men to regard themselves as righteous in slaying their civic brethren was "ignorant" and not moral. Men should die for and with one another; war perverted the use and role of mortality in human life. Fatherless men, Americans obeyed the commands of "women," seeking glory, success, power, the delusion of immortality. The fervor of the War was pitiful, the vauntings of men who struggled against the human condition and man's need for his fellows. In its tragedies the War might produce "enlightenment," but only in the silent, unknowing "knowledge" of the dead, who "lay like lovers" in a common fate. Those who survived

[91] *Stories, Poems and Letters,* pp. 212–298, 21–22.

did not learn the lesson that the dead might have taught. Their own desire for survival had been gratified, only made uneasy by the falling of their comrades, and they would assuage that uneasiness in hatred of the foe. Deaths which should have rededicated the Union would likely serve to perpetuate its division.[92]

Yet Melville was never without hope. He refused to allow himself to be defeated and overborne. When men cease to struggle with evil and despair of remedy, he had written, they must first shut off their own compassion, and to do so is to lose one's own soul, to become "like people sitting up with a corpse, making merry in the house of the dead." Melville's hope was not the brittle optimism of the idea of progress. By contrast, he could hope because he denied history, seeing the operation of chance and the unforeseen and the new beginning that is each new birth. Most men might fail to learn the lessons which society and politics failed to teach, but there remained the hope of a "saving remnant," a "band of brothers" whose "lavish hearts" might enable them to see the truth and set the example that would restore the promise of an America in which fraternity would open the gates to man's pilgrim quest.[93]

[92] *Ibid.*, pp. 22–30, 315–350.
[93] *Ibid.*, pp. 338–339, 350; *Piazza Tales*, p. 42.

> There is . . . a most dangerous passage in the history of a democratic people. When the taste for physical gratifications . . . has grown more rapidly than their education and their experience of free institutions the time will come when men . . . lose all self-restraint at the sight of the new possessions they are about to lay hold upon. . . . These people think they are following the principle of self-interest, but the idea they entertain of that principle is a very rude one; and the better to look after what they call their business, they neglect their chief business, which is to remain their own masters.
>
> De Tocqueville, *Democracy in America*

CHAPTER XIV

THE GILDED AGE

"Tenting tonight . . ."

THE Civil War, Matthew Josephson observes, "had encompassed the ruin of the old regime as surely as had the laws of the . . . French convention." [1] America had taken a gigantic, decisive step into the world of industrialism. She had done so almost unaware; the transformation which American reformers and radicals struggled to bring about was moral and political, not economic. But the new industrial leaders moved under a halo won by their contributions to the Union's crusade. On the whole, they were new men, more ruthless and less cautious than their predecessors. Where the old financial leaders had held back, they had found the money and the arms to wage the War,

---

[1] *The Politicos*, p. 12.

and could plead both their risks and their devotion to justify the passage of favorable laws (and the granting of illicit favors).

These new industrial and financial leaders asked for an active government which would support their interests, rather than a passive umpire. Partly this reflected a natural desire to benefit themselves, but their claim to patriotic motives was not simply hypocrisy. The industrial magnates were moral men in the eyes of most Americans, and undoubtedly their own. Their faith in the Union was turbulent and ebullient but sincere, and it is undeniable that commerce and industry made a major contribution toward making the nation "indivisible" after the War. Some Americans felt uneasy with the growing concentration of wealth, and almost all were indignant about the crimes of a Gould or a Fisk. But such discontent was moderated by the comparative prosperity of the 1860s and 1870s, and the coups and maneuvers of the early robber barons seemed only the seamy side of change and openness. Any man, most believed, might hope to rise into the elite, and the successes of the peculators only stimulated a sense of dazzling opportunity.

Intellectuals supported the moral claims of the new industrialism. Political scientists saw the Nation as a great collective force, expanding the power of men over nature and advancing toward perfection. Religious writers like Elisha Mulford envisioned a messianic role for America in the plan of providential history. The logic of expansion seemed to lead toward a kind of Grail on which hopes and visions of many types converged.

There was, however, a radical divergence between the ideals of Puritanistic abolitionists and Mammon-serving industrialists, and most Americans were torn between the two. The country was certain to experience a "profound change of direction," but it could not do so without tension and conflict. Even though the participants recognized it only in part, the struggle between goals was the real issue of the Reconstruction era.[2]

Two great yearnings became compounded in the Reconstruction. The first, impossible in the circumstances, was the desire to return to normality, to "bind up the nation's wounds" and restore the environment which the veteran had left behind. The second, more positive

2 W. E. B. Du Bois, *Black Reconstruction*, pp. 182, 287, 346–347, 580–635; Josephson, *The Politicos*, pp. 41–42, 137.

and more possible, was the urge to give the agony of the Union a moral justification and meaning. The latter, more "idealistic," was sober realism too, for it reflected at least a partial recognition that the War had changed the lives and souls of men too much for the recuperative powers of ritual and nostalgia to overcome.

Andrew Johnson's sufferings illustrate the shortcomings of the ideal of restoration. In many ways, Lincoln's successor was the typical American: lonely, sensitive, insecure in the high status he had won, Johnson adopted the protective stance of the tough, assertive, "independent man" (though it did not keep him from delighting in flattery and from wanting to be admired).

He was, however, a pre-War American. Johnson had found solace for his loneliness in the mystic, Jacksonian Union, the faceless brotherhood of all citizens, and he sought to reestablish the old ideal in a thoroughly hostile environment. As Johnson saw it, the people, brothers by nature, could only be led astray by selfish interests; the fratricidal act of rebellion was the work, not of the public, but of the slave aristocracy. To restore "fraternal kindness," it was necessary only to destroy or counteract such interests; democracy and liberty would lead the people toward the eventual realization of the "Divinity of Man." [3]

Johnson's traditionalistic rectitude commended itself to the young Henry Adams, but his romantic nostalgia blinded him not only to the state of things before the War but to the resentments and new affections which had shattered whatever "fraternal" sentiments had preceded it. On both sides of the sectional border, his policies seemed "soft" rather than fraternal; they stimulated Southern resistance and Northern retribution, after which even the hope of restoring the old Union was lost forever.

Those who built the new order, however, had no better answers. The political ideas most Americans had inherited failed as guides, and too little new theory developed to modify the liberal creed. In the South, matters were at their worst. Andrew Johnson's fellow loyalists and the Southern lower classes generally had every interest in political and economic change and in a government which could help them escape poverty and contempt. Yet they made the Negro the object

[3] Eric McKitrick, *Andrew Johnson and the Reconstruction*, pp. 161, 183, 200, 255, 259.

of their economic anxieties and social insecurities, partly from prejudice and partly because they saw him as the vulnerable incarnation of
the shadowy power of his "ally," Northern finance. War and prejudice helped keep them blind to the fact that the financial powers were
indifferent to white and black alike. Loneliness also played a role,
driving Southern whites to cling to an illusory racial "brotherhood."
And the racism of a major element of "scientific" thought strengthened all the bases of white racial anxieties.

In the North, however, the political thought of the Reconstruction was little wiser. The major change from pre-War ideology had
moved the "Lockean" heritage in a Hobbesian direction. The sufferings of the Union and the opprobrium attached to rebellion led
many to echo Sherman's comments of 1863.

> I would not coax them or even meet them half-way, but would make
> them so sick of war that generations would pass away before they
> would again appeal to it. . . . Obedience to law, absolute—yea, even
> abject—is the lesson that this war, under Providence, will teach the
> free and enlightened American citizen.[4]

That "lesson" not only taught the Northerner to be zealous in educating Southerners in the beauties of obedience: it taught him to revere
the law and the Constitution to the edge of idolatry. That could only
result in a savage reaction against those who found the scales of justice
weighted against them, especially if they lacked the power and the
channels to make the law hear their cause.

Yet especially in the earlier days of the Reconstruction, there
existed a genuine desire for a new order of things, for a purified Union
that would be an adequate monument both to the lost past and to the
lives which had been cast away. Those who read the period simply
as one of business dominance overlook the fact that the Fourteenth
Amendment reflected its "anti-slavery origins"; the Joint Committee
of Fifteen, for example, rejected a clause which would have forbidden
states to take property without just compensation.[5]

If business leaders got most of what they wanted, it was because

---

[4] Cited in B. H. Liddell Hart, *Sherman* (New York: Praeger, 1960), p. 205.
Sherman's own attitudes toward Reconstruction were far more conciliatory, but
his earlier statement reflects the mood of many.

[5] Jacobus Ten Broek, *The Anti-Slavery Origins of the 14th Amendment*;
Josephson, *The Politicos*, pp. 50–52.

they knew their *desiderata* and steered a straight course. Jim Fisk's remark, "Nothing is lost save honor," was unusually free from cant, but it was an accurate reflection of the singlemindedness of the new captains of industry and finance.

Citizens at large, sharers also in the ambiguous culture of America, did not have any comparable clarity. Goals were contradictory, and even those who had some clear standards of value were increasingly at a loss to connect those standards to policies and events. The old precepts were dated and the old landmarks gone: without them, the American groped about his unfamiliar world, following the path of least resistance. Increasingly, politics became strange, perverse, or remote, except for the ritual moments in which party orators stirred dimly remembered feelings with the old slogans and war cries, and the American felt momentarily at home.

Forced to deal with the great forces that were centralizing national life, the political leaders were compelled to win loyalty from voters whose sentiments remained parochial and whose ideas were traditional; they felt the full impact of tension between the old culture and the new life. Despite this it was a political system of unusual stability. To be sure, the politicos delivered for their followers. They became experts in tracing the threads through the labyrinth of great interests, adjusting claims and providing a stream of rewards in the form of homestead land, pensions, spoils, protection, and subsidy.

Something more than these services, however, sent the voters to the polls to vote a "straight ticket." Many knew hard times, which the politicos did nothing to improve after 1873, and the interests of some had always been neglected in any but the most indirect sense. Stability also reflected more than the ethic of personal and party loyalty which, then as always, was the virtue most lauded by professional politicians. Political loyalty had a special meaning, which transferred it from the world of moral verities into the lives of men. It was associated with the nostalgia of citizens for the closest approach to fraternity that they had known.

The rhetoric of the "bloody shirt" and the symbolism of the Grand Army of the Republic spoke, in the North, to the experience Bruce Catton describes so well:

> They had hated war and the army and they had wanted passionately to be rid of both forever; yet now they began to see that the war and

the army had brought then one thing that might be hard to find back home—comradeship, the sharing of great things by men set apart from society's routine. . . .

"None of us," wrote a survivor, "were fond of war; but there had grown up between the boys an attachment for each other they never had nor ever will have for any other body of men." [6]

The sentiment was real and the remembered cause great, but both barred the way to understanding. Lonely and insecure men found in the G.A.R. (or in the Sons of the Confederacy) a memory of the past, and the remembered dead made it seem disloyal to think of the world in new terms, just as the temporary warmth felt with old comrades made it seem needless. The political leader looking for support, touched a true chord of sentiment—one he often shared— and was content.

James G. Blaine was perceptive enough to see that poverty in the cities was unparalleled. Men who were isolated, dependent, and humiliated lacked the hope for the future which had partially re- deemed poverty in villages and rural areas. Blaine, however, ventured no further than the safe doctrines of tariff protection and the pleasant society of obliging men of wealth.[7]

Political leaders had always guarded their interests, but in the beginning the Grand Army had given the process a glow. Slowly, with the years, "Tenting Tonight" was sung less often; the veterans died, the old bonds weakened, the immigrants and new voters swelled the rolls. More rapidly, the forces of Industrialism grew stronger. It was an unequal contest with a sure result.

The G.O.P. became more and more a broker between organized interests, its rhetoric less rotund, the pronouncements of its leaders more cynical. Realizing that the old ethics had no real applicability to the new society, a straightforward man like Mark Hanna discarded cant, contenting himself with the vocation of maximizing the "real" things: social adjustment, economic security, and material reward. The new politics grew fragile, robust enough for prosperity but unable to pass crises in which loyalty and legitimacy must fill the political void. Even in prosperous times, the rhetoric of politics found

[6] Bruce Catton, *This Hallowed Ground* (New York: Pocket Books, 1964), p. 493.

[7] James G. Blaine, *The Life and Character of James A. Garfield* (Washington: Govt. Printing Office, 1882), p. 10.

an uneasy audience which felt something wanting, and sensed that an inadequate idea of men and citizenship was dominating political life.

The reformers, however, offered only another irrelevancy. Grover Cleveland was a tower of integrity, but his virtues were those of the old personal creed, valuable enough but inadequate in the new society. His instinct in a dispute was to sit down, man-to-man and face-to-face, with the "brothers of discontent," but that idea had its limits. There was no clearer admission of moral and political bankruptcy than Cleveland's comment, as he vetoed measures for the relief of the poor, that the "friendliness and charity of our countrymen" could care for need, and that while the people owed a duty to the government, "the government should not support the people." His righteousness in what amounted to cruelty was a clear demonstration that many at least of the old virtues had become vices in the new age.

Americans were bewildered, and though some sought to find a new way, most preferred the bypaths of nostalgia. The hearts and minds of citizens were too confused and too divided to allow them to control events. That weakness left the field open, despite a skirmish or two, and the forces of industrialism almost autonomously shaped the future.

"The bitch-goddess . . ."

In the cities, a new ugliness came on the land even in prosperous times. Many made their way to the cities, not only for economic gain but to escape the lonely solitude of the farm, to "rub elbows, even if anonymously" with other men. The anonymity proved excessive in its turn, and whatever friendships men formed were hedged with transience and instability.

Moreover, the institutional pattern of the city was inadequate. The old laws were hopelessly obsolete village codes, and the frantic patchwork which grew up only confused matters. In one sense, cities lacked diversity: each was featureless and like its counterparts. Yet (especially in the mill-towns) social diversity was more marked. Residential areas became visible barriers of stratification separating men, depriving them of the intimate environment which had once forced all classes to meet in common institutions and places of public resort.

Worse, the permanence of rural employment yielded to the infrequent but appalling menace of being "out-of-work," unmitigated now by the personal and kinship relations of the small town.

The city and its citizens seemed dominated by an endless search for amusement, the effort to escape from a privacy grown excessive, an anonymity grown intolerable, a set of purposes with no emotional meaning. The urban "fleshpot" was quite real, even if traditional moralists exaggerated its "scarlet" qualities. The concern for diversion was the tolerable side of urban anomie, but the two sides were as one; more than one tie bound organized amusement, organized business, and organized politics.

Rural and small-town America, on the other hand, were no idyll, though they often seemed so to men peering out of the smoky pall of the cities. Local community had often been fragile; now men were unambiguously bound to a commercial chain which united them to the centers of industry and trade and divided them from each other. Vulnerable to changes in the market, often overmortgaged or over-expanded, both the farmer and the tradesman were caught up in all-too-Darwinian competition. The islands of quiet, the stablest of communities, all felt it; throughout the East and especially in New England, farmers were forced off the land by competition from the West, and the towns began to die. And the West itself, partly the creation of railway promotion schemes, was in little better straits.

It was the great age of the fraternal orders which sprang up across America in the townsman's search for some safe retreat from his daily life of competition, insecurity, and hostility. The lodges did not try to conquer that environment; rather they allowed men to escape from it into a world of pure affection, a momentary place of romance. Aside from a commitment to patriotism and a hostility to variously defined outsiders, the orders had no distinct values. Indeed, they made an active effort to avoid politics or "controversy"; their fraternity was too weak to compete with the other loyalties and the individualized purposes of men. (The economic "benefits" of the lodges were more a utilitarian rationalization than a cause; inefficient and productive of division, most of their insurance programs soon fell into other hands.)

The private world of affection which the lodges provided made bearable much of the townsman's life which would otherwise have been intolerable and allowed him to cling, in his public life, to the individualistic creed and the established mores. Without the orders, William Allen White noted, the towns might have joined the Populists.[8] Allowing the individual a faint, romantic echo of fraternity, they also suggested that in the gigantic and expanding nation he was not alone and insignificant, but one of a band of brothers with lodges about the land. It was some comfort, but too feeble to do more than quiet tension. The communities were passing, men were becoming small units of a great system, and more than passwords and regalia were required to remove anxiety.

It was, in short, an age disquieting to all Americans. Religion sat badly with an age that worshipped the golden calf. The hopes of the Enlightenment were threatened by growing inequality, and its faith in liberty and competition were challenged in turn by the ability of oligopoly to control the market. Worse, wealth seemed to have lost all sense of responsibility, and ideals of fraternity, whatever their source, seemed mawkish in the face of power.

"Success" had become the sole positive, practical ethic, though success was often little more than an optimist's term for survival. Traditional critics were quick to point out that it was never clear what men intended to "succeed" in gaining, other than a security which was turned to illusion by the very means employed. More modern in attitude, William James came eventually to call the ethic a "bitch-goddess." [9] Progress yielded to process; human power now seemed to govern men, rather than serving them.

It was a hard age for the intellectual, not one that shared his values or admired his achievements. Isolation from the community became a fact of life, and even the kindred spirit was only a reminder of exclusion. The perennial condition of the intellectual has rarely been more stark and unrelieved. Values of mind and spirit commanded no more than verbal allegiance from most Americans, and even doubts and discontent generated only a desire for moral and mental assurances that would leave the industrial system intact.

The enlightened classes found the instrument of reassurance in

[8] William Allen White, *Autobiography* (New York: Macmillan, 1946), pp. 181–184.

[9] *Letters of William James,* ed. H. James (Boston: Atlantic Monthly Press, 1920), vol. II, p. 260.

the doctrines of Social Darwinism. Evolution restored the eighteenth-century creed to scientificity and tied it—with a point or two of friction—to nineteenth-century industrialism. Progress was recaptured, even if human reason and social design were sacrificed to historico-biological necessity.

Its defenders often claimed that Darwinism humbled human pride. Perhaps so, though it produced some extraordinarily arrogant claims for man as a species and for particular "races" of men. Any limit it put on pride, however, was more than balanced by the justification it provided for innocence and moral unconcern. The "struggle for survival" meant that self-concern was nature's law; the "survival of the fittest" also meant that self-interest was the moral law. William Graham Sumner's famous phrases sum up the case: social classes owe each other nothing, and the "absurd attempt to make the world over" can do nothing except allow the "unfit" to survive.[10]

Sumner's rough rhetoric appealed less to Americans than did the moralizing tones of Herbert Spencer and his domestic disciples like John Fiske. Spencer pointed to a historical march from military to industrial society, predicting a future in which the problem of material want would be solved and war eliminated, and in which men, having no longer any cause for hostility, would all be brothers. Social Darwinism affirmed the eighteenth-century creed: by nature without moral defect, man needs only expanded power to progressively realize a utopian life, a universal fraternity. Sumner was less certain, fearing a time when "land hunger" might cast men back to barbarism, but for him that grim possibility emphasized that the only hope for the future lay in the unrestricted play of "evolution." Hence Sumner's vitriol toward reformers, otherwise so inconsistent with his naturalistic relativism: those who would allow the "unfittest" to survive threatened the destiny of the species in a way which would make meaningless the sacrifices of past generations.

Sumner's anger suggests the fragility of Darwinism as a creed. Warring with men's desire for affection and security and with the ethics and metaphysics of inherited religion, it offered only a "martyrdom of man" in the interest of future generations. Moreover, the

---

[10] William Graham Sumner, *What Social Classes Owe Each Other* (New York: Harper, 1884), esp. pp. 36–37, 94–95, 134–143, and *The Challenge of Facts and Other Essays* (New Haven: Yale University Press, 1914).

doctrine seemed suspect in practice. Individual "opportunity" was something less than equal, and wealth and power might even negate the theory of the market; some had an unfair edge in the "struggle to survive." Social practice lost any clear relation to the mechanism of progress which Darwinism described.

Rising doubt lay behind the powerful impact of Henry George's *Progress and Poverty*. Industrial civilization, George argued, was moving away from fraternity. In traditional society, all rejoice or suffer together; in modern society, greater wealth and greater poverty grow side by side.[11] George's book was documented by and explained the conditions men saw around them in the depression of the 1870s, yet the book and the conditions were only the catalysts of existing doubt. That symbol of an age, the Horatio Alger novel, is almost mark of growing uncertainty, rather than confidence. Fiction's contrivance alone could support the belief in opportunity against what was, more truly than any of Sumner's essays, "the challenge of facts."

Disbelief and opposition, growing together, brought a new insecurity to the industrial elites. The arrogant statements of the financiers of the late '60s disappeared from public view; many business and financial leaders showed a new concern for public opinion (foreshadowing later interest in public relations and corporate "images"). And since business leaders were often men of piety, they sought to still their own moral uncertainties.

Andrew Carnegie, for example, eschewed Darwinist rhetoric in favor of that of the eighteenth century. Men had been forced to develop competitive habits only by scarcity, and the true nature and destiny of man was one of universal brotherhood. Present scarcity makes it necessary for the business leader to act as "trustee" for mankind to guarantee the most rapid advent of the day of brotherhood; his skills enabled him to administer the resources, and he could, from time to time, mitigate competition by charity from the "trust fund" which was temporarily his. Peace, the spread of democratic institutions, and good management were the keys to destiny:

> When the Democracy obtains sway throughout the earth the nations will become friends and brothers. . . . Men will then begin to destroy customs houses . . . not altogether from the low plane of economic

11 *Progress and Poverty* (New York: Schalkenbach Foundation, 1946), pp. 3-13.

gain or loss but strongly impelled thereto from the higher standpoint of the brotherhood of man.[12]

Carnegie's doctrine had little impact on his conduct; it is important as a mark of the new insecurity of business. Certainly classical market theory no longer described the practice of the American economy, and the business leaders were in the best position to know it. From that inapplicable model, many industrialists, or their political advisors, turned to justifications based on "scientific management."

The managerialist's utopia did not differ from that of the Darwinist: both visions were drawn from the tradition of the eighteenth century. In a world of plenty, absolute individual liberty would be compatible with perfect harmony; political responsibility would be needless, as administration could adjust whatever frictional problems resulted from the free play of impulse. In such circumstances, man's fraternal instincts would "emerge."

Long an element of liberal theory, the "science of management" was less important as a rejection of market economics than as an answer to the demands of reformers for an equally liberal "science of society." Both acknowledged that classical liberalism had perished, and both shared the same utopia, differing only on the method by which it might be reached. It was to be Edward Bellamy's most impressive achievement to combine both, which accounts in part for his influence. The age of liberal confidence, however, was over: the act of legislation could not be done once and for all; progress was erratic and required the constant tinkering of science and engineering to keep from breaking down.

Progress and Poverty

Eric Goldman divided the early history of reform into movements which proceeded "from the top down" and those which grew "from the bottom up."[13] But reform movements represented a fundamental division in American culture itself. Movements from the top began with the enlightened, taking their first premises from the

[12] Andrew Carnegie, *Triumphant Democracy* (New York: Scribner's, 1887), pp. 281–282.

[13] Eric Goldman, *Rendezvous with Destiny*, perhaps the essential source for the whole post-Civil War era in American thought.

established liberal-scientific political thought of the times. Yet they touched the deeply imbedded popular stream of "irrational Lockeanism" derived from the national past. If intellectuals who responded to movements from the bottom up were fewer, they were distinguished enough; they came from those who were alienated from the fashionable doctrines, uncertain of the principles of the eighteenth as well as the practice of the nineteenth century. Sympathy, at least, existed between such thinkers and the more traditional, religious elements of the people, who had never been assimilated to the eighteenth-century creed. The crisis of belief was not specific to a class or stratum of society; it was truly national.

Organized religion was in a weak position. The established churches more and more surrendered the world of reason and practice to scientists and "practical" men, reserving a right to fill in "gaps" in the structures created by these men of the world, or to drape a first cause over them, but unwilling to interfere with the structures themselves. Most were grateful to scientists, like Joseph Le Conte, who professed to see in Spencer's ethics and analysis the plan of God for man's salvation.[14] Emerson's cosmic moralism became more popular in the pulpit, and the churches could be classed as little more than a "sacred amusement."

There was more political content in the doctrines of traditional churches, but most sought to cure modern ills by ancient therapies. The fundamentalist reaction, when it did not content itself with efforts to save the individual soul for the next life, tended to see sumptuary legislation as the chief remedy for political life. Too, attacks on materialism and crusades against alcohol, prostitution, or gambling involved the churches in no unpleasant departures from established social thought or the economic aims of their members and donors. For different reasons, perhaps, these pietistic crusades seemed meritorious to staunch Darwinians and pious entrepreneurs, a fact which contributed to their appeal among the clergy.

Phillips Brooks portrayed church fraternity as warm, affectionate, and sentimental, yet that only indicated how far it had been sundered from the purposive life of men. Brooks' concern for the meeting of "whole personalities" could come to nothing; the church

---

[14] Joseph Le Conte, *Evolution and Its Relation to Religious Thought* (New York: Appleton, 1890).

could be little more than a weekly retreat, able to create an affectionate atmosphere only by divorcing itself from the political and economic life of its members.[15] "A Christian," Ambrose Bierce commented, "believes in the teachings of Jesus Christ, insofar as they are not inconsistent with a life of sin." [16]

Bierce's remark did not imply that the religious tradition was dead. Rather, it suggested that the religious attitude toward politics and morality had become emancipated from the church. It hardly lessened Henry George's appeal that his language was often Scriptural and apocalyptic; men read in George the old words in a half-forgotten context.

Indeed, seeking to meet Herbert Spencer head on, George reached an unusual level of philosophic clarity. Evolution, he observed, is the oldest of philosophic ideas: thinkers have always asked how things came to be. Yet traditional thought had always understood that the answer to such a question demands a knowledge of the nature of being. Materialism, George wrote, cannot answer the question of the nature of things because it cannot ask it: it can at best study matter in motion. To study evolution as the "coming into being" of things requires some sense of *telos*, of the natural end of things and men.

Any moral system must distinguish between morals ("pure ethics") and changing rules of conduct ("applied ethics")—but, George argued, the limitations of Darwinism force it to make a perverse absolute of history. The only ethics of Darwinism are those of expediency, adjustment to the laws of movement; there is no place in the system for human purposes beyond the desire for comfort or gratification.[17]

Modern man, George concluded, lacks genuine moral guides. Religion has combined superstition and acquiescence in modern doctrines to produce "fatalism." Socialism, valuable as an ideal, can be achieved only through a "nihilism" which negates its promise of fraternity. Before it could be truly achieved, men would need to

---

[15] A. W. Vernon, "Later Theology," *CHAL*, III, pp. 218–225.

[16] Ambrose Bierce, *The Devil's Dictionary* (Cleveland and New York: World, n.d.), p. 49.

[17] For George's metaphysics, see *A Perplexed Philosopher* (New York: Webster, 1892), pp. 104, 140–144, 146–147, 151–155, 160–162, 193–196, 315–319, and *Progress and Poverty*, pp. 475–488.

find "new relations" in which to express the "old truths" of religion. The Darwinian theory of sacrifice for the future of the race was inadequate: "It is as certain that the race must die as it is that the individual must die. . . . Beyond these periods, science discerns a dead earth, an exhausted sun. . . ." An ideal which could truly unify men would have to reach beyond man and society:

> Shall we say that what passes from *our* sight passes into oblivion? No; not into oblivion. Far beyond our ken the eternal laws must hold their sway.[18]

George found earthly support for this traditional metaphysic in the unchanging nature of man. Human progress was not achieved by individuals but by communities and cultures; man's social and cooperative nature is attested by his willingness to sacrifice his life for his fellows. Yet George was scornful of "savagery" as a state of "mental and material poverty." The true value of community was that, by providing the individual with security, it freed his mind for thought, imagination, and creative endeavor.[19]

George's argument in favor of a withering away of the state did not imply that man was "not political"; he made it clear that what he hoped for was a decrease in the coercive functions of the state and an increase in its cooperative activities, controlled by the political fraternity and activity of all citizens. George was consistent: a loyal unionist, he held unions no more than useful devices in a corrupt society. Unions demanded centralization, discipline, and hierarchy, which made them little different from "despotism." They reflected a society in which man is only "a mere link in one enormous chain of producers, helpless to separate himself and helpless to move except as they move." Effort and virtue have little relation to reward; community is shattered as some prosper while others perish; fear and suspicion have become the normal principles of human relations. Political action, George believed, held the best prospects for labor because political life, though corrupted by a diseased society, was still regulated in part by principles closer to the nature of man.[20]

---

[18] *Progress and Poverty*, p. 564, and see generally pp. 559–565.
[19] *Ibid.*, pp. 504–505, 507–509, 513, 514.
[20] *Ibid.*, pp. 270–278, 285, 315–321, 347–357, 368–384, 462–467, 489–523.

George's moral outrage drove him in search of an answer which might reverse or transform the course of things. The desire for results, the urge to influence the "file leaders of opinion" who held the gates of access to the apathetic majority, may have influenced his argument. In any case, his "answers" were based on principles which contradicted or undermined his moral theory.

Self-interest and the lust for power were "unnatural," George contended, and arose from scarcity. The examples he chose suggested that the cause might be insecurity, a more pervasive and less soluble problem in human life, but George fixed his attention on the material problem alone. Following Locke, he saw the earth given to men in common and followed that premise to its conclusion, which denied individual property rights to land. Property, however, was a right: again following Locke, George allowed men a right to what they have made or shaped on or out of the land. This doctrine assumes that men acquire a right through the ability to impose form on matter-in-motion, a doctrine which legitimates power and contradicts the metaphysics of George's case against Spencer. Logically the doctrine should have extended to whatever is made from land: Locke's philosophy that whatever a man touches is "proper" to him was different from George's, which should have suggested to George that only a man's ideas are properly his own, and even these he owes in large measure to community.

His doctrine of property was important to George because it gave a rule of "applied ethics" for allocating resources under conditions of scarcity. That condition still prevailed. For his own times, at least, George thought it important to retain "incentives" for the individual to add to the community's wealth.

This preoccupation with scarcity is revealing. Despite his criticism of modern society, George showed no disposition to dismantle industrialism. The Single Tax prescribes no method for dealing with inequalities of power deriving from the control, let alone the ownership, of corporate resources. This omission depends on the deep conviction that scarcity alone estranges men from their fellows. He might seek to ground it in religion, but George believed that an abundant love for his fellows would emerge in man were economic scarcity once banished from the earth. His fervor as a moralist led

George to fall back on the hopes and doctrines of the eighteenth century for the fulfillment of his dream.[21]

Though his writings made their impact through his moral assault on the existing order rather than through his prescriptions, both are illustrative. George was a portent and not a prophet: his indignation and compassion softened his intellect and led him to produce a political potpourri concocted from the contradictory ingredients of American culture, a procedure that was to be the dominant habit of the age of reform.

Protest and Portent

Frederick Jackson Turner casts a long shadow, and it is no surprise that historians' discussions of the early stirrings of protest tend to assign a critical role to "the West." Protest and the West were related, but discontent and denunciation were associated with groups and attitudes in the West, not with the region itself.

The West stands out because a high percentage of its population was composed of the estranged, men who felt themselves possessed of inherited claims on the body politic and an inherent status among the body of American citizens. That status increasingly seemed denied, and the more perceptive reasoned that it was being lost to all citizens. The age, Populist orators were to declaim, was a "century of retrogression" in which, yielding to "Mammon worship," Americans "sold their birthright for a mess of pottage." [22]

The role which they imagined had been their fathers' might never have existed, but the belief created expectation, and frustrated expectation produced outrage. Immigrants were ready to expect exclusion if not to accept it; partly for this reason Engels wrote Lloyd that socialism would never be strong in America until there was a native-born working class.[23] The South, which otherwise might have led the protests, was befuddled by "the War" and the race question. Many in the West, by contrast, felt themselves robbed and set out to

---

[21] *Ibid.*, pp. xv–xvi, 25–30, 50–88, 272, 433–439, 457–462, 506–507, 526; see also *A Perplexed Philosopher*, pp. 196–214, 231, 236, 240, 260–261.

[22] C. Vann Woodward, *The Origins of the New South*, p. 251.

[23] Norman Pollack, *The Populist Response to Industrial America*, p. 84.

recapture "their own." Vachel Lindsay was accurate, whatever the demographic facts, in tracing Western revolt to

> . . . the babies born at midnight
> In the sod huts of lost hope,
> With no physician there,
> Except a Kansas prayer,
> And the Indian raid a-howling through the air.[24]

Odd symbols it had, but the culture of the West was less distinctive than American, seized by all the ambiguities of the nation at large. The newness of the region only made those ambiguities more evident than they were in the older areas. Walter Webb observed that Westerners were children of the industrial age who had left the past behind, and with it the inherited institutions and personal relations that in the older regions softened the iron logic of "opportunity." Bryce might deplore the West's haste to master nature, but its inhabitants knew that he who may rise can fall, and that to stand still was to accept defeat.[25] Poetic it might be, but for the Westerner nature was a song of despair, a great millstone that slowly wore a man down until his last husk was cast into a dusty grave. The "boom psychology" to which the West was prone bespoke its desperate need for belief in progress. Now was always forced to yield to tomorrow, and for the Westerner there was one great joy, his dream of the future, and one great burden, his present life.

All this concealed an aching loneliness—American, but more deeply felt in the West where isolation was physical as well as psychological, and men lacked even the consolation of crowd humanity. Hamlin Garland wrote that a prison—and so Garland regarded much of the East—has at least noise and sociability; the farm was solitary confinement.[26] Despite his "individualism," the Westerner developed many collective institutions, though these were always justified in

[24] Vachel Lindsay, "Bryan, Bryan, Bryan: the Campaign of 1896 as viewed at the time by a sixteen-year-old, etc.," *The Pocket Book of Modern Verse*, ed. Oscar Williams (New York: Washington Square Press, 1960), pp. 265–272.

[25] Walter P. Webb, *The Great Plains*, pp. 272–318; Bryce, *The American Commonwealth*, vol. II, pp. 891–901, 925–930.

[26] Hamlin Garland, *Prairie Songs* (Cambridge: Stone and Kimball, 1903). See also Willa Cather, *My Antonia* (Boston: Houghton Mifflin, 1918), pp. 47, 98–102.

utilitarian terms, assistance being a coin which would be repaid in help with harvesting and house-building. Yet once justified to the anxious mind, collective activity created an entirely nonutilitarian joy in its own right. Even more, the Westerner infused his dream of the future with the older, fraternal values of religion. Individualism rested on hope for the future, and when that was undermined, the desire for community and resentment against indignities and frustrations appeared dramatically from their hidden places.

Economic changes, moreover, shook both hope for the future and the tenuous institutions of collective life. Agriculture was permanently involved in an international commercial system, making the individual the direct competitor of his neighbor and at the same time threatening any sense of independence and control, smashing individualism and community alike. Webb saw that the "distinct civilization" and the "rough fraternity" of cotton and cattle kingdoms were "tributary to the masters of the Industrial Revolution," and "destroyed by the very forces which had developed them." [27] Slowly agriculture became more mechanized; and in order to survive, the farmer bought and expanded his debt. Each stage put the small producer at a disadvantage against the organized forces and owners of concentrated holdings, who could understand and master the intricacies and opportunities of the commodity and credit markets. Early cooperative movements reflected a dawning awareness that the possibility of individualism was passing from the farm as it had from the city.

The situation of the rural areas only made discontent greater, for there was a decline in agriculture vis-à-vis industry in national life. The end of the boom came earlier to the farms, and if depression was endemic in the cities, in rural areas it seemed like a continuing process. Urban workers had enough problems; real wages rose more slowly from 1860 to 1913 than in most European states, and workers felt increasingly impotent and without say in their lives, conditions which native Americans and artisans especially resented. If workers, however, had the advantage over farmers in proximity and daily contact, they were divided by the barriers of ethnicity and craft, made competitive by hopes for upward mobility, and isolated by the menace of unemployment—which the farms, serious as their condition

[27] Webb, *The Great Plains*, pp. 246–247, 271–272.

was, did not know. Labor organization grew up sporadically, but gained only in prosperous times when workers felt secure in their jobs. In bad times, the loyalties created by such organizations were too ephemeral to long resist the threat of joblessness—and protest, when it came at all, took the form of momentary outbreaks of violence against accumulated grievances, like those of 1877. Discontent in the factory was more likely to follow than to lead the anger of the farms.

The general malaise of agriculture was not enough, however, to produce movements of protest. Agrarian activism only developed where additional factors added to farm burdens and insecurities, like the single crop areas or the regions of high mortgage indebtedness, or where predisposing factors existed in the political culture. (In some areas "west of the rainfall line," where farmers had sought political solutions to the basic problem of water, both conditions existed.) In the South, the peculiar political culture partly counteracted the economic facts.

On the whole, farmers clung persistently to the belief in progress and to the institutions thought to safeguard it. Rural areas were initially suspicious of currency reform, and their faith in market economics was long-suffering. The injustices they found were blamed on monopolies, speculators, and "commission men" who were supposed to have perverted the impartial workings of the market. "Conspiracy theory" resulted not from some peculiar agrarian psychosis, but from adherence to an economic orthodoxy—impeccably academic—which did not describe the world in which men lived.[28]

It was among the intellectually inclined that there began to grow a distaste for the "system," a conviction that market commercialism was depriving all men of dignity and fraternity. Ignatius Donnelly's *Caesar's Column* was one of the first anti-utopias, picturing a future in which estranged and resentful masses destroy an industrial oligopoly. Donnelly's multitudes lacked any sense of interpersonal loyalty or political obligation and, united only by a common hatred, they could only destroy. Their "revolution" could only produce a totalitarian state, compelled by its inner dynamics into perpetual warfare.

[28] Michael Paul Rogin, *The Intellectuals and McCarthy: the Radical Spectre* (Cambridge: M.I.T. Press, 1967), p. 188.

THE IDEA OF FRATERNITY IN AMERICA

Without some means of providing men with a minimal sense of civic identity and political fraternity, Donnelly suggested, the society was on the high road to disaster.[29]

Later, Frank Norris combined, in *The Octopus*, a moving portrait of the "causes" of injustice, as California farmers saw them, with a theme in which these "causes"—the Southern Pacific and its agents —were themselves only part of a great commercial process. The "Liverpool price" was not an idealized "just price" for Norris; it was one point in the flow of trade which everywhere bent men to its will, sacrificing human relationships and lives to the impersonal "whole." [30]

Yet Hamlin Garland, closer to the religious heritage as he was to the agrarian rebels themselves, would have felt that Norris pardoned men too easily and blamed system too much. In "Up the Coulee," a successful New York actor returns to his family's depressed farm to find his brother savagely resentful. Reconciliation occurs only when he admits his guilt and abandons his pride. "Made" by good fortune and not merit, he did not share his good fortune. Yielding to the materialistic logic of his environment, he has spent his money on superfluous "necessities," neglecting his family's need. His personal reawakening softens the brother's anger, but it cannot repair lives damaged beyond recovery. Moral self-awareness is possible, Garland was arguing, but it is not an "answer." Perception alone cannot restore what is lost, nor can it destroy the effect of the environment on the spirit; logically awareness should lead men into politics to change conditions, to alter the system that crushes the individual. Only one who resisted the system could discover his brothers and himself; yet few will do so as long as resistance results in injury, and obedience in reward.[31]

The current of protest gathered slowly and far from spontaneously. Both the Grange and the Knights of Labor were organized by "outsiders" steeped in the rites of Masonry. (The originators of the Grange, like those of so many farm groups, were em-

[29] Ignatius Donnelly, *Caesar's Column* (Cambridge: Harvard University Press, 1960).

[30] Frank Norris, *The Octopus* (New York: Doubleday, 1901); see also Parrington, *Beginnings of Critical Realism*, pp. 329–334.

[31] Hamlin Garland, *Main Travelled Roads* (New York: New American Library, 1962), pp. 54–97, 141–155; see also Parrington, *Beginnings of Critical Realism*, pp. 288–300.

ployees of the Department of Agriculture.) Workers and farmers, caught in their daily struggle, had little of the time or skill needed to create organizations. Once the organizations began, however, both groups responded in ways unexpected by the founders, who seem to have conceived of lodge-like organizations, "educational" in teaching men the principles of "self-help," and providing an emotional surcease from labor and competition. The Knights and the Grange encouraged the beginnings of trust and the airing of grievances that had been inarticulate or nursed in private. Both disclaimed any religious or "political" test, thus factoring out the divisiveness of sectarian theology and established partisanship, and leaving unencumbered the fundamental ethical heritage of the community.

Reaching their maximum growth at different times—the Grange between 1872 and 1874, the Knights from 1881 to 1886—the two orders had strikingly similar doctrines. The Grange program of 1874 began with a pledge of fraternity: "In essentials, unity; in non-essentials, liberty; in all things, charity"; and the motto of the Knights, "An injury to one is an injury to all" was drawn from Solon's assertion that "the most perfect state is one in which . . ." Both rejected class war because they pursued the ideal of the *polis*, a country whose citizens were brothers.

The Grange, in the language of *Corinthians* and *Romans*, swore farmers to uphold the laws but to "avoid litigation"—not because, as *The Nation*'s Godkin believed, they desired a "class judiciary," but because they rejected the materialistic and individualistic premises of established jurisprudence. Like the Knights, the Grange excluded and condemned a long list of malefactors thought to encourage "prodigality" and Mammon—monopolists and middlemen along with the institutions of credit and fashion. Since this amounted to a rejection of American industrial life, it is no surprise that the Grange gradually drew away from a negative program—smashing monopoly, toward a positive view of government intervention.

The Knights were more explicit, demanding a fraternal citizenry in which honor and reward would follow "individual and moral worth," not wealth, and proclaiming that "duty to God" impelled them to oppose the "wages system" and market pricing. "Corporate life," impersonal and ruled by the idea of individual gain, should be opposed by a "hostile combination" of "organized manhood" in the hope of liberating all men. Labor demands dignity, the Knights asserted, but dignity cannot be won by bargains within the system; the moral basis of the established order must be changed altogether.

Of course such demands were compromised in practice; neither order was free from America's ambiguity. The moral doctrine is no less clear for that. Part of the compromise, in fact, is due to the problem that afflicted Grange and Knights alike: the ideal of the polis is impossible when the polis cannot be achieved.

Both orders expanded rapidly under the impact of economic crisis. The strength, however, lay in the relations of trust and loyalty which had grown up among members in the local branches. The fraternal standard of legitimacy, too, tied the orders to deliberation among friends, and hence to decisions locally arrived at. The rapid expansion of membership brought in men outside the local structure of friendship who demanded immediate economic benefits.

The orders had always held out the promise of economic improvement, but in their early periods, prosperity had made the demands less strident, and success more likely. Depression reversed these conditions, and the new members felt no accumulated personal or even organizational loyalty which might soften frustrations. Even had the orders grown more slowly and in better times, there would have been pressure for the national leadership to assume a stronger role. Depression and expansion almost demanded that national officials gain control of scanty resources and impose coordination on locals, in an effort to win some economic rewards.

This meant either attenuating the importance of local loyalties or facing local branches that were suspicious and resentful. In either event, national leaders could maintain allegiance only if their policies brought the promised material rewards. Those of the National Grange failed, and the membership of the organization rapidly fell away. Yet the Grange's decline was anticlimactic in a sense; centralization had radically weakened the fraternal decision-making that was the basis of its creed and the source of its impact on the members' lives. The Knights, unable or unwilling to centralize effectively, were no better off; badly timed and badly executed strikes engineered by locals forced the Knights to become committed to a series of losing causes. Early success in strikes had led to expansion, and failure led to decline. In both cases, the alternatives were stark, and testified to the impossibility of fraternal politics in the conditions of modern times.

Though "failures," the Grange and the Knights provided their members with moments of escape from isolation and with considerable experience in organization. Both, too, demonstrated considerable insight into the political and economic facts of the time. The Knights saw, as Gompers did not, that the day of the crafts was ended and new forms of organization were needed. They saw too that labor, opposed by massive business power, would require the active support of government, not merely a benevolent neutrality. The Knights and the Grange alike saw political action as encompassing economic action in one critical sense. Interest group action alone would be inadequate if Americans could not control the processes of industrialism; personal worth and interpersonal fraternity demanded that men be more than passive clay in the hands of change.

The "failure" of the orders began the teaching of that melancholy lesson which is sometimes called realism and is really a despairing lowering of hope for reform in political and public matters. Gradually, agricultural groups became more and more the spokesmen for narrow interests of specialized constituencies. Even the Farmers' Alliance, which pledged "entire harmony and good will among all mankind and brotherhood and love among ourselves," restricted its membership far more than had the Grange, and in the interests of success accepted racial segregation, which the Grange and Knights had rejected. In labor, the case is perhaps even clearer; even the radical organizations which opposed Gompers' views spoke of the solidarity of class, and even these eventually limited themselves to narrowly defined interests or perished, leaving as a fading echo a book of songs to be sung by the nostalgic. The history of the successor organizations in labor and agriculture is a tale of men who have abandoned the hope of finding brothers or of directing change, who seek at most to outpace the current, winning private gains but following the stream.

In the Gilded Age, these developments were only potentialities. The highest values of the Alliance were still civic, and even its panaceas required political action: The subtreasury is a case in point. Grange, Knights, and Alliance all hoped to achieve their ends by pressure on the major parties; but the parties, tangled in the web of complex coalitions and beguiled by laissez-faire doctrine and acquisitive values, proved unresponsive. The "two-party" Middle West (actually a "one-party dominant" area) was no better than the "single-party" South. H. L. Taubeneck, the Populist chairman, was to refer to the Grange, the Knights, and similar organizations as "industrial schools" which had served to teach the voters the need to draw together all of the disinherited. The old political institutions had been captured by the new society, and the only hope lay in a party of their own.[32]

"Against the ways of Tubal Cain . . ."

John Hicks, writing in the early 1930s, described Populism as part of a losing battle to save agricultural America, a movement whose "panaceas" now seemed too individualistic to serve as guides to policy. As Norman Pollack rightly points out, it was this thesis (for it was certainly not research) which led Richard Hofstadter to his well-known analysis of Populism as a xenophobic, simplistic, "paranoid" precursor of the quasi-totalitarian right of the 1950s. Pollack's own argument, that Populism was a "progressive" force and not a rural idyll, has been a valuable corrective.[33]

Pollack, however, contrives to miss the point. His "digression," comparing Populism to Marxism, does reveal a number of suggestive analogies. To take only one doctrine, though, the fact that both presumed the "labor theory of value" does not show a spontaneous coincidence of ideas; rather, it suggests how far John Locke had penetrated into American popular culture.[34]

In a very important sense, Populism was not "progressive" (and as Pollack shows, Populists certainly rejected the more naive forms of the idea of progress). Rejecting the ideal of American culture as they saw it, Populists denounced the failure to "adapt the legislation of the country" to new times. A "response to industrial America,"

---

[32] Hicks, *The Populist Revolt*, pp. 218, 104, 106, 110, 115, 120, 128–152; Buck, *The Granger Movement*, p. 303.

[33] Hicks, *The Populist Revolt*, pp. 237, 422; Pollack, *The Populist Response*, *passim.*

[34] Pollack, *The Populist Response*, pp. 68–84.

the Populists responded with the accents of the past; they sought new institutions to preserve old values. Vachel Lindsay caught the tone:

On the Fourth of July sky rockets went up
Over the church and the streets and the town,
Stripes and stars, riding red cars.
Each rocket wore a red-white-and-blue gown,
And I did not see one rocket come down.

Next day on the hill I found dead sticks,
Scorched like blown-out candle-wicks.
But where are the rockets? Up in the sky.
As for the sticks, let them lie.
Dead sticks are not the Fourth of July.[35]

To hold to old values is not "retrogressive" if the values are perennial, and if the obsolescence of old means to them is realized. The Populists met both conditions fairly well, and praise for them is misplaced if the nature of those values is neglected.

Certainly Pollack is wrong to find modernism and Marxism in a movement whose spokesmen could denounce materialism because it "segregates" men and destroys all relations save those of servant and master. Populists could refer to Darwinian social theory as a "satanic creation" and announce that even if it were historically accurate, men should "rise above" its precepts; for the struggle it prescribed was morally wrong. In our times, they argued, there is danger that "the soul of man will flee and the senses be left alone to reign." The only answer was to upset the entire moral and meta-physical creed of American industrialism, establishing a fraternal citizenry in which "each will be for all and all for each." Populism, declared Senator Allen of Nebraska, is the "cause of labor and the brotherhood of man." Populism drew its ideal from the Testaments, and when it made a plea for the debtor, it turned to the law of the Jubilee, just as it saw matter as the barrier which, left to itself, kept apart the spirits of men. "We vote as we pray" read a sign in more than one Populist parade.

It helped that, profiting from the work of the Grange and the Alliance, Populism had a large number of women activists. They may

[35] Vachel Lindsay, "The Rockets That Reached Saturn," *Pocket Anthology of American Verse,* ed. Oscar Williams (New York: Washington Square Press, 1955), p. 256.

have been a detriment during campaigns in the East and South, but they brought to the movement all the force of religious ethics hitherto largely confined to the home. It was moral insight, for example, that enabled Mary Ellen Lease to shatter the "logic" of economic ortho-doxy; the system, she declaimed,

> clothes rascals in robes and honesty in rags. . . . The politicians said we suffered from overproduction . . . when 10,000 little children . . . starve to death every year in the United States.[36]

America's political crisis, Populists declared, affected and in-jured more than the farmer. The industrial worker suffered deeply and the Populists led repeated efforts to find a way to a farmer–labor coalition. One of the greatest virtues of Pollack's work is to reveal that labor—or that part led by Samuel Gompers—was the barrier to a coalition, and not agrarian suspicion of city folk. There were, of course, experiential distances to overcome: Populist spokesmen had to reassure their followers who were fearful that strikes and union-ism might mean violence and anarchy, and Populist programs stressed the debt question in ways which meant much to an over-mortgaged farmer, and little to a landless worker. Certainly, how-ever, the spirit was willing. In fact, Populist orators and writers could reach the evangelical height from which they argued that the system injured all Americans, rich and poor, threatening all men with isolation and the loss of their souls. For Populism, the state was a moral order, charged with raising men to the "breadth of human-ity," and its mission required fraternity. "We declare," read the Omaha Platform of 1892,

> that this Republic can endure as a free government only when built upon the love of the whole people for each other and for the nation . . . that we must be in fact, as we are in name, one united brotherhood of freedom.

"Freedom" has its ambiguities, as did Populism itself. Charles Gleed, seeking to dispel Frank Tracy's fears that "socialism" was rising in the Middle West, wrote in 1893 that farmers simply wanted

---

[36] Hicks, *The Populist Revolt*, p. 160; see also Annie L. Diggs, "The Women of the Alliance Movement," *Arena*, VI (1892), pp. 161–179.

more money and that protests would die down if they got it.[37] Unjust in part to farmers, certainly unjust to Populist leaders, Gleed's argument had a measure of truth. As Pollack points out, Populists spoke for a constituency that had accepted—even welcomed—technology, and which, if it feared and hated the gigantism of monopoly and big business, had no intention of abolishing the industrial system.[38] Populists hoped to overcome the dehumanizing effects of industrial society without losing its benefits; they convinced themselves of the possibility by blaming the evils they saw on economic competition and maldistributed wealth. If this was a delusion, it is one many have shared, one born of the "progressive," not the nostalgic, elements of Populist thought.

Fundamental ambiguity revealed itself even more directly. Despite Populist ideas of the moral mission of politics, which he fully shared, Governor Lewelling of Kansas could proclaim the need to make the "state subservient to the individual," a "voluntary union for the common good." When government "ceases to be of advantage to the citizen," Lewelling stated, "he ceases to be bound by the social compact." That individualistic, utilitarian streak, drawn from America's "liberal tradition," was stronger in the South, where Christian notions seemed to play a smaller role, but it existed everywhere in the movement. The two traditions were held in uneasy unity by the belief that if abuses were swept away, and the economic order reformed, a fraternal spirit would spontaneously arise. Devoted to religious values, Populists more than once sought them through liberal means which were doubtfully suited to them.

If critics have ignored these problems, it has been because Hofstadter has forced their attention to the thesis that Populism was "nativistic" and proto-totalitarian. The basis of this argument, which connects Populism with McCarthyism and other quasi-fascist movements, is a simple geographical analogy; there was strength for both in the Middle West. Hofstadter made little effort to move beyond this gross analogy and show connections between McCarthyism and

---

[37] C. S. Gleed, "The True Significance of Western Unrest," *Forum*, XVI (1893), pp. 251–260; Frank Tracy, "Menacing Socialism in the Western States," *Forum*, XV (1893), pp. 332–342.
[38] Pollack, *The Populist Response*, pp. 3, 4, 10, 15–17, 22–25.

Populist groups or constituencies. Michael Rogin and Walter Nugent have, by careful empirical study, almost wholly discredited that thesis.[39] The party was, for example, always opposed to and opposed by the nativistic American Protective Association. If its orators sometimes used "anti-Semitic" metaphors, they opposed the "exclusiveness" of Jews; far from seeking to exclude, they were demanding that Jews include themselves in American civic life. Finally, the party was far advanced on the question of race, and Congressman Milford Howard of Alabama could denounce the "issues" of the War and white supremacy as a last bid for slave-power sovereignty. The Populist traced America's malaise to her economic institutions and her political life; he had no need for an ethnic or foreign scapegoat. Indeed, such would have been a luxury for a movement which had foes enough.

Writers like Donnelly sought to avoid what they saw as a totalitarian tendency in history, and Populism appealed to the ballot and not to the barricade. To be sure, those who grew up with or identified with Populism's crusade for a fraternal polity might after its demise turn to new and revolutionary means for reaching the fraternal ideal. The doctrinaire Socialist Labor Party felt itself with some justice to be competitive with Populism in a contest for members. The new revolutionary totalitarians were few at most, and their tendency was to a totalitarianism of the left, not the right. American Communist leaders in the early days were often Kansans, and William Z. Foster titled his autobiography *From Bryan to Stalin*. For the old agrarian radicals in North Dakota, as Rogin summed up, "the danger was not so much Communist phobia as Communist-philia." Populism's Christian ideals, even turned violent and messianic, were still those of a universal fraternity.[40]

Hicks avoided an error of tone into which many contemporary critics have fallen, that of overestimating Populist strength. Even locally, support was uncertain and far from overwhelming. Populism

[39] Hofstadter, *The Age of Reform*, pp. 70–81; Rogin, *The Intellectuals and McCarthy, passim*; Nugent, *The Tolerant Populists*, pp. 153–155, 163, 175–176, 199–200, 221.

[40] Rogin, *The Intellectuals vs. McCarthy*, p. 134; Pollack, *The Populist Response*, pp. 85–102; Theodore Draper, *The Roots of American Communism* (New York: Viking, 1957), pp. 38–39, 305, 323.

drew its committed members from farmers who had been shaken out of their identification with inherited and traditional groups and who turned to constructing organizations of their own, based on their highest values. Populism did not penetrate the ethnic communities of the East, in part because such conditions of alienation did not exist. Moreover, the movement never succeeded in developing a following in states where real two-party competition provided some sort of political alternative within existing institutions: it was weak in Iowa, Wisconsin, Indiana, Illinois, Ohio, and among the Southern border states, strong only in North Carolina.

Those who led the movement were under desperate pressure to get results, a pressure imposed by their own compassion and concern as much as by their voters. Theirs were gentle ears, unable to bear the cry of anguish. The need for success stimulated an attempt to build a following even at the cost of attenuating doctrine in order to appeal to an audience, an effort which resulted in phrases like "the capitalism of the many" and in the later almost exclusive emphasis on "free silver."

As Pollack argues, it was this desire for effectiveness which led Populism to take the calculated risk of fusion with the Democrats in 1896;[41] it was, he points out, a desperate effort to avoid the fate of third parties, an attempt to move into major party status. (Northerners may have been sanguine because of the success of the Anti-Nebraska movement less than half a century earlier.) If Populism failed to realize that dream, it nevertheless won a victory. In 1896, if not in retrospect, Bryan's "Popocratic" platform was radical enough, and Eastern conservatives were stirred to their frenzied alarm not by free silver, which if a heresy was at least respectable, but by the pro-labor "socialist" planks. Populism did not become a major party, but in a sense it captured one; in the elections since 1896, the Democrats have only twice (1904 and 1924) failed to carry the "reform" standard. The ideal of a fraternal polity became attenuated, something caught in a passing phrase or a rhetorical gesture, but perhaps that was inevitable. The first age of protest was dying with the slow return of prosperity and the excitement of the War with Spain. Populism, at least, left an echo, which sounds in the unwonted pas-

[41] Pollack, *The Populist Response*, p. 103.

sion with which academics dispute its nature and meaning. Lindsay may have been right even about the election of 1896:

> There were truths eternal in the gab and tittle-tattle,
> There were real heads broken in the fustian and rattle.
> There were real lines drawn:
> Not the silver and the gold,
> But Nebraska's cry went eastward against the dour and the old,
> The mean and the cold.

Parties and movements have had worse epitaphs.

Lloyd: Populist Militant

Henry Demarest Lloyd was an intellectual, and there is sometimes a reluctance to classify him with the Populists, who did not number many of the certified breed. ("Lloyd, after all," Pollack is forced to protest, "*was* a Populist.")[42] Lloyd was one of those Populist militants who eventually made their way to socialism, but in Lloyd's case at least, conversion came by default. The doctrines of class war and working-class exclusiveness—which, in attenuated form, Sam Gompers had used to reject union with "employing" farmers— did not attract him. Lloyd was severe with the fusionists of '96 because they abandoned Populism and what he saw as the need for an Independent People's Party. (Lloyd was not averse to coalitions, and even in '96 he credited the fusionists with good motives; he had also compromised to the extent of blarneying Gompers in an effort to unite reform forces.)

Lloyd's intellectuality did not make him less a Populist; it made him a Populist doctrinaire. More than any other spokesman, he gave Populism the coherence of an ideology. That coherence is somewhat artificial; Populism was entwined with ambiguities, and it is an intellectual's conceit, that of Mannheim, that there must be a single, underlying "world view" and doctrine for every political movement. Lloyd's doctrine does, though, have the virtue of showing much of Populism's dilemma, and suggests why many of the movement's leaders preferred not to face their quandary.

[42] *Ibid.,* p. 97.

Lloyd had rejected the Calvinism of his early rearing because he felt it was "fatalistic" in its acceptance of original sin, and he was even more emphatic in his dislike for doctrines like Darwinism which elevated man-made institutions into absolutes dictated by nature. Man, he wrote, is "the god of society," the "creator and redeemer of himself and of society." There was no escape from responsibility, no need to tolerate evil as a fixed condition of human life. Knowing that what appears necessary—or even rational—may not be so in fact, Lloyd asserted the need for the radical thinker who, as "poet and creator," could create visions and designs of a better society and inspire his fellows with a sense of their duty and potentiality.

The passion of Lloyd's prophetic moralism led him to arguments which were existentialistic and relativistic in an extreme sense; often, Lloyd seems to be arguing that society is a tabula rasa on which man may write at will. In a sense, this is what Lloyd meant; he rejected on principle any limits to the moral possibilities of men. In another way, however, Lloyd's argument was absolutistic. Insistent on the need for new means, he proclaimed unchanging ends. "Humanity," he wrote, "is not God, but the priesthood of God." [43]

Man could not realize himself or his destiny save in a political community of "living love" united by "faith and works." Individualism, Lloyd argued, is self-destructive; we best love ourselves when we love what is best in others. Man by himself is too weak to develop what is best in himself; the better his fellows are, the better he himself will be. Even the "freedom" of individualism is an illusion. Free trade in the conventional sense, Lloyd argued, is not "free" at all. Those who engage in it must accept its end (pecuniary gain) and its means (the "laws" of supply and demand and of comparative advantage). Genuinely free trade depends on an ability to determine the ends and means of trade, which in turn depends on men who are not isolated and impotent parts of a process but can collectively choose their goals. Free trade, in this sense, is "bottomed on a brotherhood" and guided by human needs.

[43] Henry Demarest Lloyd, *Man, the Social Creator* (New York: Doubleday, 1906), pp. 12, 220–221, and *Wealth Against Commonwealth* (New York: Harper, 1894), p. 497; C. Lloyd, *Henry Demarest Lloyd* (New York: Putnam, 1912), vol. II, p. iii.

Industrialism had broken "the brotherhoods of the old industry," shattering the common life of guilds and villages and leaving men alone. Lloyd's hope was always part lament and he nostalgically admired the Swiss government, which enabled men to form local fraternal bonds to one another. Yet when Lloyd declared that "the people is the name of an ideal," and one which cried out for realization, he was not proposing a return to traditional simplicity.[44]

Lloyd was no Luddite; he blamed not industrialism, but the concentration of wealth in the hands of "corporate Caesars," for the crisis of the times. "Nature is rich," he asserted, "but everywhere man, the heir of nature, is poor." In part that dictum differs from the scarcity that Locke and his successors had seen in nature, but it is a difference of degree only. Rousseau, whose phraseology Lloyd was obviously imitating, had, like the classical writers, assumed that there were necessary limits on man; the classics had counseled man to adjust his desires to nature's limits, Rousseau had sought to make them legitimate, but neither quarreled with the fact. Lloyd, like the theorists of the liberal Enlightenment, denied that such limits existed; if society were rightly organized, nature would yield enough to fulfill the desires of men.[45]

Hardly a materialist, Lloyd like his Enlightenment predecessors regarded physical nature as a barrier to be overcome. Material scarcity was an obstacle to freedom and to fraternity, trapping men in a narrow struggle to survive. Even the comparative comfort of most Americans, given conditions of competition and inequality, paralyzed men with the fear of loss. Lloyd prescribed a simple solution: make all Americans members of the middle class (nor, Populist that he was, was Lloyd fearful of the term). American abundance, by guaranteeing satisfactions, was enough to eliminate material anxiety, provided it was combined with relative equality.

Industrialism made that condition possible, and Lloyd could not have abandoned it if he would. In fact he felt no such inclination. Technology made possible the "evangelization of the world," the conquest of physical space and the expansion of contacts between

---

[44] *Man, the Social Creator*, pp. 100–177; see also *A Sovereign People: a Study of Swiss Democracy* (New York: Doubleday, Page, 1907) and *Newest England* (New York: Doubleday, Page, 1900).
[45] *Wealth Against Commonwealth*, pp. 1–7.

man and his fellows, and the realization of the universal fraternity which Lloyd saw as the law of human history.[46]

Like the theorists of the eighteenth century, and, for that matter, like the Spencerian Darwinists, Lloyd rested his case on the doctrine that, with the disappearance of material scarcity and of the barriers of space, an inherent brotherliness, the "living love" that was man's nature, would reveal itself in political life. In terms of theory alone, he differed from the Darwinists principally in his belief that the time was ripe for the realization of the vision.

Not for nothing did Lloyd call for a "new Newtonianism," for like the eighteenth-century theorists he did not regard the emergence of fraternal feelings as entirely automatic; it required a "science" for drawing masses of individuals together. Intermediate groups were a threat to the civic—or universal—fraternity Lloyd hoped for; despite his admiration for the Swiss, he hated party as much as monopoly, and could refer to the need to "purify" American life by replacing "politics" with education. Group loyalties functioned socially and psychologically as matter did physically; as barriers to the emergence of larger loyalties between men.

Lloyd, however, was not blind to the problem of the human emotions. As he proposed to eliminate the obstacle of material needs by fulfilling them, so he suggested that man's need for small and secure groups be met by the "neighborhood." This, as Lloyd knew, implied groups of small size with no organic life and purpose; they could satisfy an emotional need without being able to compete with society at large for individual loyalties.[47]

Like his proposal to make all Americans middle class, this last idea is bound to disquiet the contemporary mind. Elimination of economic inequality might remove some of the worst features of the suburb, our best contemporary example of the neighborhood, but it would not necessarily remove competition for status or for power. Too, suburban life might cause us to doubt that the purposeless sociability of Lloyd's neighborhoods would truly result in emotional security.

---

[46] *Man, the Social Creator*, pp. 10, 44, 67, 118–119, 135, 153–177, and *Lords of Industry* (New York: Putnam, 1910), p. 147.

[47] *Man, the Social Creator*, pp. 16, 94, 179; C. Lloyd, *Henry Demarest Lloyd*, vol. I, pp. 193, 197, 292, 296, vol. II, p. 126.

Lloyd was in many ways more sophisticated than his Enlightenment predecessors, and he was certainly wiser than most men of his time. He held to the presumption, however, that there was no necessary obstacle in man, no natural limit to his possible fraternity. When he discarded Calvinist thought and kept its ideals, Lloyd lost knowledge about human nature as a price for the freedom he won. Populists who were closer to traditional religion hesitated to go so far. If nature was abundant and man the heir of nature, Lloyd reasoned, nature must die before man could come into his estate; he must master nature, become free of her constraints. Lloyd saw nothing to master, however, in man himself; and like most men of his times, he took passage for the City on the Celestial Railroad.

> As all citizens who compose a democratic community are nearly all equal and alike, the poet cannot dwell upon any one of them; but the nation itself invites the exercise of his powers. . . . Looking at the human race as one great whole, they easily conceive that its destinies are regulated by the same design; and in the actions of every individual they are led to acknowledge a trace of that universal and eternal plan on which God rules our race. . . . (T)heir works will be admired and understood, for the imagination of their contemporaries takes this direction of its own accord.
>
> De Tocqueville, *Democracy in America*

CHAPTER XV

WHITMAN AND BELLAMY: NATIONS OF LOVERS

The Song of Myself

No American has appealed to the symbol of fraternity as often or as stridently as Walt Whitman did. Over the years, his rhetoric of brotherhood has probably added to Whitman's following. We are no longer disturbed, as his early admirers like Emerson were, by his comparative lack of verbal inhibition, and his prophecies of fraternity find ready listeners in men who feel trapped in their own loneliness.

As D. H. Lawrence recognized, however, Whitman conceived

of fraternity as a perfect unity of selves.[1] In such a relationship, the separate identity of one or both parties is destroyed; fraternity is conceived as selfless community or total tyrannical domination. Neither possibility is equivalent to fraternity, which is communion between separate selves. But even on his own terms, Whitman misleads many of his votaries. He appears to aim at total communion; when he speaks of a conflict between "my soul and I," the "I"— strong, stubborn, and assertive—is only instrumental, a mask for protecting the sensitive soul which desires love and affection.[2] The "I" was thus something to be escaped, a barrier to fraternity which arises from fear and insecurity. Even if escape from the "I" were possible, however, there would be a difference between souls, something Whitman appears not to recognize. His teachings, however, demonstrate that difference, for they hide a grandiose individualism, a self-assertion different only in degree from that of tyrants. Whitman was the prophet of himself, not of fraternity.

If Whitman appeals to us, it is partly because he knew intimately all the ambiguous symbolism of American culture. He learned religion from the Dutch Calvinism of his kind but ineffectual mother; and his father, a follower of Paine and an admirer of the Deistic Quaker, Elias Hicks, taught him the individualism of the late eighteenth century.

It was natural that Whitman should resent his father, who was cold, stern, and domineering; it was probably also inevitable that Whitman should admire his father's strength and look to him for a knowledge of the world outside the home. Both resentment and admiration set the pattern of Whitman's thought. He never deviated much from Hicks' teaching that God had so shaped men's intuitions that they needed only to follow the spontaneous promptings of such feelings for the world to be a place of joy. Nor was Whitman ever free of the distaste for sensuality that led his father to detest Frances Wright because of her advocacy of "free love" (even though the elder Whitman admired her colleague, Robert Dale Owen).[3] While

[1] "Whitman," in *Studies in Classical American Literature*, pp. 174–191.

[2] Allen, *The Solitary Singer*, pp. 138, 511, 517, 538; John Kinnaird, "Whitman: the Paradox of Identity," *PR*, XXV (1958), pp. 380–405.

[3] *Writings*, vol. I, p. xvi; *Walt Whitman: Poems and Prose*, ed. Mark Van Doren (New York: Viking, 1945), p. 487; Allen, *Solitary Singer*, pp. 7–8, 13, 15, 20, 29–30, 308.

Whitman eventually disowned his early temperance novel, *Franklin Evans*, and while he expressed an admiration for Miss Wright, Whitman also opposed her sexual doctrines and felt horror toward "selfish males" whose "unhallowed passions" led to the ruination of "gentle hearts." [4]

But Whitman rebelled against his father's lack of affectionate feeling. His early stories feature cruel fathers and sadistic schoolmasters, and there is a strong autobiographical note in his story, "A Legend of Life and Love." In that tale, a villainous father teaches his children to be competitive individualists. As a result, his obedient children are lonely and miserable, while only the rebellious son finds love and happiness. [5]

Obviously Whitman's family encouraged a sharp distinction between the ideas of "masculinity" and "femininity," masculinity being associated with his father's assertive individualism, femininity with his mother's passive warmth. And though Whitman valued affection to excess, he could never lose the association of emotionality with weakness, or that of dependence with being dominated. Loving someone was intolerably threatening unless Whitman felt himself in control of the situation; a relationship of equals was no more possible for him than one in which he felt himself reduced to weakness and helpless passivity.

He sang of brotherhood, but with all his brothers and sisters Whitman was demanding and dictatorial as well as affectionate. In one essay, he even described them as "My Boys and Girls." (His relationship with his brother Jesse was notably unfraternal.) [6] Affection was a snare, a danger more threatening because it was needed so deeply, and the more he felt the need, the more Whitman felt the necessity of protecting the soul with the shield of the "I."

Sometimes Whitman spoke of the desire for contact with women as an "effeminate longing," and though he often varied his language,

[4] *Writings*, vol. VI, pp. 15–28, 85–88; *Solitary Singer*, pp. 29–30, 37–38, 56–58, 213, 535; J. Rubin and C. R. Brown, *Walt Whitman of the New York Aurora* (State College: Pennsylvania State College Press, 1950), pp. 99–100. See also Whitman's *Franklin Evans: or, The Inebriate* (New York: Random House, 1929).

[5] *Writings*, vol. V, pp. 5–15, vol. VI, pp. 39–49. "A Legend of Life and Love" originally appeared in *USDR*, XI (1842), pp. 83–86.

[6] *Solitary Singer*, pp. 8, 15, 30–31, 308.

he always saw woman as a danger, a temptress who led men into anguish. Almost all emotion and desire became associated with his anxieties. Even when he lauded sexuality, he saw it as (of all things) proof of a "courageous soul." The cult of strength and activity which Whitman later espoused was only an attempt to protect himself from his own yearning for affection which for him was inseparably associated with his fears of dependence, desertion, and injury.[7]

His intellectual vision, as revealed in his writings, was dominated by erotic imagery; and because Whitman was a master, his tone and symbolism are moving and powerful. But it is an intellectual vision—abstract, universalized, theoretical. Whitman departed from his early idealism only to the extent of spiritualizing matter, as his appreciation of Hegel suggests:

> Roaming in thought over the Universe, I saw the little that is Good steadily hastening towards immortality,
> And the vast all that is call'd Evil I saw hastening to merge itself and become lost and dead.[8]

"They talk of his 'splendid animality,'" D. H. Lawrence taunted, ". . . he'd got it on the brain, if that's the place for animality."[9] Whitman's relations with concrete persons were shaped by a demand for perfect understanding, for a total merger that would eliminate the perils of separate selves.

While he was young—and his hope of finding a perfect love was stronger—his actions and attitudes differed from those of his later life, with which he is chiefly associated. The poet of work and workmen delighted, in his youth, to escape from work into literature, fantasy, and imagination. The celebrator of rude vitality was a savage critic of New York's "sports," its men of bravado, its gang leaders like Captain Isaiah Rynders.

That early period was the time of Whitman's association with the Art Union in Brooklyn, a small group of friends and intellectuals whose companionship Whitman found "more satisfying" than money

[7] *Ibid.*, pp. 80, 82, 158, 172; Wilson, *The Shock of Recognition*, pp. 261–262; D. G. Brinton and Horace Traubel, "A Visit to West Hills," *Papers of the Walt Whitman Fellowship*, X (1894), p. 62.

[8] *The Works of Walt Whitman* (New York: Funk and Wagnalls, 1968), vol. I, p. 258.

[9] Lawrence, "Whitman," p. 176.

or fame. His idealism was then more uncompromising, almost dia-
metrically opposed to the material world. The theme of death, later
muted in Whitman's life-anthems (so much so that Lawrence treated
it as revealingly anomalous), was dominant in his poetry in the early
1850s. Death, not life, was the lodestar, acknowledged as "brother
sleep" and the ultimate fraternity.[10]

The distance of his early political views from his later beliefs is
equally striking. Whitman, the poet of Americanism, of equality, of
mass democracy, propounded a small "ardent and radical" phalanx
of intellectuals, artists, and writers. These, he hoped, free from cant
and convention, might support one another's artistic integrity against
the pressures of the surrounding society. Fraternity implied alienation,
being "set apart." Not surprisingly, Whitman found inspiration in
Greek culture and politics and in the ideal of the small state.

All of this depended on Whitman's ability to retain hope that
somewhere in the world he might find a total love, a true "second
self." His admiration for Greece and antiquity seems premised, as
might be expected, on the belief that in those ages and places there
existed the possibility of a perfect "brotherhood of lovers." [11]

Whitman was never without a "premonition" that the perfect
unity he associated with love was not to be found. That doubt, however, did not lead Whitman to accept the imperfect but very real
bonds that the world allows among men. His inability to acknowledge
dependence, his fear of loss of control, were too great for that. Doubt
merely stimulated fear: the majority of his friendships would be
casual, temporary, and superficial. Numbers of men, known fleet-
ingly, avoided involvement and intensity.

In general, he preferred those over whom his sense of control
was greatest: the old, who could not expose his fear of physical weakness and mortality, and the "coarse, strong, self-willed men" who

[10] Rubin and Brown, *Whitman of the New York Aurora*, pp. 21, 57;
Solitary Singer, pp. 18, 24, 34, 108, 110, 117.

[11] Dutton, *Whitman*, is especially valuable on this period of Whitman's
life. See also Allen, *Walt Whitman* (New York: Grove, 1961), p. 36, and
Solitary Singer, pp. 504, 511. The "Hellenic" note in "The Base of All Metaphysics" is counteracted by the fact that it follows the promise of "For you, O
Democracy, to make the continent indissoluble." (*Works*, vol. I, pp. 135–138.)
Compare Chase, *The Democratic Vista*, and *Walt Whitman: Poems and Prose*,
pp. 397–398.

could not expose his intellectual anxieties. Whitman sought from his friendships not the encouragement to pursue his "premonitions" and insights, but the ability to flee them.[12]

At those times when Whitman convinced himself that he had found the "perfect love," he was wracked by fears of indifference, loss, and abandonment. Proclaiming a perfect merging of spirits, he was always partly aware of the imperfect fact: he sought to make song and sound cover and compensate for the defect of reality. For that reason, if no other, he shied away from the physical contacts which would make recognition of those shortcomings even more unavoidable.

Whitman escaped anxiety only when some grievous weakness in the other made him incapable of threatening Whitman. Ultimately this meant for Whitman that relations with his fellows could best be established when they lay maimed or dying. "Walt's great poems," Lawrence noted, "are really huge, fat, tomb plants." Whitman might convince himself that the perfect love had been found this side of mortality, but his "loves" were either found when he ghoulishly prowled the Civil War hospitals, or they drove him to anguished insecurity.[13]

"Each man kills the thing he loves," wrote Oscar Wilde, a sometimes wiser though less able version of Whitman, and he knew whereof he spoke. If man does not kill the thing he loves, then the eternal child in him longs to do so. That after all is the basis of the old religious doctrine which asserts that a man loves what he is not, that which convicts him of being what he is; let him therefore love immortal God, caring for his fellows only as he loves himself. That wisdom, even Wilde's despairing understanding, Whitman never learned. Either requires distinctions—between God and man, between man and his love. And the old doctrine requires judgments of quality,

[12] *Writings*, vol. I, pp. 133–134, vol. IV, pp. 23–24, vol. IX, pp. 133–134; *The Uncollected Poetry and Prose of Walt Whitman*, ed. E. Holloway (New York: Doubleday, Page, 1921), vol. II, pp. 95–96; *Solitary Singer*, pp. 16, 36, 118–121, 200.

[13] Lawrence, "Whitman," p. 177; Whitman, *Writings*, vol. II, pp. 8, 12–13; *Works*, vol. I, pp. 284–286; *Walt Whitman: Poems and Prose*, pp. 508–515, 519–523; Clark Griffith, "Sex and Death: the Significance of Whitman's Calamus Themes," *PQ*, XXXIX (1960), pp. 18–38.

the recognition of higher and lower in assessing the relations of God and man, and of man with man.

The rejection of qualitative judgment is necessary, however, to Whitman's cosmic individualism. To judge is to stand apart, to acknowledge a separation of judge and judged; it has more than a suggestion, too, of responsibility and authority. Even to judge oneself is to acknowledge that there are standards by which the self may be judged. Whitman's willingness to "accept evil" in himself was the corollary to his love for all men. There was no judgment because there was no authority to render it. There was nothing but "humanity"—which, on analysis, proves to be Whitman himself. Even God was an "elder brother," part of the great oneness of Whitman's affection.[14] As Whitman grew less hopeful of a perfect love and as his fears of involvement mounted, he did not abandon the goal: he shifted its object. Gradually widening his embrace, discarding difference and quality, he encompassed the cosmos. The always-savage element of his loves reached its logical conclusion when desire and fear led him to seek to annihilate all separate existence through song. One can be relieved at the ineffectuality of the means without overlooking the secret meaning of the hymn.

The Base of All Metaphysics

On his own terms, Whitman "loved humanity," but it would be impossible to call that love fraternity. In "The Base of All Metaphysics" in the "Calamus" poems, Whitman does assert that the love of a man for his comrade underlies everything. Yet that "basis" also includes the attraction of friends, the feeling of parents for children (and vice versa), the love of husband and wife, patriotism and civic spirit. Any emotion which ties a man to a person or thing is included: affection as such, not a specific kind of affection, was the basis of Whitman's "metaphysics." Whitman found some solace in the thought that affection anywhere in the world was in a "metaphysical" sense also affection for Whitman. Yet not only does this deprecate the affection of specific persons for each other, it em-

14 *Works,* vol. I, pp. 65–66, 343–344; *Writings,* vol. I, p. 38, vol. II, p. 196.

phasizes that Whitman's deification of warmth lacks any specific "fraternal" content. Insofar as fraternity existed, it could be no more than a part of the whole that was for Whitman the basis of all things.[15]

Lawrence denounced Whitman's idea of comradeship because it "slides over into death." [16] Of course, all human life slides over into death, and all comradeship with it, but the point is that Whitman did not accept himself as a part of the world or of life. Vacillating between his proclamations of cosmic inclusiveness and his sense of isolation, Whitman's idea of comradeship might include dying for his beloveds or a dying of those beloveds; he does not seem to have weighed a dying with them. Whitman ranged himself as either outside, or encompassing, humanity. He saw himself, in this sense, as a different order of being from ordinary humanity.

Whitman's messianic sense seems to have developed shortly after his Art Union period. It was at this time that he became a carpenter, and the thesis that he did so in order to identify himself with Jesus is persuasive to anyone who recalls Whitman's treatment of Christ as a "comrade." It was hardly a Christian religiosity which moved him. Whitman's interests at the time moved toward Egyptology, toward the Mother who is identical with the created universe, not the God who stands outside it.[17]

Whitman moved from his own mother, whose force was inadequate, to a Mother-Goddess strong enough to establish the rule of affection. It was the analogue of his vision of "athletic mothers," the strong woman who can smash the limiting barriers of life. His vision of "immortality" was, in short, less a rebirth than a flight from birth back into the womb. A perennial child, he was endowed with art enough to create in words the child's dream of incorporating whatever it finds outside itself. "The universe, in short, adds up to ONE . . . which is Walt," Lawrence remarked. Thoreau, a more contemporary and possibly more perceptive critic, was even more incisive. Whitman,

[15] *Works*, vol. I, pp. 137–138, 129, 364–365, 367–368.

[16] Lawrence, "Whitman," p. 182.

[17] *Writings*, vol. IX, pp. 104–105; *Solitary Singer*, pp. 117, 122–123, 142, 154; E. Shephard, "Possible Sources of Whitman's Ideas and Symbols," *MIQ*, XIV (1953), p. 71, n. 37.

he commented, was driven not by a love for man, but by a hatred for the natural world.[18]

Disagree with Whitman's theories: it is hard to blame Whitman himself. Whatever authority Whitman had known—his father in childhood, the much-admired Emerson in young adulthood—had commanded him to discard authority, counseled or commanded him to seek meaning in himself, argued that the intuitions of the Oversoul were the source of truth. Whitman's greatest error lay in believing his mentors.

There is in fact much that is pathetic in Whitman's writing and posing. Try as he might, Whitman could not fully believe his own songs. The obvious sublimation of Whitman's personal erotic faculties into a "love for humanity" is saddest because it was partly conscious. He wrote of his intent to "expose and use" the "passions which were threatening to consume me." The sublimated passions of Walt Whitman would be used to reconstruct society, to build a "more ardent, more general" comradeship of citizens.[19] Whitman the man became Whitman the prophet, driven by his emotions.

Yet Whitman's mind always called his attention to finitude and limitation. It was for this reason that Whitman, the young intellectual, became the panegyricist of the unthinking "natural man." His praise of unthinking response reflects a desire to escape the strictures of his own mind.

Whitman, one of the most introspective of poets, playing the part of robust, extroverted man, is alone enough to make the gods laugh. The strange masquerade, in which Whitman played at being what he was not, had only one certain result: to deny him the genuine and personal affection he so repeatedly and desperately demanded. It left him only the cadences of false joy and vitality which muffled and stifled the "mocking taunt" of the unknown—which Whitman knew, masquerades aside, waited on the open road.

[18] Lawrence, "Whitman," p. 178; Whitman, *Works*, vol. I, pp. 237–243, 426–427; R. W. B. Lewis, "The New Adam: Whitman," in *The American Adam* (Chicago: University of Chicago Press, 1955), pp. 41–53. For Thoreau's comment, see Allen, *Solitary Singer*, pp. 204–206; Thoreau later revised his ideas, but his initial remark is to the point.

[19] *Writings*, vol. I, p. 32; *Works*, vol. I, pp. 16, 140.

The City Invincible

Whitman's political ideas have appealed to intellectuals almost as much as his poetry. Despite its negative features, its tendencies toward leveling-down and toward nationalistic self-righteousness, Whitman's notions have one undeniably positive element: the insistence that democracy must be more than formal institutions and legal structures, that it must be woven together with a sense of promise, a hope for achievement of the ideal.[20]

Whitman is the supremely American poet, the mirror of the dilemmas of American democracy itself. Doubtless he would have taken this to be the supreme compliment. Whitman did observe many of the tensions and ambiguities of American life; lack of recognition would have verged on the miraculous, for his lifetime spanned the onset of industrialism, the Civil War, the Jacksonian heyday, Abraham Lincoln and the Robber Barons. Yet his faith in American life and America did not slacken. He did revise, from time to time, his notion of what America "was." But, as Perry Miller comments, though he changed the words of the song, he never ceased to "sing." Whitman's political endeavor was simple and consistent: he would discover the American identity, provide a unifying faith, merge all the diverse strands of America in a Living Ideal.[21]

Whitman's commitment to democracy, not only to a governmental system but to the Democracy—the masses as the creative force in the political order—was a very early one. Mechanics and workmen were the nation, not simply a part of it. Democracy had transferred political power to the masses. It had destroyed the old authorities and religions; and Whitman, like Lawrence, saw the dissolution of the older forms of community through individualism as the first step toward the American soul. Whitman saw nature as an irresistible force at war with the effete artificialities of civilization, and in smash-

[20] H. A. Myers, "Whitman's Concept of Spiritual Democracy, 1855–1856," AL, VI (1934), pp. 239–253. John Jay Chapman's essay, "Whitman," in Emerson and Other Essays (New York: Scribner's, 1898), pp. 111–130, is excellent precisely because it appreciates the ambivalence.

[21] Perry Miller, "The Shaping of the American Character," NEQ, XXVIII (1955), pp. 435–454; J. Stafford, The Literary Criticism of Young America (Berkeley and Los Angeles: University of California Press, 1952), pp. 67–69.

ing the old barriers America had been nature's instrument, almost identified with nature itself. Yet destruction was not enough: the divided society of individual "decision and wilfulness" created by liberty and equality needed to be "semented" by bonds between citizens.[22]

That goal demanded a great "poet of the people" who could prophesy and lead Americans toward the "city invincible" in which "all men are like brothers." This poet would need to perceive the "native nobility of the average man," and must respect the emotions that were the strength of the masses and the "sement" of unity. Emerson, for all his lofty vision, could not fill the role. He was, Whitman concluded, too "cold": he lacked the powerful faith in the masses that Whitman possessed, and though he might use terms like "friend" and "lover" as synonyms, he shrank from too open a discussion of the passions. In short, the democratic promise depended for its fulfillment on Whitman himself and on a tradition of followers which would be the democratic equivalent of a church.[23]

Much of Whitman's creed sounds revolutionary, as it did to Whitman himself. In part, though, Whitman's vision was traditional, the high ideal of the Enlightenment. The writers of *The Federalist* had shared Whitman's hope for the "city invincible" and had no less a vision of America's mission to liberate humanity, vindicating the "honor of mankind."

Whitman's prophecy was only more immediate. He spoke in the age of America's advent to confidence of power. The embattled days had passed; America the refuge could become America the liberator. That universalistic element overcame Whitman's nativism and sympathy for the Know-Nothings. In fact, Whitman's American nationalism has no specifically American content. It was merely a part of his cosmic unity, a democratic pantheism of which Whitman was prophet. "Manifest Destiny" was as logical an extension of Americanism for Whitman as it was a perversion for Thoreau.[24]

[22] *The Eighteenth Presidency*, ed. E. F. Grier (Lawrence: University of Kansas Press, 1956); *Uncollected Poetry and Prose*, vol. II, p. 63.

[23] *Works*, vol. I, pp. 134-135, 289-290; *Walt Whitman: Poems and Prose*, pp. 392-394, 454; Allen, *Solitary Singer*, pp. 128-129, 237-238; Wilson, *Shock of Recognition*, pp. 277-278, 286-287, 291-292.

[24] Rubin and Brown, *Whitman of the New York Aurora*, pp. 58, 82-83, 117; *Writings*, vol. V, p. 54; *Poems and Prose*, pp. 390-391, 453-454; *The*

The eighteenth-century Founders had lacked Whitman's seeming confidence in the spontaneous instincts of man. Yet Whitman himself had only an ambiguous faith in those instincts. Whitman's civic bond, his fraternal "sement," was hostile to any concrete bonds between men. "Amativeness" and "philoprogenitiveness," terms he drew from the lexicon of phrenology, were opposed to "adhesiveness," with its overtones of physicality.[25] It was the generalized sentiment for men as such that Whitman admired, not the feeling for particular men. For example, he could refer to the "brotherhood" between himself as newspaper editor and his readership.[26] Even when he praised sex, it was to declare that the "continent" resisted the "fusion of all Americans." [27] (Whether the pun was unconscious or not, the use of "continent" suggests how inimical Whitman's vision is to physicality.) More erotic in tone than Emerson's, Whitman's ideal equaled it in abstraction, in irrelevance to the problems of living individuals.

Whitman was certainly a critic of the Enlightenment when he proclaimed the need for an "emotional hold" of democracy on the people which would be akin to that of "feudalism and ecclesiasticism." He ignored, of course, that whatever "hold" on the emotions feudalism and clericalism possessed was founded in large measure on authority, the conviction of a standard of truth beyond the emotions and beyond men. For Whitman, the emotions are a sufficient guide, provided that they are sublimated from "adhesiveness" onto the civic "body" as a whole. Whitman's teaching suggests that poetry (or propaganda?) can elevate the physicality of men, not that it can help the spirit guide the passions.[28]

Whitman did not propose any change in the traditional institutional structure of American government or society. He did not reject individualism—which, he asserted, "gives character to the

Gathering of Forces, ed. Cleveland Rogers and John Black (New York and London: Putnam, 1920), vol. I, pp. 13, 16–17, 23; Uncollected Poetry and Prose, vol. I, pp. 105–106.

[25] E. Hungerford, "Walt Whitman and His Chart of Bumps," AL, II (1931), pp. 350–384.

[26] Uncollected Poetry and Prose, vol. I, p. 115.

[27] Wilson, Shock of Recognition, pp. 262–263.

[28] Writings, vol. V, p. 131; Poems and Prose, p. 414; Great American Liberals, ed. G. R. Mason (Boston: Beacon, 1956), pp. 83–95.

aggregate." Perhaps so, but the words are revealing: Whitman's insistence on the need to "use" the emotions is part of his conviction that society is an "aggregate," that no genuine bond of communion exists between men. Adding to Emersonian ideas the rhetoric of democracy, Whitman retained at the center of his thought the "infinitely repelling orb" united to anything else only by the mysterious vision of the cosmic whole. Whitman denies community among men: there is only the lonely "one identity" which must embrace everything or remain alone.[29]

He was devoted to the "Union" as an idea, but it meant little in concrete terms except the Constitution, the traditional process and way. His "fraternal sentiments" never led him to reject the axiom that the best government is that which governs least, and he was always an opponent of welfare legislation. His humanitarianism, otherwise so universal, did not lead him to support even the most moderate of efforts to abolish slavery. And all more radical departures, such as utopian communities or attacks on conventional morality, he was prone to call "mental deformities." [30]

Whitman's "fraternal" teaching was a buttress to individualism and isolation in practice. Whitman was aware of a tension between the two: he would assert that democracy had completed its political revolution but still awaited the change that would bring material prosperity to the masses.[31] Whitman resolved the tension, however, in terms of history, moralizing present inhumanity in terms of an eventual "human brotherhood." His conviction of the "irresistible power" with which nature tended to the good minimized the need for men to resist in the context of their own lives.[32]

The creed of progress always resolved Whitman's ambivalence and uncertainty. Less certain of unilinear progress than the theorists of

[29] *Writings*, vol. V, p. 69; *Works*, vol. I, p. 65; *Poems and Prose*, p. 405; *Uncollected Poetry and Prose*, vol. I, p. 10, vol. II, p. 64; *The Gathering of Forces*, vol. II, pp. 212–213.

[30] Allen, *Solitary Singer*, pp. 80, 89–90, 198, 213, 370, 445, 532; R. C. Beaty, "Whitman's Political Doctrine," *SAQ*, XLVI (1947), pp. 72–83.

[31] *Poems and Prose*, pp. 416, 448. "Luckily," Whitman wrote, "the seed is already well sown and has taken ineradicable root. . . . The extreme business energy, and this almost maniacal appetite for wealth . . . are parts of amelioration and progress . . ." (p. 416–417).

[32] Wilson, *Shock of Recognition*, pp. 253–258.

the eighteenth century, he was sure that culture and society "grew," that the true human being was being produced by the "evolution" of dialectic forces.[33]

In *Specimen Days*, he noted that prophecy was being narrowed to mere prediction by a technical age. Whitman did not argue that prophecy was not prediction, but that the former was a larger variety of the latter because it was not bound by present fact. His "giving Voice" to the ultimate destiny of things was Whitman's "prophecy." The firm conviction that "God's plan is enclosed in time and space," a logical deduction from his cosmology, never left him.[34]

No problem or perception would shake that faith beyond repair. He might see rioting, violence, and mass ignorance: they only proved to him that the people had "vitality" or that due to the peoples' long-term wisdom, the problems could be ignored. Finding young Westerners boring and unsociable did not upset his belief that the West was a fraternal and vital "balance" to the effeminate individualism of the older states. He could detest the materialism of the post-war years and yet adulate material and technological growth as leading to a nonmaterialistic state.

Even in the age of the Robber Barons, amid the "published shame" of the times, when he "brooded" on the contrast between public corruption and the "quiet ways" and "deep integrities" of the people, Whitman had no sense of a tradition passing or of values being lost. He retained the faith that the supply of "deep integrities" was "endless," that the ways of the people were timid but that they were certain to prevail.[35]

In content, Whitman's political prescriptions differed only slightly from those of Sumner or Herbert Spencer. His influence was more lasting than theirs because he cast over events the mantle of rhetoric, dulled the sounds of anguish with songs of love. The Darwinists ired by their scientism; Whitman changed the gods, but kept the language of religion. More than his contemporaries, Whitman ignored events, and he sang only of what he saw beyond them, his promise and dream.

[33] *Writings*, vol. V, p. 54, vol. IX, pp. 104–105.
[34] *Poems and Prose*, p. 673; *Works*, vol. I, pp. 221–223, 307–321; Allen, *Solitary Singer*, p. 460.
[35] Writings, vol. I, pp. 133–134; vol. V, pp. 166–167.

Yet what a shabby dream it was, that vision of Whitman's. Sentiment without reference to person, a profusion of superficial contacts without depth or meaning, Whitman's fraternity is typified by the "brotherhood" George Babbitt found among salesmen in railway club cars, united by process and not by choice, passively bound by the hearty but meaningless rhetoric of good fellowship. This is the misfortune of Whitman's song: that the most compelling voice in American history should have sung, not a true prophecy, but the slogans of mass society.

Big Brother

Erich Fromm wrote that those who criticized Edward Bellamy for materialism were guilty of neglecting his "religious spirit." [36] Bellamy often used religious terms and claimed a Christian basis for his political ideas (though he disparaged the idea of the after-life). God's name, however, is conferred on many idols. Bellamy was no political leader; he was almost apathetic toward the Nationalist movement, and it never became more than a fad. Edward Bellamy's impact on his contemporaries was due to his skill as a propagandist, to what Daniel Aaron calls his unfailing sense of the "average." [37] Religion was only one of his arsenal of symbols.

In another sense, though, Bellamy was a man of faith. His greatest appeal lay in his understanding of the American's need to believe that the tensions he felt within himself were merely the birth-pangs of a future order in which all would be resolved.

Bellamy, like his hero Julian West, was reared a Calvinist. Yet his family's religiosity was tainted with heterodoxy; both his father and his maternal grandfather were turned out of pulpits (the latter for adhering to Freemasonry). More important, perhaps, was that Bellamy felt the psychological desires that were impelling Americans toward individualism and the mastery of nature with an unusual intensity. Rejected by West Point because of physical deficiencies,

[36] Erich Fromm, "Introduction to Edward Bellamy, *Looking Backward*, (New York: New American Library, 1960), p. xiii. See also *The Religion of Solidarity*, ed. A. E. Morgan (Yellow Springs, Ohio: Antioch Bookplate Co., 1940).
[37] Daniel Aaron, *Men of Good Hope*, p. 94.

Bellamy either developed or confirmed a simultaneous admiration for the military and fear of physicality. Women, for example, would always have for him some of the qualities of an evil spirit; they suggested conservatism, comfort, weakness, and effeminacy.

Aaron, seeking continuities in the American tradition, discerns traces of Fourierism in Bellamy's writings, even calling his a "village mentality." [38] Yet Bellamy has none of the French theorist's feeling for small and rural community, and lacks the sense of the empirical which is the essence of villagery. Bellamy's mentality was almost a pure version of the authoritarian personality; his morals were the creed of 1984.

Bellamy's Utopia might be a place of immediate satisfactions where men, no longer obliged to provide for the morrow, were not "deprived" of good things. Yet it was not to be a place of luxury. Men were to work and work hard; his Utopians prided themselves on successful inculcation of the obligation to labor. The excessive "extravagance" and "dissipation" of the nineteenth century would disappear as the rich ceased to be debased by idleness and the poor lost the degrading qualities of poverty.

He went further than this middle-class standard. (He did, though, have a tendency to overrate middle-class morals: Dr. Leete, West's guide, would declare that even in the nineteenth century, "ladies and gentlemen" had come to "scorn falsehood".) Jewelry, ornament, and women's fashions were to be eliminated. His women would become transvestites, assuming masculine attire. All would participate in what would amount to a cult of physical fitness and a hypermasculine toughness. Bellamy might parade as the champion of a love that "knew no law but the heart," but even in his imagined year 2000 Edith Leete blushes at the suggestion of affection and is horrified to think that, having known West only a week, she has embraced him.[39]

Louis Hartz was right to refer to Bellamy's work as a "mad utopian flight from tensions." [40] Yet the flight was "mad" only as that word reflects on his own psychological dilemmas; it was not

---

[38] *Ibid.*, pp. 95, 127.
[39] Bellamy, *Looking Backward*, pp. 57, 63, 73, 96, 122, 141, 149, 153, 177–180, 198–199.
[40] Hartz, *The Liberal Tradition in America*, pp. 233, 237.

mad in the sense of being impractical. Bellamy projected into the future the dreams he found unfulfilled in nineteenth-century America; his ideals are those of his times. His future is not "unrealistic": it is a highly realistic vision of a totalitarian state, in which few fail to see some elements of our times, and the grimmer prophets of our day discern the future.

Bellamy abandoned laissez-faire; Dr. Leete's age was to discover a "science of human conduct" more "moral" than competition. This did not imply an abandonment of wealth as a goal. Bellamy's commitments were all on the side of abundance, and of organized and mechanized "efficiency" in producing it. The new science of conduct was not only more "moral" than competitive capitalism, it was also to be more "efficient" and less wasteful, economically sounder and more productive.[41]

Too, Bellamy limited the individual only in denying him the right to use his abilities to benefit himself alone, regarding such action as part of the principle that "might is right." Bellamy was a passionate advocate, however, of "freedom of choice" and the right to pursue private tastes. The foundation of his new order was to be the principle of "self-preservation," the "supreme right of all to live," differing from the older individualism only in providing a more general and surer guarantee of life.[42]

Bellamy's Boston of the year 2000 merely perfected the Madisonian dream: a government of laws replaced the rule of men. Left to choose his own path, the individual is so guided by administrators that his choices result in public virtue. That, however, placed great power in Bellamy's administrative class. If utopia reflects behavior which is "entirely voluntary . . . under rational conditions," someone must set the conditions; and Bellamy realized that, his administrators, possessed of a "science of human beings," had a great opportunity for despotism.

It disturbed him. He proposed tests, and a careful regulation of such devices as rank and hours of labor, income having been equalized. (It is characteristic that Bellamy proposed raising the hours of the more desirable jobs, not lowering those of the less appealing ones.)

[41] Bellamy, *Equality* (New York: Appleton, 1937), p. 195; *Looking Backward*, pp. 52–55, 154–166, 215.
[42] *Looking Backward*, pp. 75–76, 98, 100; *Equality*, pp. 73–74, 90, 107.

He proposed that retired civil servants elect the chiefs of the "divisions," using as analogy the government of colleges by alumni (had he more experience with that system, his enthusiasm for it might have slackened). Even that, however, raised the specter of gerontocracy, as he was well aware.[43]

Ultimately Bellamy shifted the burden to public opinion. Following the logic of all administrative-utopians, he accepted a separation of policy and administration, arguing that the administrator would "serve" the public and be guided by its will and desire. The press, acting as a "free organ of public opinion," would enforce public demands.

Conventional democratic techniques, however, would not suffice. Rule by the majority would imply a constraint on the freedom of the minority, a violation of the rule of individual freedom. The public will, consequently, must be unanimous.

Originally Bellamy planned to drive the dissenter into "service" through the economic whip, leaving him to provide for himself—a solution which suggests how deeply Bellamy accepted the premises of traditional liberalism. Later this solution came to seem too tainted with coercion. In *Equality*, Bellamy contented himself with placing the recalcitrant on a reservation with "seeds and tools" to provide for himself.[44]

Bellamy does not seem to have considered that such a threat might produce sullen conformity. He is even less concerned that the desire for approval and honor might lead to a prudential conventionality or that mass standards might encourage mediocrity. Bellamy was certain that external conformity would lead eventually to a more "noble" and willing adherence. The false, "self-seeking," egotistic self would disappear, to be replaced by a true self based on "public spirit" and "solidarity." [45]

As Hartz suggests, Bellamy believed in thoroughly Madisonian fashion that a "mechanical gadget" can solve the enigma of com-

[43] On utopia and its elite, see *Looking Backward*, pp. 59–60, 77–78, 131–132, 135; *Equality*, pp. 94, 408.
[44] *Looking Backward*, pp. 57–60, 77, 87–88, 117, 119, 150; *Equality*, pp. 2, 6–7, 9, 16, 41, 75–86, 90, 406.
[45] *Looking Backward*, pp. 77–78; *Equality*, pp. 9off.

munity and "the puzzle of Plato." [46] A believer in the liberal creed that individualism and isolation are means to the fraternal end, Bellamy went beyond Madison to strike at the "cause" of faction because, like his contemporaries, he was less sure that history would produce the good end by itself. He substituted administration for the market because he believed in the possibility of a more contemporary millennium. Nature had been improperly obeyed, and hence had escaped command; with a true "science" of human behavior, men could realize the promise of brotherhood.

"Striving to be absorbed . . ."

Competition, Bellamy argued, was only a "brutal law of survival." Human "force" was different from that of the brute, and it was the real driving power of human evolution. The theme of human history was a "striving to be absorbed or united with other lives or life." The ultimate aim of this drive was a "oneness with God," a "return to God," and a "merger with Nature." Men of the future would be "universalists" who inherited time and space.[47]

The destiny of Bellamy's history was a return to the child's cosmos, the annihilation of distinct individuality. History would return men to God, but without the means of death. "Love," the moving force of history, would eventually eliminate death as it would eliminate history itself. Bellamy's historical theory is a flight from much of what is human: time, death and self.

In that sense, it is also a flight from the "brotherhood of man." Like Whitman, Bellamy never saw human brotherhood as more than a transient good, a way station on the road to universal merger which would eliminate all difference.[48]

Even that transient human brotherhood, of course, was at odds with all the closer, more empirical loyalties of men. Bellamy sought to connect the two, but here his language became mystical. Dr. Leete assured West that the spirit of brotherhood is as "real and vital"

---

[46] *The Liberal Tradition in America*, p. 240.

[47] *Looking Backward*, pp. 49, 77, 184, 194; *Equality*, pp. ix–x, 26, 73, 267.

[48] *Looking Backward*, p. 194; *Equality*, pp. 267–269, 341; *The Religion of Solidarity*, pp. 84–85.

as it was in the smaller units of family and kindred, and that this is a "key to the mysteries of our civilization." Bellamy went no further: the "key" remains mysterious.[49]

The answer to this mystery seems to lie in the fact that Bellamy believed, with the Enlightenment, in a "fraternal instinct" which would emerge once the barriers between men fell. True to that tradition, Bellamy conceived the walls between men as due almost entirely to economic scarcity. When he spoke of removing the "fetters" on the love which "knows no law but the heart," he referred to barriers imposed by class; the emotions and minds of men were of a different order. Economic equality was almost a sufficient guarantee of fraternity and enabled Bellamy to expect the Nation (if not the world) to become "a family, a vital union, a common life."[50]

Even granting Bellamy's assumption, such a bond requires that all smaller loyalties, themselves barriers to more general feelings, be weakened or swept away. There is more than one suggestion that Bellamy envisioned such a necessity. Bellamy admired the "solidarity" of trade unions, but he feared the "selfishness" of guild and vocation and aimed at centralized control of unions.[51]

To his credit, Bellamy never applied such an idea consistently. Indeed, he argued that individuals should be protected in their right to remain near those with whom they have formed bonds of "love and friendship," though they may be forced to accept less desirable employment if they do so. Less creditably, Bellamy's universal fraternity has one gaping hole in its fabric: Bellamy denied that he intended or implied a "commingling" of the races. To avoid that consequence, he had to leave "social relations," presumably meaning the intimate relations of the family, outside this universal bond, which weakens still further his claim to have found the answer to the "mystery" of his Utopia.[52]

Bellamy seems to have relied on the military qualities and character of his system to provide the "passion for humanity" in a positive sense. He had always admired the "ardor of self-devotion" and

[49] *Looking Backward*, p. 99.
[50] *Ibid.*, pp. 28–29, 76, 113, 122, 171, 177–180, 184; *Equality*, pp. 17, 79–86.
[51] *Looking Backward*, pp. 30–31; *Equality*, p. 56.
[52] *Equality*, pp. 37, 365.

the disciplined order he saw in the army. Opponent of war that he was, Bellamy argued that since men permitted the concentration of power for the "malificent" goals of war, they should have no fear of doing so for the "good ends" of peace.[53]

This overlooks, of course, the pathos of war: that its ends appear to be and often are "better," if not "good." That war involves evil, and that what appears good may in fact be base, destroys Bellamy's case. The fact points to the complexity and confusion of moral questions and exposes Bellamy's own moral naivete.

More important, however, is the fact that the military looks different to the parade-watcher than to the soldier, especially if the former sees through the eyes of frustrated exclusion and romance. Bellamy might have realized, had his view of the military been accurate, that small group loyalties are more the roots of military courage and devotion than any supposed passion for "the whole."

It is stranger that, as a staunch environmentalist, Bellamy never considered that it might not be so easy to shift the solidarity of the Union or the army at war to "good ends" and peaceful times. He never seems to have considered that there might be something vital in the confrontation of men with death, privation, danger, or despair which contributed to feelings of communality. Had he done so, he might have shuddered: if the great dynamic of human life is a desire to be "united with other lives," and if the military organization of life best achieves that result, then the very logic of unity would impel men toward total war.

That alone suggests the monstrous folly of the Whitmans and the Bellamys, the lonely, fearful men who would seek to be "absorbed . . . in life" and the faceless, impersonal "brotherhood" of universal merger. In the event, war may prove the only means by which men may fulfill the myth of the return and lose the consciousness of their separate humanity.

[53] *Ibid.*, p. 276; *Looking Backward*, pp. 55–56.

> In democratic countries even poor men enter-
> tain a certain lofty notion of their personal
> importance: they look upon themselves with
> complacency, and are apt to suppose that
> others are looking at them too. With this dis-
> position, they watch their language and their
> actions with care, and do not lay themselves
> open so as to betray their deficiencies; to pre-
> serve their dignity, they think it necessary to
> retain their gravity.
>
> De Tocqueville, *Democracy in America*

CHAPTER XVI

MARK TWAIN: THE TEACHER

"Never tell the naked truth . . ."

CRITICS are frequently unkind to authors, but literary criticism has so often seemed to hold Mark Twain in durance vile that attempts to rescue him have become a perennial feature of the American literary scene. Prone to deprecate the writer's design in order to elevate their own insight, critics have often regarded Twain as a basically intuitive writer whose "unconscious" meanings must be ferreted out by the critic himself. Hence Dwight Macdonald, who realizes that Twain was a "two-level" writer, sees the second level as evidence that Twain was the "least conscious" of authors.[1]

Neglected by this view are the consummate craft and contrivance

[1] Dwight Macdonald, *Against the American Grain* (New York: Random House, 1962), pp. 99–100. Easily the worst critical treatment is Van Wyck Brooks, *The Ordeal of Mark Twain* (New York: Macmillan, 1955).

of Twain's lectures and writings, his researches, his concern for tone and timing. Worse, such an interpretation encourages a depressingly literal reading of Twain—an analysis which, whatever ingenious interpretations it may engender, looks only at the surface. Twain himself was a "deep diver." [2]

This is all of a piece: critics, and perhaps academics generally, are unsmiling men, knights of the dolorous tower. Before the humorist, Henry Nash Smith writes, "criticism is helpless." [3] It will remain so until it understands the nature of humor itself.

It is a fundamental rule of the art that humor is duplicitous. The joke is based on a design, known to the story-teller and unknown to the audience until the "punch line" is revealed. Humor has a democratic aim, while wit is aristocratic: where humor prepares the mind of the audience for the bon mot, wit relies on the immediate apprehension of the discerning few.

Humor is the most conscious of arts, for the humorist always knows his secret aim. Moreover, the intention is often complex. The humorist may be most serious when he seems to amuse. Twain wrote late in life that he had no use for being funny without purpose. Like the preacher who used humor to "decorate the sermon whose moral it was," Twain asserted, "I have always preached." [4] Equally, the humorist may be most amused when he seems serious: a sober tale may be only a joke with the punch line omitted or camouflaged. Democratic in intention, humor is not equalitarian: there is a sense in which the joke is always on the audience. Commenting on a puzzled reader's reaction to a passage in his "Double-Barrelled Detective Story" in which he had referred to an "esophagus" which slept on "motionless wing," Twain wrote that:

> Nothing in the paragraph disturbed him but that one treacherous word. It shows that the paragraph was most ably constructed for the deception it was intended to put upon the reader. It was my intention that it should read plausibly, and it is now plain that it does. . . . Between you and me, I was almost ashamed of having fooled that man, but for pride's sake I was not going to say so. I wrote and told him that it was

[2] Kaplan, *Mr. Clemens and Mark Twain*, p. 198; see also pp. 30, 67–68, 71, 87.

[3] *Mark Twain*, ed. Henry Nash Smith (Englewood Cliffs: Prentice-Hall, 1963), p. 1.

[4] *The Autobiography of Mark Twain*, ed. Charles Neider (New York: Washington Square Press, 1961), pp. 273, 298.

a joke. . . . And I told him to carefully read the whole paragraph, and he would find not a vestige of sense in any detail of it. . . . I am sorry —partially. I will not do so any more—for the present. Don't ask me any more questions; let the esophagus have a rest—on his same old motionless wing.[5]

Twain never conformed to the image of the alienated artist (as prevalent today as in the 1950s, when Van Wyck Brooks wrote *The Ordeal of Mark Twain*), isolated and unappreciated in his time. He was immensely popular, and even confessed that he wrote by preference for the "belly" and not the "head."

Yet as he emerges in Justin Kaplan's biography, Twain fits the picture of alienated man well enough. The "democratic" character of his art was largely the result of the fact that Twain never lost his political concern. If he ceased to believe America's political myth, he replaced belief with a sense of responsibility for the myth: political obligation was the logical consequence of alienation.

Brooks never underrated Twain's feelings of political duty; he regarded them as another proof of Twain's neurotic fixations. But his sense of obligation may suggest that Twain possessed a maturity greater than that of the literary critics and social scientists who attempt to ignore the multiple reciprocities that bind them to society. Twain made his own best case: we should pray for Satan because he needs it most, and the ignorant have a greater claim on the artist and the teacher than do the wise.[6]

The claim of the untaught is greater because they may be more willing to learn. Brooks and his epigones overlook Twain's alienation because they underestimate it; concerned with the estrangement of the intellectual from the mass, they forget that in its higher forms art is alienated from the intellectuals.

Twain was a "belly" writer—moral claims of the untaught aside —because the public was less blinded by the conceit of wisdom, and because its customs lay closer to the truth Twain hoped to teach.

[5] *The Complete Short Stories of Mark Twain*, ed. Charles Neider (Garden City: Hanover House, 1957), pp. 436–438. The letter originally appeared in *The Springfield Republican*, April 12, 1902.

[6] Brooks, *Ordeal of Mark Twain*, pp. 24–25, 35, 49; *Autobiography*, p. 28; *Mark Twain on the Damned Human Race*, ed. Janet Smith (New York: Hill and Wang, 1962), pp. 69–73; *The Twain-Howells Letters*, ed. H. N. Smith and W. M. Gibson (Cambridge: Harvard University Press, 1960), vol. II, p. 502.

Having rejected the pietistic Protestantism of his mother, Twain gradually discarded the creed of the Enlightenment as well, rejected the liberal's faith in history and technology, the Romantic's devotion to spontaneity, and the individualism which is the basic dogma of them all. His doctrine was in many ways a vaulting back to the older tradition. Paul Carter observed that it was the "darker" elements of Calvinism which moved Twain to reject pietism, and which provided the basic elements of his political thought. Twain put it characteristically: we may outgrow many things, but not the "religious folly" in which we are reared.[7]

It would be a mistake to take Twain's statement at face value, for to do so would be to neglect the personal education that formed Twain the teacher, the turbulent and diverse experience that shaped and confirmed his belief in the necessity of fraternity for the development of men. The search and need for fraternity runs through his life as a dominant theme. It unites his desperately intense commitments and loyalties, his savage reaction to fancied betrayals, his search for companions on his tours. Too, it is part of his wanderings: alienated from much of American life, he journeyed seeking new countries, lavishing on some his prodigal affection and, when they too proved defective, lashing them with his ridicule. Even the pale society of Nook Farm meant much to him, as a dim, inadequate reflection of a "community of the like-minded." The need for fraternity was the logical result of his sense of guilt, less a neurosis than a mark of the standards by which he insisted on measuring himself, which made him demand affection and encouragement and yet realize that the only valuable support comes from those who share the standard and understand the goal.[8]

Twain was painfully aware that his idea of man and fraternity was at odds with most of the creed of his century. But he knew as well that the culture of America was in conflict, that the synthesis of traditional religion and materialistic individualism was a fragile one. The instability of that synthesis, the division and discontent of the

[7] Paul J. Carter, "Mark Twain: Moralist in Disguise," *University of Colorado Studies in Literature*, no. 6 (1957), pp. 65–79; *Mark Twain's Letters*, ed. A. B. Paine (New York: Harper, 1917), vol. II, p. 440.

[8] Kaplan, *Mr. Clemens and Mark Twain*, pp. 18, 26, 139–140, 149, 168–170, 195, 275–277, 322–323, 337, 341; De Voto, *Mark Twain in Eruption*, pp. 250–252.

American mind, made possible the hope of the teacher: that out of their discontent, Americans might listen if some way could be found to evade the defenses that fear and inherited ideas erected in front of the mind.

The value of humor as an evasive method accounts in part for Twain's use of it, but humor was not his only technique. The common tactic of all Twain's work is duplicity, the effort to approach sensitive areas of the psyche without detection.[9]

His frequent defense of deceit as a social virtue would suggest as much, but Twain provided an even more direct bit of evidence in "The Legend of the Capitoline Venus." [10] The story tells of a sculptor whose art is not appreciated by his prospective father-in-law, a man of business who believes in cash value. The father refuses his consent so long as the sculptor remains poor; and the daughter, not the most romantic of women, accepts this as legitimate. The sculptor has a friend who disguises the hero's latest creation by disfiguring it and burying it at the Roman Capitol on ground the sculptor owns. Of course, it is accepted as an immensely valuable antique and true heart wins realistic lady. The moral is clear: in the age of philistines, it is proper for art to disguise and even disfigure itself in order to bring men to some appreciation of its worth. And too, it is legitimate to disguise contemporary art as "historical," a fact to be remembered when reading Twain's "historical" writings. (The tale of the Venus suggests too that if the work of naive artists is to be appreciated, they may need a "friend" who does the disguising; Twain may well have felt himself the secret and unappreciated friend of artists and intellectuals.)

Twain's duplicity was never greater than when he wrote for children. Not a romanticizer of childhood, he did come to realize that the young are more open to influence than their elders. This realization came fairly late: his wife and Howells had to convince him that *Tom Sawyer* was best viewed as a "boy's book." Even this may have been deceit. Twain was convinced rather easily, and he may have

---

[9] Twain is almost as impossible to quote as Plato. As Henry Nash Smith observes, even the "I" in the autobiographical works is a "character deliberately projected by the writer for artistic purposes" (*Mark Twain: Development of a Writer*, p. 12).

[10] *Short Stories*, pp. 22–27.

used Mrs. Clemens and Howells to see whether the public would regard the book as "proper" for children. (Twain always took great precautions on this point; even so, he was not always successful, and his books were often banned.)[11]

In any event, his mastery of children's literature results from his knowledge that the child's insecurity makes his world one of extremes, a realm of nameless terror and wild exultancy.[12] Leslie Fiedler argues that Twain reinvokes for the adult the world of the child, but his memory seems more accurate than his analysis.[13] Adults do not find Twain's works terrifying: they find them amusing, unless they recall —or reading to children, discover—that the child finds them full of horror and suspense. The difference in perspective is important: books for children are bought by adults, and must conform to adult standards of "suitability." [14] (Notably, Twain translated Heinrich Hoffman's children's book *Struwelpeter*, which adults may find a bit grim, perhaps realizing that children often find it hysterically amusing.)

Socrates argued, according to Plato, that a man who could write comedy could also write tragedy,[15] and Twain is something of a case in point. Humor and horror are the tools of the teacher; both, in Twain's writing, are used to inculcate a view of man and society, to open up the possibility of fraternity. In another sense, humor and terror are not simply tools. They are, in Twain's teaching, major facts in the condition of man.

"The chief . . . delight of God"

Man, Twain wrote, is "the fly-speck of the universe." Hardly calculated to flatter humankind, Twain's descriptions were consistent throughout his life: man is ignorant and infinitesimal, so constrained by heredity and environment as to seem subject to an iron determinism leading to an inexorable destiny.

[11] Kaplan, *Mr. Clemens and Mark Twain*, pp. 179–180, 193, 196, 268.

[12] *Ibid.*, 72, 191; *The Writings of Mark Twain*, ed. A. B. Paine (New York: Harper, 1922–1925), vol. II, pp. 330–331.

[13] Fiedler, *Love and Death in the American Novel*, p. 590.

[14] *Autobiography*, pp. 42, 159, 233; A. E. Stone, *The Innocent Eye: Childhood in Mark Twain's Imagination* (New Haven: Yale University Press, 1961).

[15] Plato, *Symposium* (W. Hamilton trans., Harmondsworth: Penguin Books, 1959), p. 113.

Yet Twain's comments were not altogether serious. Determinism, as Twain knew, can be pretentious. The future and the past alike are made uncertain by man's ignorance, and all that can be asserted safely is that critical events appear to us to be the result of chance. In one essay ("The Turning-Point of My Life"), Twain traced his development as a writer to Caesar's crossing of the Rubicon, conceding that but for practical purposes, the line should go back to Adam. It was a magnificent illustration of the *de trop* of "scientific history," as Twain knew it would be. Tracing a life to Caesar, let alone to Adam, is useless in understanding or in guiding the decisions which man feels himself to face. Worse, it is a kind of pride in which all the events of history lead to—and excuse—the self.[16]

Twain did not discard determinism; he continued to regard men as fixed by their heredity and environment. Heredity and environment, however, were complex and not simple facts. The nature of man remained a fixed limit, but more flexible than the more mechanistic historians imagined.

Man's first desire Twain took to be the desire to be the "delight of God"—the central figure in the universal drama, if not the sole inhabitant of the cosmos. Men, and especially their emotions, center on the self. Each would escape from his condition of weakness and ignorance, would be bathed in euphoria, would be free of responsibility and allowed to follow the most convenient and comfortable course.[17]

Part of the classical literature of temptation, *The Mysterious Stranger* is notable because in it Satan emerges victorious. The appeal of Satan to the boys is mystical and irresistible despite the fact that it rapidly becomes apparent that, in human terms, Satan is a monster. In the end Satan tells the truth: the mysterious stranger is no more than a creation of will, the representation of secret desires. "I, your poor servant, have revealed you to yourself. . . ." But the truth is only the preface to the final temptation: the assertion that "Nothing exists but you." Twain states the idea in the harshest terms, "useless . . . homeless . . . forlorn": he has no desire to "teach" Satan's

---

[16] *Favorite Works of Mark Twain* (Garden City: Garden City Publishing Co., 1939), pp. 1129–1135.

[17] *Short Stories*, pp. 606–611, 657, 674–676; *Letters from the Earth*, ed. Bernard De Voto (New York: Harper, 1962), pp. 17–19.

thesis. The conclusion, "I knew . . . that all he had said was true," is accurate, but only in one sense: Satan, whose purpose is to reveal the individual to himself, has spoken "truly" in revealing not the truth but the secret belief and conviction of the self, the first and last temptation of man.[18]

Twain's psychology, however, was dialectic. He was fond of arguing that men had "twins" inside them, although he varied his terms: "belly" and "head," male and female, "rest and repose," and "ripping and tearing."[19] Men were endowed with an active curiosity which sought knowledge outside the self and was willing to recognize weakness, ignorance, and folly, if this were the price of knowing. Few men developed this faculty highly. The emotions came first in time, remained dominant in most men, and left them prisoners of folly. Yet this result was not free from ambiguity.

Even so untutored a man as Huck Finn's Pap cannot attain innocence. "Head" has enough power to remind him of death, so that his efforts to escape mortality become a series of savage struggles with the phantasmic "Angel of Death," in which Pap's emotions strive to cast death out of the mind, to separate it from the self. Pap can only become bestial: to combat mortality is to battle oneself. Yet his torment is qualitatively no different from Tom's desire to attend his own funeral, or from the attempt to attain illusory security through wealth. The only difference is that, lacking the guile and guise of more "civilized" men, Pap's impulses appear without ornament.[20]

If men are to accept themselves and life, the emotions must be trained first. A deformed mind or conscience can be redeemed with comparative ease, but Twain saw the reformation of a deformed heart as a thing rarely if ever possible.[21]

Primarily, emotions are trained in childhood, and though Twain felt a growing distaste for childhood and youth, he recognized that

[18] Twain, *The Mysterious Stranger* (New York: Harper, 1916), pp. 149–151.

[19] *Short Stories*, pp. 409, 427, 523–561, 640; *The Adventures of Huckleberry Finn* (New York: Washington Square Press, 1960), p. 24.

[20] *Huckleberry Finn*, p. 39; see also *Autobiography*, pp. 208–209, 271–272, 300; *Short Stories*, pp. 32–35, 427, 470–472, 644; *Letters from the Earth*, pp. 43–44.

[21] Henry Nash Smith, *Mark Twain: Development of a Writer*, pp. 113–137; see also *Writings*, vol. XI, p. 22.

the child, hostile to all restrictions and responsibilities, lacks the comparative physical security and the comfortable rationalizations of the adult. The child is open to the direct impact of experience as his elders are not. Twain drew the moral in *Tom Sawyer* that a "miraculous" ending may follow confrontation with the deepest fears of men: death, starvation, darkness, and (symbolic) burial. *Post tenebra, lux:* if the "pot of gold" is personal growth and development, then less is to be hoped for the child who is shielded by an excessively tender respectability.[22]

Environment, including doctrines and ideas, shaped the child and direct the man. Family, habit, religion, law, and government—Twain accorded gave all these a vital role in meeting men's basic physical needs and such mental needs as language and the opportunity for communication.[23] Moreover, this socio-political environment suggests through its law and heroes the conduct that will win admiration, honor, and affection, appealing to the "heart" at its deepest level. Environment, in other words, shapes the "moral sense" and the conscience of the individual.

Conscience is a mark of man's social and political nature. Always dimly aware of ignorance, men need assurance that the course they follow is right. The "moral sense," however, is independent of law or society. Satan argues in *The Mysterious Stranger* that men are set apart from the beasts and the angels by the realization that they can do wrong. The "moral sense" is not an instinctive goodness but a barrier to innocence. It is a part of the "active" twin, the result of man's curiosity, which shows man his dependence, his needs, and his continuing ignorance.[24]

Man could satisfy his "moral sense" only by acting morally, which for Twain has a fixed meaning. Morality is acting according

---

[22] There is a fine discussion of Tom Sawyer in Walter Blair, *Mark Twain and Huck Finn* (Berkeley and Los Angeles: University of California Press, 1960), pp. 50–70, and an outstanding one in Blues, *Mark Twain and the Community*, pp. 5–10. If Blues errs, it is in failing to distinguish between what Twain thought would be likely to be Tom's end—which he said it would be "wisest" not to speak about—and what he hoped his story would teach its young readers.

[23] Salomon, *Twain and the Image of History*, pp. 142–143.

[24] *Short Stories*, pp. 555–556, 616, 625, 657, 659; *Letters from the Earth*, pp. 225–229; *Damned Human Race*, pp. 97–104.

to reality, according to the "nature of things." But these abstractions always remain riddles, emblematic of the hidden nature of truth. Moral action is always imperfect; for men, even should they be perfect judges of good results, cannot foresee the results of their own actions. They can know that kindliness may lead to unkindness, seeming cruelty to the good; yet their ignorance implies the probability of error in any effort to make the calculation. Awareness of limitation may dissuade men from pursuing absolutism or self-righteousness; Twain did not see it as absolution from obligation. The "moral sense" will not allow men to avoid the effort to act morally, however perverse the results. Man must accept the responsibility for error which is part of his lot, and attempt to find the best course from the information available to him.[25]

Political morality has the same moral basis and limitations. Politics exists to "secure manhood," to strengthen and improve the faculties of man, and error attends its judgment.[26] Even at best, however, political society is defective: it must be based on the assumption that manhood is something to be secured, but it must orient itself to the child and the imperfect man. And few societies will do that well: most, in critical areas, will be blind guides following a course which to the excellent man will seem seriously at odds with the nature of things.

"Irreverence" would always be necessary for excellent men, and patriotism no more than a secondary, largely instrumental, value. Even in the best state, as Roger Salomon writes, Twain thought man would be "trained to challenge continually and call in question the very institutions which trained him." [27]

In the best state, men would know that they owed much to society; yet Twain also thought that some debt existed even in the worst

[25] Note that for Twain the "moral sense" is not so much a sense as it is intellectual, a kind of knowledge about moral conduct which, without the right "heart," human beings cannot translate into action. (*Writings*, XXVI, pp. 89, 91.) On the "moral sense" generally, see *Short Stories*, pp. 472–488, 507, 555–556, 625, 642, 658, 659; *Twain-Howells Letters*, vol. II, pp. 689, 698–699; *Autobiography*, pp. 334–337, 385–386; *Damned Human Race*, pp. 49–52, 147–151.

[26] *Mark Twain's Letters*, vol. II, pp. 525–528; *Twain-Howells Letters*, vol. II, p. 610; *Mark Twain's Notebook*, ed. A. B. Paine (New York: Harper, 1935), p. 210.

[27] *Twain and the Image of History*, pp. 97–98; see also Blues, *Mark Twain and the Community*, p. 1.

political order. The few rose on the base provided by the many.[28] Moreover, a claim to superior excellence could be validated by a superior morality, which would require that the excellent man make conditions better, and not worse, by his conduct.

There were times when Twain regarded a given society as completely intolerable, and under such circumstances savage attack was the only recourse. For example, though he detested violence, he praised dynamite if its object were the Czar of all the Russias (with Leopold of Belgium as a probable candidate as well).

The uses of violence are rare, however. They are made necessary by the fact that (as *Puddin'head Wilson* makes clear) after a certain point the reformation of character is impossible. In the more normal case, although the rule holds, the character of men is ambiguous, and society possesses some virtues. Hence men can and should be improved through qualities which already exist in their personalities. Twain's defense of the "noble lie" which seeks to keep men from needless pain follows naturally. So does his suggestion that, given useful but false conventions, only "vague hints" of their defects are permissible.[29]

The judgment of political morality is always a calculation which partakes of the ambiguity—and responsibility—of human decision. No rule of ethics is an absolute guide. Hating imperialism, Twain wrote of the Boer War:

> This is a sordid and criminal war, and in every way shameless and excuseless. Every day I write (in my head) bitter magazine articles about it, but I have to stop with that. For England must not fall: it would mean an inundation of Russian and German political degradations. . . . Even wrong, and she is wrong—England must be upheld. He is an enemy of the human race who would speak against her now. Why *was* the human race created? [30]

The cry against the necessities of human choice is important, for Twain generally distrusted such global and long-range calculations. His prescription insisted that men follow the best immediate rule of ethics, the most defensible and simple evaluation of conduct, until

[28] Kaplan, *Mr. Clemens and Mark Twain*, p. 270.
[29] On the tactics of moral action, see *Autobiography*, pp. 154–155, 386–388; *Huckleberry Finn*, pp. 186–188; *Damned Human Race*, pp. 49–52, 84–93, 147–151, 197–201; *Short Stories*, pp. 472–488, 527, 663–664.
[30] *Twain-Howells Letters*, vol. II, pp. 715–716.

"proved guilty"—found, in a concrete case, likely to do more harm than good. But in any event, a good man will feel guilty that he, and the humanity of which he is a part, are so limited by pride and stupidity.

"You have only to find the first friend . . ."

The burden of humanity was heavy: small wonder that most men sought to pass it on, and were willing to accept the standards of tradition and society. When it was sanctioned by custom, men's acquiescence in iniquity, even in their own degradation, never surprised Twain, though it offended him. Twain realized that the individual never "outgrew" the need for community precisely because men never outgrew their emotions and the desire to shirk burdens.

The possibility of growth beyond society's constraints in ways compatible with the moral and political burden of freedom depended on the discovery of friends and brothers. Ever in need of support and reassurance, man demands communion, and the need is greater for one who confronts his own guilt and error. The child requires the hero for a model, the freeman requires fraternity, a brotherhood whose "essential attributes" exist only when a man can unite his desire for affection with his hope for understanding, making his own soul one.

"Comrades" were the only item in the list Twain made in his notebooks of the elements of man's training that depended at all on individual choice. They were also the only persons on this list, other than the mother, the rest being social institutions.[31] For Twain there was no alternative: one who ventured outside society either found a friend or his emotions—now free from any constraint—made him the center of a shadow-cosmos, a prenatal world transported into the world of men.[32]

The last danger was terribly real for Twain. Civilization, he argued, had tried for its thousands of years to extirpate the "nomadic" instinct, the desire to escape routine and responsibility, but it had

---

[31] Salomon, *Twain and the Image of History*, pp. 142–143.

[32] On the importance of friendship, see *Autobiography*, pp. 30, 32, 47–54, 84–85, 199, 291; *Short Stories*, pp. 307–314, 399–408, 642; *Huckleberry Finn*, pp. 104–111; *Letters from the Earth*, pp. 183–189.

failed. Society could sometimes suppress the nomadic instinct, but never securely. Nomadry always called to men with the siren-accents of romance, risk, and "death-defying" adventure.[33]

Nomadry was more dangerous because it could capture the language of morality. Every shortcoming of society tempted men to "go it alone," to justify lawlessness by the defects of law. The temptations of the "nomadic instinct" were greatest, as one might expect, in adolescence, for the "head" of the child is wise enough to detect social hypocrisy, but the emotions remain those of the innocent. Twain wrote his friend Will Bowen (though he later softened the tone) that the past is happily gone. The "dreaminess, melancholy . . . romance . . . (and) heroics" of adolescence were "only mental and moral masturbation" belonging "to the period usually devoted to physical masturbation." [34] If Twain's images of fraternity concentrated on the adolescent period, it was not because friendship was characteristic of the young, but because they needed it most (for many, the alternative was to be permanently fixed in a childhood state).[35]

The "nomadic instinct" leads men to wander and to seek adventure. Friendship, by contrast, Twain associated with "laziness," a relaxed affection and easy delight which amounted to putting the mind "on the shelf" so that it might "renew" its "edge." [36] Lazing was the first stage of rebirth, a euphoria with a chosen comrade (as contrasted with the unchosen mother), the first stage of a new family and society able to evaluate the purposes and conduct of those into which man was born and able to mock their shams. Just so, in *Roughing It*, Twain and a friend lazed apart from society at Lake Tahoe, eventually engaging playfully in an elaborate mock of commercialism and competition.[37]

[33] *Writings*, vol. II, pp. 333–334, vol. III, p. 192. The first paragraph of *Tom Sawyer Abroad* is worth quoting: "Do you reckon Tom Sawyer was satisfied after all them adventures? . . . No, he wasn't. It only just p'isoned him for more. That was all the effect it had. You see . . . everybody hurrah'd and shouted and made us heroes, and that was what Tom Sawyer had always been hankering to be."

[34] *Mark Twain's Letters to Will Bowen*, ed. T. Hoernberger (Austin: University of Texas, 1941), pp. 23–24.

[35] William Dean Howells, *My Mark Twain* (New York: Harper, 1910), p. 30.

[36] Kaplan, *Mr. Clemens and Mark Twain*, pp. 49–50, 135.

[37] *Roughing It* (Hartford: American Publishing Co., 1901), pp. 173–177.

Repeat the point: this "rebirth" was not something done once and for all. It was a permanent need of man, if he were to avoid both excessive involvement with society and the trap of self. Never attracted by the idea of portraying Huck and Tom as adults, Twain did toy with the idea of having them die together at sixty.[38]

One point deserves emphasis: Twain saw fraternity as a human need, but because it depends more than others on conscious choice and action, its satisfaction demands that the individual feel the need. Rightly understood, human experience taught the need for fraternity. But experience was a very uncertain teacher: Twain described the cat who, having sat on a hot stove lid, avoids stove lids hot or cold, and he drew the moral that we should get the wisdom from any experience—but only the wisdom, not the folly.[39] The discrimination, however, is obviously difficult, and the impact of even the most educational experiences could be distorted by a society which left the individual in a state of prideful egotism and allowed or encouraged him to hate and fear his fellows, making his life one of endless anxiety.

The death of beloved persons is an experience which might be expected to teach the universal finitude of the human condition. Twain saw man's ability to sacrifice, to die for his fellows, as one of the unique traits of the species, and one mark of fraternity was its ability to govern life by values higher than survival. For most men, however, Twain knew that remorse felt at the death of a brother conceals fratricidal motives. He was only too aware that his guilt at his brother's death was based on an egotistic conceit: that his brother's death had taken place to punish Twain. Such "guilt" is cherished because it insulates the individual from the fact of mortality, allowing him the illusion of a cosmos centered on an (immortal) self. That psychological tendency surely bespeaks the ability of men to escape the lessons of experience.[40]

The great attractions of nomadry, war, and violence, Twain also saw as without necessary impact on the individual character. The duel he regarded as simply absurd. In order to win admiration and honor

[38] *Mr. Clemens and Mark Twain*, p. 307.

[39] *Following the Equator* (Hartford: American Publishing Co., 1897), vol. I, p. 125.

[40] *Life on the Mississippi* (New York: Bantam, 1945), pp. 363–371; *Autobiography*, pp. 33, 44–46.

from women and from a society steeped in romantic foolery (and especially the novels of Walter Scott), men who respected one another killed rather than died for each other, and learned nothing from the event.

War had a spurious appeal. Sometimes inevitable, it did unite the individual to the political community and to his fellows momentarily, under the impact of common peril. Yet war was deforming: it made death seem routine, and the survival of one while others died broke the "community" of danger. War helped the survivors to remain isolated from experience; it preserved and encouraged the impulse which often lay behind war, the romantic's desire to defy death.[41]

Loneliness might be thought a better teacher. Not so threatening to the individual, loneliness was the supreme curse which should drive men to seek their fellows. Twain had experienced it often enough. Yet when he journeyed West seeking a kind of brotherhood, he found the gold fields populated by isolated men. The desperate loneliness of these uprooted men could not overcome the fact that the miner was engaged in a search for gold in which his fellows were competitors. There was a forced congeniality, an ephemeral community, but Twain saw through these to the rivalry and suspicion that lay beneath. The Western miners, he wrote, were the "living dead," sacrificed "on the altar of the golden calf." [42]

Before men could find brothers, they must acknowledge a need for them; this in turn demanded that men wake from the dream of self-sufficiency. Outside events were powerless in themselves to disturb the slumber of the heart. The awakening of men must begin inside: men must destroy the heart's dream for themselves. This was so painful that it could result only from desolation, a personal sense of defeat and despair that might lead men to prefer mortality to the living death of egotism, for that preference was a necessary precondition of both fraternity and humanity.

Desolation was no guarantee; it was a momentary opportunity.

---

[41] On dueling and war, see *Autobiography*, p. 295; *Life on the Mississippi*, pp. 135–149; *Huckleberry Finn*, pp. 135–149; J. M. Cox, "Walt Whitman, Mark Twain and the Civil War"; and G. H. Orians, "Walter Scott, Mark Twain and the Civil War," *SAQ*, XL (1941), pp. 342–359.

[42] *Roughing It*, pp. 310–311, and *Short Stories*, pp. 266–272. Especially useful on this period is Lynn, *Mark Twain and Southwestern Humor*.

The emotional resilience of man is great, and the lesson of futility passes quickly. The moment of desolation, however, provided a chance for the mind and moral sense to establish enough ascendancy over the heart to teach it something, if not to become sovereign over it. In the world of personal experience, Twain wrote, the "turning-point of my life" was not Caesar's crossing of the Rubicon—it came rather when Twain, as a young adolescent, was isolated to protect him from measles.

> I was a prisoner. My soul was steeped in this awful dreariness—and in fear. At some time or other every day and every night a sudden shiver shook me to the marrow and I said to myself, "There, I've got it! And I shall die." Life on these miserable terms was not worth living and at last I made up my mind to get the disease one way or the other. I escaped from the house and went to the house of a neighbor where a playmate of mine was very ill with the malady. . . . I was discovered and sent back into captivity. But I had the disease; they could not take that from me.

The central phrase is almost buried in the tale: "at last I made up my mind." Reflection leads to the realization that life as simple survival is a prison and not worth defending: better to die with one's fellows than to live alone in fear.

The world of the child and of mothers yields to the world of adults and men when mischief becomes serious action, when romantic daring becomes a courageous realism. At such a point, a wise mother realizes that the training of the heart is as complete as can be hoped: that the child that has been is ready for second birth.

> When I got well, my mother closed my school career and apprenticed me to a printer. She was tired of trying to keep me out of mischief, and the adventure of the measles decided her to put me into more masterful hands than hers.[43]

The extremity of desolation is risky at best, providing only a fumbling, unguided opportunity for self-education. At worst, it involves the threat of a final, despairing rejection of life. The situation would be better if desolation could be taught; the experience would be more certain of occurrence, more subject to guidance and control. Twain hoped for the better result through the use of his two techniques, humor and romance.

[43] *Favorite Works*, p. 1131.

Humor is ridicule, and the pointed "story" is always directed at the audience itself. To laugh is to admit, and collective laughter implies a collective ridicule of what has been admitted. The "oral tradition" of the American West employed comedy as a means of uniting men by overcoming their fears (a theme often explicit in Twain's work), and the collective element became stronger when the humorist, like Twain, made himself the butt of the joke.[44] To offer oneself as an object of ridicule is a kind of leadership, a courage by which pride is sacrificed (though hopefully only for a moment) to free the community from its anxieties. Indeed, humor is a distinct variety of ridicule: it is ridicule in which the ridiculed individual participates. The desolation of humor is not one from which he can separate himself. In the conflict of one man and a society, humor is a feeble weapon, but so are all swords in that contest; humor may be among the best.

Romance too has its uses, as Hawthorne had known. Romance tempts pride as humor beguiles it. The reader—especially the younger reader—is prone to identify with the heroes of romance, figures who seem the mirror of his own dreams. Once that psychological identification is achieved, the reader may be subjected in the person of the hero to desolation, only more useful because it is deeply felt.

Moreover, humor and romance have advantages, as weapons of attack, which Twain could hardly ignore. They are indirect, capable of disguise. They not only lessen the danger to the assailant, they permit a due regard for the virtues which may be present in a tolerably decent society. They are the best political means to achieving great ends: preserving while destroying, taking due account of the fact that revolutions are made by men shaped by the society they overthrow, and insisting that genuine revolution requires a change in the revolutionist. Humor and romance are the tools of Twain's variety of political man: the conservative revolutionary.

"We were comrades and not comrades . . ."

Twain's political behavior defies conventional categories. A reformer, he satirized civil service bureaucracy; a mugwump ("pure from the marrow out"), he supported General Grant for a third term.

---

[44] H. D. Duncan, *Culture and Democracy* (Totowa, N.J.: Bedminster, 1965), pp. 44–45.

Small wonder that the effort of critics to discover Twain's "ideology" has produced a bewildering diversity of interpretations: they cover every point in the political spectrum from Andrews' view of Twain as a reactionary anti-democrat to the school which regards him as a precursor of American Marxism.[45]

In part, these studies suffer from the worst shortcomings of criticism. Louis Budd, for example, refers to the "One Million Pound Banknote" as a homily proving that penniless young men could succeed through credit; in fact, of course, the story is a satire on men's irrational veneration of currency.[46]

A greater fault, however, is that these analyses underrate the importance of the political in Twain's thought. One who probes as deeply as Twain did into the nature of man and political things is not likely to accept passively the doctrines and categories of another thinker, much less those of a socioeconomic group. Rather, he is likely to invent his own.[47]

An experienced political reporter, Twain's insight into the workings of American politics was shrewd. He and Warner wrote in *The Gilded Age*, for example, that the citizen's neglect of primary elections forfeited effective political power. As a citizen and advocate, he praised trade unions for collective efforts to relieve oppression; he gave generous assistance to the unemployed; he ridiculed the existence of formal laws against suicide while other, more powerful, laws condemned men to "committing half-suicide and being other-half murdered by overwork." [48]

The attempt to interpret Twain by his political behavior is almost certain to fail. His sense of political obligation would compel him to fulfill the citizen's duty of participation, but increasingly he saw the alternatives offered by American politics as too narrow to achieve important results. He damned Bret Harte for his failure to vote in 1876 and for his lack of "passion for his country," but he added:

[45] For two examples, see Andrews, *Nook Farm*, pp. 110–143, and Philip Foner, *Mark Twain: Social Critic* (New York: International Publishers, 1958).

[46] Louis J. Budd, *Mark Twain: Social Philosopher* (Bloomington: University of Indiana Press, 1962), p. 158.

[47] French, *Mark Twain and the Gilded Age*, p. 240.

[48] Budd, *Mark Twain*, p. 52; Foner, *Mark Twain*, p. 165; Paul J. Carter, "Mark Twain and the American Labor Movement," *NEQ*, XXX (1957), pp. 382–388.

I was an ardent Hayes man but that was natural, for I was pretty young at the time. I have since convinced myself that the political opinions of a nation are of next to no value, in any case, but that what little rag of value they possess is to be found among the old, rather than among the young.[49]

The defect of the young is their enthusiasm, their failure to realize the limitations and the certain disappointments of political life, especially the political life of nineteenth-century America. More and more, Twain saw the evils of American life as too universal, too basic, too rooted in history and culture to be remedied by simply changing programs or men.

The bankers and industrialists appear as characters in Twain's work, but he was as interested—perhaps more interested—in the middle classes and the petty speculators who displayed the same traits as the great. Twain was, moreover, early in describing the degrading effects of poverty (and specifically, modern poverty) on the human soul.[50]

America, Twain argued, had faced its "life choice" after the Civil War in deciding how to employ the opportunities opened up by the Gold Rush, the abolition of slavery, and the end of Southern political power. Twain was certain it had chosen wrongly: Americans had opted for a life without moral limitation or direction, a dynamism whose only purpose was the filling up of open spaces, the addition of power over nature and over men.[51] More and more, Twain would see the result as almost foreordained: as he delved into the American past and its European roots, he saw not a single choice destroying an idyllic past, but a process long in the making. The idyllic prewar world became merely another dreadful present, seen through the glasses of nostalgia.

The result was a nation of increasing impersonality in which businessman and worker no longer enjoyed personal relations, both their lives being shaped by the nonhuman process of the market. Twain saw the cities—especially New York—with eyes very different

[49] *Autobiography*, pp. 330–331.
[50] French, *Mark Twain and the Gilded Age*, pp. 218–219; Foner, *Mark Twain*, pp. 158–159; Kaplan, *Mr. Clemens and Mark Twain*, pp. 158–159; Branch, *Literary Apprenticeship of Mark Twain*, p. 190.
[51] *Letters from the Earth*, pp. 107–111, *Writings*, V, pp. 176–177.

from Whitman's: men lonely among multitudes, aimless, homeless, driven by nervous tension, excited but unable to know joy.[52] As description and prescription, his account in *Roughing It* of his experience while unemployed and in debt in Gold-Rush San Francisco is graphic:

> Misery loves company. Now and then at night, in out-of-the-way, dimly lighted places, I found myself happening on another child of misfortune. He looked so seedy and forlorn, so homeless and forsaken, that I yearned toward him as a brother. I wanted to claim kinship with him and go about and enjoy our wretchedness together. The drawing toward each other must have been mutual; at any rate, we got to falling together oftener, though still seemingly by accident; and although we did not speak or evince any recognition I think the dull anxiety passed out of both of us when we saw each other, and then for several hours we would idle along contentedly, wide apart, and glancing furtively in at home lights and fireside gatherings, out of the night shadows, and very much enjoying our dumb companionship.
>   Finally we spoke, and were inseparable after that. For our woes were identical, almost. . . .[53]

Twain's complaint was that America lacked any civic communion, any real politics. She failed as a moral teacher: if anything, American life exaggerated egotism and pride. Twain did not develop elaborate schemes for social welfare, for example, because he distrusted reform when it came "from the top down." Being convinced that society is shaped and that history is made by the mass and not by the few, that power resides—if only potentially—with the many, he was convinced that men could act to remedy their own condition. More important, he was convinced that only political life and action could result in change which would develop man's humanity. Individualism and fear forced men to lock up their most human needs and feelings: the inability to combine, the fear of the other, were responsible for the human comedy which depressed Twain most, men's cooperation in their own degradation. Even then, he found some grounds for hope.

> This was depressing—to a man with the dream of a republic in his head. It reminded me of . . . the "poor whites" of the South who

---

[52] F. Walker and G. E. Dane, *Mark Twain's Travels with Mr. Brown* (New York: Knopf, 1940), pp. 259–261; *Mr. Clemens and Mark Twain*, pp. 94–96.

[53] *Roughing It*, p. 430.

were always despised and frequently insulted by the slave-lords around them, and who owed their base condition simply to the presence of slavery . . . (yet) were pusillanimously ready to side with the slave-lords in all political moves for the . . . perpetuating of slavery, and did also finally shoulder their muskets and pour out their lives in an effort to prevent the destruction of that very institution which degraded them. And there was only one redeeming feature connected with that pitiful piece of history; and that was, that secretly the "poor white" did detest the slave-lord and did feel his own shame. That feeling was not brought to the surface but the fact that it was there and could have been brought out, under favoring circumstances, was something—in fact, it was enough; for it showed that a man is at bottom a man, after all, even if it doesn't show on the outside.[54]

Twain, "with the dream of a republic in his head," stated his aim to the British readers of *The Gilded Age*. Most voters, he wrote, were decent men; corruption had aroused them, and he proposed to agitate until citizens "made it the habit of their lives to attend to the politics of the country personally." [55] The agitation did indeed continue, although the hope (largely for foreign consumption) declined almost to the vanishing point.

This orientation helps account for the paradox that Twain, the opponent of "Grantism," supported Grant. Grant was a great man to Twain, and his tragedy was that he magnified the typical vices and virtues of Americans. Intellectual, energetic, intensely loyal, with great resources of moral strength, Grant was self-imprisoned by shyness and insecurity and lacked the fraternal relations necessary for personal and political clarity of thought and purpose. Yet the door to Grant's prison could be forced, through his sense of humor, his willingness to laugh at himself.[56] Moral reform would demand citizens who would never passively allow the development of "Grantism," but such a reform might also bring about the leadership of a Grant grown to his full stature.

In one sense, the defect of American life began in the family. Like all mothers, teachers of convention, American mothers taught an ethic of success and conformity.

---

[54] *Favorite Works*, p. 807.
[55] Cited in French, *Mark Twain and the Gilded Age*, p. 227.
[56] *Mr. Clemens and Mark Twain*, p. 227.

If people found it out, they would speak of you as an odd child, a strange child, and children would be disagreeable to you and give you nicknames. In this world one must be like everybody else if he doesn't want to provoke scorn or envy or jealousy. It is a great and fine distinction which has been born to you . . . but you will keep it a secret for mamma's sake, won't you? [57]

The Middle Ages, Twain hinted, had been defective in teaching the suppression of man's "feminine" side, hiding the desire for love and affection in the interest of status and power. American society, by contrast, forced woman to conceal her "male" active and purposive qualities. That suppression leads to a feeling of resentment at injustice, and women seek to bend their sons to a vicarious "righting" of their wrongs, vengeance wrought through their children's success. Paradoxically, this produces the "medieval" result: the mother's weapon is affection—and seeking to win it, sons become wanderers and nomads, losing their own "male" capacity for direction, using their talents in the service of a secret desire for affection and admiration. Other men, especially the father, become enemies who have "wronged" the mother, rather than friends and brothers.[58]

At the opposite pole of abstraction, the moral doctrines of America reinforced the result. Twain's most savage animus was directed at the teachings of "interest morality," the doctrine that "right pays and evil loses." The foundation of the "morality" of Sunday School tracts was an appeal to vanity, to hopes for power and fame.

Such a basis might be partly justified: appeals to the desire for honor were useful in teaching the emotions. Yet the morality of the tract was individualism and not virtue. Interest morality made no effort to teach nobility, and its pale utilitarianism was easily shattered. One could all too readily determine that the good were not always rewarded in this world.

Formal moral teaching inculcated three great falsehoods: (1) the "lie of bravado," which exalted the independent individual who needed no others and ruled by his strength and will alone; (2) the "lie of silent assertion," which contended that the world inevitably

[57] *Short Stories,* p. 426.
[58] *Ibid.,* pp. 39–42, 50–56, 424–429, 434–435; *Huckleberry Finn,* pp. 26–27, 130–134, 368–369.

tends to the good, and that therefore one is safely moral in asserting his own interest and neglecting moral duties; and (3) the "lie of virtuous ecstasy" in which men were taught to seek and claim a greater "purity" than they could achieve.

Perhaps most repugnant to Twain was the "virtue" of honesty, with its indifference to the character or good of the person addressed, its unconcern with results, and its total attention to the felt purity of the speaker himself. Indeed, as Twain was at pains to show in "The Man Who Corrupted Hadleyburg," "honesty" rested on an insecure foundation. Being based entirely on self-concern and self-indulgence, the truthfulness of Hadleyburg collapsed when it conflicted with individual hopes for gain.

American "morality" rested, in fact, on a fundamental deceit. It was not based on personal character but on the fear of being found out. Hence the American's admiration for the successful banditti of commerce and statecraft whose success allowed them to vaunt their amorality before the public as a proof of their emancipation from that basic fear.[59]

Yet Twain saw the American as deserving pity more than denunciation. The life of individualistic man had many fears and few joys. Individualistic man was compelled to fear the three things most inevitably a part of life: weakness and finitude; his fellows; death. Enslaved by fear, he was "determined" not by his own nature but by the environment alone, by the greatest force that could be brought to threaten him.

In a world of movement and change, men lost the sense of a bond with community. The cemetery, symbol of the relation between living and dead, which helped to make death familiar, became an object of fear and irreverent unconcern. The dead lost their "place" in man's life: he lost his bond with the past, his sense of continuity in time, and was left more and more alone.[60]

The vauntings of American life and thought were essentially a

[59] For Twain's criticisms of American morality, see *Short Stories*, pp. 6–9, 358, 369, 380, 387, 390–399, 516, and 472–488; *Damned Human Race*, pp. 28–35, 68; and *Autobiography*, p. 35. Twain sometimes wrote moralizing tales himself; in a notable example, false friends are punished and the truly loyal rewarded (*Short Stories*, pp. 337–342).

[60] *Short Stories*, pp. 32–39.

whistling in the graveyard, a series of desperate efforts to overcome fear and find security. The pursuit of wealth was guided by no idea of the uses of wealth, and hence became an infinite pursuit, joyless and futile. It could serve only to distract man from himself.

Science, in the hand of the American, became a new dogma, a foundation for efforts to deny human ignorance and claim certain knowledge. Doctrines of racial and cultural "superiority" seemed to grow worse with the passage of time. Imperialism and racism, to Twain, were symbolic of political decay. They represented a fear so great as to demand the ability to subjugate others, and also a sad effort by individualized man to find a bond with his fellows other than the bond of fear—which, given the nature of individualism, could be found only in common crime, the domination of others. Funston the conqueror, Twain commented sadly, had displaced Washington the liberator as the characteristic American hero.[61]

All this was painfully confirmed by politics. Democratic institutions, in a state lacking citizen community or any tie between individual and public, were empty formalities. Institutions were only curtains covering savage individualism, contributing to disenchantment with and to the impoverishment of political life.[62]

The satirist is a painter of anti-utopias, not a designer of ideal cities. In their preface to *The Gilded Age*, Twain and Warner referred to the "entirely ideal state of society" portrayed in the book, apologizing for the lack of "illustrative examples" for their tale in the real life of Americans (the book relies heavily on then-current news sensations). Ridicule points the way to right: Twain and Warner followed this facetious comment with a long list of civic virtues which they attributed to Americans. The darkest of anti-utopias suggests, negatively, the outline of an ideal.

The heavenly city of the Protestant ministry did not stir Twain's imagination; nor, he noted, did it excite most men. Twain's concern was obviously with the impact of the celestial city on the earthly; his objection was that, like American morality generally, heaven of-

[61] *Damned Human Race*, pp. 6–21, 45–49, 77–93; *Autobiography*, pp. 26–27, 376–377, 295. Puddn'head Wilson is recognized only because his technique enables the identification of physical identities; his wisdom as a detective of the soul is mocked.

[62] *Short Stories*, pp. 9–16, 16–22; *Autobiography*, pp. 60–63.

fered little incentive to virtue, though hell might provide a few barriers to vice. The preachers' heaven, Twain contended, fails in three ways: (1) it lacks sexuality; (2) it is unintellectual, without debate or conflict; and (3) it is universal, lacking racial and national distinctions. As a result, it can have no genuine appeal to men.[63]

It is easy enough to infer that a good state would have some place for sex and curiosity: these, after all, are the "twins" of Twain's psychology. The third "defect" of heaven is more puzzling, implying that a good state would not be based on universal fraternity. Yet Twain was certainly universal in his theory of man. In fact, partly in reaction against his early nativism and lingering prejudice, he had become almost philo-Semitic and a consistent supporter of Negro causes. His preoccupation with the "brotherhood of man" was sufficiently great for him to have used an abbreviation ("B of M") in his notebooks.[64] Rather, Twain's rejection of an undifferentiated heaven is based on his realization that men's need for close relations and affection makes social distance inevitable: a love for everyone is not a love for me.

Deeply concerned as Twain was with the effects of imperialism on the conquered, he was more concerned with what it revealed about and inflicted on the domestic polity. The extension of empire palliated the effects of egotism and inflamed the cause: it decreased the importance of citizen relations in favor of those between master and servant. When he wrote that it was curious that patriots could claim that all Americans were blood-brothers when they acknowledged no kinship with mankind, he was not urging Americans to feel the brotherhood of man: he was ridiculing "fraternal" pretensions based on an erroneous idea of human nature, an "affection" which can only be felt by conquering others.[65]

Twain's own heavenly city, developed in "Captain Stormfield's Visit to Heaven," had a virtue the earthly state could not possibly achieve: justice of a perfect character. In heaven, men were judged by their truly personal merits and talents, not by their achievements, which were largely the results of accident and environment.[66]

Even that impossible ideal had its earthly applications. Twain was

[63] Letters from the Earth, pp. 8–13; Autobiography, pp. 385–386.
[64] Budd, Mark Twain, pp. 189–190.
[65] Ibid., p. 181; Salomon, Twain and the Image of History, pp. 43, 108.
[66] Short Stories, pp. 587–590.

no equalitarian: he always felt that talent and virtue deserved reward. (This could hardly have been otherwise, given his feeling of the child's need for models.) He did insist that, as far as possible, the barriers to talent be removed. This was more than a devotion to the free market (a point often overlooked by the critics), because Twain included environment and rearing among the barriers. Nor did Twain simply advocate a leveling down. Believing that although the mass needed the example of the few, the possibilities open to the few were limited by the character of the mass, he insisted on elevating both as high as possible. His was, as Kaplan points out, a synthesis of democracy and elitism;[67] the unifying theme of that synthesis is man's nature and perfection, a political nature requiring the good state and demanding fraternity.

"Take the . . . relics and weave . . . romance"

Twain inherited the American belief in progress but grew to doubt it more and more, eventually abandoning it altogether. The doctrine had always warred with his idea of human nature, as Roger Salomon observes; and it was the latter that stood the test of time and analysis.[68]

Twain had always detested teleological theories of history, finally identifying such creeds as "lies of silent assertion." This opposition was primarily moral, opposed to the tendency of ideas of inevitable progress to moralize indifference or justify evil. In the end, this moral position came to coincide with Twain's view of the facts: history destined men for an end far from utopian.

He had once hoped that man's unchanging nature might be improved by a perfecting of institutions, laws, and technology; progress in the human environment would mean progress in behavior and in character. Even then, his view of technology had been mixed. Americans, he wrote in *Innocents Abroad*, admired technological progress primarily because they were ignorant of art and culture.[69] With time, and with his own observations of society and research into history (he had read the major classical and modern historians with care), he

---

[67] *Mr. Clemens and Mark Twain*, p. 109.
[68] *Twain and the Image of History*, pp. 4, 58–59.
[69] *Writings*, vol. I, pp. 242, 262.

lost whatever hope he had possessed. Man's baser nature had not only survived, it was a powerful, even a guiding, force in modern history. Consequently "progress" was only providing men with increasing opportunities for iniquity.

Twain always valued the fact that modern times, as he saw them, were more open to new ideas, more receptive to imagination. Yet he saw a danger in that liberation. Rebuking the novelist Elinor Glyn, Twain said that:

> The laws of Nature . . . plainly made every human being a law unto himself, (but) we must steadfastly refuse to obey those laws, and we must as steadfastly stand by the conventions which ignore them, since the statutes furnish us peace, fairly good government, and stability and are therefore better for us than the . . . confusion and disorder and anarchy if we should adopt them. I said her book was an assault upon certain old and well-established and wise conventions and that it would not find many friends and indeed would not deserve many.[70]

However, as late as 1897, Twain could write of modern times and of the effects of technology as being uncertain, dialectic in nature. Life had become "easy and difficult, convenient and awkward, happy and horrible . . . grand and trivial, an indispensable blessing and an unimaginable curse." [71]

The uncertainty may have been calculated for its moral effect. Imperialism made clear to Twain that the power made available by civilization would be misused, that it had become servant to man's desire for dominion and to his hatred of life and the world. In his manuscript "Eddypus" he preserved the dialectic language: modern society was a "splendid nightmare" whose genesis in "hell or heaven" was still unclear. But the preface describes the manuscript as being discovered a thousand years later, with the world in an age of darkness. The forces which had created civilization would end by smashing it: material progress had "opened the road and prepared the way for the destroyer." [72]

Twain's opinions as to the nature of the final collapse varied,

---

[70] *Autobiography*, p. 386; see also *Writings*, vol. XIV, p. 201, vol. XXII, pp. 329–332.

[71] *Writings*, vol. XXIX, pp. 202–203.

[72] "Eddypus" is discussed in Salomon, *Twain and the Image of History*. On Twain's view of Mrs. Eddy, see Kaplan, *Mr. Clemens and Mark Twain*, pp. 326, 348, 366, 383.

but not his conviction that it impended (once, foretokening Orwell, he guessed it would arrive in 1985). In *Letters from the Earth* he suggested a technician dictator who would use a secret weapon to destroy himself and a continent. "Eddypus" was less conventional, perhaps more perceptive; he discerned a new barbarism dominated by Christian Science and the teachings of Mary Baker Eddy. The logic behind this improbable result was clear: it lay in the inner meaning of the human effort to conquer nature, the desire to deny the outer world and man's mortality. Eddy's teachings had the effect of denying matter and death as well as other men: they fulfilled the pattern set by *The Mysterious Stranger*, giving religious form to the temptation of Satan.[73]

Twain never published these gloomy prophecies, for the obvious reason that he doubted their moral effect. Prophecies were folly in many ways: "A prophet doesn't have to have brains." The future remained partly open, however narrow the doorway, to human intervention and action; moreover, human ignorance was a block to any certainty about future events. Notably, unlike other imaginative writers of the century (including his friend Howells), when Twain wrote of history the past and not the future was his subject.

The historical record was not of primary concern to Twain. He admitted he changed the facts where necessary, and he never doubted the justification: "The office of history is to furnish serious and important facts that *teach*," he emphasized.[74] His researches sought for style and tone more than accuracy, and his preference for the past was due to its superiority as a vehicle of moral education.

The past has passed: it cannot encourage the sort of complacency that writings about the future easily may. Moreover, the past has occurred, and men can more easily identify with and be moved by examples and environments which they know to be possible than by those they merely hope will transpire.

The danger of the past lies in the possibility that men discontented with the present may turn to ancient romance, impoverishing both

[73] Salomon, *Twain and the Image of History*, p. 138.
[74] Twain, *Joan of Arc* (New York: Harper, 1926), p. 372. On Twain's use of history, see Kaplan, *Mr. Clemens and Mark Twain*, pp. 170, 246; *Damned Human Race*, pp. 28–35, 98–99; and *The Prince and the Pauper* (Philadelphia: Winston, 1937), notes 8, p. 270, and 10, p. 271.

present and future by nostalgia. The danger was one to which American society, with its prosaic if not sordid present, was peculiarly prone; hence Twain's hostility to the misuse of romance and the perverse teaching that he attributed to Walter Scott and Fenimore Cooper.

The danger, of course, only makes a correct view of romance more necessary, for its possible uses are great. Given the unchanging nature of man, Twain saw history following a "law of periodic repetition," rising from and returning to the permanent base of human folly. This somewhat depressing theory, however, implies that most of the follies of men have taken place at some point in the past. Through the bond of identification with the tale, men (and even more, adolescents) can live out in imagination the law of repetition: it may thus be possible for them to learn lessons which it might otherwise be merely the duty of professional historians to record.

Twain's use of history is illustrated by *Joan of Arc,* otherwise one of his weakest books. Twain presents the official record of Joan's life as reliable: it is the only story in history, he asserts, that "comes to us under oath." Yet Twain was aware of the political motives which influenced the testimony and the record of Joan's trials. Moreover, Twain does not present himself as the author of the story: his ostensible role is as "translator" of the record left by the "Sieur de Conte," a childhood friend and partisan of Joan's.

Much, then, turns on the reliability of the supposed author. Early in the book, discussing an account of the appearance of a dragon, "De Conte" reveals a belief in the beasts. He is "skeptical," but his skepticism is restricted to a doubt that the dragon could have been blue: his own opinion is that since dragons have always been gold, that was certainly its color. Hence, his comment that "*evidence* (Twain's italics) is the bones of an opinion" serves only to emphasize his status as a sincere but credulous observer.[75]

For Twain uses "De Conte" to tamper with the "record" whose accuracy he has lauded. Twain took most of the historical material for *Joan* from the sentimental presentation of Janet Tuckey, often borrowing material verbatim (a fairly good sign that that side of the story did not interest him much); but he has "De Conte" explicitly dis-

[75] *Joan of Arc,* pp. 7–8.

regard it once, asserting that "Joan would not threaten a comrade's life." [76] (He also modifies other passages so as to change their effect.)

In fact, although Twain praises Joan as a "unique" and nearly "flawless" character, his feelings about her were ambiguous. He paired her once with Martin Luther as having a temperament "made of asbestos," and although she is made to express some of Twain's favorite heresies in *Joan*, she is also assigned one of the religious doctrines he hated most: that the invasion and suffering of France is a punishment for sin (even De Conte is allowed to doubt that). In his papers, he was explicit: Joan's voices were "idiots" and she herself a "heroic soul" who, given her times, could only be elevated by "base superstition." [77]

That much emerges in the book. Joan, like her playmates, is "well stocked with narrownesses and prejudices," especially in politics and religion (she shares their belief in fairies, for example). The vision which reveals her mission and its details is vitiated by the fact that Joan has already related both in a semi-conscious daydream. De Conte "sees" her vision, but his evidence has already been discounted by the dragon incident.[78]

Twain's view and intent are made clear by an otherwise pointless diversion, in which De Conte and his fellows are besought for aid against ghosts, pierce an ancient false wall, and find only a rusty sword and a rotten fan. There is no interpretation. Twain comments only: "Take the pathetic relics, and weave about them the romance of the dungeon's . . . inmates as best you can." [79] The personal element of history, its psychological and human meaning, is hidden from us in any case. It is legitimate, then, to take the bare factual outline which records provide and "weave . . . romance" for the education of contemporary men.

In *Joan*, Twain accomplishes this by the device of a double story: the chapters from the historical record are alternated with a tale of Joan and her childhood friends that is Twain's own. In this tale, one of the principal figures is Paladin, an incredible boaster who invents tales of imagined feats of valor. Yet through his faith in Joan he is able to translate these falsehoods, which he "sincerely" believes, into action.

[76] *Ibid.*, p. 228.
[77] *Ibid.*, pp. 22–23, 31–32, 491–492; *Favorite Works*, p. 1135.
[78] *Joan of Arc*, pp. 10, 11, 56–58, 76.
[79] *Ibid.*, p. 245.

De Conte comments that "We may go on half our life not knowing that such a thing was in us, when . . . all we needed was something to turn up that would call for it." Joan, he asserts, had a "seeing eye" which discerned the true abilities of men; but more important, she had the "creating mouth"—men believed her when she spoke.[80]

Joan, in other words, was able to galvanize the courage and patriotism of the French not because she saw these qualities in them, but simply because they believed her: she gave them the courage to be themselves. Notably, the expression of De Conte's poetic talent is called up not by Joan but by his love for a girl: the "power" is not something Joan possessed in herself, but because of men's relations to her.

Moreover, De Conte observes that the secret things which may be called up are both "gifts" and "diseases": as a Joan calls for the former, so a bad model or environment evokes the "disease" of the human spirit. And it is critical to Twain's argument that Joan's France was a "diseased" environment out of which she was able to move men.[81]

Twain's explanations of Joan are quite naturalistic. At one point, he explains her military "talent" with the simple comment that French troops could win whenever they had a unified command, which Joan alone was able to provide (the inefficient habit of divided command Twain traces, clearly, to court intrigue and suspicion of military leaders).[82] The critical issue is Joan's authority, her ability to inspire men and to claim a single command. Twain explains this, in part, in similar terms: Joan knew that it was essential for the king to be crowned, because consecration gave him authority in the eyes of the priests. The priests in turn were critical because they were revered and accepted as authorities by peasants, the base of the nation. The "whole story" of Joan of Arc is, in fact, that she "was a peasant": she understood the religious nature of the peasant's view of authority and the necessity of appealing to it.[83]

Yet Joan is a failure. Her aims are to infuse her followers with patriotism, but the nature of her claim to authority is such that she inspires trust only in her person. (Partly this is the nature of peasants too; Twain comments earlier that only visible, felt events, not ab-

[80] *Ibid.*, pp. 180, 182, 211.
[82] *Ibid.*, p. 290.
[81] *Ibid.*, pp. 296–297.
[83] *Ibid.*, pp. 337–338.

stractions, truly move a simple people.) Her failure is that she cannot overcome the "disease" of the environment, the problem of caste, and an inheritance of betrayal and treachery. She does not inspire men with a loyalty to each other, and her movement collapses with her own demise. (Twain delights in having De Conte make predictions about the undying gratitude of the French to Joan. Twain then notes that the pledges involved have been revoked: Joan has failed to change men, even as regards her memory.) [84]

De Conte observes, hesitantly and wonderingly, that peasants are people. He predicts—this time accurately enough—that the peasants will someday find it out and insists on being heard and counted. [85] It is Twain's way of pointing out one logical means to the fulfillment of Joan's mission: a revolution. Twain would always defend the Revolution of 1789 as a landmark in the struggle for humanity. Its excesses, he realized, reflected only the continuing "disease" of the past environment which Joan had been unable to remove. Her heroism, when properly reconstructed, is a model for the young, but the heroic individual produces no lasting change in men unless he can build for them the relations of citizens and brothers.

A Connecticut Yankee contains Twain's sharpest contrast of the two "ages," that of faith and that of modernity. Obviously, its status as "history" is dubious: the manuscript is given Twain by a dying man, and it is hardly clear that it represents more than a dream. It may in fact be no more than an extreme case of romanticism, a nostalgic withdrawal. Merlin, in the story, makes Hank Morgan sleep until the nineteenth century. But as the caricatures of the original edition make clear, Twain identified Merlin with Tennyson, author of *The Idylls of the King*: Merlin's "potion" in the story may be no more than an inversion of the fact, a reality in which Tennyson's "potions" sent men wandering in the past.

This, of course, is speculation. It is clear, however, that Twain had more than one contemporary figure in mind for his story. He drew the idea for *A Connecticut Yankee* in part from a suggestion by Andrew Carnegie in *Triumphant Democracy* that technological know-how could have transformed the ages of the past as it inevitably would, in the industrialist's view, shape the present. There

---

[84] *Ibid.*, pp. 53, 416; see also pp. 223–224, 360, 419.
[85] *Ibid.*, pp. 374–375.

is more than one analogy: Carnegie engaged in a crusade for a British Republic and against the nobles and the Church. Moreover, Morgan's first response to his Arthurian environment is to see himself as a man without competitors who can "boss the country inside three months." [86]

Morgan surely has the technological knowledge and ingenuity of a prodigy. He is also a fool—a "perfect ignoramus," Twain told his illustrator. Morgan's basic desire appears to be a need to win admiration: there are constant references to his desire to produce "effects," to be striking, to impress. (In this, of course, he fits two models: Twain's picture of the inner psyche of modern man, and that of my hypothetical picture of the "author": a frustrated modern man who turns to the past with nostalgia, seeking what the present lacks.)

His worst follies are demonstrated in his lack of knowledge of man and society. Carnegie-like, Morgan believes that Arthurian man can be reshaped in "man factories" and by technological change.[87] Only the event educates him, and that not much. He is defeated because the Church has shaped Arthurian man and because it has never surrendered control of the institutions that symbolize the highest meaning and reality of human life: the rituals of birth, marriage, and death. The technologist is blind to the facts of human nature.

Moreover, Twain explicitly departs from Malory at a critical point: it is not the guilty love of Guenever and Launcelot that produces the final tragedy. The affair only makes it come earlier: "It would have come on your own account by and by. . . ." What produces the crisis, in fact, is a modern institution: Launcelot enrages his rivals by cornering the stock market.[88]

Even Arthur's death and the kingdom's dissolution do not educate Morgan; they provide the opportunity to proclaim his desired republic. When this in turn does not move the people, science still does not concede: modern man must fight out the battle to the last pointless carnage, resting hope on the destructive power of the instruments at his command. The result is the ultimate folly and irony:

[86] *Writings,* XIV, pp. 60–61.
[87] *Writings,* XIV, p. 147.
[88] *Favorite Works,* pp. 866–867.

the very victory of technology is its defeat, for the Boss and his followers would inevitably perish from the diseases arising from the masses of dead that surround them. (Merlin's intervention is in this sense gratuitous.) The end of the effort to change the past by modern technology and modern man is a senseless apocalypse.[89] The case is equally clear, however, that, given modern man's defective understanding, little better result can be expected in the present. *A Connecticut Yankee* is in fact a version of Twain's own stark verdict on the course of modern history, thinly covered by the beguiling veil of romance.

"It's a philosophy, you see . . ."

Twain's use of history was closely connected to his idea of fraternity. He was fond of juxtaposing stories based on different periods of time, and his "Two Little Tales," for example, teaches the lesson that modern faith in formal institutions and procedures is foolish compared with an "ancient" understanding of the role of friendship and fraternity in human life.[90]

Easily the most important of these paired stories are *Huckleberry Finn* and *The Prince and the Pauper*. Written at about the same time, Twain appears to have considered printing the two inside a single cover but was dissuaded by Mrs. Clemens, who thought *The Prince* too superior to be combined with *Huck*.[91] It is because the parallelism of the two books is ignored that critics, despite their admiration for *Huckleberry Finn*, find it full of mysterious "faults" like the reintroduction of Tom Sawyer at the end of the book. As is so often the case with Twain, the "fault" illuminates his teaching and intent.

The four boys are two almost identical pairs. Huck and Tom Canty are both children of poverty, pursued by bestial fathers; Tom Sawyer and the Prince differ mainly in that the Prince is an actual

[89] Smith's suggestion that Morgan fails because he is an "American Adam" inadequate to manage a complex industrial order (*Mark Twain's Fable of Progress*, p. 104) is bizarre in view of the denouement. Blues (*Mark Twain and the Community*, p. 39) is much closer to the point.

[90] *Short Stories*, pp. 399–408.

[91] Walter Blair, "When Was Huckleberry Finn Written?," *AL*, XXX (1958), pp. 1–25; Brooks, *Ordeal of Mark Twain*, p. 124.

prince with a royal father. For most of the story, however, the Prince's regal dreams are as fantastic as Tom's.

One difference seems to exist between the books: Prince Edward and Tom Canty are said to have an uncanny resemblance to each other. The "twin" theme, frequent in Twain's writing, is almost always intended to suggest the dual quality of human nature. In *The Prince and the Pauper*, Canty dreams of princeliness amid poverty; the Prince is delighted by the "natural" existence poverty permits. The attraction of an unknown way of life which fills the shortcomings of present existence—at least in imagination—is the mainspring of romance, and Roger Salomon is perceptive in writing that Canty and the Prince are "clouded by the same chimera of false romance that fills the imagination of Tom Sawyer." [92] In fact, they suggest the two sides of Tom's divided mind: his romantic dreams, and his attraction to Huck Finn. The theme of resemblance, twinship, and identity is clearly present in *Huckleberry Finn*. Not only does Huck "pass" for Tom, as Canty does for the Prince; when identified with Tom he remarks that it was "like being born again" and that he "was so glad to find out who I really was." [93] There is, then, a strong suggestion that Canty, the Prince, and Huck are all parts of a single human being, and that person is Tom Sawyer.

The books are similar in still another detail. One of the protagonists is left alone in the world of romance. (The fact that Canty's world is real both compels and allows Twain to devote considerable attention to it.) The other is excluded from that world, left in a grim environment, accompanied by an "elder brother." The characters are reversed: the Prince plays Huck's role, but Jim is hardly Miles Hendon. For the moment, the similarity is enough: even where the stories differ, they converge. Miles Hendon, the unjustly disinherited aristocrat, is a close parallel to Tom's vision of Jim as the "man in the iron mask."

The two boys in each book represent the dual qualities of a single individual and symbolize the twin temptations that may beset a boy in middle-class and respectable American society: the retreat to nature, the flight to romance. Tom Sawyer plays an offstage role

[92] *Twain and the Image of History*, p. 158.
[93] *Writings*, vol. XIII, p. 310; see also *The Prince and the Pauper*, pp. 7–9, 17–19.

because he is the object of the lesson; Twain was surely aware that children of nature do not read books. The technique in both books is to follow the path indicated by the two idylls, hoping to transcend both by suggesting the genuine highroad to humanity.

The sharpest difference between the books is that of setting. *The Prince and the Pauper* begins with the sharp contrasts of aristocratic society, *Huckleberry Finn* with an undifferentiated, small-town, middle-class respectability. The basic motives of *Huckleberry Finn* are established by the desire of both boys to escape from the restraint and tedium of their environment.

There is no doubt of the defect of Tom Sawyer's method of escape. Fantasy is a world of dreams only, foolish when it acts out its dreams in reality. It poses no danger to society, and it is tolerated, albeit with some exasperation. Tom, like Huck, is always aware of its unreality, secretly relying on his ability to return to the security and affection of family and society; Jim is really free, and one can attend one's own funeral. Middle-class society encourages romantic dreaming, a play world without choice, responsibility, or confrontation with life. Tom Sawyer must be seen when a boy to have charm. In adulthood, he would (as several critics note) resemble Twain's brother Orion, protected by his family, dreaming ineffectual dreams of glory.[94]

Huck's flight to "natural" conditions is quite as inadequate. The world beneath respectable society is one of brutality and low cunning, where Pap struggles with his own fears and the Duke and Dauphin beguile the trusting. There is an idyllic side to nature, as there is to romance: the raft combines affection and freedom from responsibility. Yet the result of escaping responsibility in favor of what is "handiest" is a loss of direction which results in imprisonment by the forces of the environment. The raft *drifts* and is impelled "down the river" into slavery; captivity first by the Duke and Dauphin and Jim's eventual return to slavery are the results of the idyll.[95] (Notably, Twain's voyage downriver in *Life on the Missis-*

[94] *Autobiography*, pp. 92–94, 152, 240–245; *Twain-Howells Letters*, vol. I, p. 97; Blues, *Mark Twain and the Community*, pp. 1–10.
[95] On the defects of the two "escapes," see *Huckleberry Finn*, pp. 14–15, 115, 118, 248, 270–273, 279, 287–288, 296–298, 313–314, 351; Louis Leary, "Tom and Huck: Innocence on Trial," *VQ*, XXX (1954), pp. 417–430; Smith, *Mark Twain: Development of a Writer*, p. 134.

sippi reminded him increasingly of the horrors of prewar Southern society.)[96]

The "natural child" may be charming; he is less than delightful as a man. Tom Canty is not the pure child of nature (any more than Huck is); he has received affection from his mother and education from Father Andrew. Yet despite his "common-sense" wisdom and humility, Canty develops a taste for power which makes him forgetful not only of the Prince's plight but of that of his mother and sisters. Though he is redeemed by a glimpse of his mother, the moral is clear: left to himself "natural man" drifts along the channel of social forces, and the best that can be expected is the sort of decent respectability that Canty eventually acquires.[97]

This drift is a central reason for the reappearance of Tom Sawyer. Natural man comes under the governance of the man of ideas, even if the ideas are foolish: Huck accepts Tom's direction, Canty yields gladly to that of the Prince. The strength of untutored nature is in emotion and the perception of concrete cases (Tom Canty, for example, excels in judging cases-at-law). Huck's affection for Jim leads him to defy convention and to risk hell for a friend, surrendering the "handiest" course for a more human one. Yet Huck does not doubt the morality of slavery; his presumption that he will "go to Hell" bespeaks the opposite. Tom Sawyer, however, conceives the play-question of Jim's liberation in terms of moral right: an unjustly imprisoned monarch must be freed. In that sense, Sawyer's fantasy comes closer to the truth than Huck's "realism," whatever its other shortcomings.[98]

The failure of the boys' paths, however, is only half the story: taken together, *Huckleberry Finn* and *The Prince and the Pauper* suggest a better road for the American. For American society is clearly superior. The follies of regality are revealed in typical burlesque, the injustice of feudalism is portrayed vividly. America does well by the majority of men: much of *Huckleberry Finn* suggests

[96] Kaplan, *Mr. Clemens and Mark Twain*, p. 243.

[97] *The Prince and the Pauper*, pp. 231–232, 237–238. See also Robert Regan, *Unpromising Heroes: Mark Twain and His Characters* (Berkeley and Los Angeles: University of California Press, 1966), p. 149.

[98] *Huckleberry Finn*, pp. 86–87, 104–111, 148–149, 160, 351; Branch, *The Literary Apprenticeship of Mark Twain*, p. 202.

the decency and kindness of ordinary men and women, qualities that are demonstrated rarely in *The Prince and the Pauper* (notably, mostly among the middle class).[99]

However, monarchical society has definite advantages as a literary setting, besides its greater opportunity for contrast. In Twain's mythological Tudor Britain, romance exists as reality: in America, it can only appear as fantasy. Given the romantic's tendency to identify with symbols and imagined persons, Edward's England is ideal for the education of the romantic, for his initial exposure to reality.

Twain was aware, of course, that the romantic would identify with the Prince. That alone makes the change of roles necessary; casting the Prince among the poor would not be enough. Canty can expose the follies and the injustice of the court as the Prince left to himself could never do. The comfort and security which the middle-class American shares with the royal court shield both, not only from the seamy side of reality, but from actual confrontation with the shortcomings of their own world. Nature and poverty teach little, but they do force a recognition of the defects of one's environment.

The course of education is a rise from nature toward idea, from concrete knowledge of the lives and dilemmas of men, the world of injustice, passion, and need, toward an understanding of the general truths of human life and political justice. Developing his fantasy kingdom in the streets, Tom Canty gains something of a sense of justice which he is forced to test by the standard of political reality. The Prince learns quickly and learns better, but it is necessary for him to be shaken out of the insulation from reality which surrounds him. He must fall below society in order to rise above its myths and conventions while keeping a due regard for its virtues. Huck Finn learns something of the same lessons: from beneath, the shortcomings of society do not disappear, but they are set in a framework that makes them more worthy of respect. (If Huck never truly rises above society, and if he is still impelled by the desire for escape, his decision to "light out for the territory" is a clear improvement on his original course.)

[99] *The Prince and the Pauper*, General Note, pp. 273–274, *Autobiography*, p. 295.

Immersion in the subsocial world is not enough. That world extracts its toll: it slays or brutalizes. To rise above nature toward the ideal, men require fraternity. Fraternity is a lesson hard to teach in the world of romance, for it is not necessary for survival. It is a psychological necessity, though; Tom Canty's isolation, as much as any other fact, leads him to weaken in the face of power's temptations. (His only intimate, from whom he must still conceal his secret, is the Prince's Whipping Boy.) The lesson once taught in the "natural" world, however, will not be forgotten if conditions change.

Two separate "fraternities" exist: (1) the fraternity of protection and encouragement and (2) the fraternity of education and idea. Aspects of a single, true fraternity, they reflect the "twin" needs of man, either of which may dominate in a particular relation and environment.

The first fraternity characterizes the relations of Miles Hendon and the Prince. Because the Prince's "fantastic" idea is a reality, it gives his devotion to it a certain monomaniacal quality. But in the environment of poverty such devotion would lead either to his destruction or, more probably, a flagging of his belief in his own identity. Affection given and returned leads Hendon, without faith in the Prince's "fantasy," to acts of courage and devotion; it permits the Prince to continue his own pursuit of reality in the face of social hostility and disbelief.

The fraternity of Jim and Huck contains an even more general truth. Huck's weakness, which makes him a prisoner of drift, is that he considers moral questions to be "troublesome" and prefers the path of least apparent discomfort. Affection for Jim leads him to desert that path: Jim's own dream of freedom is Huck's closest approach to a general moral truth or to a political ideal. (The principle that humanity is more important than property is only partly concealed by the fact that post-1865 respectability was forced to regard freeing a slave as heroic.) Jim is in reality the Prince to Huck's Miles Hendon; the seemingly passive partner in both fraternities is the real guiding spirit. In fact, since Jim is already free, it is accurate to say that it is Jim who frees Huck, not the reverse.[100]

Both fraternities are needed for the full development of a man.

[100] J. M. Cox, "Remarks on the Sad Initiation of Huckleberry Finn," *Sewanee Review*, LXII (1954), pp. 389–405.

The distinct problem of the young American is that he is not suited for the fraternity of education and ideal. Tom Sawyer's ideal is in one sense superior to that of the Prince. Aristocratic society could provide men with a sense of identity so strong that they could resist massive forces. Yet it was a false identity, based on the ideal of "birthright," in which the status of man at birth is identified with the desire of man for right. American society does lead Tom to a romance separate from birth: as an ideal, his romance is identical to that of Tom Canty, not that of the Prince. But Sawyer's ideal is never forced to confront the "real world": romance separate from birth does not cause him to doubt the existing injustice of slavery.

The American must make the pilgrimage of Huck Finn. He must go back to the beginning, divest himself of false romance, discipline his imagination in the school of nature. The means to those results are at hand: the American needs fraternity with the strong victim. The romantic may "identify" with the victim easily; the oppressed and the victimized appear "safe," no threat to the security of the middle-class dreamer. Injury and injustice to one beloved shakes the comfort of the dream; safe identification spells idyll-shattering pain. The romantic may then become the man of idea, his discontent redirected from the world of dreams to the life of society. Affection for the victims of society maintains the erstwhile romantic's detachment; if that affection is returned, it will afford him encouragement and protection against the forces making for social conformity.

Left-wing critics have perceived the formula ("fraternity with the strong victim") and have been led with a certain justice to claim Twain for their own. Yet they overlook the fact that the strength in question is not the power of an oppressed mass, but strength of personal character and devotion. Jim is no more a symbol of "blackness" than Miles Hendon is a symbol of the lesser nobility: both are men, transcending the classes to which they belong. Twain's idea of fraternity is not an identification with an abstract group, but an emotion felt by one individual for another, a relationship which helps both in the effort to "attain full stature."

American society had not helped men to recognize their brothers; the age of gilded industrialism was inauspicious for men and for fraternity. Yet the accidents of temperament and rearing may lead some men to see what others will not, and these may teach the lesson to others, however few. Twain's weapons as a teacher of fraternity may seem weak enough when opposed to the dynamics of his age—but, as Satan observed in *The Mysterious Stranger*, they are the distinctive qualities of men: the recognition of ignorance and dependence that is the moral sense, and the boundless humor which laughs aside man's fears and pretensions, cheering him in the search for a true humanity.

> The Americans are very patriotic and wish to make their new citizens patriotic Americans. But it is the idea of making a new nation out of literally any old nation that comes along. In a word, what is unique is not America but what is called Americanization. . . . (T)he process . . . is *not* internationalization. It would be truer to say that it is the nationalization of the internationalized.
>
> G. K. Chesterton, *What I Saw in America*

CHAPTER XVII

OLD AMERICANS AND NEW

Born in Arcadia

THE late nineteenth century became increasingly difficult for middle-class America. Its ability to live easily with two juxtaposed, contradictory codes—the religious creed, confined largely to the family, and the ethics of individualism and material progress which dominated political and economic life—had depended on the existence of some bridges, of rhetoric at least, between the two. Now the contradiction became more and more apparent; Mark Hanna became the bête noire of Progressives because he admitted the fact and allowed himself the luxury of a tough-minded cynicism in his public addresses, and Hanna was only more honest and more public-spirited than most.[1]

Moral uneasiness, however, might have been endurable except that it coincided with the realization that the middle class was drift-

[1] Thomas Beer, *Hanna* (New York: Knopf, 1928), pp. 69–70, 84–92, 277.

ing toward impotence, if not being pushed to the wall. Many have overemphasized the altruism of middle-class reform because they saw only the prosperity of the period. Prosperity played some role; giving a feeling of economic security, it provided greater latitude for the luxury of reform impulses. More basic, however, was the fact of social crisis, and Gabriel Kolko's *Triumph of Conservatism* is much to the point.

The process that had undermined farmer and craftsman now threatened the independence and status of the middle class itself. The growth of corporate organization made an ever-greater number of men into employees, and still more into dependents. The middle-class virtues of thrift and frugality were threatened by both financial panic and inflation—the first wiping out savings, the second depriving them of value.

When the question had been agrarian efforts to manipulate the currency, the townsman's position had been clear. To tamper with the Gold Standard was to endanger all those institutions which he had been taught were the guarantors of progress. Free markets, free men, sound currency, and honest business all assured that denial and sacrifice would lead to a glorious future. William Allen White's "What's the Matter with Kansas?" was not only clever sarcasm; it was an outraged protest against those who, in their folly, would deprive their fellows of the fruits of their toil.[2]

To middle-class Americans, however, it became increasingly clear that progress had gone awry. Stock watering and manipulation by "robber barons" helped to produce that sentiment; the expansion of U.S. Steel and Standard Oil helped reinforce it; recognition of middle-class impotence helped solidify it. Very early in the game, some, like George Perkins Marsh, spoke of the corporation as the root of economic evil. The corporation was iniquitous, Marsh declared, because, not being owned by one individual, it had no "conscience"; but Marsh went beyond this individualistic analysis to declare that in many cases he would prefer government ownership to corporate greed and materialism.[3] Others hesitated, and economic

[2] William Allen White, *Autobiography*, pp. 280–283; on conservatism generally, see Kolko, *The Triumph of Conservatism*, and Rogin, *The Intellectuals and McCarthy*, pp. 206–211.

[3] David Lowenthal, *George Perkins Marsh*, pp. 190–193, 322–323.

concentration alone might not have been enough to shake the faith.

The new age, however, was not only the age of the corporations; it was the age of the cities. In the cities, the names and accents were more likely to be foreign, and the Irish ruled many a city hall. Divested of control of the cities, "old-stock" Americans had to rely on rural machines like that of Tom Platt in New York to defend their ethnic cause. But such machines, though the ancestry of their members might be faultless, were only too willing to disregard middle-class values.

Corruption and connivance with social crime were hardly new to the city; neither was its lack of any sense of solidarity (or of "neighborliness," as Protestant and middle-class America understood the term). Of course, such ills had increased, but more important was the fact that the towns were declining in importance or growing into cities. More urban themselves, middle-class Americans were confronted with the existence of that "other city" they had been able to ignore while they lived in towns or while it kept passively to its tenements or was controlled politically by representatives of the old order. In the new awareness, the middle classes, then as now, turned to a savagely accented demand for "law and order" that easily shaded into vigilantism; ideas of planning were by contrast only a minor note until much later in the game.

The ecology of America was changing in more than one way. The old idylls of a Howells were passing; natural resources, especially the soil and the forests, were showing the inevitable effects of unrestricted exploitation. Marsh became one of the earliest and most powerful advocates of conservation, even though Marsh's argument—separating man from nature and arguing for the need to use "science" to tame and subject nature—bore the unmistakable signs of liberalism. Science, in this area at least, was falling out of accord with laissez-faire.[4]

Marsh foreshadowed Progressivism for another reason. Old and consistent anti-Catholic that Marsh was, his interest in the economy and conservation reflected a growing conviction that anti-foreignism was not enough—not, that anti-foreignism was wrong, only that it was insufficient. There were quite enough nativist movements like

[4] *Ibid.*, pp. 270–274, 307–308, 323.

the American Protective Association, and their agitation for restricted immigration consistently gained ground and won some results.

Increasingly it became fashionable to speak of "unassimilable" groups, though that concept was impossibly imprecise; in cultural terms, the charge against Japanese immigrants was more that they were too assimilable. Certainly the idea referred in part to cultures which resisted Americanization and put themselves outside the "fraternity" of all citizens. But more often it was a racial rather than cultural concept, defining those with whom "interbreeding" was thought impermissible. Racism was open enough in the anti-Negro and anti-Oriental provisions of the Naturalization Acts of 1870 and 1875, the latter establishing that all those not "free white persons" were "aliens ineligible for citizenship." The pseudo-scientific theories of "race" and of the perils of "mongrelization" contributed much, of course, to the arguments of the day.

Yet even those who most sturdily opposed racism were likely to use variants of the same argument. P. S. Grant, for example, held that the "brotherhood of man" was a central American ideal, consequently, racial intermarriage was the only logical and moral policy. For Grant, no less than the racists, "brotherhood" could be established only through genetic bonds which physically connected man and man.[5]

Insecure and lonely men sought for some automatic kinship with their fellows, something within each isolated man that might unite him to others. Those who would not, or with whom one ought not to, interbreed with older Americans were excluded from the blood fraternity which its advocates hoped would establish or preserve some sense of unity among divided Americans. Such self-deceptions, however, not only opposed the universalism of the national creed; set against the facts of economic and social life, they seemed rather too pale to be remedies.

The early critics provided little more convincing in the way of diagnosis and therapy. E. L. Godkin or John Jay Chapman were competent observers of amorality, mediocrity, and civic corruption.

---

[5] P. S. Grant, "American Ideals and Race Mixture," *NAR*, CXCV (1912), pp. 513–535.

But when either spoke of the sordid "unforseen consequences of democracy," their diagnoses traced the ills to a lethargic mass which was surrendering to its desires for present ease and comfort. America, Chapman declared, suffered from a "prejudice against the individual"; devoted Emersonian that he was, he would hardly trace the problem to an excess of individualism (nor would the more orthodox liberal, Godkin). Aside from such individualizing reforms as civil service, nothing was to be hoped for from politics—which, as the effort of the many to impose their standards on the few, was always coercive and inferior. Chapman could only hope that the "conscience of the unknown man" would produce a heroic few able to "accept aloneness" and resist the delusory temptations of the group.[6]

More convincing arguments would be developed, but the pattern set by the early critics revealed a general tendency. For Chapman or Godkin, the cure for amoral individualism was more individuality; critics of Darwinian orthodoxy were to demand a more genuine Darwinism; those who found fault with democratic practice would demand more democracy.

The middle class had been too well trained in the liberal tradition, and had invested too much of its life and devotion in it, to abandon its precepts. Old ideas had faded, and if they reappeared, or new ones were generated, they would have to be fitted into the categories of liberal thought. Moral uncertainty and social insecurity only provided the impetus for intellectuals and political thinkers to discover a new formula which could hold together the diverging traditions of America in the disquieting present.

"The buzzing universe . . ."

Not all Americans had been swept away by the desire to make millions. There were "people who stayed home," who preferred the ties of place and kindred to the possibility of fortune. Boston, an old city suffering from what William James called the "draining off" of its best population and its economic dynamism, was their natural intellectual capital, and for those it lost it found replacements in

[6] M. Bernstein, "John Jay Chapman and the Insurgent Individual," in *American Radicals*, ed. Harvey Goldberg, pp. 21–36.

others. From interior New England and from further afield, men who admired the slower pace and the old virtues, or who found there a place where the intellectual was less alone and more appreciated, men like Royce and Howells, gravitated naturally to the city.

It was equally natural that here should begin the shaping of the doctrine of protest. Aware of being passed by in the world's rush, beset by waves of immigrants, New England's intellectuals—and her middle class—were drawn to idyllic pictures of her past, a partly imagined world of rough equality and the town meeting where "family, education, and professional repute" still won deference, and personal bonds existed between citizens. It was the image of an America where the synthesis of liberalism and Puritanism had been easy—an atmosphere that, as George Santayana pointed out, the intellectual world of Boston and Cambridge valued and struggled to keep alive.[7]

Certainly they felt discontent, those intellectuals. "Bigness," William James declared, is often "hollower" than what is small, for limits work to encourage depth. Restraint of manner was valued partly as a corollary to, partly as a substitute for, restrictions in space and social change. The intellectuals valued what Santayana called a "placid . . . brotherhood"; the "jostling" of the world, making men lonely and dependent, led to the making of "fanciful passionate demands" on the affections of others which would only end in disappointment and resentment. Fraternity demanded the measure which could separate too little from too much.[8]

In the 1880s, Geoffrey Blodgett writes, the Brahmins had enjoyed a "placid, congenial time . . . a fleeting breathing spell . . . to bring orthodoxy up to date," to discover new ways for a new time. Many turned to reform, especially at city and state levels, seeking to create communities where men would see the good of all as the true good of each, and where, in Josiah Quincy's words, "civilization in the fullest sense" could flower.[9]

It helped rouse interest in projects like Frederick Law Olm-

[7] Santayana, *Character and Opinion in the United States*, pp. 6–38.

[8] *Ibid.*, p. 96; *The Letters of William James*, ed. H. James, vol. II, p. 64.

[9] Blodgett, *The Gentle Reformers*, p. 19; Josiah Quincy, "The Development of American Cities," *Arena*, XVII (1897), pp. 529–537.

stead's crusade for parks and recreation areas, in which he hoped citizens might be able to overcome isolation and suspicion. (In much the same vein, Jane Addams would miss the "pageants and festivals" that had enlivened the medieval city.) But what Olmstead was asking, though his proposals were praiseworthy, was that the park substitute for the common, recreation and emotional expression for a common life which the city, through its size and economy, no longer possessed.[10]

In New York, W. R. Grace was more to the point, realizing that complexity and interdependence demanded a government more concerned with matters "economical." Grace contended that the city was the proper vehicle to combine economic regulation and decentralization, and he argued for an end to control by state legislatures to enable the city to assume the task. In any case, Grace argued, citizens need the "dignity of self-government," something hard to teach in the city, "the very greatness of which has a tendency to eclipse the sense of . . . responsibility." Citizens, "being lost in the crowd feel themselves to be ciphers." The task was impossible, he concluded, if institutions were outdated and irrelevant and power lay with a distant assembly whose attitudes and interests did not reflect those of city-dwellers.[11]

It was an intelligent—if somewhat partisan—argument, but one which tried to do too much. Already too large for a fraternal citizenry, the city was far too small for the task of economic regulation. The two goals Grace set were in conflict. More and more reformers looked to state and national regimes for regulation of the economy, and many of those who yearned for community lapsed into pure nostalgia. Howells pictured a utopia where "a man is born and lives and dies among his own kindred, and the sweet sense of neighborhood, of brotherhood, which blessed the first Christian republic, is ours again." Fraternity became emotion, solidarity for its own sake; it would have astonished the martyrs of that first republic to hear Howells equate their polity with neighborhood and blood-kinship,

---

[10] F. L. Olmstead, "Public Parks and the Enlargement of Towns," *JSS*, III (1870), pp. 18–29.

[11] W. R. Grace, "The Government of Cities in the State of New York," *Harper's*, LXVII (1883), pp. 609–616.

but the dream was natural for one who saw few other alternatives to loneliness.[12]

The early reformers are not to be blamed for failing to create fraternal citizenry. More important, they fell short of the goals they might have achieved because of the nature of their "orthodoxy" itself. They always remained liberals, even Spencerians, and while they could conceive of removing barriers to equality, few were able to transcend the limits of individualist doctrine. Hating industrialism and hoping to combat the "social evil," they desired to avoid any injury to "economic liberty." Concerned for citizen education and involvement, few approached the insight of William Russell, who saw the need for party to enable the "silent people" to organize—especially if government was to have a more active role. And even Russell envisioned a government concerned only to prevent special advantages being given to private industry. Those traditional liberal limitations would be part of Progressive thought until the very end, and they remained damning. The fact was that the old synthesis had come unglued; its connection had always been artificial, and in the age of industrialism, those who sought to restore it took on the labors of Sisyphus.[13]

William James undertook that labor manfully, and his philosophy was the most important legacy of the early reformers to subsequent movements, at least until the present day. James' emphasis on the plurality of the universe helped make the world seem more malleable than Darwinism admitted it to be, while his stress on the unknown enabled men to retain, "pragmatically," ideas and goals indefensible in the light of established reason. Fundamentally, pragmatism was moral philosophy, not a theory of knowledge; it freed men for activism and insisted on their responsibility for events, and it referred to effects on human life for its test of truth.

James saw enough grounds for action. He disliked bigness and hated the "success" ethic still more, and he deeply valued friends and the sense of social rootedness. Too, he was concerned by the fact that liberalism had come to lack "speed and passion" and that,

[12] William Dean Howells, *A Traveller from Altruria* (New York: Harper, 1894).

[13] Blodgett, *The Gentle Reformers,* pp. 36, 38, 41, 90, 91, 97, 104, 117–118, 127, 137–138, 140.

under the impact of positivism, "romantic spontaneity and courage are gone, the vision is materialistic and depressing." Politically, that presaged defeat for liberalism until its defects should be cured. "The Tories and the mob," he wrote, "will always pull together in the red-blood party," a reference to his own land in the era of the "bloody shirt" more than to Tories proper.[14] That in turn meant outdatedness and an obsolescence of ideas not only inhumane but powerless to guide the course of events, and James admitted to doubts about the direction of things.

> The scope of the practical control of nature put into our hands by scientific ways of thinking vastly exceeds the scope of the old control grounded on common sense. Its rate of increase accelerates so that no one can trace the limit; one may even fear that the *being* of man will be crushed by his own powers. . . . He may drown in his wealth like a child in a bathtub who has turned on the water and who cannot turn it off.[15]

Such concerns might have been enough to make James what Ralph Barton Perry called him, a "heroic, fighting partisan."[16] In fact, they combined in him with deep fears of passivity and irrelevance and a desire to avoid the paralysis of ambiguity. Pragmatism allowed him to avoid the necessity for choice between ultimate goods and first principles. And if James spoke powerfully to American intellectuals, it was because he felt more deeply and saw more clearly the dilemmas and desires they faced.

Despite his willingness to avoid such questions, James did have a metaphysic, the doctrine of liberal individualism. Man was morally complete, and "truth," evolving slowly over the ages, was the instrument by which man was enabled to change his environment and fulfill his desires. Even when James wrote of the need for a "moral alternative to war," he recommended in part that men take up the struggle with nature rather than against one another. And though James avoided stating (for James was no Thrasymachus) that whatever an individual found pleasant was true, there is no doubt that he referred the question of good and bad to the will of the individual,

---

[14] William James, *Pragmatism*, pp. 24–25; Perry, *Thought and Character of William James*, vol. II, p. 299.

[15] *Pragmatism*, p. 123.

[16] Perry, *In the Spirit of William James*, p. 130.

presuming the existence of no other tribunal. That led James to a formulation straight from the contractarian tradition: since goods are individual and plural, human life becomes a "multifarious jungle" unless men can discard "non-organizable" goods in favor of a concentration on "organizable" ones. Out of this, through progress, might come the "reign of peace and . . . the gradual advent of some sort of a socialistic equilibrium." [17]

Though James understood the need of the intellectual for a fraternal community (he described the university as a place where ideally "the lonely thinker is least alone"), that community was never an end in itself. The primary role of the intellectual was in society, his natural position that of a leader "responsible for progress." The responsibility took two forms; first, the intellectual would create new tools for men, and second, he would adjust and remove conflicts among them, "organizing" the goods of men. But the knowledge of the intellectual which allowed him to claim leadership remained technical, the servant of the ends presumably sought instinctively by every sane man.[18]

James, in fact, reflects a major characteristic of the intellectuals of the age of Progressivism. They were estranged men, but not in the Hegelian sense alienated, who sought sometimes desperately to win the admiration of those around them, to carve a place for themselves in a society which seemed to allow them none. Proving the "tough-minded," pragmatic value of their knowledge, they might escape the verdict of ineffectuality and passivity which American materialism delivered against them.

No service that could be rendered had more potential value than the restoration of unity to the troubled psyche of the American. To perform that task, James needed to find some guarantee of progress. This was difficult to find in the rational world. James knew as well as Henry Adams that the forecasts of science for the ultimate future of man ended in "death tragedy," and it was to avoid this result that he appealed to the "pragmatic" value of religion. God was

[17] William James, *Memories and Studies* (New York: Longmans Green, 1912), pp. 287–288; Perry, *Thought and Character of William James,* vol. II, pp. 263–265, 290.

[18] James, *Memories and Studies,* p. 254; *Principles of Psychology* (New York: Holt, 1890), vol. II, pp. 318–320, 323; and "Democracy and the College Bred," *McClure's* (Feb. 1908), pp. 420–422.

useful because He provided assurance of the preservation of an "ideal order." [19]

As the dangers in progress grew, James' praises grew more lyrical, but here too, the pragmatic test was enough, whatever reason might caution. In 1907 he wrote his brother that technological advances he had just observed in New York were "magnificent" in their "courage," and that in their "heaven-scaling audacity" he could feel "great pulses and bounds of progress." [20] (Henry Adams might have wept at such language.) Sober analysis could hardly support such a vision, and James appealed to a kind of political poesy. He admired Whitman's feeling for the "human crowd" and foresaw a time when "Emerson's philosophy will be in our bones, not our dramatic imaginations." [21] It was a judgment on the times, a portent for the future; the historical faith in progress, the dream of an eventual brotherhood of man, had now to appeal to "dramatic imagination" to sustain belief. The "reason" to which both had originally appealed was withdrawing into the emotions, beginning to fly its true colors. James, however, had provided a doctrine which would help it to hold the field for all of that.

In His Steps

The churches, even in their worst days as secular amusements, never lost all social concern. The YMCA and YWCA were early efforts to provide a "wholesome" religious atmosphere for migrants to the city. The Chatauqua movement, which seemed foolish to intellectuals even then, was an effort to define the relevance of religion to modern life, and consequently was related to the rise of the Social Gospel. And the missionary movement could hardly ignore altogether the discontinuity between efforts to evangelize and modernize the lives of people abroad, and indifference to conditions at home. Gradually economic and social concerns reasserted themselves in the churches, encouraged among ministers by the increasing doubts and anxieties of their congregations.

[19] *Pragmatism*, pp. 75, 77.
[20] *Letters of William James*, vol. II, p. 264.
[21] James, *Talks to Teachers of Psychology* (New York: Holt, 1899), p. 234; Perry, *Thought and Character of William James*, vol. I, p. 352.

The development of the Social Gospel came fairly late in the reform period; Rauschenbusch, the movement's most coherent theorist, published his work after the turn of the century. The importance of the movement did not rest on its theory, however. The mood the Social Gospel reflected was one which affected thousands of clergymen, a group more responsive to doctrines of moral obligation and fraternal duty than almost any other in society, however compromised with it they might be. And their position in the community enabled them to assimilate and popularize reformist notions. Bellamy's work has recently been called "influential" and "popular"; Sheldon's *In His Steps* sold a half million copies its first year. True, clergymen often reduced reformist ideas to moral abstractions; but even so, the ideas of those theorists whose ideas read persuasively and whose rhetoric appealed to the religious (like Henry George or Henry Demarest Lloyd) found their way into countless sermons.

More important, the Social Gospel concerned itself directly with urban life and brought an awareness of urban misery to the attention of the upper and middle classes in a way that the excluded and suffering could not do themselves. It was a prod to the conscience, responsible at least for a new form of charity concerned with political life, affirming an element long present in the tradition. It did not drive the churches out of other-worldliness, but it certainly forced them, even those which opposed the Social Gospel itself, into a greater concern for social conditions.

Josiah Strong was among the earliest advocates of social concern, and one who exemplified the ambiguities of the movement more than any other thinker. A believer in evolution, Strong could accept the idea that "inferior" races might have to become extinct, and he was in addition devoted to nationalism and the American "mission" to civilize others. Yet Strong objected to all opprobrious ethnic and racial names as a violation of common humanity, and when he surveyed the cities inside America he did not see "aliens" but a world of materialism, life reduced to triviality. He advocated a "brotherhood of religions" which would set aside doctrinal differences in the interest of carrying Judeo-Christian doctrine into practice and moving toward the realization of a national culture built on the "brotherhood of man." Such a nation would override racial and cultural prejudices. Strong's doctrine was often messianic, and he seemed to believe that the Church, whatever was the case with the Constitution, followed the flag. What he achieved, however, was a teaching which expanded in imagination the private world of the family to the limits of the national territory. The competitive, purposive world of the secular liberal state was outside, its duties being defense and expansion. Inside, there would be harmony, solidarity, and emotion—and little else. Strong's ideas, no less than James', stressed the avoidance and suppression of conflict—in Strong's case, to the point of an almost vacuous consensus. His theory was a grander version of the psyche of the average American, though whatever its faults, it did teach the duty of compassion and concern for one's fellows.[22]

This suggests a general theme of Social Gospel doctrine. In their reaction against the "tough" doctrines of established reason and the rigidity of absolutist ethics, the Gospellers often offered little more than sentiment and warm feeling—which, whatever its other values, lost the distinction between warmth generally and fraternity specifically. The sentimentalism which romanticized the values and virtues of the excluded enabled the Social Gospel minister to achieve identification with them. It was something he needed, an escape from felt irrelevance and isolation. Christianity had been willing to pay the price of alienation, and ministers who felt the power of their fathers' faith might be able to endure persecution, but indifference to religion on the part of society was intolerable. (The appeal of missionarism, after all, existed *because* more than in spite of the possibility of martyrdom; to heathens, God still mattered.)

Basic to the Social Gospel was a desire to achieve results, to regain some sense of participation and importance in the life of society. Concern for results, of course, also arose from ethical concerns themselves and the desire to alleviate men's pain. Both aims, however, made the Social Gospeller impatient with the limitations on human action stressed by traditional thought, and many Gospellers, zealous to achieve some result, neglected the wisdom of traditional theology and embraced theorists of reform who offered easier, more immediately practical, ideals. (Some were quite alien to the tradition; Bellamy, for example, had a considerable vogue.) In short, their pardon-

[22] Josiah Strong, *Our Country* (New York: Baker and Taylor, 1885), pp. 175–178. See also Thomas Gossett, *Race* (New York: Schocken, 1965), pp. 293–294.

able concern for the social crisis of the nineteenth century led them to lower the standard of fraternity and human excellence in order to expand the practicability of what remained. God's city, located just around the corner, loses much of its glory, and fraternity lowered to compassion loses brotherhood; the desire for effectiveness threatened the authority as well as the wisdom of religion.

Walter Rauschenbusch, the greatest of the movement's thinkers, never forgot (as the neo-orthodox sometimes imply) the fact of sin. He did, however, identify Divine Providence with the processes of history, arguing that in the nineteenth century men had been raised high enough to control their own future. Revelation, he contended, is progressive and evolving, and the past can no longer constrain the present. Men must free themselves from the past in order to realize the promise which man's victory over nature has made possible: the Kingdom of God. The next task for men, Rauschenbusch proclaimed, is nothing less than the realization in the empirical world of the spiritual vision, the fulfillment of the messianic ideal. The "excessively narrow" morality of family and social group (which Rauschenbusch identified with Judaism) and the "excessively spiritual" morality of traditional Christianity must yield to a morality of the brotherhood of all men, immediately in this life.[23]

Rauschenbusch hoped that gradual advance and historical progress would suffice. Feeling that the march of industrialism and technology was impossible to halt, he argued that only a transformation of men's attitudes and minds could make it safe. But Rauschenbusch offered few principles by which that almost apocalyptic "transformation" could be achieved. Too sophisticated to regard the elimination of material scarcity as more than a first step, he could only suggest that subsequent steps could result from democracy and the advance of "social science." Ultimately he fell back on a faith in history itself, on the belief that material and technological advance would contain in itself the answer to the problem of man's spirit and the realization of the vision of human fraternity.[24]

[23] Walter Rauschenbusch, *Christianizing the Social Order* (New York: Macmillan, 1912), pp. 3, 136ff., 209; *Christianity and the Social Crisis* (New York: Macmillan, 1907), pp. xi–xii, 17, 27–31, 45, 68, 100–105, 420–421.

[24] *Ibid.*, pp. 60–64, 209–210; *Christianizing the Social Order*, pp. 6, 114, 119, 124.

Rauschenbusch founded a small band of Christian Socialists, the "Brotherhood of the Kingdom," and he could say with pride that "we were few and shouted in the wilderness." [25] Pride, however, did not make him value that fraternity in itself. Certainly he did not accept the traditional position that the brotherhood of Christians would perennially be voices crying in the wilderness. The "Brotherhood of the Kingdom" was conceived more as a Leninist vanguard than as a Christian fraternity.

Defects of theory should not obscure virtues in practice. The Social Gospel softened the impact of industrialism and brightened the lives of many men, and the policies it recommended still have merit. It did, however, strengthen that tendency of American thought that identified fraternity simply with solidarity. By adding the prestige of religion to the old liberal vision, the Social Gospel made it more difficult for subsequent generations to understand fraternity just at the time when social and political developments made it more difficult to achieve or recognize it. And in this sense, whatever its merits, the Social Gospel became one of the myriad snares that have conspired to trap those who would discover fraternity.

"Make the world safe . . ."

Progressivism, drawing on diverse sources, composed of differing and often conflicting tendencies, still achieved a considerable degree of coherence in its doctrines. Such unity was due in great measure to the fact that its adherents shared common premises as well as common concerns; they were devoted to the task of refurbishing the Enlightenment ideal.

No longer did it seem adequate to rely on the automatic workings of a mechanical system, for something seemed to have gone wrong with the old machine. Civic responsibility was necessary, and individual self-reliance needed to be produced. But the Progressives sought those ends by the methods which the Enlightenment had developed, brought slightly up to date; in ends and means alike, they were true children of the fathers.

Progressives sought to compel the individual to accept responsi-

[25] *Ibid.*, p. 9; see also Curti, *Growth of American Thought*, p. 632.

bility and to assert his own concerns by depriving him of the shelter of the group. Progressivism had many enemies: the party, the corporation, the union, the ethnic group, even the law—for the law, too, was a source of security, an encouragement to complacency. To Progressives, measures like the recall of judges and the direct primary seemed designed to free men from constraint as well as to free them from their own cowardice and base instincts. Such measures were nonetheless designed to produce that individual isolation which the old theory had seen as a means toward the ultimate fraternal ideal.

Man, as the Progressives saw him, received whatever "nature" he possessed before society, politics, or education, and Progressive social theory was much concerned with "instincts" and innate characteristics of behavior. In this analysis, Progressivism may have had a different emphasis, but its basic ideas diverged not at all from the theory of the liberal Enlightenment.

None sought to deny that man was prone to self-seeking and the pursuit of "self-interest," nor that, brooked of his desires, he might react with ferocity. Yet the Progressives also noticed the desire of men for affection and admiration, the need for emotional security. In their eyes, in fact, this motive was so powerful that it was identical with the social good; affection and harmony in themselves remained the chief ends of man. Ross spoke of a conflict between the "natural moral motives" of man and his original combativeness, Wilson of an "altruism" and love which warred with pride and self-assertion, and Veblen realized that the "instinct of self respect," perhaps the basic instinct, could only be fulfilled through the accolade of one's neighbors.[26]

Despite the strength of man's social yearnings, conflict was at least temporarily a necessary element of human life, made so by the scarcities of the world. If the yearning for total solidarity and community did not actually compel man to fight, it certainly demanded that he change. The desires for community, transcending reason and

[26] Woodrow Wilson, *The State* (New York: Heath, 1889), pp. 605–609; *History of the American People* (New York: Harper, 1901), vol. V, pp. 212–214; and *Public Papers* (New York: Harper, 1929), vol. I, pp. 282–283, 404; Thorstein Veblen, *The Theory of the Leisure Class* (New York: Mentor, 1953), pp. 29–31, 35–37; E. A. Ross, *Social Control* (New York: Macmillan, 1914), pp. 59–60, 411–412.

the ethics of times and places, left man unsatisfied without a truly universal brotherhood of all men. It was this reaffirmation of the eighteenth-century theory of history that the Progressives turned against their stand-pat opponents. As Eric Goldman recognized, the evolutionary perspective that change in laws and institutions is inevitable could not account for Progressive fervor. That zealousness was the result of a passionate conviction that change is for the better and to be eagerly embraced, that it affirms the triumph of man over nature, and the Fraternal destiny of mankind.[27]

This faith made the Progressives insistent that men should "adjust" themselves to changes which even (or especially) the Progressives themselves found partly painful. It accounts, too, for their eager rejection of the "absolutes" of morality or society which might bar the door to progress. Men, as James had taught, developed institutions to solve proximate problems, and the only effect of absolutes—or even the quest for absolutes, for here Progressives often went far beyond James—would be to create a superstitious reverence for a historically relative state of affairs. The search for absolutes, the groping of intellectuals for some dim image of the power denied them in reality, only diverted them from the real task. The absolute, the "putative approbation of some supernatural witness" in Veblen's phrase, merely justified the interests of the already satisfied few and deluded the unsatisfied many.

The older generation, tied to the "steel chain" of liberal orthodoxy, might have agreed; but to them, the elimination of false absolutes might have seemed enough in itself.[28] The Progressives doubted to the point of irreverence. The old institutions and methods were played out, and new methods were required for the new age; in this much, Progressivism diverged from the theory of the eighteenth century.

Politics was never more than a necessary evil in Progressive thought, made necessary by scarcity and imperfection. Wilson and

[22] Goldman, *Rendezvous with Destiny*, pp. 93–94, 200. See, for example, Herbert Croly, *Progressive Democracy* (New York: Macmillan, 1914), pp. 1–2, 168, 172; Charles Cooley, *Social Process* (New York: Scribner's, 1920), pp. 103, 418.

[28] Earl Latham, "Justice Holmes Makes His Mark," *Nation*, CXCVII (July 13, 1963), pp. 36–38.

Ross both saw it as a field for conflict and self-seeking, a place of artificial and temporary distinction. (In fact, Wilson's reticence about women's suffrage came from his belief that women, devoted to the great ideals of altruism and harmony, were too pure for and should be spared the crassness of political life.)[29]

Politics was, however, short of the ideal, a means by which men could be shaped by institutions and changes in their environment so that their lower drives would impel them toward the good end. Force could compel men to act in ways conducive to the good. Herbert Croly restored the Hamiltonian vision of using reward and punishment to control the "lower man"; Ross devoted his major work to the subject of *Social Control*. The importance Progressives attached to man's desire for social approbation allowed them an almost unlimited sphere for action. New science might replace the gropings of history and the blind struggles of trial and error. In sharp contrast to Holmes, let alone the more conservative, Roscoe Pound argued that "social engineering" made it possible to achieve unheard-of results. To change the environment, later Progressives insisted, is to change man.[30]

All this confidence, however, was in part the result of a sense of desperate necessity. Progressives felt decay and degeneration in the political and social life of America. Frederick Jackson Turner set the tone; the end of the frontier means the collapse of the world built on the ethics of the frontier. While land had been abundant, the spontaneous impulses of the individual could be allowed to push him across the continent without fear that dangerous conflict would result. Now, forced into contact with other men, the frontier spirit was resulting in anarchic individualism, and it lacked the necessary civic spirit and sense of community.

In another sense, Woodrow Wilson saw in the growth of corporate organization the end of the state based on voluntary associa-

---

[29] Woodrow Wilson, "On Being Human," *AM*, LXXX (1897), pp. 321–325; E. A. Ross, *Sin and Society* (Boston: Houghton Mifflin, 1907), pp. 3–19. See also Merle Curti, "Woodrow Wilson's Theory of Human Nature," *MJPS*, I (1957), pp. 1–19.

[30] Ross, *Social Control*, pp. 49–50; Croly, *The Promise of American Life* (New York: Macmillan, 1909), pp. 2, 207–214, 279–288; Roscoe Pound, "A Theory of Social Interests," *Proceedings*, American Sociological Society, XV (1920), pp. 23–45.

tion and individual decision. He and others like J. Allen Smith, more acute than many "group theorists," saw that the corporation had become a government over men, no longer dependent on or even subject to individual decision and will. The small community and the "natural association" had given way to impersonal organizations with a life above that of their members. Men, Wilson commented, may share the prosperity which such organizations create, but they cannot initiate it. The course of things seemed productive of a new serfdom, lacking either individualism or community.[31]

The Progressives could not, however, argue for the return to a smaller and simpler society. Whatever its defects, the industrial age made possible a material prosperity that was an essential part of progress itself. The issue defined itself as a question of organization and control within the environment of modernity.

The Progressive desired to shift control from the impersonal forces of the market to the nation at large, from private to public power. Individualism had "served its purpose." For Cooley, the age of "instinctive solidarity" and the small group based on concrete affections had yielded to the age of "fragmentation" and individualism that had created the material base of civilization. It was now time to enter the age in which "universal solidarity" would be the means as well as the end of progress. Henry Jones Ford had already argued, similarly, that Darwinism was misconceived; the "undivided commune" was the true vehicle of historical evolution for the future.[32]

In the new age, the nation as a whole must control the forces which had previously shaped it. Croly's "new nationalism" envisaged a society in which each would set for the other an example of social virtue, and Turner sought an ethic of social service to replace individual assertion. J. Allen Smith denounced the "mechanical Constitution" of the Framers, with its negative ideas of liberty, as a barrier to the governance of society. Wilson's tone, however, was most representative of Progressive thought because he infused it with

[31] J. Allen Smith, *The Spirit of American Government* (New York: Macmillan, 1912), pp. 401–402; Wilson, *The State*, pp. 633–677, and *The New Freedom* (New York: Doubleday Doran, 1913); Cooley, *Social Organization*, pp. 23–28, and *Social Process*, p. 391.

[32] Cooley, *Social Process*, pp. 42, 395, 400–401, 418; Henry Jones Ford, *The Natural History of the State* (Princeton: Princeton University Press, 1915).

his usual desperation; opinion, he declared, must be able to govern the forces now at work, for otherwise they threaten destruction.[33]

Of course, it was the Progressives' ideas of human nature which enabled them to believe that the spirit of older, concrete, and voluntary organizations could be recaptured at the level of the nation as a whole. The "moral instinct" of man was a permanent force in history, independent of material conditions, striving for ever broader unity. Charles Cooley contended that although the spirit of "onwardness" which led men to seek the universal might be entrapped by various parochialities, it remained a living force that could be set free. "The whole substance of the personal ideal," he declared, "is that men exist for one another." [34]

The issue defined itself for the Progressive in simple and traditional terms: how were men to be liberated from their outdated attachment to small groups or set free from the tyranny of corporation or party? Initially the answer was negative: break up the great interest aggregates or control them, destroy the artificial barriers of class and monopoly, open "new lines of achievement for the strongest," and the individualism of the citizen would do the rest.

Later, more moderate aims envisaged only denying existing groups the power to control the whole. Herbert Croly argued for a legislature of interest associations, a new Madisonianism which would create "constantly changing majorities" which would free the individual from "any specific formulation of the law" while minimizing the risk of violence. At the same time, it would deny any group the ability to make total claims on the loyalty of any individual.[35]

Progressives were not contented, however, with so negative a procedure, especially given their growing disenchantment with citizens. Understanding proved more parochial, less willing to be "liberated" than the early Progressives had assumed, and their successors

[33] Smith, *Spirit of American Government*, pp. 265–296; Croly, *Promise of American Life*, pp. 16–26, 453–454.

[34] Cooley, *Human Nature and the Social Order* (New York: Scribner's, 1922), pp. 118–119; *Social Process*, p. 103; "Personal Competition," *Economic Studies*, IV (1899), pp. 79–86; and "The Process of Social Change," *PSQ*, XII (1897), pp. 63–87.

[35] Croly, *Promise of American Life*, pp. 117–126, 141–154, and *Progressive Democracy*, pp. 215–216, 311, and *passim*. See also Smith, *Spirit of American Government*, pp. 386–394.

explained this by the fact of social and economic complexity. The citizen could no longer be expected to know the means toward the fraternal goal of his spirit.

Consequently, the management of industrialism by the technically qualified became a political necessity. Veblen's ponderous satire did not extend to the engineer, and Croly was certain that "scientific management" could control the "dynamics" of change to fulfill the "promise of American life." In the last analysis, Progressivism returned to the program of the earliest reformers that Wilson had advocated as early as 1887. The central need of modern society was for a new administrative elite to replace the parochial and venal politician and the self-concerned businessman, neither of whom possessed adequate knowledge of society or the human goal.[36]

The Progressives argued, revealingly, that progress demanded a new reliance on the intellectual or at least on the university-trained. In Progressivism, the rising universities found a new raison d'être, a new usefulness to society. They could produce "social scientists," experts who had the skills to perform the regulatory tasks that Progressives increasingly expected of the state. The University of Wisconsin may have carried this tendency farthest, but it was hardly unique; the great public universities and the newer private ones, bastions of the middle class, found in the Progressive program a balance to the claims of the older, elite universities. And even those universities, sensing the crisis created by the advent of a new America, were not far behind in espousing the "service ideal"; from more than one elite institution came the founders of the settlement houses, progenitors of the present welfare system and of radical "projects" among the poor alike.[37]

Control of the administrator, of course, posed some problems, but the Progressive found these singularly easy. The administrator would be regulated by opinion, by the desires of the public as a whole. Given his view of human nature, the Progressive did not see estrangement as a necessary part of the bureaucratic and industrial order.

[36] Thorstein Veblen, *The Engineers and the Price System* (New York: Huebsch, 1921); Croly, *Promise of American Life*, pp. 1-2, 428-436; Woodrow Wilson, "The Study of Public Administration," *PSQ*, II (1887), pp. 197-222.

[37] Frederick Rudolph, *The American College and University*, pp. 355-372; Grant McConnell, *Private Power and American Democracy*, pp. 38-50.

Estrangement could only result from barriers between the individual and the realization of his instinctive desires for solidarity. Once groups were deprived of their control (though that might take some time), the only remaining barrier would be "communication." Parochiality would then result only from limited perception and understanding; and, Charles Cooley contended, mass communication, as it became perfected, could gradually redeem and perfect democracy. It would make possible public control without the intervention of "artificial" secondary groups, and this would allow the nation to take on many on the qualities of a "natural" primary group. The citizenry of the nation could then emerge as a fraternal, undifferentiated whole; the Progressives, in this sense, would surely have agreed that the medium is the message.[38]

Progressivism modified Enlightenment doctrine in one respect only, though that was an important one. Progressives discarded the belief in permanent legal control of the political order in favor of dynamic administrative control. The social scientist—who had yielded up his role in 1787, relying on the workings of the political mechanism—must now resume it. The distant ideal of the Framers seemed now, in a technological age, a more immediate possibility, and public resentments and stirrings against the age seemed to make some realization a more immediate necessity. Entranced and driven by the prospect of national if not universal fraternity, and the crisis of the times, Progressives may perhaps be forgiven for overlooking the grim possibilities inherent in the idea of an administration of things replacing the government of men.

New Americans, Old Memories

The Progressive had many enemies (a friend once called Hiram Johnson, admittedly an extreme case, "catholic in his hatreds"),[39] but the machine and the ethnic group were his nemeses. Not all the Progressives disliked trade unions, nor were the unions very dangerous foes for those who did oppose them. Attitudes toward the corpora-

---

[38] Cooley, *Social Organization*, pp. 90, 118; *Social Process*, p. 103, 109, 418; *Sociological Theory and Social Research* (New York: Holt, 1930), p. 258.

[39] Gladwin Hill, *Dancing Bear: An Inside Look at California Politics* (Cleveland and New York: World, 1968), p. 48.

tions were ambiguous, and the division between Wilson's followers and T. R.'s is part of conventional history. Toward the party and the machine, Progressive hostility was unanimous and intense, and Progressives felt no sympathy for ethnic groups which resisted "assimilation" into the national "fraternity." Only at the end of the period, in a new age with new problems, did writers like Horace Kallen and Randolph Bourne begin to see values in ethnic pluralism.

Hostility was only increased by the fact that ethnicity and the machine proved resistant to Progressive threats and blandishments alike, often seeming a living refutation of Progressive theory. Exposures of graft and corruption and linkage to business did not appreciably weaken the loyalty of the lower classes to the machines, and urban victories tended to be ephemeral.

The problem of ethnic resistance to assimilation is an old one, dating at least from sects like the Amish and the Hutterites who rejected the liberal Enlightenment and preferred voluntary withdrawal into largely self-contained communities.[40] Such outright rejection, however, has been rare. Most immigrants left traditional societies which were already in decay, preferring the greater opportunity they thought America provided. Too, immigration in groups was abnormal, most coming as individuals or in family units. The experience of the immigrant tended to be individualizing, part of a break with tradition; many showed a romantic belief that in a new place, problems would disappear, having been "left behind" in the old.

This does not mean that immigrants desired to abandon the things they valued in their traditional culture. Illogical as it may have been to imagine that the "bad" elements could be left behind and the "good" preserved, many did so nonetheless. The costs of change, the price of a new culture and a new way, are rarely apparent until one has paid them. A manual for Irish immigrants urged them to individualism and to efforts to succeed, but admonished them to feel "filial devotion" and the "love of friends" as well.[41]

Attachment to valued aspects of traditional culture was only made stronger by exclusion and discrimination. Subject to indignities, denied material well-being, it was natural for the immigrant to feel

[40] J. W. Eaton, "Controlled Acculturation: A Survival Technique of the Hutterites," *ASR*, 17 (1952), pp. 331–340.

[41] Callow, *The Tweed Ring*, p. 62.

nostalgia. Moreover, he found among his ethnic fellows some element of easy communion. "Ethnicity" was not identical with the loyalties felt in the Old World; the nuances of local and city culture faded in the New World, where native Americans classified immigrants in broad "national" or racial groups, and few came from the immigrant's precise locale. Old divisions became irrelevant, and once-peripheral likenesses salient; more than once, nationalism was born in the New World and exported to the Old.

Ethnic organizations developed from those new, yet nostalgic, attachments, providing the immigrant with a defensive fraternity. They consoled him for indignities by providing a shadow-world in which honor was possible and where he could find emotional release and support which helped make endurable the disappointments of a purposive society.

Such organizations were essentially ritualistic, however, despite their apparent devotion to Old World culture. They were not characterized by distinct values at odds with those of American society at large—or at least none which would survive a contest with generally held values. It was not the political or institutional values of tradition that they upheld, but its private and personal rites. Pluralism in America became increasingly, in Milton Gordon's terms, only structural, not cultural.[42]

Had it been otherwise, the ethnic organizations might have sought to found national "areas" in America where a simulacron of the old order might be created; but such areas were few, and even where an approximation existed, most adopted the patterns of established American life. Basically the ethnic organization was an urban phenomenon; its environment was modern, destructive rather than supportive of traditional ideas and institutions. In fact, one major role of ethnic organizations was the development of new social controls to replace the old which fell so rapidly away. (Repeatedly, after all, immigrants from passive, law-abiding traditional societies came—or their children did—to appear lawless and violent to native American.)

The ethnic organization had another, possibly more conscious, aim: to raise the status of the group in the eyes of Americans in general. Yet that purpose defined its methods and values in the terms

[42] Milton Gordon, "Assimilation in America: Theory and Reality," *Daedalus*, 90 (1961), pp. 263–283.

of the dominant culture which bestowed the rewards of status. It does not require Marxist analysis to realize that ethnicity divided lower-class groups, creating a competitive situation that only strengthened the desire to identify with or win the favor of native and Protestant America. Many Italians, for example, resentful of the Irish and still attracted by the anti-clericalism of the Garibaldist tradition, sympathized with the Amerian Protective Association.

If the organization did advance the status of its members, it did so only by fixing them (and many non-members with them) more firmly in the group, adding another barrier to structural assimilation. Gains were marginal, limiting as well as limited. Confronted with a new society, or with hope-sapping restrictions, the individual might accept such gains gratefully. Children, however, were likely to see ethnicity as restrictive; and parents, though they might want their children to remain in the group, were impelled by their desire to avoid falling, relative to other ethnic fellows, to impart a dose of achievement ambition to their offspring. And those motives, of course, were strengthened and magnified by society.

Conflict among members of ethnic groups became almost a rule, especially between ethnic organization leaders and the members of their "fraternities." Ethnic leaders were on the whole marginal men, "between two worlds," and like their followers accepted American institutions and values; in fact, the basis of their leadership was often a greater familiarity with American life and culture—hence the association of ethnic leadership with the "second generation." But the "power" which helped ethnic leaders advance their own status was rooted in the organization itself; their hope for position and recognition demanded an effort to maintain the "community."

To this role parents and family members would succeed, attempting to tie the individual to the group through a network of family ties which excluded or limited extra-ethnic contacts. The roles of ethnic leaders and families only reveal that advancement in America was most available along the path of disloyalty, the casting off of interpersonal obligations as well as traditional culture. For the organization leaders, or for parents who feared the loss of their children, the path might be different; but such leaders were united to members, and children to parents, only by fragile ties which could become charged with resentment. More "positive," stronger forms of unity resulted only from barriers to advancement or dignity that were imposed by the dominant elements of society. Among groups which found few such barriers, and considerable pressure to escape the group "image" (Germans especially, as a result of the two World Wars, are an obvious example), ethnic organization and formal marks of traditional culture were likely to suffer swift decline.

Younger generations—confronting the loneliness of mass industrialism, feeling a deep discontent, and exposed to a lingering guilt reinforced by ethnic jokes and social slights—may very well, as Michael Parenti argues, find a new, nostalgic attraction in ethnic "identity." But such "identity" has largely lost its roots in the traditional environment, or any organizational ties with the world outside the family, even—most notably in the suburbs—much of its reference to the interpersonal universe of the individual.[43] It becomes more and more a private romance, a retreat into pseudo-memory as a defense against the frustrations and humiliations of the outer world.

I am far from denying that the "persistence of ethnic voting" is rooted in a continuing social and psychological distance between the ethnic group and Protestant Anglo-Saxonry and its assimilated allies. Still less would I deny the existence of a deep, if largely buried, hostility between those groups. Rather I am arguing that, seen in perspective, the roots of ethnicity (and ethnic organization especially) are for the most part negative. In part, ethnic identification would exist in any case. But it is equally arguable that the frenetic attempts by Progressivism and its imitators to "assimilate" the "hyphenated American," attempts which were too often brutal psychologically if not physically, worked to strengthen ethnic identification, to intensify and preserve it as a fact of life. The distinct, traditional cultures which Progressives disliked and feared declined largely of their own accord.

The churches of the immigrants were more clearly the custodians of distinct standards of value, and perhaps for that reason have been better able than ethnic organizations to retain their membership. The churches, however, were only relatively more immune. Increasingly,

[43] Michael Parenti, "Ethnic Politics and Ethnic Identification," *APSR*, LXI (1967), pp. 717–726. See also Erich Rosenthal, "Acculturation without Assimilation," *AJS*, LXVI (1960), pp. 275–278, and Fred Greenstein and Raymond Wolfinger, "The Suburbs and Shifting Party Loyalties," *PSQ*, XXII (1958), pp. 473–482.

they too have surrendered many of their traditional values and concerns, becoming more tied to private emotions.

De Tocqueville observed the decline of distinct social and political doctrines in American Catholicism, and despite the ancient anti-materialistic and anti-individualistic heritage of Catholic thought, a contemporary Catholic theorist can declare that because "there was no political tradition hostile to Catholicism" in America, "elaborate social policy" was not needed.[44] Such statements reflect the Church's need to deal with an "open" society where the hope for material gain and the possibility of conversion as a means to increased status were permanent threats. It was natural for the Church to seek to lessen those dangers, and hardly unexpected that it should do so by attempting to minimize its differences with the surrounding society (except where, as with "anti-communism," differences as they were perceived made Catholics better Americans in the eyes of most).

Laymen's "fraternities," formed to resist calumnies against the Church, have been at pains to emphasize similarities between Catholics and their fellows. Parochial schools, doubtless helpful in maintaining organizational ties to the church, teach few distinct values and those largely private in their impact. Birth control remains the most distinctively "Catholic" issue, but this is a "social" problem which deals with the most private of the relations of men and women. And, in any case, as Msgr. John Tracy Ellis pointed out, the rise of the laity in education and status involves them more deeply in general American culture and in its pervasive liberal philosophy; effective control on issues like birth control has lapsed, and open revolt characterizes many, especially among the younger clergy. American Catholicism seems fully subject to the tendencies that have reduced the Protestant churches to their present weakness. When John Kennedy announced in 1960 that his religion would not affect his conduct in office, Catholics received the statement without comment or with praise—though to a genuinely religious man of any persuasion, such a statement would be repellent. There is no indication that Catholic votes for Kennedy were motivated by deeply religious sentiments. That Kennedy was a Democrat was more important. Protestant anxieties to the contrary, Catholics hoped for no significant religious gain.

[44] E. J. Duff, S.J., "Social Action in the American Environment," *Social Order*, IX (1959), pp. 297-308.

Judaism is by tradition "set apart," its people bound fraternally in a common citizenship in the Kingdom yet to come. That tradition helps to account for the comparatively high resistance of Jewish culture to assimilation, strongest among the East Europeans who brought with them a highly developed pre-Enlightenment culture, but noticeable in all. Cultural values, however, are only a part of the story.

Anti-Semitism was obviously vital in forging links of solidarity, and the feeling that the offer of a warm embrace was only the prelude to the pogrom, proven by too much historical experience, hardly helped to weaken unity. Equally important, however, was the fear of men and women devoted to their heritage that the embrace would be real, and that their children would be unable to resist the combination of social seduction and the desire to escape the burden of Jewishness. All these factors encouraged the development of community institutions which maximized emotional expression and warmth, and the inculcation of the belief that Jewishness, if not Judaism, is "inborn" and not to be escaped.

This transformation into gemeinschaft, however excusable, combined with a decline in the status of traditional Jewish thought in America to produce an increasing inversion of value. The supremely volitional commitment of the covenant became reduced to the automatic unity of blood. The hard demands of moral and intellectual vision were tempered in favor of security and stability.

As the fraternal ideal yielded its sway, the "community" came more and more to conflict with the need for fraternity. Many were led to cast off religion and rite, seeking a truer brotherhood in Socialism or—for those slightly less alienated—in Zionism. These, at least, kept many of the ethical concerns of the tradition; others sought to escape their inheritance altogether.

Naturally, such attempts to escape from Jewish ethnicity were greatly reduced by Nazism. It made such escape seem immoral, a coward's desertion which produced guilt even if largely successful. Moreover, Nazism and the holocaust implied that the persistence of anti-Semitism made genuine escape impossible. And memory, declining with the years, has kept such feelings alive. Too, a similar tendency to cling to ethnicity resulted from the fact that many (especially after the war) found only isolation outside the community. Unable to live without its warmth and security, such Jews attempted to recreate it.

Organization and organized action among Jews greatly expended. Yet this development only checked deculturation, it did not halt or reverse it. Increased ethnic identification has not necessarily implied devotion to Judaic culture, especially since unity in the face of Nazism was the result of external necessity (and since 1945, of the memory of such necessity, aided by the travails of the state of Israel). The desire for community reflected a yearning for warmth per se.

The loss of traditional Jewish philosophy and value is a major theme among contemporary Jewish authors. Isaac Bashevis Singer traces that process of erosion back into the Old World, seeing a slow decay developing under the impact of modernization.[45] Others, especially younger social critics, content themselves with attacks on contemporary Jewish culture, portraying Jewish life as a thing of externals like buildings, cuisine, and resorts, lacking real commitment to Judaism. These attacks on American Judaism, partly because they are meant as warnings, are excessive. Traditional values, for example, find expression in Jewish political life to an extent which is quite unusual among American religious and cultural groups. Even with this correction, however, it is nevertheless true that the process of attenuation is at work among Jews. And as Michael Selzer has argued, much that is valuable in the traditional Jewish view of political life is in danger of disappearing altogether.[46]

Certainly the general process of deculturation which has afflicted all ethnic groups in America is visible in the Jewish fraternal orders. A body like the Workmen's Circle was forced, as its membership changed, into a largely futile effort to compete with more simply utilitarian groups in the provision of "services" like insurance. The same process may be observed in the other fraternal orders: services are better provided by others, emotional expression is found in purer form in the family; the old values are passing. Most of the orders show a concern for external affairs—the state of Israel or anti-Semitism—but little attention to the internal relations of the "brethren" with one another. The Jewish fraternities seem to be seeking a foe who will

[45] Isaac Bashevis Singer, *The Manor* (New York: Dell, 1967) and *The Estate* (New York: Dell, 1969).

[46] Michael Selzer, *The Wineskin and the Wizard* (New York and London: Macmillan, 1970).

drive men out of their private retreats (an element in the zeal with which so many Jewish organizations seized on the very dubious concept of "black anti-Semitism"). In any event, although it resists with greater strength and longer, the fraternity of the Chosen falters, like all the others, under the impact of modern industrial society.

Comparatively few Progressives showed any religious bigotry; most were notably tolerant men. For the Progressives understood from the religious history of American Protestantism that the churches, left to themselves but excluded from politics, would prove little threat, and that their claims on the loyalty of men would decay. Anti-ethnic feelings might reinforce religious identification, but this was a comparatively minor problem. More dangerous than either the ethnic group or the church, in Progressive eyes, was the vehicle which made one or both politically relevant and effective, the political party.

"My God, it's Flaherty!"

"This great and glorious country," Senator Plunkitt asserted with pride, "was built up by the political parties." [47] There was accuracy in the statement. Rooted in locality and immediate group loyalties, the political party, the urban machine perhaps most strikingly, finds a need for some general values and symbols by which the diverse, sometimes hostile groups that make it up may be united. The very act of calling for a vote stresses the importance of public life as against the private world or the social universe of the ethnic group. And if the party is an amalgam of ethnic groups, the case is even stronger. The great machines, as Plunkitt pointed out with loving detail, taught and appealed to nationalism and patriotism because these were the condition of the machine's existence, and still more of its success. The machines were a vital agency of political assimilation.

To win the allegiance of men, it is necessary to prove understanding of what they see as their private emotional and material needs. All political parties, whatever their dedication to programs and the "government of laws," involve an assurance to their voters of a "gov-

[47] *Plunkitt of Tammany Hall*, ed. William Riordon (New York: Dutton, 1963), p. 13.

ernment of men" who will understand the problems of the individual and who can be allowed safely to act for him. Men, in other words, vote for others who are in some sense "like themselves"; one of the oldest conventions of American government, that a representative should reside in the district he represents, reveals an enduring belief that knowledge of "my locale" is necessary to understand "my self."

The phenomenon is most marked, most insistent, at the point of political beginning, when allegiance is first being established among groups and men. In a new and suspect world, the need for assurance is greater, the demand for likeness in rulers more insistent. Expertise, or even agreement on issues—as the Progressives never wholly understood—will not win the allegiance of men. It may seem undignified to be governed; but even if policies are left out of account, it is a mark of pride to be ruled by one who is a friend or "one of us."

The machines grew up, in fact, before the great waves of immigrants reached America. They reflected the new, impersonal world of the cities, what Mandelbaum calls the loss of the "brotherhood of free communion." Old structures of personal contact, even the newer voluntary associations, were inadequate, unable to bind together public things and private men. That tie the machines were able to provide, at least in part. The great mechanism of patronage was as much a device for making administrations responsible to their constituents as it was a vehicle for "graft." Police and the schools—two great issues in the current "urban crisis"—were transformed into agencies that were at least less alien, sometimes into institutions which the citizen felt were "his own." Boss Tweed, hardly the most admirable of the machine leaders, allowed Catholics to "de-Protestantize" the curriculum in public schools, and gave some assistance to parochial education. The machine recognized the legitimacy of ethnic subcultures, if for no other reason, because they existed as vital elements in the personalities and loyalties of men.[48]

The various reform movements have never been able to escape their own rootedness in the culture of liberal and middle-class America, even if they escaped Protestant and Anglo-Saxon labels— which the Progressive movement, on the whole did not (partly be-

[48] Mandelbaum, *Boss Tweed's New York*, pp. 5, 6, 69, n.24; Callow, *The Tweed Ring*, pp. 10, 13, 61–63, 70–75, 152–158, 193–194, 262–263.

cause its votaries were often visibly anti-Catholic). Against the liberal values of "merit" measured in terms of the ability to manipulate things and symbols, the machine included older values in its definition of merit—personal loyalty, of course, being the most salient.

There is no need to romanticize the machine. The manipulation of men's loyalties has as much potential for iniquity as any other form of manipulation, and the machine was certainly a "private business" in many important ways. Yet, as Alexander Callow observes, a business which is political is a different business. To receive social welfare because it contributes to the economy or to "political stability" is one thing; to receive it on the basis of reciprocity, as the reward of loyalty, is another. In the first case, it is always something unearned and an offense against dignity; in the second, it may be received or even demanded as a matter of right. (To receive assistance because of a threat of violence is an improvement on passivity; but it is still, after all, a bribe in nature and intent, degrading to both giver and receiver.) The power of the machine was that it promised service and assistance in the struggle for admission to American society without a loss of dignity through a kind of political kinship based on the ethics of clan and tribe.

However, the kinship between leader and voter was often a paternal one. Patronage was frequently, and always tended to become, what the word implies: it tended to reinforce patterns of dependence and division among citizens. The "fraternal" dimension of machine politics, where it existed at all, lay in the relations of leaders with one another. Like ethnic leaders, partly in and partly out of ethnic cultures, machine leaders were more alienated from tradition, less bound by the distinctive ways of the group. Because it was always necessary for the machine to transcend particular ethnicity, at least in part, it was always more purely "voluntary," more a response to the environment of the present. Like the gangs in which it sometimes originated, the machine might have ethnicity as one of its accidents, but it could exist without it.

The foundation of the machine was the association of local leaders who could agree to cooperate in the quest for political power. Local leaders, however, were tied to their localities, to voters who were fearful—from knowledge of their own bitter condition, in many cases—that leaders, once elevated to the seats of power, would "grow away" from the community. Revolts were endemic, and sensitivity to the possibility of revolt was even more pervasive.

The iron code of loyalty reflected an attempt to counter the divisive facts of the political structure. Violations of that code—and they were numerous—only testify to its necessity. When it was upheld, the code of loyalty created problems of its own, tending to keep the old in power at the expense of the young, or leaders entrenched in wards long after a change in ethnic populations. All such developments made the "leader" from "one of us" into at best a useful alien, sometimes into an enemy. And to those who had not created it, the "organization" was just that, a bureaucracy rather than a reflection of personal loyalties. It was partly for these reasons that the machines came to depend more and more on efficiency in providing material rewards (and threatening punishments) to those who made up the "organization"—and through them, to the electorate.

There was a far more basic reason, however. The normal charge against the machines is that they allowed personal loyalty to take precedence over the public good; it is quite as true that loyalty was constantly threatened by the "public good" as the machine understood it. This was no lofty vision, but the values of American society stripped of the moderating force of traditional culture and social respectability. The words "machine" and "boss" came from the factory, and Tweed—like others—called himself a "businessman." Individualism and the desire for power, if not gain, were the chief values of the machine. The intermediate status of machine leaders, alienated from an old culture and estranged from a new, was fraternal; that status was constantly undermined by the values, the direction of movement of the organization. "Catholic and Jeffersonian conservatism," Blodgett remarks, could form a temporary alliance in Boston, but the transience of that alliance was not solely due to the emotional distance between the Yankee and the Irishman.[49] The distance was itself partly a reflection of the fact that the "Jeffersonians" were unhappy with America, while the organization leaders and their voters only wanted a place in it. The doubts and the feelings of loss would come later.

The fraternal element of the machine died early, in fact. The expanding scale of American economic and political life made an

[49] Blodgett, *The Gentle Reformers*, p. 155.

organization based on semi-autonomous local leaders unviable; it was too slow, too subject to the tactics of divide and conquer, too uncertain. Centralization became the price of survival, and the "boss" became more in fact what he had been in name. There is, however, a distinct limit to the degree to which a machine can achieve bureaucratic centralization. Chicago's organization is almost unique. It is difficult if not impossible for the machine to reach beyond the personal relations of boss and follower; such is the price of allegiance.

Deprived of its old resources of allegiance, the machine became more purely dependent on its ability to deliver rewards or inflict losses. And other organizations proved themselves more competent—the unions and the Presidential parties being most notable. Too, as the old material rewards declined in value, and as the precincts and wards decayed, the machines were faced with a relative increase in status demands and with sharper conflicts between localities. In contests with independent candidates and reform movements in the twentieth century, the machines have been increasingly feeble; today, in some cities, it is an open question whether organization support is an asset or a handicap.

Perhaps the most significant impact of the machine on American thought came through its influence on the reformers who opposed it. Taught the lesson of defeat repeatedly, despite their good intentions and high hopes, many abandoned politics altogether or lapsed into anti-democratic or nativist cynicism. Others began the painful process of rethinking their whole view of man and political things.

In general, the problem of the machine heightened the Progressives' sense of the need to provide immediately what the traditional theory of progress only promised. The individual by himself could not cope with the world of industrialism. It was necessary to provide him with guarantees of greater material security; the theory of the positive state gained strength throughout the period. It was equally necessary to provide him with some emotional security, some sense of unity and community, if he was to be the responsible, "public-regarding" citizen the Progressives hoped to make him. And that would prove a difficult task.[50]

---

[50] There were, however, very real and positive results. See David Brody, *Steelworkers of America: The Non-Union Era* (Cambridge: Harvard University Press, 1960), pp. 159–164.

Huns at the Gate

Two bases for a "national fraternity" suggested themselves to
Progressive theorists within the context of their theory: the fraternity
of race and blood and the fraternity of national "mission." No better
indication exists, probably, of the Enlightenment roots of Progressivism than the fact that in this critical respect it thought in the same
terms.

Racism was prominent. Hostility toward ethnic cultures was
normal for most, and even the tolerant saw no value in those distinct
ways of life. Anti-Orientalism was the stock in trade of West Coast
Progressives, and in the South, Progressivism was based on a combined
desire to "clean up" politics and to eliminate the black from politics
altogether as the presumed "reason" for political corruption. There
are redeeming features in Populist history; the Progressives offer few
or none. Darwinism helped. Even a reformer like Lester Ward, now
so much admired, could speak of white lynching and black "rapism"
as balanced "biological imperatives." [51] Historians thoroughly revised
the history of the Reconstruction, establishing the myths that have
endured to the present day, even (or necessarily?) maligning the
courage of the black soldier. The administrations of T. R. and
Woodrow Wilson coincided with what has been, since the abolition
of slavery, the nadir of race relations in America. Roosevelt issued
his highly publicized dinner invitation to Booker T. Washington;
for the black millions, the doors of opportunity were barred.

Yet like the theorists of the Enlightenment, most Progressives felt
uncomfortable with any less-than-universal ideal. From the mis-
sionaries-turned-reformers like Josiah Strong until the end of the
movement, Progressivism hankered after a "mission" which could
synthesize nationalism and universalism. Avarice could be defeated
and fraternity discovered, Herbert Croly argued, only when Americans felt themselves part of a crusade.

Progressives tended to be imperialistic, as Populists had not been.
The vision of empire, however, was an inadequate basis for national

---

[51] Lester F. Ward, *Pure Sociology* (New York: Macmillan, 1911), pp. 76–
77, 359–360; E. A. Ross, "The Causes of Race Superiority," *Annals,* XVIII
(1901), pp. 67–89.

"fraternity." America's selected foe, Spain, threatened no one, and Filipinos were of even less concern. The agrarians might be prone to a crusade to liberate others, but they found no important gains and many costs in the establishment of American dominion abroad. The moral idealism of the "white man's burden" had few appeals. Worse, war with Catholic Spain did not recommend itself highly to ethnic groups; and the Irish, since Ireland was still enslaved, found no great cause in the struggle to liberate Cuba. Dunne's Mr. Dooley treated the war with amused contempt, while even George Washington Plunkitt's patriotism was strained by those who denied Irishmen jobs through civil service reform, yet expected those same Irishmen to fight battles abroad. Whatever glory the war seemed to provide was tarnished by the ease of victory and the stink of disease and mismanagement. In fact, the war may have divided the community to a greater extent than before. Too gentle to paralyze men by horror, it was too peripheral to resolve more than temporarily the social and moral problems of the land.

World War I was different. The menace, if somewhat remote, was satisfyingly real. Resistance to change, even the old trust-busting hostility to corporate concentration, could be broken; "hyphenated" Americans could be bludgeoned into "Americanization" with the justification provided by the need for unity in the face of the threat to "democracy."

For many Americans, not least the Progressive intellectuals, the war was deeply exciting, providing a justification for sacrifice, camaraderie, and submission to an overriding purpose. Boring routine and imposed insecurity could yield to the chosen risk of crusading. And the war provided the moral basis of a crusade, as that with Spain had not. It could even appeal to pacifists, as America, renouncing imperial ambition, announced that she aimed at a "war to end war." Moreover, the war effort allowed every citizen to feel needed, whether in battle ("Uncle Sam needs *You*," the posters read), in war production, or in making bandages and selling bonds. The impersonal abstraction, the state, seemed to disappear into the nation, a solidaristic whole which left Whitman's poetry to enter political reality. Once leaders had spoken of the war as a sad necessity; increasingly, it was seen as an unparalleled promise. Wilson argued that:

From the first, the thought of the people of the United States turned toward something more than winning this war. It turned to the establishment of the eternal principles of right and justice. . . . There is a great tide running in the hearts of men. . . . Men have never been so conscious of their brotherhood. . . .[52]

But the events of the war shattered the confidence of younger intellectuals. World War I did not fit into the nineteenth century's scheme of progress, the march from "military" to "industrial" society. The brutality of the war suggested that the "natural ferocity" of men was still alive; the passivity of the masses raised doubts about individualism and the desire for liberty, causing speculation about the "instincts of the herd."[53] The hopes of liberalism were shadowed by a recognition of irrationality and a new sense of the darker potentialities of the human animal.

Randolph Bourne was less surprised than many, for Bourne had already come to suspect the liberal tradition. He was offended by the amoral naivete of those like John Dewey who could speak of the "social purpose" of war in overcoming cultural lag and teaching cooperation; but his new outrage differed only in degree from his earlier discontent. Bourne had already spoken of the value of ethnic diversity, the need for a "trans-national" America. Influenced by philosophers like Royce and the English pluralists, oppressed by his own loneliness and his sense of injustice, Bourne had come to doubt whether whatever sense of universal brotherhood was possible for human beings could be produced without some fraternity close at hand.[54]

Pragmatism is not enough, Bourne argued; the war proves that men, intellectuals not the least, need purpose and ideal, that they will submit to a "meaning" which is folly rather than have none. Neither

[52] Cited in Gabriel, *The Course of American Democratic Thought*, p. 369; see also *ibid.*, pp. 357–370, and Arthur S. Link, *Woodrow Wilson and the Progressive Era* (New York and Evanston: Harper and Row, 1963), pp. 81–106, 252–282.

[53] A prototypic case is the vogue of W. Trotter's *The Instincts of the Herd in Peace and War* (New York: Macmillan, 1919), though much of Trotter's work had been available before the war.

[54] Randolph Bourne, *The History of a Literary Radical*, ed. Van Wyck Brooks (New York: Russell, 1956), pp. 260–284.

are material and technical progress enough, if they demand passivity. Yet, Bourne went on, as much as men need the sense of contributing to something enduring and valuable, detached idealism is also not sufficient. Insecurity in personal relations combined with insecurity in ideas are not conditions men will endure, and men need the "beloved community" if they are to be protected against the temptation to fanaticism. Every man, Bourne argued in the accents of old, always needs the support of some community as, hopefully, he advances from ethnicity to trans-nationality. The greater fraternity demands, includes, and is never the enemy of, the lesser brotherhoods of men.[55]

The final judgment on Progressivism's shortcomings came from Harold Stearns. Progressive intellectuals, he pointed out, had always desired to win the admiration of society and to prove themselves "useful" to it; they had been "pragmatic" because they lacked values of their own. In fact, Progressivism originated with intellectuals who rejected the intellect.[56] At best it had been an alliance of individuals seeking to escape themselves and one another, too insecure and lonely to accept themselves or fraternity with those who were most akin. They could not become one with America at large; they could only find a still greater alliance in war, when danger and death substitute for mind and emotion as the bonds between men. That is the final and most devastating verdict on the Progressive quest for fraternity.

[55] *Ibid.*, pp. 197–259; see also Bourne, *War and the Intellectuals* (New York: Harper, 1964).
[56] Harold Stearns, *Liberalism in America* (New York: Boni and Liveright, 1919).

> Among democratic nations new families are constantly springing up, others are constantly falling away, and all that remain change their condition; the woof of time is every instant broken and the track of the generations effaced. Those who went before are soon forgotten; of those who will come after no one has any idea. . . . Thus not only does democracy make every man forget his ancestors, but it hides his descendants and separates his contemporaries from him. It throws him back for ever upon himself alone and threatens in the end to confine him entirely within the solitude of his own heart.
>
> De Tocqueville, *Democracy in America*

CHAPTER XVIII

GENERATIONS OF THE LOST

The Parting Ways

Many things perished in the First World War, and not only on the battlefields. The liberal faith in an orderly scheme of progress and a growth toward human fraternity were among the casualties hopelessly invalided, if not slain, by the savagery whose symbols were Ypres and the Somme. It would take more to persuade men to sacrifice for a future obscured by the shadow of uncertainty.

Some, like Andre Siegfried, ventured the hope that America, forcibly deprived of her illusions, might "come of age." [1] But it would

---

[1] Siegfried, *America Comes of Age* (New York: Harcourt, Brace, 1927).

be harder, than this to discard the liberal creed. In nineteenth-century America, the doubt that had repeatedly undermined the liberal creed had left only a minority of Americans bereft and adrift. The older communities, the localities, the ethnic groups, the churches, had given Americans a second line of defense, a world of personal relations to which men might fall back when the march of progress was turned to a temporary rout. Even in prosperity the traditional communities and groups had softened the rigors of competition and the isolating effects of economic and social life; in crisis they had provided an alternative model of society, a vocabulary of protest, and a basis for political organization.

These communities had not disappeared entirely. Americans clung to the remnants of traditional communities more desperately as they felt them slipping away, so much so that Siegfried saw the crisis of the Twenties as a cultural conflict between the "new America" and its older Protestant and Anglo-Saxon enemy. The combat, however, was as much epiphenomenal as real, a familiar diversion to distract attention from the deeper, growing crisis of industrial society. What reality it had lay in the frenzied attempt to protect what had been taken for granted, but was now probably lost beyond repair. Even Bourne, who had defined a choice between "trans-national America," united by values which included but transcended cultural diversity, and sub-national America, a society of isolated and anxious mass men, had seen only half the problem. For America to be "trans-national" there would have to be "nations," lesser communities and fraternities, to serve as the ladder to any greater. Increasingly it would not be enough to let existing "nations" alone; for Bourne's alternative to exist, governmental policy would have to protect those communities that remained, and create new ones. Logically, the end of the creed of progress and the senescence of the traditional communities demanded an end to the tottery synthesis America had always managed to retain between the two halves of her culture. "Coming of age" would require a confrontation between the creed of man before society, with its visions of universal fraternity when the barriers should be swept away, and the doctrine of political man, who needed the fraternities of the world in order to reach beyond his own and the world's limitations.

This choice, painful and difficult at best, most Americans refused to make. The politics of the Twenties was a vain struggle to reestablish the old equilibrium—vain because the liberal elements of the American heritage demanded that free play be allowed the organizational and technological forces which were destroying it. The slogans of the time, like "isolation" and "back to normalcy," only masked a politics of drift. As William Allen White realized, the decade's representative political man was Calvin Coolidge. Standing for the pre-modern virtues, Coolidge's ideology combined individualism in practice with an almost completely abstract religion, the two woven into a shoddy fabric by a belief in history—a confidence that if men would "go along with events" they would achieve personal and moral greatness. It was no accident that Coolidge should be famous for taciturnity; the old creed was too vulnerable now to risk articulation and the criticism attendant on it.[2]

In fact, the old cultural synthesis—always a shaky one—tottered further toward collapse. The pursuit of wealth reached a new intensity, and the demand behind it was for immediate rather than distant rewards. "Speculation" became almost respectable, and the virtue of thrift surrendered to the ethics of credit and consumption; even Teapot Dome, the scandal of the age, represented little more than an unusually rapacious version of the doctrine of "resource use." In the effort to find justifications for current practices, business propagandists spoke in tones so exalted as to reveal their despair of any mundane alternative, as when some identified affluence with the Kingdom of Heaven, or when Bruce Barton sought to demonstrate that Christ was best regarded as a businessman.[3]

All this was one with the fevered gaiety that became the symbol of the decade. As Fitzgerald knew, men who had "lost time"—in the future as well as the past—could not endure waiting; but in the loneliness of the present, desires turned to dust and ashes at the moment of gratification.[4] If the Twenties "roared," it was because silence was intolerable and speech could not build the bridge of communion be-

---

[2] William Allen White, *A Puritan in Babylon* (New York: Macmillan, 1940), pp. 9–10, 73, 427.

[3] Schlesinger, *The Crisis of the Old Order*, pp. 71–89; J. Leonard Bates, *The Origins of Teapot Dome* (Urbana: University of Illinois Press, 1963).

[4] F. Scott Fitzgerald, *The Crack-Up* (New York: New Directions, 1945), p. 84.

tween men. Even the economically fortunate had only the destiny of Hobbes' man, whirring from desire after desire until death.

Political leaders felt obliged to promise gain without sacrifice; Herbert Hoover, ironically, was the first President to pledge an end to poverty.[5] But far more than material well-being was involved; there was a demand for at least the shadow of fraternity. Business ideologists insisted that a "spirit of brotherliness" had entered into commercial life, and many vaunted the new interest in "human relations" as proof that businessmen took their duties as their brothers' keepers seriously (so seriously that they fought savagely with the unions which sought to relieve them of the burden). Useless as a guide to practice, such panegyrics are a touchstone of the psychological needs and the cultural crisis of the time.

The quest for community was the counterpart of the pursuit of wealth, but the two aims were contradictory. Those who could not face the cultural dilemma were sometimes harmlessly quixotic, but all too often they were sinister. The most insecure turned to the effort to establish a national "blood brotherhood"; and the Klan, adding anti-Semitism and anti-Catholicism to its repertoire, expanded to nationwide proportions. Racism, however, was not the exclusive property of townsmen and backwoodsmen. Eugenics had a scientific vogue; H. L. Mencken spiced his essays with comments about the defective "blood" of various "stocks." When Walter Lippmann criticized the "scientific" racism of Charles Yerkes and Lewis Terman, the latter placed Lippmann in the same "camp" with William Jennings Bryan. In an important sense, Terman may have been right; his rhetorical comment may have struck the basic line of cultural division in America more squarely than any of the "issues" of the time.[6]

Racism, however, spoke only indirectly to the tensions of the country. Aware at least unconsciously of their own departures from both the old creeds, most Americans found a more appropriate enemy in "foreign ideas" and attempted to rivet on America a uniform adherence to the "American way." The Klan became a vocal defender of Americanism, and it was a sign of the times that the "Invisible Empire," heir to the *majestas* of the Confederacy, should become aggres-

[5] Hoover, *The New Day* (Stanford: Stanford University Press, 1928), p. 16.
[6] Thomas Gossett, *Race: the History of an Idea in America*, pp. 366–369, 377.

sively nationalistic. The old localities, the old communities were dying, and all that remained was the effort to preserve the synthetic culture of the old order. Catholics too, shaken in their own traditional loyalties, found hostility to Communist and Socialist ideas a means to gain admission to the national "fraternity."

In fact, opposition to "alien ideologies," which did not require men to change the pattern of their daily lives, provided a pale imitation of the only "brotherhood" industrial America could know, the fraternity of battle. For those who had known that fraternity, and found peace vaguely insipid without it, the Legion and the V.F.W. marched in the forefront; behind came the somewhat overlapping cohorts of the Rotary, the Elks, and the slowly dying lodges. Under the umbrella of hostility to foreign doctrines, almost all Americans (even the so-recently-suspect Germans) could gather, finding an impersonal warmth and a partial escape from guilt in the monotonous affirmation of common "faith" and resolve.

Such xenophobia was not the result of deep commitment; it followed rather from the desire to exclude any situation in which strong loyalties and commitments might be required. The tensions within the culture and within the citizen himself were too sensitive to bear such testing. Political leaders, responsive if not inspired, felt the necessity which that desire imposed. The Twenties was a decade in which politics was suppressed, in marked contrast to the liveliness of political life in the twenty years before World War I. Until Smith was nominated in 1928, even surface issues which stirred men deeply entered politics only through third-party movements; the Democratic convention of 1924, though shaped by the old two-thirds rule, revealed the true spirit—neither Smith nor McAdoo could be nominated. Voters demonstrated their extreme unenthusiasm, and were perhaps glad to do so; turnouts at elections fell, and there are few signs that the voters desired alternatives any more exciting or demanding. The felt needs of most Americans promoted a vapid but unthreatening politics, in which the instability of life and culture could be concealed by silence, enabling men to avoid the perils of political involvement, and leaving them to the safeties and illusions of private life.

It was the time when the massive movement out of the cities and into the suburbs—the "country," in the persistent euphemism—

began; in this, as in many things, the Twenties were the forerunners of our time. A strong defense can be made for the migrants; the cities were unlovely and becoming more so, and Frank Lloyd Wright probably judged them rightly as hopelessly obsolete. The suburban movement, however, was based on illusion, on the desire to recapture the atmosphere of the small town within an urban economy. "Neighborliness" became a new ethic and a general theme in the social thought of the time, but it could never touch men deeply. Communities were not knit together by an autonomous or even a common economic life; such common institutions as they possessed (and possess) centered on shopping and schools, the world of women and children and hence of the private family. Community "spirit" was a mere desire for warmth as such; consider only the fact that "public-spirited" action so often concerns itself with recreation programs. Isolated in age and class, suburbs were and remain an effort to shut out threatening reality, constantly environed by fear because of the awareness that the "community" remains hopelessly a part of the city and lacks all serious control of its own fate. And the superficiality of its interpersonal relations is best indicated by the fact that if their economic circumstances permit or require it, citizens simply move on.

In Southern California, the extreme case in which the urban center had all but vanished, the inadequacy of the new community became evident. Over the region, the art of the movie set created Potemkin villages in which, for a fee, it was possible to delight in frontier towns and fairylands (Disneyland is only among the most recent, and the most elaborate), a recreation which appealed—under the justification of fun for children—to something the adults felt missing from their own lives. Cultism was only a more direct, and extreme, expression of the same phenomenon. It was the Romantic's dream, the total fulfillment of private man. The cults relied heavily on erotic appeals, promising wealth, love, power, youth, and immortality; all spoke of a mystic "community" into which the believer entered; almost all proclaimed that physical reality could be mastered by a new "science" of the mind.

Absurd or pathetic, the play-towns and the cults reflected a more serious trend in the culture. The world threatened and choices demanded making, and all possibilities for action required that men acknowledge their own dependence on others. But threats and demands made dependence too fearful for isolated men. They fled into private worlds, and as those citadels yielded in succession, the flights became more desperate and more fantastic. Once it was possible to laugh at the old and the half-educated who peopled the cults; it is more difficult now that their places have been taken by the young and the highly schooled. Even an ironist can find little satisfaction in the analogy between the drug culture and the imagined powers of the milky fluid that filled the mysterious vial of the Ascended Master, St. Germain.

Whether Americans could bear the knowledge or not, the Lockean tradition was at a dead end. Society no longer "underlay" the state. The traditional institutions and beliefs which liberalism had taken for granted, or seen as the "instinctive" expressions of "natural man," were perishing. Only the conjugal family remained strong, and it was radically destabilized. And as man has been thrown back more and more on himself, he has given the lie to many liberal theories, not the least to the hope for an emerging brotherhood of man. For man alone is not anyone's brother; he is simply alone.

"A night of dark intent . . ."

The intellectuals of the twenties were probably no lonelier than their fellow citizens, but they were more aware of the fact, and the awareness brought pain. They were further, both psychologically and socially, from the remnants of the traditional communities, and were only too aware that nothing had appeared to replace them—let alone improve on their defects. America had never seemed tawdrier than in the Twenties; even its illusions, crabbed by fear, lacked any grandeur. And being men of ideas, the intellectuals were caught up in the crisis of belief and the decay of the Enlightenment creed. They spent much time in mercurial, jabbering pursuit of some doctrine which could provide a new answer. Freudianism and Marxism were only the most salient—and then as now, theosophy and Eastern religion had a vogue. These were the stuff of satire, but the only alternative was an alienation most found it impossible to bear.

The gap between the intellectuals and the practice of American life had grown so great that the revolutionary ideal of Bolshevism had its appeal. The example of the Soviet Union seemed to open the possibility that a violent cataclysm which swept away existing institutions might enable men (and especially intellectuals) to remake the world. Too, Leninism provided a new basis for a belief in history, a redefinition of the idea of progress; it was hardly accidental that Lincoln Steffens' delight was expressed in the phrase, "I have seen the future and it works!" Yet Moscow was guilty of too many "excesses," too many obvious departures from fraternity, to appeal to more than a few; its moment, when it came, required the assistance of fascism and the Depression. And as often as not the intellectual of the Twenties recognized that Moscow sought to become part of the modern world, and that modernity was part of his own dilemma.[7]

More characteristic were those who turned to romantic individualism, the creed of self above society. For these, H. L. Mencken was nonpareil. Mencken's critique of American life, however, though often devastating, centered on an America which was dying, the world of the backwoods and the towns. It owed much of its appeal to the fact that it did not require the intelligentsia to examine its own life and conduct. Mencken's own individualism concealed a desperate desire for recognition and status, indicated clearly enough by his elitism in an age when intellectuals were anything but an elite. Mencken had only learned the old tactic that attention is often best won by attack. Despite his aggressive individualism, Mencken, like the expatriates, showed a yearning for community and for a place that would be "his," where affection would not have to wear the mask of "toughness." In Mencken's case, it took the form of a pseudo-ethnic devotion to Germany and things German—spurious in part because Mencken read German only with difficulty and knew few Germans. In one sense, Mencken was wiser than the expatriates; he knew that the nostalgic idyll crumbles at the touch. Even so, though Mencken was too decent and too much a foe of tomfoolery to be taken in by Nazism, his inner expatriation led him to anti-Semitism and to the denunciation of exiles and German-Americans

[7] Schlesinger, *Crisis of the Old Order*, pp. 204–223.

"who turn against their own people." There are few sadder testimonies to the need of man to have some people of his own.[8]

Not very different was the "new humanism" associated with Irving Babbitt and Paul Elmer More. There was, in fact, little new about the doctrine. It was a revived form of Federalism, which elevated property and individual liberty over "equality and fraternity" but otherwise clung to the Enlightenment creed. Mencken and More were alike in holding to the doctrine that man is by nature savage—and the state, consequently, a contractarian device. Both accepted the mastery of nature as a vital human goal. There was in both a new suspicion of the supposed fraternal "instincts" of man, but it led only to the romantic affirmation of the self, void of genuine knowledge of either human personality or fraternity. The romantic individualist had no answers, and his poses only gave him a means of winning admiration from the more easily deceived conformists, desperately insecure and willing to respect those who claimed to be strong.[9]

There were others, however, who went closer to the heart of things, tracing the American problem to the defect of modern institutions. With varying degrees of insight and sophistication, cultural critics presented a characteristic set of propositions to which social criticism in our time has added little. America, the argument went, had made life over into the image of the machine; each individual lacked a sense of the whole, had become a mere "part" without feelings of responsibility. Individualism had become impossible as the basis for meaning in life. Men needed new ideals, new theories of democracy, based on interdependence and cooperation; and to make such theories a vital force, the society needed a new sense of purpose, value, and vision. Having acquired power, men had lost the perception of those ends power was meant to serve.[10]

---

[8] Charles Angoff, "Mencken as a German American," *Chicago Jewish Forum*, XXV (1966–1967), pp. 143–146.

[9] Thomas Hartshorne, *The Distorted Image*, pp. 80–85; Schlesinger, *Crisis of the Old Order*, pp. 145–152.

[10] Hartshorne, *The Distorted Image*, pp. 90–95. For examples, see Paul Mazur, *American Prosperity* (New York: Viking, 1928), and Beard, *Whither Mankind?*, pp. 287–312, 387–402.

Yet though such critics repeatedly urged the need for such a standard of value, few indeed attempted to define what it might be. For the most part, when pressed for a positive vision, the intellectual fell back on the ideals of the Enlightenment: liberty, equality, affluence, and the mastery of nature—and, ultimately, the brotherhood of man. He was concerned to demonstrate that new institutions, replacing "obsolete" existing ones, could realize the ideals of liberalism in the short term through the use of "scientific" principles.

There was a parallel popular current, and more than one bizarre doctrine incubated in the Twenties rose to prominence in the confusion and desperation of the Depression. Technocracy; the Universal Research Foundation, which promised a "social assimilative state under transcendental administration"; Utopia, Incorporated, which sought the traditional values of individualism, opportunity, and family through the equally traditional method of a secret fraternal order; each had respectable antecedents in the social thought of the Twenties. All testified to a discontent which prosperity had lulled into an uneasy quiet, a growing realization that history and "nature" could no longer be relied on and that active planning would be needed if the goals of the liberal Enlightenment were to be hoped for at all.

In greater numbers than ever, though, there were intellectuals who doubted the value of those goals. Modernity had become suspect; without the old promise of the future, costs seemed greater, possibly, than benefits. There was a new concern for community and a search for roots. "Folk art" came into fashion, and portraits of "ordinary" Americans and older communities were à la mode. The yearning for something absent from American life—or at least from the experience of intellectuals—was so strong that much of this research and writing was highly sentimental. Sherwood Anderson, convinced that America, blinded by optimism and faith in technology, had gone astray, saw a gradual decay of personal security—typified by the passing of the craftsman—and a growing fear of affection and emotion which isolated men and destroyed their capacity to resist the impersonal tendencies of the age. And under the surface, Anderson saw resentment and destructiveness, which in turn became the driving forces of modern life. Yet though Anderson was influenced by "Freudian" ideas, he tended to make emotion and affection into panaceas, goals in and of themselves. His very desperation for "brotherhood" and for an escape from isolation led him personally to the overcommitments of romanticism and, inevitably, to the jealousy and fear of betrayal that appear frequently in his letters. The romantic and sentimental adulation of warmth and community as ends in themselves was no answer to the problem of fraternity.[11]

A few, like Stuart Sherman, probed deeply enough to see the importance of religious culture in America. Sherman pointed to Puritanism, with its concern for the public and political fraternity, as a basis for genuine democracy. And Sherman saw, too, that Puritan insistence on fraternity as a means for human development, rather than a distant end, combined the need for community with the requirements of excellence.[12]

Not many, however, had Sherman's willingness to brave the antireligious current of the time, and fewer, probably, had any desire to do so. The religious tradition was increasingly distant from the world of intellectuals—and from America at large. Sherman hesitated, however, to adopt the melancholy conclusions that the old roots were lost and that advocacy was a weak weapon with which to combat the dominant forces of the time—as Robert Frost, who saw the virtues of Puritanism as clearly as Sherman, did reluctantly. Frost found little to hope for in his contemporaries and felt that wisdom lay in a "sense of mellow decay" and withdrawal into upper New England. There was, however, a guile in Frost's retreat; for his poems, in spite or because of their limited audience, aimed to preserve the old teaching for those able to hear it. The retreat was calculated: Frost had the gentle confidence that the tradition spoke too truly to vanish permanently. When their elegant illusions proved false, men would return, and they would save time and agony if the teaching remained at hand.

> For dear me, why abandon a belief
> Merely because it ceases to be true?
> Cling to it long enough, it will turn true again,
> For so it goes.
> Most of the change we think we see in life
> Is due to truths being in and out of favor.

---

[11] Sherwood Anderson, *Puzzled America* (New York: Scribner's, 1935), pp. 1–10; Edmund Wilson, *The Shock of Recognition*, pp. 1261–1264, 1284–1285, 1287.

[12] Stuart Sherman, *The Genius of America* (New York: Scribner's, 1923).

This was scarcely optimism; Frost was certain that a "night of dark intent" was in the offing. That, however, only emphasized the principle that "someone had better be prepared," a precept that has as much value now as in Frost's time for those devoted to the ideal of fraternity.[13]

The Redhead

There were, however, voices that reached a wider public. The Twenties was one of the great ages of the novel, possibly because readers were less interested in the exciting and exotic and more concerned with insight into themselves and the time. The roster of novelists is distinguished by any standard, and if Sinclair Lewis merits special consideration, it is precisely because of his literary weaknesses. Attacking Lewis as a novelist is easy; it is almost impossible to fault him as an observer of society—in fact, the most common (and probably just) criticism is that he only used the novel as a vehicle for social commentary. And the massive appeal of Lewis to the intelligentsia of the Twenties suggests that he touched a true chord, that he found common themes in the diverse experience of men.

Lewis called himself a "romantic medievalist," but no one showed less interest in the past in general or the Middle Ages in particular. His concerns were thoroughly American. Lewis felt his own bond to the land, and would-be expatriates like Mrs. Doddsworth fared rather badly in his novels. He had no doubt that the country was his, that his problems and those of the land were inseparable, that flight in space or into the reaches of time was no answer. In fact, his criticism was the more powerful because it was sympathetic, because he saw the virtues of the American alongside—and in—his defects.

Certainly, most Americans will always remember Lewis as the assailant of the small town, the dissector of the frauds and follies of Babbittry and the middle class. Lewis' criticism, however, was far more general; if anything, he was more bitter in describing the liberal intelligentsia. Lewis saw a "system" at work in America, an integrated set of beliefs, institutions, and processes which defeated the American, balked his efforts to make his dreams real, and left him the prisoner of a life devoted to material gains which had no real personal meaning. In one of his few explicitly political essays, Lewis described the situa-

[13] *Poems of Robert Frost* (New York: Modern Library, 1946), pp. 67, 272.

tion of the Southern textile industry as one in which mill owners controlled banks, which in turn controlled small businessmen and professionals and especially the clergy, who indoctrinated and controlled workers.[14] (Lewis saw the subordination of religion to business as an extreme perversion.)

The world of *Babbitt* abounds with the defeated: Babbitt, the would-be politician; Littlefield, the frustrated scholar; Chum Frink, the businessman's poet. Lewis was, however, far from suggesting that men should in some simple sense "live by the ideal" or follow the promptings of the spirit. Rather, he indicated that the frustration of dreams and visions deprived men of the necessity of testing those dreams by the standard of reality. They were allowed the luxury of the romantic's exculpatory "if only"—or, if the dreams were repressed enough, their minds were left at the mercy of infantile fantasies like the faerie of Babbitt's dreams or the adolescent romanticism of his nature idyll. America, in fact, kept men from growing up; preserving the child in the man, it ultimately denied him humanity.

Lewis' characters, as T. K. Whipple remarked, are all poseurs, whether they act as conformists or romantic rebels; they lack personal integration, the unity of ideal and physical vision, inward thought and outer action.[15] In fact, it is his romantics who are most inclined to evade that conflict, trying to delude themselves as well as others with a stance or a grand gesture. Conformist or romantic, the American is guided by the fear of being found out, perhaps most particularly by himself. If he remains a child, it is because he has never known community, let alone fraternity; fearful and alone, he can bear others only by eliminating all apparent differences between himself and others or by adopting the hauteur of superiority and affected unconcern.

Despite his criticisms, Lewis admired the virtues of the small town: the personal significance of the individual and the inevitable concern of one man for another. What he detested was the degree to which the towns were absorbed in the quest for material gain, which poisoned the small-town virtues themselves. Apparent friendliness hid a backbiting competitiveness which made trust impossible and betrayal almost universal.

[14] *Cheap and Contented Labor* (Philadelphia: Women's Trade Union League, 1929), pp. 14–19.
[15] Whipple, *Spokesmen*, pp. 214–215, 220–221.

The cities might have more diversions; socially, however, they were worse than the towns. In an early novel, *The Job*, Lewis pictured New York as a place in which employment had become the only purpose of life, which otherwise was filled with pointless routine and equally pointless amusement. The city was a place of drift, aimlessness, and personal insecurity where men who might become citizens were taught only "sharp unscrupulousness." [16]

The system tended to be self-perpetuating; comic man, attempting to escape it, only became more entrapped. Needing affection, often wishing to make a gesture of independence, the American was likely to be led—as were Babbitt and his son—into early marriage. But marriage forces—or excuses—the abandonment of early hopes, compelling the husband to "provide," the wife to establish "the home." Too often founded on the desire for affection and admiration without any common values, marriages lacked any direction other than that given by drift and the pursuit of material gain. All the frustrated hopes of the self were projected onto one's children. The cycle repeats itself; the irony of Babbitt's affirmation of unity with his son, which closes the novel, is that the son has already rejected Babbitt's dream and become entrapped, just as Babbitt himself had been. There was no great promise in the young; they were, Lewis had Doremus Jessup declare, "going 70 m.p.h., but not going anywhere, not enough imagination to *want* to go anywhere." [17]

Lewis' criticism of marriage was hardly the result of a belief in "free love." Lewis found sensuality destructive, ultimately futile, and powerless to create genuine bonds between individuals. His characters often seek to escape from the toils of conjugality, but the escape is most often only the romantic's dream. It is a rebellion not against the purposelessness of the family but against its responsibilities, or it is an attempt to assuage the fear of growing older. A false idyll, such escape leads nowhere but to indignity, and even a return to marital respectability is made to appear an elevation to reality.

Still less is Lewis' critique meant to teach man to remain alone. His *Ann Vickers* is very much the story of Carol Kennicut had she

---

[16] *The Job* (New York: Harcourt, Brace, 1917); see also *Main Street* (New York: New American Library, 1961), p. 257.

[17] Lewis, *It Can't Happen Here* (Garden City: Doubleday Doran, 1935), pp. 16-17.

never married and had she continued to pursue her youthful ambitions. Ann Vickers fears losing her independence and being trapped in marriage; and consequently her need for affection, otherwise denied expression, finds its way into social reformism. Able to "love" the victims of society without danger to herself, Ann Vickers needs and receives "love" in the form of the admiration of other reformers—and, to a degree, of society at large. Her need for that response is deep-seated (she glories, for example, in an honorary doctorate), and when it is threatened, she becomes almost paralyzed and incapable of action. She is enabled to defy society only by the encouragement and support of Pearl McKaig, a college friend who has become a Communist; her own "independence" is a sham.

Ann Vickers' own excursions into romance have been marred by injury, yet that only confirms her tendency to seek out shallow men who are easily dominated, like her first husband, a somewhat Babbittish social worker. Eventually, Ann is "cured" by her love for Barney Dolphin, a corrupt judge whose conviction also frees him from his own entrapped concern for social position. It serves to end the novel, but Lewis leaves the more basic question open; in accepting marriage to a disgraced judge, Ann Vickers may have defied social respectability, but she has surely found a personal relationship which, again, she will inevitably dominate.

Ann Vickers is important because it reveals the basis of Lewis' distaste for liberal social reform. The attempt to eliminate inhumanities is praiseworthy, but it allows the reformer to evade the more basic issue, the values and purposes of society itself. His stance permits the reformer the illusion of independence, for he is outside orthodox patterns of behavior, at the same time that he plays an established social role. Worse, the reformer is likely to need the victim as an object for his own affections and a means for winning the admiration of others. It is an ideal path for the romantic, "independent and courageous" in the eyes of most, superior to those he seeks to help, able to win affection from both but involved in genuinely personal relations with neither. And because the reformer is so likely to need both respectable society and the unfortunate, he cannot tolerate changes which would abolish either or both.[18]

[18] *Ann Vickers* (New York: Dell, 1962), pp. 94–96, 226–229, 398–399, 423.

Lewis did not believe, however, that the dangers of reformism could be avoided by adherence to revolutionary dogma. Pearl McKaig seems to show courage during Ann Vickers' crisis, but her stance is only the negation of society, and hence a pose of its own. This posing, moreover, has the additional disadvantage that it requires the reinforcement of a narrow creed. There is no virtue in either the passive acceptance of established values or the equally passive adoption of a hostile ideology. Both lack a personal standard of value, for that can only be based on an active seeking. Fundamental to the evaluation of society, that search has no stopping place; ideal values—and hence, ideal institutions—are ultimately doubtful. "The free," Lewis wrote, "are never 'free' to be anything but free." [19]

Parrington commented that Lewis, having lost faith in the machine, in technology, and in orthodox definitions of progress, fell back on the belief in science and the intellect as such. This is accurate enough, but it indicates how much Lewis' thought presupposed the alienation of the intellectual from society and from practical life, itself a significant departure from the Enlightenment creed. Moreover, Lewis conceived of science as a religious, or at least as a quasi-mystical, phenomenon. As Max Gottlieb expressed it in *Arrowsmith*, the scientific commitment is the religious passion and the prophetic vision freed from the constraints of dogma and doctrine. Martin Arrowsmith, his disciple, puts it succinctly; "God give me strength not to trust in God." Poles from the Puritans in language and tone, Lewis was no great distance from them in spirit.[20]

Science, however, demands freedom, and freedom requires the ability to stand aside without standing alone; the lonely must pose and are never free. Friendship and fraternity were Lewis' talismans, bonds between men who share common values—in the highest sense, the search for truth. These bonds give men an autonomous center of affection and criticism, distinct from established society. Science, Lewis knew, often seems pitiless and cold to outsiders. Yet Gottlieb, his scientific paragon, feels a deep affection for his own spiritual

---

[19] *Main Street*, pp. 261–263, 423–424, 433; *It Can't Happen Here* (New York: Dell, 1961), pp. 124–125.

[20] Parrington, "Our Own Diogenes," in *Sinclair Lewis*, ed. Mark Schorer, pp. 69–70; Lewis, *Arrowsmith* (New York: New American Library, 1961), pp. 267–269.

kindred, the need of the uncertain for the support of brethren. Eventually, after the vicissitudes of life and marriage, the rejection of small-town and urban "research" medicine (Lewis was an early and acute critic of the bureaucratic tendencies of foundations), Arrowsmith finds his personal answer in life with Terry Wickett—like him, an intellectual "son" of Max Gottlieb. Their retreat in the forest is Babbitt's romance perfected by purpose; science, as Lewis defined it, is not heartless, but it refuses to be guided or to form relations solely on the basis of sentiment and affectivity.

Common values were basic because, among other reasons, Lewis was so cognizant of the sad ways in which the need for fraternity can be perverted—or, denied other expression, can be so insistent as to degenerate into mere gregariousness. False fraternity is a constant theme in his novels. Babbitt's "twin brothers" are legion, including all the hosts devoted to Zip and Pep, he-manliness and the like. Fundamentally, however, all the heartiness of Babbitt's companions, all their boisterous but genuine delight in affection, is only a veneer which conceals their own fear of difference and suspicion of each other. Even more pathetic is the "brotherhood" of the smoking car, to which Babbitt introduces his son, an impersonal aggregation of drifting men united only by loneliness and by the accidental propinquity resulting from a process which will rapidly sweep them apart.

No better is Babbitt's "brotherhood" with Paul Riesling, based on a common romantic illusion. That "fraternity" serves to enable Babbitt to bear respectability, just as it is Paul's attempted murder of his wife which shakes Babbitt into the attempt to realize the romantic idyll. Their fraternity is in fact a safety valve, providing a tenuous link between social conformity and adolescent dream. It makes chains endurable, rather than setting either free. Babbitt is, as Rebecca West called him, a "bonehead Walt Whitman"; and in a fundamental sense he is the realization of much of Whitman's ideal, revealed for the tawdry thing it is.[21]

The perversion of friendship was, Lewis knew, the natural tendency of social institutions in America. The title figure of *Our Mr. Wrenn* has a friend, Harry Morton, who opens for him the path to love and freedom, but he only learns the lesson that friendship is a

---

[21] Rebecca West, "Babbitt," in *Sinclair Lewis,* ed. M. Schorer, pp. 23-26.

potentially effective motif for advertising. Yet even false friendship could have its uses. Babbitt's period as a crusader is inspired by his encounter with Seneca Doane, the radical lawyer, whom he had known in college. Doane flatters Babbitt outrageously; Babbitt is attracted by Doane's political prominence as much or more than by his cause, and subsequently wildly romanticizes their degree of intimacy. This bogus friendship, however, more closely parallels Babbitt's own ideals and gives him a moment of human admirability. Imagined friendship, however, has no staying power when confronted with social opprobrium. Resisting social pressure would require the reality of daily contact, if not the reality of fraternity. But Babbitt's moment is testimony to the need for and power of fraternity in the lives of men.

Lewis' political vision was not a clear one. Too much of his time was absorbed in "shapeless irritation" and heavy-handed satire (though even in the worst examples, like *Gideon Planish*, he showed his wonted political prescience). He lacked, too, any complete understanding of the inherent physicality of affection, and he always remained hostile to Freudianism. Yet his political vision was real, if cloudy in its lack of any precise institutions which might realize it. The defects can be excused; Lewis saw little prospect for realizing his ideal in a society whose values and practices seemed so far from his own, and his function as a moralist was necessarily secondary to his role as a critic.

In part, however, the ideal was clear enough; Lewis' standard was a fraternal citizenry based on smaller-scale organization and a simpler economy, the need for "a new people in a new land." Citizenship always ranked high with Lewis; Babbitt was not instinctively a political man for nothing. Without much strain, Lewis' political doctrine can be identified with Populism. His favored characters were never urban radicals; they were "village rebels" like Miles Bjornstrom. In the same sense, the shallowness of *Main Street* is revealed by contrast with the farms, not with the city—which was, if anything, worse than the towns.

In a sense, Lewis fought the Populist battle out of season, combating the farmer's small-town enemies and attacking foes whose power was already broken and whose way of life was passing. That, however, would ignore Lewis' efforts at prophecy, most visible in his shrill and rather incompetent *It Can't Happen Here* and in the equally dreadful *Kingsblood Royal*. The forces of modern society, as Lewis saw them, were building slowly toward a titanic crisis, one encouraged by the isolation, apathy, and self-concern of the "decent American." Those defects themselves are always traced to outside forces, and much of his work seems an attempt to shock middle-class America into some kind of awareness. *It Can't Happen Here* has more than one echo of *Caesar's Column*: when the rebellion against fascism begins, it is Midwestern and agrarian; its leader, who aims at the brotherly polity of an American Cooperative Commonwealth, is even a Republican; its backbone is the awakened small-town intelligentsia, typified by Doremus Jessup.[22] And it seems likely that Nathaneal West, who had less faith in Americans, aimed his satire, *A Cool Million*, at the rather broad target Lewis set up.

Lewis understood better than most of his contemporaries both the nature of fraternity and man's need for it. But although he could intellectually accept the requirement of alienation, he could not do so personally, possibly because, unlike Martin Arrowsmith, he never found the fraternity which would have made it endurable. As a result, he continued to search for traditional virtues and values among people who, if not as lost as West feared, were losing rapidly whatever remnants of those qualities they possessed. Lewis' critique was never enough to convince him that those virtues had disappeared; they were merely buried in hopelessness and the material concerns of a system which dwarfed men. He had some hope that they might reemerge in the moment of crisis, just as he feared that such a moment would be too late.

Lewis had far less hope than many of his fellow citizens and readers; *It Can't Happen Here* was something of an aberration produced by heightened anxiety. But that note could be struck and the whispered faith was real—and if true of Lewis, how much truer it was of his public, less rigorous mentally and more eager for consolation. That suggests one basis for the alacrity with which so many accepted the role that society, in the crisis of the Depression, was to assign them —that of refurbishing a political order which rendered fraternity less and less accessible to men. It is almost pathetic that they did so out of

[22] *It Can't Happen Here* (1961), pp. 31, 130, 196, 373; see also *The Trail of the Hawk* (New York: Harcourt, Brace, 1915).

a hope that by escaping political impotence, they could discover or create a brotherhood of citizens.

The Philosopher

There were, however, other and more positive bases for the eagerness to embrace the cause of reform. Liberal progressivism, politically in partial eclipse, recovered whatever intellectual confidence it had lost and even acquired a new kind of zeal. Of course, the doctrine did not survive unchanged. The Twenties only confirmed what the war had suggested so emphatically, that man alone was a far weaker being than had been supposed, especially given the possibilities for manipulation that existed in modern society. The fact raised dark anxieties among liberals, and many scanned the intellectual horizon, seeking a return of the light.

The preeminence of John Dewey—which maddened H. L. Mencken, for one—rested on the fact that Dewey felt those anxieties deeply and resolved them well enough to satisfy his all-too-willing liberal contemporaries. The appeal of Dewey's thought, as Eric Goldman pointed out, was extrinsic as much as intrinsic; Dewey provided a "philosophy and a psychology perfectly tailored to progressive needs." [23]

Dewey's criticism of the old liberalism, however, had much to recommend it on its own terms. Liberalism, Dewey argued, had never understood the social bases on which its political institutions had been founded. Individualistic in law and theory, liberalism had depended in fact on local communities and on the common symbols provided by religion: the first gave men security and experience in common action, the second enabled them to articulate shared experience and communality.[24]

Ignoring those foundations, Dewey continued, older liberalism had raised its individualistic propositions to the level of absolutes. Ironically, as it exalted the individual in theory, the social and tech-

[23] Eric Goldman, *Rendezvous with Destiny* (New York: Vintage, 1956), pp. 122–123.

[24] John Dewey, *The Public and Its Problems* (New York: Holt, 1927), pp. 111–115; *Individualism Old and New* (New York: Minton Balch, 1930), pp. 13–14.

nological forces it helped to set in motion were weakening and submerging him in fact. Those new forces destroyed the old communities, "freeing" the individual only to leave him helpless and alone. Liberal theory had blinded liberals to the need to create new communities to replace the old. Now the consequences were becoming evident and Americans increasingly felt their loss. The older patterns retained a "sentimental prestige in literature and religion"—but, Dewey insisted, such ideas were sentimental only; historical change had made them irrelevant to present times. Only a clear-sighted liberalism would be equal to the task of social reconstruction.[25]

Dewey's liberalism, however, was very little different in its basic premises from its predecessor. The departure from the old liberalism consisted chiefly in Dewey's affirmation that man was "naturally social," but this only emphasized the old liberal distinction between the state and society. The naturalness of association extended, for Dewey, to all groups where the "fruits of intercourse" were directly and immediately evident to the individual. The claims of such parochial, face-to-face groups, however, conflicted with those of others. Parties to a dispute, appealing to the "right of self-help," gradually escalated the conflict by involving friends and allies. These, less immediately involved, sometimes committed to both disputants, were better able to recognize a common interest in avoiding or resolving conflict, and became the basis of a "public" which created a legal and political order.[26]

That this is little more than a restatement of contractarian theory is evident; and like contractarian theory, it casts government in an essentially passive role. The foundation of all politics remains the "right of self-help," and the principal aims of government consist in caring for and regulating private interests so as to guarantee order and a greater fulfillment of private aims.[27]

However, in Dewey's analysis, the state is an intermediate term between the "natural" and "non-political" association and those relations in which contact is so infrequent, irregular, or indirect as to exclude the recognition of any common interest. The expansion of tech-

[25] *The Public and Its Problems,* pp. 87–88, 95–99, 101, 142, 152–153; *Individualism,* pp. 12, 32, 59.
[26] *The Public and Its Problems,* pp. 16–17, 22–28, 39–40, 70, 105.
[27] *Ibid.,* pp. 19, 33–34, 47, 61, 64, 71, 73.

nological and organizational power constantly pushes this second boundary back—and as it retreats, the state expands the scale and scope of its action. The change is in itself simply the result of quantitative change, and inherent in it is the possibility of political alienation. Originally, Dewey argued, the state had been a "mere shadow" on the life of society; gradually, however, the state had come to be the ruler over society, as the natural group progressively lost the capacity to govern its own life. As complex, far-reaching, and indirect processes bulked larger in the life of men, the group became more and more inadequate, the state more and more necessary. Pluralist doctrines like Laski's, which had come into vogue shortly before and during the war, were, Dewey recognized, little more than nostalgic myths. But even as myths, they addressed the danger that in the process of state expansion, men would be left helplessly behind.[28]

Dewey was not concerned, however, with slowing or restraining the process; he was interested in the means by which men might be kept in step with it. Faith in history, the old creed of progress, was central to all his thought, and it was to validate that faith that Dewey appealed to the metaphor of "evolution," the battlecry of reform Darwinism. Dewey had no doubt that the defeat of an older scheme of things proved its inferiority, whatever the defects of the new might be. And he insisted, rather tiresomely, on the need for "adjustment." Ideals were "genuine" only when they reflected "possibilities of what is now moving," and any ideal which lacked the support of or worked at odds with existing historical trends and forces was no more than "eccentricity and escape." This led of course to Dewey's insistence on a political order that would be flexible, responsive, and able to move with the times.[29]

Hence the problem for Dewey lay in overcoming "cultural lag," the persistence of old values and institutions into a new time. Dewey understood well enough that a dissonance between the requirements of successful action and the values men held created in the individual a tension which was likely to result in apathy, and contained the po-

---

[28] *Ibid.*, pp. 41, 43, 47–48.
[29] *Ibid.*, pp. 31–32, 203–204; *Individualism*, pp. 69, 124–127, 130, 143, 148; *Reconstruction in Philosophy* (New York: New American Library, 1950), pp. 62, 65, 102, 141, 147.

tential for violent conflict.[30] His prescription was a uniform one: eliminate the resistance of old standards, remove human hostility to the new order of things, adapt men to their times. History reigned as sovereign in Dewey's theory, and no man opposed it rightly.

Dewey saw quite clearly many of the defects of industrial society, especially the human estrangement that made men hopelessly weak and allowed the process of production to move in its own aimless path. He insisted, however, that the fault was not in technology or industrialism per se, but in men's "lack of will to use them as instruments," the lack of connection to considered human goals. Dewey's attraction to Marxism—of which he confessed he had read little —was due to the Marxian insistence that the evils of modern life were separable from modernity, and Dewey adopted the thesis that a new form of production based on "cooperation" rather than "pecuniary motives" would transform the character of modern life. "Economic determinism," Dewey declared, "is a fact." [31]

Economic determinism, however, sits uneasily with Dewey's insistence on the importance of "will." For Dewey was arguing that it was the will of men—ignorant, emotional, insubordinate to the commands of historically informed reason—that was at fault. Until the modern age, material scarcity had dominated human life, and men's energies had been bent to the task of overcoming it; production and acquisition and, secondarily, the "uncoordinated" struggle to preempt scarce goods at the expense of others, had been ends in themselves, acceptable in the light of history. Now it was possible for men to be freed from the old necessities, to pursue ampler goals and visions, but it was first necessary to eliminate the old habits of mind. For Dewey, mental and cultural change were the preconditions of the economic changes which would revolutionize life in industrial society; economic organization "determined" only at a second, and lower level of causation. Dewey's adoption of "Marxism," in other words, was almost entirely instrumental; his basic creed remained liberal. Dependence on the mind, however, did not lessen his faith in historical progress.

[30] *The Public and Its Problems*, pp. 31, 68, 162, 179; *Individualism*, pp. 67–68.

[31] *Ibid.*, pp. 48, 72, 119–120, 135, 157–158; *Liberalism and Social Action* (New York: Capricorn, 1963), p. 54.

Dewey insisted that, in the long term at least, industrialism and technology would produce a "free, flexible, and many-colored life" which "in the end . . . can only signify the emancipation of the individual." [32]

The process might be short or prolonged. The majority of men remained short-sighted, unable to discern the direction of things; and intellectuals, by providing "leading ideas," might guide them more efficiently on the historical path. All thought, for Dewey, was instrumental; he revered science, as Lewis did, but Lewis had seen science as a way to knowledge, a way of discerning meaning identical with the highest human goal, where Dewey saw it as a technique for obtaining the mastery of nature. Philosophy, Dewey argued, was the result of conflict among men for the possession of scarce resources or between new and old ideas within men or in society. The principal aim of philosophy was to eliminate conflict, redirecting the energies of men away from combat with each other into the conflict with nature that was the province of science. (Thus implicitly, the aim of thought, whether philosophic or scientific, was at least in principle to eliminate itself; logically, the ultimate goal of man was a society without the need for—hence, simply without—thought.) In periods when the conflicts of men rose to an intense level and they found themselves confused and baffled, as Dewey felt to be the case in his own time, philosophy could make an "initial move" in the reconstruction of a temporary equilibrium. Men might listen to philosophers when older modes of thought were in disarray.[33]

Dewey had reason enough, given the lost and baffled men of his time, to expect that moment of opportunity sometime in the near future. But as he was aware, the "initial move" is only that; the moment does not endure, and philosophy must use it to create social forces and institutions which will continue to work in the desired direction. A believer in "democracy," Dewey was no believer in the public. His confidence in democracy was rooted in the belief that democracy was more open to the "process of experience," which Dewey equated—wrongly—with scientific method, and which at a

[32] *The Public and Its Problems*, p. 217; *Individualism*, pp. 30, 46–47, 93.

[33] *The Public and Its Problems*, pp. 30–31, 174; *Individualism*, p. 139; *Human Nature and Conduct* (New York: Holt, 1944), pp. 212–213, 270, 273. See also Ralph Barton Perry, *Characteristically American* (New York: Knopf, 1949), pp. 51–52.

more basic level was identical with his faith in history and not very different from the market mechanism of traditional liberalism.[34] But it was *process*, rightly organized, that Dewey trusted, not the substantive decisions of men.

In this, Dewey's theory is strikingly similar to that enunciated in *The Federalist*. No less than Hamilton did Dewey distrust men's affections. Out of a need for security, man has attached his emotions to things—especially, given his social nature, to groups which seemed associated with his well-being. This emotional bond leads man to fear change and to cling to old loyalties even when they have become obsolescent and inferior in the fulfillment of his needs. Even when new patterns of action have been created, thoroughly destabilizing old groups and relations, men resist emotionally, and new associations are unable to create a new sense of identity. The root of cultural lag, the conservatism of the emotions, also results in a fear of new ideas; liberty as it existed, Dewey argued, was founded in the fear of others and the suspicion that repression would result in greater evils, not in any positive commitment.[35]

For Dewey, as for the authors of *The Federalist*, the task of the political order lay in overcoming the conservatism and parochiality of the affections and in harnessing them where possible to more inclusive groups and to the future. Hence Dewey argued that older liberalism, for all the defects of its analysis, had performed a useful service in liberating men from the control of local groups, thus opening the way to change. For Dewey, as for his liberal forebears, the goals of progress remained the mastery of nature and the brotherhood of man.[36]

The error of older liberalism, Dewey argued, was in imagining that it is enough to free man from older groups and loyalties, offering him the lure of self-interest in their place. Such a policy actually maximizes the resistances that result in cultural lag. A narrow individualism creates a public that feels hopelessly weak and threatened;

[34] "Creative Democracy," *John Dewey*, ed. Irwin Edman (New York: Bobbs-Merrill, 1955), p. 314.

[35] *The Public and Its Problems*, pp. 51–52, 59, 140–141, 167; *Characters and Events*, ed. Joseph Ratner (New York: Holt, 1929), p. 453.

[36] *The Public and Its Problems*, pp. 53–56, 111, 131–134; *Human Nature and Conduct* (New York: Random House, 1930), pp. 117–124, 223ff., 249ff., 265, 289.

isolated man sees the interdependence of modern society as an alien force imposed on him, lying outside his control and constantly threatening his security. Dewey was not impressed with the proliferation of interest groups in America, recognizing that most had become governments over men. Created by the processes of industrial life, such groups were not, for their members, the reflection of personal choice, because individuals rightly saw themselves as unable to create any alternative. Moreover, the closer groups were to the individual, and the more meaning they had for him, the more likely they were to be defensive and privatistic in aim. Too limited to control or regulate the whole of society, such groups lacked any hope of planning or of changing the nature of society, contenting themselves with protecting the individual's private concerns to the extent that they were able. Modern society might be orderly, but it was based on a superficial conformity that was the result of weakness and lacked any positive loyalty or commitment. Unable to fight society actively, men were engaged in what amounted to passive resistance, but the hostility was no less real.[37]

Always, Dewey conceded, there would be some tension between the private and public roles of man. The task of political wisdom, however, lay in reducing that tension, eliminating the conflict between public and private groups which was responsible for the "unreal" idea of the individual versus society. Under the best circumstances, Dewey argued, the good citizen would find that his private life "enriched" rather than opposed his civic involvement, since the two areas would "reinforce one another and their values accord." [38]

Dewey's prescription involved a radical change in the idea of constitutional government. Traditional constitutionalism had been based on the separation of an autonomous private sphere from the area of public control. Dewey proposed what amounted in effect to the abolition of that autonomy. Since society—the sphere of private relations—was inseparably related to the state, Dewey argued for a political order able to construct the kind of private loyalties that would support, or at least would not oppose, the advancement of the

[37] *Individualism*, pp. 28–29, 49, 52–55, 65, 83, 87, 114; *The Public and Its Problems*, pp. 107–108, 115–120, 134–135; *Human Nature and Conduct* (1930), pp. 116–117.
[38] *The Public and Its Problems*, pp. 75–76, 82, 148, 191.

public good. In other words, the state should provide the individual with group memberships which would give him emotional security but be unable to offer parochial, short-sighted resistance to the course of events. Groups of this character, Dewey argued, would be compatible with order, change, and openness, with history and with the growth of loyalties which would gradually approximate the brotherhood of man.[39] Old liberalism had trusted that it would be enough to break up older groups for man's true nature to "emerge" with the progress of history; Dewey contended that it was necessary to build groups that would support that nature. For both, however, the goal was the same, and the picture of man's true nature was identical. All limited groups lacked, for Dewey, any value in themselves; they were worthy or undesirable insofar as they supported or opposed the course of history. Such groups were little more than a necessary concession to the emotional and intellectual weakness of man.

The control of modern society, the kind of planning which could realize the liberative potential that Dewey saw in modern technology and organization, required the commitment and devotion of a "great community," an "inclusive and fraternally associated public" in which each would feel himself bound to all by reciprocal ties of gratitude and obligation.[40] And Dewey, no less than his liberal predecessors, was confident that such an increasingly broad fraternity was a possible goal. It was a necessary faith, for otherwise Dewey left himself open to the charge that his advocacy of manipulated private loyalties was logically a totalitarianism that would only drive men further into isolation and withdrawal.

Dewey admitted no limitations, in principle, to human fraternity. Paradoxically for a theorist who appealed so often to "evolution," Dewey denied that the "biological makeup" of man was responsible for any of the "distinctive" features of human association, insisting that human nature was modified by knowledge and history.[41] The argument, of course, is little more than desperate sophistry; biology may be vital to human association without making any distinctive contribution to it, even if one accepts Dewey's statement of the case. The

[39] *Ibid.*, pp. 73–74; *Democracy and Education* (New York: Macmillan, 1916), pp. 95–96.
[40] *The Public and Its Problems*, pp. 109, 127, 131–134; *Individualism*, p. 38.
[41] *The Public and Its Problems*, pp. 195, 197.

weakness of the argument only suggests the lengths to which Dewey would go in order to affirm the old ideal of human fraternity.

Dewey often seemed to imply that community and fraternity were simply the results of common purposive endeavor, of shared values which shaped action. "Fraternity," he wrote, "is another name for the consciously appreciated goods which accrue from an association in which all share and which give direction to the conduct of each." Dewey was too intelligent, however, not to realize that this definition was broad enough to include a "fraternity" of stockholders concerned to maximize dividends. He included the additional consideration that each should have an "energetic desire" to sustain the shared good "just because it is a good shared by all." [42] This, however, does more than introduce the problem of emotion; it reveals the kind of emotion on which Dewey relied. In the first place, the emotion in question is completely separate from any judgment of the value of the shared good ("just because . . ."); anything shared will satisfy it. And equally, it has no limitations. In other words, Dewey relied on a potentially universal, morally indifferent, "fraternal instinct" as much as the liberals of old had done. T. V. Smith, much influenced by Dewey, was to refer to fraternity as a desire for the "indefinite enlargement of friendly contacts," and to equate that desire with a yearning to recapture the "sweetness" of childhood.[43] And however articulated, such a desire is no more than the lingering dream for merger, the passion for *gemeinschaft*.

To leave it at that would do Dewey an injustice, for he was wise and honest enough to admit that physicality does impose limitation on the human emotions. Functional loyalties, he conceded, are no substitute for face-to-face contact in building feelings of solidarity, and the "final actuality" of fraternity must always be rooted in face-to-face relations.[44] (Admirers of Dewey's "empiricism" should observe that the phrase implies a "real" fraternity independent of the contact which is required for its "final actuality.") This concession, however, only reopens the gap between smaller groups, supported by the emotions, and the political order at large which they are too small to affect. And in fact, like many other writers of the time (such as the sociolo-

[42] *Ibid.*, pp. 149–155; *Individualism*, p. 34.
[43] T. V. Smith and E. C. Lindeman, *The Democratic Way of Life*, pp. 7–8, 25–28, 37.
[44] *The Public and Its Problems*, pp. 212–214, 218.

gist Robert Park, the old Progressive Herbert Croly, and the organizational evangelist, Mary Parker Follett),[45] Dewey often stressed the need for groups which, able to provide emotional warmth, would not be strong enough to oppose the historical process. He saw the family and especially the neighborhood as such groups. But dependence on these would leave unresolved precisely the malaise that Dewey set out to cure—the emotional resistance of the individual to forces outside the sphere of his immediate loyalties which he feels himself unable to control.

The dilemma did not shake Dewey's confidence in the possibility of a fraternal public, though he was aware of the problem. At times, he fell back on argument by assertion and on an uncharacteristically winged prose that bridged the gap between seeming irreconcilables with the architecture of rhetoric. "It is easy to point to many signs," he wrote (without fulfilling the implicit promise to do so),

> which indicate that unconscious agencies as well as deliberate planning are making for such an enrichment of the experience of local communities as will conduce to render them genuine centers of the attention, interest and devotion for their constituent members. The unanswered question is how far these tendencies will reestablish the void [sic] left by the disintegration of the family church and neighborhood. . . . There is nothing intrinsic in the forces which have effected uniform standardization, mobility and remote invisible relationships that is fatally obstructive to the return . . . [to] the local homes of mankind. . . . If [local communal life] can be reestablished it will manifest a fullness, variety and freedom of possession of enjoyment of meanings and goods unknown in the contiguous associations of the past. For it will be alive and flexible as well as stable, responsive to the complex and world-wide scene in which it is enmeshed. . . . Its larger relationships will provide an [in]exhaustible and flowing fund of meanings upon which to draw. . . .[46]

This almost poetic flight was not accidental. Insofar as there was a basis for his sense of possibility, it lay in the prospect of a new kind of communication that would make possible a new community, the hope on which his fellow Progressives had relied to resolve their own

[45] See Robert Park, *Human Communities* (Glencoe: Free Press, 1952), pp. 6, 24, 34, 46–48, 59–63, 68, 72–73, 218; Herbert Croly, "Surely Good Americans," *New Republic* (Nov. 15, 1922), pp. 294–296; Mary Parker Follett, *The New State* (New York: Longmans, Green, 1933), pp. 174–185, 216–226, 245–257, 296–310.

[46] *The Public and Its Problems,* pp. 215–217.

dilemmas. Communication, Dewey noted, "can alone create a great community," and fortunately technology "facilitates the rapid and easy circulation of opinion and information," vastly improving the "methods and conditions" of debate and creating a "constant and intricate interaction far beyond the limits of face-to-face communities.[47] The hope for a fraternal public, then, rested as so many of Dewey's visions did on his faith in historical progress and the process of technological growth.

But in this case, there was a note of doubt. Dewey spoke of the need for an art of communication, "subtle, delicate, vivid and responsive," which would "breathe life" into the mass media, and for an artist who could "kindle emotion" and create involvement across the seemingly impersonal lines of the media.[48] The terms are revealing. Dewey, the declared apostle of science and reason, was forced at this essential point to rely on art to close the gap between local man and the national and international order. And in this, Dewey seems to play John the Baptist to Marshall McLuhan's Messiah. It is very doubtful, however, that Dewey would find in the contemporary "art of communication" any fulfillment of his hopes. Optimistic as he was, Dewey was also a desperate man, one who saw the social bases of a life he valued slipping away, and who struggled amid that decay to cling to the inherited liberal creed of historical progress and fraternal destiny. He spoke movingly to all those who shared his desperation. But a statement in 1940, admittedly a dark time, reveals how much at odds Dewey's values were with the moving forces of the times.

> When I think of the conditions under which men and women are living in many foreign countries today, fear of espionage with danger hanging over the meeting of friends for . . . conversation . . . I am inclined to believe that the heart and final guarantee of democracy is in the free gatherings of neighbors on the street corners to discuss . . . what is read in the uncensored news of the day.[49]

These are the snows of yesteryear, and the very anachronism of the argument indicates that the old creed had died, even though its fearful votaries might still chant the old litanies, lacking any better way of holding back the dark.

[47] *Ibid.*, pp. 152–153.
[48] *Ibid.*, pp. 114, 183–184, 208–209; see also Cushing Strout, "The Twentieth Century Enlightenment," *APSR*, LIX (1955), p. 326.
[49] *John Dewey*, ed. Edman, p. 312.

> Violent political passions have but little hold on those who have devoted all their faculties to the pursuit of their well-being. . . . Men in democratic societies . . . love change, but they dread revolutions. . . . A democratic people left to itself will not easily embark in great hazards; it is only led to revolutions unawares; it may sometimes undergo them, but it does not make them and . . . when such a people has been allowed to acquire sufficient knowledge and experience, it will not suffer them to be made.
>
> De Tocqueville, *Democracy in America*

CHAPTER XIX

FEARLESSNESS AND FEAR: THE NEW DEAL AND AFTER

Excitement Amid Despair

For American intellectuals, the Great Depression was more than a time of travail and anguish. It was a moment of opportunity, a chance to break down the door of estrangement. Business leaders and established political spokesmen were pathetically uncertain, and the mass of Americans were willing to listen to any who seemed to offer a way out. Opponents might sneer at Roosevelt's "Brain Trust"; the electorate did not. To be sure, confused Americans also gave their attention to prophets like Doctor Townsend, Father Coughlin, and Huey Long, figures who hardly ranked as intellectuals. The chance to compete for a newly attentive public, however, mattered far more to the intellectuals of the Thirties than the nature of their competition.

The sense of opportunity was especially strong among the Progressives like the disciples of John Dewey. The Depression gave them their more or less expected chance to put their techniques to work, to demonstrate that only the trained expert could manage and control a modern economy. But the great crisis also excited those intellectuals who stood outside the Progressive tradition and rejected much or all of the heritage of the Enlightenment.

Such men found new company in intellectual circles, for the collapse had shaken many out of their old adherence, articulate or unthought, to the liberal tradition. Many, too, were able to exchange isolation for prominence, and estrangement for eminence. The established academics and professionals, Basil Rauch comments, could not free themselves from the old dogmas to which they had tied themselves by years of confident exposition, and the New Deal was forced to turn to marginal intellectuals for the guidance and counsel it required.[1]

Most important, the agony of the nation allowed the dissenting intellectual to overcome his own painful ambivalence. Throughout the Twenties he had felt a distaste for industrial and technological America, even if he conceded the attraction of its power and its promise of abundance. But his sense of distance from society had left him lonely, often desperately so. In the Thirties he could convince himself, often without much effort, that Americans were abandoning or doubting their old zeal for the industrial cornucopia. The misery of the unfortunate, moreover, offered him an even more powerful solvent. His inevitable human concern for the poor and the discarded conquered his suspicion of modernity and made his intellectual doubts and distastes seem over-refined, effete, and querulous. Amid suffering and starvation, in a nation where millions faced the dehumanization of unemployment and the gray indifference of economic process, no man could stand aside. Loneliness allied with compassion routed hesitancy and persuaded intellectuals that they had found, in the movements of the Thirties, genuine community and fraternity.

---

[1] Rauch, *History of the New Deal*, pp. 9-11; see also Maynard Krueger, "Economic and Political Radicalism," *AJS*, XL (1935), pp. 770-771.

For many, the crisis amounted to death and rebirth. Harvey Swados has rightly called attention to the motif of traveling in the literature of the Thirties.[2] In the previous decade, traveling had been associated with expatriation and flight into intellectual circles at home and abroad. Now, it involved escaping the seeming brittleness and artificiality of the world of the intelligentsia, a search for repatriation which explored roots, land, and people. Some embraced the cult of the elemental, a variety of romanticism which called itself "realism," in which emotion, violence, and unreason alone were accorded status as "real things." Others examined the remnants of traditional culture, finding in the outcast and the excluded both emotion and wisdom, a truer understanding of man and of human things. Steinbeck's Mexicans and hoboes in Monterey or his migrant workers in the California Valley, Agee's Southern tenants, Adamic's ethnic workers in the cities—these were not only the oppressed but the exemplars of counter-culture, possessing (often unawares) ways of knowing, valuing, and living more ancient and wise than those of modern America. Such portraits were often overdrawn, sometimes ludicrously so; but they all reflected a new intellectual attempt at self-discovery, and the best developed a cultural critique that went to the heart of the modern dilemma.

At no time, however, did such eulogies amount to a political program, and those who denounced them as "nostalgia" had a point. The islands of traditional culture survived only because flooding them and hence displacing their people had not seemed worth the cost to the leaders of established institutions. They were hopelessly weak, unable to withstand the force and temptation of modern America, and the passionate indignation of a book like *The Grapes of Wrath* memorialized a fait accompli. As Agee knew, an author could hope to do no more than raise a fitting gravestone for those who would otherwise "have no memorial." [3]

The belief in proletarian fraternity, the dream of brotherhood with the worker which is the great theme of Depression writing, was partly inspired by a desire for a movement that could hold out the promise of concrete results in alleviating suffering. But his-

[2] *The American Writer in the Great Depression,* ed. Harvey Swados, pp. xi–xxii, xxviii, xxxi–xxxiii.

[3] Agee and Evans, *Let Us Now Praise Famous Men,* p. 445.

torical "relevance" was only part of the story; equally strong was the desire for fraternity itself, so powerful in many cases as to be blinding.

The appeal of Stalinism, which drew so many for a time, was hardly intellectual. The Party was itself a simulacrum of fraternity, an embattled world where political solidarity seemed to heighten the intensity of human bonds. But at least in theory, the Party aimed at the elimination of that intensity, hoping to extend its embrace to millions. So long as the goal remained theoretical, it posed few problems, and it was possible for those who believed, as Heywood Broun did, that fraternity was essential to a "happy life for all," to sneer at intellectual "elitism" as an "extension of the college fraternity system." [4] More important was the fact that the Party could not offer genuine fraternity precisely because it demanded a sacrifice of self on the altar of historical science; personal relations are impossible where personality is absent. Some made that sacrifice willingly:

> In the jail there were some Party men. They talked to me. Everything's been a mess all my life. Their lives weren't messes. They were working toward something. I want to work toward something. I feel dead. I thought I might get alive again.[5]

Most made the sacrifices for a time only. The Party offered them a certain chance at rebirth, a place where they could find security and discover a self, if only in opposition to the Party's commands. At best, the Party was not fraternity; it was a kind of family or, ironically, a better version of the "college fraternity system," but nothing more.

Most intellectuals, however, lacked either the desperation or the hope that led men to join the Party. They found their own analogue of its embattled "fraternity" in the crusade for union organization. Here the rhetoric of brotherhood was insistent and powerful, the need compelling, and in the great strikes it was easy to feel, as Sherwood Anderson did—escaping for a moment from his long loneliness —that workers had come to a "realization of each other . . . a religion of brotherhood."

---

[4] *American Radicals*, ed. Harvey Goldberg, pp. 53–75.
[5] John Steinbeck, *In Dubious Battle* (New York: Bantam, 1961), p. 6.

Those working men I could accept as brothers. . . . They were and are closer to me, as are men everywhere who work in factories, and in shops, than any other class.[6]

It is impossible to miss the soft note of condescension—"I could accept." Of course the statement can be read more creditably as "I can persuade myself," but in either case the note of illusion and artificiality, of personal distance masked by sentiment, is strong. There was worse. For many intellectuals, what was valued in the worker was his status as a victim, the suffering which made him safe to love because he was in need. And at best, what was loved was the sheer embattlement which drove workers and intellectuals together.

> The brotherhood is not by the blood, certainly.
> But neither are men brothers by speech—by saying so!
> Men are brothers by life and are hurt for it.
> Hunger and hurt are the great begetters of brotherhood. . . .
>
> Those are brothers whose bodies have shared fear
> Or shared harm or shared hurt or indignity.
> Why are the old soldiers brothers and nearest? [7]

MacLeish, like so many of his fellows, ignored the obvious question: Are the "hurts" that intellectuals feel and suffer the same as those of their brethren? So long as the war lasts, perhaps; bullet and club impose a unity. But there must be more than these if fraternity is to survive the war; why else is the "fraternity" of old soldiers most often expressed in nostalgia?

Embattlement was a fact for the workers and the unemployed in the Thirties, but the fraternity of battle was equally necessary for the organizations which hoped to unite them. Unions and similar groups lacked money and controlled few material resources; they could be effective only by throwing human resources into the scales, and numbers are ineffective without devotion and the willingness to endure hardship. At the same time, the nature of modern industrialism made national organization necessary; local groups would be at a fatal disadvantage when pitted against nationally organized busi-

[6] Sherwood Anderson, "Elizabethton, Tennessee," *Nation*, CXXVIII (1929), p. 527; *Puzzled America*, pp. 53–83, 164.

[7] Archibald MacLeish in *The American Writer and the Great Depression*, p. 496.

ness or in dealing with economic processes which affected the entire society. With the need for national organization went the need for centralization of decision, for coordinated strategy and rapidity of response. The "self-help" organizations and the local unions based on fraternal cooperation and participant methods of decision, which grew up early in the Depression, were often innovative, but they were universally ineffective and failed to survive. The local groups where men could meet, debate, and form positive emotional bonds yielded to great organizations able to hold out the hope of success and effectiveness. But without embattlement, such mass organizations, if created at all, would have lacked the resources of commitment that made success possible. War with the enemy banished feelings of distance and difference, justified centralization, and helped make obedience seem only a reflection of personal choice. The enemy provided a negative bond where positive forms of unity were lacking; the "Bonus Army" is a useful symbol of the protest of the Thirties.

The fraternity of battle is always defined by its foe. It was a mistake to believe that workers and the poor saw industrial society, or even capitalism, as their enemy; they fought against exclusion from that society, and being deprived of access to the goods it offered, and they sought a return to the limited well-being they had known during prosperity. This alone helps account for the consistent tendency of the unions to sacrifice every other good to the attainment of economic gain, a pattern made more compelling by the desperate need of members.

The crusade to "organize the unorganized" possessed sufficient social and political merit to inspire admiration and participation—the prospect of better conditions, liberation from total helplessness, some small margin of security. There was, too, greater understanding in the drive for industrial organization than had been present in the old A.F.L., and John L. Lewis was wise enough to see, as Gompers and his followers never had, that labor was at a hopeless economic disadvantage and could only organize by winning political support from the government. Yet none of the mass unions avoided the tendency toward centralization and bureaucracy, and the intellectuals of the Thirties have suffered as their vaulting prose has been reduced to a mockery by the passing of time. Without the fraternity of battle, the impulsion of desperation, the "house of labor" became simply another "established" organization dedicated to winning private, material gains for its members; more generous and humane than most, but lacking any suggestion of fraternity beyond the soft deceits of rhetoric.

Even in the Thirties, the signs were clear enough. The mine worker served as the exemplar of proletarian brotherhood and virtue —yet the miner was himself an atavism. The U.M.W. was not a true "industrial" union, it was a civic union, reflecting a society that came close to complete community. Miners shared not only battle and the intimate presence of death, they had a pride of skill and lived in communities where home and recreation were part of a whole whose center was the mine. The community of workers was less an aspiration than a fact. The miners' union, however, was more autocratic than most and as centralized as any, and only the bitter battle in which the miner was caught up made it tolerable. The miners retain many of their admirable qualities today, but it is evident that their world, the world of early industrialism, is dying— and the union, seeking to survive by allying itself to management and mechanization, itself becomes an enemy.[8]

It could have been foreseen in the Thirties. The old bonds of craft and skill had long been decaying, and the new industrial worker was a man of the cities, not of the mill-towns which formerly tied him to his fellows in private as well as public life. The cities permitted him to escape his job and all those associated with it after hours; the job itself, increasingly devoid of any grounds for feelings of pride or importance, made him desire escape. Increasingly privatized and estranged, he found what meaning and justification he could in the private delights and material goods that his labor might win. Deprivation might force him to recognize his need for his fellows; prosperity only enabled him to escape more effectively. The suburbs flourish on the corpse of worker "fraternity."

American workers have their moments of doubt and their feelings of something lost or missing in life, but for workers as for the intellectuals who cling to the old dream, these are likely to be ex-

[8] Harvey Swados, "The Miners: Men Without Work," *Dissent*, VI (1959), pp. 389–400; Harry Caudill, *Night Comes to the Cumberlands* (Boston: Little, Brown, 1962).

pressed in the hopeless language of nostalgia, in the songs of Joe
Hill and memories of combats past. Even those reminiscences are
pathetic. In high moments, the embattled brotherhood voiced an
aspiration which depends on industrialism and prosperity for fulfil-
ment, but which has no need for fraternity.

> Oh! the buzzing of the bees
> In the cigarette trees
> By the soda-water fountain,
> And the lemonade springs
> Where the bluebird sings
> In the Big Rock Candy Mountain.

The dream is powerful because it speaks to our oldest nostalgia, to
the child in all of us, but it is a blind guide for anyone who seeks
either manhood or fraternity.

Shuffling the Deck

The New Deal drew its recruits from intellectuals and political
men whose ideas and attitudes were deeply rooted in the liberal
tradition. The administration and the movement that supported it,
however, were inevitably the children of the War and the Depression; the old foundations were shaken, the old certainties had become matters of doubt. John Dewey's reformulations won a powerful following—but other, less orthodox ideas had an audience. The
doctrines men had learned, often from the cradle, clashed with the
obvious fact of catastrophe; the exotic became possible, and the
bizarre could not be ruled out.

Confusion was written into the New Deal, especially in the early
days, a confusion of ends as well as means. Clearly it was necessary to
get America out of the Depression, but where it was to go was as
difficult to determine as how to escape at all. Roosevelt had no
articulate goal. He was against laissez-faire and the practices that
seemed to have caused the collapse; he was for some sort of "new
deal." But he failed to find a satisfactory standard for public policy
even in such vague phrases as "the brotherhood of man" ("too idealistic") and "community interest" ("too socialistic"), and his description of himself as "a Christian and a democrat" hardly clarified
matters.

If anything, his ambiguities only endeared him to the electorate; Roosevelt's ambivalence and uncertainty—and that of his administration—in many ways mirrored the situation of the nation at large. The synthesis of the liberal and religious traditions (and of the desires to which each gave coherent expression), which had been precariously preserved by prosperity and the boom, had fallen apart so dramatically that most Americans were left to face their own conflicts. Their reaction was to seek some means of eliminating those conflicts, to find some new equilibrium that would enable them to live easily with themselves and with society. (The conservatives' denial that there was any defect in the old synthesis is an even more striking instance of the same phenomenon.) More than anything else, Roosevelt personified the confidence that it was still possible to grasp both horns of the dilemma, that an American could still be both "a Christian and a democrat." And since most who joined the New Deal shared the conflicts and the desire to eliminate them, that confidence appealed quite as strongly to members of the administration.

The administration's ambivalence made it vulnerable in many ways. The uncertainty and diversity of ideas about the appropriate goal for America encouraged a concentration on the negative goal of ending the Depression, on which all agreed—regardless of the fact that the way in which it was ended would decide the shape of the future, by default if not by design. More single-minded men, especially those who promised to be effective in restoring a measure of material prosperity, often found in the administration something close to an eagerness to yield to "pressure." The "first" New Deal, in fact, amounted to little more than asking the rulers of the industrial economy—the trade associations and the industrial farmers—to cure the crisis themselves, lending them the power of government for the purpose. Commentators, then and now, have found it easy to portray the New Deal and its chief as basically passive, moving right or left in response to pressures generated in the society at large. Roosevelt, for example, was often indifferent or hostile to efforts to organize the excluded which aimed to change those pressures; as James M. Burns points out, he was cool toward the Wagner Act and almost entirely indifferent to blacks until the advent of the war.[9]

[9] James M. Burns, *Roosevelt: The Lion and the Fox*, p. 219.

Yet that picture is a defective one. Burns was right to see Roosevelt as a "lion" as well as a "fox," a moralist as well as a politician with a canny sense for the main chance. Roosevelt was no Quixote, but a moral weight always tipped the scales of calculation and compromise if they were otherwise equal. New Dealers, inside and outside the administration, knew the President was reluctant to fight, but they were confident that he would support them if he was compelled to choose. John L. Lewis adopted such a strategy when he based his organizing campaigns on the slogan, "The President wants you to join the union." (Lewis's break with Roosevelt was partly due to rage at his inability to force the President's hand.)

Roosevelt might think that the brotherhood of man was "too idealistic" to serve as an immediate guide to policy, but clearly he did regard it *as* a desirable goal. In that, he was at one with the liberal tradition. The faith in progress, however, had broken down, and it seemed cruel and possibly pointless (and certainly impolitic) to ask men, as traditional liberalism had, to wait for the long term. Keynes' maxim was a moral axiom for the New Deal, one which conceded to citizens the right to some minimal reflection of fraternity in immediate policy. Carried into practice, that idea also served to assuage the anxieties of New Dealers and Americans generally (especially the middle classes); where liberalism failed, Americans could assure themselves that they were acting according to the religious tradition. The goals of material progress and the mastery of nature, on the one hand, and community and fraternity on the other, could at least be made to walk parallel courses.

Roosevelt and his followers, however, also followed the liberal tradition in equating fraternity with compassion and simple warmth of feeling. Compassion and bonhommie became the touchstones of New Deal policy, whether in the struggle to alleviate misery at home or in the "good neighbor" policy and the aggressive internationalism that followed it in foreign affairs. Even the "brokerage" style of administration, much celebrated by political scientists, was based on the desire to substitute good feeling for animosity by satisfying, conciliating, and, in Roosevelt's case at least, charming. It was hardly by accident that when F.D.R. proclaimed a "rendezvous with destiny" in 1936, he defined the crisis and the choice in terms of compassion: "Governments can err, Presidents do make mistakes, but the immortal Dante tells us that divine justice weighs the sins of the cold-blooded and the sins of the warm-hearted in different scales." [10]

So it does, and the New Deal will doubtless receive credit for its decencies and humanities, for the thousand ways in which it made life for Americans safer and ampler. And the New Deal needs little defense against its sectarian opponents, the left which so often fed on misery and the right which blindly denied the existence of crisis. But a relative advantage in the scales of justice does not excuse faults, and the New Deal's idea of brotherhood (other faults of the administration aside) was responsible for many.

It was, in the first place, far from fraternal. Almost universally inclusive, the good will of the New Deal was radically impersonal, comprehending masses and not men. It was distant, outside the lives of most Americans, a condescending sentiment which, while it felt for the suffering of others, only rarely felt with them in their travails. The desire to avoid conflict—the need to deny its reality—led the New Deal to take a stance "above" the battle that left it open to charges of moral blindness and betrayal. When Lewis denounced Roosevelt for failing to see that "one who has supped at labor's table" ought not to "damn with fine impartiality both labor and its enemies," he was doing more than condemning disloyalty. He was arguing that one who had seen the house of labor from inside ought to see the difference between labor and its foes, ought to realize that the oppressor and the oppressed are not equivalent.

The impersonal condescension of the New Deal, allied with the doctrine of the liberal tradition, encouraged it to be satisfied with giving Americans a greater share in material goods—and even within that standard, to measure success by quantitative "indices" of well-being that masked the unevenness of the economy's performance (even when, as was often the case, New Dealers knew better in both psychological and economic terms). To the disillusioned, in fact, New Deal compassion had all the marks of a bribe designed to "pay off" those who threatened conflict in proportion to the seriousness of the threat. Perhaps it was, especially at an unconscious level; the New Dealer's desire to escape or resolve the conflct in himself by eliminating it in society certainly would suggest as much. Even

[10] Acceptance address, June 27, 1936, *Public Papers and Addresses of Franklin D. Roosevelt* (New York: Random House, 1938), vol. V, p. 235.

those who remained appropriately grateful for New Deal benefits were forced to recognize them for what they were: acts of charity which involved an offense to the dignity of the recipient. "You don't shoot Santa Claus," Al Smith remarked, thereby touching and missing the point. In fact, lower-class Americans had to transform Roosevelt into Santa Claus and something more—a reverential, paternal figure of authority—to make it tolerable to their dignity to accept New Deal assistance. The indignity, however, was redirected into resentment at "bureaucracy," the gray and impersonal figures who stood between the President and the people. That resentment slumbered while Roosevelt lived, and provided the bureaucracy with the mantle of his authority; its expression became one of the major elements in the era of McCarthy, and the rage against liberal officialdom in those years is a severe comment on its idea of fraternity.

The most serious defect of the New Deal, however, lay in the fact that its compassion was so sincere, so deeply felt, that it emphasized the need for results, for something done now, and hence for the fastest and most efficient means of eliminating material suffering. There was always a temporariness to New Deal measures; Hopkins, for example, knew the psychological costs of relief, but put off looking for a more satisfactory answer.[11] A philosopher like William Ernest Hocking might doubt that consumption was an adequate goal and ask for greater attention to means for determining what ought to be produced; most were content to raise the purchasing and consuming power of Americans and leave the broader questions aside.[12]

It was a leadership default of great magnitude. By the time the New Deal felt itself to have solved the worst problems of the Depression, the forces of the old order had reorganized and reasserted themselves, and both indignation and willingness to follow had been dulled among the unfortunate by the very prosperity the New Deal had struggled to achieve. The war, in any event, was on the horizon. The New Deal's later problems were not accidental obstacles. Compassion is a human feeling and a blind guide, hopelessly trapped by

[11] *New Deal Thought*, ed. H. Zinn, pp. 152, 295–300.
[12] William E. Hocking, "The Future of Liberalism," *Journal of Philosophy*, XXII (1935), pp. 230–247.

the short term. It can, and in the New Deal did, help to humanize history; it cannot evaluate history's direction. Paradoxically, by rejecting the "long term," the New Deal became only more dependent on history and enmeshed in a policy of drift. The paradox is not difficult. Aiming for some immediate realization of the liberal idea of fraternity, the New Deal became more dependent on the means that liberal theory prescribed for realizing that idea: the mastery of nature, material prosperity, industrialism, and technology. Striving to bring the end of history closer, the New Deal became only a more zealous agent of historical forces themselves. It was a new deal, to be sure, but with cards from the old deck.

All this analysis, of course, has neglected the differences among individual New Dealers. These were often wide, but even the most notable dissenting voices within the administration reflected, in important ways, its basic premises and assumptions. At critical moments, consequently, dissent became ineffective. The pressure of voters often seems to account for the direction of administration policy; actually, that "pressure" was ambiguous, and derived much of its power from the pressure in the mind of the New Dealer himself.

If the religious tradition had a voice in the administration, for example, it was certainly that of Henry Agard Wallace. Prosperity is not enough, Wallace argued, without a "change in the human heart" that will change Americans from the "greedy children" they have been. America, for Wallace, was a sinful land, living in plenty while the world endured privation, and seeking no higher goal than the restoration of its own well-being. Out of abundant land, which allowed Americans the luxury of being able to afford plenitude Americans had built a perverse society which was rapacious toward itself, destructive of the bonds between man and man, unable to lift its citizens above venality and self-concern.

With the passing of the frontier, Wallace went on (following Turner), Americans were forced to face the social consequences of their history. It was now necessary to return to the land as the "mother of men" and the "foundation of civilization," to build a society which would be based on the principle of harmony with the land and with itself, concerned to discover the true and the eternal. Such a society,

Wallace declaimed, would live in "international friendship" with all nations, its foreign policy becoming a reflection of its own fraternity within.[13]

Wallace's evangelical rhetoric might offend the young sophisticates who gathered around him or regarded him as a champion, but his ideas spoke to the symbols of the old tradition to which many responded. There were numbers of New Dealers who saw the administration as a chance to reestablish community or to strengthen the relations of citizen and citizen—the most articulate, perhaps, being M. L. Wilson of the Subsistence Homestead Division of the Department of Agriculture. Wilson hoped to form, out of those dislocated by the Depression, viable small farms and communities modeled on the idea of gemeinschaft. Others, like the officials of the Farm Security Administration, aimed at creating fraternity among the disadvantaged, the FSA organizing sharecroppers and tenants for political action and seeking to create unity across the racial line. And there were other experiments, some wildly utopian, proposed in counsel and carried to varying degrees of application.

All were short-lived. Wilson's projects affected only about 6500 persons before they were abandoned; the FSA lasted longer, but was scuttled to win the support of organized agriculture and related groups for the T.V.A., and it found few defenders in the last crisis. The conventional explanation is that such projects were "unrealistic"; but the FSA, at least, was realistic enough to inspire the fear and hatred of established groups in the white South (partly because, with supreme "realism," it used loan funds to pay poll taxes for tenants and sharecroppers), and enough so that, by 1939, its loans were being repaid ahead of schedule. The defeat of such projects reflects the general willingness of the New Deal to sacrifice human participation for technical efficiency wherever the two seemed to be in conflict, to prefer production of goods to the development of men. (The AAA, in fact, was so simply a reflection of the aims of industrial agriculture that it actually increased farm tenancy.)

The record of New Deal policy in agriculture is sad, and cannot be charged entirely to the account of powerful combinations and groups as against Wallace's idealism. Wallace and his allies were

[13] Henry A. Wallace, *Democracy Reborn* (New York: Reynal and Hitchcock, 1944), pp. 9, 46, 75–76, 102.

themselves ambiguous in their attitudes, accepting the material standard which they rejected in rhetoric. Wallace never doubted that production was an almost self-sufficient good and that greater productivity would result in greater "welfare for all." In fact, Wallace's principal charge against the great corporations and organizations was not that they promoted elitism or mass society. Rather, he insisted that the "selfishness" of such organizations and their concern for "profits and wages" limits productivity. He went further, arguing that if such great organizations could "cooperate," greater productivity would result, and he approved the efforts of the New Deal to provide them with the "machinery" that would enable cooperation. Wallace was, in other words, prepared to defend corporatism as a means to production. Even peace, he felt compelled to argue, is "good business." In fact, Wallace's book, *America Must Choose,* is thoroughly mistitled, for like all his works, it sought to demonstrate that Americans need *not* choose between the relations of men as citizens and the affluence of men as private individuals, merging the two by a mystical rhetoric reminiscent of Emerson. And like Emerson, whatever Wallace conceded to religion in language, he took back in practice.[14]

Thurman Arnold, by contrast, was unambiguous. The most articulate of the New Dealers who accepted the reinterpreted doctrines of the liberal tradition developed by thinkers like John Dewey, Arnold began with the premise that the nature of man was defined by his desires, emotions, and instincts, and that these led logically toward the mastery of nature. All organizations and governments, consequently, were utilitarian devices designed to "satisfy human wants." To perform their task, however, organizations required creeds which legitimated sacrifice and met the emotional needs of men for intellectual security. When organizations had outlived their usefulness, creeds tended to blind men to the fact because of the very nonutilitarian basis which made them otherwise useful; and creeds thus helped to create "cultural lag," the survival of outdated forms. Only a great crisis ordinarily sufficed to shatter old creeds and organizations, and only when they were shattered were men set free to pursue the "max-

[14] *Ibid.,* p. 36; *Technology, Corporations and the General Welfare* (Chapel Hill: University of North Carolina Press, 1937); and *America Must Choose* (Boston: Foreign Policy Assn. and World Peace Foundation, 1934).

imum production and distribution" of material goods which was the logic of human history.[15]

Creeds were, however, necessary; a truly rational order needed a "balance" between "idealism and cynicism." Arnold proposed, for his times, a "hopeful" philosophy based on "the fundamental axiom that man works only for his fellow man." It was a revealing suggestion, for Arnold's "axiom" amounted to no more or less than the "fraternal instinct" which classical liberalism had perceived as immanent in human striving, the underlying meaning of progress in history. For Arnold, as for his liberal contemporaries, that "instinct" had at best a doubtful basis in fact and was certainly not something one chose to defend by reason; far better to give it the status of an "axiom" and to remove it from argument. Such safety was purchased at a cost; the "axiom" became a nonrational premise to be accepted or rejected at will. The cost seemed small to a theorist like Arnold, however, for all ideals were essentially epiphenomenal, justified insofar as they helped production. Arnold never explained—and small wonder—how an ideal understood to have such a nature could make men secure or move them to sacrifice. Nor did he feel a need for such an explanation. The "humanitarian" idea, rooted in the American tradition, was planted in Arnold's emotions, and doubtless he felt it would have strong appeal to his fellow citizens. At the emotional level, in other words, Arnold felt his doctrine to be true, and it seemed folly to expose it to the test of reason where it would be at a disadvantage.[16]

Arnold, despite his debunking of creeds and "folklore," had the convictions of a doctrinaire. Democracy, he argued, has no right to tell men what they "ought to want"; it must limit itself to what they "want" in fact. Yet, of course, Arnold was not averse to telling his fellow citizens what they wanted, posing their "real" desires against the illusions fostered by outdated creeds. Moreover, Arnold suggested that a democracy might legitimately "improve" the wants of men— not only by unmasking old folklore, but also by removing material scarcity, and hence anxiety about material needs.[17]

---

[15] Thurman Arnold, *The Folklore of Capitalism* (New Haven: Yale University Press, 1937), pp. 10, 16, 20–24, 165–184, 350; see also *The Symbols of Government* (New Haven: Yale University Press, 1935).

[16] *New Deal Thought*, ed. H. Zinn, pp. 36–43.

[17] *Folklore of Capitalism*, pp. 44–45, 50, 110, 133–135, 185–206.

Arnold's analysis followed the Enlightenment tradition in another way which was to grow in importance in American political thought and science. Since men and organizations, if they are rational, will always follow their "interest" in seeking to maximize power, no single interest must be allowed to dominate the state, for all citizens are equal in worth (or, more consistently with Arnold's moral theory, in the lack of any special worth). In the same sense, planning is dangerous because of the power it concentrates in government. Government should be given the task of regulating the great private associations to insure that free competitive markets continue to exist among them, thus preventing either monopolies of power or "inefficiency" from existing in any one of them. Arnold had no distaste for the great organizations per se, no distrust of massification and hierarchy which was not greatly outweighed by considerations of productive efficiency. The relations among, not within, the great organizations were his central concern.

Of course, Arnold was unwilling to trust the market to "regulate" competition, much less to preserve it. Asking the government to perform the task of regulation, however, only raises the question of the control and regulation of government itself. That task Arnold left to "the people." The public was a necessary element in all New Deal thought. A theorist like David Lilienthal, much more friendly to planning than Arnold was, saw the "conscious selection by the people of successive plans" as the answer to the problem of control.[18] Arnold only introduced an intermediate step, the competition of great private associations, and limited his perspective to a shorter term than Lilienthal and the planners did. The difference between such neo-progressives was minimal; planned competition is still a plan.

The ability of the public to perform the essential task assigned to it—even the existence of a "public"—was, however, dubious in the extreme. By Arnold's own showing, organizations had developed resources which made it painfully easy for them to control large groups of individuals, especially since those individuals were increasingly isolated and assailed by feelings of weakness. And, as was to become clear, the ability to instill new, mutable "creeds" which served the interests of those organizations had also become terrifying. Paul

[18] *New Deal Thought,* p. 107.

Douglas wrote that the error of the first New Deal was in assuming "a sufficiently strong and independent force outside capitalism which can control it," pointing out that without the organization of the excluded, capitalism would shrug off control with the return of prosperity.[19] The later New Deal solved part of the problem by the organization of labor and related groups, which helps account for Douglas' own conversion, but that organization remained painfully limited. It solved not at all the problem of giant organization itself; and without such a solution, the "people" could be little more than an increasingly evanescent abstraction, part aspiration and part memory.

Arnold's own confidence in the people was expressed as a faith almost as mystic as Wallace's. "Society shows an uncanny skill in selecting the best technicians once it understands just what those technicians are doing." [20] Perhaps so, but the last clause robs such a statement of all meaning; in few areas of technical skill can society be said to understand "just what" is being done. And in politics, where the question does not lie simply in defining the best technician, but rather in deciding between kinds of technique and hence between the ends which define "skill," Arnold's formulation is hopelessly vague, depending entirely on the word "uncanny" for whatever verisimilitude it can claim.

Arnold's confidence was rooted in three assumptions, partly unvoiced. First, the collapse of the old order had shattered its "folklore" in large measure, leaving the people with unscaled eyes—seeing "just what" technicians were really doing. Second, New Deal policy could help in removing the anxiety about material welfare that separated one citizen from another. Third, given both assumptions, it would be possible to take advantage of the situation to instill Arnold's own "hopeful" philosophy of cooperation and compassion. Given all this, a fraternal citizenry might be developed if the competitive mechanism could be kept intact.[21]

Arnold's theory was true to the prescriptions and premises of

[19] *Ibid.*, pp. 55–56.
[20] *Ibid.*, p. 43.
[21] Arnold, *Bottlenecks of Business* (New York: Reynal and Hitchcock, 1940), pp. 3, 10, 11, 13–14, 121, 130, 241–242, 263–264, 274, 283, 291; *Folklore of Capitalism*, p. 122.

the liberal Enlightenment. But the old vision was wavering, the old confidence gone. At critical points, Arnold retreated immediately to the citadel of unreason and assertion, unwilling to contest the field of reason. The instincts of man, too, had proved unreliable. It was no longer enough, for Arnold, to free men from error; it seemed necessary to teach them the truth. But, as Eric Goldman points out, the philosophy which Arnold's tradition had employed to smash error denied the existence of "truth." Arnold, like the liberals, had become tangled in a mass of contradictions and withered hopes, especially in relation to the idea of fraternity.

The New Deal was never forced to face the worst of its problems. The advent of the Second World War provided it with an unambiguous goal, the defeat of an enemy whose monumental evil swept away all moral doubts—a goal which, incidentally, solved the remaining problems of the economy. But the war also suggested the nature of the modern problem and a serious defect of New Deal liberalism. In the first place, as Walter Lippmann had guessed, the whole idea of "common purpose" in industrial society can scarcely exist without the sense of embattlement which levels the differences and distance between men.[22] The Depression provided it for what amounted to a moment and no more; "unity" could not survive the first hesitant return of prosperity, and only the war served to revive it. That, in turn, suggests the defect of the New Deal's denial of conflict, its universally inclusive idea of human fraternity. Many were deluded into the belief that men so eager to avoid conflict would not fight at all. In fact, of course, that reluctance on principle could turn into savage combat against those who persisted in conflict—reaction at home, aggression abroad. Those who insisted on opposing the New Dealer's desire to avoid conflict, who rejected his conciliation and compassionate concern, could only be classified as hopelessly perverse, outside humanity, to be fought without let or hindrance. Dresden, Hiroshima, the Cold War: these are the natural children of the New Deal. So too is the inability to understand the resentment of those whose dignity has been mortally offended by liberal compassion: blacks, middle Americans, and the young. This is, of course, far too severe. The defect lies in the philosophy of the liberal Enlightenment itself, and the

[22] *New Deal Thought*, pp. 96–102.

New Deal may be the best and most humane of all the reflections of that philosophy. Modern society, indeed, may not be able to do better. Yet, when the best is said, the indictment against the liberal doctrine of human fraternity remains.

E Pluribus . . .

The years since the New Deal have been lived under a lengthening shadow. The thermonuclear cloud is only part of that pall; far darker has been the totalitarian state and with it, a new fear among men. Before the Depression, men knew totalitarianism only as a portent in the ambiguous case of Lenin's Russia and the almost operatic example of Fascist Italy. Totalitarianism flowered in the Thirties and Forties, and what little relief from its threat has been felt in recent years has been far from enough to dispel the anxieties it raised.

Totalitarianism revealed the fact that modern man is capable of evil and horror unparalleled in earlier ages, that in our times banality shades easily into brutality, civility into savagery. Men came to be seen as terrified and resentful, prevented from outbursts of terrible rage and hatred only by impotence—which itself only outraged them further. Human consciousness revealed its weakness, parochiality, and malleability. For social science, in fact, the age since the Depression has been the "age of Michels" in which the "iron law of oligarchy" has been repeatedly reconfirmed. The "administrator" can no longer be thought of as the passive agent of the "public" or even of policymakers; individual citizens seem impotent against the modern administrative state. The small groups and neighborhoods, which so many theorists had turned to in despair and admiration, proved too small to resist the state, too weak and malleable to provide the individual with any real emotional security. "Manipulation" became a catchword; "human relations" was transformed into a euphemism for removing the resistance of subordinates to managerial superiors; "social engineering" and similar phrases drawn from Progressive thought changed from promise into menace—and the dream of human fraternity seemed to vanish amid the "organizational realities" of the age.

The disillusionment has been greatest for those who gave their youthful allegiance to Marxism. The experience of socialism, in and outside the Soviet Union, made it clear that a change in ownership does not solve the problem of control. Marx had hoped that a new and fraternal "consciousness" would emerge after the revolution, a public solidarity which would enable men to control the political apparatus, transforming the "government of men" into the "administration of things." The hope did not materialize; what emerged was not a fraternal instinct but the rigidity of the "new class" of functionaries. Explanations of that failure are possible, but for any but the most dogmatic, the shortcomings of Marxism in practice were another ground for suspicion of mankind and doubt of the idea of fraternity.

During the war, in reaction to fascism, a temporary and propagandistic vogue of humanism resulted in works like Carl Friedrich's *The New Belief in the Common Man.* It did not survive much beyond the end of hostilities. "Realism," the eternal sign of the disillusioned romantic, replaced it. The "toughness" of realism, however, is only a kind of prudence. The old ideals remain as ideals, to be approximated as far as "reality" permits (even if they seem impossible of complete realization). What is involved is a new suspicion of reality, a weakening of the old confidence that the precepts of liberalism were "scientific," a conviction that "the facts" do not support, and may be at odds with, the "values" of the liberal tradition.[23]

Most have kept their allegiance to those values and ideals, reflecting the "irrational Lockeanism" derived from rearing and culture in America. The new attitude, however, has resulted in defensiveness and a need to protect one's values against the threat of rational disconfirmation. Reinhold Niebuhr, for example, constructed a complex defense of liberal political philosophy premised on "neo-orthodox" theology. It is, however, a secular age, and most liberals—while admiring Niebuhr's "political wisdom"—have preferred the this-worldly dogma of a "separation between facts and values." Whatever the philosophic status of that oft-debated proposition, it is clearly ideal for those who feel a need to shelter values from the possible assaults of fact. Moreover, it is especially suited to liberalism, a doc-

[23] Friedrich, *The New Belief in the Common Man* (Boston: Little, Brown, 1950); John H. Schaar, *Loyalty in America* (Berkeley and Los Angeles: University of California Press, 1957), pp. 116–119.

trine which has always presumed that man's aspirations and values are at war with "nature," the world of fact, with mastery as the only goal. In that sense, at least, the premises of the liberal tradition are easily concealed in the language of Carnap.

Disillusionment did not teach liberals to abandon liberalism; it only taught them to lower their sights, to plan for a more hostile reality than they had once expected. Certainly too, it made liberals more cautious in their commitment, more hesitant in acting on or sacrificing for their ideals—a phenomenon which encourages young Americans to detect hypocrisy in so limited a devotion. The convictions, however, are real enough; only the methods have changed. The Progressive vision of a state managed by technical experts and controlled by the people was abandoned, for man proved too frail a reed to support it. Liberal realism fell back on a still earlier design, the self-regulating mechanism which would achieve the desired results in spite of the defects of men. Redefined in terms of "groups," the market mechanism became once again the master concept of political thought; and, for political science if not for all political men, what Theodore Lowi calls "interest group liberalism" became a "public philosophy." [24]

Within the pluralist school, individual theorists differ, but the old themes and premises are clear: a concern for individual liberty based on the belief that man is by nature a private, apolitical being; the conviction that politics is the result of scarcity and conflict, and that the logical aim of politics lies in limiting conflict while pursuing the mastery of nature; the doctrine that the "checks and balances" of the competitive process are the best means of pursuing that aim. The "brotherhood of man," however, which was the ultimate goal of liberal planning and contrivance, has shrunk to the softest whisper (which is one reason why the young, especially, see no "meaning" in the process). But the old hope remains, however timidly it is expressed in the crabbed language of contemporary liberalism.

It may seem unjust to refer to pluralist theory as based on individualistic premises. Theorists routinely assert that man is a "social animal," and Arthur Bentley set the tone for the school, asserting with blithe dogmatism that the individual, like the state, was an "abstrac-

[24] Theodore Lowi, *The End of Liberalism,* pp. 55–97.

tion," while only the group was "real."[25] Even the theory of the social contract, however, did not assert that man in some primordial period had been able to do without families. The individualism of the liberal tradition was a moral precept. All theorists conceded that groups were necessary for the rearing of the young as well as for survival. Hobbes, the most uncompromising of individualists, gave as a proof of the "state of nature" the fact that among some primitive peoples, only families existed, "the concord of which dependeth on savage lust."[26] Liberal individualism began with a distinction between "natural" groups like the family, in which "despotical" power might be justified, and larger groups which existed by contract and should be limited by consent and reason. In Lockean ideology, the distinction became a sharp separation between the spontaneous, natural world of "society" and the artificial and contrived world of the "state."

The same distinction exists in pluralist writing. All groups cannot be treated as identical, though group theorists often adopt a usage which blurs the differences. Bentley, for example, commented that larger groups break down into smaller and "more fundamental" bodies, even arguing that in simple societies no groups are apparent and that groups become visible only under the pressure of "necessity," a contention reminiscent of Rousseau or—more significantly—Ferdinand Tönnies. So too, David Truman distinguishes between "groups" proper (primary groups) and "associations" which arise to "stabilize the relations" of groups which become "tangent." Associations, Truman contends, "evolve" from groups in order to solve more problems by commanding "wider resources."[27]

The "evolution" is hardly a peaceful one. Politics, in the pluralist view, is conflict, force the *ultima ratio*. The state, the largest of the associations, Truman comments, is created to prevent an "entirely uninhibited" group struggle from eventuating in war. Left to himself, man is a private being. States and associations arise out of necessity,

---

[25] Arthur F. Bentley, *The Process of Government* (Bloomington: Principia, 1949), pp. 83–84, 114–117, 165–178, 208, 215; David Truman, *The Governmental Process* (New York: Knopf, 1951), pp. 14–30, 45–49, 168.

[26] *Leviathan*, ed. Macpherson, p. 187.

[27] Bentley, *The Process of Government*, pp. 209–212, 243, 410; Truman, *Governmental Process*, pp. 31–43, 105–108; Earl Latham, "The Group Basis of Politics: Notes for a Theory," *APSR*, XLVI (1952), pp. 376–397. See also S. Krislov, "What Is an Interest?", *WPQ*, XVI (1963), pp. 830–843.

especially the necessity of guarding oneself against violence; they exist not "naturally" and spontaneously but by convention. The whole argument, in fact, is a graceless version of the theory of social contract.[28]

Commitment to the traditional liberal idea of the moral freedom of the individual is, if anything, even clearer in pluralist thought. Bentley began *The Process of Government* with an attack on European theorists who had discarded the principle that law is justified by its "utility to the individual" in favor of the "soul stuff" of a higher moral purpose in law and the state. Earl Latham writes that the individual "circumscribes" the group and that groups exist to "fill the needs" of their members by seeking to "control the environment," and David Truman has suggested that the group process requires the "humanistic assumption" of the "dignity of man" to work properly.[29] More than moralism is involved in such statements (and in assertions of devotion to "individual liberty" which abound in "prefaces" to works in political science). As Michael Rogin points out, pluralistic analysis has been characterized by a persistent psychologism which dissolves the group into individual attitudes which are "shared," ignoring or slighting the influence of group structures and denying the group any distinct quality.[30]

There is, however, a difference between pluralism and traditional liberal theory. Enlightenment liberalism presumed that at some point man passed from the world of the family to the rational sphere of states and associations, moving out of the necessarily despotic situation in which the body was developed, the mind trained, and the emotions disciplined into the moral freedom that was his "by nature." In fact, much liberal policy was designed to guarantee his right to do so, aiming to break up or limit the potential tyranny of groups over men. Freudianism alone, not to mention the grim experience of the age, has hopelessly undermined that assumption. To liberal pluralism, reason is never enough, even when supported by the discipline of the market.

[28] Latham, "The Group Basis of Politics," pp. 388–389; Truman, *The Governmental Process*, pp. 51–65; Bentley, *The Process of Government*, pp. 258–259. The image of man as a private being is evident in Robert A. Dahl, *Modern Political Analysis* (Englewood Cliffs: Prentice-Hall, 1963), pp. 7, 18, 50–51, 73.

[29] Bentley, *The Process of Government*, pp. 56–91; David Truman, "The Political Process and Political Maturity," public lecture, University of California, Berkeley, April 1958, and *The Governmental Process*, p. 49.

[30] Michael Paul Rogin, *The Intellectuals and McCarthy*, pp. 18–19.

Man needs the emotional discipline of the group to prevent his desires from leading either to anarchical disorder or an "escape from freedom." Consequently, many have felt the need to argue for the group as more than a utilitarian device, as a center of moral meaning and emotional security.

Such arguments, however, raise the specter of group control over the individual, and it is an indication of the liberal premises of pluralism that, at every juncture, theorists prove willing to sacrifice meaning and security in favor of utility and individual liberty. It is partly for this reason that so many group theorists have attacked the idea of a "national interest" or public good. The basis of the argument is ethical rather than empirical or logical. Truman, for example, argues that we never observe a "national interest," but only groups struggling to advance their private interests within the rules of the game. But we do not observe an "associational" interest either; we only see small groups struggling within associations. And as Plato indicated long ago, struggle is likely to exist within the smallest groups and within the individual himself. For that matter, we do not observe groups at all; we infer them from the proximity and regularity of patterns of action which characterize discrete individuals. If "shared attitudes" constitute a group, and if a group once created may be said to have an "interest," then the shared belief in and usage of terms like the "national interest," reflecting the shared belief that we are in some sense "a people," can quite as legitimately be said to create a "national interest." Truman's assertion that groups "called" political are no different from groups "called" social is belied by the fact that the state is the one group denied the right to speak of its "interest." [31]

The prescriptive character of the argument is clear. It asserts that we ought not to use or believe in terms like "the national interest," because such terms are dangerous to liberty. Some group may be able to preempt them, identifying the national good with its own. Moreover, the state elevated above other associations would endanger the self-regulating mechanism which is the pluralist's guarantee of ordered liberty. Pluralism is not laissez-faire; the state cannot simply be reduced to the status of a night watchman. Groups and associations are too few in number, too great in resources, to be reduced to the status

[31] Truman, *The Governmental Process,* pp. 51–65.

of anonymous units of the market. Pluralist theory requires a state which is active in promoting compromise and agreement, a "broker" which acts when "countervailing power" in group competition begins to approximate equilibrium. It is vital for the imperfectly competitive model of pluralist theory that the state act within the limits set by the process of group competition, that it make no moral claims beyond accommodation and the "rules of the game." If it were to do this, the state would risk social division as particular groups rejected those claims, and with such conflict would arise the threat of open combat. (For the same reason, groups must avoid any "ideology" other than the ideology of group competition itself.) Such claims would be even worse if they were accepted, for the state would then be a threat to the liberty of all.

Group theorists have been aware, moreover, that groups large enough to be effective in influencing or limiting national policy tend to be too large to have meaning for the individual or for the primary group. That, however, is only a kind of advantage, critical to the existence of individual freedom within highly organized society. Faced with psychological withdrawal of allegiance, group leaders must limit their claims on the loyalty of members, must restrict their actions to the "interest" felt by members—a rational, limited sphere. That phenomenon, in turn, helps encourage the growth of "overlapping" or multiple group membership, important because it recreates the competitive process in the mind of the individual. One loyalty "checks and balances" another, leaving the individual "free" from control by any single affiliation. By such methods a "liberal and humanistic individualism" may be preserved in an organizational age.

Critics have pointed out that this psychological fragmentation would itself so weaken the meaning of any group to the individual as to divest it of the function of providing emotional security and discipline. When combined with massive organizational size, which reduces the individual's sense of significance in the group and his willingness to commit himself to it, the charge becomes still stronger.[32]

The response to such criticisms is sometimes purely ethical. Scott Greer writes that "the theorist who wishes to emphasize the viability

---

[32] Lowi, *The End of Liberalism*, pp. 26–27; Karl Mannheim, *Freedom, Power and Democratic Planning* (New York: Oxford University Press, 1950), p. 11 and *passim*.

of democratic institutions" must "accept the formal organization as the effective subcommunity . . . capable of organizing individuals in meaningful wholes that may then participate." [33] Science becomes theodicy; ideas are justified by the fact that they support the premise of viability in American democracy. The communal or fraternal character of the group ("meaningful wholes") must be assumed, because it would otherwise be difficult to assume a representative regime and impossible to believe in a fraternal public.

But the response has other, presumably more empirical, grounds. Few pluralists can argue that the citizen, as portrayed by their researches, is capable of direct control of his own organizations. Ignorant, psychologically riven, private and parochial in concern and lacking in organizing skills and resources, the citizen appears hopelessly passive and manipulable. It is argued, however, that the competitive process forces and guarantees representativeness on the part of leaders. Truman, who virtually identifies leaders with the group, asserts that the desire of leaders to retain power or advance their own interests is "secondary." And many have followed Truman in arguing that leaders are if anything too responsive, lacking the will and power to act for the good of the whole.[34]

All this argument is based on a distorted perception of political reality. Most evidence indicates that group leaders have considerable discretion in defining group "interests," and the facile assumption that their private interests and perspectives are in accord with those of group members (or are unimportant) hardly merits consideration. It is also fairly evident that in relation to the individual citizen, the competitive mechanism works imperfectly indeed. The great organizations tend to monopolize certain specialized sectors of economic and political life, competing with one another at the boundaries of fairly well recognized spheres of influence, but rarely competing for the allegiance of individual members. And as this might suggest, overlapping membership proves to be much less characteristic of society than was once believed. In relation to government, the picture does not differ. Interest groups capture sectors of public government within their "sphere" or develop a common frame of reference with officials, transforming government from a "neutral" into a partisan of the most

[33] Scott Greer, *The Emerging City*, p. 88 (though compare pp. 100–102).
[34] Truman, *The Governmental Process*, pp. 156–159, 164, 193, 210.

organized and insistent forces within its jurisdiction. In the process of competition and compromise between "spheres of influence," as Grant McConnell demonstrates, many values get left out altogether—especially those that to eyes unscaled by pluralist dogma seem integral elements of the public good.[35]

Earlier forms of group theory presumed that the public exerted at least a passive form of control, guaranteeing that such "widely shared values" would not be wholly neglected and that some standards of fairness would be observed. Of course, group theorists avoided the use of the term "public," but their euphemisms for it were hardly obscure. Bentley referred to a "consumer's group," for example, and Truman to a "potential group" based on the "most widely shared attitudes" within the political system.[36] Such usage defined groups that in membership were identical to the traditional public; in fact, the "consumer's group" includes every citizen to some degree. The difference from traditional ideas of the public lies in the fact that Truman's and Bentley's terms suggest a body of citizens who are passive, who in Bentley's case are defined as private consumers and in Truman's by attitudes which do not require participation.

The public, in this picture, becomes important only to the extent that the competitive mechanism and the "rules of the game" are threatened or break down. For the citizenry to perform the role of protecting or restoring the system during times of crisis, however, at least three conditions must exist. First, the public must understand and support the "rules of the game"—otherwise activation becomes a serious danger in itself. Second, the public must be aware that the "rules" and/or the "widely shared attitudes" are in danger. And finally, the individuals who make up the "potential group" must feel confident that enough men and resources to give a reasonable chance of success will join in the struggle to protect rules and values. Some men are heroes, but most will refuse to run risks or suffer losses without some corresponding gain.

All these assumptions have become extremely dubious, especially to pluralists, whose citizen is privatized, parochial, and often hostile to the "system" or imperfectly aware of the relations between the values

---

[35] Grant McConnell, *Private Power and American Democracy*, pp. 336–368.
[36] Bentley, *The Process of Government*, pp. 178, 208–209, 349–350, 372; Truman, *The Governmental Process*, pp. 51–52.

he holds dear and the "rules of the game." In a recent variant of the older pluralist argument, Bernard Berelson and his associates have argued that conflicts within the system are limited by the uncommitted citizens who refuse to be led into extremes and thus presumably influence opponents to moderate demands, as a price of giving their support.[37] The sanguine tone of this analysis, however, sits badly with the fact that the uncommitted are also identified as politically ignorant, fearful, weakly committed to political democracy, and often suffering from psychological disorders.

Truman, in fact, has indicated that a "demagogue" could threaten "the system" under one of several conditions (clearly, he had the late Senator Joseph McCarthy in mind). Such a danger could arise if large numbers of citizens lacked formal organizations and the means of expressing dissent. It could also exist if they are alienated from group elites or widely "frustrated" by some condition, or if inadequate or monopolized "communication" prevented the expression of those conditions. Finally, demagogy might become a peril if group elites become parochial and concentrate on their immediate conflicts to the exclusion of concern for "the system" as a whole.[38]

This line of analysis is obviously a far cry from earlier ideas of an automatic or self-regulating system. Still presuming that the competitive mechanism will respond appropriately if citizens are organized, and if their desires are expressed, it does concede that they may not be. Moreover, it implies a tension in the role of group leader, for the leader must not fail his members—which would alienate or frustrate them—but must also not be so closely tied to their concerns (still thought of as private and parochial) as to fail in his duty to the "system"—a duty which includes responsiveness to unorganized citizens. In fact, more than one pluralist has found fault with Congress and other "group-dominated" bodies for failing to take a broad, national perspective and for being bound to particular and narrow concerns. Despairing of the public—mass movements, for almost all pluralists, have become synonymous with mob rule and totalitarian tendencies—yet facing the defects of the self-regulatory model, plu-

---

[37] B. Berelson et al., *Voting*, pp. 311–320.

[38] Truman, "The American System in Crisis," *PSQ*, LXXIV (1959), pp. 481–497, and *The Governmental Process*, pp. 500–536; Robert Dahl, *Who Governs?* (New Haven: Yale University Press, 1962), pp. 311–325.

ralist theory demands of elites the public-spirited devotion which was once expected of citizens.[39]

Yet at a critical point, pluralists still rely on the theory of self-regulatory mechanisms. When opposing any of the various "elite" theories that have grown up in imitation of C. Wright Mills, pluralists call attention to the existence of conflict and competition between elites and point out that no group "regularly prevails" in public contests with others.[40] As many critics have indicated, this argument, even if its factual basis is accepted, depends on the assumption that all "important" issues become public questions.[41] If elites, consciously or unconsciously, agree that certain values and interests shall not become the subject of debate or contest, then the competitive model may reflect nothing but epiphenomena and peripherality. (No pluralist, for example, would deny that the conflict-ridden societies of feudal Europe were characterized by an elite.)

Outside the immediate necessities of debate, however, pluralists themselves have undermined that critical assumption. The distinction between "active" and "inactive" citizens reveals a consensus among the former which does effectively exclude a number of alternatives and attitudes from public discussion. "Active citizens," of course, suggests a broader and more open group than does "elite," and by combining all Americans in a single class—"citizens," distinguished only by "activity"—the terms avoid the qualitative distinction implicit in the juxtaposition of "elite" and "mass." But the number of active citizens, taken as a percentage of the population, is scarcely larger in the United States than the membership of the Communist Party is in the Soviet Union. Moreover, the characteristics associated with "active citizenship"—higher income, better residence, higher status occupations, and the like—hardly refute "elitist" theory.[42]

[39] Peter Bachrach, *The Theory of Democratic Elitism* (Boston: Little, Brown, 1967).

[40] Robert Dahl, "A Critique of the Ruling Elite Model," *APSR*, LII (1958), pp. 463–469.

[41] Peter Bachrach and Morton Baratz, "Two Faces of Power," *APSR*, LVI (1962), pp. 947–952.

[42] Herbert McClosky, "Consensus and Ideology in American Politics," *APSR*, LVIII (1964), pp. 361–382; Dahl, *Who Governs?*, pp. 90–102, 225, 279–293. The difference in attitudes toward policy between active and inactive citizens may be less than was believed: see Sidney Verba et al., "Public Opinion and the War in Vietnam," *APSR*, LXI (1967), pp. 331–332.

For most pluralists, such considerations can be discarded because the "active citizenry" has its consensus in a greater and more coherent devotion to liberal democratic values. That, however, reveals the crucial assumption that liberal democratic doctrine cannot be the ideology of an elite. For example, when it is pointed out that "education" is the most critical variable in the distinction between "actives" and "inactives," it is never suggested that the kind of education received may be critical—that in America, education has meant training and socialization into liberal democratic theories of man and the world. The implicit assumption has been rather that with education, the truth of liberal democratic ideas (or perhaps more fashionably, their relatively lesser untruth) becomes apparent. In this sense, there remains a hint in pluralist theory of the old belief that with education, liberal values—including the "humanistic assumptions" of human dignity and fraternity—will "emerge" among men. To that extent, the "active citizen" is not only the watchdog but the "vanguard" of the citizenry as a whole.

Such language must be employed cautiously. Pluralists are far less confident in progress than were their predecessors. Bentley, as Bernard Crick points out, stood in the "tradition of the Social Darwinists" and referred to the group struggle as a process of "natural selection," and in 1939, Charles Merriam, revered by most pluralists, predicted the eventual arrival of "a new world order . . . the brotherhood of man . . . social justice . . . a new commonwealth." It goes without saying that such ideas find few vocal adherents today. In the new rhetoric, the passivity of inactive citizens is praised as "functional," and the key considerations become social coherence and stability.[43]

Weaker and partly unspoken, the belief in progress is still very real. The process of group competition, as pluralists conceive it, is moving and open-ended, producing an increasing level of satisfactions for the system as a whole. It must do so, in fact, to result in the stability pluralists admire. A periodic redistribution of the same old pie would, as pluralists know very well, result in feelings of being robbed

---

[43] Crick, *The American Science of Politics*, p. 124; Bentley, *The Process of Government*, p. 461; Charles Merriam, *Prologue to Politics* (Chicago: University of Chicago Press, 1939), pp. 74–75. See also Lewis Lipsitz, "If, as Verba says, the state functions as a religion, what are we to do then to save our souls?", *APSR*, LXII (1968), pp. 527–535.

for those who lose ("relative deprivation") and of anxiety for those who gain, and the system would accumulate a dangerous amount of frustration and fear. To be stable, the system must result in a bigger pie. After all, this is the logic of groups, for each is designed to increase "control over the environment."

It follows that as mastery of the environment increases, the need for associations becomes less immediately compelling; and conflict between groups, since basic needs have been largely satisfied, becomes less intense. The individual feels less dependent on groups and becomes less willing to respond to extreme claims on his loyalty. Increasingly able to enjoy private satisfactions, the individual will turn more and more to "expressive behavior" within spontaneous or informal groups. Privatism increasingly replaces politics as men return to an innocence which as the tradition of the liberal Enlightenment has it, was and remains the goal of man. At the same time, conflict becomes muted, pragmatism replaces ideology, groups become more similar and more agreeable, while multiple membership unites men across the erstwhile frontiers. In this sense, pluralist theory retains a measure of faith in the emergence of the "brotherhood of man."

It is, however, a very limited and balanced measure. The march of progress brings in its train growing possibilities for destruction which threaten all men; and men themselves, having more, show a greater fear of loss. The reasons for conflict, as pluralists see them, have declined; the danger and the fear of conflict have grown. In such conditions privatism proves to be a condition of insecurity, rather than the first step toward fraternity. Consequently pluralists stress the need to keep the people secure, free from "irrational" tendencies to move too fast or to attempt to eliminate the insecurities that surround them once and for all. The sanguine precept that "things could not be better" conceals—not very deeply, given the "realistic" tone in which it is enunciated—the perception that things could indeed be much worse.

Even so, many social scientists insist that the causes of suspicion and fear may be removed and men may come to see that conflict is needless. "Communication" retains some of the talismanic power it had for Progressives like Charles H. Cooley. More than one analyst traces conflict to "blockages in communication," continuing the eighteenth-century tradition in which breaking down barriers, removing technical limitations, and setting men free from parochiality is almost a sufficient condition of fraternity. There is no great difference between the prudent scientism of Karl Deutsch's warning that the communications system of nations may "rigidify" and the ecstasy of Marshall McLuhan's vision of the world become a "universal village." The difference between the two is practical, not theoretical.[44]

That difference, however, is revealing. For liberal thought, the "brotherhood of man" remains an ideal; hence the hostility to "closed" or "exclusive" groups and to coherent loyalties. But as the old groups perish, the broader fraternity which was to replace them fails to appear and dark powers gather. That part of the pluralist case which urges holding fast to what remains has practical force. But pluralists also cling to the process of technological and organizational change, the expansion of mastery, which socially destroys what pluralists otherwise value and adds to the threats they fear. The old liberal generosity of hope, born of confidence, is almost lost; liberalism has come to suspect all enthusiasms, even its own. The liberal creed, however, proves too powerful in its hold to be abandoned, perhaps because no other has appeared, perhaps because most lack the fraternity that might enable them to seek a new one or recover any which has been lost. Trapped between faith and fear, liberalism drifts in a current which erodes faith and adds to fear, toward an end which is finis— possibly for much more than liberalism. The curtain falls on the drama which began with the bright hope of human fraternity.

[44] Karl Deutsch, *Nationalism and Social Communication* (New York: Wiley, 1953) and *The Nerves of Government* (New York: Free Press, 1963); Marshall McLuhan, *Understanding Media* (New York: McGraw-Hill, 1964).

> If America undergoes great revolutions, they
> will be brought about by the presence of the
> black race on the soil of the United States—
> that is to say, they will owe their origin, not
> to the equality, but to the inequality of con-
> ditions.
>
> De Tocqueville, *Democracy in America*

CHAPTER XX

NATIVE SONS

Through a glass, darkly . . .

FOR nearly a century, American politics has been dominated by the struggle between the assimilated and the ethnic minorities. That visible battle mirrored the older, inward conflict of the American with himself, the contest between liberal modernism and the traditional, religious culture inherited from the past. Now both combats have reached a kind of Armageddon, a final battlefield. For all practical purposes, black America is the last of the minorities and the last sub-culture in which the oldest American heritage finds an articulate voice. The old story, and with it the old America, is coming to a close.

Black America, as Myrdal saw it, was a "dilemma" for whites, the creed of equality being set against the practice of racial inequality. That this thesis touched part of the truth is obvious; recently, one survey found that 94 percent of whites proclaimed their belief in the "brotherhood of man" but only 29 percent would carry this far enough to invite Negroes to dinner.[1]

Properly speaking, however, what Myrdal described was not a

---

[1] Frank Westie, "The American Dilemma: An Empirical Test," *ASR*, 30 (1965), pp. 531–538.

"dilemma" at all. It was merely a challenge to white society to make good on the liberal promise, to make social performance correspond to moral beliefs. This perception has informed the liberal whites who have devoted themselves to the cause of racial equality. Black America, from this viewpoint, is only another in the series of minorities, more difficult than its predecessors but fundamentally identical, a "problem" to be overcome by assimilation and modernization.

Possibly it is. That black protest challenges the nature of liberal industrialism is nothing new; all the minorities have invoked their ancient cultures and older wisdom in their struggle with modern America. Moreover, the protest of the excluded is always ambivalent; those who assail the established order also resent their exclusion from it. Thus, although Eldridge Cleaver declared that blacks doubt the "sanctity surrounding property," he also stated that "what they want is to figure out a way to get some of that property for themselves, to divert it to their own needs." The cult of "soul food," Cleaver says, is a diversion from the real problem of beefsteak.[2]

One after the other, the minorities that have challenged modern America have been bought and broken, and it may be that for black America, too, social criticism will only be a lever to pry open the gates of admission to society. As always, the alienated and disenchanted hear the words of the excluded with ears made too sensitive by loneliness, listening only for those sounds which will convince them that in the black masses they have found natural allies and brothers. Past disappointments only make for a more eager and desperately hopeful present, and the fact that black America seems the last hope only intensifies the dream. The left has embraced the "myth of the Black Revolution," Harold Cruse comments, out of "sheer political insolvency."[3]

Yet the sentiment that this minority is different has a solid foundation. In the first place, black America is an inner minority. The immigrant had, in his own eyes, few claims on America; blacks know that redress is owed for injustice suffered and service rendered, a conviction only made stronger by the fact that blacks are an old minority, coeval with white settlement on the land. James Baldwin writes that

[2] Eldridge Cleaver, *Soul on Ice* (New York: Dell, 1968), pp. 134–135, 29–30.
[3] Harold Cruse, *The Crisis of the Negro Intellectual* (New York: Morrow, 1967), p. 372.

"the situation of the Irish a hundred years ago and the situation of Negroes today cannot usefully be compared. . . . What manner of consolation is it to be told that emigrants arriving—voluntarily—long after you did have risen far above you?" [4] Many inner minorities, like Appalachian whites, might say the same, but here too there is a difference. Immigrants struggled to win a place in American society; native white minorities sought to recapture a place they believed had once been theirs. Unlike both, black America's "place" is intolerable and has always been. The attack on society goes further because it must; first principles become first items on the political agenda.

This is of a piece with the history of blacks in America. Problems have always presented themselves starkly; temporization and evasion have been difficult—far more so than they have been for whites—and almost always futile. That, perhaps, has been the essence of the black condition in America. That starkness is what Ralph Ellison had in mind when he referred to the "harsh discipline" of black life in America, and especially when he pointed out that such a discipline, grinding and destructive though it has been for most, is not without its advantages.[5]

Without minimizing or attempting to rationalize black suffering, it is notable that in spite of all the worst that society could and can inflict, black America has produced intellectuals of extraordinary wisdom and understanding, and its human victories are not won by intellectuals alone. Black America has a strength too often ignored, a quality more profound than the "tools" of behavioral science can reach. Politically, it may be justifiable to concentrate almost exclusively on want and deprivation; intellectually, the same concentration hints at a racism barely covered by the rhetoric of compassion. Ellison writes:

> I could escape the reduction imposed by unjust laws and customs, but not that imposed by ideas which defined me as no more than the *sum* of those laws and customs. . . . I found some of the most treacherous assaults against me committed by those who regarded themselves either as neutrals, as sympathizers, or as disinterested military advisers.[6]

[4] James Baldwin, *The Fire Next Time*, pp. 83–84.
[5] Ralph Ellison, *Shadow and Act* (New York: New American Library, 1964), p. 119.
[6] *Ibid.*, p. 128.

Repeatedly, in black America, one finds greater understanding of the problem of human identity than is characteristic among whites. The sense of dual identity, the feeling of tension between mind and body, public and private selves, is part of the nature and condition of man; but in white America the tension is blurred. Material gain and social status lead men to hide the "inner self" so well that it becomes almost hopelessly lost, a wispy memory flitting on the edge of awareness, a bad conscience which disturbs their sleeping if not their waking hours. And those who romantically seek "expression" of the "true self" have been cushioned by laws and comforts, enabled to avoid facing the full meaning of their idyll. In black America, by contrast, the tension has been stark and almost categorical. The choice lay between a social role which degraded ("denigrated") without offering much beyond bare survival, and the assertion of dignity and private selfhood bound almost inextricably to violence and death.

> It is as though one, looking out from a dark cave in a side of an impending mountain, sees the world passing and speaks to it. . . . It gradually penetrates the minds of the prisoners that the people passing do not hear; that some thick sheet of invisible but horribly tangible plate glass is between them and the world. They get excited; they talk louder; they gesticulate. Some of the passing world stop in curiosity; these gesticulations seem so pointless; they laugh and pass on. . . . Then the people within may become hysterical. They may scream and hurl themselves against the barriers. . . . They may even, here and there, break through in blood and disfigurement and find themselves faced by a horrified, implacable and quite overwhelming mob of people frightened for their own existence.[7]

The years pass, the condition remains. Ellison only echoed Du-Bois:

> I am invisible, understand, simply because people refuse to see me. . . . When they approach me they see only my surroundings, themselves, or figments of their imagination—indeed, everything and anything except me. . . . That invisibility [is] . . . a matter of the construction of their *inner* eyes. . . . You're constantly being bumped against by those of poor vision. Or again, you often doubt if you really exist. . . . It's when you feel like this that, out of resentment, you begin to bump people back. And, let me confess, you feel that

[7] W. E. B. DuBois, *Dusk of Dawn*, p. 132; see also *Souls of Black Folk*, pp. 16–17.

way most of the time. You ache with the need to convince yourself that you do exist in the real world, that you're a part of all the sound and anguish, and you strike out with your fists, you curse and you swear to make them recognize you. And, alas, it's seldom successful.[8]

All Americans, especially the ethnic minorities, have felt this invisibility at times. But for white America, society's blindness was temporary, something which could be overcome if the "invisible men" changed accent, setting, and costume. That such changes produced only a new, more serious invisibility was not immediately clear; in white America, it seems one's own fault if one is not seen, resulting from the lack of money, social prominence, or ability.

Blacks, as the literature of the day makes clear, have often felt the same sense of personal defect. But the fact that the white blindness to blacks has been permanent has made it more evident that the blame lies with society and not the self. "Achievement," even for those who are able to make it, has left the racial stereotype largely intact. An "able Negro" remains invisible; social distance remains, even if segregation disappears. Negro Americans, in other words, have been given repeated proof that whites are the "problem race" in the United States.

Each black in America has been driven, in his own way, to analyze and explain the sources of white America's disease of the inner eye. Some diagnoses have been self-destructive, some bizarre; some have chosen the easy route of explanation which sees white blindness as a result of corrupt genes. But many have discerned the anxieties and ambiguities, have understood the wild hopes and nightmare terrors that beset white America. And the process of investigation has led to a recognition of the degree to which the blindness of white America is rooted in American society.

Probably most blacks have begun the analysis with a desire to discover weaknesses in the white citadel, hidden gates that lead to the great hall. Most, perhaps, give up at some point; the fortress seems proof against assault. Others have found some partially open gate, some way to use white fears and hopes for their own advantage—though, as James Baldwin points out, to do so is to make oneself a

[8] Ralph Ellison, *The Invisible Man* (New York: New American Library, 1952), pp. 7–8.

creature of those dreams, a kind of apparition.[9] It is important, however, that those who persist in the desire to "get in" may come to discern important reasons for staying out—may see that the fortress is in many ways not a bastion but a prison. The estrangement of black America is, in other words, unique.

Not easily and not for many: black estrangement, like all exclusions, takes a toll, and in the case of black America the toll is appalling and monstrous. Shut out of society, men fall back on their private resources—on families and inherited groups or, ultimately, on themselves. For white Americans, the private world has generally been an adequate defense. Whites who are rebuffed by or at odds with society at large have usually been able to console themselves with the illusion of private sufficiency. Black America knows that folly; original sin, the desire to deny limitation and dependence, does not stop at the color line. In any event, the recalcitrance of white society combines with its individualistic ideology to encourage blacks to seek private "solutions." A failure for all Americans, the illusion has been more difficult for blacks; the price has been greater and more evident, the gains smaller when they existed at all. The history of black America testifies to the inadequacy of private man and to man's need for fraternity.

Open resistance to society in the tradition of the slave revolts, where thousands refused to surrender their dignity and struck back at the oppressor, where mothers slew their children to save them humiliation, ended only in defeat. Moreover, such defeat brought nothing but the momentary satisfaction of having resisted. At best, it offered the hope that the example, with all of its ambivalence, might provide a legend to be whispered to the young.

Even the whispers were likely to be inaudible. Those who submitted, as most did, delighted in the moments of pleasure and peace they were allowed, hoped for a better time, and sought to build a secret place beyond the reach of the enemy. This "inner migration" had successes—the movement for black liberation today is indication enough—but it exacted a price. Even for adults, survival required a deceit so perfect and a self-control so unfailing as to be beyond the resources of most men, especially since a part of their emotions re-

[9] James Baldwin, *Going to Meet the Man* (New York: Dell, 1965), p. 74.

sented and resisted the need for either. For the child, the case seemed hopeless; the armor of deception had to be made second nature. Ellison's protagonist recalled the death of his grandfather:

> On his deathbed he called my father to him and said, "Son, after I'm gone I want you to keep up the good fight. I never told you, but our life is a war and I have been a traitor all my born days, a spy in the enemy's country ever since I gave up my gun back in the Reconstruction. Live with your head in the lion's mouth . . . overcome 'em with yesses, undermine 'em with grins, agree 'em to death and destruction. . . . Learn it to the younguns," he whispered fiercely; then he died.
>
>   But my folks were more alarmed over his last words than over his dying. . . . I was warned, emphatically, to forget what he had said. . . . I could never be sure what he meant. . . . Whenever things went well for me I remembered my grandfather and felt guilty and uncomfortable. It was as though I was carrying out his advice in spite of myself.

And not all blacks were left so articulate an inheritance.[10]

It has become commonplace to observe that the hatred of Negroes for the role in which they have been cast can be translated with frightening ease into hatred for blackness. And because blackness is a thing of the flesh, that disgust becomes a hatred for the body. Parents are despised for their blackness; and the psyche, alienated from the body, identifies with whites. The zeal, so admired by white romantics, with which many blacks embrace the delights of the flesh, often reflects little more than self-destructiveness. When retreat from the body leads to the fantasy world of drugs, the case is only less ambiguous. Always, in such cases, other blacks are the mirror-image of what is hated in the self.

There may be, moreover, very little difference in those who turn to open rebellion. Blackness may cease to be despised; the enemy is more clearly identified; violence against other blacks becomes less likely. All of this is an undeniable gain, personally and politically. But what replaces the hatred for blackness can easily be a hatred for fleshliness itself. The emotions, the desire for life, the pleasures of the

---

[10] *The Invisible Man*, pp. 19–20; see also Grier and Cobbs, *Black Rage*, pp. 52, 55, 143–146. Like Ellison, Richard Wright described a character who retreats underground into a secret place filled with a kind of light. (Richard Wright, *Eight Men* [New York: Pyramid, 1969], pp. 22–74.)

body become identified as sources of self-betrayal, especially since the enemy is—in military terms as well as numbers—overpowering. One must accept death to fight at all, and avoiding the passivity of those who "play nigger" continues to demand, from many if not most, a hatred of the "feminine" qualities, too terrified and insistent to be real.[11] In Arna Bontemps' *Black Thunder,* a novel of Prosser's rebellion, the heroine taunts those who hesitate:

> Always big-talking about what booming bed-men you is. . . . Well, let's see what you is good for sure 'nough. Let's see if you knows how to go free; let's see if you knows how to die.[12]

It goes almost without saying that the fear of being "unmanned" by women is a theme of much private, as well as political, life.[13] Or consider Cleaver's comment that "to . . . take up arms against the oppressor is to step outside life itself, to step outside the structure of this world, to enter, almost alone, the no man's land of revolution." [14] If resistance is defined in terms of an older language reserved for salvation, it is hardly improper to infer that "salvation" is felt to be necessary to it.

Whatever the gains involved, self-hatred is embedded in such attitudes. Despising one's parents for the blackness of their flesh yields to despising them for having succumbed to fleshly desires. Few have recognized Cleaver's dictum, "A Slave who dies of natural causes cannot balance two flies in the Scales of Eternity," for what it is: a monstrous insult, given Cleaver's definition of slave, to the parents and ancestors of almost every black American (an insult made ironic, moreover, by Cleaver's use of a seventeenth-century orthography and rhetoric which is a legacy from that past). Perhaps more dangerous is the possibility that whites, ceasing to be the positive ideal of the self, become its negative model. It is no surprise that Cleaver, for all his insight, so often returns to the romantic's dream of the perfect and hence bloodless love ("I seek a lasting relationship, something per-

[11] It is in a special sense that white woman is the "natural recipient of projected Oedipal fantasies," or white man is "the man." (See Grier and Cobbs, *Black Rage,* pp. 76–77.)

[12] Arna Bontemps, *Black Thunder* (New York: Macmillan, 1936), p. 99.

[13] E.G., Baldwin, *Going to Meet the Man,* pp. 18, 182, 187.

[14] Eldridge Cleaver, *Post-Prison Writings and Speeches* (New York: Random House, 1967), p. 37.

manent in a world of change in which all is transitory, ephemeral, and full of pain") and the dream of total merger, an "apocalyptic fusion" which will recover the "lost unity of the primeval sphere" in a "unitary sexual image." And Cleaver has no small measure of self-knowledge. Fear of the emotions and the effort to conquer them, whatever other benefits it may confer, offers few prospects for fraternity.[15]

Fraternity is, in fact, central. It is a repeated, insistent cry through all of black history in America, and Carmichael and Hamilton are right to comment that "black communities are the only large segments of this society where people refer to each other as brother." [16] The whole character and structure of black life in America teaches the need for fraternity, for the ability to overcome, in some sphere of life at least, the bleak antithesis between inner and outer "selves," to find some social space in which expression and aspiration can be allies.

Of course, the conditions which make fraternity so great a need also militate against its realization. Men who have learned to regard almost every relationship as unstable, who have been taught by experience to anticipate betrayal, do not form deep bonds with one another in the normal course of things.

> People never really became personalities to Saul, for hardly had he ever got to know them before they vanished. So people became . . . symbols of uneasiness, of a deprivation that evoked in him a sense of the transitory quality of life, which always made him feel that some invisible, unexplainable event was about to descend on him.[17]

Add to Wright's description that events in the world—amid the virulent racism of the South or the anonymous and mobile world of the city—most often confirm and reinforce such fears. The "lessons" learned do not encourage brotherhood; at best, they teach a guarded friendliness, gregariousness within conflict, fraternization without fraternity.[18]

[15] *Soul on Ice,* pp. 148, 177, 210.
[16] Carmichael and Hamilton, *Black Power,* p. 38.
[17] Richard Wright, *Eight Men,* p. 156.
[18] Elliot Liebow, *Tally's Corner: A Study of Negro Streetcorner Men* (Boston: Little, Brown, 1967).

All this is true, and none of it is denied by the indiscriminate use of the term "brother." Yet the usage reflects a vital reality. It is the visible sign of aspiration, a goal which is continually reaffirmed and ratified by the fact that it is expressed, a covenant for fraternity even if those who make it are less than brothers. In other words, the rhetoric of fraternity is the mark of resistance to the "lessons" society "teaches."

> Too many of us have accepted a statistical interpretation of our lives and thus much of that which makes us a source of moral strength to America goes unappreciated and undefined. Now, to trace American values as they find expression in the Negro community, where do you begin? To what books do you go? How do you account for Little Rock and the sit-ins? How do you account for the strength of the kids? You can find sociological descriptions of the conditions under which they live but few indications of their moral.[19]

Today's resistance is only the continuation of a struggle as old as black America; the idea survives because it has been strengthened and preserved. The continued quest for fraternity is the theme of black political history, and it may be one result of that history that the idea of fraternity remains an articulate force in American politics.

In His Hands

Slavery in America was thorough. Having torn Africans from the context of their cultures, it dispersed them among men of different ways, shattering family and custom by policy in order for the masters to rule more easily. And the centuries were long. Trauma, isolation, time: the experience of slavery conspired to confuse and destroy the African heritage in a way other ethnic groups have not known. Even Melville Herskovits' ingenuity in discovering African influences among Negroes only indicates how inarticulate they had become. In large measure, the culture of black America was necessarily native-born.

The church gave that new culture its center. Coming early, religion was long without rivals and, consequently, shaped and gave much of the content to all the institutions that succeeded it. In

---

[19] Ellison, *Shadow and Act*, p. 35.

institution, idea, and symbol, religion became the common bond, the thread uniting Negroes in America. And it spoke to black needs in at least two critical ways.

First, it provided both the rhetoric of community and fraternity and a setting in which those values could find some partial reflection in the lives of men. In the revivalistic form in which most Negroes received religion, the sense of fraternity could become a passionate—though momentary—reality in the lives of men. (Anyone who doubts that need only read Baldwin's *Go Tell It On The Mountains.*) The church visible gave constant affirmation to men's longings for kinship, solidarity and brotherhood, an affirmation of warmth as well as words.

Second, the dignity and the fraternity which religion proclaimed were not bound by the "evidence" of the empirical and secular world, which by itself taught only worthlessness and despair. A sense of the reality and scope of humanity—of one's own humanity—could not be derived from society, which did not even trouble, as it did with whites, to provide some comforting substitute. For black Americans, it was necessary to separate essence from accident, what is from what exists; and of all the elements of life in America, religion provided the best and possibly the only means by which those distinctions could be made.

Obviously, the church was no impregnable citadel. Society not only took its toll, but invaded and influenced the church itself. Christianity does require the separation of essence and accident; it does not require that, in this life, a sharp distinction be drawn between mind and body. In America, however, encouraged by the nature of the Negro social experience and by the corruptions of later Protestantism, black Christianity *did* tend to make that separation between flesh and spirit. But even so, blacks found in religion a dimension which reflected both the desire for identity and the yearning to be known as a whole self.

> . . . it was the Lord who knew what the charged heart endured as the strap was laid to the backside; the Lord alone who knew what one *would* have said if one had had, like the Lord, the gift of the living word. It was the Lord who knew of the impossibility every parent in that room faced; how to prepare the child for the day when that child would be despised and how to *create* in the child . . . a stronger antidote to this poison than one had found for oneself. . . . It was

better to remember: *Thou knowest this man's fall; but thou knowest not his wrassling.*[20]

Faith was stronger because war with society was necessary, and faith was the best armor of the spirit. Triumphant or defeated, pure or distorted, religion provided an element of affirmation and—perhaps more important—the possibility of total victory.

Politically, religion had value in the fact that it spoke both to black hopes and white guilts. And in human affairs, hope and guilt are closely related; the guilts of whites were hopes which had been buried or put aside. Religious thought argued for a community in which material things were adapted to the needs of men, a political order organized to develop and educate the self. All men can feel the power of such ideas; but to American Negroes, they were also the soberest common sense. Living in a "dusty desert of dollars and smartness," DuBois wrote, the "vast ideal of brotherhood," which for others was only an abstraction was, for most Negroes, the most immediate aspiration and the most pressing of their interests.[21]

Black America had far less interest than whites in achieving a "synthesis" between Christianity and liberal secularism. Its claims could be met best by a victory of the first over the second. In black churches, there was less talk of the contradictions between the "real" and the "ideal," the "rational" and matters of "faith." Rather, there was a clearer understanding that what was involved was a conflict between competing definitions of the real and the rational, a choice between first principles. Spokesmen were less inclined to avoid metaphysics, more inclined to recognize the metaphysical content of all ideas of reality. The belief in equality is said to be only a faith, DuBois wrote, and it is "not more. But a pious belief outweighs an impious belief." [22]

Not all blacks accepted the teachings of religion. Martin Delany, for example, was a deistic rationalist of neo-Federalist persuasion. But it is hardly an accident that Delany was one of the first to abandon hope for the United States and to advocate emigration. More typical was Henry Highland Garnet, who envisioned a mixed race in

20 James Baldwin, *Notes of a Native Son* (New York: Bantam, 1964), pp. 88–89.
21 *Souls of Black Folk*, pp. 22, 82, 131–133, 137–138.
22 *Dusk of Dawn*, p. 146; see also pp. 154–169.

America but argued that even so thorough a physical solution was not enough unless men recognized a fraternity of spirit, a humanity above material things.[23]

Frederick Douglass, also devoted to the ideal of human fraternity, carried the argument back to the Bible and the first principle of Divine Fatherhood. For Douglass this was more than gratuitous rhetoric. Fraternity and humanity, Douglass saw, find their principal antagonists in those who accept individualism and the doctrine of "self-reliance," for these must necessarily be fearful of their fellows. Blacks, Douglass argued, are closer to a true recognition of human weakness and dependence, and understand that what is really to be feared in human affairs is isolation. Douglass' many Marxist admirers will find it disturbing that, when he felt that Darwinism threatened the foundations of faith and might provide scientific support for racism, Douglass resorted to fundamentalism, denouncing those who purveyed the "scientific moonshine that would connect men with monkeys" in place of the Divine Word.[24]

The last argument was hardly felicitous, but the fact that Douglass was willing to go to such extremes illustrates how vital religious dogma has been as a liberation from secular dogma and from the "lessons" of experience. Of course, that very quality is inseparable from the danger that religion will do no more than relieve the tensions and resentments of daily life by an appeal to "pie-in-the-sky." Certainly no one can ignore the degree to which elites found it worthwhile to encourage those evangelists, white or black, who would confine themselves to such terms. It is also evident that whites found black ministers useful, all too often, as "responsible Negroes" who would not challenge the existing order of things.

Something must be said, however, for the perspective which led Virginia to ban separate black congregations before the Civil War because of their potential as centers for conspiracy. The ear of the antebellum South was true in that much, and it would have been hard to miss the Scriptural tone of Prosser's and Nat Turner's rebellions. When black congregations eventually became a fact, it was only prudent to attempt their domestication; but even when they attended black services, whites contrived to hear only comforting things—

[23] *Negro Social and Political Thought*, ed. H. Brotz, pp. 37–111, 199–200.
[24] *Ibid.*, pp. 210–211, 223, 229–231, 242, 307, 316–317.

partly because they wished to, partly because ministers and congregations were not lacking in guile. Gentle Jesus and the next world played a powerful role, and it was that aspect of black Christianity which whites heard and immortalized among themselves. Yet the black churches spoke as often in the language of judgment and retribution, a this-worldly promise in which Jahweh and his prophets were unencumbered by the later Testament: "Pharaoh's army got drownded/ Oh, Mary, don't you weep." [25]

Even at their worst, the churches kept alive a vision of man and fraternity, a knowledge of injustice suffered and retribution due. And for long periods, given the hopeless political environment in which the Negro found himself, "other-worldliness" was the only basis on which such an understanding of the self could be maintained at all, and God's city was the only defense against the standards of white society. (It was not the church, after all, that taught the desirability of bleaching creams.) Liberalism taught equality, but equality meant either individualism—more dangerous to the possibility of political resistance—or tended to doctrines of likeness and adaptation. The Lord taught a different lesson.

In ways unrelated to doctrine, the political importance of the church is even clearer. The churches were the major schools in which blacks learned the techniques of association—and to judge from the data, the teaching was more effective than in any other ethnic culture. Even the ministry, so often the subject of criticism or satire, provided potential leaders with a sphere in which leadership skills could be developed. The very fact that whites sought to co-opt ministers gave them a political role which the white ministry had almost entirely lost.

Gradually, as it has in society at large, the influence of religion has declined in black America. Religious leaders have less prestige among the young; other-worldliness has seemed an intolerable diversion in a world where political possibilities and hopes are greater. Both tendencies, in fact, were apparent even in the rural South before the Second World War.[26] Notably, however, Negro churches responded far more rapidly and directly to such currents than did white

---

[25] Baldwin, *Notes of a Native Son*, p. 56.
[26] C. S. Johnson, *The Negro College Graduate* (Chapel Hill: University of North Carolina Press, 1938), p. 347.

ones; politicization of the white ministry in our times has consistently followed black initiatives. Increasingly, religion speaks in directly political terms. Joseph R. Washington, for example, criticized Martin Luther King for seeking "trivial gains" at the expense of the greater goals of winning whites for God and constructing the fraternal city. Such an argument would once have referred to salvation in the next world—but, as the title suggests, Washington's *The Politics of God* is both immediately political and concerned with this world.[27]

The appropriate charge against the church is that, partly from doctrine, partly from the condition of black Americans, it has devoted itself to universal fraternity so thoroughly as to leave it with only a limited understanding of the lesser fraternities of men. In a sense, this is positive, reinforcing the resistance of black culture to any counter-racism of its own. But devotion to universality wars with the emotions of men, and religious devotion to it has also reinforced the tendency to see the flesh as the foe of the spirit. And such attitudes hold no solution to the problem of identity or the need for fraternity.

Martin Luther King, Jr., was in most respects a very traditional thinker, even when he used the language of modern theologians like Martin Buber. Politics and society are necessarily a part of religion, Dr. King argued, because religion exists in two inseparably related dimensions, the relation of man to God and the relation of man to man. Since politics affects the second, it affects the first. Correspondingly, a true realization of fraternity in this world depends on a right relation to God. Human excellence and fraternity depend on an understanding of what is beyond man; for only by a knowledge of the whole can man hope to know his nature and estate as a part of that whole. Before men can establish a right relation with their fellows, they must know something of right. Hence, when a Southern Christian Leadership Conference manifesto called for a "beloved community in an America where brotherhood is a reality," it tied that vision to the existence of laws in harmony with the "moral law of the universe." [28]

Traditional as that view of man and the law of nature was, King's moral passion, his ardor for a peaceful and fraternal world,

---

[27] Joseph R. Washington, *The Politics of God* (Boston: Beacon, 1967).
[28] *Negro Protest Thought*, ed. Broderick and Meier, p. 272.

led him to slight the concept of sin implicit in his theology—the idea that evil results when man attempts to go beyond the limits of his existence. Thus, although King rejected the doctrine of historical progress, he did so primarily to combat fatalism or complacency. Despite that rejection, he affirmed that God moves in history through men, a belief which kept him from criticizing modern organization and technology beyond the moralism that men should "use rightly" the devices they had made. And that omission ignores the possibility that these devices might affect the relation of man to man in negative ways—let alone the right relation of man to God.

More serious problems lay in the doctrine of love on which King founded his ideas of nonviolence and his hope for brotherhood. King knew that the universal fraternity he aimed at could only be based on *agape*, the love for God and for his works. King knew very well that the "sentimental" counterfeits of agape, *eros* and *philia*, draw boundaries and limits around man and his love. Beyond making the distinction, however, King did not explore the relation between these three loves very deeply. His teaching implied, whatever King himself meant, that agape was a sufficient principle on which to base the relations of men. A more traditional view would understand that agape, in this world, requires the support—and takes on some of the limits— of philia, the synthesis of love-in-spirit and love-in-body. King's teaching, unfortunately, seemed to reject that alliance in rejecting the limitations it involves. In that sense, it placed spirit in a state of war with the emotions, and—with the familiar inversion of romantic transcendentalism—it is no surprise that King's doctrine that "all men are brothers" was so often defined in terms of man's involvement in a "single process," a gentle but unambiguous hint in the direction of the "all." [29]

King's faults as a theologian were more than balanced by his virtues as a political leader. In political action, King certainly understood the need of men for emotional support, and his nonviolent warriors had all the solidarity of men who are constantly able to test the devotion of their fellows and are tested by them. The word

[29] Martin Luther King, Jr., *Stride Toward Freedom* (New York: Ballantine, 1958), pp. 26–29, 67, 101–107; "Facing the Challenge of the New Age," *Phylon*, XVIII (1957), pp. 25–34; and "Let Justice Roll Down," *Nation*, CC (1965), pp. 269–274.

"warriors" is advised; King led a church militant, and the fraternity of the movement was a fraternity of battle. Those who were part of it might "hate the sin and love the sinner," but they were engaged in combat nonetheless. And, if that love for the enemy was partly genuine, it could shine at all only by the reflection of the warmer fire that burned among the crusaders themselves.

King's assassination was genuine tragedy in a country where most "tragedy" is bathos. King gave his devotion to a love beyond what is normally human, which men attain only at the end of a long personal struggle if at all, and then only imperfectly. Made the basis of action, that love visibly reveals the struggles and loves of most men as paltry and inadequate. Nietzsche wrote that he who has such knowledge of love seeks for death; to bear witness to it, to demand that men measure themselves in relation to it, is surely to court death. Some must do so, however—lest men, lacking the example, settle for a love which is illusion and a fraternity which is a shadow.

King's life taught better than his words. It epitomizes the lives of thousands and more in black America who also bore witness, but whose deaths, violent or quiet, were hidden by the shrouds of indifference. "Many thousands gone" and a moment of blazing clarity, a martyred people and a martyr: this is an old pattern in human history. And white Americans have no claim to escape judgment when confronted by the example of those whose lives so visibly conformed to the pattern of the Master.

Sinn Fein

The sense of racial community and fraternity, in contrast to the demands of religion, is rooted in the immediate experiences and feelings of black Americans. Outside the racial wall, the white world is cold, hostile, and implacable in its resolve to treat blacks as alien; inside, men find some respite, warmth, and consolation. The black world is, in part, a place of shelter, a setting which is "home."

Man's reaction to his home, however, is always a mixed one when that home results from the automatic impersonalities of birth and blood. Among blacks, of course, that ambivalence is doubled by the fact that the community is in large measure the creation of the black role as defined by white society. No one, since E. Franklin Frazier wrote *Black Bourgeoisie*, needs to be told that there are serious conflicts of interest between Negroes. The sense and fact of common destiny, the moral foundation of ideas of racial fraternity, result because the white oppressor blindly persists in clumping diverse men together (and never more than when he distinguishes between "responsible" Negroes and others). Racial community has been, in large part, as impersonal as racism itself; "invisibility" exists inside the racial barrier because it defines that boundary.

W. E. B. DuBois pointed out that while there is nothing necessarily evil in voluntary separation, the sense of volition is radically tainted in black America; in a fundamental sense, it is impossible to "choose" a community based on exclusion. Many, Dr. DuBois observed, seek to escape the race, to their own emotional cost; others, unable to endure the frustrations and anxieties of the world outside, seek to escape to it at a cost to their personal development.[30] The very solace and comfort available in black society are inseparably related to feelings of defeat, whether experienced or only anticipated. If home is a fortress to which men can repair, in black America it has also been partly a prison, a "mark of oppression."

It adds to that ambivalence that the world of the ghettos is one of violence and threat (from the "defenders" as well as the violators of the law)—crowded, with public services always minimal, education a mockery, and exploitation a basic fact of life. Recent attention to the positive aspects of ghetto life, proper enough in its own way, should not obscure the general pall; middle-class culture has an emptiness, but it is likely to seem less undesirable to those whose lives have been too full. All of this strengthens the human desire to "leave home"; and if blacks cling to the home place and its people, it is largely because wolves prowl outside the door.

This is particularly marked in the case of black interest groups and similar associations. The lodges, one of the oldest forms of organization, provided—as they did for whites—an escape from daily life into a world where different ideals could be affirmed and emotions expressed; too, they were starting points for political organization. But, also like the white lodges, they sought to justify themselves in terms of the secular, utilitarian values which shaped the daily life of

---

[30] DuBois, *Dusk of Dawn*, pp. 186–187.

society at large. And in these terms, the black lodges were decisively inferior to their white counterparts (though the performance of the latter was spotty enough). The same has been true of all specifically black interest organizations; as compared with white groups, they have been ineffective and their existence is almost solely justified by the fact of racial discrimination. The emotional security and personal importance with which they have provided their members are important, even vital; but interest groups are created to advance interests, and loyalty to such organizations is inevitably flawed. Members, at least, must suspect their leaders when a major goal of the organization is the ending of the conditions which created the need for the organization itself.

Similarly, the charge that black political leaders have been instruments of "indirect rule" is based, in part, on the realization that leaders acquire an interest in the continued existence of the situation in which their own leadership grew. It is a valid accusation in too many cases—but it is also a disguised attack on the "community" as it now exists, a reflection of the necessary ambivalence toward black society. And the impressive sophistication and unity of black voters in recent years is only additional evidence, for voting involves the relation of blacks to white society rather than to each other. Black unity—and still more, black feelings of fraternity—remain a response to white exclusiveness and hostility.

In trade unions, for example, Negro grievances center on discriminatory admission and racial bias in the selection of officers—demands for equal status within the group. John Leggett's studies indicate, in fact, that black trade unionists are more class-conscious and more militant unionists than whites; they have, in other words, differed chiefly in more thoroughly assimilating the values of the organization.[31] Militant blacks have moved in the direction of forming black caucuses within racially mixed groups; but it is vital that the context in which this takes place is interracial. The caucus allows a synthesis of the emotional advantages of separation and the purposive advantages of unity, making racial solidarity a substratum within a community of interests, rather than an alternative to it. Even extreme

[31] John C. Leggett, "Economic Insecurity and Working-Class Consciousness," *ASR*, 29 (1964), pp. 226–234.

demands, like those for "50 percent representation," are advanced as necessary to remove the sources—especially, obviously, the emotional sources—of racial inequality and tension which prevent common action. The demand for racial recognition is, in fact, a demand that others honor one's home and origin, which is not an assertion of racial fraternity but an essential precondition of genuine fraternity based on common values. Home and origin, after all, are part of what a man is; he can hardly be our brother if we are blind to them, still less if he seeks to blind himself.

Much of the struggle of black America, in fact, has been an effort to establish a home, a place of security and pride in which personal development can begin, a first covenant which is the precondition of fraternity. Parents, certainly, have waged that battle, often savagely and sometimes successfully. The great migrations—the escape North, the mass movement of 1879, the tide into the cities and out of the South—have only been a more political form of the same seeking.[32] Too, blacks have sought to influence and shape law and government, using the whole gamut of political tactics to the same end.

Each movement, each success, each change has allowed old hopes to become new expectations. For the old, perhaps, with their memories of defeat, change has been fear-producing, menacing to a perilously established equilibrium. Most, however, have seen in change—whether actively created or simply received as the result of social, political, and technological events and currents—the possibility of new things, the spring thaw that may crack the wall. Some gains may have been won, but because the hope for home and fraternity is absolute and constant, the record is one of consistent defeat and frustration.

Social mobilization, in Deutsch's terms, has not brought assimilation. That condition has produced nationalism or its equivalent the world over. Excluded from a larger society because of their origins, men turn back to that first community, seeking to glorify what has been unjustly despised, claiming and hoping that within it alone there are sufficient resources to realize a humanity equal to or higher than the one denied them. But since, as Robert Bone points out, what is involved is a "reflex toward rejection," the people whom the national-

[32] On the migration of 1879, see J. G. Van Deusen, "The Exodus of 1879," *JNH,* XXI (1936), pp. 111-129.

ist sets out to make enviable are often defined in terms of the oppressor's stereotype; only the evaluations are changed.[33] A picture drawn by the blind, however, is a poor mirror in which to view either one's home or humanity.

The danger was apparent in the early writings of Sutton Griggs, who, at the turn of the century, wrote in praise of blackness, attacked whites, and, with the fatal sign of ambivalence, deplored mixed bloods —but whose later novels were fawningly deferential to whites. With more subtlety, Paul Laurence Dunbar cast his writings in the familiar romantic form, lauding the "naturalness" and "simplicity" of blacks against a white world ruled by artifice and convention. But Dunbar's effort to dignify the flesh led him to attack those who are guided by abstraction and idea as "fanatics." Even the abolitionists received that stricture. Dunbar's image of man was a caricature, and politically his novels—though they also attacked fanatical racism—reinforced the peculiar mythology of the Old South propagated by the New.[34]

Black separatism, however, has almost never been the exact counterpart of white racism. American Negroes have suffered too much from racism not to have learned its folly; they have felt the tension between flesh and spirit too deeply to rest easily with the brotherhood of blood. Cleaver commented that:

> . . . in the black community if you tag a man as being a racist . . . a lot of black people get uptight about it. They won't relate to that. For all these hundreds of years black people have had the thrust of their hearts against racism, because racism has been murdering them.[35]

Separatism is still best understood as the attempt to build the foundations of a future, trans-racial fraternity, something asserted as a sufficient solution only when that future is despaired of. It often is; given events and history it could hardly be otherwise. Even then, however, racial separation is rarely advocated without articulate sadness that white—or human—imperfection allows no more. As Malcolm X put

---

[33] Robert A. Bone, *The Negro Novel in America* (New Haven: Yale University Press, 1968), p. 63; DuBois, *Dusk of Dawn*, pp. 195–196.

[34] Bone, *The Negro Novel*, pp. 32–35, 38–43; Dunbar, *The Fanatics* (New York: Dodd, Mead, 1901).

[35] Cleaver, *Post-Prison Writings*, p. 142. See also Grier and Cobbs, *Black Rage*, p. 127.

it, "We've got to give the man a chance. He probably won't take it, the snake. But we've got to give him a chance." [36]

Disillusionment and despair were probably never greater than in the wake of World War I. DuBois had learned early the error of trusting the rhetoric of Woodrow Wilson, but as cruel as that disappointment was, the very upheaval of the war preserved many of his hopes. For others, the illusion lingered and the vision remained unclouded. Then came the riots of 1919, white savagery let loose, followed by the resurgence of the Klan and the establishment of a new order of things which, at best, was only more of the same and often added new torments to the old.

It is no surprise that so many felt that they had no heritage in Jesse and looked for a separate home of their own. Under DuBois' leadership, Pan-Africanism gained interest and support; less directly political, but intimately related, was the "New Negro" school among writers, who adopted the new romantic "cult of the elemental," attributing to and praising in black culture spontaneity, freedom from restraint, and the "wisdom of the body." [37] These currents, however, had far less mass impact than the "Back to Africa" movement of Marcus Garvey. Garvey offered American Negroes the symbol of Africa, the "other place" and the "old home" which other Americans have always possessed as a day-dreaming retreat from the present. He both suffered from and was aided by the fact that few American blacks were concerned with the reality of Africa—and fewer still, probably, wanted to "return" to it. (Cleaver realized this in treating the "land issue" as essentially symbolic of other needs.) [38] The fact permitted Garvey to disregard many obstacles to the realization of his plan. It also trapped his movement in a contradiction, for its nominal purpose was neither practical nor much desired and, at the same time, Garvey had envisioned few, if any, other solutions. The result was bound to be a frustration of the very hopes that Garvey aroused, and the specific circumstances of his defeat—now much debated—are probably beside the point.

That contradiction, moreover, only hints at a more basic ambiva-

[36] Cited in Gene Marine, *The Black Panthers*, p. 20.

[37] Bone, *The Negro Novel*, pp. 58–61; Alain Locke, *The New Negro* (New York: Boni, 1925), pp. 11–12.

[38] *Post-Prison Writings*, p. 64.

lence in Garveyism. Garvey spoke persuasively to so many blacks because his thought encompassed all their feelings, their self-hatred as well as their conviction of and desire for dignity. His devotion to the brotherhood of man and his hope for a "Universal Confraternity" in which the rights of all races would be respected paralleled the values taught and expressed by the religious tradition. In fact, Garvey appealed to that tradition explicitly, arguing that the Creator had intended the races to develop their unique powers separately as the first step to a higher unity.

That contention led Garvey to denounce "mongrels," who presumably perverted both bloods by the fact of admixture. This was more than a defense of blackness; as should be obvious, it amounted to an assault on virtually all black Americans, branding them as inferior to both Africans and whites. As such, it addressed and reinforced deep-seated feelings of the worthlessness of the flesh, even when it allowed darker blacks to express disdain for their lighter fellows.

Most critics have also recognized Garveyism as a counsel of defeat. It would be hard to miss that element, given Garvey's assertion that the pursuit of black rights in America would only result in "riots, lynching and mob rule." It was, however, based on feelings of defeat which were more than tactical, which had become internalized to the point where they legitimized the defeat itself, proclaiming the rightness of the conqueror's cause. The backlash of the Twenties was, Garvey asserted, a basically rightful expression of white desires for "self-preservation and self-protection." If Garvey counseled escape, it was not only because he saw no tactical basis for resistance, but because he also saw no moral one. And such ideas and feelings are hardly the basis for fraternity, even for the brotherhood of blood.

Temporarily, Garveyism created an exhilaration, a sense of movement, and some feelings of pride. But it was built on the sand of self-hatred (Cleaver argues that much "ostentatious" separatism reflects the desire to deny or repress a "racial death-wish"),[39] and given the impracticality of Garvey's alternative, it fostered submission by teaching that resistance was futile if not wrongful. If Garvey has a higher place in black history, it is because memory plays strange tricks—and legends, even when false, have a logic of their own.

[39] *Soul on Ice,* pp. 101–102.

Other movements, growing out of the frustrations and betrayals of the Twenties, the Depression, the War, and the postwar world, have generally abandoned the idea of emigration. Even when physical separation of the races is advocated, the migration involved is internal to the United States, and in many cases, it is "inner" in the true sense —a change of attitude rather than one of place. "Nationalism" in this sense ceases to be specifically nationalistic; it aspires to an ethnic community, more or less sharply set apart, within the American political order.

That ambition certainly helps explain the rise of the "Black Jewish" movement in many Eastern cities; there are few better models for a people "set apart," and the appeal to the imagery of Zion is as old as the impact of Christianity among blacks. Obviously, however, the movement suffered from the presence of Jews in America, often in positions which encouraged racial hostility and always in ways which discouraged Judaism as a means to separate identity.

Islam, obviously, has no such limitations. The phrase "Black Islam" is, in the United States, almost redundant, given the paucity of white Moslems. More significantly, Islamic symbolism drew on important elements of black culture—on the rites of the lodges and, while allowing a sharp break with the "slave religion" of Christianity, on the Scripture. Too, whatever else may be charged against Islamic nations (Saudi Arabia apparently still has slaves), Islam has been an advocate of racial equality. The fascination has a long history, beginning at least with the Moorish Science Temple in 1913, continuing through the boycott organized by "The Sufi" in Harlem during the Depression, and culminating with the movement associated with Malcolm X and Elijah Mohammed in our time.

Condemnations of Islam, now somewhat in abeyance, have been frequent and insistent. Its doctrine has been denounced as bogus, a pseudo-theology based on the pseudo-history of a pseudo-people. Its racial theories have been attacked for their political implications as well as their substance. But the vehemence of the criticism is not entirely merited; more than one movement has demonstrated the utility of absurd doctrines, and more still have revealed that there are uses in violence—though that note is now very muted in Islamic propaganda.

Nor is there a clear case against "racism" in Islam. The movement speaks of, and often has achieved, a rebirth in its members, and much of its symbolism—the change of name, the use of terms like "so-called Negro"—is designed to emphasize the fact. Part of the power of Islam is that such symbols speak directly to the condition of most blacks, increasingly free from the heritage of slavery but not yet come into their own. And by freeing many from what has been, Black Islam does not necessarily define what will be. In the best cases, it removes the loneliness and unexpressed resentment which have been insuperable obstacles to personal development; no movement needs better testimony than the life of Malcolm X. In him, the emotional strength provided by Islam freed the fire of his own desire for truth and self-knowledge; Islamic fraternity encouraged him to go on to a higher knowledge of fraternity. When Cleaver calls Malcolm the incarnation of black manhood, it is hard to disagree. And only death could cut off Malcolm's pilgrimage; his was a spirit which would not rest of its own accord.

Yet it is necessary to emphasize that in cases like Malcolm's (or Cleaver's, for that matter), Islam builds better than it knows; unlike the Puritans, it does not see each covenant as a step to a higher one. For most, it is likely to become a snare, a new obstacle replacing the old. There is in Islam the same element of racial self-hatred which tainted Garveyism; one need only read Cleaver's account of the incident when a fellow Moslem denounced him because his eyes bore the "mark of the beast" to recognize that much. Too, the stern asceticism of the movement—whatever its utilitarian advantages—reflects the old hatred of the body and distrust of the flesh.

Perhaps the greatest shortcoming of Islam lies in the very utilitarian quality of the movement. It can and does improve the economic condition of its members and that fact attracts many (William McCord and his associates found it necessary to distinguish "Protestant-ethic" Moslems from racial militants within the movement). In fact, Islam has virtually no aims other than material gain and assimilation into the benefits of industrial society; its spokesmen attack neither material values nor the American Constitution—they demand, in effect, a "fair share" of both. As Islam has become more "established," it is these qualities which have gained strength, and militancy has declined in favor of emphasis on self-help.[40]

[40] Michael Parenti, "The Black Muslims: From Revolution to Institution," *SR*, XXXI (1964), pp. 175–194; McCord, *Life Styles*, pp. 117–125.

To intellectuals of both races, Islam seems increasingly "assimilationistic" in its failure to challenge the fundamental institutions of society. And those who have hoped that blacks would insist on a transformation of America see in Islam a movement which could lead blacks, like all the other minorities, to surrender to the temptations of affluence. Islam, John Barden wrote some years ago, "turns out to be an action for damages," and lawsuits are not the basis for social transformation. Still less, whatever the movement may do for particular individuals, are they the basis for fraternity.[41]

Those who have shared such doubts, or who have opposed or suspected separatism, have often been eloquent advocates of cultural nationalism. Frazier pointed out that cultural institutions could help provide group solidarity without standing as a barrier to equality, as separate interest groups could not. Moreover, he argued, a sense of cultural difference—especially given the trans-utilitarian basis of black culture in America—would prevent blacks from losing their identity, thus enabling a fundamental critique of American society and making equality something more than a blotting out of difference.[42]

There are also more basic possible virtues. Unlike most competing forms of "nationalism," cultural nationalism does not require a disowning of the black past in America. Making that heritage a matter of pride, cultural nationalism can encourage a rebirth that is into, rather than out of, the flesh, a precondition for all fraternities. And, as Frazier knew, pride in culture is separate, logically, from any suggestion of racism—though obviously the two are often tangled in the minds of men.[43]

All of these advantages, however, are possibilities only. Cultural nationalism can, and may, become only another form of romanticism —or worse, an effort to blot out and disown the black past. Even the best intellectual intentions can have that result; correction of past interpretation leads easily to overemphasis and, in any case, what matters in a movement is not what is written but what is read by the audience. And in a movement which seeks to make one's culture enviable, it is tempting to define that culture as what outsiders already

---

[41] John Barden, "Malcolm," *The Activist*, IV (1964), pp. 164–165. A different, but related idea is contained in Cleaver, *Post-Prison Writings*, pp. 13–17.

[42] *Negro Protest Thought*, ed. Broderick and Meier, p. 101; Frazier, *The Negro Church*, p. 70.

[43] *Negro Protest Thought*, p. 99.

envy. (Cleaver calls "remarkable" a passage from Kerouac's *On the Road* which Baldwin had earlier identified as the latest version of the "happy darkies" myth.) [44]

Such dangers are probably less than they were in the past. The rise of Africa in world status, and the increasing general interest in non-Western cultures, helps make them so. (Earlier Negro interest in Africa, including the Pan-Africanism of DuBois, had a distinctly paternalistic quality.) But cultural nationalism even on the best terms has political dangers.

In the first place, the appeal of the ideology is notably strong in the middle class; its intellectual respectability is far greater than that of its competitors. Too, middle-class blacks are increasingly competitive with whites rather than with Negroes, and are likely to regard their heritage as a source of emotional strength rather than something to be escaped. Drawn more and more into the amorphous world of mass society, middle-class blacks experience an "identity crisis" less specifically racial than general, parallel to that felt by all groups which have entered the suburban-affluent milieu. As no one needs to be told, this crisis is particularly strong among the young—and especially since, in a time of racial militancy, taking sides is mandatory. The danger of black culturalism is also its psychological advantage: it can allow an affirmation of racial identity without requiring any change of life-style or the surrender of material benefits.

"Culturalism" involves, as it has for every successive ethnic culture, a dangerous intellectualism—the belief that a culture can be maintained apart from the specific conditions which called it into being. Harold Cruse has pointed to one case, at least, where cultural institutions and general equalization have clashed, the case of black theater. [45] The rise of some black actors to stardom has helped weaken the older, separate institution of black drama; the fate of the Yiddish theater is a partial parallel. It is not necessary that the old institutions and practices should disappear; in a new political environment, the meaning of even those that survive is changed. The surviving ways lose their connection with the way of life in which they developed and become parts of another. And not all survive, for it is natural

---

[44] Cleaver, *Soul on Ice*, p. 72; Baldwin, *Nobody Knows My Name* (New York: Dell, 1961), p. 182.
[45] Cruse, *The Crisis of the Negro Intellectual*, pp. 73, 80–81, 86.

that men select what seems to them of value and discard those parts of the old way which seem bitter or mediocre. Old cultures endure as "fine art" among intellectuals, and in cuisine, festival, and the like among a people in general. They become exceptions, momentary departures from the way men live ("Why is this night different from all other nights?"), symbols to be admired and appreciated but not lived.

This is the pattern of ethnic history and cultural change the world over, and it is unlikely that black America will differ very much. But the old ways affect the new, as all of our history testifies. They keep alive a world of value, symbol, and metaphor that makes most uneasy in a new world and provides others with more or less easy access to an older wisdom. And in a special sense, they give men a home, a place to begin, an anchor in the past which allows more confidence in facing the future. For all of these things, cultural nationalism may prove to be essential. If it is unlikely to be more, it is precisely because the culture of black America has given its people an unusually strong awareness that man's need for fraternity always wars with the claims of all the kindreds of blood.

Rights and Revolutions

The struggle of black America must always return to politics, for the enemy of personal wholeness and fraternity lies in social conditions and attitudes which can be changed most easily through political action. Knowledge of that fact is deeply rooted in black society. Economic weakness has contrasted with comparatively greater strength in relation to the law and to politics generally; long exclusion from the vote probably added to its importance; individual impotence cried out for collective support. For whatever reasons, Negroes register and vote in higher proportion than whites of corresponding social and educational background. And even more notably, blacks demonstrate an impressive sophistication and unity in the use of the vote. Politics, however, has its own dilemmas, made sharper in black America by the black condition itself.

Consider the case of Booker T. Washington, with whose leadership modern black political history begins. Washington's were times in which the "steel chain of ideas," the interlocking "sciences" of nineteenth-century liberalism, dominated the intellectual world, and they were no less dominant in Washington's thought. Those who have seen him as a predecessor of "Black Power" doctrines miss the point; Washington's leadership was a prolonged experiment in the social philosophy of liberalism. And the failure of that experiment says much about the subsequent political life and thought of black America.

Individualism, competition, and the struggle with nature were all key principles of Washington's thought and tactics, and he was convinced that they conformed to the logic of progress which would eventuate in the brotherhood of man, a goal to which he was devoted. His concessions to racial separation were designed as temporary expedients; his advocacy of racial unity was similarly opportunistic, seeing that unity as no more than a necessary response to the slave past and to white irrationality. Both might be abandoned in the admittedly distant long term.

His promise that Negroes would agree to social separation was based on the desire to take the "nigger issue" out of Southern politics, an aim with two related bases. First, although he felt that political rights were of value Washington saw politics as secondary in human life, less important than "society" and "pre-political" phenomena like social stability and economic well-being. Given these, political rights would follow in due course; as in liberal theory, the state was the creature of society and had little, if any, creative role. Consequently, the primary task was the development of stable families with economic skills, the inculcation of Washington's doctrines of "self-reliance" and "work and money."

Second, Washington was convinced that taking the Negro "out of politics" would allay the anxieties that were the source of white unity, allowing the divisions between whites to emerge. It would then be possible to play white against white—specifically, to teach business leaders that their interests would be advanced by free competition between black and white workers. Washington was certain blacks could win that competition; his boast that "we have never disturbed the country by riots, strikes or lockouts"—ironic reading today—envisioned white elites and black workers as natural allies against those who violated the canons of law and competitive individualism.

His strategy had more than a little guile, and it may have been pardonable, given the fact that Washington had seen black craftsmen driven out of skilled trades they once dominated by whites who appealed less to skill than to racial fears and political anxieties. It was even more excusable considering the liberal orthodoxy of his day. It was also fatally in error.

Washington's faith in individualism and competition was at least out of date during a time of industrial concentration. Even if the New South, on which he pinned so many of his hopes, had not been based on marginal industries, the result would have been disastrous. Washington's strategy made conflict with white labor almost irreparable and tied blacks to industrial elites who had virtually no interest in social change and the greatest interest in using the "threat" of each race to weaken the position of the other. No Machiavelli, Washington did not recognize that two warring and weak factions are the prey of the strong.

Similarly, Washington's liberalism blinded him to the independent possibilities of politics. Economic strength can be translated into political power fairly easily, as Washington knew, but economic weakness cannot. For the economically weak, political power may be the only way of moving events. Employers may have been pleased by the complaisance of Washington's black worker, but they were compelled to listen to white workers more attentively because—apart from the employers' own racism—those workers posed a political threat. Washington's "praise" of black workers, Monroe Trotter wrote, amounted to accusing them of stupidity (and to the extent that they followed it, psychologically emasculated them); in relation to strikes, as in all professions, Trotter advised, "the Negro is safest in doing just the same and no different than his white brother." It was a charge DuBois echoed repeatedly; and if Washington's ideas always seemed reasonable in the immediate situation, he played a losing hand in the long term.[46] During Washington's leadership, the world of opportunity became, for most blacks, a narrowing rather than a widening circle.

Believing in progress, Washington was especially susceptible to that form of "realism" which consists of short-term accommodations, confident that the long term will take care of itself. Washington's be-

---

[46] *Negro Protest Thought*, ed. Broderick and Meier, p. 29; *Negro Social and Political Thought*, ed. Brotz, pp. 514–516.

lief in history, like the rest of his liberal creed, ignored the fact that since the existing system was biased against blacks, playing by the rules of the existing context—however shrewdly—was likely to lead away from rather than toward equality.

In other words, Washington was the prototype of all those political leaders who Carmichael and Hamilton classify as "indirect rulers." Concerned to win immediate gains from the existing order, they are almost bound to inculcate the idea that the existing system is "normal," a pattern to which men should adapt their lives. And faith in the mockingbird of progress hardly justifies the fact that such teaching gives a measure of legitimacy to oppression. Willy-nilly, it amounts, as Carmichael and Hamilton argue, to ruling blacks in the interest of whites, at a cost probably beyond the value of any immediate gains—if, in fact, it results in any gains at all.[47]

But, as DuBois knew, that criticism does not end the matter. Certain as he was of the need for constant assertion and affirmation of ultimate goals, lest the way be lost in a pragmatic maze (and sure as he was that Washington had lost his sense of direction, if indeed he had ever known the goal), DuBois knew too that the belief that a "series of brilliant assaults" will bring down the enemy citadel is in all probability a dangerous delusion. Moreover, DuBois knew that a community desperately in need cannot and will not forego immediate benefits, and that it cannot morally be asked to—even if one is aware that those rewards will have little perceptible effect on the structure of repression. Those who would make such a request, hoping for greater militancy amid worse conditions, demonstrate a cruelty which impeaches their right to lead—and it is unlikely that they will be allowed to lead for long. Hence DuBois' prescription: "Negroes must live and eat and strive and still hold unfailing commerce with the stars." [48]

DuBois understood better than most how very precarious that balance is. To keep it would require the judgment and skills of a supreme statesman—perhaps, given the difficulties which beset blacks and the temptations which beguile black leaders, one even beyond the

---

[47] *Black Power*, pp. 11–15.

[48] DuBois, *Dusk of Dawn*, pp. 6–7. Compare Baldwin, *Notes of a Native Son*, pp. 6–7, and Michael Walzer, *Obligations* (Cambridge: Harvard University Press, 1970), pp. 53–70.

statesman of Plato's imagining. That is one major element of DuBois' dispute with Washington, for DuBois felt and insisted that the burden was too great to be borne by any man alone. It required a fraternal political leadership, able to encourage and reprove.

That belief in the necessity of a fraternal "vanguard" was behind the dispute with Washington over the "talented tenth," for Washington did not oppose higher education for the gifted—he merely insisted that those so educated follow the course he set. DuBois was arguing, in effect, for the autonomy of the "tenth," its status as a fraternal body.[49] The same theme unites DuBois' career, with all its varied changes of political front. His early ideas yielded to doctrines like his hope for a cooperative movement—more mass-based and more explicitly fraternal—and ultimately, to the Communist Party—more elitist than the "tenth" even, but more insistent on comradely fraternity than any of the earlier alternatives.[50] Always, for DuBois, the way to general fraternity—"the vast ideal of human brotherhood"— lay through a narrower and more immediate bond.

DuBois' life also reflects an increasing radicalism, a growing doubt of the possibilities for change within the existing order of things in America, a greater sympathy for militancy. That, more than ideology, accounts for his joining the Party (the aftermath of Hungary was hardly a propitious time to do so). But oddly, as DuBois became more militant, his tactics became less based on blacks alone, which is a partial measure of the passion of his own devotion to the fraternal ideal he served. And his "radicalization" was no more than an ever sharper perception of the condition of black America.

In fact, the most characteristic thought of black America has always been "revolutionary." Those who called to and waited for the Lord understood that only radical, even miraculous, change could make the blind see, and that nothing less was required. Black religion, in its gentle and harsh visions alike, knew that the entire structure of perception in American culture might have to be transformed before justice could be done. Nor is there anything new about acts of violent rebellion; Richard Wright saw that almost the only choice open to a

[49] W. E. B. DuBois, "The Talented Tenth," in *The Negro Problem*, ed. Booker T. Washington et al. (New York: James Pott, 1903), pp. 33–75; *Dusk of Dawn*, pp. 70, 132.

[50] *Dusk of Dawn*, pp. 197–202, 209–216.

black who did not choose to be a victim was to become a rebel.[51] But historically, the two qualities were more or less distinct. The religious waited for "the time," the rebels struck individual blows which, sadly, fell more often on their fellows than on the oppressor. In our time, however, the two currents seem more and more to merge into a torrent.

By the end of World War I, many Negroes proclaimed themselves Socialists and it was only to be expected that the Depression—which hit blacks so much harder than whites—would attract others toward the Communists. (It was also an advantage that the Communists had a smaller white working-class following, and hence less racial ambivalence to deal with, as well as better discipline with which to control whatever bigotry did appear.)

For blacks, the Old Left had at least two advantages. The first was, simply, that it treated race and racism as epiphenomenal, which not only ranged it on the "right side" but provided those Negroes who joined it with a psychological escape from race. Second, insistence on comradely solidarity, especially the Communist Party's demand for total commitment, appealed because it amounted to a rebirth out of loneliness into the organizational image of fraternity. Ellison's protagonist found that:

> Brotherhood was something to which men could give themselves completely; that was its strength and my strength, and it was this sense of wholeness that guaranteed that it would change the course of history.

Richard Wright commented that the Party said, ". . . speak out what you are, you will find that you are not alone." Angelo Herndon, one of the Scottsboro defendants, may have summed it all up.

> My family had told me not to come back. What did I care? My real family was the organization. I'd found that I had brothers and sisters in every corner of the world, I knew that we were all fighting for one thing and that they'd stick by me. I never lost that feeling . . .[52]

Most did, however. Resolutely doctrinaire, the Party never developed much of a mass following, partly because its doctrine made it

[51] Richard Wright, *Twelve Million Black Voices* (New York: Viking, 1941).

[52] Ellison, *Invisible Man*, p. 351; Wright, "I Tried to Be a Communist," *AM*, CLXXIV (1944), p. 68; *Negro Protest Thought*, ed. Broderick and Meier, p. 128 (see also pp. 67–70, 118–133, 197–201).

difficult or impossible to address feelings of racial resentment. Those who joined soon began to suspect, and then to be certain, that there was a note of patronizing racism within the fold, and especially in the hierarchy. Too, there was the knowledge that whatever the interracial future of proletarian solidarity, the present was rather another matter. Also, with marvelous ineptitude, the Party advocated a form of black separatism until 1957 defending it when it had little appeal and discarding it precisely when it was about to come into vogue. Finally, as with white members, events raised the question of whether all the brethren were in fact fighting for "one thing"; it appeared as if some were only the instruments of others. Important as it was in the lives of its members, the Party was only an interlude, one which left behind a legacy of disillusionment and bitterness.[53]

But the Party was far from the only disappointment; blacks have rarely had to look far to find causes for that feeling. From the era of the New Deal, the War, and the post-war crises have come social changes which resulted in marginal gains. New white awareness of blacks led to repeated political promises, which sometimes became embodied in law, most often through court decisions. Both aroused a hope which was only more vaulting because of repeated frustration. Such hopes were probably doomed to some partial disappointment. That, however, is less significant than the fact that, in many areas of life, the Negro's position has actually grown worse. Residential segregation has increased, and federal policy, far from correcting matters, has all too often been manipulated by those who—inadvertently or not—worked to produce greater separation. Technology put new pressure on unskilled workers, and industries have left cities in increasing numbers, leaving many blacks only the possibility of marginal employment, at best.

In such conditions, the argument that black militancy results from greater "relative injustice"—greater hopes which far outrun gains—is altogether too weak.[54] More appropriately, militancy can be traced to a feeling of injustice combined with the belief that, politically, the situation in the United States is no longer hopeless. Activism and

[53] Wilson Record, *The Negro and the Communist Party* (Chapel Hill: University of North Carolina Press, 1951), pp. 54–183.

[54] R. W. Friedrichs, "Interpretation of Black Aggression," *Yale Review*, LVII (1968), pp. 358–374.

optimism are closely related, but optimism does not involve a lessened militancy. Militancy, insofar as it reflects a sense of political possibility (though not necessarily through "normal" channels), implies a compliment to whites, a belief that—though blundering and unwilling—they are not utterly recalcitrant. Part of Eldridge Cleaver's rather considerable faith in America rests with the young, but it is not a matter of youth alone.

> . . . if it does come to massive repression of blacks, I don't think the majority of whites are going to either approve it or remain silent. . . . It could go on for awhile, but at some point, we think that large numbers of whites would become so revolted that leaders would arise . . . and offer other solutions.[55]

Mingling glory and defeat, the Civil Rights Movement set the tone of contemporary black politics more than any competing force or event. The successes of the movement created the sense of political possibility (and it may not be excessive to say that the movement created that possibility); the fact that those successes proved hollow suggested the need for a "new politics."

Partly because of its Southern origin, the movement was preoccupied with removing abuses of the law and with winning for the Negro, where it did not exist, procedural and legal equality. Vital as this task remains—for it is far from complete—it was only a "negative liberty" that was won, the old promise of liberalism made social fact. No one now needs to be told that formal rights are mockeries to those without the means to make use of them; this teaching, at least, is ingrained in contemporary liberalism. In fact, there is nothing very new in the demand for "Black Power"; DuBois anticipated it as early as 1915, and only the realization has been lacking.[56] The phrase, and the mood of militancy behind it, reflect a demand for substantive justice and equality rather than their procedural imitators, for positive as well as negative liberty. All that is surprising is that so many liberals remain so wedded to the old procedural and negative ideas that they fail to grasp that if some men begin with an artificial advantage, it is less than just—and certainly less than equal—to insist that others "compete equally" with them. Horse racing is in this respect, ahead

[55] Cleaver, *Post-Prison Writings*, p. 176.

[56] DuBois, "The Immediate Program of the American Negro," *The Crisis*, IX (1915), pp. 310–312.

of social thought; where inequalities exist, those who have been deprived must be preferred if there is to be equal freedom. But horse racing does not have to grapple with racism.

"Black Power" and similar ideologies, however, are not simply programs for the distribution of material rewards and benefits; they are often maddeningly vague on economic issues beyond a general commitment to equalization. "Black Power" advocates have, in fact, regarded material rewards as secondary. The movement has been explicitly political, more concerned with how rewards are won than whether they are won. Its spokesmen know very well that unless gains are made collectively and through political action, they are likely to be no more than shams. Not only is it true that charity is literally cheap—what is donated is not likely to upset the established social scale—but rewards which are won by individuals or conceded by compassion reinforce the existing social pattern and, with it, the psychological damage of racism. That much is especially clear to the "para-intellectuals" who have seen at first hand the havoc wreaked by welfare bureaucracies, but others have—or should have—known it before.

To speak of blacks as a "colonial society," though partly correct, is a very misleading metaphor. There is no advocacy of political secession; militancy speaks very much within the context of American life. And, in concrete terms, "Black Power" advocates speak in distinctly reformist tones (consider only Carmichael and Hamilton's concern with gerrymandering), so much so that the far-from-discerning ears of political scientists have detected "system-supportive attitudes" among the militant.[57] If such doctrines are "revolutionary," it is only because racism is more deeply rooted in America than their proponents hope—though not, perhaps, more than they fear.

In fact, the thesis in Carmichael and Hamilton's *Black Power* is, up to a point, distinctly orthodox. It is that the United States is, in some vital sense, a pluralistic "open society" in which group unity is

[57] Carmichael and Hamilton, *Black Power*, pp. 15, 44; Charles Hamilton, "An Advocate of Black Power Defends It," *New York Times Magazine* (April 14, 1968), pp. 22ff.; and the following papers presented to the American Political Science Association, New York, Sept. 1969: Lester Milbrath, "Individual Change During a Period of Community Interventions for Change"; Lyman A. Kellstedt, "Riot Propensity and System Dissaffection"; and—much more pessimistic—Joel Auerbach and Jack L. Walker, "Political Trust and Racial Ideology."

an essential of access and effectiveness. Explicitly, they draw an analogy, which in other respects they would reject, between blacks and the immigrants of the past; group unity, it is argued, was politically effective for the latter and constitutes an essential means for the former. If this analysis were presented in another context, white radicals would reject it out of hand. There is, however, a decisive departure from orthodoxy. In black militant thought, community and unity are not merely devices, tactical means to win admission to the "open society" and then to be abandoned. Community becomes a permanent principle, a constant political need.[58]

This is as one might expect. The immigrant communities were more or less ready-made, and the political institutions of the time were, in the age of the great machines, tailored to fit community demands. Even if men valued those communities, it was easy to take them for granted and to allow them to slip away imperceptibly. For blacks, community has been something to be created, and the bureaucratic state combats it, rather than giving it aid. All of the highly publicized demands—control of schools, police, and the like—are an insistence on creating in a hostile environment what white Americans once possessed as a birthright. Circumstances—culture, the advanced industrial environment, the aching fact of loneliness—have given black political actors a knowledge that man is in truth a political animal, that he needs community as well as the formal state.

However "extreme" its tone, the Black Panther Party has more than a few resemblances to the old machine. The central principle of Panther doctrine is community control and service, and those who remember machine judges and prosecutors will find a refreshing honesty—not to mention greater justice—in the demand that black prisoners, convicted by outsiders, all be freed. Even the demand for military exemption may recall protests during the Civil War. It is not hard to see the Panthers engaged in the attempt, made necessarily explicit and bitter both by black history and by the rise of the bureaucratic state, to create a new form of the old politics. Perhaps whites would understand Panther statements better if they read them as a "first hurrah." [59]

[58] *Black Power*, pp. 45–49, 55, 164–177; Cruse, *Crisis of the Negro Intellectual*, pp. 13, 29, 452, 458.
[59] Marine, *The Black Panthers*, esp. pp. 73–75.

It should be emphasized that concern for racial community is not racism. The Panthers, again, have been consistently anti-racist, sometimes to their political cost, and Panther spokesmen have called attention to the need of many groups among whites (as well as other races) for substantive justice. In almost all militancy, in fact, there is a desire to free whites from their own prison of loneliness and anxiety, to teach them the need for community and fraternity in political life. Even critics like Bayard Rustin, who doubt the efficacy of attempting to save whites by "traumatizing" them, concede that much.[60] Concern for community represents only the wise understanding that the lesser fraternities of birth and blood can help rather than hinder ascent into the higher brotherhoods of men.

No group has raised fraternity to a higher status, or been more rigorous in demanding it, than the Black Panthers. Panther understanding of fraternity, however, is far from faultless. Like so many movements, it has suffered from rapid, media-induced expansion which has strained discipline and weakened interpersonal solidarity. In this case, however, expansion is not the result of the liberal faith that human brotherhood emerges when man is set free. It is partly the result of political necessity, the desire to be effective on a national scale. And in part it is due to the battle fraternity which the Panthers take as their model and what that fraternity reveals—both about those who choose it and the society in which they live.

The fraternity of battle suggests violence, and it is necessary to point out that Panthers have been far more likely to suffer violence than inflict it, whatever their words may imply to a fearful mind. In any case, political violence—in threats or action—has more than a few uses. Most simply, violence is an expression of the intensity of feelings and commitment, which helps compensate for inferiority of numbers and resources, making up for some of the otherwise inherent weakness of blacks in political coalitions. Radicals, in this at least, are the best allies of moderates.

Violence is also an aid to solidarity, partly because it dissolves the possibility of an ambivalent stance between camps. More im-

---

[60] Cleaver, *Post-Prison Writings*, pp. 117, 135; Cruse, *Crisis of the Negro Intellectual*, p. 458; Bayard Rustin in *Negro Protest Thought*, ed. Broderick and Meier, p. 413; E. C. Ladd, "The Negro as 'Cause,'" *Nation*, CC (1965), pp. 161–165.

portantly, violence involves a testing, an extreme situation which permits men to measure the depth and sincerity of their fellows' loyalty and to give proof of their own. Among men who have learned to regard human bonds as unreliable, to scent betrayal even in words of affirmation, violence may be almost essential for even a shadow of fraternity.[61]

"Nonviolence," by producing an extreme situation, can give the same proofs, but an environment of indifference and unconcern like that of the urban North denies nonviolence the means of creating such a situation. A major advantage of violence is that it is noticed, it defeats invisibility, it becomes an affirmation of self precisely because it forces others to acknowledge the existence of that self. This after all, is the psychological side of the violence and rage that all acknowledge are built into the ghetto.[62]

Especially among blacks—though hardly exclusively—violence is also an assertion of masculinity, an escape from social ineffectuality and from the taunts of women. Once freed, even temporarily, men may acquire the confidence to go on; not for nothing did the old initiation rites almost always require a crime against the blood. Cleaver, for example, describes his own days of violence as an iconoclastic stage in which he was "enamored of sin, yet appalled by the sins of others" (the Augustinian cadence is both notable and appropriate). It is significant, moreover, that Cleaver defines the enemy of those days as white *woman*, and that he asserts that his "self" then was largely defined by "feedback" through the admiration of women. Rape failed as an "insurrectionary act," not because it was violent, but because "maleness" cannot be proved by violence against women; it must be demonstrated in the world of men. And for Cleaver, encountering Huey Newton and the Panthers was vital because they provided a fraternity which helped strengthen his own resolution.[63]

That, however, hints at a major limitation of Panther fraternity and of all the fraternities of battle: that so often such brotherhoods

---

[61] McCord, *Life Styles*, pp. 87–89; B. J. Siegel, "Defensive Cultural Adaptation," in *The History of Violence in America*, ed. H. D. Graham and T. R. Gurr (New York: Bantam, 1969), pp. 764–787.

[62] McCord, *Life Styles*, pp. 32, 62, 272–274; Ellison, *Shadow and Act*, p. 37; Baldwin, *Notes of a Native Son*, pp. 92, 93, 79, 81; *Nobody Knows My Name*, pp. 61, 63; Cleaver, *Soul on Ice*, pp. 106, 125, 220.

[63] *Soul on Ice*, pp. 5, 6, 12–15, 28–29; *Post-Prison Writings*, pp. 23–39.

are bound up with the fear of fleshliness, and their logic is self-destructive. The best hope of such fraternity, in fact, is that it may give men something in the world which they love enough to overcome that fear. It is to be hoped that they do overcome it before, with the familiar logic of battle fraternity, the war which was needed to create the bond slays so many as to leave those who remain with an insuperable burden of guilt.

Too, the secret of violence is always that it is the enemy who is loved and admired; the contemptible do not merit hatred. The aim of violence is often external, the desire to win the enemy's admiration in turn; and in any case, the logic of combat demands that we create ourselves in the image of our enemies. Fanon's thesis suggests that combat with the colonial power is useful because it does just that: it overcomes traditional resistance to the modern ways of the outsider. That note is hardly lacking in black militancy. Cleaver, momentarily abandoning his Hawthornesque racial/sexual classification, speaks of the ultimate fraternity of Paul Bunyan and John Henry and, in a still more illustrative phrase addressed to black women, asserts that "the white man was your man and my man." [64]

Partly this is to the good, for violent confrontation, as the prophets and the theorists of social contract both knew, may be the first step to a new unity, a covenant previously impossible. There is no fraternity without reciprocity, and in human affairs, reciprocity rarely results without conflict.

But there also lies the danger. More than once, conflict in America has only resulted in removing the last barriers, on both sides, to assimilation into industrial society—if only because the challengers have so often made themselves into the image of the challenged. Conflict may lead to covenant; it may also result in the liberal "contract" between private men (to say nothing of grimmer possibilities). If the latter is the result of the racial confrontation, it would add symmetry to our history and subtract the hope for a politics based on community. When Baldwin wrote that much violence results from the rage of the disesteemed against the modern world, he recognized in ways Fanon did not that such a world is itself the ultimate oppressor, because it makes indignity ubiquitous. It was out of wisdom that Baldwin urged that the ability to forgive is part of the human birthright, one never to be surrendered.[65] Forgiving, too, is a kind of violence, but one which refuses to do the honor of treating as enemies those who are merely lost.

Priest and Prophet

Baldwin and Ellison have made critics uneasy; each has been the object of impassioned political attack and hostilities that are suspiciously strong. Irving Howe's critical faculties have rarely been better employed than when he grouped the two together, suggesting that both were less authentically Negro than Richard Wright.[66] It was, in an odd sense, a compliment. The "Negro writer" is the reflection of an intellectual Jim Crow; there is a marked distance between him and his white reader that allows his work to be read as a sociological document or a case study in psychology. It is harder to keep Baldwin and Ellison "in their place." For all they say about black life, their real subject is man, and no reader can escape the disturbing awareness that he is reading about himself.

Baldwin's ideas of man are ancient; they could hardly be otherwise, given his acceptance, after a long personal struggle, of his father's Scriptural texts as his own "legacy." Man desires, with part of his spirit, to deny the world and its limitations, wills himself to illusion, delights in the suffering of others because it helps him to forget his own. But at the same time, man wills to know himself and struggles fumblingly for the good.[67] The imagery of blindness and illumination suggests how similar Ellison's ideas are, even if different in origin or detail.

Preoccupied as both are with the inner struggles of men, both know very well that man is always a social and political being, shaped —whether aided or hindered, improved or damaged—by "that cage of reality bequeathed to us at our birth." Society reflects man's need for security, his ineluctable dependence on others for all the foundations of life and personality; children, Baldwin commented, always imitate parents if only by negation. Hence Baldwin's insistence that *la vie*

---

[65] *Notes of a Native Son,* pp. 104, 140.

[66] Irving Howe, "Native Sons and Black Boys," *Dissent,* X (1963), pp. 353–368.

[67] *Notes of a Native Son,* pp. 94–95, 117–134; *Nobody Knows My Name,* p. 108.

bohème is a delusion, a desire to deny the bond between a man and his society, part of the human attempt to escape the world. "Shapelessness," the idea of freedom from restraint, is not human freedom, because the illusion of freedom from society—from political time and space—can be purchased only by dissolving life into a series of presents, a succession of sensations, at the cost of personality and genuine identity.[68]

As essential as society is, both Baldwin and Ellison insist that it never fully accounts for man; in fact, in the ultimate sense, all societies are at odds with him. Man, for both, is more than social; he always seeks, and in the best cases is able to go beyond society—a triumph related to his experience in society but not of it. Man, Baldwin wrote,

> . . . is not, after all, merely a member of a Society or a Group or a deplorable conundrum to be explained by Science. He is—and how old-fashioned the words sound!—something more than that, something resolutely indefinable, unpredictable.[69]

The words have differed, but Ellison has expressed the same sentiment repeatedly. The self-knowledge possible for men requires attention to both dimensions of human life, man in relation to his time and his fellows (not for nothing did Baldwin stress the importance of listening in becoming free) and in his quest for a truth which has no such limits.[70]

Man always needs support, and where society cannot or does not provide it, in the great crises of his life and in his striving to see and know better than society, he needs fraternity. Baldwin's short story, "The Outing," is a tale of boys who are estranged from authority, "fatherless" in lacking a safe guide or certainty. The need for support in the search for self helps drive them into fraternity; reciprocally, the fact of fraternity helps move the quest for self. Specifically, fraternity helps preserve alienation, provides the emotional support necessary to resist the warmth—and the restricted perception—of society and community. Woman seems a threat to that fraternity, symboliz-

[68] *Notes of a Native Son*, pp. 114–115; *Nobody Knows My Name*, p. 59.
[69] *Notes of a Native Son*, p. 11.
[70] *Ibid.*, pp. 3, 88–89; *Nobody Knows My Name*, pp. 23, 108; *Going to Meet the Man*, p. 122; Ellison, *Shadow and Act*, pp. 120, 128.

ing the attractions of society and the menace of sexual rivalry. But, as Baldwin has argued, "sexism" is also a delusion. To love one another, to have genuine fraternity, men must love what is "feminine" in themselves (and vice versa, in the case of sorority); the world of fraternity must be free of sexual Jim Crow. That it has not been is, for Baldwin, a stricture on the barriers which America sets in the way of man's search for fraternity and for self.[71]

It is typical of Baldwin to stress the feelings, the need for purging men of emotional blindness. While Ellison would certainly agree, he has been more inclined to emphasize conscious decision and will,[72] for his picture of America is, if anything, bleaker than Baldwin's; men will have to endure without communion or create it themselves, and their emotions will provide little if any support.

Until recently, Ellison observed, America was able to have her two moralities "kept in balance by social science," but no more. The great writers of the nineteenth century had a political dimension to their vision, an understanding that "real fraternal . . . values" were the essence of democracy, and this knowledge led them to take the Negro as a symbol of mankind and of the American crisis. In our times, authors have been increasingly inclined to concern with private, individual problems; apolitical men, their perception is distorted and their understanding is defective. (Contrasting Twain and Hemingway, Ellison points out that blacks are almost wholly absent from the latter's work.) Lack of faith in democracy, which Ellison sees in later writers, reflects despair of fraternity, the sense of isolation, insecurity, and unimportance which besets Americans, and which has so often driven them into a terrified optimism in flight from an insecure and pastless present. Modern America has, in fact, become a place of terror for all races.[73]

Similarly, Baldwin has observed the decay of the older white culture under the impact of industrialism, social change, and instability. As the old communities collapsed, lonely men became ever more eager for some sense of mastery. The white South—competitive, dynastic, sensitive to affront, furiously seeking some sense of control and con-

---

[71] *Going to Meet the Man*, pp. 33, 38, 41, 47, 100–101; *Nobody Knows My Name*, p. 132.

[72] *Shadow and Act*, pp. 104, 137.

[73] *Ibid.*, pp. 39, 42–60, 112, 200, 243, 300.

tinuity—is only the extreme case of white America.[74] The "aggressive" white, as Baldwin and Ellison both know, is desperately in need of emotional support or simply attention; that, as blacks have always known, is a weakness which can be used—but only by degrading the self. Blacks may appear more at ease with emotionality, but—again, both writers have been graphic—they are tempted to retreat into private visions, the dark world of the movies or of drugs, in a desperate attempt to control at least inner space, to make it yield what the outer world will not.[75] American society makes a whole man something of a miracle.

Those conditions are at least part of Baldwin's increasing alarm. The last comforting illusion left to whites was the belief in material well-being, a myth exposed now as hollow, and rejected by the young.[76] In the past, whites have always compensated for their own insecurity by keeping blacks at the bottom of the scale, making them the one fixed point in a universe of change. Racism was and remains a feeble compensation for the lack of community. It follows, for Baldwin, that as white conditions grow worse, the psychological need for racism increases, whatever the prevailing racial ideology. And faced with expanding black claims, resistance and repression may became more bitter, even, than in the past. (It should be added that a more equalitarian ideology might itself increase savagery if repression occurs, given the tricks guilt plays in the human mind.)

All Americans are threatened by invisibility, the loss of identity and the lack of even the shadow of community. We face, Baldwin and Ellison argue, a national "identity crisis," the result of the collapse of the old synthesis with all its comforting illusions and the resulting confrontation between the two cultures of America. Race is more than an event in, or even an occasion for, that crisis. For Baldwin and Ellison alike, it provides the possibility of transferring the struggle between those cultures, and their respective ideas of fraternity, from the mind of the individual to the world of politics.[77]

Both regard it as essential that black Americans should resist de-

---

[74] *Going to Meet the Man*, pp. 48–67; *Nobody Knows My Name*, pp. 108–110, 113.

[75] *Going to Meet the Man*, pp. 74, 85, 87, 104, 107, 113–115, 194–195, 197.

[76] *Nobody Knows My Name*, p. 87.

[77] *Ibid.*, pp. 18, 19, 22, 114; *Notes of a Native Son*, pp. 19, 22, 102–103, 149; *Shadow and Act*, pp. xvii–xviii, 39–41, 60, 68–69, 246.

fining themselves—however pridefully—as the negation of whiteness. The image of blacks in America is only the mirror of what whites fear and long for in themselves, their terror of and attraction toward emotion, violence, and fleshliness. Surrendering to that image, especially by lauding it, is to accept the radically defective idea of human nature on which it is based. And it would be false to black history and experience, ignoring the complex world of black life which white men did not know. For both, black estrangement has never been more than partial; blacks were and are in white society, though not of it, a condition which—however painful—Baldwin and Ellison see as essential to the mission which each envisages for black America in the contemporary crisis.[78]

Here, as might be expected, the analyses differ. Both criticized Richard Wright for accepting, in his novels, the white man's image of the black. Baldwin argued that Wright's work might be accurate as a portrayal of what existed, but that it abandoned the struggle for a fuller humanity by confusing essence and accident. In other words, Baldwin charged that Wright failed as a political teacher; his picture lacked a dimension, the true nature of black manhood behind appearances. But Ellison quarreled with Wright's depiction of black life, while conceding that Wright might have a political justification in attempting to shock whites into awareness. Wright had omitted all that was strong and valuable in black life Ellison argued; in a telling point, he noted that Wright's analysis could never account for the triumphant survival of Wright himself. In terms rather too simple, Ellison was arguing that Wright had been false to the Negro past in the interests of what he took to be the future; Baldwin was concerned that he had betrayed the future, failing to set a true course toward the perennial human reality.[79]

This is of a piece with their differences in general. Baldwin, by thought and temperament, is a prophet, a man concerned with the moral transformation of society. Ellison is more secular, inclined to take that society as it is and to find ways of humanizing it. Hence Ellison's great concern is the loss of the virtues which characterized black society in the past. Movement to the North, increasing involve-

[78] *Notes of a Native Son*, pp. 4, 28, 33, 93, 104, 142; *Nobody Knows My Name*, pp. 24–41; *Shadow and Act*, pp. 45, 97, 267.
[79] *Notes of a Native Son*, pp. 17, 27–31; *Nobody Knows My Name*, p. 151; *Shadow and Act*, pp. 35, 94–95, 121.

ment with the main currents of society, the possible decline or end of exclusion—all have drawn blacks into the rootless, amorphous world of mass society, which encompasses men's minds and lives in its dreary compass and, at the same time, leaves them alone.[80]

Black life has always been severe, Ellison argues, but the "harsh discipline" it involved was not without merit. It demanded that blacks find ways to preserve aspiration while knowing limitation, and black culture—Ellison particularly notes the blues—is a response to that condition. The knowledge of limitation is precisely what white culture—specifically, liberal culture—has never accepted; and consequently, its aspirations were and remain infantile and without depth. The black condition, in other words, led black culture into an understanding of the human condition, to the only American expressions of tragedy. When conditions change, and Ellison certainly hopes that they will, it will be difficult to keep that understanding alive.[81]

Ellison also argues that there was in the black condition a kind of freedom, a necessary emancipation from society. Uninvolved with or excluded from existing social forms, blacks were given a unique ability to formulate differing ideals, fantasies, and social visions. If many retreated into those private visions, others shared them with their fellows. In any case, this development of ideals involved setting personal standards, higher standards of manhood in most cases than was characteristic of society at large. The mere fact that those standards were so exalted broke many, and helped lead to a willed invisibility. But for some it was an almost unparalleled opportunity to enhance creativity and critical understanding of society.[82]

In other words, Ellison's concern is that there be new ways for all Americans to be "in but not of" society. The old black world is probably passing, but the existence of that world has given an understanding of the need for community and for distinctness, for lesser communities and for fraternities which set limits without being prisons of the spirit. Accepting modernity as a given, Ellison hopes for a "new synthesis," and his argument is closer than many realize to the new pluralism of the advocates of Black Power.[83] The difference, perhaps, is that Ellison would stress Black Wisdom, a knowledge which helps

---

[80] *Shadow and Act*, pp. 39–41, 99, 232, 255, 285, 287.
[81] *Ibid.*, pp. 119, 121, 209, 239, 249–250.
[82] *Ibid.*, pp. xii–xv, 31.
[83] *Ibid.*, p. 256.

define those powers which are needful, as against those which are destructive, to human excellence and fraternity.

Baldwin recognizes and would agree with the importance of the sense of limitation in black culture. His own concern, however, is more fixed on aspiration, on the belief that "when life has done its worst, they will be enabled to rise above themselves and triumph over life" which he discerns among blacks, especially in the churches. In vital ways, however, that belief requires society and polity to be made real. The black churches, as Baldwin sees them, confronted the "power of nature" with the "power of revelation," but this dichotomization was artificial, a reflection both of racial oppression and the false ideas and institutions of white society. It lost the real meaning of the churches, the communion of members, the sense of a fraternal dimension where "nature" allied itself to, rather than opposing, "revelation." Baldwin's argument, in fact, is Puritan in very important ways; the best society seeks to make nature contribute to an understanding of what is beyond nature, to give what is original its place and no more in the teleological order.[84]

Much of that view is embodied in *Another Country*. Experience, Baldwin asserts, is always a torment. Men must, however, resist both the seductions of ease—which his anti-hero, Richard Silenski, finds more than tempting—and the dreams of mastery, which Silenski cannot combat at all. The best life is bound up with its limitations, even with its agonies. Dependence is often torture, involving fears of loss, misuse, or betrayal; but men are dependent, and without the strength of others' support are worse than lost. Life is, in the old idiom, a good which is inadequate for man's spirit, one which fraternity helps men love without being enslaved to.

Rufus Scott begins as a kind of incarnate Eros, a man of violence and carnality, who gives expression to all the desires that are normally repressed, including his desire for and hatred of white women. Yet Scott's is also a struggle of spirit, a quest for self, for dignity and understanding. The desires, satisfied in turn, prove no solution, and his life becomes a restless pilgrimage which ends in suicide. Cleaver criticized Baldwin for having Scott engage in the "white man's pastime" of suicide; but he missed the point. Even in its most diseased

---

[84] *Notes of a Native Son*, p. 145; *Going to Meet the Man*, p. 38; *Nobody Knows My Name*, pp. 113–114.

forms, suicide involves a sense of importance, a conviction that one's death will matter. If the suicide rate has been lower among blacks, it is in part because that conviction is lacking (and notably, the rate has been rising among young black males). In many ways, I suspect that Cleaver protested too much. Rufus Scott is similar to his description of his own life in too many ways, and it hardly strains the point to see in Cleaver's willingness—and that of his fellows—to undertake a struggle against seemingly hopeless odds a more political, but undeniably suicidal, quality.

Rufus Scott is, in fact, a black Christ, convinced at least in part that his death matters to God if not to man. If Baldwin seems to be asserting the simplistic and erroneous proposition that all that is needed in human life is to let the emotions express themselves, it is because Scott is in part an allegorical figure, the representation of blacks as a whole, struggling out of a world of violence and Eros toward a fuller humanity. In the process, Scott sets free those whites whom his life has touched deeply enough for them to read the lesson. He is an ultimate brother, who teaches the old lesson that the world is not a home, that the logic of life is a growing away from roots, from the country where we all begin, toward "Another Country." And in that pilgrimage, men find no small help in fraternity.[85]

In a narrow sense, Ellison is more "political" than Baldwin. In an equally narrow sense, Baldwin may be more "visionary." Especially in his later works, Baldwin seems to ignore complexity, to portray too simply and possibly too starkly—a measure of his desperation and of our crisis. And in a time of crisis, Ellison is sure to be regarded as too complacent, or at least too silent, by the highly involved. Such differences, however, are to be valued. The racial crisis is a crisis of identity, an American Armageddon in which the old hosts muster for what may be the last time against the life and thought of liberalism and mass society. The stakes, for man and for fraternity in America, demand the highest statesmanship, and, as Achad Ha'am knew, priest and prophet are both needed for statecraft in its most exalted form. The great arts of politics seem even more essential when one reflects that in this battle, unlike the Lord's last combat, there are no promises of victory; and more than one shadow of defeat hangs over the hope that Americans may win a measure of fraternity.

[85] For an explicitly political development of the theme, see Baldwin, "Mass Society and the Creative Artist," *Daedalus*, 89 (1960), pp. 373–376.

> I never dared be radical when young
> For fear it would make me conservative when
> old.
>
> Robert Frost, "Precaution"

EPILOGUE:
A NOTE ON
GENERATION AND
REGENERATION

A POLITICAL era—or *the* political era—in American history is ending. Earlier, Americans knew or felt that when liberalism and modernity failed them, there was another world to which they could repair. Made most visible by the churches, the ethnic groups, and the small communities, it was what Americans meant when they spoke of "home." Its invisible side, the values and symbols and the culture these reflected, helped intellectuals to organize and clarify their own discontent and, in politics, allowed them the warm illusion of a fraternity between the excluded and the alienated. Now, however, the groups which supported that tradition are dead or dying, as liberal society comes more and more to resemble that blank sheet which its great prophet asserted was the natural beginning of men. And the ideas which our older culture reflected and kept partly alive have been banished by fashion to odd corners—to dusty alcoves and the minds of the eccentric or fortunate—and have become distant from the life of men.

Intellectuals have felt the change. Christopher Lasch has described the "new radicalism" as born of the knowledge that intellectuals are alone, a distinct "class"; the old myth of brotherhood between the excluded, oppressed victims of industrial society and those who are self-consciously alienated and seek to escape from society or transform it is no longer believed.[1] Even those radicals who cling to it refer to an "alliance," not a brotherhood, between students and workers, and the language hints at a sophisticated but sad foreknowledge: alliances rarely outlast the enemy they are intended to defeat. The estranged wander in a deepening discontent, but one which for most is formless, uncomprehending, and alone, painfully malleable in anger which falls, more often than not, on those who share their discontent or whom they love most. At the same time, the more intellectual, especially the young, are in little better condition. Lacking an articulate alternative, lacking too the communal basis of alienation, theirs is frequently a vague search for something missing; but they are without knowledge of what the needed thing might be or resemble, which raises not only the danger of passing it by but of anger which is objectless—as lonely and universal as society itself. We seem, in fact, to be given the alternatives Frost saw some time ago between being "prudes" and "pukes."

> It seems a narrow choice the age insists on.
> How about being a good Greek, for instance?
> That course, they tell me, isn't offered this year.[2]

Many, Lasch and Herbert Marcuse being salient, have hoped that the new intellectual awareness of being alone, at least for the moment, and the sense of class, would lead to the discovery or creation of a new alternative—one sharpened by the new clarity about the intellectual's status.[3] There is a validity in that hope. Certainly students and intellectuals possess the tools and skills by which a new alternative can be found or an old one recreated; economically, the idea of intellectuals as a "class" has much to be said for it.

The limitation, however, is suggested by the truth of the idea. Students and intellectuals generally belong to the most mobile, the least socially stable, elements of society. More deeply than any other Americans, their feelings have been shaped by the experience of iso-

---

[1] Christopher Lasch, *The New Radicalism in America* (New York: Vintage, 1965).

[2] *The Poems of Robert Frost*, p. 193.

[3] Compare Lasch, *The Agony of the American Left* (New York: Vintage, 1969).

lation, the expectation of loss, the logic of withdrawal. Even the term "class" suggests a problem: that intellectuals and students are rooted in and a part of the structure of liberal industrialism, even when they reject it; for the most part, they lack the prerequisites of alienation.

John Schaar and Sheldon Wolin have pointed out that the new rebellion draws its legions from those who feel America never had a place for them, not even a "place" which deserves rejection.[4] Socially and politically, of course, this is true, yet for that reason it is misleading psychologically and intellectually. American society formed the emotions and informed the mind of the young; what it denied was precisely the "home"—the community and the alternate tradition which might have made resistance to those feelings and ideas easier and more autonomous. It is no surprise that few advocates recognize the contradiction involved in arguing that, while the United States is a "sick society" (as indeed it is), the young—who have little or no experience of any other—have mysteriously escaped the infection. It is an old philosophic truth that even those who recognize their illness may have problems in diagnosing it, and even more in selecting the physician of the soul. The "counter-culture," as Theodore Roszak very ably describes it, is still no more than that—a negation which is bound up with the affirmation it rejects, the underside of liberalism rather than an alternative to it.[5]

Brotherhood has become a major theme, an impassioned assertion and a rallying cry, a fact that reflects man's need for fraternity and his knowledge of that need. But as the movements acquire a greater mass base, they become more subject to the general currents of thought in America. Increasingly, fraternity is identified with the immediate realization of the old liberal utopia, a world of total private liberty and the ability to gratify desires in which a fraternal "instinct" will emerge. And as always, that utopia, blind to the nature of communion, is rooted in hatred of the self and fear of the other, a desire to blot out separate identity—revealed, all too clearly, in hostility to the "ego."

There is more hope in movements for "liberation" than this may

[4] Sheldon Wolin and John Schaar, "Where We Are Now," *New York Review of Books*, May 7, 1970.

[5] Theodore Roszak, *The Making of a Counter Culture* (Garden City: Doubleday, 1969).

imply. But the yearning for "liberation," apart from its obvious roots in liberal individualism, indicates that fraternity in the "counter-culture" is a bond of embattlement, of unity against oppression. It suggests how "unfree" most really are in relation to society, and that they sense their condition as one of restriction and exclusion. The generosity that led alienated men to imagine that they had "chosen comradeship" with the oppressed is replaced by the doctrine that the oppressed are free. And both ideas help to restrict the possibility of fraternity.

Less hopeful, even, is the belief that a common "life style" provides the basis for brotherhood. That notion is integrally related to the externalism and to the product and commodity orientation of industrial society (a truth which leads advertisers to adopt the argument rather than repressing it). It implies that what is visible, one's "style," is somehow the essence of community, a political behavioralism which looks no better when adopted by the left than when employed by orthodoxy. Taken literally, it would suggest that the common life style of the suburbs reflects "community." Perhaps it means to make that suggestion. The belief in the community of "life style" reflects the liberal doctrine of private man, for whom community is always an illusion, a "superstition" to which he is subjected or which he induces in others. It is sad that men who feel a desperate need for communion have been so deeply affected by a society whose life and thought deny it, that they can conceive of community only as an "image," an illusion no less ephemeral for being willed.

As always, the danger of the rebellions of the excluded and the fraternity of the embattled is that victory may be won—that men may create a place for themselves within the existing order without changing it, especially a nook of private gratification which helps conceal the knowledge of public indignity. It is already possible to hear the familiar tones, the belief that politics can be abolished in favor of a world of total private liberty and gratification under a society ordered and arranged by computers. That many fear such a society (in 1968, one man attempted to assassinate a computer) is not sufficient to dispel the liberal hope that policy, and the choices and restraints it involves, can be replaced by administration. In this, as in other things, the age does not lack prophets to whom "brave new worlds" are really that—who are cheered by the prospect of a time when the government of men yields to an administration not *of*, but *by*, things.[6] Which, in part, may be what Frost had in mind:

> The trouble with a total revolution
> (Ask any reputable Rosicrucian)
> Is that it brings the same class up on top.
> Executives of skillful execution
> Will therefore plan to go half-way and stop.[7]

All of this is too critical, however. It reflects my own lover's-quarrel with the left, my belief that there are genuine possibilities in the "new radicalism" which, given the frightful portents of our time, cannot be lost nor allowed the luxury of folly. At worst, the seeking and the protest of the day—sometimes bizarre, sometimes naive, often deluded, and always desperate—reflects a knowledge of something wrong, and a quest for and experiment with ways to put it right. And the ferment sometimes reaches the level of wisdom and often succeeds in the difficult task of forcing political orthodoxy to begin to think again.[8]

Under modern conditions, general political fraternity is impossible, and Robert Pranger was right to speak of the "eclipse of citizenship." [9] Doubly right, in fact: what has been eclipsed may reemerge. If men can recognize both the need for political fraternity and the fact that modern society makes it impossible, they will not necessarily discard that society. Compassion will probably forbid it; without the powers and resources of modern life, millions now living would be doomed not only to frustration but to death. Men can, however, attempt to provide the greatest approximations possible; they can make communities and fraternities more possible, more likely rather than less. And there may for some be the possibility of political fraternity in a different sense and a different polity.

[6] See, for example, Robert Boguslaw, *The New Utopians* (Englewood Cliffs: Prentice-Hall, 1965).

[7] *The Poems of Robert Frost*, p. 423.

[8] See Martin Duberman, "The Agony of the American Left," *New York Times Book Review* (March 23, 1969), p. 34. For an example of new ideas among the "establishment," see Robert Dahl, "The City and the Future of Democracy," *APSR*, LXI (1967), pp. 953–970.

[9] Robert Pranger, *The Eclipse of Citizenship* (New York: Holt, Rinehart and Winston, 1968).

The loss of the old tradition is to be regretted, and not only because it possessed experience which might save men from the path of folly. It understood, as liberalism and reactive anti-liberalism do not, the need for discipline, the fact that a way of life involves constraint as well as support. It is a stern word, but in the modern world and especially in modern America, the mind needs sternness to keep its freedom and autonomy. And the old words—obligation, honor, authority—involve more than constraint; as they imply, constraints are involved whenever affection matters, whenever one is deeply bound to other human beings. The constraints are never more vital than for intellectuals, whose characteristic vice is the sin of pride, and especially when intellectuals begin alone. The old tradition, in a word, understood fraternity, and we suffer when it becomes a strangled whisper.

For a real revolution, a turning back in human affairs away from the needless limitations and threats which liberal modernity has inflicted on mankind, time is needed—a long series of partial moves and shrewd compromises that demands a clear sense of direction.[10] No one need be told, in America, how easy it is for men to lose the way. The only hope for that direction, the only hope too for an end to the "eclipse," lies in the "inner city" in the true sense. Such a fraternal city can exist within an unfraternal polity only if men know the dangers that beset it and the possibilities it offers. To build a city amid strangers, it is necessary to recognize one's fellow citizens when chance casts them in the way, and to find means for affirming a mutual patriotism.

If I have spoken much of tradition in this book, it is because the American tradition seems to me to offer both encouragement and caution, and a great deal of wise counsel, in that difficult task. In a vital sense, human time is changeless, and the American past and the American future are not separable. This only emphasizes that tradition once had a beginning, a heritage its time of creation; and if America has lost, for the moment, the strength of her earliest tradition, she only comes full circle to the *Alpha* which is each new generation. It is fearful to know that one has been born, for the first lesson is loneliness. The highest possibilities and the lowest coexist alike, and the latter—

[10] Andrea Caffi, *A Critique of Violence* (Indianapolis and New York: Bobbs-Merrill, 1970), p. 51.

this is the teaching of prudence—are always more likely. But likelihood is never the sole language of men, especially in a time when the incredible is the stuff of daily life. Some minds turn to, and other voices speak, the old language of fraternity, and that is only testimony to the fact which the idea expresses: that fraternity is a need because, at a level no less true because ultimately beyond human imagining, all men are kinsmen and brothers.

BIBLIOGRAPHIC NOTES

GENERAL

Throughout the chapter, I have drawn material from Ernest Crawley, *The Mystic Rose* (London: MacMillan, 1902; and ed. T. Besterman, London: Methuen, 1927); Arnold van Gennep, *Rites of Passage*, trans. M. Vizadom and G. Caffee (London: Routledge and Kegan Paul, 1960); John Bright, *A History of Israel* (London: SCM Press, 1967); James G. Frazer, *The Golden Bough* (New York: Macmillan, 1955); W. Robertson-Smith, *The Religion of the Semites* (New York: Meridian, 1957); Sigmund Freud, *Totem and Taboo*, in *The Basic Works of Sigmund Freud*, trans. A. Brill (New York: Modern Library, 1938); Ferdinand Tönnies, *Custom: An Essay in Social Codes*, trans. A. Borenstein (Glencoe: Free Press, 1961); Geza Roheim, *The Gates of the Dream* (New York: International Universities Press, 1961); I. Schapera, *Government and Politics in Tribal Societies* (London: Watts, 1956); and Graham Clark and Stuart Piggott, *Prehistoric Societies* (New York and London: Knopf, 1966).

BETWEEN WORLDS

On the influence of values and ideas of kinship in traditional societies, see Robert Marsh, "Formal Organization in Pre-Industrial Society," *ASR*, 26 (1961), pp. 547–556, and Talcott Parsons, *The Social System* (Glencoe: Free Press, 1951), esp. pp. 301–306. For traditional ideas of kinship, see E. Leach, "On Certain Unconsidered Aspects of Double Descent Groups," *Man*, LXII (1962), pp. 130–134; B. Malinowski, "Kinship," *Encyclopedia Britannica*, XIII (1929), pp. 403–409; Robert Lowie, *The Crow Indians* (New York: Farrar and Rinehart, 1935), pp. 329–334; Fred Gearing, *Priests and Warriors*, American Anthropological Assn. Memoir 93, *AA*, 64 (1962), part V, no. 2, pp. 18–26; M. Embree, "Political Authority and Kinship in Samoa," *AA* (1962), pp. 964–971; and W. Davenport, "Non-Unilinear Descent and Descent Groups," *AA*, 61 (1959), pp. 557–572.

Maternal and paternal imagery and ideas of sex role generally are discussed in Norman Kelman, "Social and Psychoanalytical Reflections on the Father," *AS*, 29 (1960), pp. 335–358; Joseph Campbell, *The Hero with a Thousand Faces* (New York: Meridian, 1956); E. S. Hartland, *The Legend of Perseus* (London: Nutt, 1894–1896); Bruno Bettelheim, *Symbolic Wounds* (New York: Collier, 1962); Felix Boehm, "The Femininity Complex in Men," *IJP*, XI (1930), pp. 444–469; J. Honigman, "Cultural Dynamics of Sex," *P*, X (1947), pp. 37–47; and Alan Dundes, "The Earth Diver," *AA*, 64 (1962), pp. 423–438.

On the function of sexual solidarity, see Theodor Reik, *Ritual* (New York: Grove, 1962), pp. 27–91, 123; Hutton Webster, *Primitive Secret Societies* (New York: Macmillan, 1908), pp. 1–19; Sigmund Freud, "The Taboo of Virginity," *Collected Papers* (London: Hogarth, 1924–1925), IV, pp. 217–243; S. Eisenstadt, "African Age Groups," *Africa*, XXIV (1954), pp. 105–106; and F. W. Young, "The Function of Male Initiation Ceremonies," *AJS*, LXVII (1962), pp. 379–391.

On the relation between fraternity and lineage systems, see Lewis H. Morgan, *The League of the Ho-de-no-sau-nee or Iroquois* (New York: Dodd, Mead, 1904); Reik, *Ritual*, pp. 143–163; Meyer Fortes, "Primitive Kinship," *Scientific American*, 200 (1959), pp. 146–158; Bernard Campbell, *Human Evolution* (Chicago: Aldine, 1967); J. H. Goody, "Mother's Brother and Sister's Son in West Africa," *JAI*, LXXXIX (1959), pp. 61–88; R. Murphy, "Intergroup Hostility and Social Cohesion," *AA*, 59 (1957), pp. 1018–1035; H. van Welzen and W. Watering, "Residence, Power Groups and Intra-Societal Aggression," *International Archives of Ethnography*, 49 (1960), pp. 169–200; and Sigmund Freud, *Leonardo da Vinci*, trans. A. Brill (New York: Random House, 1947), pp. 47, 65–84, 97–110.

SOULS AND SECRETS

On the principle of reciprocity, see Claude Lévi-Strauss, *Structures Elementaires de la Parenté* (Paris: Presses Universitaires, 1949); R. G. Patai, *Society and the Family in the Bible and Middle East* (Garden City: Dolphin, 1959), pp. 92–99, 149–159, 168–173, 197–206; Webster, *Primitive Secret Societies*, pp. 40–43; and M. E. Durham, *Some Tribal Origins, Laws and Customs of the Balkans* (New York: Macmillan, 1929), p. 157.

The relation between traditional psychological theory and fraternity is discussed in both Crawley and Roheim. See also Webster, *Primitive Secret Societies*, pp. 1–48, 153; Erik Eriksen, "Childhood and Tradition in Two American Societies," *The Psychoanalytic Study of the Child*, ed. Otto Fenichel (New York: International Universities Press, 1945), pp. 319–350; and C. H. Wedgwood, "The Function of Secret Societies," *Oceania*, XI (1930), pp. 128–145.

On the limits of fraternity and the alienation from society implied by fraternal rituals, see Lorenz, *On Aggression*, pp. 252–253; Webster, *Primitive Secret Societies*, pp. 20–73, 115, 164–168; Durham, *Some Tribal Origins*, pp. 120–123, 131–141; S. E. Washburn, *The Social Life of Early Man* (Chicago: Aldine, 1961), pp. 11–15; Margaret Stevenson, *The Rites of the Twice Born* (London and New York: Oxford University Press, 1920); Karl Pearson, *The Chances of Death and Other Essays* (London: Arnold, 1897), pp. 159–160; Van Gennep, *passim;* Sigmund Freud, *Civilization and its Discontents* (New York: Vintage, 1951), pp. 44–56; Henry Clay Trumbull, *The Blood Covenant* (New York: Scribner's, 1885); P. H. Hamilton-Grierson, "Brotherhood: Artificial," in *Encyclopedia of Religion and Ethics,* ed. J. Hastings (New York: Scribner's, 1918), pp. 857–870; R. E. Renla, "Two Patterns of Friendship in a Guatemalan Community," *AA,* 61 (1959), pp. 44–50; and S. Eisenstadt, "Archetypal Patterns of Youth," *Daedalus,* 91 (1962), pp. 28–46.

POLITICS AND FRATERNITY

On the general problem of the relation between fraternal solidarity and politics, see Max Weber, *The City* (New York: Collier, 1962), ch. 2; Bertrand de Jouvenel, *On Power* (New York: Viking, 1949), pp. 40–43, 63–76, 89, 116–118, and *Sovereignty* (Chicago: University of Chicago Press, 1957), pp. 2–6, 18–24, 34–39, 60–62, 99–103, 116–118, 300–304; Werner Jaeger, *Paideia: Ideals of Greek Culture* (New York: Oxford University Press, 1945), vol. I, pp. 159–160, 167–171, vol. II, p. 27; Leo Strauss, *Natural Right and History* (Chicago: University of Chicago Press, 1953), pp. 81–92; Sebastian de Grazia, *Political Community* (Chicago: University of Chicago Press, 1948); Richard Kuhns, *The House, the City and the Judge* (New York and Indianapolis: Bobbs-Merrill, 1962); and H. W. Wright, "Intellect vs. Emotion in Political Cooperation," *Ethics,* LVI (1945), pp. 19–29.

On fraternity and politics in classical political theory, see Plato in *The Republic,* 442a–b, 469c, 473d, 501b, 504a–b, 516b, 532a–b; *Symposium,* 177c, 191a–193a, 199d–f, 202b–203c, 204d–205c, 208a–209a, 211b–d; *Phaedrus,* 257b; *Statesman,* 303a; and *Epistles,* VII, 325d. See Aristotle's *Ethics,* Bk. V, chs. 6–7, Bk. VI, ch. 2, Bk. VIII, chs. 1–4, 8, 9, 12, Bk. IX, ch. 7–9, and *Politics,* ed. E. Barker (Oxford: Clarendon Press, 1952), pp. 1–2, 92–110, 279–292. Also see Jaeger, *Paideia,* vol. I, pp. 84, 97, 131–132, vol. II, pp. 35–36, 58, 149–158, 174, 239, 274, 322–323; Fustel de Coulanges, *The Ancient City,* trans. W. Small (Boston: Lee and Shepard, 1901), Bk. III, chs. 7, 8, 12, 13, 16, 17; and John Wild, *Plato's Theory of Man* (Cambridge: Harvard University Press, 1946), pp. 74, 143, 188, 203.

LESSONS AND LEGACIES

On the problem of universal fraternity, see Strauss, *Natural Right and History,* pp. 149–151; Jaeger, *Paideia,* vol. II, pp. 356–364; and W. Tarn, *Alexander* (London: Cambridge University Press, 1950), vol. II, pp. 63–127, 262–265, 298–326, 399–449. On the relation between war and fraternity, see De Jouvenel, *On Power,* pp. 43–59, 254–279, and *Sovereignty,* pp. 19–33, 117–118; Gearing, *Priests and Warriors,* pp. 60–61; Morgan, *League of the Ho-de-no-sau-nee,* pp. 53–68, 88, 95–97; Engels, *The Origin of the Family, Private Property and the State* (Chicago: Kerr, 1902), pp.

78–89; and H. V. Routh, *God, Man and Epic Poetry* (Cambridge: Cambridge University Press, 1927), vol. II, pp. 49–50. (An excellent commentary on the issue is *I Samuel*: 8.)

On fraternity in relation to kingship and to large states, see Webster, *Primitive Secret Societies*, pp. 121–153; Schapera, *Government and Politics*, pp. 167–170, 174–178; and G. M. Calhoun, *Athenian Clubs in Politics and Literature* (Austin: University of Texas Press, 1913). A fine comment on the resistance of traditional fraternities to change is Margaret Murray, *The God of the Witches* (Garden City: Doubleday, 1960), pp. 33–35, 68–75.

CHAPTER II

GENERAL

Basic references for this chapter are Sigmund Freud, *Civilization and its Discontents and Totem and Taboo*; Erik Erikson, "The Roots of Virtue," in *The Humanist Frame*, ed. Julian Huxley (London: Allen and Unwin, 1961), pp. 145–166, and *Insight and Responsibility* (New York: Norton, 1964); Werner Wolff, *The Personality of the Pre-School Child: The Child's Search for His Self* (New York: Grune and Stratton, 1946); Wilhelm Stekel, *Patterns of Psychosexual Infantilism* (New York: Washington Square Press, 1966); Ernest G. Schachtel, "On Memory and Childhood Amnesia," *P*, X (1947), pp. 1–26; and *The Sociology of Georg Simmel*, ed. Kurt Wolff (Glencoe: Free Press, 1951).

EROS AND COMMUNITY

On egotism and enmity in childhood, see Sigmund Freud, *The Interpretation of Dreams*, in *Basic Writings*, trans. A. Brill, pp. 297–316; Jean Piaget, *The Moral Judgment of the Child* (Glencoe: Free Press, 1951), pp. 401–441; W. Stern, *Psychologie der Fruhen Kindheit bis zum sechtsen Lebensjahre* (Leipzig: Quelle and Meÿer, 1914); and A. Lang, *Magic and Religion* (London: Longmans, 1901), pp. 32, 35, 274–276.

On eros and isolation, see Sigmund Freud, *The Ego and the Id* (London: Hogarth, 1949), pp. 55–56, and "Thoughts for the Times on War and Death," *On Creativity and the Unconscious*, ed. B. Nelson (New York: Harper, 1958), pp. 117–118; *The Sociology of Georg Simmel*, pp. 320–324; Frazer, *The Golden Bough*, pp. 158–161; Crawley, *The Mystic Rose* (1902), vol. I, pp. 163, 214–215; and Kingsley Davis, "Jealousy and Sexual Property," *SF*, XIV (1936), pp. 395–405. (It is useful to compare these ideas with Hume's comment in *Dialogues Concerning Natural Religion*; see *Hume: Selections*, ed. Charles Hendel (New York: Scribner's, 1927), pp. 367–368.)

On repression, blood-kinship, and the market orientation, see Werner Wolff, *Personality of the Pre-School Child*; F. A. Weiss, "Self-Alienation," *AJP*, XXI (1961), pp. 207–218; Ernest G. Schachtel, "On Alienated

Concepts of Identity," *AJP*, XXI (1961), pp. 120–131; John C. Gustin, "The Revolt of Youth," *PPR*, XLVIII (1961), pp. 88–90; Geza Roheim, "Psychoanalysis and Folktale," *IJP*, III (1922), pp. 180–186; Robert W. Shirley and A. Kimball Romney, "Love Magic and Socialized Anxiety," *AA*, 64 (1962), pp. 1028–1031. (For a very similar, and very contemporary, argument, see Rudolph Troike, "The Origins of Plains Mescalism," *AA*, 64 (1962), pp. 946–963.)

On the defects of various theories of community, see Richard Adams, "The Community in Latin America: A Changing Myth," *CR*, VI (1962), pp. 409–434; Paul Wallace, *Indians in Pennsylvania* (Harrisburg: Pennsylvania State Historical Society, 1961); M. J. Field, *The Search for Security* (Evanston: Northwestern University Press, 1960); and Crawley, *The Mystic Rose* (1902), vol. I, pp. 30–38, 64–66, 74–75, 140–141, 178–180, 227, 283. (An excellent essay on the development of codes of custom is J. Johnson, "Rudimentary Society Among Boys," *Johns Hopkins Studies in Historical and Political Science*, II (1884), pp. 522–531.)

THE DYING ANIMAL

On the relation between identity and moral freedom and the discovery of the limits of the self, especially mortality, see Eriksen, *Insight and Responsibility*, Karl Menninger, *Man Against Himself* (New York: Harcourt, Brace, 1938); Frazer, *The Golden Bough*, pp. 63–69, 107; Alfred Alder, *The Theory and Practice of Individual Psychology* (Paterson, N.J.: Littlefield and Adams, 1959), pp. 1–15; John Macmurray, *The Self as Agent* (New York: Harper, 1957); Anthony Storr, *Human Aggression* (London: Penguin, 1968); and H. F. Searles, "Schizophrenia and the Inevitability of Death," *Psychiatric Quarterly*, XXXV (1961), pp. 631–635.

Purposive behavior as a divisive force is discussed in Josephine Klein, *The Study of Groups* (London: Routledge and Kegan Paul, 1956), pp. 1–11, 76–142, and Gregory Bateson, "The Frustration-Aggression Hypothesis and Culture," *Psy. R.*, LXVIII (1941), pp. 350–355. Values and interpersonal solidarity are related in C. E. Izard, "Personality, Similarity and Friendship," *JASP*, LXI (1960), pp. 47–51, and Donn Byrne, "Interpersonal Attraction and Attitude Similarity," *JASP*, LXII (1961), pp. 713–715.

MY BROTHER, MY ENEMY

Throughout this section, I have relied on *The Sociology of Georg Simmel*, see esp. pp. 181–186, 307–329, 402–424. On the phenomenon of rivalry, see Robert K. Merton, "The Ambivalence of Scientists," *The Dynamics of Modern Society*, ed. W. J. Goode (New York: Atherton, 1966), pp. 283–296, and Yves Simon, "Work and the Workman," *RP*, II (1940), pp. 63–86. The role of a sense of defect in solidarity may be seen in Freud, *Leonardo da Vinci: A Study in Psychosexuality*, trans. A. A. Brill (New York: Random House, 1947), pp. 47–54, 65–84, 97–110.

For rivalry and its uses, see L. Solomon, "Power, Game Strategies and Interpersonal Trust," *JASP*, LXI (1960), pp. 223–230; Gustin, "The Revolt of Youth," pp. 86–88; and Anthony Lauria, "Respeto, Relajo and Interpersonal Relations in Puerto Rico," *AQ*, XXXVII (1964), pp. 53–67.

On the problem of romanticism and total dependence, see Denis de Rougemont, *Passion and Society* (London: Faber and Faber, 1956), pp. 207, 260, 285, 311–318; K. Davis, "Jealousy and Sexual Property," in Geza Roheim, ed., *Psychoanalysis and the Social Sciences* (New York: International Universities Press, 1947), pp. 313–336; and E. B. Reuter, "The Sociology of Adolescence," *AJS*, XLII (1937), pp. 414–427.

The danger of dehumanization in devotion to abstract and universal doctrines is discussed in Albert Camus, *The Rebel* (New York: Knopf, 1954); Vladimir Nahirny, "Some Observations on Ideological Groups," *AJS*, LXVII (1962), pp. 397–405; J. L. Rubens, "The Self-Concept, Identity and Alienation from Self," *AJP*, XXI (1961), pp. 132–143; and J. Vollmerhausen, "Alienation in the Light of Karen Horney's Theory of Neuroses," *AJP*, XXI (1961), pp. 144–155. (Compare James Fitzjames Stephen, *Liberty, Equality, Fraternity*.)

SCIENCES AND SENTIMENTS

The limitations of group extensiveness and the role of sensed difference from other salient groups are discussed in Mancur Olson, *The Logic of Collective Action* (Cambridge: Harvard University Press, 1965); *The Sociology of Georg Simmel*, pp. 402–408; and J. H. Schaar and W. C. McWilliams, "Uncle Sam Vanishes," *New University Thought*, I (1961), pp. 61–68.

The combination of shortcoming (or frustration) and need for support can be seen in the articles by Rubens and Vollmerhausen cited in the previous section; E. D. Hutchinson, "The Period of Frustration in Creative Endeavor," *P*, III (1940), pp. 351–359, and "The Period of Elaboration in Creative Endeavor," *P*, V (1942), pp. 165–176; Klein, *The Study of Groups*, pp. 76–142; Anton T. Boisen, "The Sense of Isolation in Mental Disorder," *AJS*, XXXIII (1928), pp. 555–567, and "Onset in Acute Schizophrenia," *P*, X (1947), pp. 159–166; and Herbert Read, "The Dereliction of the Artist," *Confluence*, I (1952), pp. 45–51. (Compare Unamuno's comments: "Fighting one another, men learn to love, to have compassion. . . . But note well that the war which accomplishes is that war one plans against himself, against the mystery of our lives and destiny," in *Perplexities and Paradoxes* (New York, Philosophical Library, 1945), pp. 27, 48.)

On the flight from purpose, see John H. Schaar, *Escape from*

Authority (New York: Basic Books, 1961), and Glenn Tinder, "Modern Society and the Realms of the Spirit," *RP*, XXIII (1961), pp. 20–36. The ubiquity of frustration, given the diversity of human goals, may be seen in Norman R. F. Maier, *Frustration* (Ann Arbor: University of Michigan Press, 1963), and E. H. Powell, "Occupation, Status and Suicide: Toward a Redefinition of Anomie," *ASR*, XXIII (1958), pp. 131–139. It is useful to compare the numerous other findings which suggest that personal integration involves some sort of "balancing" between goals—e.g., G. H. Mead, *Mind, Self and Society* (Chicago: University of Chicago Press, 1935), pp. 173–178, and Gordon Allport, "The Psychology of Participation," *Psy. R.*, LII (1945), pp. 117–132.

The necessity for a dynamic understanding of human personality and identity is presented in A. H. Maslow, "A Theory of Human Motivation," *Psy. R.*, L (1943), pp. 370–396; see also Kenneth Keniston, "Alienation and the Decline of Utopia," *AS*, 29 (1960), pp. 181–200, and Edward Sapir, *Culture, Language and Personality* (Berkeley and Los Angeles: University of California Press, 1958), pp. 99–100.

The substitution of historical for personal development is presented in Bertrand de Jouvenel, *On Power*, pp. 119–135, 193–214, 301–317; Benjamin Nelson, *The Idea of Usury: from Tribal Brotherhood to Universal Otherhood*; and Reinhard Bendix, "The Cultural Setting of Economic Rationality in Western Europe," in *Value and Plan*, ed. G. Grossman (Berkeley and Los Angeles: University of California Press, 1960), pp. 245–261.

Comments on Weber's ideas include Peter Blau, "Critical Remarks on Weber's Theory of Authority," *APSR*, LVII (1963), pp. 305–316, and Peter Berger, "Charisma, Religious Innovation and Israelite Prophecy," *ASR*, XXVIII (1963), pp. 940–950. For the necessity of facing relevant insecurity, see Bruno Bettelheim, "Individual and Mass Behavior in Extreme Situations," *JASP*, XXXVIII (1943), pp. 417–452, and "The Ignored Lesson of Anne Frank," *Harper's*, CCXXI (Nov. 1960), pp. 45–50.

"THE SECRET SITS . . ."

The need for "assurance of identity" provided by a fraternal group is based on material drawn from Erik Erikson, "Youth: Fidelity and Diversity," *Daedalus*, 91 (1962), pp. 5–27; G. H. Mead, *Mind, Self and Society*, pp. 152–165; Bertrand de Jouvenel, *The Pure Theory of Politics* (New Haven: Yale University Press, 1963); *The Sociology of Georg Simmel*, pp. 307–316; Karen Horney, *New Ways in Psychoanalysis* (New York: Norton, 1939), esp. pp. 99, 230; E. G. Jaco, "The Social Isolation Hypothesis," *ASR*, 19 (1954), pp. 567–577; M. L. Kohn and J. A. Clausen, "Social Isolation and Schizophrenia," *ASR*, 20 (1955), pp. 265–275; M. M. Gordon, "Social Structure and Goals in Group Relations," in *Freedom and Control in Modern Society*, ed. M. Berger et al. (New

York: Van Nostrand, 1954), pp. 141–157; and Robert E. Lane, "The Fear of Equality," *APSR*, LIII (1959), pp. 35–57.

On secrecy and secret societies, see *The Sociology of Georg Simmel*, pp. 334–344, 356–366; Gaetano Mosca, *The Ruling Class* (New York: McGraw-Hill, 1939), pp. 173–176, 207–210; and Louis Wirth, *The Ghetto* (Chicago: University of Chicago Press, 1956), pp. 51–62. The need to recreate tradition is expressed well by Herbert Marcuse, who says of the classics that "coming to life as classics, they come to life only as other than themselves," in *One Dimensional Man* (Boston: Beacon, 1968), p. 64. See also Jose Ortega y Gasset, *Man in Crisis* (New York: Norton, 1963).

CHAPTER III

GENERAL

Throughout this chapter, I have drawn on *The Sociology of Georg Simmel*, ed. Kurt Wolff; Bertrand de Jouvenel's three works—*On Power, Sovereignty*, and *The Pure Theory of Politics*; Sheldon S. Wolin, *Politics and Vision* (Boston: Little, Brown, 1960); Karl Mannheim, *Man and Society in an Age of Reconstruction* (New York: Harcourt, Brace, 1951); Sigmund Freud, *Civilization and its Discontents*; Herbert Marcuse, *One Dimensional Man*; Jacques Ellul, *The Technological Society* (New York: Knopf, 1964), and *The Political Illusion* (New York: Knopf, 1967); and Phillip Green and Sanford Levinson, eds., *Power and Community* (New York: Pantheon, 1970).

ALIENS AND STRANGERS

For some examples of the literature on alienation and estrangement, see Sebastian de Grazia, *Political Community*; William Kornhauser, *The Politics of Mass Society* (Glencoe: Free Press, 1959); Angus Campbell et al., *The Voter Decides* (Evanston: Row, Peterson, 1954), pp. 83–87, 187–194; Wayne Thompson and J. C. Horton, "Political Alienation as a Force in Political Action," *SF*, XXXVIII (1960), pp. 190–195; J. C. Horton and Wayne Thompson, "Powerlessness and Political Negativism," *AJS*, LXVII (1962), pp. 485–495; Frederic Templeton, "Alienation and Political Participation," *POQ*, XXX (1966), pp. 252–256; James Gusfield, "Mass Society and Extremist Politics," *ASR*, 27 (1962), pp. 19–30; Christian Bay, "Politics and Pseudopolitics," *APSR*, LIX (1965), pp. 39–51; Jack L. Walker, "A Critique of the Elitist Theory of Democracy," *APSR*, LX (1966), pp. 285–295; and Joel Auerbach, "Alienation and Political Behavior," *APSR*, LXIII (1969), pp. 86–99.

On privatization and forms of resentment in modern society, see Karen Horney, *The Neurotic Personality of Our Time* (New York: Norton, 1937); Morris Rosenberg, "Some Determinants of Political Apathy," *POQ*, XVIII (1954), pp. 349–366; John H. Schaar, *Loyalty in America* (Berkeley and Los Angeles, 1957), pp. 35–37; Joseph Schumpeter, *Capitalism, Socialism and Democracy* (New York: Harper, 1950), pp. 121–163, 269–283; Robert Lane, *Political Life* (Glencoe: Free Press, 1959), pp. 124–128; and J. P. Gibbs and W. R. Martin, "A Theory of Status Integration and its Relation to Suicide," *ASR*, 23 (1958), pp. 140–147.

The necessary passivity of most citizens in modern society, especially given the size of political units, can be seen in Robert Michels, *Political Parties* (New York: Collier, 1963); Mancur Olson, *The Logic of Collective Action* (Cambridge: Harvard University Press, 1965); Bertrand de Jouvenel, "The Technocratic Age," *Bulletin of Atomic Scientists*, XX (Oct. 1964), pp. 27–29; Walter D. Burnham, "The Changing Shape of the American Political Universe," *APSR*, LIX (1965), pp. 7–28; Scott Greer, *The Emerging City* (New York: Free Press, 1962), pp. 37–40, 52–54, 76–77, 100–102, 186–189; E. J. Thomas, "Role Conceptions and Organization Size," *ASR*, 24 (1959), pp. 30–37; H. Wechsler, "Community Growth, Depressive Disorders, and Suicide," *ASR*, 26 (1961), pp. 9–16; and E. E. Raphael, "Power Structure and Membership Dispersion," *AJS*, LXXI (1965), pp. 274–283.

Pluralist attitudes toward interest group leadership can be found in David Truman, *The Governmental Process* (New York: Knopf, 1951), pp. 112, 156–165, 193, and Robert Dahl, *Who Governs?* (New Haven: Yale University Press, 1962), pp. 311–325. Critical comment on the relation of leaders and followers includes V. O. Key, *Public Opinion and American Democracy* (New York: Wiley, 1960), pp. 168–215, 536ff.; Grant McConnell, *Private Power and American Democracy* (New York: Knopf, 1966); Peter Bachrach, "Elite Consensus and Democracy," *JP*, XXIX (1962), pp. 439–452; and Norman Luttbeg and Harmon Zeigler, "Attitude Consensus and Conflict in an Interest Group," *APSR*, LX (1966), pp. 655–666.

On tensions of loyalty and the decline of meaning in organized activity, see Georges Friedmann, *Industrial Society* (Glencoe: Free Press, 1945); E. Friedman and R. Havighurst, *The Meaning of Work and Retirement* (Chicago: University of Chicago Press, 1954), pp. 65, 90–91, 178; Andre Philip, "Socialism and Social Classes," *Dissent*, V (1958), pp. 20–31; E. F. Jackson, "Status Inconsistency and Systems of Stress," *ASR*, 27 (1962), pp. 469–479; H. Wilensky, "Orderly Careers and Social Participation," *ASR*, 26 (1961), pp. 521–539; Gerhard Lenski, "Social Participation and Status Crystallization," *ASR*, 21 (1956), pp. 456–464; and Clement Greenberg, "Work and Leisure under Industrialism," *Commentary*, XVI (July 1953), pp. 57–61. An excellent overview is Henry S. Kariel, *The Decline of American Pluralism* (Stanford: Stanford University Press, 1961).

On membership in associations, see David Sills, *The Volunteers* (Glencoe: Free Press, 1957); Scott Greer, "Urbanism Reconsidered," *ASR*, 21 (1956), pp. 19–25; J. Scott, "Membership and Participation in

Voluntary Associations," *ASR*, 22 (1957), pp. 315–326; C. Wright Mills and H. Hyman, "Voluntary Association Memberships of American Adults," *ASR*, 23 (1958), pp. 284–294; and Leonard Reissman, "Class, Leisure and Social Participation," *ASR*, 19 (1954), pp. 76–84.

On political parties and their problems, see V. O. Key, *Politics, Parties and Pressure Groups* (New York: Crowell, 1958), pp. 218–219, 702–741; Otto Kirchheimer, "The Party in Mass Society," *WP*, X (1958), pp. 289–294, and "Majorities and Minorities in Western European Government," *WPQ*, XII (1959), pp. 492–510; Sigmund Neumann, "Toward a Theory of Political Parties," *WP*, VI (1954), pp. 549–563; Bernard Berelson et al., *Voting* (Chicago: University of Chicago Press, 1954); Schumpeter, *Capitalism, Socialism and Democracy*, pp. 284–302; Edward Shils, "The Legislator and His Environment," *University of Chicago Law Review*, XVIII (1950), pp. 571–584; Robert Salisbury, "The Urban Party Organization Member," *POQ*, XXIX (1965–1966), pp. 550–564; Raymond Wolfinger, "The Influence of Precinct Work on Voting Behavior," *POQ*, XXVII (1963), pp. 872–885; W. T. Martin, "The Structure of Social Relationships Engendered by Suburban Residents," *ASR*, 21 (1956), pp. 34–37; John H. Schaar and W. C. McWilliams, "Uncle Sam Vanishes," *New University Thought*, I (1961), pp. 61–68; Walter Dean Burnham, "The End of American Party Politics," *Trans-Action*, 7 (December 1969), pp. 12–22; and Jack Dennis, "Support for the Party System by the Mass Public," *APSR*, LX (1966), p. 614.

RESISTANCE

The pluralist view may be found in Berelson et al., *Voting*, pp. 310–320. For critical comments, see Theodore J. Lowi, "Interest Group Liberalism: the New Public Philosophy," *APSR*, LXI (1967), pp. 5–24; Lane Davis, "The Cost of Realism: Contemporary Restatements of Democracy," *WPQ*, XVII (1964), pp. 37–46; J. C. Horton et al., "Order and Conflict Theories of Social Problems as Conflicting Ideologies," *AJS*, LXXI (1966), pp. 701–713; and Lewis Lipsitz, "If, as Verba says, the state functions as a religion, what are we to do then to save our souls?" in *APSR*, LXII (1968), pp. 527–535.

On intellectuals and intellectual life in modern society, see Friedrich Nietzsche, *Beyond Good and Evil*, in *The Philosophy of Nietzsche*, esp. pp. 525–532, 549–551, 571–582, 597–598, 606; John H. Schaar, *Escape from Authority* (New York: Basic Books, 1961); Reinhold Niebuhr, "The Unity and Depth of Our Culture," *Sewanee Review*, LII (1944), pp. 193–198; Edward Shils, "The Intellectuals and the Powers," in *The Intellectuals*, ed. George Huszar (Glencoe: Free Press, 1960), pp. 55–61; Maurice Postan, "The Revulsion from Thought," *Cambridge Journal*, I (1948), pp. 395–408; and S. M. Lipset, "American Intellectuals: Their Politics and Status," *Daedalus*, 89 (1959), pp. 460–486.

On traditionalistic resistance and its decline, see Talcott Parsons,

"Certain Primary Sources and Patterns of Aggression in the Social Structure of the Western World," *P*, X (1947), pp. 167–181; Adam Ulam, *The Unfinished Revolution* (New York: Random House, 1960); Harold Lasswell, *Politics: Who Gets What, When and How* (Glencoe: Free Press, 1936), pp. 442–456; Reinhard Bendix, "Industrialization, Ideologies and Social Structure," *ASR*, 24 (1959), pp. 613–623; and Kenneth Little, *West African Urbanisation: A Study of Voluntary Associations in Social Change* (London: Cambridge University Press, 1965).

GENERATION

On the modern family, see Talcott Parsons, "The Kinship System in the Contemporary United States," *AA*, 45 (1943), pp. 22–38; Arnold Green, "The Middle-Class Male Child and Neurosis," *ASR*, 11 (1946), pp. 31–41; Evelyn M. Duvall, "The Concept of Parenthood," *AJS*, LII (1946), pp. 193–203; Martha Wolfenstein, "The Emergence of Fun Morality," *JSI*, VII (1951), pp. 15–24; M. L. Kohn, "Social Class and Parent-Child Relations," *AJS*, LVIII (1963), pp. 471–480, and "Social Class and the Exercise of Authority," *ASR*, 24 (1959), pp. 353–366; E. H. Bell, "Age-Group Conflict and Our Changing Culture," *SF*, XII (1933), pp. 237–243; E. Litwak, "Occupational Mobility and Extended Family Cohesion," *ASR*, 25 (1960), pp. 9–21; and R. P. Stuckert, "Occupational Mobility and Family Relationships," *SF*, XLI (1963), pp. 301–307.

Various aspects of fraternal relationships in the family may be found in E. Cumming and D. Schneider, "Sibling Solidarity in the American Family," *AA*, 58 (1961), pp. 498–507; Karen Horney, *Our Inner Conflicts* (New York: Norton, 1945); Kingsley Davis, "The Sociology of Parent-Youth Conflict," *ASR*, 5 (1940), pp. 523–535; Ruth Hartley, "Sex Role Pressure and the Socialization of the Male Child," *Psychological Reports*, V (1959), pp. 457–468; and D. Miller and G. Swanson, *The Changing American Parent* (New York: Wiley, 1958).

On gangs, see Frederic Thrasher, *The Gang* (Chicago: University of Chicago Press, 1960); J. Margolis, "Juvenile Delinquents: Latter-Day Knights?," *AS*, 29 (1960), pp. 211–218; Joseph Adelson, "The Mystique of Adolescence," *P*, XXVII (1964), pp. 1–5; David Matza, "Subterranean Values and Juvenile Delinquency," *ASR*, 26 (1961), pp. 712–719; Lewis Yablonsky, "The Violent Gang," *Commentary*, XXX (1960), pp. 125–130; and Michael Harrington, "Slums New and Old," *Commentary*, XXX (1960), pp. 118–124.

On youth culture generally and in its contemporary forms, see Peter Blos, *On Adolescence* (New York: Free Press, 1962); Kenneth Keniston, *The Uncommitted* (New York: Harcourt, Brace, 1967), *The Young Radicals* (New York: Harcourt, Brace, 1968), and "Youth and Social Change," *Daedalus*, 91 (1962), pp. 145–171; George Goethals and Dennis Klos, *Experiencing Youth* (Boston: Little, Brown, 1970); Jonathan Eisen, ed., *Altamont* (New York: Avon, 1970); Phillip Nobile, ed., *The Con III*

Controversy (New York: Pocket Books, 1971); J. Milton Yinger, "Contraculture and Subculture," *ASR*, 25 (1960), pp. 625–635; W. J. Goode, "The Theoretical Importance of Love," *ASR*, 24 (1959), pp. 38–47; Edgar Z. Friedenberg, *The Vanishing Adolescent* (Boston: Beacon, 1959), and *The Dignity of Youth and Other Atavisms* (Boston: Beacon, 1965).

The decline of the New Left is best indicated by comparing current rhetoric with Mitchell Cohen and Dennis Hale, eds., *The New Student Left* (Boston: Beacon, 1966); on the theoretical problem, see Mancur Olson, "Rapid Growth as a Destabilizing Force," *JEH*, XXVII (1963), pp. 529–552.

RECOGNITION

On interpersonal knowledge and relations in modern society, see especially *The Sociology of Georg Simmel*, pp. 307–326, 334–338, 415–416; Georg Simmel, *The Web of Group Affiliations*, ed. Reinhard Bendix (New York: Free Press, 1955), pp. 162–163; Emil Lederer, *The State of the Masses* (New York; Norton, 1940), pp. 47–68; J. Hadja, "Alienation and Integration of Student Intellectuals," *ASR*, 26 (1961), pp. 758–777; Ernest G. Schachtel, "On Alienated Concepts of Identity," *AJP*, XXI (1961), pp. 120–131; and Charles Kadushin, "The Friends and Supporters of Psychotherapy: On Social Circles in Urban Life," *ASR*, 31 (1966), pp. 786–801.

On the temptations of violence and war in modern states, see Hans Speier, *The Social Order and the Risks of War* (New York: George Stewart, 1952), pp. 112–128; Sebastian de Grazia, *Political Community*, pp. 176–190; Harold Lasswell, "The Garrison State," *AJS*, XLVI (1941), pp. 455–468; W. C. McWilliams, "On Violence and Legitimacy," *Yale Law Journal*, 79 (1970), pp. 623–646; and Lewis Coser, *Continuities in the Study of Social Conflict* (Stanford: Stanford University Press, 1967).

On battle fraternity and its defects, see Freud, "Thoughts for the Times on War and Death," *On Creativity and the Unconscious*, ed. B. Nelson; Edward Shils and Morris Janowitz, "Cohesion and Disintegration in the Wehrmacht," *POQ*, XII (1948), pp. 280–315; and E. A. Weinstein, "The Function of Interpersonal Relations in the Neuroses of Combat," *P*, X (1947), pp. 307–321.

CHAPTER IV

GENERAL

Useful works on American politics and culture, which I have relied on but not specifically cited in the notes, include: James Bryce, *The American Commonwealth* (New York: Macmillan, 1913); Morris R. Cohen, *American Thought* (New York: Collier, 1962); Bernard Crick, *The American Science of Politics* (Berkeley and Los Angeles: University of California Press, 1959); Merle Curti, *The Growth of American Thought* (New York: Harper, 1943), and *The Roots of American Loyalty* (New

York: Columbia University Press, 1946); Ralph Henry Gabriel, *The Course of American Democratic Thought* (New York: Ronald, 1940); Oscar Handlin, *The Uprooted* (New York: Grosset and Dunlap, 1961); Hans Kohn, *American Nationalism* (New York: Collier, 1961); Harold J. Laski, *The American Democracy* (New York: Viking, 1948); Paul Mazur, *American Prosperity* (New York: Viking, 1928); Clinton Rossiter, *Conservatism in America* (New York: Knopf, 1955); George Santayana, *Character and Opinion in the United States* (New York: Braziller, 1955); John H. Schaar, *Loyalty in America*; Harold Stearns, *Liberalism in America* (New York: Boni and Liveright, 1919); Norman Jacobson, "Political Science and Political Education," *APSR*, LVII (1963), pp. 561–569; Abraham Kaplan, "American Ethics and Public Policy," in *The American Style*, ed. E. E. Morison (Cambridge: M.I.T. Press, 1958), pp. 11–14; Ewart K. Lewis, "The Contribution of Medieval Thought to the American Political Tradition," *APSR*, L (1956), pp. 462–474; and J. Livingstone, "Alexander Hamilton and the American Tradition," *MJPS*, I (1957), pp. 209–224.

On the influence of religion, see H. Richard Niebuhr, *The Kingdom of God in America* (Chicago: Willet, 1937); Ralph Barton Perry, *Puritanism and Democracy* (New York: Vanguard, 1944); Paul Carter, *The Decline and Revival of the Social Gospel* (Ithaca: Cornell University Press, 1954); and E. W. Embree, *Brown America* (New York: Viking, 1931), pp. 208–209.

Various pietistic corruptions are discussed in Laski, *American Democracy*, pp. 264–322, and H. Richard Niebuhr, *The Social Sources of Denominationalism* (New York: Meridian, 1957), pp. 54–76, 106–134.

CHAPTER V

GENERAL

The field of American Puritan thought is almost preempted by Perry Miller's two-volume *The New England Mind* (Boston: Beacon, 1961). Also highly valuable are Edmund S. Morgan's *The Puritan Family* (New York: Harper, 1966) and *The Puritan Dilemma* (Boston: Little, Brown, 1958).

The best study of Calvinistic political thought is S. S. Wolin, *Politics and Vision* (Boston: Little, Brown, 1960). Obviously essential is John Calvin, *Institutes of the Christian Religion*, ed. J. T. McNeill (Philadelphia: Westminster, 1960). See also J. W. Allen, *Political Thought of the Sixteenth Century* (London: Methuen, 1928); William Haller, *The Rise of Puritanism* (New York: Harper, 1957), John T. McNeill, *The History and Character of Calvinism* (New York: Oxford University Press, 1954); H. Richard Niebuhr, *The Kingdom of God in America* and *The Social Sources of Denominationalism*; and Michael Walzer, *The Revolution of the Saints* (Cambridge: Harvard University Press, 1965).

Typical of sources highly critical of Puritanism are Brooks Adams, *The Emancipation of Massachusetts* (Boston: Houghton Mifflin, 1887), and Thomas Wertenbaker, *The Puritan Oligarchy* (New York: Scribner's, 1947).

"THE FAULT OF DULLNESS IS WITHIN US . . ."

On the goodness of creation and the remnants of excellence in humanity, see Calvin, *Institutes*, I:i: 1–2, iii: 3, iv: 4, xi: 2, xiv: 3, xv, xvii: 9, II:ii: 12–22, iii.1 III:vii, viii, xix: 15, 16; Miller, *The New England Mind*, vol. I, pp. 132–149, 155, 162–169, 173, 177–187, 194, 198, 220, 262, 397, vol. II, pp. 437–438; Haller, *The Rise of Puritanism*, pp. 23–33, 308; and Cotton Mather, *Magnalia Christi Americana* (Hartford: Silas Andrus, 1855), vol. II, pp. 196–197. Perhaps the best single statement of the doctrine of sin is Thomas Hooker, "A True Sight of Sin," in *The American Puritans*, ed. Perry Miller (New York: Doubleday, 1956), pp. 153–164; see also Calvin, *Institutes*, I:i: 4, v: 3, 4, 11, 14, xiv: 3, 16, xv: 7, 8, II:i, ii, vii, III:iii: 12, 14, v; Miller, *The New England Mind*, vol. I, pp. 42, 254–262, 395, 400–401; Haller, *The Rise of Puritanism*, pp. 123, 154.

On uncertainty and its relation to Scriptural interpretation, see Calvin, *Institutes*, I:v: 7, 9, 10–12, vii: 4, 5, xiii: 5, xiv: 4, xvi, xvii: 1–6, xviii, II:ii: 18–26, iii: 7, 8, III:ii: 18, vii: 8, xxi–xxiv, IV:i, xvii: 20, 25; Miller, *The New England Mind*, vol. I, pp. 15, 26–27, 32, 35–38, 49, 53–67, 112–114, 242, 279, 282, 287, 426–430, 461–462, 490–491, vol. II, pp. 19–20, 42, 143, 144; Haller, *The Rise of Puritanism*, pp. 14, 83, 175, 197, 240; and J. S. Whale, *The Protestant Tradition* (Cambridge: Cambridge University Press, 1959), pp. 129–134, 143–144. For a conservative view, see J. I. Packer, "Calvin the Theologian," in *John Calvin*, ed. F. L. Battles et al. (Grand Rapids: Eerdmans, n.d.), pp. 162–167.

"NO NEGLECT OF MEANS . . ."

On determinism, action, and "social therapy" in Calvinism and Puritanism, see Walzer, *Revolution of the Saints*, esp. p. 27; Richard Baxter, *The Holy Commonwealth* (London, 1659); Calvin, *Institutes*, III:vii–x, xvi, xix; Morgan, *The Puritan Family*, pp. 2, 14–16; Miller, *The New England Mind*, vol. I, pp. 45–48, 102, 162–163, 177–187, 191, 198, 270–273, 286–287; Haller, *The Rise of Puritanism*, pp. 23–33, 115–116, 152, 154; Richard Schlatter, *Richard Baxter and Puritan Politics* (New Brunswick: Rutgers University Press, 1957); and E. Battis, *Saints and Sectaries: Anne Hutchinson and the Anti-Nomian Controversy in Massachusetts* (Chapel Hill: University of North Carolina Press, 1962).

On the emotions and social discipline, see Calvin, *Institutes*, I:xiii: 5, II:vii: 1, 6, 10, viii: 6, III:iii, iv: 6, x, IV:i: 13, 16, x, xi, xii; Miller, *The New England Mind*, vol. I, pp 53–67, 250–253, 260, 390, vol. II, p. 59; Edmund S. Morgan, "The Puritans and Sex," *NEQ*, XV (1942), pp. 591–607;

Albert-Marie Schmidt, *Calvin* (New York: Harper, 1960), pp. 76–77; and George Mosse, "Puritanism and Reason of State in Old and New England," *WMQ*, IX (1952), pp. 67–80.

On the concept of pilgrimage, see Calvin, *Institutes*, I:xvii:10, 11, III: ix, x; Charles Drelincourt, *La Bourgeoisie du Ciel* (Charenton, France, 1657) and *The Christian's Defence against the Fears of Death* (Trenton: J. Oram, 1808); and Lewis Feuer, "What Is Alienation: the Career of a Concept," *New Politics*, I (1962), pp. 116–117.

On the nature and role of community, see Morgan, *The Puritan Dilemma*; Calvin, *Institutes*, II:ii:13–16, iii:1, 6, 10, III:xix:10, IV:xx:2, 9; Miller, *The New England Mind*, vol. I, pp. 49–53, 59; and Allen, *Political Thought of the 16th Century*, pp. 6–11, 29–34. An excellent discussion of Puritan community planning and its origins is S. C. Powell, *Puritan Village* (Middletown: Wesleyan University Press, 1963), esp. ch. 10, pp. 178–186.

"WITHOUT DESPISING LIFE . . ."

On the theory of covenants, see Miller, *The New England Mind*, vol. I, pp. 49, 121–122, 177, 250, 282, 287, 298, 300, 375–386, 392, 398–399, 405–409, 414–419, 429, 442–449, 452–453, 462, vol. II, pp. 41–54, 267; Calvin, *Institutes*, II:vi:1, xi:11, xii; Haller, *The Rise of Puritanism*, pp. 84, 115–117, 123, 128–175, 193, 268–269; John Cotton, *The Way of the Churches of Christ in New England* (London: Matthew Simmons, 1645), *The Pouring out of the Seven Vials, or an Exposition of the XVIth Chapter of Revelations* (London: R. S., 1645), and *An Abstract of the Lawes of New England* (London: F. Coules and W. Ley, 1641); Walzer, *Revolution of the Saints*, pp. 14, 48–50, 188–189, 193–195; Niebuhr, *The Kindom of God*, pp. 70–71, 98–99; Morgan, *The Puritan Family*, pp. 7, 19, 25–26, 153–154; Ralph Barton Perry, *Puritanism and Democracy* (New York: Vanguard, 1944), pp. 330–333; Perry Miller, "Preparation for Salvation in 17th Century New England," *JHI*, IV (1943), pp. 253–286; and E. H. Emerson, "Calvin and Covenant Theology," *Church History*, XXV (1956), pp. 136–144.

"INTEGRAL AND CONSERVANT CAUSES . . ."

On the role of the church in society, see Calvin, *Institutes*, III:xix, IV:xi: 1–4, xii:7, 17, xx:1–12; Walzer, *Revolution of the Saints*, pp. 115, 116, 122, 123, 128, 130, 134; Haller, *The Rise of Puritanism*, pp. 11–12; and F. Wendel, *Calvin: The Origins and Development of His Religious Thought* (New York: Harper and Row, 1963), pp. 79–80, 309:310.

On economic doctrine, see Miller, *The New England Mind*, vol. I, pp. 418–419, 429, vol. II, pp. 42, 50–51, 150; Schlatter, *Richard Baxter*, pp. 39, 121; Walzer, *Revolution of the Saints*, pp. 43, 226; McNeill, *History and Character of Calvinism*, pp. 221–223, 418–421; and B. A. Gerrish,

"Capitalism and the Decline of Religion," *McCormick Quarterly*, XVIII (1965), pp. 12–19.

On egalitarian elements in Calvinistic and Puritan thought, see Calvin, *Institutes*, IV:iv, v, vi, xi:6, xiii:1–2, xx:8; Perry, *Puritanism and Democracy*; Miller, *The New England Mind*, vol. I, pp. 121–122, 412; and J. T. McNeill, "The Democratic Element in Calvin's Thought," *Church History*, XVIII (1949), pp. 153–171. The similarity to Aristotle's ideas is evident in Baxter, who disliked democracy in the Commons because most men were sensual, but also distrusted the pride of the Lords, preferring rule by "sober men of middle rank." (Schlatter, *Richard Baxter*, pp. 26, 28, 31.)

On the doctrine of resistance, see Calvin, *Institutes*, IV:xx:8, 12, 22–23, 31, and G. H. Laird, *Calvinism and the Political Order* (Philadelphia: Westminster, 1965).

Chapter VI

GENERAL

For Winthrop's writings, see *The Winthrop Papers* (Boston: Massachusetts Historical Society, 1929–1947); *The Life and Letters of John Winthrop*, ed. R. C. Winthrop (Boston: Little, Brown, 1869); and *Winthrop's Journal: A History of New England, 1630–1649*, ed. J. K. Hosmer (New York: Scribner's, 1908). Critical sources include Edmund S. Morgan, *The Puritan Dilemma: the Story of John Winthrop*; Vernon L. Parrington, *Main Currents in American Thought* (New York: Harcourt, Brace, 1954), vol. I, pp. 37–50; and Stanley Gray, "The Political Thought of John Winthrop," *NEQ*, III (1930), pp. 681–705.

"MORE THAN NATURE DEMANDS . . ."

On the human need for love and society, see *Winthrop Papers*, vol. II, pp. 288–292. Winthrop's emphasis on likeness made his arguments more egalitarian and fraternal than those of Puritans like Hooker, who portrayed the covenants hierarchically. (See Miller, *The New England Mind*, vol. I, pp. 408, 413, 448.) Winthrop's ideal cases were David and Jonathan and Ruth and Naomi. The need for closeness is indicated in *Winthrop Papers*, vol. II, p. 283, and *Life and Letters*, vol. I, pp. 397–398, 416. On the natural law and Christian justice, see *Winthrop Papers*, vol. II, pp. 112, 115, 118, 120, 136, 139–141, 283–286, 294–295, vol. III, pp. 341–343, vol. IV, pp. 100, 102, 391–392, 405–406, 478, 481, 486. (Note the comments on separatism, *Winthrop Papers*, vol. III, pp. 12–14.)

CITIZENS AND MAGISTRATES

On political knowledge and political vocation, see *Winthrop Papers*, vol. III, pp. 505–507, vol. IV, pp. 348, 380–392, 477, vol. V, p. 32; *Life and*

Letters, vol. I, p. 451, vol. II, pp. 211–214, 236; Morgan, *The Puritan Dilemma*, pp. 17–18, 95–96; G. L. Mosse, *The Holy Pretense: A Study in Christianity and Reason of State from William Perkins to John Winthrop* (Oxford: Blackwell, 1957); and A. Seidman, "Church and State in the Early Years of Massachusetts Bay Colony," *NEQ*, XVIII (1945), pp. 211–233.

On relationships between rulers, see *Winthrop Papers*, vol. IV, pp. 360–361, 402–411, 493. (Opposition, however, may be useful if it does not challenge the sense of fraternal unity. See *Winthrop Papers*, vol. II, p. 175, IV, p. 386.) On magisterial power and its limits, see *Winthrop Papers*, vol. I, pp. 201–202, vol. II, pp. 133, 285, vol. III, p. 507, vol. IV, pp. 360, 380–392, 402–411, 468–488; *Life and Letters*, vol. I, pp. 421, 451, vol. II, pp. 416, 432; Morgan, *The Puritan Dilemma*, pp. 90–95, 110; and Miller, *The New England Mind*, vol. I, pp. 424–428.

PROFESSION AND ACTION

For Winthrop's economic ideas, see *Winthrop Papers*, vol. I, pp. 295–311, vol. II, p. 124; Morgan, *The Puritan Dilemma*, pp. 21, 67; and E. A. Johnson, "Economic Ideas of John Winthrop," *NEQ*, III (1930), pp. 235–240. For the idea of possible example in New England, see *Winthrop Papers*, vol. II, pp. 89–90, 112, 115; Morgan, *The Puritan Dilemma*, p. 43. Other justifications for migration were few and often weak; see *Winthrop Papers*, vol. II, pp. 111–112, 114, 117, 120, 127, 133, 142, 145, 147, and Morgan, *The Puritan Dilemma*, pp. 31–33, 40–43.

New England's opportunity is presented in *Winthrop Papers*, vol. II, pp. 115, 125, 287, 293–295, vol. IV, pp. 100, 203; *Life and Letters*, vol. I, pp. 397–398; and Miller, *The American Puritans*, pp. 40–43. See the similar ideas of John Cotton in George L. Haskins, *Law and Authority in Early Massachusetts* (New York: Macmillan, 1960), p. 187.

PROMISE AND PERIL

On the dangers in the American environment which threatened Puritan political ideas, see *Winthrop Papers*, vol. II, pp. 116, 119, 285, 287; Miller, *The New England Mind*, vol. II, pp. 36–37, 50, 143–144, 307–313; Christopher Hill, *Society and Puritanism in Pre-Revolutionary England* (New York: Schocken, 1964); chs. 12–14; Morgan, *The Puritan Family*, pp. 175–186; Alan Simpson, *Puritanism in Old and New England* (Chicago: University of Chicago Press, 1961); and A. Heimert, "Puritanism, the Wilderness and the Frontier," *NEQ*, XXXV (1963), pp. 361–382.

On the problem of political obligation and its relation to dissenters, see Morgan, *The Puritan Dilemma*, esp. pp. 134–154; Miller, *The New England Mind*, vol. I, p. 429, vol. II, pp. 117–118, 143–145; *Winthrop Papers*, vol. II, pp. 284, 287, 293–295; and Perry Miller, "The Shaping of the American Character," *NEQ*, XXVIII (1955), pp. 435–454.

ROGER WILLIAMS AND ANTI-POLITICS

Absolutely essential is Perry Miller, *Roger Williams: His Contribution to the American Tradition* (New York: Atheneum, 1962). Two useful studies are Alan Simpson, "How Democratic Was Roger Williams?," *WMQ*, XIII (1956), pp. 53–67, and M. Calamandrei, "Neglected Aspects of Roger Williams' Thought," *Church History*, XXI (1952), pp. 239–258. Typical of traditional interpretations which see Williams as the precursor of modern ideologies are S. Brockunier, *The Irrepressible Democrat* (New York: Ronald, 1940), and T. T. Treadwell, *Roger Williams: Prophetic Legislator* (Providence: Greene, 1872).

CHAPTER VII

GENERAL

Most of the works relied on in this chapter are cited in the general bibliography of Chapter Five. However, see also Herbert Schneider, *The Puritan Mind* (Ann Arbor: University of Michigan Press, 1958); Perry Miller, *Errand into the Wilderness* (Cambridge: Harvard University Press, 1956); H. Richard Niebuhr, *The Social Sources of Denominationalism*; C. H. Faust, "The Decline of Puritanism," in *Transitions in American Literary History*, ed. H. H. Clark (Durham: Duke University Press, 1953), pp. 1–48; and Alan Heimert, *Religion and the American Mind: from the Great Awakening to the Revolution* (Cambridge: Harvard University Press, 1966).

"SAY NOT, I AM A CHILD . . ."

On the problem of political decay and its relation to inherited loyalties, see Miller, *The New England Mind*, vol. I, pp. 396–397, 432–433, 458–459, 473–478, 486–491, vol. II, pp. 12–15, 28–34, 53–67, 82–128, 145, 168, 242, 248, 267, 426–430, 461–478; Niebuhr, *The Kingdom of God*, pp. 18–39; and Haller, *The Rise of Puritanism*, pp. 49–82.

On the sense of political superiority, isolation, and related phenomena, see *The New England Mind*, vol. I, pp. 464–470, 482–487, vol. II, pp. 5–9, 25–26, 36–41, 50, 117–119, 123–128, 139–145, 307–313; Morgan, *The Puritan Dilemma*, pp. 98–99, 179–180; Ralph Barton Perry, *Puritanism and Democracy*, pp. 310–319; and A. H. Buffington, "The Isolationist Policy of Colonial New England," *NEQ*, I (1928), pp. 158–179. Winthrop's discovery of obscure providences and his scorn of success as a test of merit can be seen in *The Winthrop Papers*, vol. II, pp. 116, 120, 134–138, 145.

The changes in attitude culminating in and resulting from the witch trials are described in *The New England Mind*, vol. II, pp. 145–146, 168, 179–182, 191–208, 212, 227, 269–273, 279, 281, 368–370, 464–468. It is intriguing that a major part of the opposition to the trials came from fundamentalists who found no warrant for the trials in Scripture; see *The New England Mind*, vol. II, p. 252.

CAMELS AND NEEDLES

On the doctrine of "special providences" and the rise of a new, acquisitive economic ethic, see *The New England Mind*, vol. I, pp. 400–401, 464–466, 473–481, vol. II, pp. 5–15, 41–51, 324–327, 397–402; Perry Miller, "Declension in a Bible Commonwealth," in *Nature's Nation*, ed. E. Miller (Cambridge: Harvard University Press, 1967), pp. 14–49; Haskins, *Law and Authority in Early Massachusetts*, pp. 69–72; and Wertenbaker, *The Puritan Oligarchy*, pp. 53, 183–184. Nelson, *The Idea of Usury* is generally useful on economic issues.

The relation between new economic doctrines and economic and social change, especially the development of class distinctions, is discussed in *The New England Mind*, vol. II, pp. 120, 141–142, 150, 254–255, 315, 401–402; Haskins, *Law and Authority*, pp. 108–109, 220; K. Murdock, *Increase Mather* (Cambridge: Harvard University Press, 1925), pp. 258ff.; M. Gottfried, "The First Depression in Massachusetts," *NEQ*, IX (1936), pp. 655–678; and C. S. Grant, *Democracy in the Connecticut Frontier Town of Kent* (New York: Columbia University Press, 1961), pp. 128–140.

For Cotton Mather's scientific concerns and his attitudes in relation to Lockean epistemology, see *The New England Mind*, vol. II, pp. 345, 369–370, 404–405, 417–424, 426–427, 437–446, 460–462, 478, and T. Hornburger, "The Data, Sources and Significance of Cotton Mather's Interest in Science," *AL*, VI (1935), pp. 413–420. Mather's own *The Christian Philosopher*, ed. J. K. Piercy (Gainesville: Scholars' Facsimiles and Reprints, 1968), and *A Man of Reason* (Boston: John Edwards, 1718) are illustrative, especially of Mather's tendency when seeking "scientific" arguments to naturalize Deity. (For the smallpox episode, easily the most creditable of Mather's ventures, see *The New England Mind*, vol. II, pp. 345–366.)

On Mather's doctrine of voluntarism and his abandonment of the political order, see his *Bonifacius: An Essay to do Good*, ed. J. K. Piercy (Gainesville: Scholars' Facsimiles and Reprints, 1967), and *Brethren Dwelling Together in Unity* (Boston: S. Gerrish, 1718), as well as *The New England Mind*, vol. II, pp. 397, 402–409, 412–416; Niebuhr, *Kingdom of God*, pp. 171–172; and L. Boas, *Cotton Mather: Keeper of the Puritan Conscience* (New York: Harper, 1928). On Stoddard and centralization, see *The New England Mind*, vol. II, pp. 248–269, 277–281.

JOHN WISE: STATECRAFT REVISITED

For Wise's political ideas, see *A Vindication of the Government of New England Churches* and *The Churches' Quarrel Espoused* (published in a single edition by the Congregational Board of Publications, Boston, 1860), and *The Law of Nature and Government*, Old South Leaflet #165 (Boston: Old South Association, 1905). Useful critical literature includes Vernon Louis Parrington, *Main Currents in American Thought*, vol. I, pp. 119–126; *The New England Mind*, vol. II, pp. 288–302; G. A. Cooke, *John Wise: Early American Democrat* (New York: Kings Crown, 1952); Alan Heimert, "Puritanism, the Wilderness and the Frontier"; and J. L. Wolf, *The Significance of John Wise* (unpublished master's thesis, Graduate School of Theology, Oberlin College, 1946).

The relation between traditionalism and populism can be seen in *The New England Mind*, vol. II, pp. 50–51, 105–112, 150, 178, 299–301, 307–315, and L. B. Wright, *The Cultural Life of the American Colonies* (New York: Harper, 1962), pp. 26–28.

EDWARDS: "GOD MUST BE NEAR . . ."

Edwards' writings are cited from *The Works of President Edwards*, ed. S. Dwight (New York: S. Converse, 1829–1830), though I have relied on the more recent editions edited by Perry Miller, John E. Smith, and Clyde A. Holbrook (New Haven: Yale University Press, 1955, 1959, and 1970, respectively). Especially useful critical sources include Faust, "The Decline of Puritanism," and Miller's books: *Errand into the Wilderness*, pp. 153–203; *Nature's Nation*, pp. 78–120; and *Jonathan Edwards* (New York: Sloane, 1949).

For the influence on Edwards of science and the new doctrine of reason and Lockeanism, see *Jonathan Edwards*, ed. C. H. Faust and T. H. Johnson (New York: Hill and Wang, 1962), pp. 11, 12, 18–23, 27–37; Schneider, *The Puritan Mind*, pp. 106–142; T. Hornburger, "The Effect of the New Science upon the Thought of Jonathan Edwards," *AL*, IX (1937), pp. 196–207; H. N. Gardiner, "The Early Idealism of Jonathan Edwards," *Phil. R.*, IX (1900), pp. 573–596; and C. Gohdes, "Aspects of Idealism in Early New England," *Phil. R.*, XXXIX (1930), pp. 537–575. The general argument made here is disputed by Rufus Suter, "The Strange Universe of Jonathan Edwards," *Harvard Theological Review*, LIV (1961), pp. 125–128, but with arguments which at best qualify the major thesis. It is useful in relation to the whole issue to compare Locke, *Essay on Human Understanding*, II:xii:8, to Edwards' doctrines.

Edwards' doctrine of original sin is best found in *Original Sin*, ed. Clyde Holbrook (New Haven: Yale University Press, 1970). See also Faust and Johnson, *Jonathan Edwards*, pp. 27–37, 254, 349–371, and C. H. Shafer, "Jonathan Edwards and the Principle of Self-Love," *Papers of the Michigan Academy of Science*, XXXV (1951), pp. 341–348.

On the doctrine of the senses, see Faust and Johnson, *Jonathan Edwards*, pp. 238–254; Miller, *The New England Mind*, vol. II, pp. 214–215, 279, 282–287, and "The Rhetoric of Sensation" in *Errand into the Wilderness*, pp. 167–183; Niebuhr, *The Kingdom of God*, pp. 110–111;

and E. H. Cady, "The Artistry of Jonathan Edwards," *NEQ*, XXII (1949), pp. 61–72. For Edwards' dilemmas in relation to his own congregation, see his *Works*, vol. I, pp. 640–651.

Edwards' ideas on charity and community can be found in Faust and Johnson, *Jonathan Edwards*, pp. 240–254, 372–374. Note that Edwards saw the glory of Christ in his "condescension" to men; the only imitation of Christ suggested is far from fraternal.

For Edwards' ideas of history and the American mission, see Schneider, *The Puritan Mind*, pp. 127, 223–232; Edwards, *Works*, vol. IV, pp. 128–132; and Perry, *Puritanism and Democracy*, pp. 102–103, 314–315, 363. For the works of Jonathan Mayhew, see Schneider, *The Puritan Mind*, pp. 192–198; Charles W. Akers, *Called unto Liberty: A Life of Jonathan Mayhew* (Cambridge: Harvard University Press, 1964); and the similar work of Joseph Bellamy, *Four Sermons on the Wisdom of God in the Permission of Sin* (Morristown, N.J.: H. Russell, 1804).

CHAPTER VIII

GENERAL

The essential work will always be Hamilton, Madison, and Jay, *The Federalist*, ed. Max Beloff (Oxford: Blackwell, 1948). Useful discussions of the period include Edmund S. Morgan, *The Birth of the Republic, 1763–1789* (Chicago: University of Chicago Press, 1956); Bernard Bailyn, *The Ideological Origins of the American Revolution* (Cambridge: Harvard University Press, 1967) and *The Origins of American Politics* (New York: Knopf, 1968); L. B. Wright, *Cultural Life in the American Colonies*; Merle Curti, *Growth of American Thought, Roots of American Loyalty and American Paradox: the Conflict of Thought and Action* (New Brunswick: Rutgers University Press, 1956); C. H. Van Tyne, *The War of Independence* (Boston: Houghton Mifflin, 1929); Carl L. Becker, *The Declaration of Independence* (New York: Vintage, 1958); and Clinton Rossiter, *The First American Revolution* (New York: Harcourt, Brace and World, 1956).

OLD AND NEW

The Enlightenment and its impact in America are discussed in Carl L. Becker, *The Heavenly City of the 18th Century Philosophers* (New Haven: Yale University Press, 1932); Daniel Boorstin, *The Genius of American Politics* (Chicago: University of Chicago Press, 1953); Hans Kohn, *The Idea of Nationalism* (New York: Macmillan, 1961), pp. 265–286; Phillip Schorr, *Science and Superstition in the 18th Century* (New York: Columbia University Press, 1940); and Gilbert Chinard, "Eighteenth Century Theories on America as a Human Habitat," *Proceedings, American Philosophical Society*, XCI (1947), pp. 25–57.

On scientific theories, see J. A. Robinson, "Newtonianism and the

Constitution," *MJPS*, I (1957), pp. 252-266; J. G. Crowther, *Famous American Men of Science* (New York: Norton, 1937); and John Adams, *Works*, ed. C. F. Adams (Boston: Little, Brown, 1856), vol. IV, pp. 93, 416-420, 427-434, vol. VI, pp. 479-481, vol. IX, pp. 339-512.

On the change from old to new theories generally, see Ewart K. Lewis, "The Contribution of Medieval Thought to the American Political Tradition," *APSR*, L (1956), pp. 462-474; Benjamin F. Wright, *American Interpretations of Natural Law* (Cambridge: Harvard University Press, 1931); Arthur Lovejoy, "The Theory of Human Nature in the American Constitution and the Method of Counterpoise" in *Reflections on Human Nature* (Baltimore: Johns Hopkins University Press, 1961), pp. 37-66; Henry S. Commager, "Leadership in 18th Century America and Today," *Daedalus*, 90 (1961), pp. 652-673; Hannah Arendt, *On Revolution* (New York: Viking, 1963); and T. V. Smith, *The American Philosophy of Equality* (Chicago: University of Chicago Press, 1927), pp. 1-43, 142-152, 198.

HEREDITY: THE BONDS OF RACE

On racial ideas in the eighteenth century, see David B. Davis, *The Problem of Slavery in Western Culture* (Ithaca: Cornell University Press, 1966), pp. 178-182, 404, 426-427, 440, 452-459; William Stanton, *The Leopard's Spots: Scientific Attitudes toward Race in America* (Chicago: University of Chicago Press, 1966), pp. 15-19; Eric Voegelin, "The Growth of the Race Idea," *JP*, II (1940), pp. 301-302; J. C. Greene, "The American Debate on the Negro's Place in Nature," *JHI*, XV (1954), pp. 384-396; and Oscar Handlin, *Race and Nationality in American Life* (New York: Doubleday, 1957), pp. 13-17, 32-34.

For traditional resistance to slavery and racism, see Samuel Willard, *A Compleat Body of Divinity* (Boston: B. Eliot and D. Henchman, 1726), pp. 613-616, 646, and *The Journal and Essays of John Woolman*, ed. A. H. Gummere (New York: Macmillan, 1922).

ENVIRONMENT: THE BROTHERHOOD OF PLACE

On "natural man" and the ambivalence of Enlightenment theorists in relation to man in the "state of nature," see Geoffrey Clive, *The Romantic Enlightenment* (New York: Meridian, 1960), pp. 19-38; S. I. Bredvolt, *The Brave New World of the Enlightenment* (Ann Arbor: University of Michigan Press, 1961); H. M. Fairchild, *The Noble Savage* (New York: Columbia University Press, 1928); and Paul Wallace, *Indians in Pennsylvania*.

THE BROTHERHOOD OF MAN

Samuel L. Mintz, *The Hunting of Leviathan* (Cambridge: Cambridge University Press, 1962), describes the origin of the theory of "moral sentiments," aimed at refuting Hobbes. Whether in its original form or in terms of the idea of "moral intuition," the theory had great currency in the eighteenth century and through partisans like Adam Smith or Richard Price was a major part of political discourse in the English-speaking world. See Alfred Cobban, *In Search of Humanity* (New York: Braziller, 1960), pp. 86–89. For a contemporary criticism of the theory, see Adam Ferguson, *Principles of Moral and Political Science* (London: Strahan and Cadell, and Edinburgh: Creech, 1792), vol. I, pp. 159–161, vol. II, pp. 120–127; see also vol. II, p. 143, for Ferguson's own partial compromise with the doctrine.

In general, see E. Tuveson, *Milennium and Utopia: A Study in the Background of the Idea of Progress* (Berkeley and Los Angeles: University of California Press, 1949); Curti, *Growth of American Thought*, pp. 120–122, 161, and *Roots of American Loyalty*, pp. 80–91; H. Morais, *Deism in 18th Century America* (New York: Columbia University Press, 1934); and David G. Smith, *The Convention and the Constitution* (New York: St. Martin's, 1965), pp. 143–145, 154–162, 177, 188, 207. An excellent essay on Franklin and his influence is L. B. Wright, "Franklin's Legacy to the Gilded Age," *VQ*, XXII (1946), pp. 268–277.

POLITICS AS MECHANICS

For this and the succeeding section, useful secondary sources include Smith, *The Convention and the Constitution*, pp. 4–55, 58, 62–64, 75–76, 79, 91; Martin Diamond, "Democracy and the Federalist," *APSR*, LIII (1959), pp. 52–68; Ralph Ketcham, "James Madison and T. V. Smith: A Study in the Politics of Privacy," *AR*, XX (1960), pp. 261–281 (especially useful in noting the concern of both for "fraternity"); M. Smith, "Reason, Passion and Political Freedom in The Federalist," *JP*, XXII (1960), pp. 525–544; Adrienne Koch, "Hamilton, Adams and the Pursuit of Power," *RP*, XVI (1954), pp. 6off.; and Cecilia Kenyon, "Men of Little Faith," *WMQ*, XII (1955), pp. 3–46, and "An Economic Interpretation of the Constitution After Fifty Years," *CR*, VII (1963), pp. 327–352. Useful comments on the Constitution in relation to contemporary issues include E. E. Schattschneider, *Party Government* (New York: Rinehart, 1942), pp. 4–13, and T. Payne, "The Effect of Federalism on Interest Groups," *WPQ*, XIII (1960), Supplement, pp. 78–79.

JAMES WILSON: THE MORAL INSTINCT

There are few general studies of Wilson as a political thinker. However, see C. P. Smith, *James Wilson: Founding Father* (Chapel Hill: University of North Carolina Press, 1956), and A. C. McLaughlin, "James Wilson and the Philadelphia Convention," *PSQ*, XII (1897), pp. 1–20, as well as more general intellectual histories of the period.

CHAPTER IX

GENERAL

The works cited in the bibliography for Chapter Eight are useful. See also Henry Adams, *History of the United States during the Administrations of Thomas Jefferson and James Madison* (New York: Scribner's, 1889–1891); William N. Chambers, *Political Parties in a New Nation: the American Experience, 1776–1809* (New York: Oxford University Press, 1963); Charles A. Beard, *The Economic Origins of Jeffersonian Democracy* (New York: Macmillan, 1915); Daniel Boorstin, *The Lost World of Thomas Jefferson* (Boston: Beacon, 1960); James Woodress, *A Yankee's Odyssey: the Life of Joel Barlow* (Philadelphia and New York: Lippincott, 1958); and C. H. Wiltse, *The Jeffersonian Tradition in American Democracy* (Chapel Hill: University of North Carolina Press, 1935).

"LIMITED TO A NARROW SPACE . . ."

For elements of commonness in the American experience, see Richard L. Merritt, *Symbols of American Community, 1773–1775* (New Haven: Yale University Press, 1966); the parochiality of American life is emphasized by D. C. North, *The Economic Growth of the United States* (New York: Norton, 1966), p. 35. Elements of political and social change are indicated in Curti, *Growth of American Thought* (see also bibliography for Awakenings and Architects, below).

Pre-revolutionary divisions in American political culture, and their continuity, are indicated by John C. Miller, *The Origins of the American Revolution* (Boston: Little, Brown, 1943); J. F. Jameson, *The American Revolution Considered as a Social Movement* (Boston: Beacon, 1956); Smith, *The Convention and the Constitution*, pp. 35–43; and especially Jack P. Greene, *The Quest for Power* (Chapel Hill: University of North Carolina Press, 1963).

Popular culture is described in Wright, *Cultural Life in the American Colonies*; Curti, *Growth of American Thought*, pp. 36–37, 113, 266–267; Norman Jacobson, "Class and Ideology in the American Revolution," in *Class, Status and Power*, ed. Reinhard Bendix and S. M. Lipset (Glencoe: Free Press, 1956), pp. 547–554; Alice Baldwin, *The American Clergy and the American Revolution* (Durham: Duke University Press, 1928); Michael Kammen, *Deputyes and Libertyes: the Origins of Representative Government in Colonial America* (New York: Knopf, 1969); and J. R. Poole, "Historians and the Problem of Early American Democracy," *AHR*, LXVII (1962), pp. 626–646. A traditional view which is still intriguing is C. H. McIlwain, *The American Revolution: A Constitutional Interpretation* (New York: Macmillan, 1923).

Anti-Federalist ideas may be found in *The Anti-Federalists*, ed. Cecilia Kenyon (Indianapolis, Kansas City, and New York: Bobbs-

Merrill, 1966), pp. xxvii–xlii, xlv–xlviii, li–liii, 6, 7, 39, 91, 133, 135, 151, 154, 251, 308–310, and *Federalists vs. Anti-Federalists*, ed. John D. Lewis (San Francisco: Chandler, 1967), pp. 2, 13–15, 20–21, 28, 59–62.

AWAKENINGS AND ARCHITECTS

On the Great Awakening, see Perry Miller, *Nature's Nation*, pp. 78–89; Wright, *Cultural Life*, pp. 98–125; C. H. Maxson, *The Great Awakening in the Middle Colonies* (Chicago: University of Chicago Press, 1920); and W. M. Gewehr, *The Great Awakening in Virginia* (Durham: Duke University Press, 1930).

On Thomas Cooper and the political ideas of evangelists generally, see C. C. Cole, *Social Ideas of the Evangelists* (New York: Columbia University Press, 1954), pp. 166, 181, 186–189, and D. Malone, *The Public Life of Thomas Cooper* (New Haven: Yale University Press, 1926). Friendly societies are described in W. Dawson, "Friendly Societies," *ESS*, III (1931), pp. 494–498; urban social change is noted in Foster R. Dulles, *Labor in America* (New York: Crowell, 1960), pp. 20–31, and Mary Beard, *A Short History of American Labor* (New York: Harcourt, Brace, 1920), pp. 3–28.

On Masonry and the Cincinnati, see Curti, *Growth of American Thought*, pp. 48, 110–113, 159–161, 199–200; Morais, *Deism in 18th Century America*, pp. 14, 20, 27, 28, 72, 130–133; Vernon Stauffer, *New England and the Bavarian Illuminati* (New York: Columbia University Press, 1918); and E. E. Hume, "The Role of the Society of the Cincinnati in the Birth of the Constitution of the United States," *Pennsylvania History*, V (1938), pp. 101–107.

"WE ARE ALL REPUBLICANS . . ."

On the embryonic growth of political parties, see Chambers, *Political Parties*; Carl L. Becker, *The History of Political Parties in the Province of New York, 1760–1776* (Madison: University of Wisconsin Press, 1960); N. E. Cunningham, *The Jeffersonian Republicans: the Formation of Party Organization, 1789–1801* (Chapel Hill: University of North Carolina Press, 1957), and "John Beckley: An Early American Party Manager," *WMQ*, XIII (1956), pp. 40–52; W. A. Robinson, *Jeffersonian Democracy in New England* (New Haven: Yale University Press, 1916); Claude Bowers, *Jefferson and Hamilton* (Boston and New York: Houghton Mifflin, 1944), pp. 145–151, 223–224, 261–264; and C. S. Snydor, "The One-Party Period of American History," *AHR*, LI (1946), pp. 439–451.

JEFFERSON: "THE GREAT PRINCIPLES . . ."

Useful secondary sources on Jefferson include M. D. Peterson, *The Jefferson Image in the American Mind* (New York: Oxford, 1962); Gilbert Chinard, *Thomas Jefferson: Apostle of Americanism* (Boston: Little, Brown, 1929); Adrienne Koch, "Power, Morals and the Founding Fathers:

Jefferson," *RP*, XV (1953), pp. 470–490; Charles E. Merriam, "The Political Theory of Thomas Jefferson," *PSQ*, XVII (1902), pp. 24–45; and Claude Bowers, *Jefferson and Hamilton* and *Jefferson in Power* (Boston: Houghton Mifflin, 1936).

CHAPTER X

GENERAL

An extremely valuable history of the period is Roy Nichols, *The Disruption of American Democracy* (New York: Macmillan, 1948); a more traditional picture, which makes a useful contrast to Nichols' analysis, is Carl R. Fish, *The Rise of the Common Man, 1830–1850* (New York: Macmillan, 1933). Also valuable are Perry Miller, *The Life of the Mind in America* (New York: Harcourt, Brace and World, 1965)—as usual, Miller is nonpareil; Arthur Schlesinger, Jr., *The Age of Jackson* (Boston: Little, Brown, 1946); Alan Nevins, *The Emergence of Lincoln* (New York: Scribner's, 1950); and Hans Trefousse, *The Radical Republicans* (New York: Knopf, 1969). Woodrow Wilson's *Division and Reunion* (New York: Longmans, Green, 1893) continues to be useful on many counts.

EXCELSIOR

On economic and social change during the period, see George R. Taylor, *The Transportation Revolution, 1815–1860* (New York: Holt, Rinehart and Winston, 1951); Richard C. Wade, *The Urban Frontier: the Rise of Western Cities, 1790–1830* (Cambridge: Harvard University Press, 1959); D. C. North, *The Economic Growth of the United States*, esp. pp. 143, 193; Curti, *Growth of American Thought*, pp. 344–367; A. M. Simons, *Social Forces in American History* (New York; Macmillan, 1913), pp. 191–215; and *Farmers in a Changing World* (Washington: U.S. Dept. of Agriculture, 1940), pp. 116–123, 213–221.

On change in New England specifically, a valuable essay is T. D. S. Bassett, "A Case Study of Urban Impact on Rural Society: Vermont, 1840–1880," *Agricultural History*, XXX (1956), pp. 28–34; see also H. Harris, *American Labor* (New Haven: Yale University Press, 1945), pp. 307–313; A. B. Hart, *The Formation of the Union* (New York: Longmans, Green, 1901), p. 261; and Van Wyck Brooks, *The Flowering of New England* (New York: Dutton, 1952), pp. 179, 348, 416, 497, 522, 539–542. The problems of Western cities may be seen in Wade, *The Urban Frontier*, pp. 28–30, 73–77, 80–82.

ROMANCE AND TRANSCENDENCE

On intellectuals in America, see De Tocqueville, *Democracy in America*, vol. II, pp. 65–72; Brooks, *Flowering of New England*, pp. 1–12, 16, 40–42, 82, 110, 116, 164, 168, 188–190, 197–198, 206, 253, 291, 389; Edith R. Curtis, *A Season in Utopia* (New York: Nelson, 1961), pp. 21–22, 94–95;

and Octavius B. Frothingham, *Transcendentalism in New England* (New York: Harper, 1959), pp. 101–145.

On romanticism, see George Boas, *Romanticism in America* (Baltimore: Johns Hopkins University Press, 1940); Brooks, *Flowering of New England*, pp. 48, 185–191, 418–422, 480–489; and Leslie Fiedler, *Love and Death in the American Novel* (New York: Criterion, 1960). James Fenimore Cooper's ideas are discussed most ably in Marvin Meyers, *The Jacksonian Persuasion; Politics and Belief* (New York: Vintage, 1960), pp. 57–100; see also D. H. Lawrence, *Studies in Classical American Literature* (New York: Doubleday, 1951), pp. 43–72, and R. E. Spiller, *James Fenimore Cooper: Critic of His Times* (New York: Balch, 1931).

On transcendentalism, see Frothingham, *Transcendentalism*, pp. 147–150, 157, 291–299; Brooks, *Flowering of New England*, pp. 64–73, 97, 102, 180–184, 465, 475–476, 497; Curtis, *Season in Utopia*, pp. 91–92, 129; George Santayana, *Character and Opinion in the United States* (New York: Braziller, 1955), pp. 12–14; and C. Griffin, *Their Brothers' Keepers* (New Brunswick: Rutgers University Press, 1960), pp. 198–214.

"BROTHERS WILL YOU MEET ME . . . ?"

On religion and political culture, see Ralph H. Gabriel, *The Course of American Democratic Thought* (New York: Ronald, 1940), pp. 26–38; Curti, *Growth of American Thought*, pp. 307–311, 372, 376–378; Miller, *Life of the Mind*, pp. 40–43, 49–58, 69; Clara Sears, *Days of Delusion* (Boston: Houghton Mifflin, 1924); Ralph Fletcher, *A History of Oberlin College* (Oberlin: Oberlin College, 1943); and T. I. Smith, *Revivalism and Social Reform in 19th Century America* (Nashville and New York: Abingdon, 1957).

On Mormonism, see Bernard de Voto, *1846: Year of Decision* (Boston: Houghton Mifflin, 1943), pp. 81–84, 466–469; Richard T. Ely, "Economic Aspects of Mormonism," *Harper's*, CVI (1903), pp. 667–678; and G. H. Durham, "A Political Interpretation of Mormon History," *Pacific Historical Review*, XIII (1944), pp. 139–140.

On utopians, see Charles Madison, *Critics and Crusaders* (New York: Holt, 1947), pp. 85–132; Curtis, *A Season in Utopia, passim.*; Brooks, *Flowering of New England*, pp. 251–260; and Frothingham, *Transcendentalism*, pp. 160, 167–168, 174–180, 328–334. Noyes' ideas are best approached through his own *History of American Socialisms* (New York: Hilary House, 1961), esp. pp. 27, 48–55.

OLD ROMANS, NEW LIBERALS

On the bases of the Jacksonian movement, see Richard P. McCormick, *The Second American Party System* (Chapel Hill: University of North Carolina Press, 1966), pp. 14, 15, 30, 104–124, 134–147, 178–198, 222–236, 258–270; Harry Stevens, *The Early Jackson Party in Ohio* (Durham: Duke University Press, 1957); Wade, *The Urban Frontier*, pp. 112–120,

129–134, 174, 176, 203–205, 211–212, 217; Henry Adams, *History of the United States*, vol. IX, pp. 175–242; Wilson, *Division and Reunion*, pp. 18–21, 25, 32–34, 37–38, 211–212; and Joseph Dorfman, "The Jacksonian Wage Earner Thesis," *AHR*, LIV (1949), pp. 296–306.

Among useful biographies of Jackson are Marquis James, *Andrew Jackson: Border Captain* (New York: Grosset and Dunlap, 1933) and *Andrew Jackson: Portrait of a President* (New York: Grosset and Dunlap, 1937). Still valuable is James Parton, *Life of Andrew Jackson* (Boston: Houghton Mifflin, 1888).

On Jacksonian doctrine, see Meyers, *Jacksonian Persuasion*, esp. pp. 101–162; *Social Theories of Jacksonian Democracy*, ed. Joseph L. Blau (New York: Hafner, 1947); Robert V. Remini, *Andrew Jackson* (New York: Twayne, 1966); Bray Hammond, *Banks and Politics in America* (Princeton: Princeton University Press, 1957); James, *Border Captain*, pp. 93–94, 123, 130, 332, 334, 357, and *Portrait of a President*, pp. 21, 78–79, 145, 220, 313, 395, 415, 424, 440–442; and Thomas P. Abernathy, *From Frontier to Plantation in Tennessee: A Study of Frontier Democracy* (Memphis: Memphis State College Press, 1955). On Brownson, see Gabriel, *Course of American Democratic Thought*, pp. 52–66; Schlesinger, *Age of Jackson* pp. 299–304, 380–382, 400–408, 417–421, 495, 502; and G. C. Hellis, "Brownson on George Bancroft," *SAQ*, LX (1950), pp. 42–52.

On Bancroft, see Russell B. Nye, *George Bancroft* (New York: Washington Square Press, 1964), and David Levin, *History as Romantic Art: Bancroft, Prescott and Parkman* (Stanford: Stanford University Press, 1959), as well as Bancroft's own *History of the United States* (New York: Appleton, 1883–1885); *History of the Formation of the Constitution of the United States* (New York: Appleton, 1882); "The Place of Abraham Lincoln in History," *AM*, XV (1866), pp. 757–770; and *Literary and Historical Miscellanies* (New York: Harper, 1855).

CRIES OF RACE AND CLAN

On Anti-Masonry, see Lee Benson, *The Concept of Jacksonian Democracy: New York as a Test Case* (Princeton: Princeton University Press, 1961); Gustavus Myers, *A History of Bigotry in the United States* (New York: Capricorn, 1960), pp. 73–83; Oliver Wendell Holmes, *The Professor at the Breakfast Table* (Boston: Houghton Mifflin, 1891), pp. 372–376, and *The Poet at the Breakfast Table* (Boston: Houghton Mifflin, 1891), pp. 321–325; McCormick, *The Second American Party System*, pp. 47–49, 75, 84; R. N. Current, *Old Thad Stevens* (Madison: University of Wisconsin Press, 1942), pp. 34, 40–43, 51; and Frederick Rudolph, *The American College and University* (New York: Knopf, 1962), pp. 144–150.

Anti-foreignism is described in R. A. Billington, *The Protestant Crusade: A Study in the Origins of American Nativism* (New York:

Macmillan, 1938), and Myers, *A History of Bigotry*, pp. 84–130, 133, 143–154; see also Griffin, *Their Brothers' Keepers*, pp. 214–218, and W. J. Bromwell, *History of Immigration to The United States* (New York: Redfield, 1856).

George Perkins Marsh and the Gothic origins theory are discussed in David Lowenthal, *George Perkins Marsh: Versatile Vermonter* (New York: Columbia University Press, 1958), and Samuel Klieger, "George Marsh and the Gothic Tradition in New England," *NEQ*, XIX (1946), pp. 524–531. See also Marsh's later essay, "The Catholic Church and Modern Civilization," *Nation*, V (1867), pp. 229–231.

Various aspects of the new fascination with the Indian and related phenomena are observed in D. C. Allen, *The Legend of Noah* (Urbana: University of Illinois Press, 1949), pp. 113–149; see also Bernard de Voto, *1846*, pp. 81–84.

On scientific racism, see Stanton, *The Leopard's Spots*, pp. 25–36, 40–41, 52–53, 61–70, 77, 80, 112, 154, 177–179, 189–191.

WHITE HOPES, DARK PRESENCES

On society and change in the South, see W. J. Cash, *The Mind of the South* (New York: Doubleday, 1954), pp. 22–27, 34–39, 44–49, 53, 77–78; Wright, *Cultural Life*, pp. 19–22; Schlesinger, *Age of Jackson*, pp. 22–23, 242–250; Clement Eaton, *The Growth of Southern Civilization, 1790–1860* (New York: Harper, 1860); Jesse Carpenter, *The South as a Conscious Minority* (New York: N.Y.U. Press, 1930); C. G. Sellers, "Who Were The Southern Whigs?" *AHR*, LIX (1954), pp. 335–342; and W. B. Hesseltine, "Some New Aspects of Pro-Slavery Arguments," *JNH*, XXI (1936), pp. 1–14.

The role of non-slave-holding whites in Southern politics may be seen in Cash, *Mind of the South*, pp. 28–33, 39–41, 72, 86; F. L. and H. C. Owsley, "The Economic Basis of Society in the Ante-Bellum South," *JSH*, VI (1940), pp. 24–45; Hinton R. Helper, *The Impending Crisis, Antebellum*, ed. Harvey Wish (New York: Putnam, 1860), pp. 157–255. Kenneth Stampp, *And the War Came* (Chicago: University of Chicago Press, 1965) is excellent, but may underestimate underlying Unionist sympathies; the fact that Confederate elites felt a need to throw the blame for "striking first" on the North—which may have cost them the war —is illustrative (Stampp, p. 134). On the general crisis, Walter Webb, in *The Great Plains* (New York: Grosset and Dunlap, n.d.), writes that after the annexation of Texas, "the whole chapter was closed. But the South could not admit that this was true" (p. 192).

On white unity, see Stampp, *And the War Came*, pp. 2, 5, 50; Cash, *Mind of the South*, pp. 46, 53–54, 73–79, 82–90; Carpenter, *The South as a Conscious Minority*, pp. 17–21; North, *Economic Growth of the United States*, pp. 69–71, 122, 252; W. S. Jenkins, *Pro-Slavery Thought in the Old South* (Chapel Hill: University of North Carolina Press,

1935), pp. 192, 286; and Clement Eaton, *Freedom of Thought in the Old South* (Durham: Duke University Press, 1940).

On various Southern ideologies, see especially Louis Hartz, *The Liberal Tradition*, pp. 145–201; John Taylor, *Inquiry into the Principles and Policy of the Government of the United States* (New Haven: Yale University Press, 1950); Cash, *Mind of the South*, pp. 66–73, 91–100; Eaton, *Freedom of Thought*; Elizabeth Merritt, *James Henry Hammond* (Baltimore: Johns Hopkins University Press, 1923); and *Cotton Is King*, ed. E. Elliott (Augusta: Pritchard, Abbott and Loomis, 1860).

On race and glory in Southern psychology, see Cash, *Mind of the South*, pp. 56, 63–67, 78, 86, 94–97, 141–143; Gilbert Stephenson, *Race Distinctions in American Law* (New York: Appleton, 1910), pp. 36ff.; and David Davis, *The Problem of Slavery*, pp. 277–279. For a contemporary comment, see *Life and Correspondence of John A. Quitman*, ed. J. Claiborne (New York: Harper, 1861), vol. II, p. 110.

BATTLECRIES OF FREEDOM

On working-class movements generally, see Harris, *American Labor*, pp. 17, 30–39, 48; John R. Commons, *History of Labor in the United States* (New York: Macmillan, 1918), vol. I, pp. 4–8, 388–389; Gerald N. Grob, *Workers and Utopia* (Evanston: Northwestern University Press, 1961); N. Ware, *The Industrial Workers, 1840–1860* (Boston: Houghton Mifflin, 1924); W. A. Sullivan, "Did Labor Support Jackson?" *PSQ*, LXII (1947), pp. 569–580; and Edward Pessen, "The Workingmen's Movement of the Jacksonian Era," *MVHR*, XLIII (1956), pp. 428–443. On Evans, see Harris, *American Labor*, pp. 43–55; F. T. Carlton, *Organized Labor in American History* (New York: Appleton, 1920), pp. 78–107, and Benjamin H. Hibbard, *A History of Public Land Policies* (New York: Macmillan, 1924).

The best single work on anti-slavery thought is *The Anti-Slavery Vanguard*, ed. Martin Duberman (Princeton: Princeton University Press, 1965). See also Gilbert Barnes, *The Antislavery Impulse* (New York: Appleton, 1933); B. P. Thomas, *Theodore Dwight Weld* (New Brunswick: Rutgers University Press, 1950); C. C. Cole, *Social Ideas of the Northern Evangelists* (New York: Columbia University Press, 1954); Betty Fladeland, *James G. Birney: Slaveholder to Abolitionist* (Ithaca: Cornell University Press, 1955); and Griffin, *Their Brothers' Keepers*, pp. 162, 177–197.

Zeal for the Civil War and its manifestation among pacifists may be seen in Edmund Wilson, *Patriotic Gore* (New York: Oxford University Press, 1962); Fletcher, *History of Oberlin College*, vol. II, pp. 87–88, 843–885; Griffin, *Their Brothers' Keepers*, pp. 242–264; and Merle Curti, *The American Peace Crusade, 1815–1860* (Durham: Duke University Press, 1929).

CHAPTER XI

GENERAL

There are excellent critical comments on Emerson in George Santayana, *The Interpretation of Poetry and Religion* (New York: Scribner's, 1900). Other valuable sources on Emerson's work include Daniel Aaron, *Men of Good Hope* (New York: Oxford University Press, 1951), pp. 3–20; Sherman Paul, *Emerson's Angle of Vision* (Cambridge: Harvard University Press, 1952); Perry Miller, "Jonathan Edwards to Emerson," *Errand into the Wilderness*, pp. 184–203, and "The Emersonian Genius and American Democracy," *NEQ*, XXVI (1953), pp. 27–44; Paul Elmer More, "Emerson," *CHAL*, I, pp. 354–361; Saul K. Padover, "Emerson: the Moral Voice in Politics," *PSQ*, LXXIV (1959), pp. 334–350; Stuart Sherman, *Americans* (New York: Scribner's, 1923), esp. pp. 136–137; Frothingham, *Transcendentalism*, pp. 142–143, 150–157, 221–230, 237, 239, 363–380; and A. C. Kern, "Emerson and Economics," *NEQ*, XIII (1940), pp. 678–696.

On both Emerson and Thoreau, see Brooks, *The Flowering of New England*, and Edmund Wilson, *The Shock of Recognition* (New York: Farrar, Strauss and Cudahy, 1955). On Thoreau, see *Thoreau*, ed. Sherman Paul (Englewood Cliffs: Prentice-Hall, 1962), esp. pp. 142–160; Paul, *Emerson's Angle of Vision*, pp. 100–116; R. W. B. Lewis, *The American Adam* (Chicago: University of Chicago Press, 1955); Lewis Mumford, *The Golden Day* (New York: Liveright, 1926); Leo Staller, "Thoreau's Doctrine of Simplicity," *NEQ*, XXIX (1946), pp. 443–461; Richard Groff, *Thoreau and the Prophetic Tradition* (Los Angeles: Manas, 1961); Max Lerner, "Thoreau: No Hermit," *Ideas Are Weapons* (New York: Viking, 1939), pp. 45–47; Heinz Eulau, "Wayside Challenger: Some Remarks on the Politics of Henry David Thoreau," *AR*, IX (1950), pp. 509–522; and S. E. Hyman, "Henry Thoreau in Our Time," *AM*, CLXXVIII (1946), pp. 137–146.

CHAPTER XII

GENERAL

Critical studies of Hawthorne and his work on which I have relied include Mark van Doren, *Nathaniel Hawthorne: A Critical Biography* (New York: Viking, 1957); Brooks, *The Flowering of New England*; Fiedler, *Love and Death in the American Novel*; Irving Howe, *Politics and the Novel* (New York: Horizon, 1957); and E. H. Davidson, *Hawthorne's Last Phase* (New Haven: Yale University Press, 1949).

Among more specialized studies, see, for Hawthorne's relation to religion and religious sources, Joseph Schwartz, "Three Aspects of Hawthorne's Puritanism," *NEQ*, XXXVI (1963), pp. 192–208; W. R. Thompson, "The Biblical Sources of Hawthorne's Roger Malvin,"

PMLA, LXXVII (1962), pp. 192–196; and R. Stanton, "Hawthorne, Bunyan and the American Romances," *PMLA*, LXXI (1956), pp. 155–165.

On Hawthorne's idea of sin, see J. E. Miller, "Hawthorne and Melville: the Unpardonable Sin," *PMLA*, LXX (1955), pp. 91–114. His general view of human nature is discussed in J. Mathews, "Hawthorne and the Chain of Being," *MLQ*, XVII (1957), pp. 283–294, and H. G. Fairbank, "Man's Separation from Nature: Hawthorne's Philosophy of Suffering and Death," *Christian Scholar*, XLII (1959), pp. 51–65.

For Hawthorne's ideas about science and technology, see Leo Marx, "The Machine in the Garden," *NEQ*, XXVII (1946), pp. 27–42; E. H. Rosenberry, "Hawthorne's Allegory of Science: Rappacini's Daughter," *AL*, XXXII (1960), pp. 39–46; and H. G. Fairbank, "Hawthorne and the Machine Age," *AL*, XXVIII (1956), pp. 155–163.

Hawthorne's political views are discussed in S. L. Gross, "Hawthorne and the Shakers," *AL*, XXIX (1958), pp. 457–463; M. Hawthorne, "Hawthorne and Utopian Socialism," *NEQ*, XII (1939), pp. 726–730; Alex Gottfried and Sue Davidson, "Utopia's Children: An Interpretation of Three Political Novels," *WPQ*, XVI (1962), p. 21; Arlin Turner, "Hawthorne and Reform," *NEQ*, XV (1942), pp. 700–714; and M. Fisher, "The Pattern of Conservatism in Johnson's Rasselas and Hawthorne's Tales," *JHI*, XIX (1958), pp. 173–196.

Nationalism and patriotism in Hawthorne's work are illustrated in Randall Stewart, "Hawthorne in England: the Patriotic Motive," *NEQ*, VIII (1935), pp. 3–13, and N. Doubleday, "Hawthorne and Literary Nationalism," *AL*, XII (1941), pp. 447–453.

Other critical works are also cited in the notes. Unless otherwise indicated, all citations from Hawthorne are from *Hawthorne's Works* (Boston: Houghton Mifflin, 1880).

CHAPTER XIII

GENERAL

Critical literature which I have found useful includes D. H. Lawrence, *Studies in Classical American Literature*, pp. 142–156; R. H. Gabriel, *The Course of American Democratic Thought*, pp. 67–77; Parrington, *Main Currents in American Thought*, vol. II, pp. 249ff., Richard Chase, *Herman Melville* (New York: Macmillan, 1949); Lewis Mumford, *Herman Melville* (New York: Harcourt Brace, 1929); Leslie Fiedler, *Love and Death in the American Novel*; Jean Mayoux, *Melville* (New York: Grove, 1960); *Herman Melville*, ed. Newton Arvin (New York: Viking, 1957); Nathalia Wright, *Melville's Use of the Bible* (Durham: Duke University Press, 1949); Merlin Bowen, *The Long Encounter* (Chicago: University of Chicago Press, 1960); A. R. Humphreys, *Herman Melville* (New York: Grove, 1962); Milton R. Stern, *The Fine Hammered Steel of Her-*

man Melville (Urbana: University of Illinois Press, 1957); C. H. Holman, "The Reconciliation of Ishmael: Moby Dick and the Book of Job," *SAQ*, LVII (1958), pp. 447–490; and H. B. Franklin, "Apparent Symbolism of Despotic Command: Melville's Benito Cereno," *NEQ*, XXXIV (1961), pp. 462–477.

Other critical works are also cited in the notes. Unless otherwise indicated, citations from Melville's own work are taken from the Standard Edition (London: Constable, 1922–1924). On Melville's life and its relation to his work, see Charles Olson, *Call Me Ishmael* (New York: Grove, 1958), and E. M. Metcalf, *Herman Melville: Cycle and Epicycle* (Cambridge: Harvard University Press, 1953). The image of fatherless men occurs, for example, in *Redburn* as well as other works; Redburn is called a "sort of Ishmael" (*Redburn*, p. 181). Man's paternity, Melville wrote, is secret. See *Moby Dick: Centennial Essays*, ed. T. Hillway and L. S. Mansfield (Dallas: S.M.U. Press, 1953), p. 66.

CHAPTER XIV

GENERAL

Works generally consulted for this chapter include Matthew Josephson, *The Robber Barons* (New York: Harcourt, Brace, 1934) and *The Politicos* (New York: Harcourt, Brace, 1938); R. H. Gabriel, *The Course of American Democratic Thought*, pp. 132–289; C. Vann Woodward, *Reunion and Reaction* (New York: Doubleday, 1956) and *The Origins of the New South* (Baton Rouge: Louisiana State University Press, 1951); Vernon Louis Parrington, *The Beginnings of Critical Realism* (New York: Harcourt, Brace, 1958); Ray Ginger, *Altgeld's America* (New York: Funk and Wagnalls, 1958); James Bryce, *The American Commonwealth* (New York: Macmillan, 1913); Merle Curti, *Roots of American Loyalty*, pp. 173–199; Arthur Schlesinger, *The Rise of the Cities* (New York: Macmillan, 1933); and Alan Nevins, *The Evolution of Modern America* (New York: Macmillan, 1927).

"TENTING TONIGHT . . ."

On the Reconstruction and ideas relating to it, see Eric McKitrick, *Andrew Johnson and the Reconstruction* (Chicago: University of Chicago Press, 1964); W. E. B. du Bois, *Black Reconstruction in America, 1860–1880* (Cleveland: World, 1965); H. J. Graham, "The Conspiracy Theory of the 14th Amendment," *Yale Law Journal*, XLVII (1938), p. 371, and XLVIII (1939), pp. 171ff.; and Jacobus Ten Broek, *The Anti-Slavery Origins of the 14th Amendment* (Berkeley and Los Angeles: University of California Press, 1951).

Descriptions of the politics of the period include Gabriel, *Course of American Democratic Thought*, pp. 132–140; Josephson, *The Politicos*; William Allen White, *Masks in a Pageant* (New York: Macmillan, 1928);

J. T. Salter, *Boss Rule* (New York: McGraw-Hill, 1935); N. W. Stephenson, *Nelson W. Aldrich* (New York: Scribner, 1930); Thomas Beer, *Hanna* (New York: Knopf, 1929); R. M. McElroy, *Grover Cleveland: the Man and the Statesman* (New York: Harper, 1923); and V. de Sanctis, "American Politics in the Gilded Age," *RP*, XXV (1963), pp. 551–561.

"THE BITCH-GODDESS . . ."

On social change, see Schlesinger, *The Rise of the Cities*; Van Wyck Brooks, *New England's Indian Summer* (New York: Dutton, 1940); Fred Cottrell, *Energy and Society* (New York: McGraw-Hill, 1955); L. S. Rowe, "The Political Consequences of Urban Growth," *YR*, IX (1900), pp. 20–32; and A. F. Sanborn, "The Future of Rural New England," *AM*, LXXX (1897), pp. 74–83.

The rise of the lodges is treated in Noel P. Gist, *Secret Societies* (Columbia: University of Missouri Press, 1940); C. M. Harger, "The Lodge," *AM*, XCVII (1906), pp. 488–494; and W. B. Hill, "The Great American Safety Valve," *Century*, XLIV (1892), pp. 383–384. (For an essay expressing traditional fears of secret societies, see J. M. Foster, "Secret Societies and the State," *Arena*, XIX (1898), pp. 229–239.)

New economic ethics are described in Robert G. McCloskey, *American Conservatism in the Age of Enterprise* (Cambridge: Harvard University Press, 1951); Gabriel, *The Course of American Democratic Thought*, pp. 143–172; and Andrew Carnegie, *The Gospel of Wealth* (New York: Doubleday, 1933).

For Social Darwinism, see *Evolutionary Thought in America*, ed. Stow Persons (New York: Braziller, 1956), and Richard Hofstadter, *Social Darwinism in American Thought* (Boston: Beacon, 1955). The ideology of scientific management and related notions are discussed in Dwight Waldo, *The Administrative State* (New York: Ronald, 1946), pp. 51–59; Frederick T. Martin, *The Passing of the Idle Rich* (New York: Doubleday, 1911); and F. A. Walker, "Democracy and Wealth," *Forum*, X (1890), pp. 251–254.

Utopian aspects of thought, especially in relation to fraternity, may be seen in Elihu Root, "Human Brotherhood and the World Order," *JAH*, IV (1910), p. 156; R. L. Sherter, "The Utopian Novel in America," *SAQ*, XXXIV (1935), pp. 137–174; A. Forbes, "The Literary Quest for Utopia, 1880–1900," *SF*, VI (1927), pp. 179–189; and C. L. Sanford, *The Quest for Paradise* (Urbana: University of Illinois Press, 1961).

PROGRESS AND POVERTY

The best work on the churches in the industrial era is H. F. May, *The Protestant Churches and Industrial America* (New York: Harper, 1949). See also Herbert W. Schneider, "Evolution and Theology in America,"

JHI, VI (1945), pp. 3–18; R. Albright, *Focus on Infinity: A Life of Phillips Brooks* (New York: Macmillan, 1961); and Henry Drummond, *The Ascent of Man* (New York: Pott, 1894). For an example of the connections between religious anxieties and nativism, see H. D. Sedgwick, "The United States and Rome," *AM*, LXXXIV (1899), pp. 445–458.

On Henry George, see George R. Geiger, *The Philosophy of Henry George* (New York: Macmillan, 1933) and Henry George, Jr., *The Life of Henry George* (New York: Doubleday and McClure, 1900).

PROTEST AND PORTENT

On agrarian discontent and the nature of Western society, see Solon J. Buck, *The Granger Movement* (Cambridge: Harvard University Press, 1913) and *The Agrarian Crusade* (New Haven: Yale University Press, 1920); Howard Lamar, *Dakota Territory* (New Haven: Yale University Press, 1957); Grant McConnell, *The Decline of Agrarian Democracy* (Berkeley and Los Angeles: University of California Press, 1953), pp. 3–18; E. V. Smalley, "The Isolation of Life on Prairie Farms," *AM*, LXXII (1893), pp. 378–382; and Fred Shannon, "The Status of the Middle Western Farmer in 1900," *MVHR*, XXXVII (1950), p. 506.

Contemporary ideological statements include William Peffer, "The Farmers' Defensive Movement," *Forum*, VIII (1889), pp. 464–473; Washington Gladden, "The Embattled Farmer," *Forum*, X (1890), pp. 315–322; and Hamlin Garland, "The West in Literature," *Arena*, VI (1892), pp. 669–676. A recent study of Donnelly is Sidney Warren's "Ignatius Donnelly and the Populists," *Current History*, XXVIII (1955), pp. 336–342.

On industrial workers, see N. Ware, *The Labor Movement in the United States, 1860–1895* (New York: Appleton, 1929); M. Karson, *Labor Unions and Politics* (Carbondale: Southern Illinois University Press, 1958), pp. 284–300; and R. V. Bruce, *1877: Year of Violence* (Indianapolis: Bobbs-Merrill, 1959).

On the Grange and the Knights, see Gabriel, *The Course of American Democratic Thought*, pp. 187–197; John R. Commons, *A History of Labor in the United States* (New York: Macmillan, 1918), vol. II, pp. 40–43, 342–343, 381, 413–423, 482–488; Gerald N. Grob, *Workers and Utopia*, pp. 38–43, 79–98; Theodore Saloutos and John D. Hicks, *Agricultural Discontent in the Middle West* (Madison: University of Wisconsin Press, 1951), pp. 56–86; Terence V. Powderly, *Thirty Years of Labor* (New York: Columbia University Press, 1889); C. D. Wright, "A Historical Sketch of the Knights of Labor," *QJE*, I (1887), pp. 137–168; C. Birdsall, "The Problem of Structure in the Knights of Labor," *Industrial and Labor Relations Review*, VI (1953), pp. 532–546; and H. J. Carman, "Terence V. Powderly: An Appraisal," *JEH*, I (1941), pp. 83–87.

"AGAINST THE WAYS OF TUBAL CAIN . . ."

The essential works on Populism are John D. Hicks, *The Populist Revolt* (Lincoln: University of Nebraska Press, 1961); Norman Pollack, *The Populist Response to Industrial America* (New York: Norton, 1966) and *The Populist Mind* (New York and Indianapolis: Bobbs-Merrill, 1967); Richard Hofstadter, *The Age of Reform* (New York: Knopf, 1955); and Walter T. K. Nugent, *The Tolerant Populists* (Chicago: University of Chicago Press, 1963).

Also useful are R. F. Durden, *The Climax of Populism* (Lexington: University of Kentucky Press, 1965); L. W. Fuller, "Colorado's Revolt against Capitalism," *MVHR*, XI (1934), pp. 355–357; P. S. Holbo, "Wheat or What: Populism and American Fascism," *WPQ*, XIV (1961), pp. 727–736; and Shlomo Bergman, "Some Methodological Errors in the Study of Anti-Semitism," *Jewish Social Studies*, V (1943), p. 47. Among contemporary comments, see William Peffer, *The Farmers' Side* (New York: Appleton, 1891).

William Jennings Bryan and his relation to Populism have finally been given adequate description by Louis W. Koenig, *Bryan* (New York: Putnam, 1971); see also P. W. Glad, *The Trumpet Soundeth: William Jennings Bryan and His Democracy* (Lincoln: University of Nebraska Press, 1960).

LLOYD: POPULIST MILITANT

See Chester Destler, *Henry Demarest Lloyd and the Empire of Reform* (Philadelphia: University of Pennsylvania Press, 1963); Harvey O'Connor, "Henry D. Lloyd: the Prophetic Tradition," in *American Radicals*, ed. H. Goldberg (New York: Monthly Review Press, 1957), pp. 78–89; Daniel Aaron, *Men of Good Hope*, pp. 133–171; D. Noble, *The Paradox of Progressive Thought* (Minneapolis: University of Minnesota Press, 1958), pp. 138–147; and Lloyd's own "The New Conscience," *NAR*, CXLVIII (1888), pp. 325–339.

CHAPTER XV

GENERAL

On Whitman, see Gay Wilson Allen, *The Solitary Singer* (New York: Grove, 1955) and "Walt Whitman, Cosmos-Inspired," in *New World Writing*, 8th ed. (New York: Mentor, 1955), pp. 266–280; Geoffrey Dutton, *Whitman* (New York: Grove, 1961); Henry S. Canby, *Walt Whitman: An American* (Boston: Houghton Mifflin, 1943); John A. Symonds, *Walt Whitman: A Study* (London: Nimmo, 1893); Vernon Louis Parrington, *The Beginnings of Critical Realism*, pp. 69–86; R. H. Gabriel, *The Course of American Democratic Thought*, pp. 123–131; Clarence Gohdes and R. G. Silver, *Faint Clews and Indirections* (Durham: Duke University Press, 1949); Richard Chase, *The Democratic Vista*

(New York: Doubleday, 1958), pp. 104–115; Benjamin Shapiro, *The Quest for Nationality* (Syracuse: Syracuse University Press, 1957), pp. 219–241; Joseph Beaver, *Walt Whitman: Poet of Science* (New York: King's Crown, 1951); J. M. Cox, "Walt Whitman, Mark Twain and the Civil War," *Sewanee Review*, LXIX (1961), pp. 185–204; Clarence Gohdes, "Whitman and Emerson," *Sewanee Review*, XXXVII (1929), pp. 79–93; David Goodale, "Some of Walt Whitman's Borrowings," *AL*, X (1938), pp. 202–213; G. Paine, "The Literary Relation of Whitman and Carlyle," *SP*, XXXVI (1939), pp. 560–563; and R. H. Pearce, "Whitman Justified: The Poet in 1860," *Minnesota Review*, I (1961), pp. 261–294. Other critical sources are cited in the notes. Unless otherwise noted, citations from Whitman are from *The Complete Writings of Walt Whitman*, ed. R. M. Bucke et al. (New York: Putnam, 1902).

On Bellamy, see A. E. Morgan, *The Philosophy of Edward Bellamy* (New York: King's Crown, 1945); Vernon Parrington, Jr., *American Dreams* (Providence: Brown University Press, 1947), pp. 69–97; Charles Madison, *Critics and Crusaders* (New York: Holt, 1947), pp. 134–153; J. H. Franklin, "Edward Bellamy and the Nationalist Movement," *NEQ*, XI (1938), pp. 739–772; and Elizabeth Sadler, "One Man's Influence: Edward Bellamy's *Looking Backward*," *NEQ*, XVII (1944), pp. 530–555. Other critical sources are cited in the notes.

Chapter XVI

GENERAL

The works on Twain I have found most useful in general are Justin Kaplan, *Mr. Clemens and Mark Twain* (New York: Simon and Schuster, 1966), and Henry Nash Smith, *Mark Twain: Development of a Writer* (Cambridge: Harvard University Press, 1962). See also K. R. Andrews, *Nook Farm: Mark Twain's Hartford Circle* (Cambridge: Harvard University Press, 1950); G. C. Bellamy, *Mark Twain as a Literary Artist* (Norman: University of Oklahoma Press, 1950); E. M. Branch, *The Literary Apprenticeship of Mark Twain* (Urbana: University of Illinois Press, 1950); G. A. Caldwell, *Twins of Genius* (East Lansing: Michigan State University Press, 1953); Bernard De Voto, *Mark Twain in Eruption* (New York: Harper, 1940) and *Mark Twain at Work* (Cambridge: Harvard University Press, 1942); Leslie Fiedler, *Love and Death in the American Novel*; Bryant M. French, *Mark Twain and the Gilded Age* (Dallas: Southern Methodist University Press, 1965); Dewey A. Ganzel, *Mark Twain Abroad* (Chicago: University of Chicago Press, 1968); and Kenneth Lynn, *Mark Twain and Southwestern Humor* (Boston: Little, Brown, 1959).

Other pertinent writings include R. T. Bell, "How Mark Twain Comments on Society Through the Use of Folklore," *MTJ*, X (1955), pp. 1–8, 24–25; B. A. Booth, "Mark Twain's Comments on Holmes' *Auto-*

crat," *AL*, XXI (1950), pp. 346–353; Bernard De Voto, "Fenimore Cooper's Further Literary Offenses," *NEQ*, XIX (1946), pp. 291–301; Theodore Dreiser, "Mark, the Double Twainer," *English Journal*, XXIV (1935), pp. 615–627; Otto Friedrich, "Mark Twain and the Nature of Humor," *Discourse*, II (1959), pp. 67–86; J. C. Gerber, "Mark Twain's Use of the Comic Pose," *PMLA*, LXXVII (1962), pp. 299–304; A. E. Jones, "Mark Twain and the Determinism of *What Is Man?*," *AL*, XXIX (1957), pp. 1–17; and W. F. Taylor, "Mark Twain and the Machine Age," *SAQ*, XXXVII (1938), pp. 384–394. Other critical sources are cited in the notes.

"TAKE THE . . . RELICS AND WEAVE . . . ROMANCE"

A Connecticut Yankee deserves separate bibliographic discussion. Easily the most useful work is Roger Salomon, *Twain and the Image of History* (New Haven: Yale University Press, 1957). Henry Nash Smith, *Mark Twain's Fable of Progress: Political and Economic Ideas in A Connecticut Yankee* (New Brunswick: Rutgers University Press, 1964), is one of the less fortunate works by a gifted critic. Like many critics, Smith is persuaded, partly by the details of the story's composition, that Twain was unable to give as positive an image of the virtues of technology and modern man as he had hoped. But this neglects the fact that Twain chose as his vehicle a classic tragedy. His ending is no more inconsistent with his beginning than are the cheerful first chapters of T. H. White's *Once and Future King* (New York: Dell, 1958) with White's powerful development of the tragic theme. Thomas Blues, *Mark Twain and the Community* (Lexington: University of Kentucky Press, 1970) is preferable. Another useful source is J. M. Cox, "*A Connecticut Yankee in King Arthur's Court*: The Machinery of Self-Preservation," *YR*, L (1960), pp. 89–102.

CHAPTER XVII

GENERAL

Many of the works on which I depended in writing this chapter are cited in the bibliography for Chapter Fourteen. In addition, see Claude Bowers, *Beveridge and the Progressive Era* (New York: Literary Guild, 1932); Harold Faulkner, *Politics, Reform and Expansion* (New York: Harper and Row, 1963); Sidney Fine, *Laissez-Faire and the General Welfare State* (Ann Arbor: University of Michigan Press, 1964); Harry K. Girvetz, *From Wealth to Welfare* (Stanford: Stanford University Press, 1950); George Mowry, *The Era of Theodore Roosevelt* (New York: Harper and Row, 1962); D. W. Noble, *The Paradox of Progressive Thought* (Minneapolis: University of Minnesota Press, 1958); Russel B. Nye, *Midwestern Progressive Politics* (East Lansing: Michigan State College

Press, 1951); and William Allen White, *Autobiography* and *Forty Years on Main Street* (New York and Toronto: Farrar and Rinehart, 1937).

BORN IN ARCADIA

An invaluable work is Josiah Royce, *Race Questions, Provincialism and Other American Problems* (New York: Macmillan, 1908). Among recent works, see Gabriel Kolko, *The Triumph of Conservatism* (New York: Free Press, 1963); Edward Chase Kirkland, *Dream and Thought in the Business Community* (Ithaca: Cornell University Press, 1956); and Henry Steele Commager, *The American Mind* (New Haven: Yale University Press, 1954), pp. 3–195.

On racial issues, see C. Vann Woodward, *The Origins of the New South*, pp. 321–395, and John Higham, *Strangers in a Strange Land* (New Brunswick: Rutgers University Press, 1955), pp. 131ff.

"THE BUZZING UNIVERSE . . ."

Among many works on New England, see Geoffrey Blodgett, *The Gentle Reformers: Massachusetts Democrats in the Cleveland Era* (Cambridge: Harvard University Press, 1966); Edward Chase Kirkland, *Charles Francis Adams, Jr.*; Van Wyck Brooks, *New England's Indian Summer*; Ernest Samuels, *Henry Adams: the Middle Years* (Cambridge: Harvard University Press, 1965) and *Henry Adams: the Major Phase* (Cambridge: Harvard University Press, 1964); Moorfield Storey, *Politics as a Duty and a Career* (New York: Putnam, 1899); Kenneth S. Lynn, *William Dean Howells: An American Life* (New York: Harcourt Brace Jovanovich, 1971), and E. M. Cady, *The Realist at War: The Mature Years, 1885–1920* (Syracuse: Syracuse University Press, 1956).

The essential work on philosophic thought in New England is George Santayana, *Character and Opinion in the United States* (New York: Braziller, 1955). On William James, see Ralph Barton Perry, *The Thought and Character of William James* (Boston: Little, Brown, 1935) and *In the Spirit of William James* (Bloomington: University of Indiana Press, 1958).

IN HIS STEPS

On the churches and social crisis, see Gabriel, *The Course of American Democratic Thought*, pp. 308–330; H. F. May, *The Protestant Church and Social Action* (New York: Harper, 1949); J. Dombrowski, *The Early Days of Christian Socialism* (New York: Columbia University Press, 1936); J. W. Pratt, *Expansionists of 1898* (Chicago: Quadrangle, 1964), pp. 279–316; Charles M. Sheldon, *In His Steps* (Philadelphia: Universal Book and Bible House, 1937); Josiah Strong, *The New Era* (New York: Baker and Taylor, 1893), and Walter Rauschenbusch, *Theology for the Social Gospel* (New York: Macmillan, 1917).

"MAKE THE WORLD SAFE . . ."

One of the most incisive studies of progressive ideology is Morton White, *Social Thought in America: The Revolt Against Formalism* (Boston: Beacon, 1964). Walter Lippmann, *Drift and Mastery* (Englewood Cliffs: Prentice-Hall, 1961), expresses so many themes in Progressivism that it amounts to a text. Also useful, in addition to the works cited in the notes, are Walter Weyl, *The New Democracy* (New York: Harper, 1964); George Mowry, *The California Progressives* (Berkeley and Los Angeles: University of California Press, 1951); Frederick Howe, *The Confessions of a Reformer* (New York: Scribner's, 1925); Melvin Holli, *Reform in Detroit: Hazen Pingree and Urban Politics* (New York: Oxford University Press, 1969); Gabriel, *The Course of American Democratic Thought*, pp. 293–370; and, as always, Eric Goldman, *Rendezvous with Destiny*.

NEW AMERICANS, OLD MEMORIES

On the experience of immigrants and ethnic groups, see Herbert Gans, *The Urban Villagers* (New York: Free Press, 1962); Oscar Handlin, *The Uprooted* (New York: Grosset and Dunlap, 1961); Marcus Hansen, *The Great Migration, 1607–1860* (Cambridge: Harvard University Press, 1940); Melville Herskovits, *Acculturation* (New York: Augustin, 1938); Bradford Smith, *Americans from Japan* (Philadelphia: Lippincott, 1948); Carey McWilliams, *Prejudice* (Boston: Little, Brown, 1944) and *North from Mexico* (Philadelphia: Lippincott, 1949); M. R. Stein, *The Eclipse of Community* (Princeton: Princeton University Press, 1960); W. F. Whyte, *Street Corner Society* (Chicago: University of Chicago Press, 1955); Nathan Glazer, "Ethnic Groups in America: From National Culture to Ideology," in M. Berger et al., *Freedom and Control in Modern Society*, pp. 160–167; C. Gulick, "The Transition from Familism to Nationalism among the Chinese of Hawaii," *AJS*, XLIII (1948), pp. 734–743; and Daniel Moynihan and James Q. Wilson, "Patronage in New York State," *APSR*, LVIII (1964), pp. 289–300.

On Catholics, see especially John Tracy Ellis, *American Catholicism* (Chicago: University of Chicago Press, 1961). On Jews, see Louis Wirth, *The Ghetto* (Chicago: University of Chicago Press, 1956); C. B. Sherman, *The Jews Within American Society* (Detroit: Wayne State University Press, 1961); Carey McWilliams, *A Mask for Privilege* (Boston: Little, Brown, 1948); Eugene Borowitz, "Crisis Theology and the Jewish Community," *Commentary*, XXXII (1961), pp. 36–42; Daniel Bell, "Reflections on Jewish Identity," *Commentary*, XXXI (1961), pp. 471–478; L. Fuchs, "The American Jews and the Presidential Vote," in *American Ethnic Politics*, ed. L. Fuchs (New York and Evanston: Harper and Row, 1968), pp. 10–31; N. Miller, "The Jewish Leadership of Lakeport," in *Studies in Leadership*, ed. Alvin Gouldner (New York: Harper, 1950), pp. 195–227; and Israel Knox et al., *The Jewish Labor Movement in America* (New York: Workmen's Circle, 1958). Comments on Jewish fraternal orders are drawn from official publications furnished by B'rith Abraham, The Free Sons of Israel, and The Workmen's Circle.

"MY GOD, IT'S FLAHERTY!"

On machine politics and related phenomena, see Alexander Callow, *The Tweed Ring* (New York: Oxford University Press, 1966); Bryce, *The American Commonwealth*, vol. II, pp. 93–119; Raymond Fosdick, *American Police Systems* (New York: Century, 1920), pp. 76–90; Ari Hoogenboom, *Outlawing the Spoils* (Urbana: University of Illinois Press, 1961); V. O. Kev, *Politics, Parties and Pressure Groups*, pp. 250–279; Seymour Mandelbaum, *Boss Tweed's New York* (New York: Wiley, 1965); Roy V. Peel, *Political Clubs of the City of New York* (New York: Putnam, 1935); James Reichley, *The Art of Government* (Philadelphia: Fund for the Republic, 1959); Brand Whitlock, *Forty Years of It* (New York: Appleton, 1925); Robert A. Woods, "The Roots of Political Power," in *The City Wilderness* (Boston: Houghton Mifflin, 1898), pp. 114–147; Marvin Gettleman, "Charity and Social Classes in the United States," *American Journal of Economics and Sociology*, XXII (1963), pp. 313–329, 417–426; Harold Gosnell, "Political Meetings in the Chicago Black Belt," *APSR*, XXVIII (1934), pp. 254–258; H. C. Merwin, "Tammany Hall," *AM*, LXIII (1894), pp. 240–251; J. P. Salter, "The Pattern of Politics," *JP*, I (1939), pp. 258–277; Mary K. Simkhovitch, "Friendship and Politics," *PSQ*, VII (1902), pp. 189–205; and Raymond Wolfinger, "The Development and Persistence of Ethnic Voting," *APSR*, LIX (1965), pp. 896–908.

HUNS AT THE GATE

On racism and racist ideology, see especially Thomas Hartshorne, *The Distorted Image* (Cleveland: Case Western Reserve University Press, 1968), pp. 35–78. On imperialism, expansionism, and the war crusade, see Gabriel, *The Course of American Democratic Thought*, pp. 339–356; Walter Millis, *The Martial Spirit* (Boston: Literary Guild, 1929); Pratt, *Expansionists of 1898*, pp. 230–278; Harley Notter, *The Origins of the Foreign Policy of Woodrow Wilson* (Baltimore: Johns Hopkins University, 1937); F. H. Harrington, "The Anti-Imperialist Movement in the United States," *MVHR*, XXII (1935), pp. 211–230; W. E. Leuchtenberg, "Progressivism and Imperialism: the Progressive Movement and Foreign Policy, 1896–1916," *MVHR*, XXXIX (1952), pp. 483–504; Christopher Lasch, "The Anti-Imperialists, The Philippines and the Inequality of Man," *JSH*, XXIV (1958), pp. 319–331; and Walter Lippmann, *The Political Scene* (New York: Holt, 1919).

Chapter XVIII

GENERAL

There are valuable discussions of the 1920's in Goldman, *Rendezvous with Destiny*, pp. 202–247; Arthur Schlesinger, Jr., *The Crisis of the Old Order* (Boston: Houghton Mifflin, 1957); Frederick Lewis Allen, *Only Yesterday* (New York: Bantam, 1952); George Soule, *Prosperity Decade* (London: Pilot, 1947); Irving Bernstein, *The Lean Years* (Baltimore: Penguin, 1966); P. W. Slosson, *The Great Crusade and After* (New York: Macmillan, 1928); *Whither Mankind?*, ed. Charles A. Beard (New York: Longmans Green, 1928); and Henry S. Kariel, *The Decline of American Pluralism.*

THE PARTING WAYS

On business, see E. C. Lindeman, *Wealth and Culture* (New York: Harcourt, Brace, 1935), and Bernstein, *The Lean Years*, pp. 144–189.

The Klan is discussed in David Chalmers, *Hooded Americanism* (Garden City: Doubleday, 1955), and J. A. Mecklin, *The Ku Klux Klan* (New York: Harcourt, Brace, 1924). The fear of foreign ideologies may be seen in Curti, *Roots of American Loyalty*, pp. 236–248; I. B. Berkson, *Theories of Americanization* (New York: Columbia University Press, 1920); and R. K. Murray, *Red Scare* (Minneapolis: University of Minnesota Press, 1955).

The politics of the period are ably treated by Arthur S. Link, "What Happened to the Progressive Movement in the 1920's?" *AHR*, LXIV (1959), pp. 833–851; the struggle to find new alternatives may be seen in Nye, *Midwestern Progressive Politics*, pp. 310–350, and Robert Morlan, *Political Prairie Fire* (Minneapolis: University of Minnesota Press, 1955).

On suburbs, see Arensberg and Kimball, *Culture and Community*, pp. 114–115, 146–147, 165; Greer, *The Emerging City*, pp. 146–151, 163, 186–189; White and White, *The Intellectual vs. The City*, pp. 190–199, 203–204; and David Gottlieb, "The Neighborhood Tavern and the Cocktail Lounge," *AJS*, LXII (1957), pp. 559–562.

On Southern California, see Carey McWilliams, *Southern California Country* (New York: Duell, Sloan and Pierce, 1946).

"A NIGHT OF DARK INTENT . . ."

Intellectuals and intellectual life are treated in Matthew Josephson, *Portrait of the Artist as an American* (New York: Harcourt, Brace, 1930); Harold Stearns, *America and the Young Intellectual* (New York: Doran, 1928) and *Civilization in the United States* (New York: Harcourt, Brace, 1922); Caroline Ware, *Greenwich Village* (Boston: Houghton Mifflin, 1935); and Oscar Cargill, *Intellectual America* (New York: Macmillan, 1941).

On various writers and currents, see Edgar Kemler, *The Irreverent*

Mr. Mencken (Boston: Little, Brown, 1950); H. L. Mencken, *Notes on Democracy* (New York: Knopf, 1926); Irving Babbitt, *Democracy and Leadership* (Boston: Houghton Mifflin, 1924); and Ralph Barsodi, *This Ugly Civilization* (New York: Harper, 1929).

Political cults of various sorts are described in Carey McWilliams, *Southern California Country*, pp. 293–303, and "Utopia, Incorporated," *New Republic*, 79 (1934), pp. 255–259; see also Harry Elsner, *The Technocrats* (Syracuse: Syracuse University Press, 1967).

One of the more illustrative of Sherwood Anderson's works is *Poor White* (New York: Huebsch, 1920). On Anderson and Frost, see T. K. Whipple, *Spokesmen* (Berkeley and Los Angeles: University of California Press, 1963), pp. 94–138.

THE REDHEAD

Of the many critical studies of Lewis, see especially Whipple, *Spokesmen*, pp. 208–229; *Sinclair Lewis*, ed. Mark Schorer (Englewood Cliffs: Prentice-Hall, 1962); *After the Genteel Tradition*, ed. Malcolm Cowley (New York: Norton, 1937); *The Young Rebel in American Literature*, ed. Carl Bode (New York: Praeger, 1960); Walter Lippmann, *Men of Destiny* (New York: Macmillan, 1927); Alfred Kazin, *On Native Grounds* (New York: Harcourt, Brace, 1942); and the relevant comments in Sherwood Anderson, *Sherwood Anderson's Notebook* (New York: Boni and Liveright, 1926).

THE PHILOSOPHER

A useful collection of articles on Dewey is *The Philosophy of John Dewey*, ed. Paul A. Schilpp (Evanston and Chicago: Northwestern University Press, 1939). More critical comments may be found in Morris R. Cohen, *American Thought*, pp. 366–376; Morton G. White, *The Origins of Dewey's Instrumentalism* (New York: Columbia University Press, 1943); Phillip Wiener, *Evolution and the Founders of Pragmatism* (Cambridge: Harvard University Press, 1949); Reinhold Niebuhr, *Human Nature and Destiny* (New York: Scribner's, 1951); and Robert Horwitz, "John Dewey," *History of Political Philosophy*, ed. Leo Strauss and Joseph Cropsey (Chicago: Rand McNally, 1963), pp. 746–764.

CHAPTER XIX

GENERAL

The literature on Roosevelt and the New Deal is vast and constantly expanding. The discussion of New Deal thought in Hartz, *The Liberal Tradition in America*, pp. 259–283, is very fine, as is that in Goldman, *Rendezvous with Destiny* (1956), pp. 269–347. See also Arthur Schlesinger, Jr., *The Coming of the New Deal* (Boston: Houghton Mifflin, 1959) and *The Politics of Upheaval* (Boston: Houghton Mifflin,

1960); Rexford G. Tugwell, *The Democratic Roosevelt* (Garden City: Doubleday, 1957); James M. Burns, *Roosevelt: the Lion and the Fox* (New York: Harcourt, Brace, 1956); Harold L. Ickes, *Secret Diary* (New York, Simon and Schuster, 1954, 3 vols.); Robert E. Sherwood, *Roosevelt and Hopkins* (New York: Harper, 1948); Basil Rauch, *A History of the New Deal, 1933–1938* (New York: Creative Age, 1941); and Charles A. Beard and George Smith, *The Old Deal and the New* (New York: Macmillan, 1940).

EXCITEMENT AMID DESPAIR

A very valuable recent study of one "extreme" movement is T. Harry Williams, *Huey Long* (New York: Knopf, 1969). On currents among intellectuals, see *The American Writer in the Great Depression*, ed. Harvey Swados (New York and Indianapolis: Bobbs-Merrill, 1966); W. L. Dusenberry, *The Theme of Loneliness in Modern American Drama* (Gainesville: University of Florida Press, 1960); Alfred Kazin, *On Native Grounds*; James Agee and Walker Evans, *Let Us Now Praise Famous Men* (Boston: Houghton Mifflin, 1940); Louis Adamic, *My Native Land* (New York: Harper, 1938); and Carey McWilliams, *Louis Adamic and Shadow America* (Los Angeles: Whipple, 1935).

On trade unions and organizations of the poor, see Irving Bernstein, *The Lean Years*, pp. 11, 41, 53, 59–60, 83–143, 287–300, 416–418, 437–455; H. Harris, *American Labor*, pp. 97–148, 334–335, 356–364; C. Wright Mills, *New Men of Power* (New York: Harcourt, Brace, 1948); Jesse Steiner, "Community Organization," *AJS*, XL (1935), pp. 788–795; Lloyd Fisher and Grant McConnell, "Internal Conflict and Trade Union Solidarity," in *Industrial Conflict*, ed. A. Kornhauser (New York: McGraw-Hill, 1954), pp. 132–144; and M. J. Nadworny, *Scientific Management and the Unions, 1900–1932* (Cambridge: Harvard University Press, 1955).

SHUFFLING THE DECK

The ideas of the New Deal are discussed in Hartz, Goldman, and other works cited in the general section. See also *New Deal Thought*, ed. Howard Zinn (New York and Indianapolis: Bobbs-Merrill, 1966); T. H. Greer, *What Roosevelt Thought: the Social and Political Ideas of Franklin D. Roosevelt* (East Lansing: Michigan State University Press, 1958); Rexford G. Tugwell, "The Principle of Planning and the Institutions of Laissez-Faire," *American Economic Review*, XXII (1932), pp. 75–92; Reinhold Niebuhr, "After Capitalism, What?," *World Tomorrow*, XVI (1933), p. 205; and Max Lerner, *Ideas for the Ice Age*, pp. 376–381.

On Henry Wallace, see Wallace's own *New Frontiers* (New York: Reynal and Hitchcock, 1934) and *Whose Constitution?* (New York: Reynal and Hitchcock, 1936). A useful though very inadequate study is Edward L. and Frederick H. Schapsmeier, *Henry Wallace of Iowa: the*

Agrarian Years, 1910–1940 (Ames: Iowa State University Press, 1968). On agricultural policy, see John D. Lewis, "Democratic Planning in Agriculture," *APSR*, XXXV (1941), pp. 232–249, 254–269; Phillip A. Selznick, *TVA and the Grass Roots* (Berkeley and Los Angeles: University of California Press, 1953); David Conrad, *Forgotten Farmers* (Urbana: University of Illinois Press, 1965); Russell Lord and P. H. Johnstone, *A Place on the Earth* (Washington: Bureau of Agricultural Economics, 1942); Carey McWilliams, *Ill Fares the Land* (Boston: Little, Brown, 1942); and R. S. Kirkendall, *Social Scientists and Farm Politics in the Age of Roosevelt* (Columbia: University of Missouri Press, 1966).

A recent study of Thurman Arnold is Edward Kearny, *Thurman Arnold: Social Critic* (Albuquerque: University of New Mexico Press, 1970).

E PLURIBUS . . .

One useful text in pluralist thought not otherwise cited is John Kenneth Galbraith, *American Capitalism: the Concept of Countervailing Power* (Boston: Houghton Mifflin, 1952). Critical studies and comments include Walter Adams and Horace Gray, *Monopoly in America* (New York: Macmillan, 1955); *The Bias of Pluralism*, ed. William Connolly (New York: Atherton, 1969); Bernard Crick, *The American Science of Politics* (Berkeley and Los Angeles: University of California Press, 1960); Green and Levinson, *Power and Community*; V. O. Key, *Public Opinion and American Democracy* (New York: Knopf, 1961), pp. 153–201; Theodore J. Lowi, *The End of Liberalism* (New York: Norton, 1969); C. Wright Mills, *The Power Elite* (New York: Oxford University Press, 1956), pp. 242–268; H. Mark Roelofs, *The Tensions of Citizenship* (New York: Rinehart, 1957); E. E. Schattschneider, *The Semi-Sovereign People* (New York: Holt, 1960); Christian Bay, "The Cheerful Science of Dismal Politics," *The Dissenting Academy*, ed. T. Roszak (New York: Pantheon, 1967), pp. 208–230; R. E. Dowling, "Group Theory: Its Methodological Range," *APSR*, LIV (1960), pp. 944–954; Myron Q. Hale, "The Cosmology of Arthur F. Bentley," *APSR*, LIV (1960), pp. 955–961; Bruno Leoni, "The Meaning of 'Political' in Political Decisions," *Political Studies*, V (1951), pp. 225–239; Peter H. Odegard, "The Group Basis of Politics: New Name for an Old Myth," *WPQ*, XI (1958), pp. 689–702; Jack L. Walker, "A Critique of the Elitist Theory of Democracy," *APSR*, LX (1966), pp. 285–295; and Stanley Rothman, "Systematic Political Theory: the Group Approach," *APSR*, LIV (1960), pp. 15–33.

For a discussion of Niebuhr's "realism" and related ideas, see my "Reinhold Niebuhr: New Orthodoxy for Old Liberalism," *APSR*, LVI (1962), pp. 874–885.

CHAPTER XX

GENERAL

Among the most useful books on life and thought in Black America are
Gunnar Myrdal, *An American Dilemma*; E. Franklin Frazier, *Black
Bourgeoisie* (New York: Free Press, 1962) and *The Negro in America*,
(New York: Macmillan, 1957); W. E. B. DuBois, *Souls of Black Folk*
(Greenwich: Fawcett, 1961); John Hope Franklin, *From Slavery to
Freedom* (New York: Knopf, 1967); Charles Silberman, *Crisis in Black
and White* (New York: Random House, 1964); Stokely Carmichael and
Charles Hamilton, *Black Power: The Politics of Liberation in America*
(New York: Random House, 1967); Richard Wright, *Black Power: A
Record of Reaction in a Land of Pathos* (New York: Harper and Row,
1954); Kenneth Clark, *Dark Ghetto* (New York: Harper, 1955); Louis
Masotti et al., *A Time to Burn?* (Chicago: Rand McNally, 1969); and
Rayford W. Logan, *The Negro in American Life and Thought* (New
York: Dial, 1954).

THROUGH A GLASS, DARKLY . . .

General views of American blacks include Abram Kardiner and Lionel
Ovesey, *The Mark of Oppression* (New York: Norton, 1951); William
H. Grier and Price M. Cobbs, *Black Rage* (New York: Bantam, 1968);
T. F. Pettigrew, *A Profile of the Negro American* (Princeton: Van
Nostrand, 1964); *The Negro American*, ed. Talcott Parsons and Kenneth
Clark (Boston: Houghton Mifflin, 1966); Bertram Karom, *The Negro
Personality* (New York: Springer, 1959); and M. R. Yarrow, "Inter-
personal Dynamics in a Desegregation Process," *JSI*, XIV (1958), pp.
3–63.

On life styles, see William McCord et al., *Life Styles in the Black
Ghetto* (New York: Norton, 1969), and Horace Cayton and St. Clair
Drake, *Black Metropolis* (New York: Harper and Row, 1962).

Resistance to slavery is described in Martin Kilson, "Towards Freedom: an Analysis of Slave Revolts in the United States," *Phylon*, XXV
(1964), pp. 175–187, and Raymond and Alice Bauer, "Day to Day Resistance to Slavery," *JNH*, XXVII (1942), pp. 388–419.

IN HIS HANDS

On religion in black America, see E. Franklin Frazier, *The Negro Church
in America* (New York: Schocken, 1963); Kyle Haselden, *The Racial
Problem in Christian Perspective* (New York: Harper, 1959); *Negro
Social and Political Thought*, ed. Howard Brotz (New York: Basic
Books, 1966), pp. 483–491; Hortense Powdermaker, *After Freedom*
(New York: Viking, 1939); Richard Wright, *Twelve Million Black
Voices* (New York: Viking, 1941), pp. 130–133; Hylan Lewis, *Blackways
of Kent* (Chapel Hill: University of North Carolina Press, 1955); Ruby

F. Johnston, *The Development of Negro Religion* (New York: Philosophical Library, 1954); and Charles Wesley, "The Religious Attitudes of Negro Youth," *JNH*, XXI (1936), pp. 376–393. Also relevant is E. Barth's finding that blacks employ the language of emotions and ultimate values more than whites and are less inclined to speak in utilitarian terms. ("The Language Behavior of Negroes and Whites," *Pacific Sociological Review*, IV, 1961, pp. 69–72.)

SINN FEIN

Probably no book gives a better description of the formation of nationalist and separatist feelings than Frantz Fanon, *The Wretched of the Earth* (New York: Grove, 1963).

On Negro organizations and associations, see Frazier, *The Negro in America*, pp. 366–386; E. N. Palmer, "Negro Secret Societies," *SF*, XXIII (1944–1945), pp. 209ff.; G. B. Johnson, "Some Factors in the Development of Negro Social Institutions in the United States," *AJS*, XXX (1934), pp. 329–337; W. Gulley, "Relative Effectiveness of Negro and White Voluntary Associations," *Phylon*, XXIV (1963), pp. 172–183; G. Franklin Edwards, *The Negro Professional Class* (Glencoe: Free Press, 1949); James Weldon Johnson, *Black Manhattan* (New York: Knopf, 1930), pp. 283ff.; and D. C. Thompson, *The Negro Leadership Class* (Englewood Cliffs: Prentice-Hall, 1963).

Negro disillusionment in the 1920's is described in W. E. B. DuBois, *Dusk of Dawn* (New York: Schocken, 1968), pp. 221–268, 274–279. On Garvey and Garveyism, see *Negro Protest Thought in the Twentieth Century*, ed. Francis L. Broderick and August Meier (Indianapolis: Bobbs-Merrill, 1965), pp. 83–91; E. D. Cronon, *Black Moses: The Story of Marcus Garvey* (Madison: University of Wisconsin Press, 1962); E. Franklin Frazier, "Garvey: A Mass Leader," *Nation*, CXXIII (1926), pp. 147–148; and T. Standing, "Nationalism and Negro Leadership," *AJS*, XL (1934), pp. 180–192.

On Islam, see Malcolm X, *Autobiography* (New York: Grove, 1965); E. Essien-Udom, *Black Nationalism* (Chicago: University of Chicago Press, 1962); James Baldwin, *The Fire Next Time* (New York: Dell, 1963), pp. 67–113; J. H. Laue, "A Contemporary Revitalization Movement in American Race Relations: the Black Muslims," *SF*, XLII (1964), pp. 315–323; Claude McKay, *Harlem* (New York: Dutton, 1940), pp. 185–196; and Samuel Weiss, "The Ordeal of Malcolm X," *SAQ*, LXVII (1968), pp. 53–63.

On African culturalism in America, see Harold Isaacs, *The New World of the Negro American* (New York: Wiley, 1963); Seymour Parker and Robert Kleiner, "Status Position, Mobility and Ethnic Identification of the Negro," *JSI*, XX (1964), pp. 85–102; Clement Vontress, "The Negro Suburban Retreat and Its Implications," *Chicago Jewish Forum*, XXV (1966), pp. 18–22; and Ruth Searles and J. A. Williams,

"Negro College Students' Participation," *SF*, XL (1962), pp. 215–220. Some political problems in cultural nationalism are suggested in Gene Marine, *The Black Panthers* (New York: New American Library, 1969), pp. 21–27.

RIGHTS AND REVOLUTIONS

On black politics generally, see William Keech, *The Impact of Negro Voting* (Chicago: Rand McNally, 1968); Donald Matthews and James Prothro, *Negroes and the New Southern Politics* (New York: Harcourt, Brace, 1966); E. S. Ladd, *Negro Political Leadership in the South* (Ithaca: Cornell University Press, 1966); A. M. Crum, "A Reappraisal of the Social and Political Participation of Negroes," *AJS*, LXXII (1966), pp. 32–46; Jack L. Walker, "Negro Voting in Atlanta," *Phylon*, XXIV (1963), pp. 379–387; and, at a much lower level of value, James Q. Wilson, *Negro Politics* (Glencoe: Free Press, 1960).

On Booker T. Washington and his times, see *Negro Social and Political Thought*, pp. 13–15, 357, 359, 371, 411, 422–423, 447; Booker T. Washington, "The Negro and the Labor Movement," *AM*, CXI (1913), p. 756; C. S. Johnson, "The Social Philosophy of Booker T. Washington," *Opportunity*, VI (1928), pp. 102–105; August Meier, "Negro Class Structure and Ideology in the Age of Booker T. Washington," *Phylon*, XXIII (1962), pp. 258–266; and B. G. Mandel, "Samuel Gompers and Negro Workers," *JNH*, XL (1955), pp. 34–60. (Mandel is useful in indicating the limitations which Washington faced.)

On the decay of conditions during and after the Second World War, see Lowi, *The End of Liberalism*, pp. 250–266; McCord, *Life Styles in the Black Ghetto*, pp. 28–29, 54; Silberman, *Crisis in Black and White*, pp. 40–41, 60–65; G. Osofsky, *Harlem: the Making of a Ghetto* (New York: Harper and Row, 1966); and Peter Rossi and Robert Dentler, *The Politics of Urban Renewal* (New York: Free Press, 1961).

Various militant protests are discussed in Ralph Bunche, "A Critical Analysis of the Tactics and Program of Minority Groups," *Journal, of Negro Education*, IV (1935), pp. 308–320; Tom Hayden, *Rebellion in Newark* (New York: Random House, 1967); Gene Marine, *The Black Panthers*; Gary Marx, *Protest and Prejudice* (New York: Harper, 1967); Loren Miller, "Farewell to the Liberals," *Nation*, CXCV (Oct. 20, 1962), pp. 235–238; Bayard Rustin, "From Protest to Politics," *Commentary*, XXXIX (1965), pp. 25–31; and Fred Powledge, *Black Power, White Resistance* (Cleveland: World, 1967). On violence, see H. L. Nieburg, *Political Violence*, and my "On Violence and Legitimacy," *Yale Law Journal*, LXXIX (1970), pp. 623–646.

INDEX